T0181878

Lecture Notes of the Institute for Computer Sciences, Social Informatics and Telecommunications Engineering 407

More information about this series at https://link.springer.com/bookseries/8197

Honghao Gao · Xinheng Wang (Eds.)

Collaborative Computing: Networking, Applications and Worksharing

17th EAI International Conference, CollaborateCom 2021
Virtual Event, October 16–18, 2021
Proceedings, Part II

 Springer

Editors
Honghao Gao
Shanghai University
Shanghai, China

Xinheng Wang
Xi'an Jiaotong-Liverpool University
Suzhou, China

ISSN 1867-8211 ISSN 1867-822X (electronic)
Lecture Notes of the Institute for Computer Sciences, Social Informatics
and Telecommunications Engineering
ISBN 978-3-030-92637-3 ISBN 978-3-030-92638-0 (eBook)
https://doi.org/10.1007/978-3-030-92638-0

This Springer imprint is published by the registered company Springer Nature Switzerland AG
The registered company address is: Gewerbestrasse 11, 6330 Cham, Switzerland

Preface

We are delighted to introduce the proceedings of the 17th European Alliance for Innovation (EAI) International Conference on Collaborative Computing: Networking, Applications and Worksharing (CollaborateCom 2021). This conference has brought together researchers, developers, and practitioners around the world who are interested in fully realizing the promises of electronic collaboration from the aspects of networking, technology and systems, user interfaces and interaction paradigms, and interoperation with application-specific components and tools.

This year's conference attracted 206 submissions. Each submission was reviewed by an average of three reviewers. After a rigorous review process, 69 papers were accepted, including 62 full papers and seven short papers in oral presentation sessions at the main conference tracks. The conference sessions covered optimization, UAV and traffic systems, recommendation systems, network and security, IOT and social networks, image handling and human recognition, edge computing, collaborative working, and deep learning and its applications. Apart from the high-quality technical paper presentations, the technical program also featured two keynote speeches and two technical workshops. The two keynote speeches were delivered by Jie Wu from Temple University and Dan Feng from Huazhong University of Science and Technology. The two workshops organized were Securing IoT Networks (SITN) and Data-driven Fault Diagnosis with Collaborative Computing. The SITN workshop aims to bring together expertise from academia and industry to build secure IoT infrastructures for smart society. The workshop on Data-driven Fault Diagnosis with Collaborative Computing aims to provide a forum for researchers and industrial practitioners to exchange their latest results on data-driven fault diagnosis techniques with collaborative computing.

Coordination with the steering chair, Imrich Chlamtac, and the steering committee members was essential for the success of the conference. We sincerely appreciate their constant support and guidance. It was also a great pleasure to work with such an excellent organizing committee team for their hard work in organizing and supporting the conference. In particular, we are grateful to the Technical Program Committee who completed the peer-review process for technical papers and helped to put together a high-quality technical program. We are also grateful to the conference manager, Karolina Marcinova, for her support and all the authors who submitted their papers to the CollaborateCom 2021 conference and workshops.

We strongly believe that the CollaborateCom conference provides a good forum for all researchers, developers, and practitioners to discuss all science and technology aspects that are relevant to collaborative computing. We also expect that the future

CollaborateCom conferences will be as successful and stimulating as this year's, as indicated by the contributions presented in this volume.

October 2021

Honghao Gao
Xinheng Wang
Yuanyuan Yang
Kaizhu Huang
Tun Lu

Organization

Steering Committee

Chair

Imrich Chlamtac   University of Trento, Italy

Members

Song Guo   University of Aizu, Japan
Bo Li   Hong Kong University of Science and
Technology, China
Xiaofei Liao   Huazhong University of Science and Technology,
China
Xinheng Wang   Xi'an Jiaotong-Liverpool University, China
Honghao Gao   Shanghai University, China

Organizing Committee

General Chairs

Eng Gee Lim   Xi'an Jiaotong-Liverpool University, China
Yuanyuan Yang   State University of New York, USA
Honghao Gao   Shanghai University, China
Xinheng Wang   Xi'an Jiaotong-Liverpool University, China

Technical Program Committee Co-chairs

Kaizhu Huang   Xi'an Jiaotong-Liverpool University, China
Tun Lu   Fudan University, China

Web Chair

Fei Cheng   Xi'an Jiaotong-Liverpool University, China

Publicity and Social Media Chairs

Li Kuang   Central South University, China
Andrei Tchernykh   CICESE Research Center, Mexico

Workshops Chairs

Yusheng Xu	Xidian University, China
Shahid Mumtaz	Instituto de Telecomunicações, Portugal

Publications Chairs

Youhuizi Li	Hangzhou Dianzi University, China
Azah Kamilah Binti Draman	University Teknikal Malaysia Melaka, Malaysia
Xiaoxian Yang	Shanghai Polytechnic University, China

Panels Chair

Kyeongsoo (Joseph) Kim	Xi'an Jiaotong-Liverpool University, China

Tutorials Chair

Yuyu Yin	Hangzhou Dianzi University, China

Local Chairs

Junyao Duan	Xi'an Jiaotong-Liverpool University, China
Xiaoyi Wu	Xi'an Jiaotong-Liverpool University, China

Technical Program Committee

Anwer Al-Dulaimi	University of Toronto, Canada
Amjad Ali	Korea University, South Korea
Junaid Arshad	University of West London, UK
Zhongqin Bi	Shanghai University of Electric Power, China
Bin Cao	Zhejiang University of Technology, China
Buqing Cao	Hunan University of Science and Technology, China
Liang Chen	University of West London, UK
Shizhan Chen	Tianjing University, China
Yihai Chen	Shanghai University, China
Ying Chen	Beijing University of Information Technology, China
Fei Dai	Yunnan University, China
Yucong Duan	Hainan University, China
Xiaoliang Fan	Fuzhou University, China
Shucun Fu	Nanjing University of Information Science and Technology, China
Fekade Getahun	Addis Ababa University, Ethiopia
Jiwei Huang	China University of Petroleum, Beijing, China

Tao Huang   Silicon Lake University, China
Congfeng Jiang   Hangzhou Dianzi University, China
Malik Ahmad Kamran   COMSATS University Islamabad, Pakistan
Li Kuang   Central South University, China
Rui Li   Xidian University, China
Youhuizi Li   Hangzhou Dianzi University, China
Wenmin Lin   Hangzhou Dianzi University, China
Jianxun Liu   Hunan University of Science and Technology,
                             China
Shijun Liu   Shandong University, China
Xihua Liu   Nanjing University of Information Science and
                             Technology, China
Xuan Liu   Southeast University, China
Yutao Ma   Wuhan University, China
Lin Meng   Ritsumeikan University, Japan
Shunmei Meng   Nanjing University of Science and Technology,
                             China
Elahe Naserianhanzaei   University of Exeter, UK
Yu-Chun Pan   University of West London, UK
Shanchen Pang   China University of Petroleum, China
Lianyong Qi   Qufu Normal University, China
Kuangyu Qin   Wuhan University, China
Stephan Reiff-Marganiec   University of Leicester, UK
Imed Romdhani   Edinburgh Napier University, UK
Changai Sun   University of Science and Technology, China
Xiaobing Sun   Yangzhou University, China
Wenda Tang   Lancaster University, UK
George Ubakanma   London South Bank University, UK
Shaohua Wan   Zhongnan University of Economics and Law,
                             China
Dongjing Wang   Hangzhou Dianzi University, China
Jian Wang   Wuhan University, China
Junhao Wen   Chongqing University, China
Yiping Wen   Hunan University of Science and Technology,
                             China
Yu Weng   Minzu University of China, China
Yirui Wu   Hohai University, China
Yunni Xia   Chongqing University, China
Haolong Xiang   University of Auckland, New Zealand
Jiuyun Xu   China University of Petroleum, China
Xiaolong Xu   Nanjing University of Information Science and
                             Technology, China

Contents – Part II

Edge Computing

Energy-Efficient Cooperative Offloading for Multi-AP MEC in IoT
Networks 3
    Zhihui Cao, Haifeng Sun, Ning Zhang, and Xiang Lv

Multi-truth Discovery with Correlations of Candidates in Crowdsourcing
Systems 18
    Hongyu Huang, Guijun Fan, Yantao Li, and Nankun Mu

D2D-Based Multi-relay-Assisted Computation Offloading in Edge
Computing Network 33
    Xuan Zhao, Song Zhang, Bowen Liu, Xutong Jiang, and Wanchun Dou

Delay-Sensitive Slicing Resources Scheduling Based on Multi-MEC
Collaboration in IoV 50
    Yan Liang, Xin Chen, Shengcheng Ma, and Libo Jiao

An OO-Based Approach of Computing Offloading and Resource
Allocation for Large-Scale Mobile Edge Computing Systems 65
    Yufu Tan, Sikandar Ali, Haotian Wang, and Jiwei Huang

Edge Computing and Collaborative Working

Joint Location-Value Privacy Protection for Spatiotemporal Data
Collection via Mobile Crowdsensing 87
    Tong Liu, Dan Li, Chenhong Cao, Honghao Gao, Chengfan Li,
    and Zhenni Feng

Hybrid Semantic Conflict Prevention in Real-Time Collaborative
Programming 104
    Wenhua Xu, Yiteng Zhang, Brian Chiu, Dong Chen, Jinfeng Jiang,
    Bowen Du, and Hongfei Fan

Supporting Cross-Platform Real-Time Collaborative Programming:
Architecture, Techniques, and Prototype System 124
    Yifan Ma, Zichao Yang, Brian Chiu, Yiteng Zhang, Jinfeng Jiang,
    Bowen Du, and Hongfei Fan

Collaborative Computing Based on Truthful Online Auction Mechanism
in Internet of Things 144
  Bilian Wu, Xin Chen, and Libo Jiao

A Hashgraph-Based Knowledge Sharing Approach for Mobile Robot
Swarm 158
  Xiao Shu, Bo Ding, Jie Luo, Xiang Fu, Min Xie, and Zhen Li

Collaborative Working and Deep Learning and Application

CASE: Predict User Behaviors via Collaborative Assistant Sequence
Embedding Model 175
  Fei He, Canghong Jin, and Minghui Wu

A Collaborative Optimization-Guided Entity Extraction Scheme 190
  *Qiaojuan Peng, Xiong Luo, Hailun Shen, Ziyang Huang,
  and Maojian Chen*

A Safe Topological Waypoints Searching-Based Conservative Adaptive
Motion Planner in Unknown Cluttered Environment 206
  *Jiachi Xu, Jiefu Tan, Chao Xue, Yaqianwen Su, Xionghui He,
  and Yongjun Zhang*

Multi-D3QN: A Multi-strategy Deep Reinforcement Learning for Service
Composition in Cloud Manufacturing 225
  Jun Zeng, Juan Yao, Yang Yu, and Yingbo Wu

Transfer Knowledge Between Cities by Incremental Few-Shot Learning 241
  Jiahao Wang, Wenxiong Li, Xiuxiu Qi, and Yuheng Ren

Deep Learning and Application

Multi-view Representation Learning with Deep Features for Offline
Signature Verification 261
  *Xingbiao Zhao, Changzheng Liu, Benzhuang Zhang, Limengzi Yuan,
  and Yuchen Zheng*

Backdoor Attack of Graph Neural Networks Based on Subgraph Trigger 276
  Yu Sheng, Rong Chen, Guanyu Cai, and Li Kuang

A UniverApproCNN with Universal Approximation and Explicit Training
Strategy 297
  Yin Yang, Yifeng Wang, and Senqiao Yang

MS-BERT: A Multi-layer Self-distillation Approach for BERT
Compression Based on Earth Mover's Distance 316
  Jiahui Huang, Bin Cao, Jiaxing Wang, and Jing Fan

Smart Contract Vulnerability Detection Based on Dual Attention Graph
Convolutional Network 335
  Yuqi Fan, Siyuan Shang, and Xu Ding

Crowdturfing Detection in Online Review System: A Graph-Based
Modeling 352
  Qilong Feng, Yue Zhang, and Li Kuang

Attention-Aware Actor for Cooperative Multi-agent Reinforcement
Learning 370
  Chenran Zhao, Dianxi Shi, Yaowen Zhang, Yaqianwen Su,
  Yongjun Zhang, and Shaowu Yang

Geographic and Temporal Deep Learning Method for Traffic Flow
Prediction in Highway Network 385
  Tianpu Zhang, Weilong Ding, Mengda Xing, Jun Chen, Yongkang Du,
  and Ying Liang

How are You Affected? A Structural Graph Neural Network Model
Predicting Individual Social Influence Status 401
  Jiajie Du and Li Pan

Multi-order Proximity Graph Structure Embedding 416
  Wang Zhang, Lei Jiang, Huailiang Peng, Qiong Dai, and Xu Bai

Deep Learning and Application and UVA

PATR: A Novel Poisoning Attack Based on Triangle Relations Against
Deep Learning-Based Recommender Systems 435
  Meiling Chao, Min Gao, Junwei Zhang, Zongwei Wang, Quanwu Zhao,
  and Yulin He

Low-Cost LiDAR-Based Vehicle Detection for Self-driving Container
Trucks at Seaport 451
  Changjie Zhang, Zhenchao Ouyang, Lu Ren, and Yu Liu

Author Index 467

Contents – Part I

Optimization for Collaborate System (Workshop Papers)

Chinese Named Entity Recognition Based on Dynamically Adjusting
Feature Weights 3
   Qing Lv, Limin Zheng, and Miao Wang

Location Differential Privacy Protection in Task Allocation for Mobile
Crowdsensing Over Road Networks 20
   Mohan Fang, Juan Yu, Jianmin Han, Xin Yao, Hao Peng, Jianfeng Lu,
   and Ngounou Bernard

"Failure" Service Pattern Mining for Exploratory Service Composition 38
   Yunjing Yuan, Jing Wang, Yanbo Han, Qianwen Li, Gaojian Chen,
   and Boyang Jiao

Optimal Control and Reinforcement Learning for Robot: A Survey 54
   Haodong Feng, Lei Yu, and Yuqing Chen

KTOBS: An Approach of Bayesian Network Learning Based on K-tree
Optimizing Ordering-Based Search 67
   Qingwang Zhang, Sihang Liu, Ruihong Xu, Zemeng Yang,
   and Jianxiao Liu

Recommendation Model Based on Social Homogeneity Factor and Social
Influence Factor 83
   Weizhi Ying, Qing Yu, and Zuohua Wang

Attention Based Spatial-Temporal Graph Convolutional Networks
for RSU Communication Load Forecasting 99
   Hang Zheng, Xu Ding, Yang Wang, and Chong Zhao

UVA and Traffic System

Mobile Encrypted Traffic Classification Based on Message Type Inference 117
   Yige Chen, Tianning Zang, Yongzheng Zhang, Yuan Zhou, and Peng Yang

Fine-Grained Spatial-Temporal Representation Learning with Missing
Data Completion for Traffic Flow Prediction 138
   Shiqi Wang, Min Gao, Zongwei Wang, Jia Wang, Fan Wu, and Junhao Wen

Underwater Information Sensing Method Based on Improved
Dual-Coupled Duffing Oscillator Under Lévy Noise Description   156
  Hanwen Zhang, Zhen Qin, and Dajiang Chen

Unpaired Learning of Roadway-Level Traffic Paths from Trajectories   171
  Weixing Jia, Guiling Wang, Xuankai Yang, and Fengquan Zhang

Multi-UAV Cooperative Exploring for the Unknown Indoor Environment
Based on Dynamic Target Tracking   191
  Ning Li, Jiefu Tan, Yunlong Wu, Jiachi Xu, Huan Wang, and Wendi Wu

Recommendation System

MR-FI: Mobile Application Recommendation Based on Feature
Importance and Bilinear Feature Interaction   213
  Mi Peng, Buqing Cao, Junjie Chen, Jianxun Liu, and Rong Hu

The Missing POI Completion Based on Bidirectional Masked Trajectory
Model   229
  Jun Zeng, Yizhu Zhao, Yang Yu, Min Gao, and Wei Zhou

Dual-Channel Graph Contextual Self-Attention Network for Session-Based
Recommendation   244
  Teng Huang, Huiqun Yu, and Guisheng Fan

Context-aware Graph Collaborative Recommendation Without Feature
Entanglement   259
  Tianyi Gu, Ping Li, and Kaiwen Huang

Improving Recommender System via Personalized Reconstruction
of Reviews   277
  *Zunfu Huang, Bo Wang, Hongtao Liu, Qinxue Jiang, Naixue Xiong,
  and Yuexian Hou*

Recommendation System and Network and Security

Dynamic Traffic Network Based Multi-Modal Travel Mode Fusion
Recommendation   299
  *Nannan Jia, Mengmeng Chang, Zhiming Ding, Zunhao Liu,
  Bowen Yang, Lei Yuan, and Lutong Li*

Improving Personalized Project Recommendation on GitHub Based
on Deep Matrix Factorization   318
  Huan Yang, Song Sun, Junhao Wen, Haini Cai, and Muhammad Mateen

An Intelligent SDN DDoS Detection Framework 333
  Xiang Zhang, Chaokui Zhang, Zhenyang Zhong, and Peng Ye

Inspector: A Semantics-Driven Approach to Automatic Protocol Reverse
Engineering 348
  *Yige Chen, Tianning Zang, Yongzheng Zhang, Yuan Zhou, Peng Yang,
  and Yipeng Wang*

MFF-AMD: Multivariate Feature Fusion for Android Malware Detection 368
  *Guangquan Xu, Meiqi Feng, Litao Jiao, Jian Liu, Hong-Ning Dai,
  Ding Wang, Emmanouil Panaousis, and Xi Zheng*

Network and Security

PSG: Local Privacy Preserving Synthetic Social Graph Generation 389
  Hongyu Huang, Yao Yang, and Yantao Li

Topology Self-optimization for Anti-tracking Network via Nodes
Distributed Computing 405
  Changbo Tian, Yongzheng Zhang, and Tao Yin

An Empirical Study of Model-Agnostic Interpretation Technique
for Just-in-Time Software Defect Prediction 420
  *Xingguang Yang, Huiqun Yu, Guisheng Fan, Zijie Huang, Kang Yang,
  and Ziyi Zhou*

Yet Another Traffic Black Hole: Amplifying CDN Fetching Traffic
with RangeFragAmp Attacks 439
  Chi Xu, Juanru Li, and Junrong Liu

DCNMF: Dynamic Community Discovery with Improved Convex-NMF
in Temporal Networks 460
  Limengzi Yuan, Yuxian Ke, Yujian Xie, Qingzhan Zhao, and Yuchen Zheng

Network and Security and IoT and Social Networks

Loopster++: Termination Analysis for Multi-path Linear Loop 479
  Hui Jin, Weimin Ge, Yao Zhang, Xiaohong Li, and Zhidong Deng

A Stepwise Path Selection Scheme Based on Multiple QoS Parameters
Evaluation in SDN 498
  Lin Liu, Jian-Tao Zhou, Hai-Feng Xing, and Xiao-Yong Guo

A Novel Approach to Taxi-GPS-Trace-Aware Bus Network Planning 520
  Liangyao Tang, Peng Chen, Ruilong Yang, Yunni Xia, Ning Jiang,
  Yin Li, and Hong Xie

Community Influence Maximization Based on Flexible Budget in Social
Networks 534
  Mengdi Xiao, Peng Li, Weiyi Huang, Junlei Xiao, and Lei Nie

An Online Truthful Auction for IoT Data Trading with Dynamic Data
Owners 554
  Zhenni Feng, Junchang Chen, and Tong Liu

**IoT and Social Networks and Images Handling and Human
Recognition**

Exploiting Heterogeneous Information for IoT Device Identification Using
Graph Convolutional Network 575
  Jisong Yang, Yafei Sang, Yongzheng Zhang, Peng Chang,
  and Chengwei Peng

Data-Driven Influential Nodes Identification in Dynamic Social Networks 592
  Ye Qian and Li Pan

Human Motion Recognition Based on Wi-Fi Imaging 608
  Liangliang Lin, Kun Zhao, Xiaoyu Ma, Wei Xi, Chen Yang, Hui He,
  and Jizhong Zhao

A Pervasive Multi-physiological Signal-Based Emotion Classification
with Shapelet Transformation and Decision Fusion 628
  Shichao Zhang, Xiangwei Zheng, Mingzhe Zhang, Gengyuan Guo,
  and Cun Ji

A Novel and Efficient Distance Detection Based on Monocular Images
for Grasp and Handover 642
  Dianwen Liu, Pengfei Yi, Dongsheng Zhou, Qiang Zhang,
  Xiaopeng Wei, Rui Liu, and Jing Dong

Images Handling and Human Recognition and Edge Computing

A Novel Gaze-Point-Driven HRI Framework for Single-Person 661
  Wei Li, Pengfei Yi, Dongsheng Zhou, Qiang Zhang, Xiaopeng Wei,
  Rui Liu, and Jing Dong

Semi-automatic Segmentation of Tissue Regions in Digital
Histopathological Image 678
  Xin He, Kairun Chen, and Mengning Yang

T-UNet: A Novel TC-Based Point Cloud Super-Resolution Model
for Mechanical LiDAR 697
  Lu Ren, Deyi Li, Zhenchao Ouyang, Jianwei Niu, and Wen He

Computation Offloading for Multi-user Sequential Tasks in Heterogeneous
Mobile Edge Computing 713
  Huanhuan Xu, Jingya Zhou, and Fei Gu

Model-Based Evaluation and Optimization of Dependability for Edge
Computing Systems 728
  Jingyu Liang, Bowen Ma, Sikandar Ali, and Jiwei Huang

Author Index 749

Edge Computing

Energy-Efficient Cooperative Offloading for Multi-AP MEC in IoT Networks

Zhihui Cao[1], Haifeng Sun[1(✉)] ⓘ, Ning Zhang[2], and Xiang Lv[1]

[1] School of Computer Science and Technology,
Southwest University of Science and Technology, Mianyang 621010, China
[2] University of Windsor, Windsor, Canada

Abstract. Mobile Edge Computing (MEC) technology is used for offloading local application tasks on Mobile Devices (MDs) to the edge server to decrease task processing time and reduce energy consumption in Internet of Things (IoTs) networks. In this paper, we investigate a scenario consisting of a local MD adjacent with a group of other MDs, one of which can act as the offloading cooperator. All the MDs are surrounded by multiple Access Points (APs), and each AP is deployed an MEC server providing abundant computation resources. Based on this scenario, we propose a cooperative energy-efficient offloading scheme under delay constraint. The local MD can offload part of the application task to a cooperative relay MD or the MEC server, and the relay MD can also offload part of the segment to an AP. By solving the proposed energy-efficient cooperative offloading problem under the constraint of computing delay, the most energy-efficient cooperative offloading MD and the AP as well as the task segmentation to minimize the energy consumption are determined. Numerical analysis shows that our proposed scheme significantly outperforms the benchmark schemes in the aspect of energy consumption and the supported task length in maximum.

Keywords: Mobile Edge Computing · Cooperative offloading · Multiple-AP · Energy efficient

1 Introduction

The continuous development of Internet of Things (IoTs) technology in the fifth generation (5G) communication systems has boosted an impact on a variety of applications in different fields. The IoT integrating people's lives and work, has a huge impact on the world economy, military, politics, culture and other aspects, and makes people's way of life change dramatically. The future world will be interconnected and globally intelligent [11]. Industrial IoT applications are in the explosive growth stage, on the other hand the computing power and latency feedback required by these applications are extremely strict and require a certain

This work was supported in part by the Applied Basic Research Programs of Science & Technology Committee Foundation of Sichuan Province (2019YJ0309).

amount of massive application resources to handle computation-intensive application tasks. At present, the high-performance Central Processing Unit (CPU) chips on the terminal devices keep on constantly being updated, but still can't meet the requirement of dealing the huge application tasks under a limited delay constraint. The quite finite battery life of the Mobile Device (MD) is also a difficult problem to solve today. The energy consumption required by a large number of computing undoubtedly shortens the working time of the MD, which greatly affects the user experience [2]. Cloud computing can transfer the application tasks to the servers in the cloud center [16]. However, a large number of MDs in different area locations will cause heavy bandwidth load and high transmission delay, which makes cloud computing incompetent for the delay-sensitive applications.

Mobile Edge Computing (MEC) is a promising technology. In recent years, mobile computing has been shifting from centralized cloud computing to MEC, driven by 5G communication technologies. The main feature of MEC is offloading computation-intensive and high-latency constraint application data to the edge of the network near the MD, as well as reducing the pressure on the cloud-centric server, which significantly reduces energy consumption and computing latency at MDs [9].

In the MEC-based IoT network, we consider a scenario of an MD adjacent with many other MDs, one of which can act as the offloading cooperator. All the MDs are surrounded by a group of Access Points (APs), and each AP is deployed an MEC server providing abundant computation resources. It is of great significance to select a neighboring MD as the offloading relay to optimize the energy consumption in the whole task computing process with delay constraints [10]. In some cases, an application task is supported to be divided into several segments in different sizes, so we can select multiple adjacent relay MDs for offloading. But there are other cases where the application task is indivisible, or only supported to be divided into limited number of segments, so we can select a most energy-efficient relay MD for cooperative offloading. According to some research results that not all the task offloading can save energy [7]. Communication links, communication modes and so on can all affect the energy consumption. If an MD has a long distance from the AP accompanied by poor communication channel, offloading of tasks will use further energy than processing them locally. However, some studies have shown that the use of cooperative offloading by relay MDs can save communication energy [17].

We propose an efficient cooperative task offloading scheme for multi-AP MEC under delay constraint in the IoT network. By selecting an appropriate relay MD and the AP as well as the task segmentation for cooperative task offloading, the energy consumption of the whole task computing process is minimized. For this purpose, we first setup the system model, then we present the task offloading process with the relay MD. Next, we give the computation latency and energy consumption for each process on the local MD, the relay MD as well as the MEC server, respectively. Therefore we get a minimum energy consumption optimization problem in total for the whole process of task computing and offloading, prove the problem is convex and solve it by the convex optimization toolbox CVX [4]. Finally, the conducted simulation results indicate the proposed scheme outperforms the benchmark schemes. The contribution of this paper is summarized below.

1) We consider a multi-AP offloading scenario that a local MD is adjacent with a group of other MDs, one of which can act as the offloading cooperator. All the MDs are surrounded by some APs, and each AP is deployed an MEC server with abundant computation resources. An application task can be partitioned into finite segments, and one adjacent MD can be selected as the collaborative offloading relay MD.
2) A scheme is proposed with energy-efficient cooperative task offloading for multi-AP MEC under delay constraint in IoT networks. The scheme minimizes the energy consumption under delay constraint by selecting the appropriate relay MD and the AP for cooperative task offloading.
3) By solving the optimization problem, the selection of the relay MD and the AP as well as the task segmentation were determined. A large number of numerical experimental results verified the advantages of our proposed scheme.

The rest of this paper is described as follows. In Sect. 2, we review MEC works in the MEC-based IoT. Section 3 presents the system model. Section 4 formulates the delay constrained energy minimization problem and presents the optimal solutions. Section 5 performs the numerical experiments. We conclude our work in Sect. 6.

2   Related Work

MEC can effectively reduce computing latency in computation-intensive applications. When processed by local MDs, delay sensitive tasks have to take a lot of time to wait, and the user demand is not satisfied [20]. Most of today's MDs are hardly to meet the computing requirements of a large number of delay-sensitive applications. The traditional method is to offload the application tasks to the cloud center server for computing. However, faced with numerous IoT devices, the cloud center server bears too much pressure, which greatly increases the task transmission time and computing latency. But in the MEC mode, the offloading of application tasks to the network edge for computing reduces the pressure at the cloud-centric server, solves the problem of high task transmission delay, and attracts widespread concern in academia and industry [19].

Some studies have shown that co-offloading can help reduce energy consumption compared with direct offloading. Baidas et al. maximized the network and offloading efficiency of all user clusters through power allocation and computing resource allocation [1]. Sun et al. introduced a scenario where an MD is surrounded by multiple MDs and an AP integrated with an MEC server, and proposed an optimal neighbor aided cooperative offloading scheme [15]. Li et al. proposed an artificial intelligence (AI) based single AP collaborative offloading computing approach to determine the task offloading, computing, and result delivery policy [8]. Wei *et al.* studied single AP partial offloading of application tasks. The authors in [18] proposed an energy-saving optimization problem of MDs with separable tasks, and solved it using greedy algorithm. Pan *et al.* proposed an iterative algorithm implemented by successive convex approximation, and got the task offloading partition and time allocation [13]. But these works only support one AP scenario. Fan *et al.* investigated the cooperations of multiple mobile edge computing enabled-base station (MEC-BS), and proposed a novel scheme to enhance the computation offloading service of a MEC-BS through further offloading the extra tasks to other MEC-BSs connected to it [3], but this work did not consider cooperative offloading. Different from previous works, we investigate the scenario of an local MD adjacent with a group of other MDs, one of which can act as the offloading cooperator. Some APs randomly locate around, and each AP deployed an MEC server with abundant computation resources. The optimization problem with minimized energy consumption in the multi-AP offloading process, the selection of the offloading cooperator and APs, as well as the optimized task segmentation were solved.

3   System Model

In this section, firstly we set up an application scenario in the IoT network. Then, the delay constraint and energy consumption of an MD in local processing, relay MD processing and MEC server processing phases are respectively explored. Because of the particularity of application tasks, we consider tasks can be divided only into limited segments, and only one MD can be selected as a cooperative offloading assistant.

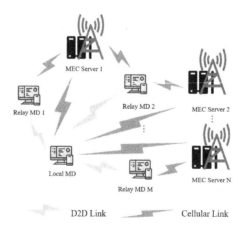

Fig. 1. System model.

As shown in Fig. 1, we set up a local MD u adjacent to multiple MDs $\mathcal{M} = \{1, 2, \ldots, M\}$, one of which can act as an relay MD $m_i, i \in \mathcal{M}$ to help the local MD u offload application tasks to the randomly surrounded APs $\mathcal{N} = \{1, 2, \ldots, N\}$, each one deployed an MEC server, which provides a abundant of computing resources. The offloading collaborative MD m_i can computing the offloaded segment locally, or select one AP $s_j, j \in \mathcal{N}$ deployed with an MEC server for offloading the sub-segment through cellular links. On the other hand, the task segment in the local MD u can also be directly offloaded to the AP $s_k, k \in \mathcal{N}$ through cellular links. In summary, each segment of the task can be processed on the local MD, the relay MD and the MEC server, separately [12]. The D2D link is used to transmit the offloading data between MDs. After the task computing is completed, the result will be returned to the local MD. Each MD can request the cooperative offloading, and we can consider the scenario of one task cooperative offloading.

In this network, we consider that cellular links as well as D2D links are deployed at different frequencies, so that all nodes do not affect each other when transferring data. We assume that the channel follows the decline of quasi-static blocks. In other words, during the offloading of a task segment, the channel state keeps constant [6]. In addition, due to the short length of the result, the delay and energy consumption of the result feedback are not considered.

We denote the application task length as $L > 0$, and the delay constraint as $T \geq 0$. For the total task length L of applications, it can be divided into four different segments. Let $l_u \geq 0, l_u^{s_k} \geq 0, l_u^{m_i} \geq 0$ and $l_{m_i}^{s_j} \geq 0$ represent the length of the computing segment at the local MD u, offloading from u to the AP s_k, offloading from u to the relay MD m_i, and offloading from m_i to the AP s_j, respectively. Then we have

$$L = l_u + l_u^{s_k} + l_u^{m_i} + l_{m_i}^{s_j}. \tag{1}$$

In particular, the task segment performed on the relay MD m_i is $l_u^{m_i}$, and the task segment $l_{m_i}^{s_j}$ is offloaded from m_i to the MEC server s_j, so the total task segment length that is offloaded from the local MD u to the relay MD m_i is $l_u^{m_i} + l_{m_i}^{s_j}$.

The whole process of task computing and offloading in the model include three phases. The first is the local processing phase, the second is the relay MD cooperative offloading processing phase, and the third is the MEC server processing phase. We will explore the computing delay, the offloading delay, together with energy consumption at each phase in detail.

3.1 Local Processing Phase

The local processing phase includes the self-computing of segment l_u at the local MD u, offloading one segment $l_u^{s_k}$ from u to the AP s_k, and offloading one segment $l_u^{m_i} + l_{m_i}^{s_j}$ from u to the relay MD m_i.

Local Computing. During the local processing phase, the segment of l_u will be executed on the local MD. Let c_u represent the number of local MD CPU cycles used for each bit, f_u represent the maximum computing capability (CPU cycles/second) of the local MD CPU. f'_u represent the computing capability required by the local MD for l_u. Then the computing time of l_u is

$$T^C_u = \frac{c_u l_u}{f'_u}. \tag{2}$$

Because the task should be executed under the delay constraint T, the task segment of each phase will be completed within T, namely the processing time T^C_u of l_u need to meet the delay constraint $T \geq T^C_u$. Put Eq. (2) into the constraint and we get $\frac{c_u l_u}{f'_u} \leq T$, and because $f'_u \leq f_u$, we get that the time constraint for the local processing phase is

$$\frac{c_u l_u}{f_u} \leq T. \tag{3}$$

The energy consumption E^C_u for the local MD computing can be described as

$$E^C_u = \gamma_u c_u f'^2_u l_u, \tag{4}$$

where γ_u is the effective CPU capacitance coefficient on the local MD. For achieving the minimum energy consumption at the local MD, we set the computing time T^C_u equal to the delay constraint T, thus we obtain $T = T^C_u = \frac{c_u l_u}{f'_u}$, i.e. $f'_u = \frac{c_u l_u}{T}$. Substituting it into Eq. (4), we get

$$E^C_u = \frac{\gamma_u c^3_u l^3_u}{T^2}. \tag{5}$$

Offloading to the MEC Server for Processing. The local MD offloads part of the task $l^{s_k}_u$ to the MEC server s_k through cellular links, in which the transmission power of the MD is expressed as $P_{u,s_k} \geq 0$. Suppose the channel power gain between them be $h_{u,s_k} \geq 0$, $\sigma^2_{s_k}$ denote the noise power at the AP intergrated with s_k and $\omega_k, k \in \mathcal{N}$ denote the cellular channel bandwidth from the local MD to the AP, so the data transmission rate (bits/second) from the local MD to the MEC server s_k is

$$r(P_{u,s_k}) = \omega_k \log_2 \left(1 + \frac{p_{u,s_k} h_{u,s_k}}{\sigma^2_{s_k}} \right). \tag{6}$$

By Eq. (6), we can get the offloading delay T^O_{u,s_k} and offloading energy consumption E^O_{u,s_k} from the local MD to the MEC server s_k as

$$T^O_{u,s_k} = \frac{l^{s_k}_u}{r(P_{u,s_k})}, \tag{7}$$

$$E^O_{u,s_k} = \frac{P_{u,s_k} l^{s_k}_u}{r(P_{u,s_k})}. \tag{8}$$

Offloading to the Relay MD for Cooperative Processing. The relay MD m_i receives the segment with the length of $l_u^{m_i} + l_{m_i}^{s_j}$ sent by the local MD through D2D links on the transmit power $P_{u,m_i} \geq 0$. Let the channel power gain from the local MD to the relay MD m_i be $h_{u,m_i} \geq 0$, $\sigma_{m_i}^2$ denote the noise power at the relay MD m_i, and $\omega_i, i \in \mathcal{M}$ denote the cellular channel bandwidth from the local MD to the relay MD m_i, then the data transmission rate (bits/second) offloading from the local MD to the relay MD m_i is

$$r\left(P_{u,m_i}\right) = \omega_i \log_2 \left(1 + \frac{p_{u,m_i} h_{u,m_i}}{\sigma_{m_i}^2}\right). \tag{9}$$

From Eq. (9), we can get the offloading delay T_{u,m_i}^O from the MD to the relay MD m_i and the energy consumption E_{u,m_i}^O for offloading as

$$T_{u,m_i}^O = \frac{l_u^{m_i} + l_{m_i}^{s_j}}{r\left(P_{u,m_i}\right)}, \tag{10}$$

$$E_{u,m_i}^O = \frac{P_{u,m_i} \left(l_u^{m_i} + l_{m_i}^{s_j}\right)}{r\left(P_{u,m_i}\right)}. \tag{11}$$

3.2 Relay MD Processing Phase

The relay MD cooperative offloading processing phase consists of two parts, one is the relay MD m_i computing of the segment $l_u^{m_i}$ that is offloaded from the local MD, and the other is the segment $l_{m_i}^{s_j}$ that is offloaded from m_i to the MEC server s_j.

Computing at the Relay MD. Choosing the properly relay MD with minimal energy consumption for offloading is significant [5,14,21]. We use c_{m_i} to represent the number of CPU cycles of each computing bit at the relay MD m_i, f_{m_i} to represent the maximum CPU computing capacity of the relay MD m_i, and f_{m_i}' to represent the computing capacity required by m_i according to the application segment. Thus, the computing delay at the relay MD m_i is

$$T_{u,m_i}^C = \frac{c_{m_i} l_u^{m_i}}{f_{m_i}'}. \tag{12}$$

For the relay MD m_i, the delay constraint includes the offloading delay from the local MD and the segment computing time, so we have

$$T_{u,m_i}^O + T_{u,m_i}^C \leq T. \tag{13}$$

Same as the local processing phase, since $f_{m_i} \geq f_{m_i}'$, substitute Eq. (10) and Eq. (12) into Eq. (13), we obtain the delay constraint of the relay MD m_i as

$$\frac{l_u^{m_i} + l_{m_i}^{s_j}}{r\left(P_{u,m_i}\right)} + \frac{c_{m_i} l_u^{m_i}}{f_{m_i}} \leq T. \tag{14}$$

The energy consumption for computing at the relay MD m_i is

$$E_{m_i}^C = \gamma_{m_i} c_{m_i} f_{m_i}'^2 l_{m_i}, \tag{15}$$

where γ_{m_i} is the effective capacitance coefficient at the CPU of the relay MD m_i. Substitute Eq. (12) into Eq. (15), similar to Eq. (5), we can obtain the energy consumption for computing at the relay MD m_i as

$$E_{m_i}^C = \frac{\gamma_{m_i} c_{m_i}^3 l_u^{m_i}{}^3}{\left(T - T_{u,m_i}^O\right)^2}. \tag{16}$$

Offloading to the MEC Server. The relay MD m_i offloads the segment $l_{m_i}^{s_j}$ through cellular links to the MEC server with sufficient computing resources for computing. Let the transmission power of the relay MD m_i offloading to the AP integrated with an MEC server s_j be $P_{m_i,s_j} \geq 0$, the channel power gain be $h_{m_i,s_j} \geq 0$, the noise power at the AP be $\sigma_{s_j}^2$, and $\omega_j, j \in \mathcal{N}$ denote the cellular channel bandwidth from the relay MD m_i to the AP integrated with an MEC server s_j. Therefore, the data transmission rate (bits/second) from the relay MD m_i to the MEC server s_j is

$$r\left(P_{m_i,s_j}\right) = \omega_j \log_2\left(1 + \frac{p_{m_i,s_j} h_{m_i,s_j}}{\sigma_{s_j}^2}\right). \tag{17}$$

Then, from Eq. (17), we can describe the offloading delay T_{m_i,s_j}^O of the relay MD m_i to the AP integrated with an MEC server s_j and the energy consumption E_{m_i,s_j}^O for offloading as

$$T_{m_i,s_j}^O = \frac{l_{m_i}^{s_j}}{r\left(P_{m_i,s_j}\right)}, \tag{18}$$

$$E_{m_i,s_j}^O = \frac{P_{m_i,s_j} l_{m_i}^{s_j}}{r\left(P_{m_i,s_j}\right)}. \tag{19}$$

3.3   MEC Server Processing Phase

Since the computing result is usually short, we ignore its feed back time from the MEC server to the local MD. The computing resources of the MEC server are strong enough, so we do not consider the energy consumption for computing at the MEC server. Therefore, the MEC server processing phase consists of computing the directly offloaded segment from the local MD and the indirectly offloaded segment from the relay MD m_i. Let c_s represent the number of CPU cycles used by the MEC server s for each task bit, f_s represent the maximum CPU computing capacity of s, and f_s' represent the computing capacity required by s for the application task. Then the computing delay T_{u,s_k}^C for the directly offloaded segment from the local MD and the computing delay T_{m_i,s_j}^C for the indirectly offloaded segment form the relay MD at the MEC server s can be described as

$$T^C_{u,s_k} = \frac{c_{s_k} l^{s_k}_u}{f'_{s_k}}, \tag{20}$$

$$T^C_{m_i,s_j} = \frac{c_{s_j} l^{s_j}_{m_i}}{f'_{s_j}}. \tag{21}$$

The delay constraint for the directly offloaded segment on the MEC server includes the offloading delay from the local MD and the computing delay at the MEC server. Then, we have

$$T^O_{u,s_k} + T^C_{u,s_k} \leq T. \tag{22}$$

The delay constraint for the indirectly offloaded segment includes the offloading delay from the local MD to the relay MD and then to the MEC server, as well as the computing delay at the MEC server. Then we get

$$T^O_{u,m_i} + T^O_{m_i,s_j} + T^C_{m_i,s_j} \leq T. \tag{23}$$

Substitute Eq. (7) and Eq. (20) into Eq. (22), and substitute Eq. (10), Eq. (12), Eq. (18) and Eq. (21) into Eq. (23), so we get

$$\frac{l^{s_k}_u}{r\left(P_{u,s_k}\right)} + \frac{c_{s_k} l^{s_k}_u}{f_{s_k}} \leq T, \tag{24}$$

$$\frac{l^{m_i}_u + l^{s_j}_{m_i}}{r\left(P_{u,m_j}\right)} + \frac{l^{s_j}_{m_i}}{r\left(P_{m_i,s_j}\right)} + \frac{c_{s_j} l^{s_j}_{m_i}}{f_{s_j}} \leq T. \tag{25}$$

4   Problem Formulation and Optimal Solution

In this section, we pursue the energy-efficient problem in the process of AP selection and relay selection as well as the task segmentation in an IoT network based on MEC under delay constraint. We also propose and solve the supported maximum task length problem in the scenario.

4.1   Energy Efficient Problem and Optimal Solution

We use $\theta_i = \{0, 1\}$ to represent the single selected offloading relay MD m_i by the local MD, $\theta_j = \{0, 1\}$ to represent the single selected AP s_j by the relay MD, and $\theta_k = \{0, 1\}$ to represent the single selected AP s_k by the local MD for direct offloading, thus we have

$$\sum_{i=1}^M \theta_i = 1, \sum_{j=1}^N \theta_j = 1, \sum_{k=1}^N \theta_k = 1. \tag{26}$$

The process of energy consumption is mainly consist of the following parts: the local MD computing, a relay MD m_i computing, the local MD offloading to the relay MD m_i, the local MD offloading to the AP s_k, and the relay MD offloading to the AP s_j. Let E represent the total energy consumption generated in the whole process, so we have

$$E = E_u^C + \sum_{i=1}^{M}\sum_{j=1}^{N}\sum_{k=1}^{N}\left(\theta_i\left(E_{u,m_i}^O + E_{m_i}^C\right) + \theta_k E_{u,s_k}^O + \theta_j E_{m,s_j}^O\right). \tag{27}$$

Substitute Eq. (5), Eq. (8), Eq. (10), Eq. (11), Eq. (16) and Eq. (19) into Eq. (27) then we get

$$E = \frac{\gamma_u c_u^3 l_u^3}{T^2}$$
$$+ \sum_{i=1}^{M}\sum_{j=1}^{N}\sum_{k=1}^{N}\theta_i\left(\frac{P_{u,m_i}\left(l_u^{m_i} + l_{m_i}^{s_j}\right)}{r\left(P_{u,m_i}\right)} + \frac{r\left(P_{u,s_k}\right)^2 \gamma_{m_i} c_{m_i}^3 l_u^{m_i^3}}{\left(Tr\left(P_{u,m_i}\right) - \left(l_u^{m_i} + l_{m_i}^{s_j}\right)\right)^2}\right) \tag{28}$$
$$+ \theta_k \frac{P_{u,s_k} l_u^{s_k}}{r\left(P_{u,s_k}\right)} + \theta_j \frac{P_{m_i,s_j} l_{m_i}^{s_j}}{r\left(P_{m_i,s_j}\right)}.$$

By designing a variable of the local MD's task partition vector $l \triangleq [l_u, l_u^{s_k}, l_u^{m_i}, l_{m_i}^{s_j}]$, the energy minimization problem can be expressed as

$$(P1): \min_{l,i,j,k} E$$

$$\text{s.t. } T \geq 0,$$
$$l_u \geq 0, l_u^{s_k} \geq 0, l_u^{m_i} \geq 0, l_{m_i}^{s_j} \geq 0, \tag{29}$$
$$\theta_i = \{0,1\}, \theta_j = \{0,1\}, \theta_k = \{0,1\},$$
$$(1),(3),(14),(24),(25) \text{ and } (26).$$

In problem $(P1)$, $\frac{P_{u,m_i}\left(l_u^{m_i}+l_{m_i}^{s_j}\right)}{r\left(P_{u,m_i}\right)} + \frac{P_{u,s_k} l_u^{s_k}}{r\left(P_{u,s_k}\right)} + \frac{P_{m_i,s_j} l_{m_i}^{s_j}}{r\left(P_{m_i,s_j}\right)}$ is a linear problem. $\frac{l_u^{m_i^3}}{\left(l_u^{m_i}+l_{m_i}^{s_j}\right)^2}$ is convex with $l_u^{m_i} \geq 0$ and $l_u^{m_i} + l_{m_i}^{s_j} \geq 0$, then the term $\frac{r\left(P_{u,s_k}\right)^2 \gamma_{m_i} c_{m_i}^3 l_u^{m_i^3}}{\left(Tr\left(P_{u,m_i}\right)-\left(l_u^{m_i}+l_{m_i}^{s_j}\right)\right)^2}$ in problem $(P1)$ is jointly convex as $l_u^{m_i} \geq 0$ and $\frac{l_u^{m_i}+l_{m_i}^{s_j}}{r(P(u,m_i))} < T$. Therefore, it can be concluded that problem $(P1)$ is a convex problem, which can be solved by the convex optimization toolbox.

According to problem $(P1)$, we can get the minimum value of energy consumption based on the cooperative offloading of relay MDs, solve the values of i, j and k to determine the selection of relay MD and the AP and determine each segment length of the application task.

4.2 Supported Maximum Task Length

In the IoT networks, we define the supported maximum task length as the number of data bits supported most by a task under a given delay constraint T. We then formulate the problem as

$$(P2): \max_{l} l_u + l_u^{s_k} + l_u^{m_i} + l_{m_i}^{s_j}$$

$$\text{s.t. } T \geq 0, \tag{30}$$

$$l_u \geq 0, l_u^{s_k} \geq 0, l_u^{m_i} \geq 0, l_{m_i}^{s_j} \geq 0$$

$$(3), (14), (24) \text{ and} (25).$$

Problem $(P2)$ is linear that can be solved effectively through standard convex optimization techniques when m_i, s_j and s_k are confirmed by problem $(P1)$.

5 Numerical Analysis

In this section, we propose two benchmark schemes for comparison with our cooperative offloading scheme through numerical experiments. Our benchmark schemes include

1) Local computing only: The local MD will finish all task computing. From Eq. (3), the maximum application task of the local MD can be described as $\frac{f_u T}{c_u}$. From Eq. (5), the energy consumption of the local MD is $E_u^C = \frac{\gamma_u c_u^3 l_u^3}{T^2}$.

2) Direct offloading: The local MD offloads application tasks directly to the MEC server without the help of the relay MD. Like our proposed cooperative offloading scheme, this scheme maximizes the task length and minimizes the energy consumption by setting $l_u^{m_i} + l_{m_i}^{s_j} = 0$ to solve problem $(P1)$ and problem $(P2)$.

In the numerical experiment, we set a spatial Cartesian coordinate system with a range of $(0 \leq x \leq 500, 0 \leq y \leq 300, 0 \leq z \leq 200)$, and randomly placed a group of relay MDs and a group of AP nodes at different positions in the system. Set the location of the local MD at $(300, 100, 100)$, and randomly place 200 relay MDs and 5 AP nodes in the system.

In order to facilitate the processing of numerical experimental results, we set $\omega_i = \omega_j = \omega_k = 1\,\text{MHz}$, $\sigma_{m_i}^2 = \sigma_{s_j}^2 = \sigma_{s_k}^2 = -70\,\text{dBm}$, $c_u = c_{m_i} = c_{s_j} = c_{s_k} = 10^3\,\text{cycles/bit}$, $P_{u,m_i} = P_{u,s_k} = P_{m_i,s_j} = 40\,\text{dBm}$, $\gamma_u = \gamma_{m_i} = 10^{-26}$, $f_u = f_{m_i} = 1\,\text{GHz}$ and $f_{s_j} = f_{s_k} = 5\,\text{GHz}$. In addition, we assume that the distance from node A to node B is represented by x, and the path loss is $\beta_0 = -60\,\text{db}$ corresponding to the reference distance $x_0 = 10\,\text{m}$, then the path-loss between two MDs is $\beta_0 (x/x_0)^{-\zeta}$, where $\zeta = 3$ is the path-loss exponent [15].

Figure 2 shows the relationship of the supported maximum task length in average versus delay constraint. As the delay constraint increases, so does the maximum length of the corresponding computational task. The supported maximum task length of our proposed scheme is much longer than the other two schemes because the relay MD can help offloading more additional data bits of the task especially for longer delay constraint. Compared with the direct offloading scheme, the local computing only scheme supports less data with the same delay constraint. While the length of the input task exceeds the maximum length, the task will not be completed within the delay constraint, which means that the longer the supported maximum length by the proposed cooperative offloading scheme with the local MD, the greater the computing capacities it has.

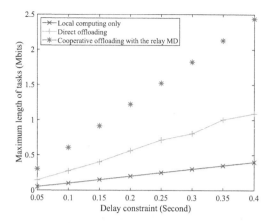

Fig. 2. Supported maximum task length versus the delay constraint T.

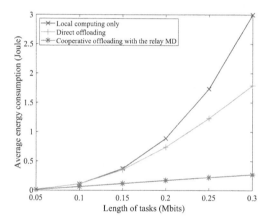

Fig. 3. Average energy consumption under different task length.

Figure 3 shows the relationship between the task length and the average energy consumption under the delay constraint T is set to be $0.3s$. Experimental results show the average energy consumption increases when the application task length becomes longer. By selecting an optimal relay MD, the energy consumption of the proposed scheme significantly outperforms the other two benchmark schemes under different task length. When the input application task is smaller, it will not occupy too much computing resources of the device because tasks will be done at lower CPU frequency, and the performance of the local computing only scheme is similar with other solutions. But the local computing only scheme consumes more energy as the input task length of the application increases, due to the increase of CPU execution frequency. Our proposed scheme consumes relatively much less energy because part of the task can be offloaded to its relay MD and MEC servers for execution.

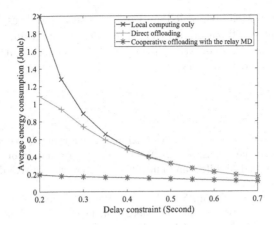

Fig. 4. Average energy consumption under different delay constraints.

Figure 4 shows the relationship between the average minimum energy and the delay constraint when the application task is $L = 0.02$ Mbits. The experimental results show that the energy consumption decreases with the increase of time constraints, which means that the shorter time of the delay constraint, the greater energy consumed by the computation task. Compared with the benchmark schemes, our proposed scheme has the smallest energy consumption at each delay constraint setting, while the local computing only scheme has the largest energy consumption for all tasks are placed on the local MD. However, with the increase of delay constraint, the energy consumption of the three schemes gradually tends to the same scale. When the delay constraint $T = 0.45$ s, the energy consumption of the benchmark schemes gradually becomes the same, because the time constraint becomes loose. Especially when $T = 0.7$ s, the energy consumption of the three schemes differs little, which suggests that our proposed scheme is quite suitable at the condition of strict delay constraint.

6   Conclusions

In this paper, we propose a cooperative energy-efficient offloading scheme under delay constraint for multi-AP MEC in IoT networks. We consider a scenario of a local MD adjacent with many other MDs, one of which can act as the offloading cooperator of the local MD. All the MDs are surrounded by a group of APs, and each AP is deployed an MEC server with abundant computing resources. After building the system model, the computing time, the offloading delay and the energy consumption of local MD processing, relay MD cooperative offloading processing together with the MEC server processing are presented as well. By solving the derived energy-efficient cooperative offloading problem under delay constraint, we can select the most energy-efficient neighbor MD as a relay MD as well as the AP to minimize total energy consumption for task processing. In addition, we formulate and solve a maximum application task length problem that is supported in MEC-based IoT networks. Experimental results confirm the proposed cooperative offloading scheme under delay constraint achieves better performance than the benchmark schemes with less energy consumption while supports longer application tasks.

References

1. Baidas, M.W.: Offloading-efficiency maximization for mobile edge computing in clustered NOMA networks. In: 2020 11th IEEE Annual Information Technology, Electronics and Mobile Communication Conference (IEMCON), pp. 101–107 (2020)
2. Chen, Y., Zhang, N., Zhang, Y., Chen, X., Wu, W., Shen, X.S.: TOFFEE: task offloading and frequency scaling for energy efficiency of mobile devices in mobile edge computing. IEEE Trans. Cloud Comput., 1 (2019)
3. Fan, W., Liu, Y., Tang, B., Wu, F., Wang, Z.: Computation offloading based on cooperations of mobile edge computing-enabled base stations. IEEE Access **6**, 22622–22633 (2018)
4. Grant, M.: CVX: Matlab software for disciplined convex programming. http:// cvxr.com/cvx (2008)
5. Guo, S., Liu, J., Yang, Y., Xiao, B., Li, Z.: Energy-efficient dynamic computation offloading and cooperative task scheduling in mobile cloud computing. IEEE Trans. Mob. Comput. **18**(2), 319–333 (2019)
6. Hu, G., Jia, Y., Chen, Z.: Multi-user computation offloading with D2D for mobile edge computing. In: 2018 IEEE Global Communications Conference (GLOBE-COM), pp. 1–6 (2018)
7. Kumar, K., Lu, Y.H.: Cloud computing for mobile users: can offloading computation save energy? Computer **43**(4), 51–56 (2010)
8. Li, M.S., Gao, J., Zhao, L., Shen, X.M.: Deep reinforcement learning for collaborative edge computing in vehicular networks. IEEE Trans. Cogn. Commun. Netw. **6**(4), 1122–1135 (2020)
9. Mao, Y., You, C., Zhang, J., Huang, K., Letaief, K.B.: A survey on mobile edge computing: the communication perspective. IEEE Commun. Surv. Tutorials **19**(4), 2322–2358 (2017)
10. Ning, Z., Dong, P., Kong, X., Xia, F.: A cooperative partial computation offloading scheme for mobile edge computing enabled internet of things. IEEE Internet Things J. **6**(3), 4804–4814 (2019)
11. Niyato, D., Maso, M., Kim, D.I., Xhafa, A., Zorzi, M., Dutta, A.: Practical perspectives on IoT in 5G networks: from theory to industrial challenges and business opportunities. IEEE Commun. Mag. **55**(2), 68–69 (2017)
12. Opadere, J., Liu, Q., Zhang, N., Han, T.: Joint computation and communication resource allocation for energy-efficient mobile edge networks. In: ICC 2019–2019 IEEE International Conference on Communications (ICC), pp. 1–6 (2019)
13. Pan, Y., Chen, M., Yang, Z., Huang, N., Shikh-Bahaei, M.: Energy-efficient NOMA-based mobile edge computing offloading. IEEE Commun. Lett. **23**(2), 310–313 (2019)
14. Saleem, U., Liu, Y., Jangsher, S., Li, Y., Jiang, T.: Mobility-aware joint task scheduling and resource allocation for cooperative mobile edge computing. IEEE Trans. Wireless Commun. **20**(1), 360–374 (2021)

15. Sun, H., Wang, J., Peng, H., Song, L., Qin, M.: Delay constraint energy efficient cooperative offloading in MEC for IoT. In: Gao, H., Wang, X., Iqbal, M., Yin, Y., Yin, J., Gu, N. (eds.) CollaborateCom 2020. LNICST, vol. 349, pp. 671–685. Springer, Cham (2021). https://doi.org/10.1007/978-3-030-67537-0_40
16. Tsai, J.F., Huang, C.H., Lin, M.H.: An optimal task assignment strategy in cloud-fog computing environment. Appl. Sci. 11(4), 1909–2006 (2021)
17. Wang, S., Guo, Y., Zhang, N., Yang, P., Zhou, A., Shen, X.: Delay-aware microservice coordination in mobile edge computing: a reinforcement learning approach. IEEE Trans. Mob. Comput. 20(3), 939–951 (2021)
18. Wei, F., Chen, S., Zou, W.: SCADS: simultaneous computing and distribution strategy for task offloading in mobile-edge computing system. China Commun. 15(11), 149–157 (2018)
19. Xl, A., Liang, Z.B., Ky, C., Ma, D., Yj, E.: A cooperative resource allocation model for IoT applications in mobile edge computing. Comput. Commun. 173, 183–191 (2021)
20. Zhang, N., Wu, R., Yuan, S., Yuan, C., Chen, D.: RAV: relay aided vectorized secure transmission in physical layer security for internet of things under active attacks. IEEE Internet Things J. 6(5), 8496–8506 (2019)
21. Zhang, T., Wen, H., Jie, T., Song, H., Xie, F.: Cooperative jamming secure scheme for IWNs random mobile users aided by edge computing intelligent node selection. IEEE Trans. Industr. Inf. 17(7), 4999–5009 (2021)

Multi-truth Discovery with Correlations of Candidates in Crowdsourcing Systems

Hongyu Huang, Guijun Fan, Yantao Li$^{(\boxtimes)}$, and Nankun Mu

College of Computer Science, Chongqing University, Chongqing 400044, China
yantaoli@cqu.edu.cn

Abstract. In the past decade, crowdsourcing has emerged as a popular internet-based collaborative computing paradigm. In crowdsourcing systems, requesters can ask users ('sources') for true values ('truths') of objects or events. Generally, an object may have multiple truths and sources could provide inconsistent or even conflicting answers ('candidates') about the object. For this scenario, the multi-truth discovery is a promising technique to deal with various candidates provided by different sources. However, most of the existing multi-truth discovery methods ignore the correlation between candidates so that the inferred truth could be different from the ground truth. In order to solve this problem, we propose MTD-CC, a <u>M</u>ulti-<u>T</u>ruth <u>D</u>iscovery with <u>C</u>andidate <u>C</u>orrelations. Specifically, we first design a metric of potential function to measure the correlation between each pair of candidates based on sources' votes and reliabilities. Then, we construct a Markov Random Field (MRF) to represent these correlations. Next, we transform the MRF into a directed graph and cut it based on the Min-cut theorem to infer which candidates are truths. Last, we evaluate the proposed method on both real and synthetic datasets and experimental results demonstrate that the accuracy of MTD-CC outperforms existing solutions.

Keywords: Crowdsourcing systems · Multi-truth discovery · Candidate correlations · Markov random field

1 Introduction

Crowdsourcing, as a popular internet-based collaborative computing paradigm, can utilize the intelligence of internet users to solve some problems that are difficult for machines. At present, there are many successful crowdsourcing platforms, such as Wikipedia, Zhihu and Baidu Zhidao. In crowdsourcing systems, people can raise a question to the public and then obtain its answers according to the responses from different users which are usually called 'data sources' or 'sources'. For examples, a patient may ask other people about his symptoms through crowdsourcing platforms before going to see a doctor, or a traveller may enquire a hotel condition before setting off. After receiving responses from

H. Gao and X. Wang (Eds.): CollaborateCom 2021, LNICST 407, pp. 18–32, 2021.
https://doi.org/10.1007/978-3-030-92638-0_2

sources, the requester can extract some 'candidates' to further infer the true answers or 'truths' of the question. Due to the diversity of sources, however, the extracted candidates are often inconsistent or even conflicting.

A simple but widely used method for aggregating different data is majority voting, where the most frequently voted candidates are regarded as truths. However, this approach ignores the quality of candidates from different sources, which leads to low accuracy of data aggregation. To address this problem, the truth discovery, which infers the truth more efficiently and accurately, has emerged as a hot topic and been applied in many domains [11], such as healthcare [14], knowledge base [1], and crowd sensing [2]. The intuition of truth discovery is that if a source provides accurate candidates frequently, it will be rewarded with high reliability. On the other side, if a candidate is supported by reliable sources, it will be highly inferred as a truth.

Most of the existing truth discovery methods are applied to single-truth scenarios. In real applications, however, it is common that an object has one or more truths, such as the side effects of a medicine, and the authors of a book. There are a few works focusing on the multi-truth discovery problem. Zhao et al. first observe that each source may have two types of errors, i.e., false positive and false negative. Therefore, they model two different aspects of source reliability to improve the accuracy of truth discovery [21]. Lin et al. propose an integrated Bayesian approach incorporating sources' domain expertise and confidence scores of value sets to find possible truths [12]. Fang et al. adopt a graph model that incorporates source relations, object popularity, loose mutual exclusion, and long-tail phenomenon to estimate the truth [4]. The aforementioned approaches assume that candidates are independent, but they might be correlated in real applications and their correlations could be used to further improve the inference accuracy.

Inspired by this observation, we attempt to discover multi-truth from different candidates utilizing their correlations. Therefore, we propose MTD-CC, a Multi-Truth Discovery with Candidate Correlations in this paper. Specifically, we first design a metric of potential function to quantify the correlation of candidates, which satisfies submodularity, i.e., if both candidates are supported or not supported by a source, their correlations will be increased. Then, we utilize an undirected graph model, i.e., the Markov Random Field (MRF), to construct the candidate correlation network. Next, we assign each edge of the MRF with a direction by two additional vertexes, i.e., a source vertex and a sink vertex, and the related directed edges are also added into the network. Last, we cut the network into two partitions based on the Min-cut theorem. The candidates who are connected with the sink vertex are regarded as truths. We finally evaluate MTD-CC on both real and synthetic datasets and the experimental results show that MTD-CC is notably more accurate than baseline methods.

The rest of the paper is organized as follows. Section 2 reviews the state-of-the-art. Section 3 introduces the key concepts of our problem. Section 4 presents MTD-CC in detail. Performance evaluation on real and synthetic datasets is conducted in Sect. 5. Last, we conclude our work in Sect. 6.

2   Related Work

There are state-of-the-art approaches proposed to solving the truth discovery problem and multi-truth discovery problem respectively.

2.1   Truth Discovery

There have been various methods to solve the truth discovery problem. Truth finder is the first work to formulate the truth discovery problem, and it utilizes a Bayesian-based method to compute the source reliability and object truth iteratively [19]. Li *et al.* consider the long-tail phenomenon on source coverage for objects, and confidence interval is used to represent the source reliability [9]. Liu *et al.* employ a probabilistic model to characterize the reliability of sources and propose an user recruitment algorithm, aiming to guarantee the accuracy of results in truth discovery [13]. Zheng *et al.* model the reliability of sources based on the difficulty of objects dynamically to estimate the true value [22].

However, these methods ignore correlations among sources, objects, or answers, which are helpful to improve the performance.

2.2   Truth Discovery with Different Correlations

Different kinds of correlations are often considered in the process of truth discovery. In [17], the authors propose a probabilistic graph model considering object correlations and the correlations among objects can be measured by spatial distance. Li *et al.* study the existence of clusters in sources, and divide clusters based on sources' relative locations [3]. In [18], CTD captures correlations of attributes through life experience. For example, departure time of the flight must precede its landing time. The authors in [10] measures the similarity of answers by capturing key words in different objects.

Nevertheless, the above works ignore correlations between candidates. Therefore, even if we can directly use these methods into multi-truth discovery scenario, the performance is not competitive.

2.3   Multi-truth Discovery

There are a few approaches addressing the multi-truth discovery problem. Wang *et al.* adopt a probabilistic graph model to infer true values and the source reliability and improve the performance by assuming a prior distribution of the truths [16]. In [12,15], the authors propose integrated Bayesian approaches to jointly reason about truths and the source reliability. Wang *et al.* consider the source confidence and finer-grained copy detection [15]. Lin *et al.* take domain expertise of sources into account and assign reasonable scores to value sets [12]. Fang *et al.* utilize a Markov chain to build the relations among sources and incorporate four important implications to achieve better accuracy [4].

We notice that the above approaches assume that candidates are independent so they do not measure the correlation between these candidates. Different from the aforementioned works, we consider the correlation of candidates to further improve the accuracy of multi-truth discovery.

3   Preliminaries

In this section, we first describe the key concepts of the source, candidates, and truths, and then utilize an illustrative example to give an insight understanding of these concepts.

Source. In this work, we regard the source as an entity which provides the information of an object or event. In a crowd-sensing scenario, the source could be a person who takes a sensing task and submits data to the server. In a data analysis scenario, the source could be a website which provides the authors of a book or the symptoms of a disease. Formally, we use $S = \{s_1, s_2, ..., s_N\}$ to represent the set of sources, where N is the total number of sources. Considering the trustworthiness of each source, we use $R = \{r_1, r_2, ..., r_N\}$ to denote sources' reliabilities. A source with higher reliability indicates that the corresponding data are more reliable.

Candidates. Given a certain object, different sources may provide various information about it. We assume that, before truth discovery, the information has been preprocessed by some techniques and thus we can obtain a set of key words or values about the object. For each key word, we define a binary random variable, i.e., candidate, to represent whether it is the true value of the object. Formally, we define $c_i \in \{0, 1\}$ as the ith candidate. Let $c_i = 1$ or simply as c_i^1 indicate that the ith key word related to c_i is a true value, where c_i^0 indicates that it is a false value. Let $C = \{c_1, c_2, ..., c_M\}$ denote the set of candidates, where M is the total number of candidates.

Truths. We assume that each object has one or more true values, i.e., ground truths, which are unknown to us. Based on the data submitted by sources, the goal is to compute the inferred truth, i.e., to infer each c_i is c_i^1 or c_i^0.

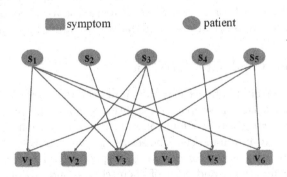

Fig. 1. Five patients report their symptoms about the side effects of a new medicine. Each directed edge represents that a patient has a certain symptom.

Example. We take an example, as shown in Fig. 1 and Table 1, to further illustrate the aforementioned concepts. Supposing we attempt to know the side effects of a new medicine from five patients ($s_1 \sim s_5$), we need to require them to provide their symptoms ($v_1 \sim v_6$) to us. Each patient supports part of the symptoms, e.g., patient s_1 reports symptoms $\{v_1, v_3, v_5, v_6\}$. We assign each symptom to a candidate and convert each patient's report as a vector of candidates, i.e., $<c_1, c_2, c_3, c_4, c_5, c_6>$, where c_i belongs to c_i^0 or c_i^1. Then, we can list each patient's report in Table 1.

Table 1. The binary representation of each patient's report.

Patients	Candidates					
	c_1	c_2	c_3	c_4	c_5	c_6
s_1	1	0	1	0	1	1
s_2	0	0	1	0	0	0
s_3	0	1	1	1	0	0
s_4	0	0	0	0	1	0
s_5	1	0	1	0	0	1

4   The Design of MTD-CC

In this section, we introduce the details of our proposed multi-truth discovery method, MTD-CC. Our method is based on a probabilistic graph model, i.e., the MRF, where each vertex represents a candidate taking value in $\{0, 1\}$. The edges stand for correlations between pairs of candidates. We first design a metric of potential function to measure these correlations. Since we regard each candidate as a random binary variable, the goal is to find an assignment for each candidate so that their joint probability is optimal. To achieve this goal, we convert the MRF into an undirected graph and then separate the graph into two partitions based on the Min-cut theorem, where one partition is assigned with 1 and the other with 0. Last, we regard those candidates with value 1 as truths.

4.1   Metric for Candidate Correlations

To measure the correlation between each pair of candidates, we design the potential function that takes the sources' reliabilities into account. Given two candidates c_j and c_k ($j \neq k$), there are four cases of their combination. Accordingly, we can separate sources into four sets. The set $S_{(x,y)}$, where $x, y \in \{0, 1\}$, has those sources who support x and y for c_j and c_k, respectively. Therefore, there could be four specific functions, and each of them corresponds to one case. Table 2 describes how to compute the potential function for each case.

The intuition of the potential function is that if a source votes two candidates as 1 or 0 simultaneously, we should add its reliability into the correlation. On the contrary, if a source votes two candidates differently, an intermediate weight is reasonable. Moreover, the case with double 1s has more weights than that with double 0s because two positive votes show more significant correlation than negative votes.

Table 2. The potential function $\psi(c_j, c_k)$ of two candidates.

$\psi(c_j^0, c_k^0)$	$\sum_{i \in S_{(0,0)}} (1 - r_i)$
$\psi(c_j^0, c_k^1)$	$\sum_{i \in S_{(0,1)}} 0.5$
$\psi(c_j^1, c_k^0)$	$\sum_{i \in S_{(1,0)}} 0.5$
$\psi(c_j^1, c_k^1)$	$\sum_{i \in S_{(1,1)}} r_i$

4.2   Construction of MRF

MRF is an undirected graphical model, where each vertex depicts a random variable and the edge between them indicates their relation. In our problem, each vertex is a candidate. We define a parameter δ to determine whether two vertexes have an edge. Let $\delta_{j,k} = \psi(c_j^0, c_k^0) + \psi(c_j^1, c_k^1) - \psi(c_j^0, c_k^1) - \psi(c_j^1, c_k^0)$. Two vertexes c_j and c_k are connected with an edge if and only if $\delta_{j,k} > 0$. For two connected vertexes, Table 2 is also used to be the edge potential function of MRF.

Take c_1 and c_3 in Table 1 as an example. We can see that s_1 and s_5 vote two 1s, s_4 votes two 0s, and s_2 and s_3 vote a 1 and a 0. We assume that all sources' reliabilities are equal to 0.6, that is, $\delta_{1,3} = 0.6 + 0.6 + 0.4 - 0.5 - 0.5 = 0.6 > 0$. So we connect c_1 and c_3 with an edge. In this way, using the data in Table 1, we build an MRF which is shown in Fig. 2.

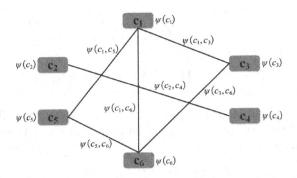

Fig. 2. MRF on a new medicine's side effects based on values provided by patients.

Next, we define the vertex potential function to quantify the extent of how a candidate is supported or opposed by sources. Similar to the edge potential function, we use a table to define the vertex potential function, as shown in Table 3. To compute the potential function for a candidate, e.g., c_j, we first separate sources into two sets by their votes. The sets $S_{(0)}$ and $S_{(1)}$ have those sources whose votes on c_j are 0 and 1, respectively. Then, we use the sum of the square roots of their reliabilities, $\sum_{i \in S_{(0)}} \sqrt{1 - r_i}$ or $\sum_{i \in S_{(1)}} \sqrt{r_i}$, as the $\psi(c_j)$.

Table 3. The potential function $\psi(c_j)$ of a candidate.

$\psi(c_j^0)$	$\sum_{i \in S_{(0)}} \sqrt{1 - r_i}$
$\psi(c_j^1)$	$\sum_{i \in S_{(1)}} \sqrt{r_i}$

We can see that both potential functions of edges and vertexes depend on the sources' reliabilites. Initially, we assume that each source has the same reliability. When obtaining the inferred truths, we can update the sources' reliabilites by Eq. (1), and use them to iteratively infer truths.

$$r_i = g(\frac{\sum_{j \in M} I(c_{i,j}, t_j)}{M}), \tag{1}$$

where $g(\cdot)$ is a monotonically increasing function, and $I(\cdot, \cdot)$ is an indicator function. Parameter $c_{i,j}$ is the binary vote from the ith source for the jth candidate, and t_j represents the inferred truth for the jth candidate. If the vote $c_{i,j}$ agrees with the inferred truth t_j, then $I(c_{i,j}, t_j) = 1$. Otherwise, $I(c_{i,j}, t_j) = 0$. Last, parameter M represents the number of candidates.

4.3 Transformation of MRF

Since we regard candidates as random binary variables, there are 2^M cases of their combinations in total. For each case, we can compute its probability as:

$$P(c_1, ..., c_M) = \frac{1}{Z} \prod_{c_j \in U} \psi(c_j) \prod_{(c_j, c_k) \in E} \psi(c_j, c_k), \tag{2}$$

where 'Z' is a normalized factor:

$$Z = \sum_{c_1, ..., c_M} \prod_{c_j \in U} \psi(c_j) \prod_{(c_j, c_k) \in E} \psi(c_j, c_k). \tag{3}$$

The intuition of our inference approach is to find the most possible truths by maximizing the joint probability. Then we utilize Maximum A Posteriori (MAP) estimation to infer truths T:

$$T = arg \max_{c_1, ..., c_M} P(c_1, ..., c_M) \tag{4}$$

The MAP problem is usually transformed into an energy minimization problem [7], which has two advantages. First, it avoids the numerical problems associated with multiplying a lot of small numbers. More importantly, the multiplication can be transformed into a linear computation. The energy function f is computed as the negative likelihood of the joint probability:

$$f(c_1, ..., c_M) = -\ln(arg \max_{c_1,...,c_M} P(c_1, ..., c_M))$$
$$\propto arg \min_{c_1,...,c_M} \sum_{c_j \in U} \theta(c_j) + \sum_{(c_j, c_k) \in E} \theta(c_j, c_k) \qquad (5)$$

where $\theta(c_j) = -\ln \psi(c_j)$ and $\theta(c_j, c_k) = -\ln \psi(c_j, c_k)$. Obviously, a brute-force algorithm that checks all possible joint assignments is inefficient, and thus we need to find a more efficient inference algorithm.

Our method is inspired by the Min-cut theorem, which is widely used to solve the optimization problem. For energy functions that satisfy graph-representable [8], the Min-cut can guarantee that the optimal solution will be obtained in polynomial time regardless of the number of vertexes and edges. Assume that a directed graph $\hat{G}$ with nonnegative edge weights has two terminals, i.e., a source vertex $\hat{s}$ and a sink vertex $\hat{t}$. When we divide vertexes of the graph into two disjoint subsets $\hat{S}$ and $\hat{T}$, where $\hat{s} \in \hat{S}$ and $\hat{t} \in \hat{T}$, the Min-cut requires that the sum of the edges in the cut set is minimum.

In order to utilize the Min-cut to solve the energy minimization problem, we need to construct a directed graph $\hat{G}(\hat{U}, \hat{E})$, where $\hat{U} = \{c_1, ..., c_M, \hat{s}, \hat{t}\}$ and $\hat{E}$ is transformed from the edges in the MRF. The process includes two steps. First, we design a method to transform each edge in the MRF into a directed one and assign weights. The second step is to add new directed edges with weights between the original vertexes and the added terminal vertexes. After cutting the graph $\hat{G}$ into two disjoint subsets $\hat{S}$ and $\hat{T}$, we assign 0 to vertexes which connect with $\hat{s}$ and 1 to vertexes which connect with $\hat{t}$, respectively.

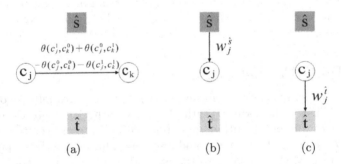

(a)   (b)   (c)

Fig. 3. Transform an MRF into a directed graph. (a) Transform an undirected edge of the MRF into a directed edge. (b) Connect the source vertex $\hat{s}$ with c_j. (c) Connect c_j with the sink vertex $\hat{t}$.

Now we introduce these two steps in detail. First, we consider two candidates c_j and c_k, where $j < k$, connected by an edge in the MRF. We transform the undirected edge to a directed one from c_j to c_k, i.e., (c_j, c_k). The weight of this edge is equal to $\theta(c_j^1, c_k^0) + \theta(c_j^0, c_k^1) - \theta(c_j^0, c_k^0) - \theta(c_j^1, c_k^1)$, as shown in Fig. 3(a).

Second, we investigate how to connect original vertexes with two terminal vertexes. Consider the vertex energy function $\theta(c_j)$. If $\theta(c_j^0) < \theta(c_j^1)$, it indicates that candidate c_j is more likely to be 0. Thus we add an edge $(\hat{s}, c_j)$ from $\hat{s}$ to c_j and record a weight $w_j^{\hat{s}} = \theta(c_j^1) - \theta(c_j^0)$, as is shown in Fig. 3(b). Otherwise, we add edge $(c_j, \hat{t})$ from c_j to $\hat{t}$ and record a weight $w_j^{\hat{t}} = \theta(c_j^0) - \theta(c_j^1)$, as is shown in Fig. 3(c). Furthermore, we notice that the edge energy function also affects the connections between c_j and terminal vertexes. For each edge which goes out from c_j, e.g., (c_j, c_k), $j < k$, we compute $w = \theta(c_j^1, c_k^0) - \theta(c_j^0, c_k^0)$. If $w > 0$, it also indicates that candidate c_j is more likely to be 0. Then we connect $\hat{s}$ with c_j and set the weight as $w_j^{\hat{s}} = w$. If there is already an edge $(\hat{s}, c_j)$, then we update its weight as $w_j^{\hat{s}} = w_j^{\hat{s}} + w$. If $w < 0$, then we connect c_j with $\hat{t}$ and set the weight as $w_j^{\hat{t}} = -w$. Similarly, if there is already an edge $(c_j, \hat{t})$, then we update its weight as $w_j^{\hat{t}} = w_j^{\hat{t}} - w$. For each edge which goes to c_j, e.g., (c_i, c_j), $i < j$, we compute $w = \theta(c_i^1, c_j^1) - \theta(c_i^1, c_j^0)$. We check whether $w > 0$, and repeat the same process as mentioned above.

4.4   Min-cut Based Graph Separation

After we obtain the directed graph, as the last step of our method, we cut the graph to separate vertexes into two partitions. It is proved in literature [5] that the minimum cut problem is equivalent to the maximum flow problem from a source vertex to a sink vertex. In this work, we utilize the widely-used Edmonds-Karp (EK) algorithm [20] to cut the graph. Briefly, EK utilizes Breadth-First-Search (BFS) to find augmented paths iteratively and then updates the weights along the path until there is no new augmented path. When EK stops, we remove all edges whose weights are 0s and all vertexes that can be reached from $\hat{s}$. Last, the remaining vertexes, i.e., candidates that can be reached from $\hat{t}$, are our inferred truths.

4.5   MTD-CC Algorithm

To this end, we summarize the above mentioned procedures into Algorithm 1, named as MTD-CC, i.e., Multi-Truth Discovery with Candidate Correlations. The main body of the algorithm runs iteratively. For each iteration, we first store T to T', increase the counter, and reset the value of T to be empty. Then, we construct an MRF according to the method presented in Sect. 4.1 and 4.2. Also, we transform G into a directed graph $\hat{G}$ according to rules presented in Sect. 4.3. Next, we separate the graph $\hat{G}$ into two partitions based on the Min-cut theorem. Only those candidates who can be reached from the sink vertex $\hat{t}$ are regarded as truths. Last, we apply Eq. (1) to update all sources' reliabilities which will be used to compute truths in the next iteration. This algorithm converges when inferred truths of the current iteration agree with previous truths or the number of iterations exceeds a predefined threshold θ. It is worth noting that this algorithm only outputs truths obtained in the last iteration while all previous truths are used for updating sources' reliabilities.

Algorithm 1. MTD-CC

Input: A set of sources S, a set of candidates C.
Output: Inferred truths T, sources' reliabilities R.
1: Initialize r_i for all $s_i \in S$, counter= 0, $T = \emptyset$, $\theta \leftarrow$ predefined value.
2:**Repeat**
3:    $T' = T$, counter++.
4:    $T = \emptyset$.
5:    Construct an MRF $G(U, E)$.
6:    Transform $G(U, E)$ into a directed graph $\hat{G}(\hat{U}, \hat{E})$.
7:    Cut $\hat{G}$ using EK.
8:    $T = T \cup \{c_i\}$ if c_i can be reached from $\hat{t}$.
9:    Update all r_i using eq.(1).
10: **Until** $T == T'$ or counter $>= \theta$.
11: **Return** T, R.

---

5   Performance Evaluation

5.1   Metrics and Baselines

Metrics. In order to evaluate the performance of our proposed algorithm, we take three general metrics which are often used for evaluating classification algorithms.

- *Precision.* The number of inferred truths which agree with the ground truths over the number of inferred truths.
- *Recall.* The number of inferred truths which agree with the ground truths over the number of ground truths.
- *F_1 score.* The harmonic mean of precision and recall, i.e., $F_1 = \frac{2 \cdot precision \cdot recall}{precision + recall}$.

Baselines. We compare MTD-CC with five truth and multi-truth discovery methods, which are summarized as follows:

- *Majority Voting (MV).* For each candidate, it is regarded as a truth if more than a half of sources vote for it.
- *Truth Finder (TF)* [19]. TF investigates the relationship among different sources' answers, where each answer may include multiple candidates. It computes the score for each answer and the truth could be the answer with the highest score.
- *2-Estimates* [6]. It updates the weights of candidates and sources' reliabilities iteratively. One candidate is regarded as the truth if its weight exceeds a threshold.
- *LTM* [21]. LTM constructs a probabilistic graph to model the relations between truths and sources' reliabilities. It uses a sampling method to estimate the probability that a candidate is the truth. Those candidates whose probabilities exceed a threshold are treated as the truths.

– *DART* [12]. The Bayesian theorem is used in this method to update the scores of candidates and sources' reliabilities. A predefined threshold is also used to determine whether a candidate can be the truth.

To ensure the fair comparison, we run a series of experiments to warm up the initial parameter settings of baselines. As for our method, we initialize the source reliability as 0.6.

5.2   Experiment on Real Dataset

In order to evaluate MTD-CC and baseline methods in real applications, we run simulations on the book-author dataset [19]. This dataset includes 33,971 book-author records crawled from www.abebooks.com. Each record represents a bookstore's claim about the authors of a book. After removing redundant and invalid claims, we obtain 10,013 distinctive claims which are collected from 499 sources who report the authors of 483 books. We further select 100 books which we know the ground truths from the 483 books. We regard each book as an individual object and all performance results are presented by their averages.

Table 4. Comparison with different algorithms on the book-author dataset. The best performance values are in bold.

Methods	Book-author dataset		
	Precision	Recall	F_1 score
Majority Voting	0.883	0.633	0.738
Truth Finder	**0.9**	0.681	0.775
2-Estimates	0.867	0.675	0.759
LTM	0.803	0.856	0.828
DART	0.822	0.783	0.802
MTD-CC	0.825	**0.897**	**0.861**

Table 4 shows the performance of different algorithms on the book-author dataset in terms of precision, recall and F_1 score. We can see that MTD-CC achieves the best recall and F_1 score among all baseline methods. The reasons are two folds. First, the vertex and edge potential functions give advantages to our method to discover some truths which only have a few votes. For example, assume that the candidate c_j obtain 20 votes and c_k receives only 5 votes. If 4 votes for c_k also support c_j simultaneously, then c_k is more likely to be determined as a truth by MTD-CC. Second, given a certain object, the value of recall only depends on the number of inferred truths that agree with ground truths, so a method which discovers more ground truths will outperform other methods which discover less ground truths. This also explains why MTD-CC only achieves average result on the precision. Considering the overall performance, including F_1 score, the MTD-CC is still better than the baseline methods.

We can also see from Table 4 that the difference between precision and recall could be very large, e.g., Majority Voting, Truth Finder, and 2-Estimates. This shows that they omit some ground truths, even though their inferred truths are very likely to be correct. On the contrary, MTD-CC, along with LTM and DART, has a balance between the precision and recall. Among these three methods, MTD-CC is also the best on all metrics.

5.3   Experiment on Synthetic Dataset

To further evaluate the performance of MTD-CC, we conduct experiments on a synthetic dataset. We investigate the influence of two factors: the number of ground truths and the number of candidates.

In the following experiments, we generate 100 sources. Each source is assigned with ground truths. However, in order to simulate the diversity of different sources, we allow each source to add noise to their votes. Specifically, when obtaining the ground truths, a source generates two probabilities, denoted as p_0 and p_1, where p_0 represents the probability of switching 0 to 1, and p_1 indicates the reverse switch.

Effect of the Number of Ground Truths. We evaluate how the performance varies with different number of ground truths. We fix the number of candidates to be 10 in this experiment. The number of ground truths ranges from 1 to 9, and the corresponding truths are randomly selected from these 10 candidates.

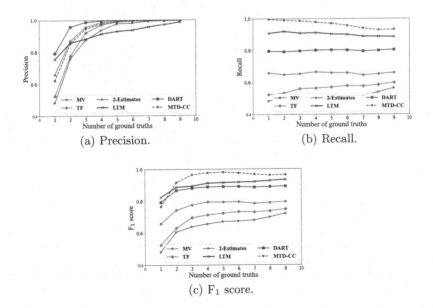

(a) Precision.   (b) Recall.

(c) F_1 score.

Fig. 4. Comparison of precision, recall and F_1 score on the synthetic dataset under different number of ground truths.

Investigating Fig. 4(a), we find that all methods show poor performance when the number of ground truths is 1, which corresponds to the single truth discovery. In this case, MTD-CC cannot guarantee to discover the ground truth precisely. In fact, MTD-CC often infers two truths. If one of them hits the ground truth, then the precision is 0.5.

Figure 4(b) shows that no matter how many ground truths, MTD-CC always shows the best recall. This result validates that the performance of MTD-CC is adaptable with the number of ground truths. Meanwhile, Fig. 4(c) shows that MTD-CC maintains the best F_1 score except the number of ground truth 1.

Effect of the Number of Candidates. We evaluate how the number of candidates to affect the performance of MTD-CC. We increase the number of candidates from 5 to 45, and set the number of ground truths to be half of the number of candidates. At this time, we can see from Fig. 5 that MTD-CC is always compelling and stable on all three metrics. We notice that there are 2 ground truths when the number of candidates is 5. At this point, the precision in Fig. 5(a) is much better than that in Fig. 4(a). The reason lies in the ratio of the number of ground truths to the number of candidates. We can see that the ratio is 2/5 in Fig. 5(a) and 2/10 in Fig. 4(a), which means all methods have more chance to infer ground truths.

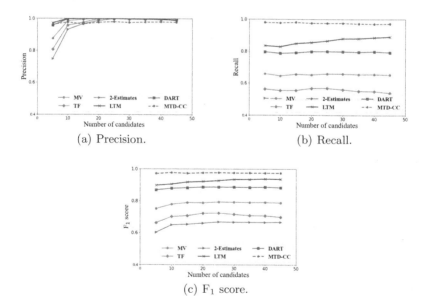

(a) Precision.   (b) Recall.

(c) F_1 score.

Fig. 5. Comparison of precision, recall and F_1 score on the synthetic dataset under different number of candidates.

6   Conclusion

In this paper, we study the problem of how to discover multiple truths from different sources' data. Our intuition is to improve the inference accuracy by utilizing correlations among different candidates. We design a metric to measure correlations between each pair of candidates based on sources' reliabilities and votes. Then, we use these correlations to construct an MRF and transform it into a directed graph with two additional terminal vertexes. Next, we separate the graph into two partitions based on the Min-cut theorem so that the truths can be directly inferred. Finally, experiment results on both real and synthetic datasets demonstrate that MTD-CC is notably more accurate than baseline methods.

Acknowledgements. This work was partially supported by the National Natural Science Foundation of China under Grants 62072061 and U20A20176, and by the Fundamental Research Funds for the Central Universities under Grant 2021CDJQY-026.

References

1. Dong, X., et al.: Knowledge vault: a web-scale approach to probabilistic knowledge fusion. In: Proceedings of the 20th ACM SIGKDD International Conference on Knowledge Discovery and Data Mining, pp. 601–610 (2014)
2. Du, Y., et al.: Bayesian co-clustering truth discovery for mobile crowd sensing systems. IEEE Trans. Industr. Inf. **16**(2), 1045–1057 (2019)
3. Du, Y., Xu, H., Sun, Y.-E., Huang, L.: A general fine-grained truth discovery approach for crowdsourced data aggregation. In: Candan, S., Chen, L., Pedersen, T.B., Chang, L., Hua, W. (eds.) DASFAA 2017. LNCS, vol. 10177, pp. 3–18. Springer, Cham (2017). https://doi.org/10.1007/978-3-319-55753-3_1
4. Fang, X.S., Sheng, Q.Z., Wang, X., Chu, D., Ngu, A.H.: SmartVote: a full-fledged graph-based model for multi-valued truth discovery. World Wide Web **22**(4), 1855–1885 (2019)
5. Ford, L.R., Jr., Fulkerson, D.R.: Flows in Networks, vol. 54. Princeton University Press, Princeton (2015)
6. Galland, A., Abiteboul, S., Marian, A., Senellart, P.: Corroborating information from disagreeing views. In: Proceedings of the Third ACM International Conference on Web Search and Data Mining, pp. 131–140 (2010)
7. Koller, D., Friedman, N.: Probabilistic Graphical Models: Principles and Techniques. MIT Press, Cambridge (2009)
8. Kolmogorov, V., Zabin, R.: What energy functions can be minimized via graph cuts? IEEE Trans. Pattern Anal. Mach. Intell. **26**(2), 147–159 (2004)
9. Li, Q., et al.: A confidence-aware approach for truth discovery on long-tail data. Proc. VLDB Endowment **8**(4), 425–436 (2014)
10. Li, Y., et al.: Reliable medical diagnosis from crowdsourcing: discover trustworthy answers from non-experts. In: Proceedings of the Tenth ACM International Conference on Web Search and Data Mining, pp. 253–261 (2017)
11. Li, Y., et al.: A survey on truth discovery. ACM SIGKDD Explor. Newsl. **17**(2), 1–16 (2016)
12. Lin, X., Chen, L.: Domain-aware multi-truth discovery from conflicting sources. Proc. VLDB Endowment **11**(5), 635–647 (2018)

13. Liu, T., Wu, W., Zhu, Y., Tong, W.: Accuracy-guaranteed event detection via collaborative mobile crowdsensing with unreliable users. In: Wang, X., Gao, H., Iqbal, M., Min, G. (eds.) CollaborateCom 2019. LNICST, vol. 292, pp. 729–744. Springer, Cham (2019). https://doi.org/10.1007/978-3-030-30146-0_49

14. Ma, F., et al.: Unsupervised discovery of drug side-effects from heterogeneous data sources. In: Proceedings of the 23rd ACM SIGKDD International Conference on Knowledge Discovery and Data Mining, pp. 967–976 (2017)

15. Wang, X., Sheng, Q.Z., Fang, X.S., Yao, L., Xu, X., Li, X.: An integrated Bayesian approach for effective multi-truth discovery. In: Proceedings of the 24th ACM International on Conference on Information and Knowledge Management, pp. 493–502 (2015)

16. Wang, X., et al.: Truth discovery via exploiting implications from multi-source data. In: Proceedings of the 25th ACM International on Conference on Information and Knowledge Management, pp. 861–870 (2016)

17. Yang, Y., Bai, Q., Liu, Q.: A probabilistic model for truth discovery with object correlations. Knowl. Based Syst. **165**, 360–373 (2019)

18. Ye, C., et al.: Constrained truth discovery. IEEE Trans. Knowl. Data Eng. (2020)

19. Yin, X., Han, J., Philip, S.Y.: Truth discovery with multiple conflicting information providers on the web. IEEE Trans. Knowl. Data Eng. **20**(6), 796–808 (2008)

20. Zadeh, N.: Theoretical efficiency of the Edmonds-Karp algorithm for computing maximal flows. J. ACM (JACM) **19**(1), 184–192 (1972)

21. Zhao, B., Rubinstein, B.I., Gemmell, J., Han, J.: A Bayesian approach to discovering truth from conflicting sources for data integration. arXiv preprint arXiv:1203.0058 (2012)

22. Zheng, M., Cui, L., He, W., Guo, W., Lu, X.: A dynamic difficulty-sensitive worker distribution model for crowdsourcing quality management. In: Wang, X., Gao, H., Iqbal, M., Min, G. (eds.) CollaborateCom 2019. LNICST, vol. 292, pp. 12–27. Springer, Cham (2019). https://doi.org/10.1007/978-3-030-30146-0_2

D2D-Based Multi-relay-Assisted Computation Offloading in Edge Computing Network

Xuan Zhao, Song Zhang, Bowen Liu, Xutong Jiang, and Wanchun Dou[✉]

State Key Laboratory for Novel Software Technology, Nanjing University, Nanjing 210023, China
{xzhao,songzhang,liubw,jiangxutong}@smail.nju.edu.cn, douwc@nju.edu.cn

Abstract. With the rapid development of edge computing, a large number of compute-intensive tasks are offloaded to the edge server, and computation offloading strategy has become a hot research topic. Because the deployment of edge servers is still in its infancy, there would be some service blind area. Through D2D technology, mobile devices in the blind area can obtain edge services with the help of relays. However, the existing methods usually select single relay to transmit tasks, and seldom consider the sensitivity of processing delay for compute-intensive tasks. When the available bandwidth of single relay is not enough to complete the data transmission in a limited time, it will produce a large delay, which seriously affects the quality of user experience. In view of this challenge, a D2D-based multi-relay-assisted computation offloading method is proposed. Technically, multiple mobile devices in the available area of edge service are used as the relays. Based on D2D technology, mobile devices in the blind area use the relays to transmit the computing task to the edge server to improve the application computing efficiency. A large number of experiments with real-world datasets have proved the feasibility and effectiveness of our method.

Keywords: Compute-intensive task · Computation offloading · Edge computing · D2D · Multi-relay

1 Introduction

With the rapid development of electronic technology and the large-scale popularization of mobile devices, complex applications to achieve various functions have sprung up. Compute-intensive applications characterized by high demand for computing resources, such as AR/VR, online games and so on, have received extensive attention [1,2]. However, due to the lack of computing resources and high energy consumption of mobile devices, the promotion of compute-intensive applications is facing great challenges [3]. Although traditional cloud computing can provide nearly unlimited computing resources for these applications, due to

© ICST Institute for Computer Sciences, Social Informatics and Telecommunications Engineering 2021
Published by Springer Nature Switzerland AG 2021. All Rights Reserved
H. Gao and X. Wang (Eds.): CollaborateCom 2021, LNICST 407, pp. 33–49, 2021.
https://doi.org/10.1007/978-3-030-92638-0_3

the time delay caused by physical distance and complex network links, some delay-sensitive compute-intensive tasks cannot be effectively handled [4,5].

Edge computing is a new computing model proposed in recent years. As a supplement to cloud computing, edge computing places part of the computing and storage resources on the edge of the network close to users [6]. This makes the computing tasks that need to be offloaded to the cloud can be directly processed at the edge of the network, which greatly reduces the task processing time and meets the demand of delay sensitive applications for low latency [7]. Therefore, the problem of computing offloading in edge computing environment has become the focus of industry and academia [8,9].

Because the deployment of edge devices is still in its infancy, there are a lot of edge service blind areas in real life. If the mobile devices in these blind areas want to use the computing and storage resources of the edge server, they can only use other mobile devices in the service scope of the edge server to assist the transmission. By establishing a direct network connection between devices, D2D technology can help mobile devices and relays in the blind area to establish a D2D transmission link and obtain edge service. At present, a lot of work has been done based on D2D technology [9–12].

However, the existing methods usually select single relay to transmit tasks, and seldom consider the sensitivity of processing delay for compute-intensive tasks. When the available bandwidth of single relay is not enough to complete the data transmission in a limited time, it will cause a large network delay at the application end, which seriously affects the quality of user experience [13]. Therefore, it is necessary to select multiple relays among the candidate relays and select the most reasonable computing task to be offloaded to the edge server for processing, so as to minimize the energy consumption of mobile devices and task execution time.

In view of this challenge, a D2D-Based multi-Relay-Assisted Computation Offloading method (named DRACO) is proposed. In this method, multiple mobile devices in the available area of edge service are used as the relays, and the mobile devices in the blind area use the relays to transmit the task data, and then offload the compute-intensive task to the edge server to improve the performance of compute-intensive tasks. A large number of experiments using real-world datasets are conducted and the results proved the feasibility and effectiveness of our method. The main contributions are summarized as follows.

- We study the task processing in the local and in th edge server and incentive mechanism for the relays, and build the task processing edge system model.
- We fully consider the energy consumption of system devices, the revenue of relays and task processing time, and design a multi-relay selection method to select the best relay set.
- A large number of experiments using real-world datasets are conducted and the results proved that our method significantly improved the satisfaction of helper devices while ensuring video quality of requester devices.

The remainder of the paper is organized as follows. In Sect. 2, a motivating example is introduced. In Sect. 3, we present the system model and problem formulation of our computation offloading scenario. Section 4 describes our offloading method DRACO. Experimental results are presented in Sect. 5 to demonstrate the performance of our method, followed by Sect. 6 summarizing related work. Finally, Sect. 7 concludes the paper.

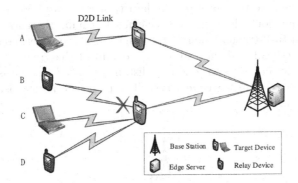

Fig. 1. Single relay cannot transmit multiple tasks at the same time.

2   Motivating Example

This section takes online games as an example to explore the motivation of our method. Large online games need high bandwidth to support the normal operation, especially AR/VR games. These games need to be rendered in real-time and the results are fed back to mobile users. At this time, the mobile device will continue to collect the data of the surrounding environment and transmit the data to the edge server for processing through the wireless network.

When the mobile device is in the blind area, it needs to use the relay to assist data transmission. However, AR/VR games receive and process the surrounding environment data in real-time. Therefore, it needs sufficient bandwidth resources to ensure the real-time completion of computing tasks. However, as a mobile device, the relay not only needs to assist the target device to transmit data, but also needs to process its local tasks, or transmit the local tasks to the edge server for processing. Therefore, it is very likely that a single relay can not complete the huge data transmission of compute-intensive tasks within the specified time, which will lead to task timeout.

Moreover, in the actual edge computing environment, there may be more than one mobile device in the blind area at the same time. As shown in Fig. 1, there are mobile devices A, B, C and D in the blind area, all of which need to transmit the computing task through the relay. Mobile devices B, C and D choose the same relay. At this time, since the compute-intensive task being executed by device B is a VR/AR game, it has a higher bandwidth requirement. However, the bandwidth provided by the relay is difficult to meet the needs of the task in device B. Therefore, the relay selection for device B is unreasonable. Multiple relays can provide more bandwidth resources.

In view of the above challenges, a D2D-based multi-relay-assisted computation offloading method is proposed. As shown in Fig. 2, when the target device in the blind area needs to offload the compute-intensive task to the edge server, the mobile device that can directly communicate with the edge server will be selected as the relay. However, the bandwidth resources provided by a single relay may not be able to complete the data transmission of compute-intensive applications. Therefore, the target device can select multiple relays to assist the target device in task transmission at the same time. Moreover, considering the transmission overhead and data allocation overhead that may be brought by relays, we only select relays for one hop distance assisted transmission, that is, target device –> relay(s) –> edge server. The relay will not transmit the data to other ralays for help.

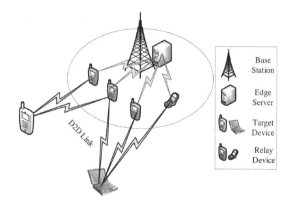

Fig. 2. D2D-based multi-relay-assisted computation offloading.

3 System Model and Problem Formulation

3.1 Local Model

In D2D computation offloading supporting compute-intensive tasks, the target device can select multiple relays to assist it in transmitting task data. In the process of assisting the target device to transmit data, the relays not only provide bandwidth resources but also consume the energy of target devices in the local.

The compute-intensive task to be processed in the target device is recorded as $m_i = (d_i, r_i, D_i)$. d_i is the amount of raw data of the m_i, r_i represents the CPU processing cycle required by m_i. D_i represents the expected completion time of m_i. The target device will divide the task m_i, part of which are offloaded to the edge server and others are executed locally. We use $\alpha_i \in [0, 1]$ to represent the proportion of task m_i that is offloaded to the edge server.

The time consumed by the local execution is not only affected by the computing power of the local device, but also related to the calculation backlog of the local device. For task m_i, the part to be executed locally is: $\mathcal{A}_i = (1 - \alpha_i)r_i$.

The computing tasks run at a fixed interval t_{in} continuously arrive at the target device. If the target device is limited by the computing performance of the local device and cannot be processed in time, these tasks will be overstocked locally, affecting the execution time of the tasks arriving later. When task m_i arrives, the target device's calculation backlog Q_i is:

$$Q_i = \begin{cases} 0, & i = 0 \\ \frac{maxQ_{i-1} + A_{i-1} - f_D t_{in}, 0}{f_D}, & i > 0 \end{cases} \tag{1}$$

Here, f^D is the computing power of the target device. The locally execution time

$$t_i^L = (1 - \alpha_i)\frac{r_i}{f^D} + Q_i \tag{2}$$

3.2 Edge Model

In the edge computing network, each base station is equipped with an edge server. Mobile devices need to go through the base station to access the edge server. Time of task m_i executed on the edge server is:

$$t_i^E = \alpha_i \frac{r_i}{\sum_k x_k^E f_k^E} \tag{3}$$

where f_k^E represents the computing power of the edge server accessed through base station k. $x_k^E = 1$ indicates that the edge server accessed through base station k is selected, otherwise, $x_k^E = 0$.

The relay set is $D^r = \{D_1, D_2, \cdots, D_j, \cdots, D_N\}$. For each relay, $D_j = \{\varphi_j, b_j, n_j\}$ where φ_j is the cost per unit time of using relay j to transmit compute-intensive tasks; b_j represents the bandwidth owned by relay j; n_j represents the number of tasks currently being transmitted by relay j.

When relay j is used to transmit task m_i, the transmission rate of relay j is

$$s_j = \frac{b_j}{n_j + 1} log_2(1 + \frac{p_j H_j}{\sigma^2}) \tag{4}$$

Here, p_j is the transmission power of relay j, H_j is the channel gain between the relay and the base station, and σ is the noise power. $\frac{b_j}{n_j+1}$ indicates that the tasks transmitted by the relay evenly divide the bandwidth of the relay. The transmission time for task m_i by relay j is

$$t_{i,j} = \frac{d_{i,j}}{s_j} + \frac{d_{i,j}}{s_{i,j}} \tag{5}$$

where $d_{i,j}$ denotes the amount of data of compute-intensive task m_i transmitted on relay j, and $\sum_{j=1}^N d_{i,j} = d_i$. $N = |D^r|$ indicates the number of relays in the relay set. $s_{i,j}$ is the transmission rate between the target device and relay j,

$$s_{i,j} = \frac{b_i}{N + 1} log_2(1 + \frac{p_i H_{i,j}}{\sigma^2}) \tag{6}$$

Here, b_i and p_i are the bandwidth and transmission power of the target device. $H_{i,j}$ is the channel gain between the target device and the relay.

The relay sets the transmission time of all relay to form the relay transmission time set $T^r = t_{i,1}, t_{i,2}, \cdots, t_{i,N}$. Therefore, the uplink transmission time for the target device to offload the task is: $t_i^r = \max\{T^r\}$. At the same time, we also need to consider the current backlog of transmission data in the transmission of compute-intensive tasks. This paper takes δ_i represents the transmission backlog, which is defined as when task m_i arrive, it takes time to wait for transmission, which is related to $i - 1$ and previous tasks. Based on this, the time for task transmission can be calculated when the target device offloads the task:

$$t_i^T = x_i((1-y)\frac{d_i}{s_i} + yt_i^r + \delta_i) \tag{7}$$

where x_i is 0(if $\alpha_i = 0$) or 1(if $\alpha_i > 0$). y indicates whether a relay is selected. If the target device can complete the transmission without a relay, $y = 0$; Otherwise, $y = 1$. s_i is the transmission rate to the base station and can be calculated by $s_i = b_i \log_2\left(1 + \frac{p_i H_i}{\sigma^2}\right)$ where H_i is the channel gain between the target device and the base station. It should be noted that when task m_i after reaching the target device, δ_i is a constant.

3.3 Incentive Model

As a relay, mobile devices not only occupy bandwidth resources, but also consume power. Therefore, in order to encourage more mobile devices to join the transmission process, the incentive model is considered for the transmission of relays. During the offloading, the relay can benefit from the transmission:

$$E^R = x_i \sum_{j=1}^{N} \varphi_j \frac{d_{i,j}}{s_j} \tag{8}$$

where φ_j is the cost per unit time when using relay j to transmit.

There is also a payment for the usage of edge servers. The cost for renting the computing resources is:

$$E^E = \varphi_k t_i^E \tag{9}$$

where φ_k is the cost of unit time when the task is offloaded to the edge server through base station k. The overall cost for task processing is $E^R + E^C$.

3.4 Computation Offloading Model

In computation offloading, the task m_i in the target device is to be processed execute in parallel locally and at the edge. Therefore, the task completion time

$$t_i = \max\{t_i^E + t_i^T, t_i^L\} \tag{10}$$

The energy consumed by the target device can be divided into two parts: 1) the energy consumed by local computing; 2) the energy consumed by transmitting data. Therefore, the local energy consumption for m_i can be calculated by

$$E^C = \alpha_i \varphi_i r_i + x_i p_i \frac{d_i}{S_i} \tag{11}$$

where φ_i is the energy consumed by local processing in one cycling time. p_i represents the energy consumed by task transmission.

We use μ_i and ψ_i to represent sensitivity of user to the task m_i and power consumption, respectively. Then the target device offloading utility for task m_i can be calculated as

$$U_i(\alpha_i, d_{i,j}, x_k^E) = \mu_i(D_i - t_i) - E^R - E^E - \psi_i E^C \qquad (12)$$

Therefore, the optimization problems can be obtained

$$\max_{(x \in \{0,1\}, y \in \{0,1\}, 0 < d_{i,j} < d_i, x_k^E \in \{0,1\})} U_i(\alpha_i, d_{i,j}, x_k^E) \qquad (13a)$$

$$\text{s.t.} \quad dist(j) \le l(0 < j \le N) \qquad (13b)$$

$$\sum_{j=1}^{N} d_{i,j} = d_i \qquad (13c)$$

$$\sum_{k} x_k^E = 1 \qquad (13d)$$

Formula (13b) indicates that the distance between the target device and the relay j cannot exceed the maximum distance l of D2D communication. Formula (13c) represents collaborative transmission for the compute-intensive tasks by all relays. Formula (13d) ensures that only one edge server will be selected.

4   D2D-Based Multi-relay-Assisted Computation Offloading Method

4.1   Relay Selection Algorithm

When the target device is in the blind area, it needs to establish a D2D connection with the relay that can access the edge server to obtain the service of the edge server. Therefore, the target device needs to first confirm whether it is in the blind area, that is, whether it is within the service coverage of the edge server. This paper considers the case of edge server damage or downtime. In this case, although the mobile device can connect with the base station, the edge server equipped with the base station is difficult to provide external services. In this paper, base stations are denoted as $K = \{k_1, k_2, \cdots, k_m\}$. Algorithm 1 gives the specific process.

Algorithm 1 outputs the relay information ω. Specifically, the target device will traverse the base station set K. If the target device can connect to the base station, it will further test whether the edge server is available. If no edge server is available, return $y = 1$ and the relay set D. If the target device finds an available edge server, return $y = 0$ and $D = \emptyset$. At this time, the target device can directly access the edge server through the base station.

The target device obtains the relay set D through Algorithm 1. The target device will select one or more mobile devices according to the bandwidth and

---

Algorithm 1. Candidate relay sets construction

Require: Target device, relay set, base station set
Ensure: $\omega = \{y, D\}$
1: $y = 1$
2: **for** $k \in K$ **do**
3:     **if** Target device can connect to the base station k **then**
4:         **if** The edge server connected to base station k is available **then**
5:             $y = 0$
6: **if** $y == 0$ **then**
7:     $D = \emptyset$
8: **else**
9:     The target device obtains the information D_i of the mobile device that can establish a D2D connection
10:     Construct relay set $D = \{D_1, D_2, \cdots, D_M\}$
11: **return** ω

---

price of each relay to form the final relay set D_r, and $D_r \in D$. The target device will allocate the amount of data to each relay in the relay set, which is related to the utility that the target device can obtain.

We allocate the amount of data according to the scheme of minimum transmission time. The average speed of data transmission through relay j can be reached by

$$\bar{v}_j = \frac{d_{i,j}}{\frac{d_{i,j}}{s_j} + \frac{d_{i,j}}{s_{i,j}}} = \frac{s_j s_{i,j}}{s_j + s_{i,j}} \tag{14}$$

where $d_{i,j} = \frac{\bar{v}_j}{\sum_{k=1}^N \bar{v}_k} d_i$. In this way, the profit for relay j is

$$E^R = \sum_{j=1}^N \varphi_j \frac{d_{i,j}}{\bar{v}_j} = \sum_{j=1}^N \varphi_j \frac{d_i}{\sum_{k=1}^N \bar{v}_k} \tag{15}$$

If the target device adjusts the devices in the relay set and the amount of data transmitted, it needs to meet the requirement that the utility value improvement obtained by the target device after adjustment is greater than the cost of adjustment:

$$\Delta u^r = \mu_i \Delta t_i^T - \Delta E^R > 0 \tag{16}$$

where Δt_i^T represents the difference between the transmission time after policy adjustment and that before policy adjustment; ΔE^R represents the difference between the revenue of the relay after policy adjustment and that before policy adjustment.

Based on the strategy of transmission delay minimization, the data allocation $d_{i,j}$ of each relay can be obtained, but also need to get the final relay set D_r. Algorithm 2 gives an greedy-based iterative strategy. Based on this strategy, Algorithm 3 gives the relays selection algorithm. In Algorithm 3, D^i is used to represent the data allocation set: $D^i = \{d_{i,1}, d_{i,2}, \cdots, d_{i,N}\}$.

Algorithm 2. Greedy-based relay selection algorithm

Require: D, current utility u^r, transmission time t_i^T
Ensure: Relay set D_k
1: $\Delta u^r = -\infty, D^r = D, D_k = \emptyset$
2: **for** $D_i \in D^r$ **do**
3:     Calculate the utility improvement Δu_{temp}^r and time cost t_{temp}^T based on u^r
4:     **if** $\Delta u_{temp}^r > \Delta u^r$ **then**
5:         $D_k = D_i$; $t_i^T = t_{temp}^T$; $\Delta u^r = \Delta u_{temp}^r$
6:     **if** $\Delta u_{temp}^r == \Delta u^r$ and $t_{temp}^T < t_i^T$ **then**
7:         $D_k = D_i$; $t_i^T = t_{temp}^T$; $\Delta u^r = \Delta u_{temp}^r$
8: **return** D_k

Algorithm 3 gives the steps of selecting a relay set. The relay set selection algorithm allocates the transmission data intending to minimize the transmission time, and then selects the relay set based on the utility value. Initially, the algorithm takes the whole set of relays to be selected as the set of relays to calculate the transmission data allocation corresponding to the minimum transmission time. After that, the algorithm will remove the mobile devices with the least utility improvement in the set of relays to be selected in a greedy way every iteration, and calculate again until the set is empty. Finally, the target device selects the set with the largest utility value as the relay set.

Algorithm 3. Relay Set Selection Algorithm

Require: y, candidate relay set D
Ensure: Information of relay set $r = \{y, D^{max}, D^i, t_i^T\}$
1: $t_i^T = +\infty$; $D^r = D$
2: **if** $y == 0$ **then**
3:     $t_i^T = \frac{d_i}{s_i}$; $D^r = \emptyset$; $D^i = \emptyset$
4: **else**
5:     **while** $D^r \neq \emptyset$ **do**
6:         **for** $D_i \in D^r$ **do**
7:             $d_{i,j} = \frac{\bar{v_j}}{\sum_{k=1}^N \bar{v_k}} d_i$
8:             $t_{temp}^T = \frac{d_{i,j}}{\bar{v_j}}$; $E^R = \sum_{j=1}^N \varphi_j \frac{d_{i,j}}{\bar{v_j}}$
9:         **if** $D^r == D$ or $\mu_i \Delta t_i^T > \Delta E^R$ **then**
10:            $t_i^T = t_{temp}^T$; $D^{max} = D^r$; record D^i; $E_{temp}^R = E^R$
11:         **else**
12:            **if** $\mu_i \Delta t_i^T == \Delta E^R$ and $t_{temp}^T < t_i^T$ **then**
13:               $t_i^T = t_{temp}^T$; $D^{max} = D^r$; record D^i; $E_{temp}^R = E^R$
14:         Get D_k by Algorithm 2
15:         $D^r = D^r - D_k$
16: **return** r

4.2   D2D-Based Multi-relay-Assisted Computation Offloading

The construction method of candidate relay set is given in the previous. In this way, the target device can get the relay set D^r, as well as the transmission data amount D^i allocated by each relay. Considering the intensive deployment of edge servers, relays may be in the service coverage of multiple edge servers at the same time. Therefore, the target device also needs to determine the proportion of data uploaded to the edge server α_i and edge server K.

According to the connection between the relay to be selected and the edge server, the relay to be selected is divided first. For the set D of relays to be selected, it is divided into k subsets d according to the connection between the relays to be selected and the edge server $D_1^E, D_2^E, \cdots, D_K^E$. For the edge server equipped on the base station k, All mobile devices in D_k^E are accessible. K is the number of base stations that can be accessed by the selected relay. This chapter assumes that each base station is equipped with only one edge server, so K is also the number of edge servers. After partition, the set of relays to be selected meets the requirement of $\bigcup_{k=1}^K D_k^K = D$. Moreover, for any two subsets $D_{k_1}^K, D_{k_2}^K$ The intersection of the two is not necessarily empty.

After the division, the combination set $D^E = \{\{1, D_1^E\}, \{2, D_2^E\}, \cdots, \{k, D_k^E\}, \cdots, \{K, D_K^E\}\}$. $\{k, D_k^E\}\}$ represents the base station k and the set of relays to be selected that can access the edge server equipped on the base station k. To obtain the offloading strategy, the target device can traverse D^E to calculate the maximum utility that the target device can obtain by offloading the compute-intensive task to the edge server in D2D mode under the current situation. In this case, the edge server to be offloaded by the target device is determined, and the relay set and the transmission data assigned to each relay can be obtained by using Algorithm 3. Formula (12) is transformed into

$$f(\alpha_i) = \mu_i t_i^D - \mu_i t_i - E^E - E^R - \psi_i E^C \tag{17}$$

After determining the relay, C is a constant. We define

$$f_1(\alpha_i) = \mu_i t_i^D - \mu_i(t_i^E + t_i^{T'}) - E^E - E^{R'} - \psi_i E^{C'}(t_i^E + t_i^T \ge t_i^L) \tag{18}$$

$$f_2(\alpha_i) = \mu_i t_i^D - \mu_i(t_i^E + t_i^{T'}) - E^E - E^{R'} - \psi_i E^{C'} \quad (t_i^E + t_i^T \le t_i^L) \tag{19}$$

$$f_3(\alpha_i) = \mu_i t_i^D - \mu_i(t_i^E + t_i^T) - E^E - E^{R'} - \psi_i E^C \quad (t_i^E + t_i^T \le t_i^L) \tag{20}$$

where $t_i^{T'} = (1-y)\frac{d_i}{s_i} + y t_i^r$, $E^{R'} = \sum_{j=1}^N \varphi_j \frac{d_{i,j}}{s_j}$, $E^{C'} = \alpha_i \varphi_i r_i + p_i \frac{d_i}{S_i}$. Then we can get

$$\max f(\alpha_i) = \max\left(\max f_1(\alpha_i), \max f_2(\alpha_i), f_3(0)\right) \tag{21}$$

The utility maximization problem is transformed into the maximum problem of $f_1(\alpha_i)$, $f_2(\alpha_i)$ and $f_3(0)$. Moreover, from the definition of function, $f_1(\alpha_i)$ and $f_2(\alpha_i)$ are continuous. Furthermore, we decompose the above maximum problem into two subproblems: (1) If $t_i^E + t_i^T \ge t_i^L$, find the maximum value of $f_1(\alpha_i)$; (2) If $t_i^E + t_i^T \le t_i^L$, find the maximum value of $f_2(\alpha_i)$. In the following section, we will discuss the maximum problem in these two cases in turn. For ease of expression, we set $\alpha_1 = (Q_i + \frac{r_i}{f^D} - t_i^T)/r_i(\frac{1}{f_k^E} + \frac{1}{f^D})$.

For subproblem (1), we first calculate

$$f_1'(\alpha_i) = \frac{df_1(\alpha_i)}{d\alpha_i} = -\mu_i \frac{r_i}{f_k^E} - \varphi_k \frac{r_i}{f_k^E} - \psi_i \varphi_i r_i \tag{22}$$

From the definition of each variable in the formula, we can see that $f_1'(\alpha_i) \leq 0$. As $t_i^E + t_i^T \geq t_i^L$, $\alpha_i \geq \alpha_1$. If $\alpha_1 \in (0,1]$, $\max f_1(\alpha_i) = f_1(\alpha_1)$.

For subproblem (2), we first calculate

$$f_2'(\alpha_i) = \frac{df_2(\alpha_i)}{d\alpha_i} = \mu_i \frac{r_i}{f^D} - \varphi_k \frac{r_i}{f_k^E} - \psi_i \varphi_i r_i \tag{23}$$

By $t_i^E + t_i^T \leq t_i^L$, we can get $\alpha_i \leq \alpha_1$. If $f_2'(\alpha_i) \geq 0$, $\max f_2(\alpha_i) = f_2(\alpha_1)$. If $f_2'(\alpha_i) < 0$, $\max f_2(\alpha_i) = f_2(0)$.

Through the above process, we can get the maximum value of $f_1(\alpha_i)$ and $f_2(\alpha_i)$ and further get the utility value $f(\alpha_i)$. Based on this process, a D2D-based multi-relay-assisted offloading strategy can be obtained. Algorithm 4 shows the process of solving the problem.

Algorithm 4. D2D-Based Multi-Relay-Assisted Computation Offloading

---

Require: m_i, μ_i, f^D, y_{final}, D
Ensure: Offloading strategy $\Omega = \{\alpha_{final}, D_{final}, k_{final}\}$
1: $u_{final} = -\infty$, $k_{final} = \emptyset$, task processing time t_i
2: **if** $y_{final} == 0$ **then**
3:      $D^E = \{k, \emptyset\}$
4: **else**
5:      D^E is obtained by dividing the candidate relays set
6: **for** $D_k^E \in D^E$ **do**
7:      Execute Algorithm 3 to obtain relay set D_i and data allocation set D^i
8:      Obtain the currently available base station k
9:      $\alpha = \dfrac{Q_i + \frac{r_i}{f^D} - t_i^T}{r_i(\frac{1}{f_k^E} + \frac{1}{f^D})}$
10:      Calculate the maximal value u of $f(\alpha_i)$ and task processing delay t
11:      **if** $u_{final} < u$ or ($u_{final} = u$ and $t_i < t$) **then**
12:          $u_{final} = u$, $t_i = t$, $\alpha_{final} = \alpha$, $D_{final} = D_i$
13: **return** Ω

Algorithm 4 will traverse the relay partition set, and each time, it will select the current local optimal solution based on maximum utility value, and then obtain the global optimal strategy Ω. The strategy includes task m_i's offloading ratio α_{final}, relay set D_{final}, base station k_{final}.

4.3   Complexity Analysis

In Sect 4.1, we first give the algorithm for constructing the candidate relay sets. The algorithm will traverse the surrounding base station that may establish communication with the target device, so the complexity is $O(|K|)$. Greedy-based device selection algorithm is a part of the relay set selection algorithm. The algorithm will traverse the candidate relay set, so the complexity is $O(|D|)$. The relay set selection algorithm also traverses the candidate relay set. In each round of traversal, greedy-based device selection algorithm also needs to select the devices that are not in the relay set, so the complexity is $O(|K| + |D|^2)$.

In Sect 4.2, we present a computation offloading algorithm to support compute-intensive tasks. The algorithm will first execute the construction algorithm to obtain the candidate relay sets. After that, the algorithm will divide the candidate relay sets. Based on the divided set D^E, the algorithm will find the final offloading strategy. During the execution of the algorithm, it will traverse the base station set, and the complexity of the algorithm can be obtained as $O(|K| + |D| + |D|^2|K|)$.

5   Performance Evaluation

5.1   Simulation Setting

We select the Australian base station distribution dataset [14] which is derived from the radio communication license dataset issued by the Australian Communications and Media Authority. Twenty edge servers are chosen and the coverage radius of each edge server is randomly set to [450, 750]. Within the coverage of each edge server, there will be 10 randomly generated mobile devices for transmission assistance.

This experiment uses the following indicators to evaluate the performance of the three methods: (1) the proportion of tasks completed before the expected completion time; (2) The energy consumption of mobile devices accounts for the proportion of local execution energy consumption.

The task data transmission time in $[\frac{r_i}{f^D}, \frac{1.5r_i}{f^D}]$. We set $t_{bench} = \frac{r_i}{f^D} + \frac{2d_i}{S_i}$, and $50\% - 140\%$ of t_{bench} are expected completion time by tasks. The arrival of the task obeys Poisson distribution, and $\lambda = 1$. This experiment will first calculate the index value of each target device in turn, and finally calculate the average value of 10 target devices.

We compare our method with the following two methods: (1) Random Single Relay-Assisted Offloading (RSRO): it will randomly select a device from the set of relays as the relay. The target device will determine the offloading ratio according to the strategy of maximizing utility value. (2) Greedy-Based Single Relay-Assisted Offloading (GSRO): it will sort the devices and select the device with the highest transmission rate as the relay. The target device will determine the offload ratio according to the strategy of minimizing execution time.

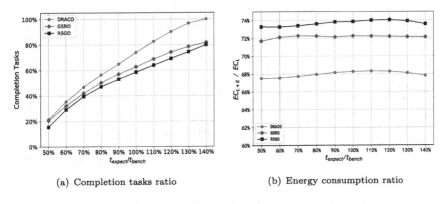

(a) Completion tasks ratio   (b) Energy consumption ratio

Fig. 3. Impact of the expected completion time.

5.2 Experimental Results

We first change the expected completion time. Figure 3(a) shows the number of tasks completed before the expected completion time of the user. With the increasing expected completion time, the performance of DRACO, GSRO and RSRO are constantly improving, but the number of tasks that the method DRACO has completed is always the most. Figure 3(b) shows the ratio of energy consumption of considering to un-considering computation offloading. The energy consumed by local devices using different methods is not related to the expected time change of task users, but the energy consumption of method DRACO is always the lowest of the three methods. As can be seen from Figs. 3(a) and 3(b), the performance of DRACO is always better than the other two methods, because a single relay may not be able to complete task processing before the user expected completion time.

Then we change the number of relays to be selected from 2 to 20. Figure 4(a) shows that the proportion of completion tasks before the expected completion time. With the increasing number of relays to be selected, the number of tasks completed before the expected completion time with DRACO is gradually increasing. However, the number of tasks completed by GSRO and RSRO before the expected completion time has little change. The performance of DRACO is always the best. Figure 4(b) shows the ratio of energy consumption of considering to un-considering computation offloading. The energy consumption of DRACO is decreasing and remains the lowest at all times, but the energy consumption of GSRO and RSRO is unchanged. This is because GSRO and RSRO can only select one relay, so the improvement of the number of relays will not improve the performance of the algorithm. However, DRACO can use multiple relays for parallel data transmission at the same time, which greatly improves the performance of compute-intensive tasks.

Finally, we test the impact of the number of available edge servers. Figure 5(a) shows the completion tasks before the expected completion time. As the number of available edge servers is decreasing, the performance of DRACO, GSRO and

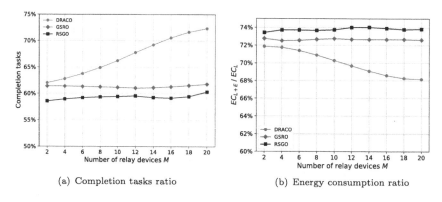

(a) Completion tasks ratio   (b) Energy consumption ratio

Fig. 4. Impact of the number of relays.

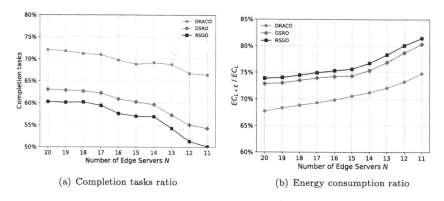

(a) Completion tasks ratio   (b) Energy consumption ratio

Fig. 5. Impact of the number of edge servers.

RSRO is decreasing, and the number of tasks completed before the expected completion time decreases. But the performance of DRACO is always the best. Figure 5(b) shows the ratio of energy consumption of considering to un-considering computation offloading. With the decrease of the number of available edge servers, the energy consumption of DRACO, GSRO and RSRO for target devices is increasing, but the energy consumption of DRACO is always the lowest among the three methods. The reason for the above phenomenon is that with the decrease of the number of available edge servers, the single relay assisted offloading method is difficult to support more compute-intensive tasks, while the DRACO with multi-relay strategy can. Moreover, the continuous reduction of the number of available edge servers makes the target devices put more tasks on the local execution, so the energy consumption of mobile devices will continue to increase. However, DRACO is still superior to the other two methods.

6   Related Work and Comparison Analysis

Low latency, high bandwidth, close to users and other advantages make edge computing receive a lot of attention and research. With the rapid development of edge computing, more and more service providers try to offload large-scale computing tasks to edge servers. Computing offload strategy has become a research hotspot. Wang et al. [15] introduced a dynamic edge computing model and conducted the first study on robust task offloading which is tolerant to h server failures. Deng et al. [16] designed a user-centered joint optimization offloading scheme to minimize the weighted cost of time delay, energy consumption and price under the constraint of satisfying the advanced personalized needs of users. Song et al. [17] proposed a scheme in which tasks are offloaded to servers with the aim of maximizing a reward within a limited power budget, server processing capacities, and wireless network coverage. Yan et al. [18] proposed an MEC service pricing scheme to coordinate with the service caching decisions and control wireless devices' task offloading behavior in a cellular network. Based on the available bandwidth of heterogeneous edge severs and the location of mobile devices, Yang et al. [19] formulated an optimal offloading node selection strategy as a Markov decision process (MDP), and solved by employing the value iteration algorithm (VIA). Zhan et al. [7] investigated the problem of offloading decision and resource allocation among multiple users served by one base station to achieve the optimal system-wide user utility, which is defined as a trade-off between task latency and energy consumption. However, these methods seldom consider the devices in blind area that cannot communicate with the edge server directly. We use D2D technology to solve this problem by using multiple devices as relays. If the devices in blind area want to use edge services, they could offload computing tasks to edge servers through relay devices.

D2D technology improves the communication efficiency through the direct connection between devices, and also provides a new idea for data transmission. The establishment of efficient D2D connection plays an important role in the calculation of offloading efficiency. Sun et al. [20] studied device-to-device enabled traffic offloading scheme by employing non-orthogonal multiple access (NOMA) and unlicensed access technologies to maximize the capacity of the D2D network by optimizing sub-channel assignment and power control while guaranteeing the capacity of NOMA-based cellular links and the WiFi system. Pan et al. [21] investigated the caching strategy to maximize the D2D offloading gain with the comprehensive consideration of user collaborative characteristics as well as the physical transmission conditions. Feng et al. [22] proposed a device-to-device communications-assisted traffic offloading scheme to improve the amount of traffic offloaded from cellular to WiFi in integrated cellular and WiFi networks. Peng et al. [23] discussed joint multi-user cooperative partial offloading, transmission scheduling and computation allocating for device-to-device underlay mobile edge computing. Ko et al. [12] proposed a distributed device-to-device offloading system (DDOS) in which a task owner opportunistically broadcasts an offloading request that includes its mobility level and task completion deadline. After receiving the request, mobile devices in the vicinity of the task owner employ a constraint stochastic game to decide, in a distributed manner, whether to accept the request or not. However, these methods rarely consider that single relay may not be able to meet the response time requirements of compute-intensive tasks. We fully consider the available bandwidth and choose multiple relays to complete the transmission and ensure that the application is completed in the effective time.

7   Conclusion

In order to support the computation offloading of compute-intensive tasks in blind area, this paper proposes a computation offloading method, DRACO. Specifically, DRACO will select multiple mobile devices that can communicate with edge servers as relays, and target devices will establish D2D connection with these devices in turn. The compute-intensive tasks in blind area are offloaded to edge servers by parallel transmission of multiple relays. A large number of experiments with the real-world datasets have proved the feasibility and effectiveness of our method.

Acknowledgments. This work was supported in part by the National Key Research and Development Program of China (No. 2020YFB1707600), the Key Research and Development Program of Jiangsu Province (No. BE2019104), and the Collaborative Innovation Center of Novel Software Technology and Industrialization, Nanjing University.

References

1. Josilo, S., Dán, G.: Selfish decentralized computation offloading for mobile cloud computing in dense wireless networks. IEEE Trans. Mob. Comput. **18**(1), 207–220 (2019)
2. Josilo, S., Dán, G.: Wireless and computing resource allocation for selfish computation offloading in edge computing. In: 2019 IEEE Conference on Computer Communications, INFOCOM 2019, pp. 2467–2475. IEEE (2019)
3. Sun, H., Wang, J., Peng, H., Song, L., Qin, M.: Delay constraint energy efficient cooperative offloading in MEC for IoT. In: Collaborative Computing: Networking, Applications and Worksharing, pp. 671–685 (2021)
4. Liang, Y., Ge, J., Zhang, S., Wu, J., Tang, Z., Luo, B.: A utility-based optimization framework for edge service entity caching. IEEE Trans. Parallel Distributed Syst. **30**(11), 2384–2395 (2019)
5. Malik, R., Vu, M.: Energy-efficient computation offloading in delay-constrained massive MIMO enabled edge network using data partitioning. IEEE Trans. Wireless Commun. **19**(10), 6977–6991 (2020)
6. Peng, Q., He, Q., Xia, Y., Wu, C., Wang, S.: Collaborative workflow scheduling over MANET, a user position prediction-based approach. In: Gao, H., Wang, X., Yin, Y., Iqbal, M. (eds.) CollaborateCom 2018. LNICSSITE, vol. 268, pp. 33–52. Springer, Cham (2019). https://doi.org/10.1007/978-3-030-12981-1_3
7. Zhan, W., Luo, C., Min, G., Wang, C., Zhu, Q., Duan, H.: Mobility-aware multi-user offloading optimization for mobile edge computing. IEEE Trans. Veh. Technol. **69**(3), 3341–3356 (2020)

8. Liu, L., Chang, Z., Guo, X., Mao, S., Ristaniemi, T.: Multiobjective optimization for computation offloading in fog computing. IEEE Internet Things J. **5**(1), 283–294 (2018)
9. Yang, Y., Long, C., Wu, J., Peng, S., Li, B.: D2D-enabled mobile-edge computation offloading for multi-user IoT network. IEEE Internet Things J. **8**, 12490–12504 (2021)
10. Zhang, X., Zhu, Q.: D2D offloading for statistical QoS provisionings over 5G multimedia mobile wireless networks. In: IEEE INFOCOM 2019 - IEEE Conference on Computer Communications, pp. 82–90 (2019)
11. Saleem, U., Liu, Y., Jangsher, S., Tao, X., Li, Y.: Latency minimization for D2D-enabled partial computation offloading in mobile edge computing. IEEE Trans. Veh. Technol. **69**(4), 4472–4486 (2020)
12. Ko, H., Pack, S.: Distributed device-to-device offloading system: design and performance optimization. IEEE Trans. Mob. Comput. **20**, 2949–2960 (2020)
13. Lagar-Cavilla, H.A., Tolia, N., de Lara, E., Satyanarayanan, M., O'Hallaron, D.: Interactive resource-intensive applications made easy. In: Cerqueira, R., Campbell, R.H. (eds.) Middleware 2007. LNCS, vol. 4834, pp. 143–163. Springer, Heidelberg (2007). https://doi.org/10.1007/978-3-540-76778-7_8
14. Lai, P., et al.: Optimal edge user allocation in edge computing with variable sized vector bin packing. In: Pahl, C., Vukovic, M., Yin, J., Yu, Q. (eds.) ICSOC 2018. LNCS, vol. 11236, pp. 230–245. Springer, Cham (2018). https://doi.org/10.1007/978-3-030-03596-9_15
15. Wang, H., Xu, H., Huang, H., Chen, M., Chen, S.: Robust task offloading in dynamic edge computing. IEEE Trans. Mob. Comput., 1 (2021)
16. Deng, X., Sun, Z., Li, D., Luo, J., Wan, S.: User-centric computation offloading for edge computing. IEEE Internet Things J. **8**, 12559–12568 (2021)
17. Song, M., Lee, Y., Kim, K.: Reward-oriented task offloading under limited edge server power for multi-access edge computing. IEEE Internet Things J. **8**, 13425–13438 (2021)
18. Yan, J., Bi, S., Duan, L., Zhang, Y.J.A.: Pricing-driven service caching and task offloading in mobile edge computing. IEEE Trans. Wireless Commun. **20**, 4495–4512 (2021)
19. Yang, G., Hou, L., He, X., He, D., Chan, S., Guizani, M.: Offloading time optimization via Markov decision process in mobile-edge computing. IEEE Internet Things J. **8**(4), 2483–2493 (2021)
20. Sun, M., Xu, X., Tao, X., Zhang, P., Leung, V.C.M.: NOMA-based D2D-enabled traffic offloading for 5G and beyond networks employing licensed and unlicensed access. IEEE Trans. Wireless Commun. **19**, 4109–4124 (2020)
21. Pan, Y., Pan, C., Yang, Z., Chen, M., Wang, J.: A caching strategy towards maximal D2D assisted offloading gain. IEEE Trans. Mob. Comput. **19**(11), 2489–2504 (2020)
22. Feng, B., Zhang, C., Liu, J., Fang, Y.: D2D communications-assisted traffic offloading in integrated cellular-WiFi networks. IEEE Internet Things J. **6**(5), 8670–8680 (2019)
23. Peng, J., Qiu, H., Cai, J., Xu, W., Wang, J.: D2D-assisted multi-user cooperative partial offloading, transmission scheduling and computation allocating for MEC. IEEE Trans. Wireless Commun. **20**, 4858–4873 (2021)

Delay-Sensitive Slicing Resources Scheduling Based on Multi-MEC Collaboration in IoV

Yan Liang[1], Xin Chen[1(✉)], Shengcheng Ma[2], and Libo Jiao[1]

[1] School of Computer Science, Beijing Information Science and Technology University, Beijing 100101, China
{chenxin,jiaolibo}@bistu.edu.cn
[2] School of Computer Science and Engineering, Beihang University, Beijing 100191, China
mashengcheng@buaa.edu.cn

Abstract. The emerging Vehicle to Infrastructure (V2I) technology supports the service of task offloading under the Internet of vehicle (IoV), which improves the computational efficiency of the task. Facing tasks with different demands, network slicing technology builds a variety of logic private networks on a unified infrastructure, divides and allocates resources according to different user needs, which improves the vehicle transmission efficiency. Nevertheless, the diversity of demand resources and the randomness of tasks make the network scenario of IoV more complex. It is still a challenge to consider how to combine the network slicing technology to reduce the cost of offloading the computing task. In this paper, we study the scenario of autonomous vehicle offloading the computing task to Roadside Units (RSUs), and consider the multi-Mobile Edge Computing (multi-MEC) collaborative computing task to ensure that the task can be completed within tolerable delay. We consider the computing power and resource occupancy rate of MEC servers to ensure the user experience, and formulate a resource pricing scheme. Then, we propose a Performance-Price Ratio Task Scheduling (PPRTS) algorithm, which aims to complete the computing task within the maximum tolerable delay and reduce the cost of user. Simulation results show that the algorithm can effectively reduce the cost of the user.

Keywords: Internet of Vehicle (IoV) · Vehicle to Infrastructure (V2I) · Network slicing · Mobile Edge Computing (MEC) · Resource scheduling

1 Introduction

With the evolution of cellular network, the transmission rate of the network has been greatly improved, which provides technical support for the information interaction between vehicle information and external traffic elements [1]. V2I

© ICST Institute for Computer Sciences, Social Informatics and Telecommunications Engineering 2021
Published by Springer Nature Switzerland AG 2021. All Rights Reserved
H. Gao and X. Wang (Eds.): CollaborateCom 2021, LNICST 407, pp. 50–64, 2021.
https://doi.org/10.1007/978-3-030-92638-0_4

communication is an important form of Vehicle to Everything (V2X), which is considered to improve the roadside safety and traffic system in the Intelligent Transportation System (ITS) [2]. When the network of RSU equipment is dense enough, it can act as the orientation point and provide the vehicle with relevant information about the dangerous situation on the road, such as traffic jam ahead, traffic accidents and other risks. In addition, the vehicles offload the computing task to the MEC server of RSU, which can process the data faster.

In V2I communication scenario, it mainly refers to the interactive communication between vehicles and RSUs. V2I can facilitate the vehicle to quickly obtain the surrounding facilities information and process the computing tasks. By connecting the RSU with the Internet, the RSU can be turned into a relay point, which reduces the dependence of communication between vehicles and base stations, vehicles and other vehicles in the Internet of vehicles network. Compared with vehicle to base station communication, V2I can reduce the transmission delay and the processing delay of computing tasks [3].

Moreover, RSU combined with Mobile Edge Computing (MEC) technology is used to improve the efficiency of task processing. As a new deployment scheme, MEC can reduce the core network load and data transmission delay by deploying small data centers or nodes with cache and computing capabilities at the edge of the network, which is closely connected with mobile devices and users [4]. The mobile terminal can judge whether it needs offloading service according to the delay tolerance of the task, processing capacity, energy consumption, and other factors. By employing offloading service, the computing-intensive and delay-sensitive tasks can be processed on MEC servers to meet the performance requirements of tasks [5].

However, Multiple users request and share resources from MEC server at the same time, which causes congestion and slow response speed. In addition, different users have different requirements for data capacity and computing resources, which leads to inefficient resource allocation. In order to solve this problem, network slicing technology is used to divide the data capacity and computing resource of MEC server into multiple slices. These slices are respectively allocated to multiple users, and they are isolated from each other [6]. Network slicing technology provides a powerful guarantee to solve the problem of different requirements in network capacity, delay, reliability, speed and other aspects in diversified application scenarios [7]. And it builds corresponding logical networks for different types of resource requirements on the same physical infrastructure, and ensures mutual isolation [8].

Resource pricing scheme can affect the cost and resource utilization strategy of users, which is an important part. In [9], Baek B. et al. considered three dynamic pricing mechanisms for edge computing resource allocation in the Internet of Things environment: bid-proportional allocation mechanism, uniform pricing mechanism, and fairness-seeking differentiated pricing mechanism. In [10], Cardellini V. et al. studied the resource pricing and Provisioning Strategies in cloud systems, and found that the dynamic pricing scheme for different customers can give network operator higher income. By exploring the relationship between resource efficiency and profit maximization, Wang G. et al. studied the dimensioning of network slicing with resource pricing strategy in [11], and improved the profit of network slicing in [12]. However, most of these pricing schemes aim at improving profits of operator, without considering resource utilization and user competition, so we adopt dynamic asymmetric pricing strategy to improve resource utilization.

At present, some authors consider some strategies and methods to complete computing tasks. In [13], Liu M. *et al.* considered the edge cloud with limited computing power, divided the spectrum resources and computing resources of the edge cloud MEC server, and sold them to multiple users. And the partial offloading strategy was adopted to divide the user's computing tasks into different parts for local computing and offloading at the same time. In [14], Liu Y. *et al.* introduced the non-orthogonal multiple access function, which ensured that multiple users can offload computing tasks to the same fog node, so that a fog node can serve multiple users. On this basis, the total system cost of energy and user delay are minimized. In [15], Wang C. *et al.* chose some user equipments to offload their computing tasks, while others execute their computing tasks locally. However, this does not take into account users's willingness to offload, so a reasonable pricing scheme should be made to guide users to choose offloading when the resource utilization rate is low, otherwise choose local computing.

Many authors think that cloud computing in core network may cause too much delay, and consider offloading computing tasks to RSU to provide low delay services. In [16], Huang C. *et al.* considered that the computing task is offloaded from the vehicle to the base station, which leads to the increase of data transmission time, so the computing task is offloaded to RSU. In [17], Chen C. *et al.* used the idle resources between vehicles for collaborative computing. Computing tasks can also be offloaded to a single RSU, but the collaborative computing of multiple RSUs is not considered, which causes great pressure on a single RSU.

Based on the above, in this paper we build a multi-RSU collaborative slicing resources scheduling model to solve the delay sensitive computing task demand problem of IoV users. Facing the situation that users choose local computing or offload the task to MEC servers, we use performance-price ratio strategy to reduce user cost, and the evaluation results show that the user cost of the algorithm is lower than the other three algorithms. The main contributions are as follows,

- We study the scenario in which the computing task is offloaded to RSU by the automatic driving vehicle, and consider the multi-MEC collaborative computing task to ensure that the task can be completed within the tolerable delay.
- We use network slicing to segment MEC server resources, so that one RSU can serve multiple users, and multiple RSUs can also cooperate with each other in the computing task.
- We propose a Performance-Price Ratio Task Scheduling (PPRTS) algorithm, which aims to complete the computing task within the maximum tolerable delay and reduces the cost of user. Compared with the other three algorithms, PPRTS always ensures the lowest cost of the user when the computing task is completed within the tolerable delay.

The rest of the paper is organized as follows. In Sect. 2, we introduce the system model and problem formulation. In Sect. 3 is our proposed solution strategy. In Sect. 4, we compare the performance of different algorithms and analyze the different parameters of PPRTS algorithm followed by the conclusion in Sect. 5.

2 System Model

In this section, we first introduce the application scenario and the slicing resources model. Next, we propose mobility and communication model to describe the condition of the vehicle and task. Then, under appropriate assumptions, we give the slicing resources pricing model and design the specific pricing function. Finally, we integrate the above three models to propose the optimization objectives and related constraints.

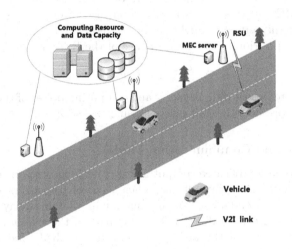

Fig. 1. Computational offloading of Multi-MEC collaboration.

2.1 Slicing Resources Model

As shown in Fig. 1, we consider that in the automatic driving scenario, some vehicles are driving on the straight road, and they can communicate with RSUs equipped with the MEC server through V2I link. We denote RSU set as $\mathcal{R} = \{1, 2, ..., N\}$. It is assumed that there is a certain distance between RSUs and the coverage is contiguous but not overlapping. Each RSU is equipped with the MEC server, which has limited data capacity and computing power. We mark the i-th RSU of vehicle connection as RSU_i, whose total data capacity is C_i and total computing power is A_i.

For vehicles, they have data capacity c_v, weak computing power a_v and low unit price p_v. Following [18], we use a triplet $\langle \delta, M, d \rangle$ to describe the task that the vehicle need to compute, where δ represents the complexity factor of the task, M represents the data size, and d represents maximum tolerable delay of the task. The computing tasks of vehicles are different in the form of text, voice or video, so the computing complexity factor of these tasks is different.

For RSUs, the computing resources and data capacity of multiple MEC servers are composed of network slices, which can be dynamically allocated to multiple vehicles. When the vehicle enters the coverage area of RSU, diversified logical private network services can be realized by accessing the network slicing. In this way, there is no need to build a physical private network and avoid the extra cost and waste of resources.

For the urgent computing tasks of vehicles, due to the weak local computing power, it may not be able to complete within the tolerable delay, which is an undesirable result for users. When a part of the tasks are offloaded to RSU and multiple MEC servers with strong computing power are used to process it simultaneously, the computing delay can be saved.

And the composition of the network slice of the RSU_i is

$$S_i = \{c_i, a_i, p_i\}, \tag{1}$$

where c_i and a_i represent data capacity and computing power of the slice respectively, and p_i represents the unit price of using this slice.

2.2 Mobility and Communication Model

There will be some complicated computing tasks in the process of vehicle driving to meet the safety, entertainment and other needs of passengers. According to the complexity factor δ, data size M and maximum tolerable delay d of the task, the computing task can be divided [19]. One part of the task m_v is computed locally, the other part of the task m_i is offloaded to RSU and computed by utilizing MEC servers slicing resources. The task local execution delay is as

$$t^v = \frac{\delta m_v}{a_v}, \tag{2}$$

where m_v is the data size computed locally by the vehicle, and a_v is the local computing power of the vehicle.

In the case of offloading the task to RSU and receiving the returned result, the vehicle location is different, and the vehicle mobility needs to be considered. Suppose there are T slots, set $\mathcal{T} = \{1, 2, ..., T\}$. At time t, we mark the coordinate of the vehicle as (x_t^v, y_t^v), and the RSU_i is (x_i, y_i), where $i \in \{1, 2, ..., N\}$. The distance between the vehicle and RSU_i can be calculated by Euclidean Distance as

$$d_i(t) = \sqrt{(x_t^v - x_i)^2 + (y_t^v - y_i)^2}, \forall i \in N. \tag{3}$$

And the channel gain between them is

$$g_i(t) = g_0 \rho^2 d_i(t)^{-\alpha_h}, \forall i \in N, \tag{4}$$

where g_0 is the channel gain at the reference distance, ρ is an exponential random variable with an mean value, d_i is the distance between the vehicle and the RSU_i, and α_h is the path loss index in the V2I link.

When K vehicles offload tasks to the same RSU through the shared channel, the signal-to-interference-plus-noise ratio (SINR) between the vehicle and RSU_i is

$$\gamma_i(t) = \frac{pg_i(t)}{\sigma^2 + \sum_{j=1}^{K-1} q_j h_j}, \forall i \in N, \tag{5}$$

where p is the transmission power of the current vehicle, g is the channel gain between the current vehicle and RSU; q is the transmission power of other vehicles, and h is the channel gain between other vehicles and RSU. And σ^2 is the power of additive white Gaussian noise.

Thus, the instantaneous data transmission rate between vehicle and RSU_i is

$$R_i(t) = W log_2 \left(1 + \gamma_i(t)\right), \forall i \in N, \tag{6}$$

where W represents the channel bandwidth. The instantaneous data transmission rate of vehicle is measured once in each time slot, and the average transmission rate can be calculated as

$$\bar{R} = \frac{\sum_{t=1}^{T} R_i(t)}{T}, \forall i \in N. \tag{7}$$

We denote β^u and β^d as transmission overhead of uplink and downlink respectively. Then, the uplink t^u and downlink t^d transmission delay of vehicle remaining computing task offloaded to RSU are respectively represented as follows

$$t^u = \frac{\beta^u (M - m_v)}{\bar{R}}, \tag{8}$$

$$t^d = \frac{\beta^d (M - m_v)}{\bar{R}}. \tag{9}$$

Short distance optical fiber communication is used between RSUs, and the transmission delay between them can be ignored. After receiving the computing task of vehicle offloading, RSU_i will assign the task to the next RSUs, which will execute the computing task at the same time. So the task execution delay in MEC is

$$t^m = \max \left(\frac{\delta m_i}{a_i}\right), \forall i \in N, \tag{10}$$

where m_i is the data size computed by slice of the i-th MEC, and a_i is computing power of slice of the i-th MEC. After MEC servers cooperatively processes the data, the network slice transmits the task results from the nearest RSU to the vehicle. Thus, the total execution delay of the vehicle computing task is

$$t^{total} = \max \left(t^v, t^u + t^m + t^d\right). \tag{11}$$

We divide the computing task into two parts: one part is executed locally on the vehicle, the other part is offloaded to MEC servers on RSUs for execution. The two parts of the task are carried out at the same time, so the total delay depends on the part that takes more time.

2.3 Pricing Model

For vehicles, local processing of computing task requires energy consumption, and the unit price p_v is a low fixed value. For RSUs, MEC servers have different computing power. In industries with high fixed equipment cost and low marginal cost, dynamic pricing of resources can improve the enthusiasm of users to use resources and ensure the efficiency of resource utilization. Similar to [20], we consider the computing power and resource occupancy rate of MEC to ensure the user experience. Thus, we propose the unit price function of slicing resources as

$$P^{unit} = \lambda e^{\mu x} + \nu, \tag{12}$$

where x is related to computing resource occupancy rate of MEC. λ is the initial unit price of slicing resources. Its value is dynamic, and it is the proportion of the current MEC server and the largest server computing power. μ represents the degree of unit price change, which affects how fast the unit price changes with x. ν represents the minimum unit price provided by infrastructure provider. And λ and ν jointly determine the starting price of resources. All the above parameters are positive.

In order to complete the computing task, the cost of local processing on the vehicle is

$$P_v = p_v t^v. \tag{13}$$

Because multiple MEC slicing resources are used to cooperatively process the computing task, the processing cost of the task offloaded to RSUs is

$$P_m = \sum_{i=1}^{N} p_i^{unit} \frac{\delta m_i}{a_i}, \tag{14}$$

where p_i is the unit price of the i-th MEC slice according to (12), and $\frac{\delta m_i}{a_i}$ is the usage time of the i-th MEC slice. The total cost of computing task offloaded to RSUs is the sum of slicing resources costs.

By integrating the above three models, the user's computing task cost can be defined as a constrained optimization problem, as follows:

$$
\begin{aligned}
\textbf{P1:} \quad &\min \quad P_v + P_m \\
s.t. \quad &C1 : m_v + \sum_{i=1}^{N} m_i = M, \\
&C2 : a_v + \sum_{i=1}^{N} a_i \geqslant \frac{M}{d - t^u - t^d}, \\
&C3 : t^{total} \leqslant d, \\
&C4 : m_v \leqslant c_v, \\
&C5 : m_i \leqslant c_i, \forall i \in N
\end{aligned}
\tag{15}
$$

where $C1$ represents that the total the task assigned to vehicle and MEC servers is certain. $C2$ represents that the computing power of the vehicle and slices of

MEC servers can complete the computing task. $C3$ represents that the maximum delay for processing the computing task locally or MEC shall not exceed maximum tolerable delay of the task. $C4$ and $C5$ ensure that the data size of the task assigned to the vehicle or each slice does not exceed the data capacity of them, otherwise the task data will be lost.

3   Proposed Solution Strategy

In this section, we discuss the solution, and propose algorithm based on greedy algorithm to solve **P1** quickly.

Firstly, we analyze the trend of the pricing function in problem **P1**. The pricing function is a monotonically increasing function. Its characteristic is that the higher the occupancy rate of computing resource, the higher the unit price, and the larger the slope. Such a mechanism can reduce congestion caused by high resource occupancy rate, which is helpful to improve user experience.

Next, we consider a special case of problem **P1**: the vehicle and all MEC servers are isomorphic, so the computing power, data capacity and resources price of the vehicle and MEC servers are the same. For problem **P1**, the task can be divided into multiple items according to the data capacity of MEC servers, and the MEC server can be seen as a bin. Thus, the cost of user can be minimized by reasonably dividing the task, processing it locally or offloading it to the MEC servers. In this case, problem **P1** can be regarded as: minimizing the number of bins used by reasonably placing items.

In fact, each MEC server has different computing power, data capacity and resource price. In order to get more computing power at a cheaper price, we consider designing a greedy algorithm based on performance-price ratio strategy to reduce the cost of resource utilization.

Initialization: Recording the vehicle coordinates, judging which RSU the vehicle is in and select the RSU to offload. If the distance between the vehicle and RSU is less than the radius, it means that it is within its coverage, as follows

$$d_i(t) \leqslant R_r, \forall i \in N. \tag{16}$$

Stage 1: Selecting bins according to performance-price ratio and dividing the task by data capacity of each bin. We regard the vehicle and N MEC servers as a bins set $\mathcal{B} = \{b_1, ..., b_i, ..., b_{n+1}\}$, which have data capacity c_i, computing power a_i and unit price p_i. In order to minimize the cost of user, we try to use bin with high performance-price ratio under the premise of satisfying the constraints. The performance-price ratio is calculated as

$$r_i = \frac{a_i}{p_i}, \forall i \in N + 1. \tag{17}$$

Then direct performance-price strategy reorder the bin set $\mathcal{B}$ in descending order of the performance-price ratio.

Sometimes the amount of task data is too large, which will lead to large transmission delay. At this time, the offload data takes up a large part of the

---

Algorithm 1. Performance-Price Ratio Task Scheduling (PPRTS) Algorithm

---

Input:

 Coordinates of RSUs and vehicle, RSU coverage radius Rr, vehicle speed Sv;
 complexity factor, data size and maximum tolerable delay of the task $\langle \delta, M, d \rangle$;
 data capacity, computing power and unit price of MEC servers slicing resources
 $\{c_i, a_i, p_i\}, \forall i \in N$ and the vehicle $\{c_v, a_v, p_v\}$.

Output:

 Computation task scheduling scheme and minimum cost of the vehicle user $\mathcal{P}_v + \mathcal{P}_m$.

1: Determine which RSU the vehicle is located in according to (16), and the RSU to
 be offloaded is selected;
2: Create a bins set $\mathcal{B} = \{b_1, ..., b_i, ..., b_{n+1}\}$ of vehicle and MEC servers resources;
3: **if** direct performance-price strategy **then**
4: Sort the set $\mathcal{B}$ in descending order according to (17);
5: **else**
6: The local vehicle ranks first, and the rest sorts the set $\mathcal{B}$ in descending order
  according to (17);
7: **end if**
8: **while** the task is not fully divided **do**
9: **for** $i \in N + 1$ **do**
10:   Check the data capacity c_i of b_i;
11:   $m_i \Leftarrow c_i$;
12:   Assign the task amount with data size m_i to b_i;
13:   $b_i \Leftarrow b_{i+1}$;
14: **end for**
15: **end while**
16: The total delay t^{total} is calculated according to (11);
17: **while** $t^{total} > d$ **do**
18: Assign the task amount $m_i \leqslant c_i$ that can be completed by b_{i+1} within d;
19: $b_i \Leftarrow b_{i+1}$;
20: **end while**
21: According to the vehicle speed S_v and task uplink t^u and processing t^m delay, the
 new vehicle coordinates are calculated as $(x_t + S_v(t^u + t^m), y_t)$, and the RSU of
 the returned results is selected.
22: Generate task scheduling scheme and the user cost according to (13), (14).

---

time, and the final task is difficult to complete. In this case, the amount of data offloaded to MEC should be reduced, and the local computing resources should be utilized to reduce the transmission delay. Thus, for the task with large amount of data and high delay requirement, we adopt a local priority strategy, which makes maximum use of the local computing resources, and the rest part of the task is offloaded to the MEC servers according to the performance-price ratio.

 The algorithm divides the task into many parts, checks the data capacity of $b1$, fills the data capacity of it, and loads the rest into $b2$ and $b3$ by analogy until the task assignment is completed. Next, the algorithm checks whether the delay of the scheme does not exceed maximum tolerable delay d. if not, the algorithm divides a part of the data m_{i+1} that can be completed in time d to b_{i+1}, and so on; otherwise, the scheme is generated and the minimum user cost is calculated according to (13) and (14). Then, we compare the direct performance-price ratio strategy with the local priority strategy, and the task scheduling scheme adopts the one with lower user cost within the maximum tolerable delay.

Stage 2: Processing the computation task and returning the computation result. After formulating the task scheduling scheme, one part of the task is offloaded to MEC servers for cooperative processing, and the other part is processed locally. According to the vehicle speed and task uplink and processing delay, vehicle coordinates are calculated. Similar to (16), the RSU in coverage range is selected and the computation result is returned to the vehicle. And our proposed performance-price ratio task scheduling (PPRTS) algorithm is shown in Algorithm 1.

Finally, we analyze the time complexity of PPRTS algorithm. For the line 3 and 4 in Algorithm 1, specifically it will take $O(nlog_2(n))$ operations to sort all the bin in this line in descending order according to performance-price ratio. For lines 8–15 and 17–20 of the loop, each set will traverse once and then terminate within $O(n)$ operations in the worst case. In conclusion, the overall time complexity of PPRTS algorithm is $O(nlog_2(n))$.

4 Simulation Results

In this section, we present simulation results of the PPRTS algorithm and show its performance. In addition, compared with the other three schemes, we verify that the proposed scheme can complete the task within the maximum tolerable delay and the user cost is the lowest. Then, we analyze the influence of different parameters on the scheme through parameter experiment.

Table 1. Simulation parameters

Parameter	Value
Vehicle available data capacity c_v	100 GB
Vehicle computing capacity a_v	500 MHz
Local computing unit price p_v	100
Vehicle transmitting power p	37 dBm
Vehicle bandwidth W	100 MHz
Vehicle speed S_v	60 km/h
RSU coverage radius R_r	500 m
White Gaussian noise power σ^2	−118 dBm
Transmission overhead of uplink β^u and downlink β^d	1, 0.05
Number of vehicles K and MEC servers N	5, 3
Total data capacity of each MEC server	100 GB, 300 GB, 500 GB
Total computing power of each MEC server	1 GHz, 3 GHz, 5 GHz
Coefficient μ of pricing function	0.1
Minimum price ν of pricing function	10

4.1 Simulation Settings

We randomly simulate the usage of computing resource in MEC servers and conduct lots of experiments to verify the performance of PPRTS algorithm. Some parameters are listed in Table 1. It is worth noting that more MEC server cooperation is not always better, nor is shorter latency always better. Because our optimization goal is to complete the computing task within the maximum tolerable delay and minimize the cost of users. Too many MEC collaborative computing tasks can reduce the delay, but the cost of users will increase, which is not what users expect. According to the simulation experiment task data, the total computing resource of the three MEC servers are 1GHz, 3GHz and 5GHz respectively. In each experiment, the computing resource used and occupancy rate of three MEC servers are shown in Table 2. The tolerable delay of vehicle is strict, and low delay ensures normal driving. In the experiment, the total delay of computing task offloading to MEC, server processing task and result return is millisecond level. And the complexity factor, data size and maximum tolerable delay of vehicle computing task are shown in Table 3.

Table 2. Usage of MEC servers computing resource in each experiment

		MEC1	MEC2	MEC3
Set1	CR used (MHz)	772.10	1780.46	1646.73
	CR occupancy (%)	77.21	59.35	32.93
Set2	CR used (MHz)	615.18	771.56	4746.14
	CR occupancy(%)	61.52	25.72	94.92
Set3	CR used (MHz)	722.64	1332.38	1439.44
	CR occupancy (%)	72.26	44.41	28.79
Set4	CR used (MHz)	551.88	2535.63	3574.18
	CR occupancy (%)	55.19	84.52	71.48
Set5	CR used (MHz)	803.38	515.66	1932.10
	CR occupancy (%)	80.34	17.19	38.64

Table 3. Task status in each experiment

Task	Complexity factor δ	Data size $\mathcal{M}$	Tolerable delay d
Set1	1	12.5 MB	200 ms
Set2	1.5	25 MB	400 ms
Set3	1	50 MB	600 ms
Set4	2	37.5 MB	650 ms
Set5	2	50 MB	800 ms

4.2 Parametric Analysis

The unit price of resources is a noticeable factor, which determines the strategy of selecting MEC resources. Thus, we conduct simulation experiments to observe the impact of MEC server computing power and resource occupancy on unit price.

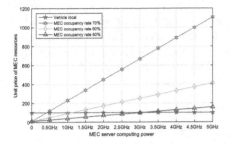 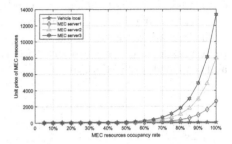

Fig. 2. Comparison of different MEC occupancy rates.

Fig. 3. Comparison of different MEC servers.

As shown in Fig. 2, the abscissa is the computing power of the MEC server, and the ordinate is the unit price of MEC resources. Taking the preset fixed vehicle local price as a reference, the influence of three MEC resource occupancy rates on resource unit price is compared. When the remaining computing power of MEC server is weak, the unit price is lower than vehicle local resources. With the enhancement of the remaining computing power of MEC server, the unit price also exceeds the vehicle. Under the same MEC computing capacity, the higher the occupancy rate, the higher the unit price, and the greater the growth rate of unit price. In this case, the MEC server with low resource occupancy and relatively strong computing power should be selected on the premise that the task can be completed within the tolerable delay.

Then, we compare the resource unit prices of heterogeneous MEC servers. Taking the preset fixed vehicle local price as a reference, three MEC servers use all the computing power, and the specific resources are shown in Table II. As shown in Fig. 3, the abscissa is the resource occupancy rate calculated by MEC, and the ordinate is the unit price of MEC resources. The unit price gap of each MEC server is small before 50%, and gradually widens after 60%, which is a protection mechanism. The high cost makes the user choose the server with relatively idle resources, ensuring the user experience and dispersing the server pressure of operator.

4.3 Scheme Comparison

We count the task delay, and use MEC resource pricing function under the same parameters to calculate the user cost of four task scheduling schemes in these five Sets. The four task scheduling schemes are *PPRTS, PLRRO, All random offloading* and *Completely random.*

PPRTS uses our proposed Performance-Price Ratio Task Scheduling Algorithm. In other words, within the maximum tolerable delay, the scheme chooses the one with lower user cost between the direct performance-price ratio strategy and the local priority strategy. *PLRRO* means priority local residual random offloading. In this scheme, local computing task is considered first, and the rest of the task is randomly offloaded to multiple MEC servers. *All random offloading* represents that the task does not consider local computing at all, and all parts of the task are randomly offloaded to multiple MEC servers. *Completely random* represents a completely random proportion of the task being computed locally and offloaded to MEC servers.

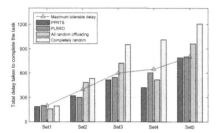 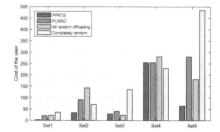

Fig. 4. Total delay of different schemes.   **Fig. 5.** Cost of different schemes.

The total delay of different schemes is shown in Fig. 4, and should not exceed the maximum tolerable delay. The abscissa is the MEC computing resource usage in five sets, and the ordinate is total delay of four schemes to complete the task. From the experimental results, not every scheme can complete the computing task within the maximum tolerable delay.

In these five Sets, *PLRRO* once, *All random offloading* three times, and *Completely random* four times failed to complete the computing task within the maximum tolerable delay. And Each experiment of *PPRTS* can complete the task within the tolerable delay. In Set 2, we find that the delay of *PLRRO* is lower than that of *PPRTS*, but it is not that the lower the delay is, the cheaper the price is. It may be that the *PLRRO* uses better computing resources to complete the computing task with lower delay, but the user cost is not necessarily the lowest. Our goal is to minimize the user cost within the tolerable delay of the task, so we only need to complete the task within the tolerable delay.

The user cost comparison of the four schemes is shown in Fig. 5. The abscissa is the MEC computing resource usage in these five sets, and the ordinate is user cost of four schemes to complete the task.

Due to the randomness, the user cost of *Completely random* is sometimes high and sometimes low, and the performance is unstable in these five Sets. If the task data is large and all parts of the task are offloaded to MEC, most of the delay is spent on transmission, leaving less computing time, and the performance of *All random offloading* without considering local computing is not ideal. Although the cost of *All random offloading* is lowest in Set 3, it can not complete the task within the tolerance delay, so it is not desirable. Relatively speaking, *PLRRO* gives priority to the local cheap computing resources processing the task, so the user cost is lower than the two random schemes. However, MEC resources are relatively idle and cheap in Set 5, and the cost of preferentially computing task locally is high. *PPRTS* selects resources according to performance-price ratio, and the user cost is always the lowest among the four schemes.

5 Conclusion

In this paper, we study the cost of the user computing task for vehicle in autonomous driving scenario. In order to minimize the cost of user, we use network slicing to segment MEC server resources, and propose PPRTS algorithm, which offloads the computing task to multi-MEC servers according to performance-price ratio of slicing resources. Simulation results show that the algorithm can complete the task within the maximum tolerable delay, and effectively reduce the cost of user.

Acknowledgement. This work is partly supported by the National Natural Science Foundation of China (Nos. 61872044, 61902029), The Key Research and Cultivation Projects at Beijing Information Science and Technology University (No. 5211823411).

References

1. Dai, C., Liu, X., et al.: A low-latency object detection algorithm for the edge devices of IoV systems. IEEE Trans. Veh. Technol. **69**(10), 11169–11178 (2020)
2. Tang, X., Geng, Z., Chen, W.: Safety message propagation using vehicle-infrastructure cooperation in urban vehicular networks. In: Gao, H., Wang, X., Yin, Y., Iqbal, M. (eds.) CollaborateCom 2018. LNICST, vol. 268, pp. 235–251. Springer, Cham (2019). https://doi.org/10.1007/978-3-030-12981-1_17
3. Lien, S., Hung, S., et al.: Low latency radio access in 3GPP local area data networks for V2X: stochastic optimization and learning. IEEE Internet Things J. **6**(3), 4867–4879 (2019)
4. Xiao, X., Li, Y., Xia, Y., Ma, Y., Jiang, C., Zhong, X.: Location-aware edge service migration for mobile user reallocation in crowded scenes. In: Gao, H., Wang, X., Iqbal, M., Yin, Y., Yin, J., Gu, N. (eds.) CollaborateCom 2020, Part I. LNICST, vol. 349, pp. 441–457. Springer, Cham (2021). https://doi.org/10.1007/978-3-030-67537-0_27
5. Campolo C., Iera A., et al.: MEC support for 5G–V2X use cases through docker containers. In: IEEE Wireless Communications and Networking Conference (WCNC), pp. 1–6 (2019)
6. Feng, J., Pei, Q., et al.: Dynamic network slicing and resource allocation in mobile edge computing systems. IEEE Trans. Veh. Technol. **69**(7), 7863–7878 (2020)
7. Liu, Y., Peng, M., et al.: Toward edge intelligence: multiaccess edge computing for 5G and internet of things. IEEE Internet Things J. **7**(8), 6722–6747 (2020)

8. Coronado E., Riggio R.: Flow-based network slicing: mapping the future mobile radio access networks. In: IEEE The 28th International Conference on Computer Communications and Networks (ICCCN), pp. 1–9 (2019)
9. Baek, B., Lee, J., et al.: Three dynamic pricing schemes for resource allocation of edge computing for iot environment. IEEE Internet Things J. **7**(5), 4292–4303 (2020)
10. Cardellini, V., Valerio, V.D., et al.: Game-theoretic resource pricing and provisioning strategies in cloud systems. IEEE Trans. Serv. Comput. **13**(1), 86–98 (2020)
11. Wang G., Feng G., et al.: Resource allocation for network slices in 5G with network resource pricing. In: IEEE Global Communications Conference (GLOBECOM), pp. 1–6 (2017)
12. Wang, G., Feng, G., et al.: Reconfiguration in network slicing–optimizing the profit and performance. IEEE Trans. Netw. Serv. Manag. **16**(2), 591–605 (2019)
13. Liu, M., Liu, Y.: Price-based distributed offloading for mobile-edge computing with computation capacity constraints. IEEE Wirel. Commun. Lett. **7**(3), 420–423 (2018)
14. Liu, Y., Yu, F.R., et al.: Distributed resource allocation and computation offloading in fog and cloud networks with non-orthogonal multiple access. IEEE Trans. Veh. Technol. **67**(12), 12137–12151 (2018)
15. Wang, C., Liang, C., et al.: Computation offloading and resource allocation in wireless cellular networks with mobile edge computing. IEEE Trans. Wirel. Commun. **16**(8), 4924–4938 (2017)
16. Huang, C., Lin, T., et al.: Data dissemination of application service by using member-centric routing protocol in a platoon of internet of vehicle (IoV). IEEE Access **7**, 127713–127727 (2019)
17. Chen, C., Chen, L., et al.: Delay-optimized V2V-based computation offloading in urban vehicular edge computing and networks. IEEE Access **8**, 18863–18873 (2020)
18. Wang, Y., Lang, P., et al.: A game-based computation offloading method in vehicular multiaccess edge computing networks. IEEE Internet Things J. **7**(6), 4987–4996 (2020)
19. Lan Y., Wang X., et al.: Mobile-edge computation offloading and resource allocation in heterogeneous wireless networks. In: IEEE Wireless Communications and Networking Conference (WCNC), pp. 1–6 (2019)
20. Liang Y., Chen X., et al.: Cooperative resource sharing strategy with eMBB cellular and C-V2X slices. In: IEEE 26th International Conference on Parallel and Distributed Systems (ICPADS), pp. 716–721 (2020)

An OO-Based Approach of Computing Offloading and Resource Allocation for Large-Scale Mobile Edge Computing Systems

Yufu Tan, Sikandar Ali, Haotian Wang, and Jiwei Huang[✉]

Beijing Key Laboratory of Petroleum Data Mining, China University of Petroleum - Beijing, Beijing 102249, China
{2019211243,2018011122}@student.cup.edu.cn,
{sikandar,huangjw}@cup.edu.cn

Abstract. Mobile edge computing (MEC) is an emerging paradigm to meet the increasing real-time performance demands for Internet of Things and mobile applications. By offloading the computationally intensive workloads to edge servers, the quality of service (QoS) could be greatly improved. However, with the growing popularity of MEC, the MEC systems grow extremely large, and thus the QoS optimization suffers from search space explosion problem, making it impractical in real-life scenarios. To attack this challenge, this paper studies the joint optimization of task offloading and computational resource allocation for large-scale MEC systems. We formulate this problem as a cost minimization problem and illustrate the NP-hardness of this problem. In order to solve this problem, we divide the original problem into two sub-problems and introduce the theory of Ordinal Optimization (OO) to search for a near-optimal computing offloading and resource allocation policy within a significantly reduced search space. Finally, the efficacy of our approach is validated by simulation experiments.

Keywords: Mobile Edge Computing (MEC) · Computing offloading · Resource allocation · Ordinal optimization · Large-scale MEC systems

1 Introduction

With the rapid development of Internet of Things (IoT) and Mobile Internet, the amount of mobile data traffic and the number of mobile devices have surged. According to the forecast [1], by 2022, mobile will account for 20% of total IP traffic and the world's mobile data traffic will almost reach to one zettabyte. Moreover, there will be 12.3 billion mobile devices including M2M modules by 2022, which outnumber the estimated global population (8 billion) at that moment by 1.5 times. At the same time, more and more innovative applications

© ICST Institute for Computer Sciences, Social Informatics and Telecommunications Engineering 2021
Published by Springer Nature Switzerland AG 2021. All Rights Reserved
H. Gao and X. Wang (Eds.): CollaborateCom 2021, LNICST 407, pp. 65–83, 2021.
https://doi.org/10.1007/978-3-030-92638-0_5

are emerging, such as Augmented Reality (AR) [2], Natural Language Processing (NLP) [3], Virtual Reality (VR) [4] and self-driving [5]. These applications are all computing-intensive, time-sensitive, and energy-intensive. However, due to limited resources of the mobile devices (i.e., computational resources and battery capacity), these applications are difficult to achieve a satisfactory experience for users. Therefore, due to the contradiction between the huge demand for computational resources as well as energy consumption of these emerging applications and limited resources of mobile devices, the advance of future mobile platforms becomes a major challenge.

Mobile Cloud Computing (MCC) is a traditional architecture which is deemed to be able to address the above challenges [6]. Mobile devices are able to offload computationally intensive workloads to a central cloud for execution by MCC. Without sacrificing the mobility and convenience of mobile devices, the rich computing resources of the central cloud can be utilized to enhance the support of mobile devices for these emerging applications. However, MCC also introduces high latency as data has to be transferred to remote cloud servers for processing [7].

Mobile Edge Computing (MEC) is an innovative paradigm designed to offer an IT service environment as well as cloud computing capabilities at the edge of the mobile network that is geographically close to mobile users [8]. On the one hand, like MCC, MEC is able to provide rich computational resources for mobile devices. On the other hand, MEC can achieve less latency as well as network load and offer an improved user experience compared to MCC.

Since the era of cloud computing, task scheduling and resource management have always been a high-profile issue in the academic as well as industrial community [9]. Furthermore, as one of the most important issues in MEC, how to get an excellent task offloading policy which decides whether a task is executed locally or offloaded to the edge server has attracted attention in recent years. A majority of the existing researches focus on the optimization of latency or energy consumption.

In [10], the authors studied a single-user MEC system that allows parallel processing of computationally intensive tasks at the local device as well as at the edge server to reduce the average latency of each task. In order to find the optimal offloading policy, they presented a one-dimensional search policy based on the theory of Markov Decision Process. Numerical results shown that the proposed policy is significantly better than the greedy scheduling policy. For multi-user MEC system, Kan et al. [6] formulated the multi-user offloading decision as a cost minimization problem. By classifying and prioritizing mobile devices, they developed a heuristic algorithm considering both computation and radio resource allocation. Furthermore, they also considered the variety of latency requirements of tasks. Mao et al. [11] considered a multi-user MEC system where tasks arrive stochastically. They formulated a power consumption minimization problem with task buffer stability constraints. Based on the theory of Lyapunov optimization, they developed an online algorithm to decide the CPU-cycle frequencies for execution locally as well as the transmission power and bandwidth allocation for execution remotely. Numerical results showed that the proposed algorithm is capable to keep the balance between the quality of computation experience and the energy consumption of mobile devices. In a dynamic MEC system, it is very challenging to find an excellent offloading policy. To attack this problem, the theory of Reinforcement Learning (RL) has been introduced [12]. Li et al. [13] presented an offloading method based on RL in a multi-user MEC system. In the beginning, they developed an offloading method based on Q-learning algorithm. But numerical results shown that the number of possible actions may surge as the users increases. In that case, the action-value Q would be too complicated to be computed and stored. Therefore, to solve this problem, they presented to use a Deep Q-Network (DQN) to estimate the Q-table. Simulation results shown that, under different system parameters, the proposed methods perform better than other two methods. In our previous work [14], we studied the problems of dynamic task scheduling and resource management in MEC system to maximize revenue of the edge service providers. While the discrete nature of our problem makes it is formulated as an integer programming (IP) problem, which is NP-hard. To tackle this problem, we researched the totally unimodular constraints of the problem, which help us convert the original problem into a linear programming (LP) problem. Then, experiments was conducted to verify this approach.

All of the above studies just focused on optimizing the execution latency or the energy consumption of mobile devices while neglecting the energy consumption of the edge servers. However, reducing the energy consumption of edge servers is critical because it not only reduces carbon dioxide emissions but also cuts down the costs for service providers. Furthermore, the Fifth Generation Mobile Communication Technology has become a research hotspot in the communications industry and academia in recent years. In order to achieving seamless coverage, it is necessary to densely deploy vast quantities of small cells. Consequently, the ultra-dense cellular network becomes a core feature of 5G cellular networks [15]. Therefore, it is essential to focus on multi-user computing offloading in the ultra-dense network. Chen et al. [16] propose a novel framework of task offloading for MEC in ultra-dense networks. They studied the problem of computational offloading in ultra-dense network to optimize the average latency and save the battery of mobile devices. They propose an efficient offloading policy, however, the final offloading policy is too dependent on the given initial task placement policy.

This paper proposes a method based on Ordinal Optimization (OO) to minimize latency and energy consumption of edge servers in large-scale MEC systems. The main contributions of the work are listed as follows.

- We propose large-scale MEC systems offloading problem, which aims to minimize the execution latency and energy consumption of edge servers in the ultra-dense network with multiple users by joint optimization of offload policy and computation resource allocation. Further, the problem is formulated as an NP-hard problem.

- In order to attack the above NP-hard problem, the original problem is divided into two sub-problem: i.e., the task placement problem and the resource allocation problem. Furthermore, we obtain the closed-form solution of the optimal resource allocation under an arbitrary given task placement policy.
- We introduce the theory of Ordinal Optimization intending to get a near-optimal task placement policy. Then, an efficient offloading algorithm is proposed and its efficiency is verified.

The rest of the paper is organized as follows. Section 2 describes the system model definition and the problem formulation. In Sect. 3, we develop a near-optimal offloading policy based on the theory of Ordinal Optimization. In Sect. 4, we compare the performance of our novel policy with three baseline policies. Finally, Sect. 5 concludes the paper.

2   System Model and Problem Formulation

In this section, we first introduce the large-scale MEC systems. Then, we formulate the problem and show that this problem is NP-hard. The scenario, we are considering is shown in Fig. 1. In the large-scale MEC systems, we assume that there exists n wireless base station, labeled as $\mathcal{B} = \{b_1, b_2, ..., b_n\}$. Each base station is equipped with an edge server, and thus we can also use $\mathcal{B}$ to denote the set of edge servers. We denote the set of mobile users as $\mathcal{U} = \{u_1, u_2, ...u_m\}$, and consider that each mobile user u_i has a computation task $T_i = (\omega_i, s_i)$ that can be processed locally or offloaded to one of the edge servers via the wireless channel. Similarly, we also use $\mathcal{U}$ to denote the set of mobile devices. Here, ω_i denotes the CPU cycles required to accomplish the task T_i, and s_i represents the data size of task T_i. Each server can provide services to multiple users within its signal coverage. Naturally, each user also can offload computation task to any edge server whose signal coverage includes the user's location. The system model denote $\mathcal{A}(u_i)$ as the set of edge servers that can provide services for the user u_i.

2.1   Communication Model

When the computation task of mobile user u_i is offloaded to edge server b_j, the uplink data rate can be expressed as follows:

$$r_{i,j} = B \log_2(1 + \frac{p_i^T g_{i,j}}{\sigma^2}) \tag{1}$$

here B is channel bandwidth, p_i^T is the transmission power of user u_i and σ^2 is noise power of the mobile device. Since the duration of data transmission is short, we assume that the users are not moving during the task offloading. So the channel gain between user u_i and base station b_j which is denoted as $g_{i,j}$

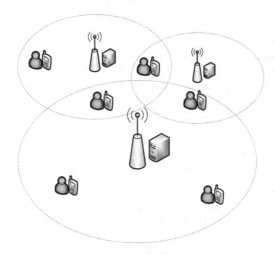

Fig. 1. Model of the large-scale MEC systems

can be regarded as a constant. Therefore, the transmission latency from mobile device u_i to base station b_j can be expressed as follows:

$$t_{i,j}^T = \frac{s_i}{r_{i,j}} \qquad (2)$$

Furthermore, the transmission energy consumption of mobile device u_i can be also attained as follows:

$$\epsilon_{i,j}^T = p_i^T t_{i,j}^T \qquad (3)$$

2.2 Computing Model

It is obvious that, task can be executed locally or remotely. Therefore, the two models are discussed separately.

Local Computing. For local computing, the computation capability of mobile device u_i is defined as f_i^L (cycles/second). Therefore, the local latency of task T_i is:

$$t_i^L = \frac{\omega_i}{f_i^L} \qquad (4)$$

Moreover, the computation energy consumption for processing locally can be obtain as:

$$\epsilon_i^L = p_i^L t_i^L \qquad (5)$$

where p_i^L is the computation power of mobile device u_i.

Table 1. Notation table

Symbol	Example
n	The number of base stations (edge servers)
m	The number of mobile users (tasks)
$\mathcal{B}$	The set of base stations (edge servers)
b_j	j^{th} base station (edge server)
$\mathcal{U}$	The set of mobile users (mobile devices)
u_i	i^{th} mobile user (mobile device)
T_i	i^{th} task
s_i	The data size of T_i
ω_i	The CPU cycles of T_i
$\mathcal{A}(u_i)$	The set of edge server that can provide services to mobile user u_i
$r_{i,j}$	The uplink data rate between u_i and b_j
σ^2	The noise power of the mobile device
B	The channel bandwidth
$g_{i,j}$	The channel gain between u_i and b_j
$t_{i,j}^T$	The transmission latency from u_i to b_j
t_i^L	The local computing latency of u_i
p_i^T	The transmission power of u_i
p_i^L	The computing power of u_i
$\epsilon_{i,j}^T$	The transmission energy consumption for transferring T_i to transfer to b_j
ϵ_i^L	The local computation energy consumption of T_i
$\mathbf{f}^E$	The set of edge server frequencies
f_j^E	The frequency of edge server b_j
f_i^L	The frequency of mobile device b_i
$\kappa_{j,i}$	The proportion of edge server b_j computation resources allocated to task T_i
p_j^E	The power of edge server b_j
p_j^{max}	The max power of edge server b_j
p_j^{idle}	The idle power of edge server b_j
u_j	The utilization of edge server b_j
$p_{i,j}^E$	The extra power consumed to process task T_i on the server b_j
$\epsilon_{i,j}^E$	The extra energy consumed to process task T_i on the server b_j
E_i^{max}	The total battery capacity of mobile device u_i
α_i	The remainder energy consumption relative to the total battery capacity E_i^{max}

Mobile Edge Computing. The computation resources of edge servers can
be denoted as $\mathbf{f}^E = (f_1^E, f_2^E, \cdots, f_n^E)$, where f_j^E denotes the computational
resource of jth edge server. The latency of task T_i processed on edge server b_j
consists of transmission latency and computation latency. Thus, the edge latency
can be obtained as follows:

$$t_{i,j}^E = \frac{\omega_i}{\kappa_{j,i} f_j^E} + t_{i,j}^T \tag{6}$$

where $\kappa_{j,i}$ is the proportion of computation resource of edge server b_j allocated
to task T_i. It should be noted that the transmission delay of returning processed
result from edge server to mobile device is ignored here. Since, the output data

is usually very small and the downlink rate is much higher than uplink rate, therefore, its impact on the overall computation overhead is negligible.

To calculate the power consumed by an edge server b_j, a simple utilization-based model that proved to be very accurate is used [17,18]:

$$p_j^E = (p_j^{max} - p_j^{idle})u_j + p_j^{idle} \tag{7}$$

where u_j denote CPU utilization of the edge server b_j, p_j^{idle} and p_j^{max} are the respective average power values when the edge server b_j is idle or fully utilized. It can be seen from the above equation that p_j^E consists of two parts: The former is the extra power consumed when processing tasks, which is related to the workload of the server b_j. While the latter is the power consumed regardless of whether the server is working, which is irrelevant to the workload of the server. Thus, for the sake of convenience, we only consider the former. Therefore, the extra power of edge server b_j consumed by task T_i is:

$$p_{i,j}^E = (p_j^{max} - p_j^{idle})\kappa_{j,i} \tag{8}$$

Consequently, the energy consumption of the task T_i processed on the edge server b_j is:

$$\epsilon_{i,j}^E = \frac{\omega_i}{\kappa_i^j f_j^E} \cdot P_{i,j}^E = \frac{\omega_i}{f_j^E}(p_j^{max} - p_j^{idle}) \tag{9}$$

(9) indicates that $\epsilon_{i,j}^E$ is irrelevant to $\kappa_{j,i}$. Table 1 shows the notation in this paper.

2.3 Problem Formulation

In this paper, a simple additive weighting (SAW) method to minimize the task latency and the extra energy consumption of edge servers has been incorporated. Therefore, we can formulate the problem as follows:

$$\min_{\boldsymbol{x},\boldsymbol{\kappa}} f(\boldsymbol{x},\boldsymbol{\kappa}) = \beta_1 \sum_{i=1}^{m}[x_{i,0}t_i^L + \sum_{j=1}^{n}x_{i,j}t_{i,j}^E] + \beta_2 \sum_{i=1}^{m}\sum_{j=1}^{n}x_{i,j}\epsilon_{i,j}^E$$

$$\text{s.t.} \quad C1: x_{i,j} \in \{0,1\}, \forall i = 1,2,\cdots,m, \forall j = 0,1,2,...,n$$

$$C2: \sum_{j=0}^{n} x_{i,j} = 1, \forall i = 1,2,\cdots,m$$

$$C3: 0 \le \kappa_{j,i} \le 1, \forall i = 1,2,\cdots,m, \forall j = 1,2,...,n \tag{10}$$

$$C4: 0 \le \sum_{i=1}^{n} x_{i,j}\kappa_{j,i} \le 1, \forall j = 1,2,\cdots,n$$

$$C5: x_i\epsilon_i^L \le \alpha_i E_i^{max}, \forall i = 1,2,\cdots,m$$

$$C6: (1-x_i)\epsilon_i^T \le \alpha_i E_i^{max}, \forall i = 1,2,\cdots,m$$

$$C7: \sum_{j \in \mathcal{A}(u_i)\cup\{u_i\}} x_{i,j} = 1, \forall i = 1,2,\cdots,m$$

where $x_{i,0} = 1$ ($x_{i,0} = 0$) represents that task T_i will be computed on local mobile device (edge server), $x_{i,j} = 1$ ($j = 1, 2, \cdots, n$) represents task T_i will be computed on edge server b_j, otherwise, $x_{i,j} = 0$. $\kappa_{j,i}$ represents the computation resources allocated to the task T_i by the edge server b_j, β_1 and β_2 are weight factors, and $\beta_1 + \beta_2 = 1$. The constraint C1 and C2 indicate that tasks can only be computed on the local device or one of the edge servers. The constraint C3 and C4 state that the total computation resources allocated from an edge server must not exceed its computation capacity. The constraint C5 and C6 indicate that the energy consumption for computing and transmission task cannot exceed the remaining energy of the mobile device. The last constraint C7 indicates task can only be computed locally or offloaded to edge servers whose signal coverage includes the user's location. Obviously, (10) is a mixed-integer non-linear programming problem, which is NP-hard [19, 20].

3   An Efficient Offloading Algorithm Based on Ordinal Optimization

In this section, we demonstrate an efficient offloading algorithm based on Ordinal Optimization to tackle the problem mentioned in (10). We solve the problem by dividing the original problem into two sub-problems as follows:

- **Computation resource allocation problem**: This problem aims to decide how much computation resource, an edge server allocate to each task offloaded to the edge server.
- **Task placement problem**: This problem aims to decide whether each task will be processed locally or remotely, and if offloaded, to which edge server it will be offloaded.

3.1   Computation Resource Allocation Problem

Theorem 1. *Given* $\boldsymbol{x} = \boldsymbol{x}^0$, *using* $\mathcal{T}(b_j)$ *to represent the set of tasks offloaded to the edge server* b_j, *then the optimal resources allocated by edge server* b_j *for the ith task is given by* $\dfrac{\sqrt{\omega_i}}{\sum_{m=1}^{|\mathcal{T}(b_j)|} \sqrt{\omega_m}}$.

Proof. Given $\boldsymbol{x} = \boldsymbol{x}^0$, the objective function of (10) can be expressed as follows:

$$
\begin{aligned}
f(\boldsymbol{\kappa}) = f(\boldsymbol{x}^0, \boldsymbol{\kappa}) &= \beta_1 \sum_{i=1}^{m} [x_{i,0}^0 \frac{\omega_i}{f_i^L} + \sum_{j=1}^{n} x_{i,j}^0 (\frac{\omega_i}{\kappa_{j,i} f_j^E} + \frac{s_i}{r_{i,j}})] \\
&+ \beta_2 \sum_{i=1}^{m} \sum_{j=1}^{n} x_{i,j}^0 \frac{\omega_i}{f_j^E} (p_j^{max} - p_j^{idle}) \\
&= \beta_1 \sum_{i=1}^{m} \sum_{j=1}^{n} x_{i,j}^0 \frac{\omega_i}{\kappa_{j,i} f_j^E} + C
\end{aligned}
\tag{11}
$$

where $C = \beta_1 \sum_{i=1}^{m} x_{i,0}^0 \frac{\omega_i}{f_i^L} + \beta_1 \sum_{i=1}^{m} \sum_{j=1}^{n} x_{i,j}^0 \frac{s_i}{r_{i,j}} + \beta_2 \sum_{i=1}^{m} \sum_{j=1}^{n} x_{i,j}^0 \frac{\omega_i}{f_j^E}$
$(p_j^{max} - p_j^{idle})$ is a constant. We denote the set of offloaded tasks is $\mathcal{T}$ and the set of edge servers which there are tasks place on is $\mathcal{E}$. For convenience, we assume $\mathcal{T} = \{T_1, T_2, \cdots, T_{|\mathcal{T}|}\}$ and $\mathcal{E} = \{b_1, b_2, \cdots, b_{|\mathcal{E}|}\}$. So (10) can be converted as follows:

$$\min_{\boldsymbol{\kappa}} \quad f(\boldsymbol{\kappa}) = \beta_1 \sum_{i=1}^{|\mathcal{T}|} \frac{\omega_i}{\kappa_{j_i,i} f_{j_i}^E} + C$$

$$\text{s.t.} \quad C1: 0 < \kappa_{j_i,i} \leq 1, \forall i = 1, 2, \cdots, |\mathcal{T}|, b_{j_i} \in \mathcal{E}$$
$$C2: 0 < \sum_{i \in \mathcal{T}(b_j)} \kappa_{j,i} \leq 1, \forall j \in \mathcal{E}$$

(12)

where b_{j_i} represents the edge server to which task T_i will be offloaded, $\mathcal{T}(b_j)$ is the set of tasks offloaded to the edge server b_j. We noticed that the resource allocation of one server does not effect the resource allocation of another server, therefore, the objective function of (12) can be expressed as a combination of n independent minimization problems. Thus, (12) can be transform as follows:

$$\min_{\boldsymbol{\kappa}} \quad f(\boldsymbol{\kappa}) = \beta_1 \min_{\kappa_{1,\cdot}} \sum_{i \in \mathcal{T}(b_1)} \frac{\omega_i}{\kappa_{1,i} f_1^E} + \beta_1 \min_{\kappa_{2,\cdot}} \sum_{i \in \mathcal{T}(b_2)} \frac{\omega_i}{\kappa_{2,i} f_2^E}$$

$$+ \cdots + \beta_1 \min_{\kappa_{n,\cdot}} \sum_{i \in \mathcal{T}(b_n)} \frac{\omega_i}{\kappa_{n,i} f_n^E} + C$$

$$\text{s.t.} \quad C1: 0 < \kappa_{j,i} \leq 1, \forall j \in \mathcal{E}, i \in \mathcal{T}(b_j)$$
$$C2: 0 < \sum_{i \in \mathcal{T}(b_j)} \kappa_{j,i} \leq 1, \forall b_j \in \mathcal{E}$$

(13)

where $|\mathcal{T}(b_1)| + |\mathcal{T}(b_2)| + \cdots + |\mathcal{T}(b_n)| = |\mathcal{T}|$. As for one minimization problem in objective function of (13), it is not difficult to see that $\sum_{i=1}^{l^j} \kappa_i^j = 1$ must be hold to minimize the objective function. Finally, the original problem is converted into $|\mathcal{E}|$ minimization problems, jth of which is as follows:

$$\min_{\kappa_{j,\cdot}} \quad f(\kappa_{j,\cdot}) = \sum_{i \in \mathcal{T}(b_j)} \frac{a_i}{\kappa_{j,i}}$$

$$\text{s.t.} \quad C1: \kappa_{j,i} > 0, \forall i \in \mathcal{T}(b_j)$$
$$C2: \sum_{i \in \mathcal{T}(b_j)} \kappa_{j,i} = 1$$

(14)

where $a_i = \frac{\omega_i}{f_j^E}$. Resorting to Inequality of Arithmetic and Geometric Means, we can get the closed-form of the optimal resource allocation:

$$\sum_{i \in T(b_j)} \frac{a_i}{\kappa_{j,i}} = \sum_{i \in T(b_j)} \frac{a_i \sum\limits_{i \in T(b_j)} \kappa_{j,i}}{\kappa_{j,i}}$$

$$= \sum_{i \in T(b_j)} a_i + \sum_{i \in T(b_j)} \sum_{\substack{m \in T(b_j) \\ m \neq i}} \frac{a_i \kappa_{j,m}}{\kappa_{j,i}}$$

$$= \sum_{i \in T(b_j)} a_i + \frac{1}{2} \sum_{i \in T(b_j)} \sum_{\substack{m \in T(b_j) \\ m \neq i}} \left(\frac{a_i \kappa_{j,m}}{\kappa_{j,i}} + \frac{a_m \kappa_{j,i}}{\kappa_{j,m}} \right) \quad (15)$$

$$\geq \sum_{i \in T(b_j)} a_i + \frac{1}{2} \sum_{i \in T(b_j)} \sum_{\substack{m \in T(b_j) \\ m \neq i}} \sqrt{2 \frac{a_i \kappa_{j,m}}{\kappa_{j,i}} \cdot \frac{a_m \kappa_{j,i}}{\kappa_{j,m}}}$$

$$= \sum_{i \in T(b_j)} a_i + \frac{1}{2} \sum_{i \in T(b_j)} \sum_{\substack{m \in T(b_j) \\ m \neq i}} \sqrt{2 a_i a_m}$$

if and only if $\kappa_{j,i} = \frac{\sqrt{a_i}}{\sum\limits_{m \in T(b_j)} \sqrt{a_m}}$, $\sum\limits_{m \in T(b_j)} \frac{a_i}{\kappa_i^j} = \sum\limits_{i \in T(b_j)} a_i + \frac{1}{2} \sum\limits_{i \in T(b_j)}$ $\sum\limits_{\substack{m \in T(b_j) \\ m \neq i}} \sqrt{2 a_i a_m}$. So, the optimal allocation of resources for ith task offloaded to the edge server b_j is:

$$\kappa_{j,i} = \frac{\sqrt{\omega_i / f_j^E}}{\sum\limits_{m \in T(b_j)} \sqrt{\omega_m / f_j^E}} = \frac{\sqrt{\omega_i}}{\sum\limits_{m \in T(b_j)} \sqrt{\omega_m}} \quad (16)$$

3.2 Task Placement Problem and An OO-Based Offloading Algorithm

We have got the optimal resource allocation of the edge servers under an arbitrary given task placement policy. Thus, the original problem is converted into getting the optimal task placement policy, which means we should decide whether each task is processed locally or remotely and to which edge server task should be placed on. In other words, if we obtain the optimal task placement policy, the optimal resource allocation under this policy must be the optimal solution to the original problem. Unfortunately, the decision space of the task placement problem might be $\Theta = \{b \mid b \in \mathcal{A}(u_1) \text{ or } b = u_1\} \times \{b \mid b \in \mathcal{A}(u_2) \text{ or } b = u_2\} \times \cdots \times \{b \mid b \in \mathcal{A}(u_m) \text{ or } b = u_m\}$, which is extremely large. Hence, we consider introducing the concept of Ordinal Optimization (OO) to solve this problem.

Ordinal Optimization (OO) was first proposed by Ho *et al.* [21] to address the stochastic complex simulation-based optimization problems (SCP). Moreover, OO has also been proved to be suitable for solving deterministic complex problems (DCP) and gets some successful applications. "Soft optimization for hard problems" is the quintessence of OO, which means after softening the goal, the hard problem can be tackled within a tolerable time. It is highly impracticable to find the global optimal solution, so, we seek to find a near-optimal solution instead with high probability. The objective can be formed as:

$$Pr(|G \cap S| \geq k) \geq \alpha \qquad (17)$$

Here, G denotes the good enough set (i.e., the top-$|G|$ solutions of the problem). S denotes the set of selected solutions (i.e., the estimated top-$|S|$ solutions selected by simulation experiments). $Pr(|G \cap S| \geq k)$ called alignment probability denotes the probability that the number of good enough solutions in S is no less than k, and k is called the alignment level. OO can pick out S to ensure that (17) holds under the $|G|$, k and α specified by the user. The Horse Race rule is a commonly used method for selecting set S in OO. The rule is as follows:

1. Select N samples uniformly and randomly from Θ.
2. Use a crude but computationally fast model to estimate the performances of these N samples.
3. Estimate the Ordered Performance Curve (OPC) class and the error level of the crude model.
4. Use the table in [22] to get $|S|$, the size of S.
5. Use the crude model to select the estimated top-$|S|$ samples to form S.
6. Evaluate each sample in S with a precise model.
7. Apply the best sample from the evaluation results in Step 6.

Therefore, we design an OO-based offloading algorithm by combining the Ordinal Optimization with Theorem 1. The specific offloading algorithm is shown in Algorithm 1, where Line 1 aims to replace Θ with Θ_N. According to [23], when $N \geq 1000$, we can treat Θ_N as a reasonable representative of Θ, Lines 2–3 estimate the performance of each sample in Θ_N roughly, Lines 4–6 aim to find the set S, Lines 7–8 evaluate the performance of each sample in S precisely. Finally, the sample with the best performance as the good enough offloading policy is found.

Algorithm 1: OO-based offloading algorithm

Input: Θ, k, g, α
Output: a good enough offloading policy
1 select N samples uniformly and randomly from Θ to form set Θ_N
2 **foreach** *sample in Θ_N* **do**
3 | use a crude but computationally fast model to estimate the performances of
   | the sample

4 estimate the Ordered Performance Curve (OPC) class and the noise level of the
   crude model
5 use the table presented in [22] to calculate the size of selected set s
6 pick out the top-s samples to form set S
7 **foreach** *sample in S* **do**
8 | use a precise model to evaluate the performances of the sample

9 pick out the sample with best performance as the good enough offloading policy
   we found

---

4 Performance Evaluation

In this section, we discuss the performance of the OO-based offloading algorithm
we proposed.

4.1 Simulation Setup

Consider a 700 m × 300 m² area in which 16 base station are evenly distributed,
and each base station are equipped with an edge server. The overage radius of
each base station is set as 100 m. The computation capability and full state
power of each edge server are set as 5 GHz and 500 W, respectively. According
to the survey result in [24], the idle power of the edge server accounts for 60%
of the full state power. The mobile devices are randomly scattered in the area,
and the computation capability of each mobile device is 1 GHz. The size of tasks
is randomly chosen from [0.5, 1] MB, and the processing density of tasks is 500
cycles/bit, which means 500 CPU cycles are required to process each bit of the
task. Besides, the channel gain $g_{i,j}$ is modeled by $(d_{i,j})^{-\alpha}$, where $\alpha = 4$ denotes
the path loss factor and $d_{i,j}$ denotes the distance between user u_i and edge server
b_j [25]. The other simulation parameters are given in Table 2.

Table 2. Simulation parameters

Parameter	Value
Number of users, m	{30, 40, 50, 60, 70, 80, 90}
Number of edge servers, n	16
Channel bandwidth, B	10 MHz
Transmission power of mobile device u_i, p_i^T	0.5 W
Computing power of mobile device u_i, p_i^L	0.5 W
Noise power, σ^2	10^{-13} W
Size of task T_i, s_i	[0.5, 1] MB
Frequency of mobile device u_i, f_i^L	1 GHz
Frequency of edge server b_j, f_j^E,	5 GHz
Remaining energy of the mobile device u_i, $\alpha_i E_i^{max}$	1000 mAh
Idle power of edge server b_j, p_j^{idle}	300 W
Max power of edge server b_j, p_j^{max}	500 W [26]

4.2 Determine Crude Model and OPC Class

In the crude model, the transmission rate $r_{i,j}$ is replaced by the overall average transmission rate $r_{average}$. For each sample, we denote the number of offloaded tasks as $m^{offload}$, then set $\kappa_{j,i}(\forall i, j)$ to $\kappa = \min\{\frac{n}{m^{offload}}, 1\}$. So the crude model can be expressed as follows:

$$\hat{f}(\boldsymbol{x}, \boldsymbol{\kappa}) = \beta_1 \sum_{i=1}^{m} [x_{i,0} \frac{\omega_i}{f_i^L} + \sum_{j=1}^{n} x_{i,j} (\frac{\omega_i}{\kappa f_j^E} + \frac{s_i}{r_{average}})]$$
$$+ \beta_2 \sum_{i=1}^{m} \sum_{j=1}^{n} x_{i,j} \frac{\omega_i}{\kappa f_j^E} (p_j^{max} - p_j^{idle})$$

(18)

Then, we select 1000 samples uniformly from Θ to form set Θ_N, which is a reasonable representative of Θ. Next, with the $g = 50$, $\alpha = 0.95$ and $k = 5$, we estimate the OPC class and calculate s. The OPC is shown in Fig. 2. As we can see, no matter what the β_1, β_2, and the number of users are, the OPC class is Bell [23]. According to [22], when the error level is a large error, medium error, or small error, s is 40, 80, and 140 respectively.

Just like [13,27], we compare the OO-based offloading policy with other three offloading policies:

- **Local computing policy:** This policy involves no offloading. All computation tasks are executed locally on mobile devices.
- **Edge computing policy:** In this policy, all mobile device user offload their tasks to one edge server.
- **Random offloading policy:** In this policy, all computation tasks are randomly decided whether to offload.

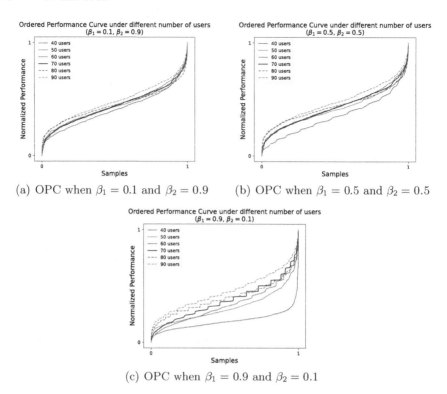

(a) OPC when $\beta_1 = 0.1$ and $\beta_2 = 0.9$ (b) OPC when $\beta_1 = 0.5$ and $\beta_2 = 0.5$

(c) OPC when $\beta_1 = 0.9$ and $\beta_2 = 0.1$

Fig. 2. Ordered performance curve

For the four offloading policies, we evaluate performance in terms of average latency and average extra energy consumption of all edge servers.

4.3   Comparison with Baseline Methods

The average task latency and average extra edge server energy consumption of OO-based policy with different error levels and the other three baseline offloading policies under different weights are shown in Figs. 3, 4 and 5 respectively. It can be observe that different β_1 and β_2 do not affect the performance of the three baseline policies (i.e., the performance curves of three baseline policies under different β_1 and β_2 are the same). In other words, the OO-based offloading policy proposed in this paper is more adaptable to different situations. For edge computing policy, as the number of users increases, the average latency increases rapidly, while the average extra energy consumption remains constant but actually the highest of all offloading policies. This is because all tasks consume as much energy as shown in (9) and the increase in the number of users leads to the reduction of computing resources allocated to each task. For local computing policy, since all task processed locally, the average extra consumption is always 0 and the latency of each task is local computation latency. This is the reason

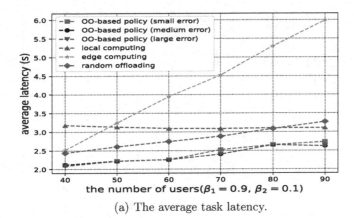

(a) The average task latency.

(b) The average extra energy consumption.

Fig. 3. The performance of different offloading policies when $\beta_1 = 0.9$ and $\beta_2 = 0.1$.

that there is little fluctuation in average task latency. As for the performance of the random offloading policy, as the average result of 1000 random trials, if the number of users increases, the average task latency tends to increase while the average extra energy consumption remaining stable. Furthermore, the performance of OO-based policy under different error levels are extremely close to each other, which means the error level of the crude model is small noise. So, we just need to evaluate the performance of the top-40 samples selected by the crude model to get a good-enough policy.

In Fig. 3, we compared the performance of the aforementioned policies when $\beta_1 = 0.9$ and $\beta_2 = 0.1$. In this case, we are more concerned about the average latency rather than the average extra edge server consumption. It can be observed that no matter how many user is, the OO-based policy always achieves significantly lower latency than other policies. In this case, although more attention is paid to average task latency, still, in most cases (i.e., $m \geq 50$), the average

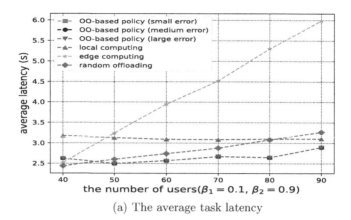

(a) The average task latency

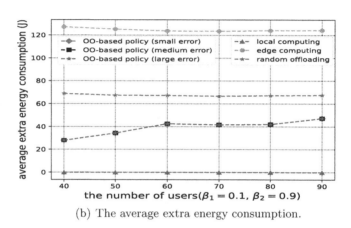

(b) The average extra energy consumption.

Fig. 4. The performance of different offloading policies when $\beta_1 = 0.1$ and $\beta_2 = 0.9$.

extra energy consumption of OO-based policy is better than random offloading policy and edge computing policy.

Figure 4 illustrates the performance of four offloading policies when $\beta_1 = 0.1$ and $\beta_2 = 0.9$. Contrary to the above situation, in this case, we are more concerned about extra energy consumption than task latency. As for energy consumption, OO-based policy is significantly better than edge computing policy and random offloading policy. Similar to the situation above, in most cases (i.e., $m \geq 50$), the average task latency of OO-based policy is the best.

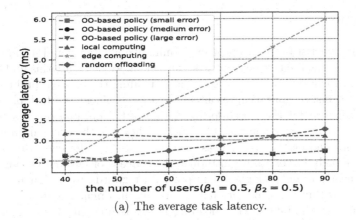

(a) The average task latency.

(b) The average energy consumption of four offloading policies

Fig. 5. The performance of different offloading policies when $\beta_1 = 0.5$ and $\beta_2 = 0.5$.

Figure 5 illustrates the performance of four offloading policies when $\beta_1 = 0.5$ and $\beta_2 = 0.5$. In this case, we considered offloading task and extra energy consumption equally important. At this time, OO-based policy has achieved good results in reducing task latency and extra energy consumption. It can be observed that although the latency of OO-based policy is slightly higher than that of random offloading policy and edge computing policy, the extra energy consumption of OO-based policy is significantly better when the number of users is 40. Besides, when $m \geq 50$, both the average task latency and average extra energy consumption of OO-based are best except the extra energy consumption of local computing (i.e., 0).

5   Conclusion

In this paper, we first propose a problem of minimizing latency and server energy consumption in the large-scale MEC systems. Then, we illustrate this problem as NP-hard. To solve this problem, we consider dividing the original problem into two sub-problems: computation resource allocation problem and task placement problem. Next, we get the closed-form solution of the optimal resource allocation under an arbitrary given task placement policy. So, the original problem is converted into finding the optimal task placement policy. However, the decision space is extremely large. So, we introduce the concept of Ordinal Optimization to find the near-optimal task placement policy. Afterwards, we design an efficient offloading algorithm based on Ordinal Optimization. Finally, simulation results have shown that the OO-based offloading policy is not only more efficient as compared to the other three baseline policies, but also more adaptable to different situations. In the future work, real-world mobility data will be employed to validate our proposed offloading algorithm.

Acknowledgment. This work is supported by Beijing Nova Program (No. Z201100 006820082), National Natural Science Foundation of China (No. 61972414), National Key Research and Development Plan (No. 2016YFC0303700), Beijing Natural Science Foundation (No. 4202066), and the Fundamental Research Funds for Central Universities (Nos. 2462018YJRC040 and 2462020YJRC001).

References

1. Forecast, G.: Cisco visual networking index: global mobile data traffic forecast update, 2017–2022. Update **2017**, 2022 (2019)
2. Azuma, R.T.: A survey of augmented reality. Presence Teleoperators Virtual Environ. **6**(4), 355–385 (1997)
3. Ranjan, N., Mundada, K., Phaltane, K., Ahmad, S.: A survey on techniques in NLP. Int. J. Comput. Appl. **134**(8), 6–9 (2016)
4. Zhao, Q.: A survey on virtual reality. Sci. China Ser. F Inf. Sci. **52**(3), 348–400 (2009)
5. Badue, C., et al.: Self-driving cars: a survey. Expert Syst. Appli. **165**, 113816 (2020)
6. Kan, T.Y., Chiang, Y., Wei, H.Y.: Task offloading and resource allocation in mobile-edge computing system. In: 2018 27th Wireless and Optical Communication Conference (WOCC), pp. 1–4. IEEE (2018)
7. Mach, P., Becvar, Z.: Mobile edge computing: a survey on architecture and computation offloading. IEEE Commun. Surv. Tutorials **19**(3), 1628–1656 (2017)
8. Hu, Y.C., Patel, M., Sabella, D., Sprecher, N., Young, V.: Mobile edge computing-a key technology towards 5G. ETSI White Paper **11**(11), 1–16 (2015)
9. Huang, J., Zhang, C., Zhang, J.: A multi-queue approach of energy efficient task scheduling for sensor hubs. Chin. J. Electron. **29**(2), 242–247 (2020)
10. Liu, J., Mao, Y., Zhang, J., Letaief, K.B.: Delay-optimal computation task scheduling for mobile-edge computing systems. In: 2016 IEEE International Symposium on Information Theory (ISIT), pp. 1451–1455. IEEE (2016)

11. Mao, Y., Zhang, J., Song, S., Letaief, K.B.: Power-delay tradeoff in multi-user mobile-edge computing systems. In: 2016 IEEE Global Communications Conference (GLOBECOM), pp. 1–6. IEEE (2016)
12. Xu, Z., Wang, Y., Tang, J., Wang, J., Gursoy, M.C.: A deep reinforcement learning based framework for power-efficient resource allocation in cloud rans. In: 2017 IEEE International Conference on Communications (ICC), pp. 1–6. IEEE (2017)
13. Li, J., Gao, H., Lv, T., Lu, Y.: Deep reinforcement learning based computation offloading and resource allocation for mec. In: 2018 IEEE Wireless Communications and Networking Conference (WCNC), pp. 1–6. IEEE (2018)
14. Huang, J., Li, S., Chen, Y.: Revenue-optimal task scheduling and resource management for IoT batch jobs in mobile edge computing. Peer-to-Peer Netw. Appl. 13(5), 1776–1787 (2020)
15. Ge, X., Tu, S., Mao, G., Wang, C.X., Han, T.: 5G ultra-dense cellular networks. IEEE Wirel. Commun. 23(1), 72–79 (2016). https://doi.org/10.1109/MWC.2016.7422408
16. Chen, M., Hao, Y.: Task offloading for mobile edge computing in software defined ultra-dense network. IEEE J. Sel. Areas Commun. 36(3), 587–597 (2018)
17. Gao, Y., Guan, H., Qi, Z., Wang, B., Liu, L.: Quality of service aware power management for virtualized data centers. J. Syst. Archit. 59(4–5), 245–259 (2013)
18. Fan, X., Weber, W.D., Barroso, L.A.: Power provisioning for a warehouse-sized computer. ACM SIGARCH Comput. Archit. News 35(2), 13–23 (2007)
19. Pochet, Y., Wolsey, L.A.: Production Planning by Mixed Integer Programming. Springer Science and Business Media, Heidelberg (2006)
20. Vu, T.T., Van Huynh, N., Hoang, D.T., Nguyen, D.N., Dutkiewicz, E.: Offloading energy efficiency with delay constraint for cooperative mobile edge computing networks. In: 2018 IEEE Global Communications Conference (GLOBECOM), pp. 1–6. IEEE (2018)
21. Ho, Y.C., Sreenivas, R., Vakili, P.: Ordinal optimization of DEDS. Discrete Event Dyn. Syst. 2(1), 61–88 (1992)
22. Lau, T.E., Ho, Y.C.: Universal alignment probabilities and subset selection for ordinal optimization. J. Optim. Theory Appl. 93(3), 455–489 (1997)
23. Ho, Y.C., Zhao, Q.C., Jia, Q.S.: Ordinal Optimization: Soft Optimization for Hard Problems. Springer Science & Business Media, Heidelberg (2008)
24. Dayarathna, M., Wen, Y., Fan, R.: Data center energy consumption modeling: a survey. IEEE Commun. Surv Tutorials 18(1), 732–794 (2015)
25. Liu, Z., Yang, Y., Wang, K., Shao, Z., Zhang, J.: Post: parallel offloading of splittable tasks in heterogeneous fog networks. IEEE Internet Things J. 7(4), 3170–3183 (2020)
26. Li, Y., Wang, S.: An energy-aware edge server placement algorithm in mobile edge computing. In: 2018 IEEE International Conference on Edge Computing (EDGE), pp. 66–73. IEEE (2018)
27. Zhang, Y., Niyato, D., Wang, P.: Offloading in mobile cloudlet systems with intermittent connectivity. IEEE Trans. Mob. Comput. 14(12), 2516–2529 (2015)

Edge Computing and Collaborative Working

Joint Location-Value Privacy Protection for Spatiotemporal Data Collection via Mobile Crowdsensing

Tong Liu[1,2($\boxtimes$)], Dan Li[1], Chenhong Cao[1], Honghao Gao[1], Chengfan Li[1,2], and Zhenni Feng[3]

[1] School of Computer Engineering and Science, Shanghai University, Shanghai, China
{tong_liu,ld19721539,caoch,gaohonghao}@shu.edu.cn
[2] Shanghai Engineering Research Center of Intelligent Computing System, Shanghai, China
[3] School of Computer Science and Technology, Donghua University, Shanghai, China
fzn@dhu.edu.cn

Abstract. Due to the development of the Internet of Things, mobile crowdsensing has emerged as a promising pervasive sensing paradigm for online spatiotemporal data collection, by leveraging ubiquitous mobile devices. However, privacy leakage of device users is a crucial problem, especially when an untrusted central platform in mobile crowdsensing is considered. Moreover, private information of users like trajectories contained in both location tags and sensed values of their sensing data may be unexpectedly revealed to the platform. In order to solve this problem, we proposed a joint location-value privacy protection approach, which consists of two privacy preserving mechanisms to perturb the locations and sensed values of users, respectively. The approach can be performed by each user locally and independently. The privacy of users can be well preserved, as we theoretically prove that the two mechanisms satisfy local differential privacy. In addition, extensive simulations are conducted, and the results show that accurate estimated values can be derived based on perturbed locations and sanitized sensed values, by adopting the truth discovery method.

Keywords: Mobile crowdsensing · Privacy protection · Local differential privacy · Truth discovery

1 Introduction

With the rapid development of the Internet of Things, mobile devices equipped with diverse embedded sensors (e.g., camera, accelerometer, compass) are pervasive. Mobile crowdsensing (MCS) [4,13] has emerged recently as a promising pervasive sensing paradigm to enable the Internet of Things, which facilitates spatiotemporal data collection in large urban areas like transportation monitoring [28], air

© ICST Institute for Computer Sciences, Social Informatics and Telecommunications Engineering 2021
Published by Springer Nature Switzerland AG 2021. All Rights Reserved
H. Gao and X. Wang (Eds.): CollaborateCom 2021, LNICST 407, pp. 87–103, 2021.
https://doi.org/10.1007/978-3-030-92638-0_6

monitoring [12] and noise mapping [14]. A typical MCS system consists of a central platform resided in cloud and plenty of distributed mobile device users. According to the sensing requests of the platform, users collect location-based sensing data continuously and submit them to the platform for extracting useful information.

A major concern in spatiotemporal data collection via MCS is privacy leakage [7,16], as spatiotemporal sensing data collected by users contain their private information, such as their trajectories and preferences. Moreover, an untrusted platform in the MCS system should be considered, and hence privacy protection should be conducted by each user independently. Note that both location tags and sensed values contained in the sensing data of users should be perturbed, before they are submitted to the platform. On one hand, the trajectory privacy of a user will be exposed to the untrusted platform, if sensing data with unperturbed location tags of the user are continuously submitted. On the other hand, sensed values also leak location privacy of users unexpectedly, since the location of a user may be inferred according to the values of collected data by adopting truth discovery methods. The intuition of inferring locations of users is that sensing data collected in the same location always have close values, while the values of sensing data collected in different locations may be discrepant. Thus, the sensed values of sensing data collected by users should be sanitized before they are submitted to the platform.

To solve the privacy concern in MCS, some privacy preserving approaches [5,11,18,21,22,27] have been proposed based on differential privacy (DP)[2,15] which is an effective tool to provide valid privacy protection and ensure the usability of aggregated sensing data at the same time. These DP-based approaches always assume that the platform is a trusted third party for users, which is responsible to sanitize collected sensing data and limit the disclosure of private information of users. However, the assumption is not true in reality, as the platform may leak the privacy of users for commercial benefits or be attacked by adversaries. Some other approaches [9,10,17,19,20,23,25] are proposed based on local differential privacy (LDP) [3,6], in which users perturb their sensing data locally and independently before submitting sensing data to the platform. Hence, private information of users are protected. Moreover, truth discovery methods [8] can be adopted by the platform to extract true values from the perturbed data. However, there are few works considering preserving the privacy contained in both locations and sensed values of users at the same time.

In this work, we consider a MCS system with an untrusted platform, in which location-based sensing data are collected from mobile users continuously. Each datum submitted by a user consists of the identity of the user, the sensed value of a monitored object, the location tag and the time stamp. With sensed values collected by multiple users in an interested location, the platform applies a truth discovery method to obtain the estimated value of the monitored object. Obviously, the trajectory of the user can be released to the untrusted platform over the time, which is a succession of the timestamped locations. Moreover, even if the locations of users are perturbed, we consider that the platform can also infer the trajectories of users from their sensed values in the submitted data. Considering that there are few work considering the problem that sensing data of users may lead to unexpected location privacy leakage, we try to design a privacy protection approach for online spatiotemporal data collection, which protects the location privacy of participating users by perturbing both sensed values and locations in their submitted data.

However, the joint location-value privacy protection problem in MCS is particularly difficult due to the existence of the following challenges. *Firstly*, the locations of users contained in sensing data submitted to the platform should be perturbed to protect their privacy, which will lead to the platform mismatches the collected sensing data to a wrong location. Furthermore, the accuracy of values estimated based on sanitized sensing data with perturbed locations is impacted. *Secondly*, considering there is no trusted third party, the joint location-value privacy protection approach should be performed by each user locally and independently. It makes the truth discovery conducted by the platform becomes particularly difficult. *Finally*, there exists a natural intrinsic tradeoff between the level of privacy protection and the utility of perturbed data. In other words, a high-level privacy protection approach inevitably decreases the utility of sensing data, i.e., the accuracy of estimated values.

In response to these challenges, we propose a privacy protection approach for online spatiotemporal data collection via MCS, in which a location privacy preserving mechanism and a value privacy preserving mechanism are provided respectively. Specially, the location privacy preserving mechanism is designed based on random response that each user can perturb their locations locally. In the Gaussian-mechanism-based value privacy preserving mechanism, each user sanitizes the collected sensed values by adding random Gaussian noise independently. Spatiotemporal sensing data with perturbed locations and sanitized sensed values are submitted to the platform continuously.

The main contributions of this work can be summarized as follows:

- We consider the privacy preserving problem in a MCS system to collect location-based sensing data over time, in which we observe that not only location tags but also sensed values submitted to an untrusted platform will expose the private information of users.
- We propose a LDP-based privacy protection approach, which includes two privacy preserving mechanisms to perturb location tags and sensed values respectively. The approach can be performed by each user locally and independently. We theoretically prove that the two mechanisms achieve certain local differential privacy.
- Extensive simulations are conducted to validate the performance of our proposed privacy protection approach. The simulation results show that the privacy of users is well preserved and the estimated values obtained by the truth discovery method is relatively accurate.

This paper is organized as follows. We first discuss related works in Sect. 2, and present the motivation of joint location-value privacy protection in Sect. 3. Then, we present our system model and some preliminaries in Sect. 4. Section 5 and Sect. 6 elaborate our proposed privacy protection approach and the theoretical analysis, respectively. Finally, simulation results are presented in Sect. 7, and the paper is concluded in Sect. 8.

2   Related Work

Privacy protection has received a lot of attention in MCS, while differential privacy is seen as a promising technology in recent studies [5, 9–11, 17–23, 25, 27]. These privacy protection approaches in MCS can be classified into two categories, i.e., DP-based approaches and LDP-based approaches.

2.1   DP-Based Approaches in MCS

DP-based privacy preserving approaches assume there exists a trusted third party(e.g., a platform or a central server) has been widely adopted and used in many areas [1, 26]. In the MCS system, there are some DP-based approaches [5, 11, 18, 21, 22, 27] which sanitize the sensing data collected from mobile users for privacy protection.

To *et al.* [18] introduce a framework for protecting location privacy of works participating spatial crowdsourcing tasks, which needs users' cellular service providers to take coordination role between users and MCS platforms. Wang *et al.* [22] study the privacy protection problem in a crowd-sourced system for continuous real-time spatiotemporal data publishing, and an online privacy preserving scheme is proposed to monitor population statistics over infinite streams. Then, an enhanced RescueDP framework in [21] is proposed which leverages neural networks to accurately predict the values of statistics and improve the utility of released data. In [5, 11, 27], privacy preserving auction-based incentive mechanisms are designed to preserve the users' bid privacy. Specifically, the mechanism designed by Jin *et al.* [5] approximately minimizes the platform's total payment with a guaranteed approximation ratio. Besides, Lin *et al.* [11] propose two score functions to realize frameworks for privacy-preserving aution-based incentive mechanisms which achieves approximate social cost minimization. Differently, the joint effect of users privacy concerns and the positive network effect are considered in [27].

However, the assumption of a trusted third party is unpractical sometimes, as the platform may leak the privacy of users for commercial interests or be attacked by adversaries.

2.2   LDP-Based Approaches in MCS

Recently, some LDP-based approaches toward data statistics and analysis in MCS are widely adopted to alleviate the privacy concerns caused by untrusted third party [24]. Mobile users can sanitize their private sensing data locally and submitting the perturbed data to the platform.

There are some works [17, 23] focus on studying the privacy preserving data distribution estimation with LDP in MCS. Wang *et al.* [23] provide an optimal LDP-based privacy preserving mechanism for distribution estimation over user-contributed data, in which the private information of users contained in both qualitative data and discrete quantitative data can be protected. Ren *et al.* [17] develop LDP-based privacy-preserving algorithms for multi-dimensional data

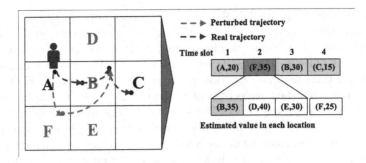

Fig. 1. An example of inferring the real location of a user based on sensed values, even though the location is perturbed.

distribution estimation and data publication, which achieve high computation efficiency and data utility.

[19,20,25] design privacy-preserving frameworks to satisfy the privacy demands of users. In order to protect the location privacy of users, [20] design a LDP-based privacy-preserving framework which consists of a data adjustment function and an optimal location obfuscation, and they propose an inference algorithm to improve the inference accuracy of obfuscated data. While [19] leverage distortion privacy with differential privacy together to provide more comprehensive protection for users' location privacy. Differently, a privacy-preserving task allocation framework in MCS is proposed in [25], in which provides personalized location privacy protection to meet different demands of users. Moreover, Lin *et al.* [10] propose a randomized response-based privacy-preserving crowd-sensing data collection and analysis method to ensure users' privacy, and Li *et al.* [9] provide a privacy preserving truth discovery mechanism with theoretical guarantees of both utility and privacy.

Unfortunately, there are few works considering both location tags and sensed values contained in sensing data may unexpectedly disclose the private information of users and further proposing a joint location-value privacy protection approach accordingly.

3   Motivation

In this section, we aim to emphasize that joint location-value privacy protection is necessary for spatiotemporal data collection via MCS. Only perturbing the locations contained in sensing data collected by a user is not enough, as the platform can infer the real locations of users according to the sensed values. Here, we give a simple example to illustrate how the platform infers the real location of a user based on his/her sensed values, even though the location in submitted sensing data is perturbed.

Example: Suppose there is a platform requiring users to collect ambient noise from various interested locations. A location privacy preserving mechanism is provided to perturb their original locations to other possible locations with a certain probability. Assume there is a mobile user who collects 20 dB, 35 dB, 30 dB, and 15 dB of ambient noise in location A, B, and C over four time slots, where ambient noise is collected twice at location B. The location of the user at the second time slot (i.e., location B) is perturbed to location F. The real trajectory and perturbed trajectory of the user are $A \rightarrow B \rightarrow B \rightarrow C$ and $A \rightarrow F \rightarrow B \rightarrow C$, respectively. The sensing data of users submitted to the platform are shown in Fig. 1. In addition, we assume the platform can obtain relatively accurate estimations of the ambient noise in each location over time.

According to the estimated values in the second time slot, the platform can easily find F is not the real location of the user. In addition, according to the locations of the user in the first and third time slot, the platform can infer that the possible location of the user in the second time slot can be D, B, or E. Then, by comparing the estimated values of these three locations with the sensed values collected by the user in the second time slot, the platform can successfully infer that the real location of the user in the second time slot is B.

4   System Model and Preliminaries

In this section, we present the model of online spatiotemporal data collection in MCS, and introduce some preliminaries including truth discovery and local differential privacy.

4.1   System Model

In this work, we consider a typical crowdsensing system consists of a central platform located in cloud and a set of registered users equipped with smart devices. We denote the set of users by $\mathcal{U} = \{u_1, u_2, \cdots, u_n\}$. Users are mobile and distributed in an urban area. The platform requires users to collect location-based and time-sensitive sensing data around several interested locations continuously. The locations of interested points in the urban area are represented as $\mathcal{L} = \{L_1, L_2, \cdots, L_m\}$, where m is the number of interested locations. For convenience, we divide time into equal-interval time slots, i.e., $\mathcal{T} = \{t_1, t_2, \cdots, t_\tau, \cdots\}$. In each time slot t_τ, the subset of users located around location $L_j \in \mathcal{L}$ is denoted as $\mathcal{U}_j^\tau \subseteq \mathcal{U}$.

Let u_i denote a user located around interested point L_j in time slot t_τ (i.e., $u_i \in \mathcal{U}_j^\tau$). We denote the location of user u_i in t_τ as l_i^τ, and we use the location of his/her nearby interested point to replace it, i.e., $l_i^\tau = L_j$. The sensed value of sensing data collected by user u_i in time slot t_τ is represented by v_i^τ. Each user submits the identity, the sensed value, the location tag, and the time stamp to the platform in real time.

Submitting original sensed values and locations of users will expose their private information (e.g., trajectories) to the platform and adversaries, since an untrusted platform may leak privacy of users for commercial interests and financial benefits or be attacked by adversaries. In this work, we consider users preserve their private information by submitting sanitized values of sensing data and perturbed locations to the platform. Specially, the perturbed location and the sanitized value of user u_i in time slot t_τ is denoted by $\tilde{l}_i^\tau$ and $\tilde{v}_i^\tau$, respectively. Note that we assume $\tilde{l}_i^\tau \in \mathcal{L}$.

With receiving all sensing data collected in t_τ, the platform aggregates the sanitized value $\tilde{v}_i^\tau$ of user u_i according to perturbed location $\tilde{l}_i^\tau$. Specially, we define the set of users whose perturbed location is L_j as $\tilde{\mathcal{U}}_j^\tau = \{u_i \in \mathcal{U}|\tilde{l}_i^\tau = L_j\}$. According to the sanitized values $\{\tilde{v}_i^\tau|u_i \in \tilde{\mathcal{U}}_j^\tau\}$ collected in L_j, the platform can obtain the estimated value $\bar{V}_j^\tau$ in location L_j by employing truth estimation as follows,

$$\bar{V}_j^\tau = \frac{\sum_{u_i \in \tilde{\mathcal{U}}_j^\tau} \tilde{w}_i^\tau \cdot \tilde{v}_i^\tau}{\sum_{u_i \in \tilde{\mathcal{U}}_j^\tau} \tilde{w}_i^\tau}, \tag{1}$$

where $\tilde{w}_i^\tau$ is the weight of user u_i, calculated based on sanitized value at time slot t_τ. Correspondingly, we denote w_i^τ as the weight of user u_i calculated based on the original sensed value at time slot t_τ.

4.2   Preliminaries

Truth Discovery [8]: Given an initialization of the weights of users, the truth discovery method iteratively conducts the following steps until the estimated value converges.

- **Truth estimation:** Given the weights of users and sanitized values collected in location L_j at time slot t_τ, the estimated value $\bar{V}_j^\tau$ is calculated as (1).
- **Weight update:** According to difference between sanitized values submitted to the platform and estimated value $\bar{V}^\tau$ of the monitored object, the weight of user u_i can be updated as

$$\tilde{w}_i^\tau = \log \left(\frac{\sum_{u_r \in \tilde{\mathcal{U}}_j^\tau} (\tilde{v}_r^\tau - \bar{V}_j^\tau)^2}{(\tilde{v}_i^\tau - \bar{V}_j^\tau)^2} \right). \tag{2}$$

Local Differential Privacy [3]: LDP is a promising technology used to provide privacy protection with a quantified guarantee, which is applied to the systems without a trusted third party.

Let $M(x)$ denote the perturbed output of a randomization mechanism M given an input x. M achieves (ϵ, δ)-LDP if it satisfies the following definition.

Definition 1 $((\epsilon, \delta)$-LDP). *A randomization mechanism M with its output domain $range(M)$ achieves (ϵ, δ)-LDP, if for an arbitrary pair of inputs x, y and any possible subset $S \subseteq range(M)$, there exists*

$$Pr\{M(x) \in S\} \le \exp(\epsilon) \cdot Pr\{M(y) \in S\} + \delta, \tag{3}$$

where $\epsilon > 0$ is privacy budget and $\delta \ge 0$ is relaxation variable.

Specially, randomization mechanism M is called ϵ-differential privacy when $\delta = 0$. Note that a lower value of privacy budget ϵ and δ indicates a stronger privacy protection level can be achieved, vice versa.

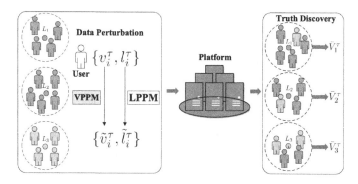

Fig. 2. An illustration of the MCS system and our proposed privacy protection approach.

5 Methodology

In this section, we first introduce the overview of our proposed privacy protection approach, which includes two mechanisms for preserving location privacy and sensed value privacy of users, respectively. Then, we describe the detailed designs of these two mechanisms in the next two subsections.

5.1 Overview

As shown in Fig. 2, our MCS system consists of a central platform resided in cloud and a set of mobile smart device users distributed in an urban area. Sensing data around interested locations are continuously collected by the users nearby and submitted to the platform. In each time slot, the operations conducted by each user and the platform are illustrated in the following.

Each user first collects the sensed value v_i^τ of the monitored object in his/her current location l_i^τ. Then, each user performs the LPPM and VPPM locally and independently, to perturb the location and sanitize the sensed value as $\tilde{l}_i^\tau$ and $\tilde{v}_i^\tau$, respectively. Finally, the perturbed location and sanitized sensed value, as well as the identity of the user and the time stamp, are submitted to the platform.

The platform first aggregates sanitized values according to the perturbed locations of users after receiving all sanitized sensing data. Then, based on the sanitized values $\{\tilde{v}_i^\tau | u_i \in \tilde{\mathcal{U}}_j^\tau\}$ in each location, the platform conducts the truth discovery method to estimate the true value of the monitored object $\bar{V}_j^\tau$ in location L_j at time slot t_τ.

By conducting our privacy protection approach online in a MCS system, we can guarantee that the private information of users can be preserved and the value of the monitored object can be estimated accurately.

5.2   Location Privacy Preserving Mechanism (LPPM)

Original location tags contained in sensing data collected by users over time will disclose their trajectories to the platform or adversaries, which may pose severe threats to their real life and public security. In order to protect the location information of users, we provide a LPPM based on random response [3]. The main idea of this mechanism is that the original location of a user is perturbed to another interested location with a certain probability. The details are illustrated in the following.

We represent our LPPM by a function A, whose both input domain and output range are $\mathcal{L}$. Given a predefined probability $p \in (0, 1)$, we perturb the original location $l_i^\tau = L_j \in \mathcal{L}$ of user u_i in time slot t_τ as follows,

$$\tilde{l}_i^\tau = A(l_i^\tau, p) = \begin{cases} L_j, & \text{with probability } 1 - p, \\ L_r \in \mathcal{L} \setminus \{L_j\}, & \text{with probability } \frac{p}{m-1}. \end{cases}$$

In Sect. 6, we prove that our location privacy preserving mechanism satisfies LDP. Note that although the location tags of users are perturbed, the platform can still extract accurate estimated values in different locations by applying the truth discovery method. Because the sensed value with a mismatched location will be assigned a low weight in truth discovery, and there could be less impact on the accuracy of the estimated result.

5.3   Value Privacy Preserving Mechanism (VPPM)

The trajectory of a user can be still inferred by the platform or adversaries, through comparing the sensed values collected by the user over time and the estimated true values obtained by truth discovery. Thus, besides perturbing locations of users, their sensed values should be sanitized as well. In this subsection, we propose a LDP-Gaussian-based VPPM to sanitize sensed values of users. The main idea of this mechanism is adding noise on sensed values to obtain a sanitized version of them, where the noise is sampled by users from their private Gaussian distributions. The details of this mechanism are illustrated as follows.

In each time slot t_τ, the platform first publishes a predefined parameter λ to all users, where λ is determined by specific privacy demands (i.e., privacy budget ϵ_2 and δ). Then, each user u_i generates a private Gaussian distribution $\mathcal{N}(0, \sigma_i^2)$ locally, where σ_i^2 is sampled from the exponential distribution $\mathcal{E}(\lambda)$, according to the parameter published by the platform. Finally, user u_i independently samples noise ζ_i^τ from his/her private Gaussian distribution and adds the noise on the sensed value. Summarily, letting function B denote the VPPM, the process can be formulated as

$$\tilde{v}_i^\tau = B(v_i^\tau, \sigma_i^2) = v_i^\tau + \zeta_i^\tau, \tag{4}$$
$$\text{where } \zeta_i^\tau \sim \mathcal{N}(0, \sigma_i^2) \text{ and } \sigma_i^2 \sim \mathcal{E}(\lambda).$$

Intuitively, a larger value of parameter λ indicates a smaller expectation of σ_i^2, which leads to a smaller expectation of noise added to sensed values and a lower privacy protection level accordingly.

Algorithm 1. Joint location-value privacy protection approach for spatiotemporal data collection

---

Input: Set of interested locations $\mathcal{L}$, the locations $\{l_i^\tau\}_{i=1}^n$ and sensed values $\{v_i^\tau\}_{i=1}^n$ of all participating users at time slot t_τ, predefined parameters p and λ

Output: Estimated values $\{\bar{V}_j^\tau\}_{j=1}^m$ of all interested locations at time slot t_τ

1: **for** each user u_i, $(i = 1, \cdots, n)$ independently **do**

2:     perturbs his/her location l_i^τ as

$$\tilde{l}_i^\tau = \begin{cases} L_j, & \text{with probability } 1 - p, \\ L_r \in \mathcal{L} \setminus \{L_j\}, & \text{with probability } \frac{p}{m-1}. \end{cases}$$

3:     generates a private Gaussian distribution $\mathcal{N}(0, \sigma_i^2)$, where σ_i^2 is sampled from exponential distribution $\mathcal{E}(\lambda)$.

4:     samples a noise ζ_i^τ from $\mathcal{N}(0, \sigma_i^2)$, and obtains the sanitized sensed value as

$$\tilde{v}_i^\tau = v_i^\tau + \zeta_i^\tau.$$

5:     submits the perturbed location $\tilde{l}_i^\tau$ and sanitized value $\tilde{v}_i^\tau$ to the platform.

6: **end for**

7: The platform aggregates sanitized values based on perturbed locations submitted by users.

8: **for** each interested location $L_j \in \mathcal{L}$ **do**

9:     conducts truth discovery to obtain the estimated value of location L_j.

10: **end for**

11: **return** Estimated values $\{\bar{V}_j^\tau\}_{j=1}^m$ of all interested locations at time slot t_τ

So far, the locations and sensed values of users submitted to the platform are perturbed. Then, the platform can use the aforementioned truth discovery method to estimate the true values in different locations. Our privacy protection approach is summarized in Algorithm 1.

6   Theoretical Analysis

In the following, we theoretically analyze that both the location and value privacy preserving mechanisms satisfy LDP.

Theorem 1. *Given a set of locations whose size is m, the LPPM with perturbation probability p satisfies ϵ_1-local differential privacy, where $\epsilon_1 = \ln((1 - p)(m - 1)/p)$.*

Proof. According to Eq. (3), for any two possible locations L_j and L_r, the LPPM satisfies LDP if we could calculate the probability ratio $Pr\{A(L_j) = \tilde{l}_i^\tau\}/Pr\{A(L_r) = \tilde{l}_i^\tau\}$ and find its maximum. Accordingly, the ratio is maximized when function A outputs perturbed location $\tilde{l}_i^\tau$ which is identical to one of the input locations. Mathematically, when $L_j \neq L_r$ and $\tilde{l}_i^\tau = L_j$, the ratio reaches its maximum. Then we have,

$$\frac{Pr\{A(L_j) = \tilde{l}_i^\tau\}}{Pr\{A(L_r) = \tilde{l}_i^\tau\}} \leq \frac{Pr\{A(L_j) = L_j\}}{Pr\{A(L_r) = L_j\}} = \frac{1-p}{\frac{p}{m-1}}$$

Thus, the LPPM satisfies ϵ_1-LDP with $\epsilon_1 = \ln((1-p)(m-1)/p)$.

From Theorem 1, we can observe that when perturbation probability becomes larger or the size of location set becomes smaller, the value of ϵ_1 will become smaller, which indicates low level of privacy protection, vice versa.

In what follows, we present the theoretical analysis on the VPPM in each location at each time slot. We first introduce some parameters just for theoretical analysis. Generally, value v_i^τ of sensing data collected by user u_i in location L_j follows Gaussian distribution $\mathcal{N}(V_{j_{truth}}^\tau, \rho_j^{\tau 2})$ [29], where $V_{j_{truth}}^\tau$ and $\rho_j^{\tau 2}$ represent the ground truth and the error variance at L_j, respectively. Then, we give the definition of L1-Sensitivity as follows.

Definition 2 (L1-Sensitivity). *L1-Sensitivity Δ_j^τ of a user in L_j at time slot t_τ is defined as*

$$\Delta_j^\tau = \max_{v_i^\tau, \check{v}_i^\tau \in \mathcal{D}_j^\tau} |v_i^\tau - \check{v}_i^\tau|,$$

where $\mathcal{D}_j^\tau$ is the range of values that may be sensed by users in L_j at t_τ, and v_i^τ and $\check{v}_i^\tau$ are two possible values of sensing data collected by u_i.

Obviously, Δ_j^τ depends on ρ_j^τ. We present the relation between the ρ_j^τ and Δ_j^τ in the following lemma.

Lemma 1. *The value of sensitive information Δ_j^τ is smaller than $a\sqrt{2}\rho_j^\tau$ with probability at least $1 - \frac{1}{a}e^{\frac{-a^2}{2}}$, where $a \geq 0$ and decided by the sensed values collected by the users.*

Proof. According to the description mentioned, the error between sensed value v_i^τ and $V_{j_{truth}}^\tau$ follows Gaussian distribution $\mathcal{N}(0, \rho_j^{\tau 2})$, and $v_i^\tau \sim \mathcal{N}(V_{j_{truth}}^\tau, \rho_j^{\tau 2})$. Hence, for any two possible values v_i^τ and $\check{v}_i^\tau$ may sensed by u_i, the difference between v_i^τ and $\check{v}_i^\tau$ follows Gaussian distribution $\mathcal{N}(0, 2\rho_j^{\tau 2})$. Based on the Gaussian tail bounds, we have,

$$Pr\{|v_i^\tau - \check{v}_i^\tau| > a\sqrt{2}\rho_j^\tau\} \leq \frac{1}{a}e^{\frac{-a^2}{2}}, \tag{5}$$

where $a \geq 0$ and a is decided by values of sensing data collected by users. Thus, the lemma is proved.

Next, we take $\Delta_j^\tau = a\sqrt{2}\rho_j^\tau$ to analyze the LDP property achieved by the VPPM.

Theorem 2. *Given L1-Sensitivity Δ_j^τ and an exponential distribution with parameter with λ, the VPPM is (ϵ_2, δ)-local differential private, where $\epsilon_2 \geq \frac{\Delta_j^{\tau 2}}{2\sigma_i^2}$ and $\delta > 1 - e^{\frac{-\lambda \Delta_j^{\tau 2}}{2\epsilon_2}}$.*

Proof. According to Eq. (4), user u_i adopts VPPM to add noise sampled from Gaussian distribution $\mathcal{N}(0, \sigma_i^2)$ on v_i^τ to obtain sanitized value $\tilde{v}_i^\tau$. Besides, noise variance σ_i^2 is sampled from an exponential distribution with parameter λ. For any two possible sensed values v_i^τ and $\hat{v}_i^\tau$, we have,

$$\frac{Pr\{B(v_i^\tau, \sigma_i^2) = \tilde{v}_i^\tau\}}{Pr\{B(\hat{v}_i^\tau, \sigma_i^2) = \tilde{v}_i^\tau\}} = \frac{\frac{1}{\sqrt{2\pi}\sigma_i} e^{-\frac{(\tilde{v}_i^\tau - v_i^\tau)^2}{2\sigma_i^2}}}{\frac{1}{\sqrt{2\pi}\sigma_i} e^{-\frac{(\tilde{v}_i^\tau - \hat{v}_i^\tau)^2}{2\sigma_i^2}}} \tag{6}$$

$$= e^{\frac{(\tilde{v}_i^\tau - \hat{v}_i^\tau)^2 - (\tilde{v}_i^\tau - v_i^\tau)^2}{2\sigma_i^2}} \leq e^{\frac{(v_i^\tau - \hat{v}_i^\tau)^2}{2\sigma_i^2}} \leq e^{\frac{\Delta_j^{\tau 2}}{2\sigma_i^2}} \leq e^{\epsilon_2}$$

According to Eq. (6), when $\sigma_i^2 \geq \frac{\Delta_j^{\tau 2}}{2\epsilon_2}$, mechanism B meets ϵ_2-local differential privacy. As σ_i^2 follows the exponential distribution with parameter λ, and we constrain the probability of event $\{\sigma_i^2 : \sigma_i^2 \geq \frac{\Delta_j^{\tau 2}}{2\epsilon_2}\}$ happens with at least $1 - \delta$. Thus, $Pr\{\sigma_i^2 \geq \frac{\Delta_j^{\tau 2}}{2\epsilon_2}\} = e^{-\frac{\lambda \Delta_j^{\tau 2}}{2\epsilon_2}} \geq 1 - \delta$. Therefore, $\lambda \leq \frac{2\epsilon_2 \ln(\frac{1}{1-\delta})}{\Delta_j^{\tau 2}}$.

Next we partition $\mathbb{R}^+$, the domain of noise variance, as $\mathbb{R}^+ = R_1 \cup R_2$, where $R_1 = \{\sigma_i^2 \in \mathbb{R}^+ : \sigma_i^2 \geq \frac{\Delta_j^{\tau 2}}{2\epsilon_2}\}$ and $R_2 = \{\sigma_i^2 \in \mathbb{R}^+ : \sigma_i^2 \leq \frac{\Delta_j^{\tau 2}}{2\epsilon_2}\}$. For subset $S_1 \in \mathbb{S}$ and $S_2 \in \mathbb{S}$, where $\mathbb{S}$ is the range of $B(v_i^\tau, \sigma_i^2)$, we define $S_1 = \{B(v_i^\tau, \sigma_i^2) | \sigma_i^2 \in R_1\}$ and $S_2 = \{B(v_i^\tau, \sigma_i^2) | \sigma_i^2 \in R_2\}$. Then we have,

$$\Pr_{\sigma_i^2 \in \mathbb{R}^+} \{B(v_i^\tau, \sigma_i^2) \in S\}$$

$$= \Pr_{\sigma_i^2 \in R_1} \{B(v_i^\tau, \sigma_i^2) \in S_1\} + \Pr_{\sigma_i^2 \in R_2} \{B(v_i^\tau, \sigma_i^2) \in S_2\}$$

$$\leq \Pr_{\sigma_i^2 \in R_1} \{B(v_i^\tau, \sigma_i^2) \in S_1\} + \delta$$

$$\leq e^{\epsilon_2} (\Pr_{\sigma_i^2 \in R_1} \{B(\hat{v}_i^\tau, \sigma_i^2) \in S_1\}) + \delta$$

$$\leq e^{\epsilon_2} (\Pr_{\sigma_i^2 \in \mathbb{R}^+} \{B(\hat{v}_i^\tau, \sigma_i^2) \in S\}) + \delta,$$

Thus, mechanism B yields (ϵ_2, δ)-local differential privacy, where $\epsilon_2 \geq \frac{\Delta_j^{\tau 2}}{2\sigma_i^2}$ and $\delta > 1 - e^{\frac{-\lambda \Delta_j^{\tau 2}}{2\epsilon_2}}$.

From Theorem 2, we can find that when σ_i^2 becomes larger, the lower bound of ϵ_2 becomes smaller. In addition, the lower bound of δ will be smaller when the value of λ is smaller. When ϵ_2 and δ have smaller values, higher privacy protection can be achieved.

7   Performance Evaluation

7.1   Simulation Setup

The default settings in our simulations are set as follows. We consider there is an urban area consists of 10 interested locations that need to monitor ambient noise, and the total number of users is 400. The sensed values of users are simulated by a Gaussian distribution $\mathcal{N}(V_{j_{truth}}^\tau, 3)$, where $V_{j_{truth}}^\tau$ represents the ground truth and is uniformly distributed in $[20, 100]$dB. We set perturbation probability p as 0.3 (i.e., $\epsilon_1 = 3.004$), privacy budget ϵ_2 as 0.7, and relaxation variable $\delta = 0.3$. Besides, the weight of each user are equally initialized to 1 at the beginning of each time slot.

We compare our proposed approach with two baselines:

- *No Privacy Protection(NPP)*: Each user submits the original sensing data. Then the estimated values obtained by truth discovery.
- *Original Location with Sanitized Value (OLSV)*: Each user submits the original locations and sanitized values obtained by value privacy preserving mechanism to the platform. Then the estimated values obtained by truth discovery.
- *Perturbed Location with Original Value (PLOV)*: Each user submits the perturbed locations obtained by location privacy preserving mechanism and original sensed values to the platform. Then the estimated values obtained by truth discovery.
- *Privacy Protection with Mean (PPM)*: Each user submits the perturbed locations and sanitized values obtained by our privacy preserving mechanisms to the platform. Then the estimated values obtained by taking the average of the sanitized values submitted by the user in each interested location.

In order to measure the performance achieved by different approaches, we first adopt the commonly used Mean Absolute Error (MAE) as our metric, which calculates the differences between ground truth and estimated values as

$$\text{MAE} = \frac{1}{m} \sum_{j=1}^{m} \left| V_{j_{truth}}^\tau - \bar{V}_j^\tau \right|.$$

The smaller values of MAE indicate that the perturbation and sanitization have little impact on the accuracy of estimated results for the monitored object in all interested locations.

Besides, we compare the average accuracy of estimated values under different settings, which is calculated as

$$Accuracy = \frac{1}{m} \sum_{j=1}^{m} \left(1 - \frac{|V_{j_{truth}}^\tau - \bar{V}_j^\tau|}{V_{j_{truth}}^\tau} \right).$$

7.2 Performance Evaluation

In the following, we take different numbers of interested locations into consideration to compare the MAE achieved by our privacy preserving approach and other baselines first. We plot the MAE and the accuracy achieved by five approaches when the number of locations varies from 5 to 25 in Fig. 3 and Fig. 6. It can be found that the MAE and the accuracy of our approach remain stable, which indicates that our approach is scalable to the amount of interested points.

Specially, when our approach can achieve about 94.61% accuracy of estimated values, which is only 8.13%, 7.26% and 1.94% lower than NPP, OLSV and PLOV but 4.67% higher than PMM, respectively.

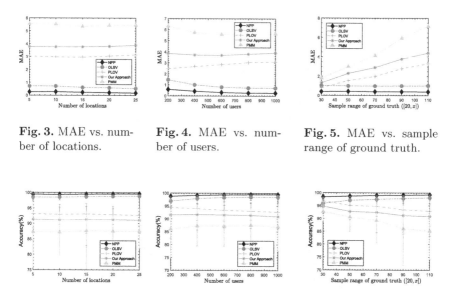

Fig. 3. MAE vs. number of locations.

Fig. 4. MAE vs. number of users.

Fig. 5. MAE vs. sample range of ground truth.

Fig. 6. MAE vs. number of locations.

Fig. 7. MAE vs. number of users.

Fig. 8. MAE vs. sample range of ground truth.

As shown in Fig. 4 and Fig. 7, we evaluate the performance of five approaches, by varying the total number of users from 200 to 1000. It can be observed that the MAE and the accuracy achieved by our approach keeps stable regardless of the number of users, which indicates that our approach applies to a large-scale MCS system with plenty of users. Specially, when there are 600 users, our approach achieves 91.68% accuracy, which is only 7.51%, 6.36% and 3.41% lower than NPP, OLSV and PLOV, respectively.

For further studying the performance of our privacy preserving mechanisms on estimation quality, we change the range of user sensed values, i.e., adjusting the range of $V_{j_{truth}}^{\tau}$. The sampling interval of $V_{j_{truth}}^{\tau}$ is $[20, x]$ and we vary x from 30dB to 110dB. In Fig. 5 and Fig. 8, the MAE increases but the accuracy decreases, when x becomes larger. This is because as the sample range of $V_{j_{truth}}^{\tau}$ increasing, sensed values of users becomes more diverse. Specifically, our approach can achieve about 92.39% average accuracy of estimated values when varies the sample range of $V_{j_{truth}}^{\tau}$, which is only 6.38%, 4.82% and 1.02% lower than NPP, OLSV and PLOV but 2.97% higher than PMM, respectively.

To summarize, although the performance of our approach is inevitably worse than NPP, OLSV and PLOV, our approach still achieves relatively high accuracy of estimated values and provides joint location-value privacy protection for users. Moreover, our approach always outperforms PMM, since we adopt a more reliable truth discovery method to eliminate the influence of unreliable or protected sensing data on the truth estimation.

8   Conclusion

In this work, we consider the joint location-value privacy protection problem in a MCS system with an untrusted platform, since not only location tags but also sensed values of users contained in their spatiotemporal sensing data will expose the privacy. Therefore, we propose a privacy protection approach, comprising of two privacy preserving mechanisms to perturb the locations and sensed values of users respectively. Specially, the LPPM is designed based on random response, and the VPPM is designed based on Gaussian mechanism. Both of the two mechanisms are proved to satisfy local differential privacy. Moreover, we conduct extensive simulations to show that the true values in interested locations can be accurately estimated based on perturbed locations and sanitized sensed values, by adopting the truth discovery method.

Acknowledgements. This research is supported by Grant No. 61802245 from NSFC and Grant No. 20CG47 from Shanghai Chen Guang Program. We also appreciate the High Performance Computing Center of Shanghai University and Shanghai Engineering Research Center of Intelligent Computing System (No. 19DZ2252600) for providing the computing resources.

References

1. Abowd, J.M.: The US census Bureau adopts differential privacy. In: Proceedings of the 24th ACM SIGKDD International Conference on Knowledge Discovery and Data Mining, p. 2867 (2018)
2. Dwork, C.: Differential privacy. In: Henk, C., van Tilborg, A., Jajodia, S. (eds.) Encyclopedia of Cryptography and Security pp. 338–340 (2011). https://doi.org/10.1007/978-1-4419-5906-5_752
3. Dwork, C., Roth, A., et al.: The algorithmic foundations of differential privacy. Found. Trends® Theor. Comput. Sci. **9**(3–4), 211–407 (2014)
4. Ganti, R.K., Ye, F., Lei, H.: Mobile crowdsensing: current state and future challenges. IEEE Commun. Mag. **49**(11), 32–39 (2011)
5. Jin, H., Su, L., Ding, B., Nahrstedt, K., Borisov, N.: Enabling privacy-preserving incentives for mobile crowd sensing systems. In: 2016 IEEE 36th International Conference on Distributed Computing Systems (ICDCS), pp. 344–353. IEEE (2016)
6. Kairouz, P., Oh, S., Viswanath, P.: Extremal mechanisms for local differential privacy. In: Advances in neural information processing systems, pp. 2879–2887 (2014)
7. Kouicem, D.E., Bouabdallah, A., Lakhlef, H.: Internet of things security: A top-down survey. Comput. Netw. **141**, 199–221 (2018)
8. Li, Q., Li, Y., Gao, J., Zhao, B., Fan, W., Han, J.: Resolving conflicts in heterogeneous data by truth discovery and source reliability estimation. In: Proceedings of the 2014 ACM SIGMOD International Conference on Management of Data, pp. 1187–1198. ACM (2014)

9. Li, Y., et al.: Towards differentially private truth discovery for crowd sensing systems. arXiv preprint arXiv:1810.04760 (2018)
10. Lin, B.C., Wu, S.H., Tsou, Y.T., Huang, Y.: PPDCA: privacy-preserving crowd-sensing data collection and analysis with randomized response. In: 2018 IEEE Wireless Communications and Networking Conference (WCNC), pp. 1–6. IEEE (2018)
11. Lin, J., Yang, D., Li, M., Xu, J., Xue, G.: Frameworks for privacy-preserving mobile crowdsensing incentive mechanisms. IEEE Trans. Mob. Comput. **17**(8), 1851–1864 (2017)
12. Liu, L., Liu, W., Zheng, Y., Ma, H., Zhang, C.: Third-eye: a mobilephone-enabled crowdsensing system for air quality monitoring. Proc. ACM Interact. Mob. Wearable Ubiquit. Technol. **2**(1), 20 (2018)
13. Ma, H., Zhao, D., Yuan, P.: Opportunities in mobile crowd sensing. IEEE Commun. Mag. **52**(8), 29–35 (2014)
14. Maisonneuve, N., Stevens, M., Niessen, M.E., Steels, L.: NoiseTube: measuring and mapping noise pollution with mobile phones. In: Athanasiadis, I.N., Rizzoli, A.E., Mitkas, P.A., Gómez, J.M. (eds.) Information Technologies in Environmental Engineering. Environmental Science and Engineering, pp. 215–228. Springer, Heidelberg (2009). https://doi.org/10.1007/978-3-540-88351-7_16
15. McSherry, F., Talwar, K.: Mechanism design via differential privacy. In: FOCS, vol. 7, pp. 94–103 (2007)
16. Pournajaf, L., Garcia-Ulloa, D.A., Xiong, L., Sunderam, V.: Participant privacy in mobile crowd sensing task management: a survey of methods and challenges. ACM Sigmod Record **44**(4), 23–34 (2016)
17. Ren, X., et al.: LoPub: high-dimensional crowdsourced data publication with local differential privacy. IEEE Trans. Inf. Forensics Secur. **13**(9), 2151–2166 (2018)
18. To, H., Ghinita, G., Shahabi, C.: A framework for protecting worker location privacy in spatial crowdsourcing. Proc. VLDB Endow. **7**(10), 919–930 (2014)
19. Wang, L., Zhang, D., Yang, D., Lim, B.Y., Han, X., Ma, X.: Sparse mobile crowd-sensing with differential and distortion location privacy. IEEE Trans. Inf. Forensics Secur. **15**, 2735–2749 (2020)
20. Wang, L., Zhang, D., Yang, D., Lim, B.Y., Ma, X.: Differential location privacy for sparse mobile crowdsensing. In: 2016 IEEE 16th International Conference on Data Mining (ICDM), pp. 1257–1262. IEEE (2016)
21. Wang, Q., Zhang, Y., Lu, X., Wang, Z., Qin, Z., Ren, K.: Real-time and spatio-temporal crowd-sourced social network data publishing with differential privacy. IEEE Trans. Dependable Secure Comput. **15**(4), 591–606 (2016)
22. Wang, Q., Zhang, Y., Lu, X., Wang, Z., Qin, Z., Ren, K.: RescueDP: real-time spatio-temporal crowd-sourced data publishing with differential privacy. In: IEEE INFOCOM 2016-The 35th Annual IEEE International Conference on Computer Communications, pp. 1–9. IEEE (2016)
23. Wang, S., et al.: Local differential private data aggregation for discrete distribution estimation. IEEE Trans. Parallel Distrib. Syst. **30**, 2046–2059 (2019)
24. Wang, T., Zhao, J., Zhang, X., Yang, X.: A comprehensive survey on local differential privacy toward data statistics and analysis in crowdsensing. arXiv preprint arXiv:2010.05253 (2020)
25. Wang, Z., et al.: Personalized privacy-preserving task allocation for mobile crowd-sensing. IEEE Trans. Mob. Comput. **18**(6), 1330–1341 (2018)
26. Yang, X., Wang, T., Ren, X., Yu, W.: Survey on improving data utility in differentially private sequential data publishing. IEEE Trans. Big Data **7**, 729–749 (2017)

27. Zhang, M., Yang, L., Gong, X., Zhang, J.: Privacy-preserving crowdsensing: privacy valuation, network effect, and profit maximization. In: 2016 IEEE Global Communications Conference (GLOBECOM), pp. 1–6. IEEE (2016)
28. Zhang, X., Yang, Z., Liu, Y.: Vehicle-based bi-objective crowdsourcing. IEEE Trans. Intell. Transp. Syst. **99**, 1–9 (2018)
29. Zhao, B., Rubinstein, B.I., Gemmell, J., Han, J.: A Bayesian approach to discovering truth from conflicting sources for data integration. Proc. VLDB Endow. **5**(6), 550–561 (2012)

Hybrid Semantic Conflict Prevention in Real-Time Collaborative Programming

Wenhua Xu[1], Yiteng Zhang[1], Brian Chiu[1], Dong Chen[2], Jinfeng Jiang[1],
Bowen Du[3(✉)], and Hongfei Fan[1(✉)]

[1] School of Software Engineering, Tongji University, Shanghai, China
{2031534,1852137,1850250,1751047,fanhongfei}@tongji.edu.cn
[2] SAP Labs China, Shanghai, China
dong.chen03@sap.com
[3] Department of Computer Science, University of Warwick, Coventry, UK
B.Du@warwick.ac.uk

Abstract. Real-time collaborative programming allows a group of programmers to edit the same source code at the same time. To support
semantic conflict prevention in real-time collaboration, a dependency-
based automatic locking (DAL) approach was proposed in prior work.
The DAL mechanism automatically detects programming elements with
dependency relationships, and prohibits concurrent editing on the inter-
dependent source code regions by locking. However, the prior DAL
scheme is too restrictive, which leads to an unnecessarily large locking
scope and seriously impacts the concurrent work. To address this issue,
we propose a novel hybrid semantic conflict prevention (HSCP) scheme,
to achieve a better balance between conflict prevention and concurrent
work. The scheme enforces locking on the working and strongly-depended
regions, while applies awareness highlight on weakly-depended regions.
The depth of locking scope can be customized by each programmer
in a fine-grained manner. A three-level awareness mechanism has been
designed for programmers to intuitively distinguish working, strongly-
depended and weakly-depended regions. In supporting the scheme, we
have devised techniques and solutions, and implemented a prototype
that supports programmers to enjoy hybrid semantic conflict prevention
in real-time collaborative programming over Eclipse and IntelliJ IDEA
platforms. Experimental evaluations have confirmed the satisfactory performance of the scheme in complex real-world scenarios.

Keywords: Real-time collaborative programming · Hybrid Semantic
Conflict Prevention (HSCP) · Dependency-Based Automatic Locking
(DAL) · Customizable locking scope determination · Collaboration
awareness mechanism

1 Introduction

Software development requires effective collaboration by multiple programmers.
In general, there are two approaches for collaborative programming, namely non-

© ICST Institute for Computer Sciences, Social Informatics and Telecommunications Engineering 2021
Published by Springer Nature Switzerland AG 2021. All Rights Reserved
H. Gao and X. Wang (Eds.): CollaborateCom 2021, LNICST 407, pp. 104–123, 2021.
https://doi.org/10.1007/978-3-030-92638-0_7

real-time collaborative programming and real-time collaborative programming [5]. Non-real-time collaborative programming has been widely applied in the industry as a traditional and mature collaboration approach, which is commonly supported by version control systems like Git. In contrast, real-time collaborative programming is an emerging collaborative programming approach that has attracted increasing attention and interests in the recent years [1–3,8–13,16,17]. · In a real-time collaborative programming session, each programmer's editing operations will be immediately propagated to all other collaborators' sites [15]. Real-time collaborative programming allows each collaborator to clearly know the work progress of others, reduces the cost of communication, and increases the efficiency of work. In addition, there is no need to manually merge concurrent work, and conflicts due to communication problems could be reduced. As an emerging approach, real-time collaborative programming is an effective supplement to the traditional non-real-time collaborative programming, and both approaches collectively meet diverse collaboration needs at different stages of software development processes [6].

The generic real-time collaborative editing technique is an essential part of implementing collaborative programming systems. In order to allow collaborators to edit freely in a session without being affected by network factors, real-time collaborative editing systems have commonly been designed with a *replicated architecture*, where each collaborating site maintains a distributed copy of the shared document. Under such architecture, each user's local editing operation will be immediately executed at the local site and sent to other collaborators. Consequently, there arises a classic problem called *syntactic consistency* [14], which is concerned with maintaining the consistency of all distributed copies of the document after all editing operations have been propagated and executed remotely. In order to solve this problem, a sophisticated *operational transformation* (OT) technique has been proposed and widely adopted [14,15]. By transforming the remote operations under certain conditions, the syntactic consistency of the replicated document can be guaranteed at all collaborators' sites.

In addition, there is another higher-level consistency problem, named *semantic consistency*. Syntactic consistency considers the consistency of the replicated code, whereas semantic consistency emphasizes the consistency of coding logic [4,7,14]. For supporting semantic consistency maintenance (also regarded as semantic conflict prevention), prior work proposed a *dependency-based automatic locking* (DAL) scheme [7], which prevents concurrent editing work on the same and inter-dependent source code regions. However, the existing DAL scheme is too restrictive: whenever a user is editing a basic region, all depended regions will be locked by the user until he/she finishes, and concurrent work is seriously impacted by the extremely large locking scope.

To better balance semantic conflict prevention and concurrent programming work, we contribute a novel *Hybrid Semantic Conflict Prevention* (HSCP) approach in this study. Under the HSCP scheme, the depended regions of each programmer are divided into strongly-depended and weakly-depended regions. Locking is enforced in working regions and strongly-depended regions, whereas awareness highlight is applied in weakly-depended regions. In addition, the depth of the scope of strongly-depended regions (i.e. locking scope) can be customized by each individual programmer in a fine-grained manner. The HSCP scheme also employs a three-level awareness mechanism, which assists collaborating programmers to intuitively distinguish working regions, strongly-depended regions, and weakly-depended regions, helping programmers to assess the risk of semantic conflicts. All approaches, mechanisms and techniques have been successfully implemented in prototype systems, while user evaluations and experimental evaluations have confirmed the feasibility, effectiveness, efficiency and usability of the system.

The rest of this paper is organized as follows. Firstly, we briefly review prior work on semantic conflict prevention with the DAL scheme in Sect. 2. Secondly, we provide detailed analysis on the constraints of the previous DAL scheme in Sect. 3. Thirdly, we propose the HSCP scheme in Sect. 4. Consequently, we present major technical issues and solutions for implementing the HSCP scheme in Sect. 5. We demonstrate the prototype implementation, experimental evaluations, and preliminary user evaluations in Sect. 6. Finally, we summarize this study in Sect. 7.

2   Related Work: Review of Prior Work on Semantic Conflict Prevention with Dependency-Based Automatic Locking (DAL)

Based on investigations, when multiple programmers are working in a real-time collaborative programming session, semantic conflicts may occur. Different from other collaborative work such as text editing, programming work requires strict consistency and continuity in terms of coding logic. Due to these characteristics of programming work, it is easy for programmers to unintentionally modify the logic of other programmer's code in a real-time collaborative programming session. When collaborative programmers are working in the same source code region or multiple source code regions with dependency relationships, semantic conflicts may occur [4, 7]. For example, when two programmers P_1 and P_2 are concurrently editing the same Java source code document (*Queue* implementation) as shown in Fig. 1, semantic conflicts may occur if P_1 and P_2 are concurrently editing method *offer*. In addition, semantic conflicts may also occur when two programmers are editing different regions with a dependency relationship (e.g., P_1 is editing the method *isEmpty*, while P_2 is editing the method *poll* which invokes *isEmpty*.).

For the convenience of discussion, we firstly introduce several terms as follows [4, 7]:

1. In object-oriented programming languages (such as Java), a class can be divided into *open areas* and *basic regions*. A basic region is a self-contained logical unit, which can refer to a *field* or a *method*; while all other spaces can be regarded as open areas.

2. In a source code document, if basic region A depends on region B in terms of semantics, then there is a *dependency relationship* from A to B, denoted as $A{\rightarrow}B$, and B is called a depended region of A. If $A{\nrightarrow}B$ and $B{\nrightarrow}A$, A and B are independent. The dependency relationship is transitive, when $A{\rightarrow}B$, $B{\rightarrow}C$, then $A{\rightarrow}C$. For example, if A is a method, the field B is referenced in A, $A{\rightarrow}B$, the method C invoking A, $C{\rightarrow}A$, and then $C{\rightarrow}B$.

3. Given a source code document, we can obtain a *dependency graph* (DG) by analyzing the dependency relationship among all basic regions. In the DG, a node represents a basic region, and an edge from node A to node B represents a dependency relationship from node A to node B, denoted as $A{\rightarrow}B$.

The source code *Queue.class* can be parsed into a DG with 7 open areas and 10 basic regions as shown in Fig. 1. It is worth further mentioning that any piece of source code that cannot form a valid basic region will be treated as an open area, including those intended but uncompleted regions. For example, when a Java method is being created but not completed yet (e.g. a brace is missing), the code segment will be regarded as an open area until it is syntactically completed.

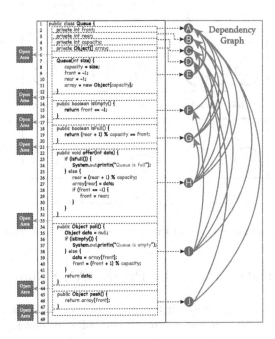

Fig. 1. Basic regions, dependency relationships and dependency graph (DG)

In prior work, to solve the problem of semantic conflict, a *Dependency-based Automatic Locking* (DAL) approach was proposed [4,7]. Whenever a programmer attempts to edit a region, the DAL scheme automatically detects the working region, derives the depended regions, requests and grants locks on them for this programmer, and finally releases locks when the work is completed. The whole mechanism works without any manual effort from the programmers. After each local or remote editing operation is executed, a *Contextualization and Full Derivation Locking State Update* (CFD_LSU) procedure will be executed [7], which ensures correct locking on the latest working region and depended regions for each programmer at any time, based on the programmers' latest editing positions and the latest DG structure. Under the DAL scheme, the *CheckPermission* procedure can prevent programmers from accidentally working on the regions which may cause semantic conflicts [7]. When a programmer selects a basic region to start working, if the basic region is locked by other programmers, or there is another user's working region within the depended regions, the editing operation will be rejected along with a UI notification as shown in Fig. 2.

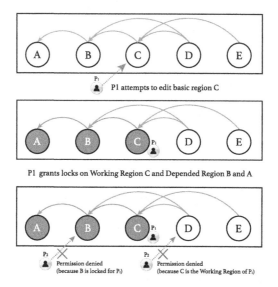

Fig. 2. A simple example of the DAL permission check mechanism

3   Major Constraints of the Prior DAL Scheme

The prior DAL scheme focused on the prevention of semantic conflicts without considering user experience in a real-world software development scenario. Whenever a programmer starts to work on a non-locked basic region, the working region and all depended regions will be locked. Due to the transitivity of dependency relationships, it is easy to produce extremely large locking scope. Consequently, any other programmer's editing operation on the locked regions will be rejected, which greatly affects the concurrency of collaborative work among programmers, especially for small-scale software development scenarios (e.g. multiple programmers working in the same class or package).

On the one hand, an extremely large locking scope may not be necessary for semantic conflict prevention. It is intuitive that semantic conflicts are more likely to occur among regions with stronger dependency relationships, which form a relatively small locking scope. Given a working region, it is possible that most depended regions are indirectly depended by the working region, which are far away from the working region along the dependency paths. Locking these weakly-depended regions does not make much sense, but greatly reduces the concurrency of programming work. On the other hand, shrinking the locking scope will inevitably weaken the capability of semantic conflict prevention. In certain cases, semantic conflicts may occur even if programmers work in regions with weak dependency relationships. It is not worth locking basic regions with weak dependency relationships; however, if no measure is taken, semantic conflicts may still occur.

Based on these observations, it is preferable if the locking scope could be reasonably reduced for better balancing concurrent work and conflict prevention, while at the same time, a weaker measure of semantic conflict prevention (weaker than locking) could be applied on those weakly-depended regions. It is also beneficial if the DAL scheme could support a general mechanism for more fine-grained locking scope determination where the depth of locking scope can be customized by each collaborating programmer.

4   HSCP: Hybrid Semantic Conflict Prevention

To solve the various constraints in the prior DAL scheme and improve the usability of semantic conflict prevention, we propose a *Hybrid Semantic Conflict Prevention* (HSCP) scheme, which employs a hybrid approach combining locking and awareness.

For the convenience of discussion, we introduce a term named dependency depth and a concept of three type regions as follows:

- In the DG, the *dependency depth* from node A to node B refers to the minimum number of edges from node A to node B in the DG. For example, $A{\rightarrow}B{\rightarrow}C$ and $A{\rightarrow}E{\rightarrow}F{\rightarrow}C$, and then the dependency depth from $A{\rightarrow}C$ is 2. If $A{\nrightarrow}D$, then the dependency depth of A to D is regarded as infinite. A simple example of dependency depth is presented in Fig. 3.

Based on investigations, it is observed that the risk of semantic conflicts is closely related to the dependency depth. Given a working region, semantic conflicts are more likely to occur in depended regions with smaller dependency depths from that working region, while semantic conflicts are less likely to occur in regions with larger dependency depths. It is necessary to determine a limited locking scope by locking regions within a reasonable dependency depth. Due to the complexity of software development, it is impossible to specify a general locking depth for all occasions, and it is preferable that the DAL scheme provides a generic working mechanism but leaving the setting of dependency depth up to the collaborating programmers. For example, if collaborating programmers

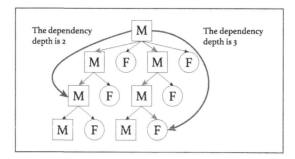

Fig. 3. A simple example of dependency depth

judge that there is less risk of semantic conflicts in the current session and more concurrent work is needed to speed up the work progress, the programmers may appropriately choose a smaller locking scope by setting a smaller dependency depth.

Therefore, we propose a customizable locking scope determination mechanism, where each programmer can customize his/her depth of the locking scope freely by setting the locking scope policy. Within the policy setting, there are two important arguments, namely F-depth and M-depth, which can precisely determine the locking scope of depended regions. All arguments of the policy setting are presented in Table 1 below.

Table 1. Arguments of customizable locking scope policy setting

Argument	Description
Locking Depth Switch	If it is turned on, the locking scope is determined according to F-depth and M-depth;
	If it is turned off, all depended regions will be locked (similar to the prior DAL scheme).
F-depth	Locking all field regions with dependency depth $\leq$ F-depth
M-depth	Locking all method regions with dependency depth $\leq$ M-depth

In addition, we define three types of regions which have different risk of semantic conflicts. When a programmer is editing a basic region, the set of depended regions of this region can be divided into the working regions, depended regions within the locking scope (denoted as *strongly-depended regions*), and the depended regions outside the locking scope (denoted as *weakly-depended regions*).

In real-world scenarios, each collaborating programmer can customize F-depth and M-depth in the user interface to dynamically adjust the locking scope. The change of locking scope can be immediately propagated to all collaborators' sites. It is worth pointing out that each collaborating programmer has his/her own locking scope policy and can only be decided by himself/herself. This implies that in a collaborative programming session, there may be different locking scope policies corresponding to different users at the same time. Although the customizable locking scope mechanism is much more complicated than a global locking scope policy (i.e. all users having the same locking scope policy), it is more fine-grained and has the following two advantages.

1. A global policy setting may not comply with the nature of collaborative work. If one user modifies the global policy setting, the locking scope of all users will be changed, which may interrupt the work of others and cause the originally-locked depended regions to be unlocked and modified by others.
2. A global policy setting is not flexible enough. The programming preferences of programmers may be diverse and variant. Some programmers may prefer a larger locking scope (with less risk of semantic conflicts), whereas other programmers may choose a small locking scope with more concurrency of work. A global policy setting obviously cannot satisfy all programmers.

For the above reasons, the customizable locking scope determination is very flexible and can well enhance the user experience. To intuitively explain the customizable locking scope determination, we present a simple example as shown in Fig. 4. In the figure, two programmers are concurrently working in the same document and have different locking scope policy settings. Under the prior DAL scheme, multiple programmers were certainly not allowed to work at the same time (because each user needs to lock all depended regions).

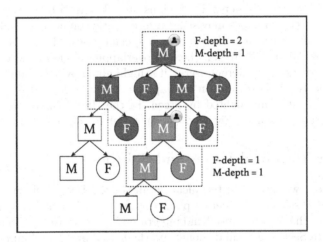

Fig. 4. A simple example of customizable locking scope determination

In addition, we have further devised a three-level awareness mechanism for distinguishing the working region (locked and highlighted), strongly-depended regions (locked and highlighted), and weakly-depended region (unlocked but also highlighted). Programmers can intuitively observe and assess the risk of semantic conflicts based on the awareness highlight of a basic region. These three types of regions correspond to different semantic conflict risk. Based on the risk level of semantic conflicts, the working region, strongly-depended regions, and weakly-depended regions are highlighted by a series of colors from darker to lighter (e.g., dark blue, normal blue, and light blue). As shown in the Fig. 5, when F-depth = 1 and M-depth = 2, the regions enclosed by the dotted line are locked and the darker colors are applied (the color of the working region is the darkest), and the regions outside the dotted line are the weakly-depended regions with the lighter color.

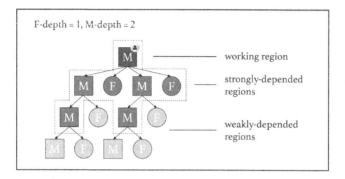

Fig. 5. Example of HSCP scheme

As mentioned, weakly-depended regions are allowed to be edited by others, but working on these regions may still raise semantic conflicts. Therefore, under the HSCP coloring scheme, there are two special cases: (1) whenever a basic region is currently a W-D region (i.e., an overlapping region of working region and depended region by different users), it is highlighted by red; and (2) whenever a basic region is a D-D region (an overlapping region of depended regions from different users), it is highlighted by green. In the HSCP three-level awareness mechanism, the example in Fig. 4 will be turn out to Fig. 6.

5   Major Technical Issues and Solutions

In this section, we introduce technical details of the HSCP scheme. To implement the HSCP scheme on different platforms, we have designed a set of common functionalities that can be reused and integrated into platform-specific collaboration clients. In Sect. 6, we will demonstrate the HSCP prototype implementation respectively on the Eclipse and IDEA platforms.

5.1   Customizable Locking Scope Determination

There are two major data structures in the HSCP scheme: the region state table and the user table. The user table stores all users' latest information for deriving right depended regions. The region state table stores all regions' state information. The function of the region state table is (1) to display the right awareness highlights of the regions (2) to judge whether the local user's editing operations should be allowed.

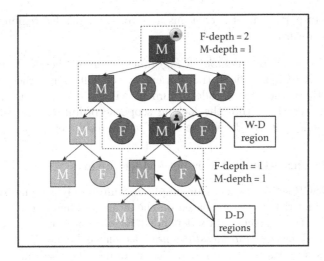

Fig. 6. Two users working under the HSCP three-level awareness mechanism

To implement the customizable locking scope determination, we have added a locking scope policy setting for each user. Each user can configure the local policy setting at any time. In the prior DAL scheme, the *Local Operation Processor* (LOP) and the *Remote Operation Processor* (ROP) have been proposed. For each local user's editing operation, the LOP firstly checks whether the user's operation should be allowed, and then processes the permitted operation, and finally, the operation will be sent to the server for real-time propagation to other sites. For each local and remote editing operation, the region state table will be updated, and the user's locks will be added to all depended basic regions.

Under the HSCP scheme, each user site has a user table that stores all users' latest editing operations and locking scope policy settings. The *CheckPermission* procedure determines the permission for each local editing operation. For each permitted local editing operation, the local locking scope policy setting will be loaded for granting locks with the correct locking scope, and then the policy setting will be sent to the server together with the editing operation. When the ROP receives a message from the server, it retrieves the remote user's editing operation together with the corresponding locking scope policy setting to grant correct locks for the remote user. All editing operations which are permitted in the LOP will not be checked again after being propagated to remote sites. Since each user can receive the policy setting of other users along with the editing operations and all editing operations will only be checked once at their original sites, the global locking state consistency can be ensured by nature.

In order to determine the correct strongly-depended regions according to the user's policy setting, we have re-designed the *DeriveDependedRegionSet* utility function as follows.

- *DeriveDependedRegionSet(R, PS)*: to retrieve the basic regions (as a set) with respect to the user's locking scope policy setting PS and the given source code region R. In particular, if R contains no strongly-depended region, an empty set will be returned.

The *DeriveDependedRegionSet(R,PS)* function firstly checks the type of the basic regions R. If it is a field, then an empty set will be returned; otherwise, if it is a method, the source code document will be parsed to DG, and then the depended regions within the locking scope according to the F-depth and M-depth of policy setting PS will be added to the result set.

5.2   HSCP Three-Level Awareness Mechanism

Under the HSCP scheme, users can simply and intuitively distinguish different semantic conflict risk of regions based on the awareness highlight.

To retrieve the correct weakly-depended regions, we propose a new utility function named *DeriveAwarenessRegionSet* as shown below. Correspondingly, an *awareness flag* has been proposed. The awareness flags will not be involved in the *CheckPermission* procedure [7], and therefore the local user's editing operations in the regions which are granted awareness flags will not be rejected. The only use of the awareness flags are to provide the correct color of the targeted region.

– *DeriveAwarenessRegionSet(R,PS)*: to retrieve the basic regions (as a set) outside the user's locking scope according to policy setting PS with respect to the given source code region R. In particular, if R has no weakly-depended region, an empty set will be returned.

The *DerieveAwarenessRegionSet(R,PS)* function firstly checks the type of the basic regions R. If it is a field, then an empty set will be returned; otherwise, if it is a method, the source code document will be parsed to a DG, and then all depended regions outside the locking scope according to the F-depth and M-depth of policy setting PS will be added to the result set.

Correspondingly, we have re-defined the *CFD_LSU* utility function as follows. The CFD_LSU is invoked after each local or remote editing operation has been executed.

To retrieve the highlight color of a basic region according to the region state table, a utility function *GetHSCPAwareness* is devised as follows.

– *GetHSCPAwareness(R)*: to retrieve the highlight color of basic region R. If there is only one lock or awareness flag associated with R, return the corresponding color of the owner. If there are multiple locks or awareness flags in the basic region R, when there are any working region locks, return a W-D color (red); otherwise, return a D-D color (green).

5.3   HSCP Implementation: Architecture and Components

Under the HSCP scheme, each collaborating site maintains a user table and a region state table as shown in Fig. 7 below. The HSCP user table is used to store

---

Algorithm 1. CFD_LSU(O)

1: **for** each site i in the session **do**
2:     ReleaseLocks(i);
3:     Contextualize(O, i);
4:     W := DetectTargetedRegion(EP(i));
5:     **if** W != OA **then**
6:         DRS := DeriveDependedRegionSet(W, PS(i));
7:         DARS := DeriveAwarenessRegionSet(W, PS(i));
8:         GrantLocks(i, W, DRS);
9:         GrantAwarenessFlags(i, DARS);
10:    **end if**;
11: **end for**;

---

the latest editing positions and locking scope policy settings of all collaborators and the region state table is used to record the locks and awareness flags of all basic regions in the current document.

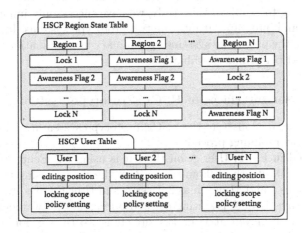

Fig. 7. The major data structures of the HSCP scheme

In software development processes, programmers may prefer different programming IDEs. To implement the HSCP scheme on different platforms (IDEs) without redundant work, we have designed an architecture that has separated a set of common functionalities from platform-specific client components. The overview of the HSCP architecture is presented in Fig. 8. The HSCP Core Module provides common functionalities, while the *HSCP Cross-platform Interfaces* define platform-specific components. Under this architecture, dependency-related information can be retrieved by implementing the platform-specific interfaces. After being processed by the *HSCP Core Module*, the information will be transmitted to other collaborators and stored in the local *HSCP Data Structures*.

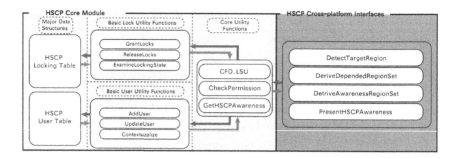

Fig. 8. The overview architecture of HSCP scheme

6   Prototype Implementation and Evaluations

CoEclipse and CoIDEA are two real-time collaborative programming systems proposed and implemented in prior work, which transparently converted the single-user Eclipse and IntelliJ IDEA IDEs into multi-user real-time collaborative programming tools [3]. In this study, we have successfully implemented the HSCP scheme and integrated it into the two prototype systems. In this section, we demonstrate the prototype systems, preliminary user evaluations, and a comprehensive set of performance evaluations.

6.1   Major User Interfaces of HSCP Prototype System

In this section, we demonstrate the HSCP prototype system used in a real-time collaborative programming process.

As presented in Fig. 9, User A on the left is using the Eclipse IDE, setting F-depth as 1 and M-depth as 0; and User B on the right is using IntelliJ IDEA, setting F-depth as 1 and M-depth as 2. User A and User B are editing the source code of *Queue.java*. User A is editing method *offer*, and the awareness highlights are immediately displayed at User B's site. It is worth mentioning that User A's working and depended regions are currently highlighted with three colors: the working region (method *offer*) is highlighted by dark blue, the strongly-depended region (field *rear*) is highlighted by blue, and the weakly-depended region (method *isFull*) is highlighted by light blue.

When User B is editing method *poll*, B's locks and awareness highlights will immediately appear on User A's site as shown in Fig. 10. The M-depth of B is 2, and the method *isEmpty* is a strongly-depended region. It can be seen from the figure that there are three fields (field *front*, *capacity*, and *array*) which are overlapping depended regions, and presenting the D-D color (green). From the figure, we can intuitively observe the risk of semantic conflicts in different regions based on the highlight colors. If User B clicks on User A's working region, a rejection notification will pop up, and the system prevents User A from working in this basic region.

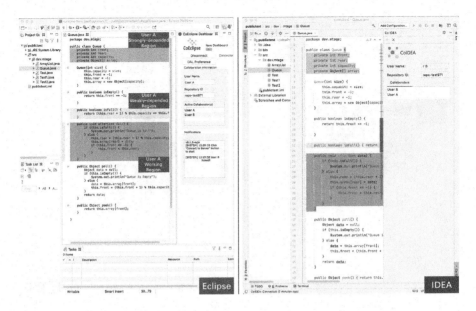

Fig. 9. The three-level awareness of HSCP scheme

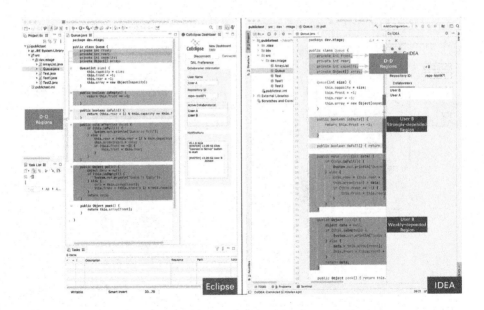

Fig. 10. Programming concurrently under the HSCP scheme

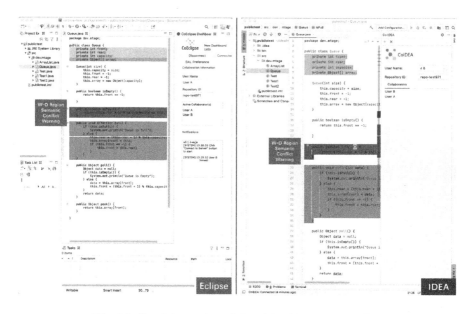

Fig. 11. Special warning of the risk of semantic conflict

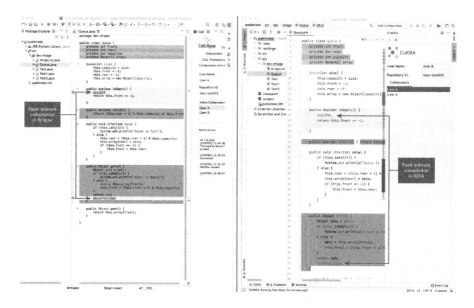

Fig. 12. Fault-tolerant source code analysis mechanism in supporting DAL

When User B is ready to work in method *isFull* which is a weakly-depended region of User A, there will be no rejection, but the region will be highlighted by the W-D color (red) as a special warning, as shown in Fig. 11.

It is worth pointing out that the underlying source code analysis mechanism (for deriving the DG, i.e. basic regions and dependency relationships) has the capability of fault-tolerant parsing. Given any uncompleted code which is syntactically invalid, the above mechanism can always generate basic regions and dependency relationships as much as possible. For example, as illustrated in Fig. 12, there are syntactical errors in both the working region and the depended region, but the DAL mechanism still behaves correctly (with correct highlight awareness and locks).

6.2   Preliminary User Evaluations

The prototype implementation has validated the feasibility of the proposed HSCP approach and techniques. A group of programmers participated in preliminary user evaluations (Fig. 13 illustrates a picture taken during the experiment) and provided positive feedback on semantic conflict prevention features based on the HSCP scheme. Firstly, the programmers selected basic regions, and the HSCP awareness could be immediately displayed on all collaborators' screens. Secondly, when programmers modified the DG structure, the HSCP awareness of all programmers also changed accordingly. Thirdly, when a programmer selected the region locked by others, a UI notification will pop up and the programmer's editing operation were rejected. Finally, when a programmer works in another collaborator's depended region, the highlight of the region became the W-D color to indicate the risk of semantic conflict. During the collaboration process, the syntactic consistency of the shared source code has always been maintained, based on the implementation of the OT algorithm. In addition, we also invited several groups of students to use the prototype system in their programming projects, and received positive feedback as well.

Fig. 13. A picture taken in a laboratory at Tongji University

6.3   Experimental Evaluations

In addition to preliminary user evaluations, we further conducted a comprehensive set of performance evaluations. We evaluated the HSCP core module and the cross-platform interface implementations respectively on CoEclipse and CoIDEA platforms.

Under the HSCP scheme, the amount of basic regions and dependency relationships in a source code document is a key factor that can determinate the performance of the HSCP mechanism. In order to systematically and comprehensively evaluate the performance of the HSCP system, we have developed a utility tool that can generate source code documents based on customizable parameters such as the amount of basic regions and dependency relationships. With multiple documents as input, a comprehensive set of performance evaluation can be conducted. The experimental platform is a laptop with a processor of Intel Core i5-7200U @ 2.5 GHz and 8 GB of RAM.

Firstly, we have evaluated the performance of the implementations of platform-specific components *DetectTargetedRegion*, *DeriveDependedRegionSet* and *DeriveAwarenessRegionSet* on the CoEclipse and CoIDEA platforms, respectively. The performance of these three utility functions depends on the amount of basic regions (denoted as N) and the amount of dependency relationships (denoted as M). Due to the different implementations of AST analyzers on different platforms, the performance of these functions on different platforms is also different. Table 2 and Table 3 present the evaluation results of these utility functions on the CoEclipse and CoIDEA platforms, respectively. The F-depth and M-depth of the customizable policy setting are both 3. As presented, the execution time in the two tables grows steadily with the increase of N and M values. In these utility functions, because *DeriveAwarenessRegionSet* needs to traverse all dependency relationships, it takes the longest time. When the N is 800 and the M is 32000, which is almost impossible in a real scenario, the *DeriveAwarenessRegionSet* function costs 9.84124×10^{-2} s on the CoIDEA platform and costs 2.511987×10^{-1} s on the CoEclipse platform.

Table 2. Performance evaluation of HSCP platform-specific components on the CoEclipse platform

Utility function	N = 50 M = 2,000	N = 100 M = 4,000	N = 200 M = 8,000	N = 400 M = 16,000	N = 800 M = 32,000
DetectTargetRegion	0.044 ms	0.098 ms	0.228 ms	0.237 ms	0.525 ms
DeriveDependedRegionSet	7.289 ms	10.668 ms	16.633 ms	24.435 ms	56.553 ms
DeriveAwarenessRegionSet	7.409 ms	17.128 ms	46.291 ms	92.605 ms	251.199 ms

N: amount of basic regions (i.e., fields and methods)
M: amount of field references and method invocations

Secondly, we have evaluated the performance of major procedures within the core module of the HSCP scheme, namely *CFD_LSU* and *CheckPermission*.

Table 3. Performance evaluation of HSCP platform-specific components on the CoIDEA platform

Utility function	N = 50 M = 2,000	N = 100 M = 4,000	N = 200 M = 8,000	N = 400 M = 16,000	N = 800 M = 32,000
DetectTargetRegion	0.002 ms	0.002 ms	0.003 ms	0.003 ms	0.004 ms
DeriveDependedRegionSet	0.241 ms	0.428 ms	0.511 ms	0.643 ms	0.699 ms
DeriveAwarenessRegionSet	5.830 ms	11.545 ms	24.022 ms	46.077 ms	98.412 ms

N: amount of basic regions (i.e., fields and methods)
M: amount of field references and method invocations

The performance of these utility functions also depends on the amount of collaborating programmers (denoted as P). Accordingly, by specifying the amount of collaborating programmers (P), the amount of basic regions (N), and the amount of dependency relationships (M), 20 groups of experiments for each procedure have been conducted. Since we are evaluating the platform-independent core module, we ignore the time spent on platform-specific components. Table 4 presents the experimental results, which have confirmed the good performance of the core module. As presented, the execution time grows steadily with the increase of N, M and P values. When the N is 800, the M is 32000 and the P is 16, which is almost impossible in a real scenario, the *CheckPermission* function costs only 2.3658×10^{-3} s and *CFD_LSU* function costs only 6.3966×10^{-2} s.

Table 4. Performance evaluation of the HSCP core module

P	Utility function	N = 50 M = 2,000	N = 100 M = 4,000	N = 200 M = 8,000	N = 400 M = 16,000	N = 800 M = 32,000
2	*CheckPermission*	0.005 ms	0.021 ms	0.065 ms	0.111 ms	0.347 ms
	CFD_LSU	0.063 ms	0.195 ms	0.654 ms	2.549 ms	7.312 ms
4	*CheckPermission*	0.012 ms	0.022 ms	0.099 ms	0.214 ms	0.661 ms
	CFD_LSU	0.245 ms	0.686 ms	2.396 ms	5.179 ms	17.206 ms
8	*CheckPermission*	0.027 ms	0.031 ms	0.180 ms	0.665 ms	1.232 ms
	CFD_LSU	0.897 ms	2.786 ms	7.526 ms	8.415 ms	35.449 ms
16	*CheckPermission*	0.028 ms	0.037 ms	0.208 ms	1.151 ms	2.366 ms
	CFD_LSU	4.009 ms	8.995 ms	17.668 ms	25.129 ms	63.966 ms

P: amount of collaborating programmers
N: amount of basic regions (i.e, fields and methods)
M: amount of field references and method invocations

7   Conclusions and Future Work

Dependency-based automatic locking (DAL) is an approach for supporting semantic conflict prevention in real-time collaborative programming. However, the prior DAL scheme produces extremely and unnecessarily large locking scope, which seriously impacts the concurrent programming work. To better balance concurrent work and semantic conflict prevention, we have proposed a novel Hybrid Semantic Conflict Prevention (HSCP), which combines locking and awareness approaches. Locking is enforced on the working regions and strongly-depended regions, whereas awareness highlight is applied on weakly-depended regions. Each programmer can customize the depth of the locking scope freely with a fine-grained locking scope policy setting. In addition, a three-level awareness mechanism has been devised, and the conflict risk on different regions can be intuitively distinguished by collaborating programmers. Compared with previous DAL schemes, this work provides users with customization options, and improves the flexibility of semantic conflict prevention.

For implementing the HSCP scheme on different platforms, we have designed a system architecture that separates HSCP's common functionalities from platform-specific components. As examples, we have successfully implemented the HSCP scheme and functionalities on two prototype systems named CoEclipse and CoIDEA, which support programmers to conduct real-time collaborative programming work while enjoying semantic conflict prevention over Eclipse and IntelliJ IDEA. A comprehensive set of experiments have confirmed the responsiveness, efficiency, effectiveness and usability of the HSCP scheme and solution in real-world scenarios.

We have been continuously working in the field of semantic conflict prevention for real-time collaborative programming, and our future work includes (a) supporting multiple locking groups (with multiple working regions) for an individual programmer in the session; and (b) achieving semantic conflict prevention across multiple source code documents. We are continuously developing and improving the research prototype, and planning to release the programs and source code for the community to utilize, with more in-depth evaluations.

Acknowledgment. This study has been sponsored by the Natural Science Foundation of Shanghai (No. 21ZR1465100), the National Natural Science Foundation of China (No. 61772371, No. 62172301, No. 62173248, No. 62073245, and No. 61702374), and the Fundamental Research Funds for the Central Universities.

References

1. Chen, Y., Lee, S.W., Xie, Y., Yang, Y., Lasecki, W.S., Oney, S.: Codeon: on-demand software development assistance. In: Proceedings of the 2017 CHI Conference on Human Factors in Computing Systems, CHI 2017, pp. 6220–6231 Association for Computing Machinery, New York (2017)
2. Fan, H., et al.: CoVSCode: a novel real-time collaborative programming environment for lightweight ide. Appl. Sci. **9**(21), 4642 (2019)
3. Fan, H., Sun, C.: Achieving integrated consistency maintenance and awareness in real-time collaborative programming environments: the CoEclipse approach. In: Proceedings of the 2012 IEEE 16th International Conference on Computer Supported Cooperative Work in Design (CSCWD), pp. 94–101 (2012)

4. Fan, H., Sun, C.: Dependency-based automatic locking for semantic conflict prevention in real-time collaborative programming. In: Proceedings of the 27th Annual ACM Symposium on Applied Computing, SAC 2012, pp. 737–742. Association for Computing Machinery, New York (2012)

5. Fan, H., Sun, C., Shen, H.: ATCoPE: any-time collaborative programming environment for seamless integration of real-time and non-real-time teamwork in software development. In: Proceedings of the 17th ACM International Conference on Supporting Group Work. p. 107–116. GROUP '12, Association for Computing Machinery, New York (2012)

6. Fan, H., Sun, C., Shen, H.: ATCoPE: any-time collaborative programming environment for seamless integration of real-time and non-real-time teamwork in software development. In: Proceedings of the 17th ACM International Conference on Supporting Group Work, pp. 107–116 (2012)

7. Fan, H., Zhu, H., Liu, Q., Shi, Y., Sun, C.: A novel dal scheme with shared-locking for semantic conflict prevention in unconstrained real-time collaborative programming. IEEE Access **5**, 22566–22583 (2017)

8. Feldman, M.: CodeSync: a collaborative coding environment for novice web developers. Wellesley College, Wellesley (2014)

9. Goldman, M., Little, G., Miller, R.C.: Real-time collaborative coding in a web IDE. In: Proceedings of the 24th Annual ACM Symposium on User Interface Software and Technology, pp. 155–164 (2011)

10. Guo, P.J., White, J., Zanelatto, R.: Codechella: Multi-user program visualizations for real-time tutoring and collaborative learning. In: 2015 IEEE Symposium on Visual Languages and Human-Centric Computing (VL/HCC), pp. 79–87. IEEE (2015)

11. Kurniawan, A., Soesanto, C., Wijaya, J.E.C.: Coder: real-time code editor application for collaborative programming. Procedia Comput. Sci. **59**, 510–519 (2015)

12. Lautamäki, J., Nieminen, A., Koskinen, J., Aho, T., Mikkonen, T., Englund, M.: Cored: browser-based collaborative real-time editor for java web applications. In: Proceedings of the ACM 2012 conference on Computer Supported Cooperative Work, pp. 1307–1316 (2012)

13. Nguyen, V., Dang, H.H., Do, N.K., Tran, D.T.: Enhancing team collaboration through integrating social interactions in a web-based development environment. Comput. Appl. Eng. Educ. **24**(4), 529–545 (2016)

14. Sun, C.: OTFAQ: Operational Transformation Frequently Asked Questions and Answers. Nanyang Technological University (2015)

15. Sun, C., Jia, X., Zhang, Y., Yang, Y., Chen, D.: Achieving convergence, causality preservation, and intention preservation in real-time cooperative editing systems. ACM Trans. Comput. Hum. Interact. **5**(1), 63–108 (1998)

16. Wang, Y., Wagstrom, P., Duesterwald, E., Redmiles, D.: New opportunities for extracting insights from cloud based IDEs. In: Companion Proceedings of the 36th International Conference on Software Engineering, pp. 408–411 (2014)

17. Warner, J., Guo, P.J.: CodePilot: scaffolding end-to-end collaborative software development for novice programmers. In: Proceedings of the 2017 CHI Conference on Human Factors in Computing Systems, pp. 1136–1141 (2017)

Supporting Cross-Platform Real-Time Collaborative Programming: Architecture, Techniques, and Prototype System

Yifan Ma[1], Zichao Yang[2], Brian Chiu[1], Yiteng Zhang[1], Jinfeng Jiang[1], Bowen Du[3(✉)], and Hongfei Fan[1(✉)]

[1] School of Software Engineering, Tongji University, Shanghai, China
{mtage,1850250,1852137,1751047,fanhongfei}@tongji.edu.cn
[2] Institute of Software, Chinese Academy of Sciences, Beijing, China
yangzichao21@otcaix.iscas.ac.cn
[3] Department of Computer Science, University of Warwick, Coventry, UK
B.Du@warwick.ac.uk

Abstract. Real-time collaborative programming supports a group of programmers to edit shared source code concurrently across geographically-distributed sites and collaborate in a closely-coupled fashion. There exists a number of problems and limitations for this emerging approach to be applied in real-world scenarios, and two critical issues are the lack of support on cross-platform collaboration and multi-level consistency maintenance. In this study, we have proposed, designed and implemented a novel Cross-Platform Real-time Collaborative Framework (CP-ROOF), and meanwhile achieved conflict resolution of multi-level editing operations. Based on the proposed framework, we have successfully implemented two collaboration clients that have realized cross-platform real-time collaboration over Eclipse and IntelliJ IDEA, two of the most popular Java programming environments. In this paper, we present design objectives and rationales, workflow and functional design, CP-ROOF's architecture and components, and major technical issues and solutions. Preliminary user evaluations and performance experiments have demonstrated the feasibility of the framework and the satisfactory performance of the prototype systems in a wide range of scenarios.

Keywords: Real-time collaborative programming · Cross-platform collaboration · Multi-level consistency maintenance · Operational transformation

1 Introduction

Software development requires effective collaboration among programmers with diverse skills and expertise. In general, there are two categories of approaches

H. Gao and X. Wang (Eds.): CollaborateCom 2021, LNICST 407, pp. 124–143, 2021.
https://doi.org/10.1007/978-3-030-92638-0_8

in supporting collaboration during the programming process, namely *non-real-time collaborative programming* and *real-time collaborative programming* [13,14]. Non-real-time collaborative programming is a traditional and mature approach that has been widely applied in the industry, which is always based on version control systems such as *Git* [1]. Programmers edit source code in their private workspaces and manually merge other programmers' work when necessary. In contrast, real-time collaborative programming supports a group of programmers to view and edit the shared source code at the same time, while changes performed by collaborators are transmitted and merged instantly [11]. Operation conflicts caused by concurrent editing are resolved automatically, which ensures the consistency of distributed source code after all remote editing operations have been replayed locally.

Real-time collaborative programming is beneficial in various scenarios. As presented in [11,13,21], such novel approach achieves closely-coupled collaboration in agile software development, supports distributed pair programming, enables remote diagnoses and troubleshooting, and many more. As an emerging approach, *real-time collaborative programming* has attracted increasing interests from both academia and industry in recent years [9,11,13,15,23].

There exists a variety of problems and limitations with existing real-time collaborative programming environments. One critical issue is the lack of support for cross-platform collaboration. Most existing real-time collaborative programming tools have been designed for single environments only. For example, *Code With Me* [2] provides real-time collaboration features on IntelliJ IDEA only, and *CoVSCode* [13] supports real-time collaboration on Visual Studio Code only. Detailed analysis on the limitations of existing real-time programming environments will be presented in Sect. 2.

To address the above mentioned issue in real-time collaborative programming, we propose, design and implement a novel Cross-Platform Real-time Collaborative Programming Framework (CP-ROOF), as well as two client prototype systems based on the CP-ROOF. The framework has been proposed with generic approaches and design. Based on CP-ROOF, specific collaboration clients on different platforms can be designed and implemented with little effort. In this study, we have implemented two client prototypes based on CP-ROOF, namely CoIDEA and CoEclipse, which have enabled real-time collaboration over IntelliJ IDEA and Eclipse, two of the most popular Java IDEs. We present the design objectives, workflow and functional design, system architecture and components, major technical issues and solutions, and a set of experimental evaluations.

The rest of this paper is organized as follows. Firstly, in Sect. 2, we review related studies, and present problems and limitations on existing real-time collaboration environments and tools. In Sect. 3, we introduce and explain three design objectives for the proposed solution. In Sect. 4, we present the design of collaboration functionalities and the proposed framework in detail. In Sect. 5, we discuss major technical issues and solutions in implementing the framework. In Sect. 6, we demonstrate the prototype system, and present performance evaluations. Finally, we summarize this study and identify potential issues for future work in Sect. 7.

2   Related Work

Real-time collaborative programming benefits programmers a lot in multiple scenarios. There exist several research prototypes and preliminary products for supporting real-time collaborative programming, such as *CoEclipse* [11], *CoVS-Code* [13], *Teletype for Atom* [6] and *Code With Me* [2]. However, none of these systems has been widely applied in real-world software industry, because there exists a variety of problems and limitations with existing real-time collaborative programming techniques. In this study, we aim to address two critical issues among them, which are discussed as follows.

Firstly, existing tools and environments have been designed for supporting single programming environments, and none of them supports cross-platform collaboration. For example, *Code With Me* [2] supports real-time collaboration with IntelliJ IDEA only; *CoEclipse* [11] supports Eclipse only; *Teletype for Atom* [6] provides real-time collaboration features for Atom only; and *CoVSCode* [13] supports real-time collaboration on *Visual Studio Code* only. *Saros* [3] was claimed to support real-time collaboration for both IntelliJ IDEA and Eclipse, but its versions for the two platforms are not compatible with each other, and the version for IntelliJ IDEA (Saros/I) is restricted to two-participant sessions. In conclusion, none of these systems really permits programmers to freely collaborate in an unconstrained manner using different IDEs. The lack of cross-platform support impedes the application of real-time collaborative programming.

Secondly, existing prototypes only support file-level consistency maintenance of the source code, ignoring folder-level conflicts. To achieve rapid local responsiveness in the sense that a user's local editing operation can be applied in the document without noticeable delay, real-time collaborative editing systems have commonly been designed with a *replicated architecture* [19]: the shared document is replicated at all collaborating sites. Consequently, one critical issue is to ensure the consistency of the distributed documents. *Operational Transformation (OT)* [8,16–18,22] is a well-established consistency maintenance technique, where the basic idea is to transform a remote operation into a new form according to the effects of previously executed concurrent operations. OT has been widely adopted in a wide range of real-time collaborative applications [10,11,13,14,16]. Most of the existing real-time collaborative programming solutions like [3,11,13] can transform and resolve conflicts between file-level editing operations (i.e. inserting or deleting a string in a file). However, concurrent folder-level editing operations (i.e. creating, deleting and renaming folders/files) may also conflict, and most of existing solutions miss support for it. For example, suppose there are two collaborators, namely A and B. At one moment, A creates a file and B deletes the whole parent folder concurrently. Their development environment may be inconsistent after the two operations have been propagated and replayed at remote sites. B has the file created by A whereas the folder including its content is deleted in site A. *Cloud Storage Operational Transformation(CSOT)* [16] is inspiring for designing transformation functions for folder-level editing operations. However, CSOT does not achieve seamless integration between folder-level editing operations and file-level editing operations.

To address the above mentioned limitations, we propose a novel solution for supporting real-time collaborative programming which will be described in the following sections.

3   Design Objectives and Rationales

In this study, we aim to address the two major limitations of existing real-time collaborative programming environments as presented above. We firstly present three design objectives of the proposed solution in this section.

3.1   Design Objective A: Supporting Cross-Platform Real-Time Collaborative Programming

Integrated Development Environment (IDE) is an essential part in programmers' lives. Each IDE delivers its unique features and benefits, and studies have shown that most programmers are satisfied with the IDE they are using [7]. For Java programmers, IntelliJ IDEA is used most, but there are still more than 20% of the programmers using other IDEs as a result of considerations on license cost, usability and collaboration-related capabilities [4,5,7]. As explained in Sect. 2, most of existing real-time collaborative programming environments support single IDEs or editors only. To achieve real-time collaboration in programming, some programmers are forced to adapt to another IDE which they may not be familiar with.

Our proposed solution must be capable of supporting cross-platform real-time collaboration, in the sense that programmers would be enabled to use different IDEs in the same real-time collaboration session. For example, with our solution, several Java programmers would be able to use both IntelliJ IDEA and Eclipse for real-time collaboration, so that each of them may continue to use the most preferred IDE without change. The solution would employ an architecture where the essential and generic functions are designed independently, and each platform-specific collaboration adaptor (i.e. collaboration client plugin for a specific IDE) could be implemented with least effort by following the same set of interface and process.

3.2   Design Objective B: Supporting Unconstrained Multi-level Consistency Maintenance

As presented in Sect. 2, existing real-time collaborative programming environments ignore folder-level consistency maintenance. Concurrent folder-level editing operations may also conflict and cause inconsistency like file-level editing operations. Integrating file-level and folder-level editing operations is also a challenge. For example, we have to consider when a file-level operation and a folder-level conflict with each other and how to resolve it. We have to consider the mechanism to define the relationship between file-level operations and folder-level operations and coordinate them.

The proposed solution should support unconstrained multi-level consistency maintenance, in the sense that collaborators can create, delete or rename files or folders in the shared project at any time while others are editing files and/or folders concurrently. The system should be capable of identifying the context of each operation and resolving conflicts between multi-level editing operations internally and automatically.

3.3   Design Objective C: Supporting Flexible Extensibility and Reusability in Design and Implementation

In addition to addressing the two limitations mentioned in Sect. 2, the proposed framework and system should be extensible and adaptable for multi-language and multi-functional support. Firstly, the proposed framework should be language-neutral, which can be applicable for supporting real-time collaboration with any programming language. For example, the design of the general workflow should accommodate common collaboration requirements from programmers using different programming languages. Secondly, the proposed solution should be extensible for diverse collaboration functionalities. For example, it should provide interfaces for easily integrating other functionalities such as collaboration awareness support, audio and video calls, and higher-level semantic conflict prevention support like DAL [12].

4   CP-ROOF: A Novel and Generic Cross-Platform Real-Time Collaborative Programming Framework

To achieve the above mentioned design objectives, we propose a novel Cross-Platform Real-time Collaborative Programming Framework (CP-ROOF), which serves as an essential part of our solution. In this section, we firstly present the design of the generic workflow and functionalities of real-time collaboration based on CP-ROOF from end-users' perspective, and then describe the architectural design of CP-ROOF in detail, which consists of three components named CP-ROOF Core (fundamental real-time collaborative programming support), CP-ROOF Server (collaboration coordinator) and CP-ROOF Client (transparent collaboration client adaptor).

4.1   Workflow and Functional Design

Although different programmers may prefer different IDEs and tools, the collaboration workflow can be unified. We extract common elements from the collaboration processes, and design the CP-ROOF framework based on the unified workflow as requirements. CP-ROOF provides out-of-the-box support for realizing this generic workflow, while specific collaboration clients may provide additional functionalities as appropriate.

Firstly, to initialize a collaboration session, a programmer may choose to create a brand new repository (i.e. the project including files and folders that programmers will edit collaboratively). Local folders and files in the repository will be synchronized to the server, which serve as the base version for the real-time collaboration session. When there is only him/her working in the session, the only difference from the single-user programming work is that the editing operations are also transmitted to the server to maintain the source code copy on the server. When other programmers choose to collaborate with the programmer, they can join the session by the identity. The server transmits the copy of the repository including all folders and files to each collaborator in a short time.

After collaborators join the same collaboration session, they can start to work in the real-time collaboration style. According to Design Objective B, collaborators can edit source code files, create new files or folders, and delete any file or folder in the shared repository. The client will detect every editing operation and transmit it immediately to the server through the CP-ROOF framework. The editing operation will then be propagated to all other clients within the session. Each client of CP-ROOF will receive, transform and execute remote operations in the local environment. The conflicts between multi-level operations will be resolved by CP-ROOF automatically and transparently. As illustrated in Fig. 1, each collaborator is aware of the presence of others.

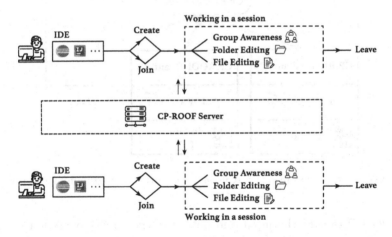

Fig. 1. The workflow design of CP-ROOF based real-time collaboration

A collaborator may leave from the session at any time, and other collaborators will be notified when a programmer leaves. CP-ROOF will maintain the latest collaboration repository even if all collaborators have left from the session. The repository will serve as the basis of programming work when the next session is initialized.

4.2   Architectural Overview of CP-ROOF

Based on the workflow and functional design above, we propose and design the Cross-Platform Real-time Collaborative Programming Framework (CP-ROOF) as follows. We will firstly present an overview with responsibilities of components and layers in this section.

As a generic cross-platform framework, CP-ROOF does not capture or apply editing operation from users directly. Instead, specific adaptors are responsible for interacting with collaborators and handling operations from users directly based on the common components provided by CP-ROOF. We have designed and implemented two specific adaptors in Java platforms named CoEclipse and CoIDEA in the form of plugins on Eclipse and IDEA respectively as illustrated in Fig. 2. Editing operations will be processed by CP-ROOF after being captured by plugins. CP-ROOF consists of three components, i.e. CP-ROOF Core, CP-ROOF Client, and CP-ROOF Server as illustrated in Fig. 3.

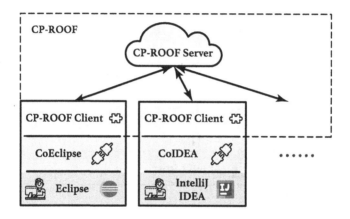

Fig. 2. Overview of cross-platform real-time collaborative programming environments

Under CP-ROOF, the input and output of each user's operation are processed by a hierarchy of layers. Each module has several layers according to its responsibility. CP-ROOF Core locates at the center of CP-ROOF as illustrated in Fig. 3. It is responsible for providing the most fundamental collaborative programming support. It includes the models of operations that users can perform, utilities and other messages transmitted between CP-ROOF Client and CP-ROOF Server. We also design and implement multi-level transforming functions for editing operations in CP-ROOF Core. The details of CP-ROOF Core will be presented in Sect. 4.3.

CP-ROOF Client provides common interfaces and classes for the design and implementation of concrete real-time collaboration adaptors. CP-ROOF Client is also responsible for controlling the transformation and execution of remote editing operations at each collaborating site.

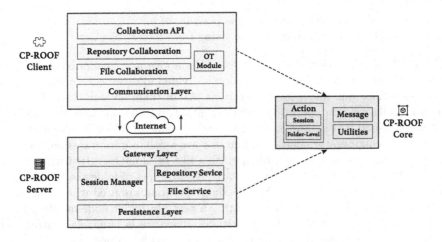

Fig. 3. CP-ROOF architecture and components

After a user chooses to create or join a real-time collaboration session, CP-ROOF Client will attempt to establish a persistent connection with the CP-ROOF Server. The connection is based on WebSocket by default and all messages and editing operations are transmitted via such persistent connection. CP-ROOF Server is responsible for managing all connections with clients on different platforms and broadcasting editing operations and messages to them. Design details and rationals of CP-ROOF Server and CP-ROOF Client will be presented in Sect. 4.4 and Sect. 4.5, respectively.

4.3 CP-ROOF Core: Fundamental Real-Time Collaborative Programming Support

According to Design Objective A, the proposed framework should support common collaboration operations in cross-platform real-time collaborative programming. To devise the framework, it is necessary to formally define what operations users can perform on a shared repository. A replicated repository in real-time collaborative programming can be described as a hierarchical file tree. After a user performs an operation of joining or creating a collaboration session, there are four folder-level operations that users can perform on the replicated repository:

1. $CR(p, T_p)$: to create a subtree T_p with a pathname p. A T_p can be a single file or a folder node.
2. $DL(p)$: to delete the subtree rooted with node p.
3. $RN(p, q)$: to change the name of node p to q.
4. $UP(p, d)$: to update the content of a file node(p) with file-level operation d.

Each $UP(p, d)$ embeds a specific file-level editing operation. There are two string-wise file-level operations that users can perform to update the content of a file:

1. $Insert(p, s)$: to insert string s at the position of p.
2. $Delete(lower, upper)$: to delete the string from $lower$ to $upper$.

CP-ROOF Core provides the model of the above user-generated operation. The user's operation during collaboration is divided into two categories, session-level operations and folder-level operations. All of them are sub-class of CoOperation (collaboration operation), which contains information about which collaborator issued it. File-level operations are sub-class of folder-level operations.

When a collaborator chooses to join or leave a collaboration session, a corresponding sub-type of session-level operation like InitJoinOperation will be created and transmitted to the server. Relatively, sub-types of folder-level operation like NodeCreateOperation and NodeUpdateOperation are used when collaborators are working in a session and creating a new file/folder node or editing the content of an existing file. This inheritance structure is language-neutral and highly extensible to support more diverse operations when necessary.

To provide multi-level consistency maintenance, CP-ROOF Core includes an integrated transformation function for creating, deleting, renaming and updating operations in both folder-level and file-level which will be presented in detail in Sect. 5.1.

4.4 CP-ROOF Server: Collaboration Coordinator

In real-time collaborative programming, collaborators will receive editing operations from others instantly. CP-ROOF Server is the central coordinator to receive and broadcast source code files, editing operations and various notifications. CP-ROOF Server is responsible for maintaining all files in working sessions and managing all persistent connections with clients. It will notify others about the operations when a collaborator creates, joins a session or modifies the file tree inner the working repository. The central document server works not only for notification but also for consistency maintenance. CP-ROOF Server serializes editing operations and allocates a total order which helps ensure correct transformation and execution ordering.

Each user operation will be collected by CP-ROOF Client and sent to CP-ROOF Server as a request. The request will be processed by multiple layers in CP-ROOF Server. In the gateway layer, requests are deserialized and distributed to different service layers. In real-time collaboration, collaborators may produce a mass of operations which have to be synchronized in a short time and servers have to notify others frequently. Consequently, persistent connections between clients and servers are maintained to save network overhead. Necessary files and information are stored in and read from the persistence layer which is advantageous to maintain collaboration sessions and recover from a breakdown.

4.5 CP-ROOF Client: Transparent Collaboration Client Adaptor

As a part of the cross-platform framework, CP-ROOF Client does not interact with users directly. It supplies out-of-the-box design and implementation for supporting real-time collaborative programming. Depending on CP-ROOF Client, specific IDE plugins can support the whole workflow in Sect. 4.1 with little effort.

Based on the operations model in CP-ROOF Core, CP-ROOF Client provides collaboration API for both session-level and folder-level. Each call from collaboration plugins on different platforms will be transformed into universal formats and transmitted to CP-ROOF Server. Remote operations received from CP-ROOF Server will also be transformed meticulously and executed in the local environment. The repository collaboration layer and file collaboration layer are in charge of above transformation. And the communication layer is responsible for establishing a connection and exchanging messages with CP-ROOF Server. CP-ROOF Client uses WebSocket to connect to server by default and it is extensible to use a different protocol. Only if the protocol supports specific means of information interchange defined by CP-ROOF.

5 Major Technical Issues and Solutions

In this section, we present major technical issues and solutions involved in the design and implementation of CP-ROOF, as well as the implementation of two concrete collaboration clients based on CP-ROOF.

5.1 Multi-level Operational Transformation

Transformation Control in Multi-level Editing Operations. As presented in Sect. 2, Operational Transformation (OT) is widely used to support consistency maintenance in the replicated architecture. Studies have shown one basic strategy to apply OT is to separate the high-level transformation control algorithms from the low-level transformation functions [17,20]. Control algorithms like [20,22] are responsible for controlling the order, target and reference of transformation. To reduce the complexity, we have adopted and implemented *Context-Based Operational Transformation(COT)* [20] in CP-ROOF. As for file-level transformation functions, the design of string-wise transformation functions for individual files can be found in prior work [17].

The Context-Based Operational Transformation (COT) [20] algorithm provides efficient solutions to control transformation and execution of local and remote operations. To combine COT algorithm with cross-platform collaborative programming, we have to consider how to perceive editing operations from users and coordinate local operations and remote operations. Firstly, we have to ensure processors that handle local operations and remote operations compete orderly for the execution of COT module. Secondly, we have to ensure that the context of the editing operation being executed is the same as the state of the document that is being changed. In other words, if another thread changes the document after a transformation and before the execution of the operation, the transformation based on old context will become invalid and the execution may modify the document wrongly. Only by ensuring these two conditions can we ensure the consistency between document replicates over collaboration sites.

For example, as presented in Fig. 4, there are two operation processors running on different threads to handle local and remote operations respectively. At one moment, the remote operation processor (ROP) receives a remote operation and the transformed operation is *Insert* (7, "*a*") (to insert the text "*a*" at the position 7 of the document). Unfortunately, the local operation processor (LOP) receives a local editing event and the document is changed before execution. The transformation becomes obsolete and the execution will modify the document wrongly due to the inconsistency between the context of remote operation and local document state.

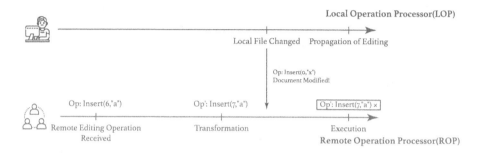

Fig. 4. An example scenario for illustrating execution competition

To ensure the conditions derived above, we have designed two strategies to maintain the consistency of document content and the structure of file tree respectively.

Firstly, when a local file-level editing operation is detected by the system, before it is applied in the document, LOP will request a lock in the OT module of CP-ROOF Client as illustrated in Fig. 5. If there is currently a remote editing operation being transformed and executed, LOP will be blocked until ROP completes the transformation and the document state is changed. The opposite is similar when ROP receives a remote editing operation. In this way, the OT module is invoked orderly, and editing operations will be transformed and executed based on the current document state strictly. Technically, the detection of local editing operation could be achieved by implementing handlers associated with particular events. For example, in Eclipse and IntelliJ IDEA IDEs, a local editing operation can be detected in the form of a keyboard press event that is about to change the document.

Secondly, things become different when it comes to folder-level operations. Existing IDEs provide a mass of ways to change local file tree. Collaborators may click buttons, move folder nodes by mouse or even create and delete files through file explorer. It is hard for CP-ROOF and specific client plugins to detect local editing and request the lock before local operation execution

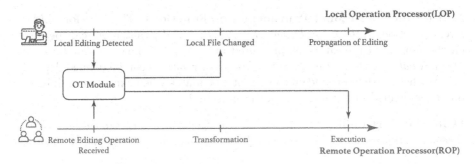

Fig. 5. Integrated processors for file-level editing

as described in file content editing. Therefore, we propose a novel coordination strategy for folder-level editing operation transformation control.

As presented in Fig. 6, ROP requests the lock when it receives a remote editing operation. But LOP will not try to acquire the lock until it detects the local file tree has been changed. If any remote editing operation is executed in a different file-tree state after transformation, a conflict will be perceived. The OT module will try to fetch the updated file-tree, transform and execute the remote operation again. We have derived that the OT module can detect the conflict in the form of *IOException* in Java. For example, if one site detects a folder-level change *DeleteFile("src/A.java")* (to delete the file in *src/* named *A.java*), ROP transforms a remote operation into *Rename("src/A.java", "src/Action.java")* (to rename file *src/A.java* to *src/Action.java*) concurrently. The execution of *Rename* operation will fail due to the file deletion and an *IOException* will be thrown. The OT module will catch the exception and a new transformation process will be conducted. In this way, local and remote operations are coordinated to be transformed and executed correctly. This control process is implemented in CP-ROOF and transparent to both plugin developers and collaborators.

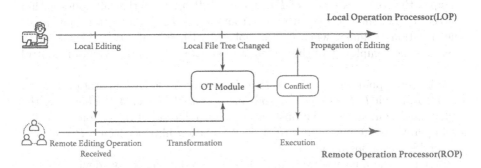

Fig. 6. Integrated processors for folder-level editing

Multi-level Operational Transformation Functions. There are four folder-level operations, $CR(p, T_p), DL(p), RN(p, q), UP(p, d)$, that users can perform on the replicated repository as presented in Sect. 4.3. Following *Cloud Storage Operational Transformation (CSOT)* [16], their relations can be defined depending on whether they produce inconsistent tree states when executed in different orders as defined in Definition 1 and Definition 2.

Definition 1 (Conflict "$\otimes$"). *Given two operations, they are conflict only if these operations are concurrent and different execution orders result in inconsistent file-tree states.*

Definition 2 (Compatible "$\odot$"). *Given two operations, they are compatible only if they do not have a conflict relation.*

In order to integrate file-level and folder-level OT algorithms supporting transformation control mentioned in Sect. 5.1 and reduce the complexity of the system, we devise a new set of conflict and compatible relations between editing operations as shown in Table 1.

Table 1. Conflict and compatible relations.

	$CR(p_2, Tp_2)$	$DL(p_2)$	$RN(p_2, q_2)$	$UP(p_2, d_2)$
$CR(p_1, Tp_1)$	$\otimes \leftrightarrow (p_1 = p_2)$	$\otimes \leftrightarrow (p_2 \subset p_1)$	$\otimes \leftrightarrow (p_2 \subset p_1) \vee$ $((parent(p_1) = parent(p_2))$ $\wedge(nodename(p_1) = q_2))$	$\odot$
$DL(p_1)$		$\odot$	$\otimes \leftrightarrow (p_2 \subseteq p_1) \vee (p_1 \subset p_2)$	$\otimes \leftrightarrow (p_1 \subseteq p_2)$
$RN(p_1, q_1)$			$\otimes \leftrightarrow (p_1 \subseteq p_2) \vee (p_2 \subset p_1) \vee$ $((parent(p_1) = parent(p_2))$ $\wedge(q_1 = q_2)$	$\otimes \leftrightarrow (p_1 \subseteq p_2)$
$UP(p_1, d_1)$				$\otimes \leftrightarrow (p_1 = p_2)$

Take the conflict relation of $DL(p_1)$ and $UP(p_2, d_2)$ when $p_1 \subseteq p_2$ as an example, the combined-effect of $DL(p_1)$ and $UP(p_2, d_2)$ is that all nodes within $subtree(p_1)$(i.e. the subtree with p_1 as root) are deleted, no matter what p_2 is. The situation is similar when UP is replaced with RN and CR. This solution simplifies the complexity of the system and supports the transformation control well.

It is worth pointing out that $UP(p, d)$ embeds a file-level operation (i.e. an *Insert(p, s)* or a *Delete(lower, upper)*) as presented in Sect. 4.3. Therefore, the conflict and compatible relationships between folder-level operations and file-level operations are inherited directly from relationships between $UP(p, d)$ and other folder-level operations.

Based on the above conflict and compatible relationship, we devise a set of new transformation functions which are different from CSOT [16]. The basic idea of designing transformation functions is to define another operation so that the transformed operation can be correctly executed and achieve document consistency in face of concurrent operations. For example, to integrate folder-level editing operations with file-level editing operations, our solution defines UP with a nested file-level editing operation. Whenever a conflict of two UP happens, the folder-level transformation function does nothing. The transformation control algorithm takes out the internal file-level operation of UP and passes it to the file-level operational transformation functions for processing. This solution easily supports multilevel operational transformations and it performs well. It also satisfies the *Convergence Property 1 (CP1)*, which ensures the same repository is produced by executing two concurrent and mutually transformed operations in different orders. *CP1* is required when designing transformation functions combined with COT and has been discussed in detail in [20, 22].

5.2 Client Design and Implementations

This section shows how the specific collaboration clients are designed and implemented based on CP-ROOF. These clients can be implemented in the form of plugins of IDEs which help programmers conduct real-time collaboration based on their preferred environments. We have implemented two clients named CoEclipse and CoIDEA as the reference implementations, based on the Eclipse and IntelliJ IDEA platforms, respectively.

With the full use of the components provided by CP-ROOF, the process of developing a new collaborative programming client simply involves three steps: (1) identifying the mechanism of listening for editing operations on a different platform, (2) implementing direct editing of local files and folders, (3) invoking the common components from CP-ROOF to receive editing events and displaying collaboration notifications. During the first step, the designer has to identify how to detect file editing operations on the specific IDE. After that, the designer has to implement classes that help the CP-ROOF Client apply remote operations locally. The designer has to follow the process of locking described in Sect. 5.1. The result of this activity is the implementation of two interfaces defined in the CP-ROOF Client. As illustrated in Fig. 7, interfaces named *ILocalFileEditor* and *ILocalRepositoryEditor* are the protocol between the CP-ROOF Client and collaboration plugins. During the third step, the client can receive collaboration events from remote sites and present them on the user interface finally.

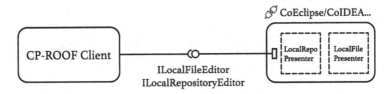

Fig. 7. Integration of CP-ROOF Client and specific IDE platform

Following the above design Steps 5.2, we have designed and implemented two prototype client systems, namely CoEclipse and CoIDEA, which are IDE plugins to support real-time collaborative programming in Eclipse and IntelliJ IDEA, respectively. They can support the whole workflow presented in Sect. 4.1. Both of them fully reuse components provided by CP-ROOF and their design follows the Model-View-Presenter pattern. To support CP-ROOF Client especially implement interfaces $ILocalFileEditor$ and $ILocalRepositoryEditor$, CoEclipse and CoIDEA require a collection of plugin APIs, which depend on the concrete platform. For example, CoEclipse utilizes $IWorkspace.addResourceChangeListener$ $(IResourceChangeListener):void$ to detect folder-level editing operations on Eclipse. We will demonstrate their UI and cross-platform collaboration based on CoEclipse and CoIDEA in Sect. 6.1.

6   Experimental Evaluations

In this section, we demonstrate the cross-platform collaboration based on the proposed framework along with preliminary user evaluations and performance evaluations.

6.1   Cross-Platform Collaboration and Evaluations

Figure 8 presents CoEclipse UI for a programmer to start a real-time collaborative programming session. The user interface is similar to original Eclipse and existing single-user functionalities are preserved. Once clicking the *"Connect to Server"* button, a configuration dialog is displayed. The programmer needs to choose to create a brand new collaborative repository or join an existing session. Necessary parameters like the identity of the repository are required. Local source code will be uploaded to CP-ROOF server if a new repository is created. The initialization process is similar in CoIDEA.

Fig. 8. UI snapshot of CoEclipse client's initialization panel

When programmers are working on the same repository in a collaboration session, all folder-level and file-level editing operations from other collaborators will be synchronized and replayed locally. As presented in Fig. 9 and Fig. 10, the collaborator using CoIDEA is working on the static method *copyOf* and the CoEclipse user is editing the constructor of class *CoUser*. The CoIDEA user is notified about the deletion of a file performed by the CoEclipse user. Both of them can see each other's work in real-time. The CoEclipse and CoIDEA prototype implementation have confirmed the feasibility of cross-platform real-time collaborative programming based on the CP-ROOF framework.

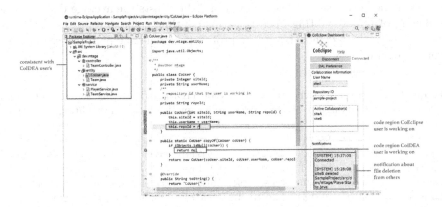

Fig. 9. UI snapshot of CoEclipse client in a real-time collaboration session

Fig. 10. UI snapshot of CoIDEA client in a real-time collaboration session

6.2 Performance of Major Procedures During Collaboration

In addition to the above user evaluations, we have conducted a set of performance evaluations on key procedures critical to user experience. Firstly, whenever a collaborator creates a new collaboration session, CP-ROOF Client will upload the initial source code copy. A replication of source code will be transmitted to local when other collaborators join an existing session. We selected several repositories to evaluate the performance of the initialization of real-time collaboration session.

The repositories were fetched from GitHub with diversity in project sizes to reflect real-world Java programming scenarios as much as possible. Table 2 presents the names, branches, and initialization times of each project. The experimental computer was equipped with an Intel Core i7@2.6 GHz processor and 64 GB of RAM, while the operating system was macOS 10.15.7. As illustrated in Table 2, even for large-size projects, the time cost for initialization was still acceptable.

Table 2 also presents the average processing times of local and remote editing operations in real-time collaboration sessions. It can be observed that local editing operations are always captured and applied instantly. The duration from an operation's generation to its remote replay mainly depends on its transmission over the network. The last column of Table 2 lists the average delay of the replaying of remote editing operations in real-time collaboration sessions over the Internet, which demonstrates the prototype's real-time performance in real-world scenarios.

Table 2. Average processing times of session creation (involving source code copy upload), session joining (involving source code copy download) and editing operations

Repository	Branches	Commit	Size	Items	Creation	Joining	Local editing	Remote editing
Halo	Master	bec10e9	2.0 MB	579	605 ms	1448 ms	1.33 ms	16.50 ms
Apollo	Master	b0173d7	6.3 MB	1214	911 ms	3307 ms	1.26 ms	20.92 ms
Lombok	Master	1a15270	6.9 MB	1946	1086 ms	4897 ms	1.28 ms	24.25 ms
Commons-lang	Master	d1e9e59	7.9 MB	472	870 ms	2151 ms	1.64 ms	25.83 ms
Netty	4.1	df53de5	18.6 MB	3109	2029 ms	6911 ms	1.36 ms	34.08 ms
Spring boot	Master	e1ad2cd	26.9 MB	7644	4461 ms	16138 ms	1.23 ms	40.83 ms

Moreover, we conducted further experiments to confirm the scalability of CP-ROOF in supporting real-time collaboration by a large number of participants. In a real-time session, whenever a remote operation is received, CP-ROOF Client will attempt to acquire the lock in OT module, and transform and replay the operation as presented in Sect. 5.1. Regardless of the network transmission delay (which is completely out of our control), the process of transformation and replaying is the most critical and time-consuming element that affects the user experience. The execution duration of such process is highly dependent on the number of sites and operations in the session, which affects the system's scalability. During our experiment, we simulated multiple sets of concurrent editing operations and measured the processing times of transformation. The most recently created version (MRCV) scheme is an effective buffering mechanism for operational transformation proposed in [20]. We have evaluated the processing times of CP-ROOF without MRCV and with MRCV respectively.

We have designed two simulation scenarios. In the first scenario, there is one local site and n remote collaborators working in the same session. Each remote site performs an editing operation concurrently. The local site receives n editing operations, transforms and replays them. Table 3 presents the processing times of transformation of n operations on average. The percentages of each row present the percentage of remote folder-level operations. The rest are file-level operations that edit the same file concurrently.

Table 3. Times of transformation in n-collaborator sessions

Scenario A	n = 5	n = 10	n = 20	n = 30	n = 100
No MRCV (20%)	2.45 ms	5.02 ms	238.79 ms	31045.81 ms	(Timeout)
MRCV (20%)	2.33 ms	4.58 ms	8.57 ms	14.25 ms	46.61 ms
No MRCV (30%)	2.30 ms	3.33 ms	64.27 ms	8349.77 ms	(Timeout)
MRCV (30%)	1.44 ms	2.74 ms	5.31 ms	9.14 ms	44.173 ms

In the second scenario, there is a local site and a remote site working in the same session. Each site performs $n/2$ editing operations and local processing times of transformation are measured as presented in Table 4. The percentages of folder-level operations are still 20% and 30% respectively.

Table 4. Times of transforming n operations in two-collaborator sessions

Scenario B	n = 6	n = 10	n = 20	n = 30
No MRCV (20%)	2.04 ms	3.98 ms	681.57 ms	(Timeout)
MRCV (20%)	2.08 ms	2.48 ms	7.20 ms	11.33 ms
No MRCV (30%)	1.04 ms	2.97 ms	534.45 ms	(Timeout)
MRCV (30%)	1.03 ms	2.58 ms	5.05 ms	11.62 ms

It can be observed that even for a large amount of collaborators, the proposed framework can transform multilevel operations with acceptable time costs with MRCV regardless of the percentage of folder-level operations. Such time cost for transformation is only incurred when receiving remote operations, whereas the processing of local operations mainly depends on the original IDE and can be completed locally and instantly. Experimental results have demonstrated the good scalability of the CP-ROOF system in supporting large-scale collaborations by a large number of sites.

7 Conclusions and Further Work

Real-time collaborative programming is an emerging approach that enables a team of programmers to edit shared source code concurrently. However, the lack of cross-platform collaboration support and multi-level consistency maintenance impedes the real-world application of real-time collaborative programming. In this paper, we have contributed a novel Cross-Platform Real-time Collaborative Programming Framework (CP-ROOF), which supports real-time collaboration for programmers using different IDEs. Both file-level and folder-level consistency maintenance have been supported and integrated. We presented a set of design objectives and rationales, proposed the architecture of CP-ROOF, and designed the three components of CP-ROOF (namely CP-ROOF Core, CP-ROOF Server, and CP-ROOF Client) in detail. We have also presented major technical issues and solutions in supporting the implementation of CP-ROOF. Following the CP-ROOF framework, we have successfully implemented two client prototypes named CoEclipse and CoIDEA to support cross-platform real-time collaboration over Eclipse and IntelliJ IDEA. Preliminary user evaluations have confirmed that all design objectives have been met, and performance evaluations have demonstrated the high efficiency of the implemented prototype system.

We are continuously working in the domain of real-time collaborative programming environments, and there are several issues identified for future work. Firstly, we plan to support more IDEs for real-time collaboration based on the proposed framework. During that process, we will invent more functionalities to assist programmers in collaboration awareness. Secondly, we will further improve and validate the proposed lock and transformation control to ensure consistence maintenance under complex situations in long-term collaboration. Thirdly, the CoEclipse and CoIDEA prototype systems will be continuously developed and improved, and the programs and source code will be released for the community to utilize when appropriate. Consequently, more in-depth evaluations will be conducted with more diverse scenarios.

Acknowledgment. This study has been sponsored by the National Natural Science Foundation of China (No. 62172301, No. 61772371, No. 62173248, No. 62073245, and No. 61702374), the Natural Science Foundation of Shanghai (No. 21ZR1465100), and the Fundamental Research Funds for the Central Universities.

References

1. Git. https://git-scm.com/. Accessed 12 Apr 2021
2. Code With Me: The ultimate collaborative development service by JetBrains. https://www.jetbrains.com/code-with-me/. Accessed 12 Apr 2021
3. Saros. https://www.saros-project.org/. Accessed 12 Apr 2021
4. Stack Overflow Developer Survey 2019. https://insights.stackoverflow.com/survey/2019#development-environments-and-tools/. Accessed 12 Apr 2021
5. Java Programming - The State of Developer Ecosystem in 2020 Infographic — JetBrains: Developer Tools for Professionals and Teams. https://www.jetbrains.com/lp/devecosystem-2020/java/. Accessed 12 Apr 2021
6. Teletype for Atom. https://teletype.atom.io/. Accessed 12 Apr 2021
7. Bergström, A.: A survey on developers' preferences in integrated development environments (2018). https://www.diva-portal.org/smash/get/diva2:1177860/FULLTEXT01.pdf
8. Cai, W., He, F., Lv, X., Cheng, Y.: A semi-transparent selective undo algorithm for multi-user collaborative editors. Front. Comput. Sci. **15**(5), 1–17 (2021). https://doi.org/10.1007/s11704-020-9518-x

9. Chen, Y., Lee, S.W., Xie, Y., Yang, Y., Lasecki, W.S., Oney, S.: Codeon: on-demand software development assistance. In: Proceedings of the 2017 CHI Conference on Human Factors in Computing Systems, pp. 6220–6231 (2017)
10. Cho, B., Sun, C., Ng, A.: Issues and experiences in building heterogeneous co-editing systems. Proc. ACM Hum.-Comput. Interact. 3(GROUP) (2019). https://doi.org/10.1145/3361126
11. Fan, H., Sun, C.: Achieving integrated consistency maintenance and awareness in real-time collaborative programming environments: the CoEclipse approach. In: Proceedings of the 2012 IEEE 16th International Conference on Computer Supported Cooperative Work in Design (CSCWD), pp. 94–101 (2012)
12. Fan, H., Zhu, H., Liu, Q., Shi, Y., Sun, C.: A novel DAL scheme with shared-locking for semantic conflict prevention in unconstrained real-time collaborative programming. IEEE Access 5, 22566–22583 (2017)
13. Fan, H., et al.: CoVSCode: a novel real-time collaborative programming environment for lightweight IDE. Appl. Sci. 9(21), 4642 (2019). https://www.mdpi.com/2076-3417/9/21/4642
14. Fan, H., Sun, C., Shen, H.: ATCoPE: Any-time collaborative programming environment for seamless integration of real-time and non-real-time teamwork in software development, pp. 107–116 (10 2012)
15. Kurniawan, A., Soesanto, C., Wijaya, J.: CodeR: real-time code editor application for collaborative programming. Procedia Comput. Sci. 59, 510–519 (2015)
16. Ng, A., Sun, C.: Operational transformation for real-time synchronization of shared workspace in cloud storage. In: Proceedings of the 19th International Conference on Supporting Group Work, GROUP 2016, pp. 61–70. Association for Computing Machinery, New York (2016)
17. Sun, C.: OT FAQ: Operational transformation frequently asked questions and answers. https://www3.ntu.edu.sg/scse/staff/czsun/projects/otfaq/. Accessed 12 Apr 2021
18. Sun, C., Chen, D., Jia, X.: Reversible inclusion and exclusion transformation for string-wise operations in cooperative editing systems. In: Proceedings of the 21st Australasian Computer Science Conference, pp. 441–452. Citeseer (1998)
19. Sun, C., Xia, S., Sun, D., Chen, D., Shen, H., Cai, W.: Transparent adaptation of single-user applications for multi-user real-time collaboration. ACM Trans. Comput.-Hum. Interact. (TOCHI) 13(4), 531–582 (2006)
20. Sun, D., Sun, C.: Context-based operational transformation in distributed collaborative editing systems. IEEE Trans. Parallel Distrib. Syst. 20(10), 1454–1470 (2009)
21. Wang, A.Y., Mittal, A., Brooks, C., Oney, S.: How data scientists use computational notebooks for real-time collaboration. Proc. ACM Hum.-Comput. Interact. 3(CSCW), 1–30 (2019)
22. Xu, Y., Sun, C.: Conditions and patterns for achieving convergence in ot-based co-editors. IEEE Trans. Parallel Distrib. Syst. 27(3), 695–709 (2016)
23. Zhang, J.: An Investigation of Technology Design Features for Supporting Real-Time Collaborative Programming in an Educational Environment. Master's thesis, Pennsylvania State University, State College, PA, USA (2018)

Collaborative Computing Based on Truthful Online Auction Mechanism in Internet of Things

Bilian Wu, Xin Chen$^{(\boxtimes)}$, and Libo Jiao

School of Computer Science, Beijing Information Science and Technology University, Beijing 100101, China
{wubilian,chenxin,jiaolibo}@bistu.edu.cn

Abstract. With the increasingly diverse and complex demands of the Internet of Things (IoT) devices, terminal equipments have been unable to effectively meet their quality of service (QoS). To resolve this issue, the resource allocation strategy for edge-cloud collaborative computing has been seen as a promising scheme by offloading computation-intensive tasks from IoT devices to edge servers or cloud data center. In this paper, we study the resource collaborative scheduling problem and formulate a truthful online auction mechanism in the mobile edge computing (MEC) system. We propose the objective problem of maximizing the long-term average revenue, subjecting to the task queue stability constraint. Furthermore, we apply Lyapunov optimization techniques to deal with this objective problem, which can be solved without prior information. So as to derive subproblems optimal solutions and obtain effective resource allocation strategy, a revenue maximization online auction (RMOA) algorithm is designed. Theoretical analysis shows that the RMOA algorithm can achieve optimal system revenue approximately while ensuring the stability of the MEC system. In addition, simulation results indicate the effectiveness of the RMOA algorithm and verify the influence of various parameters.

Keywords: Collaborative computing · Internet of Things · Resource allocation · Auction mechanism · Lyapunov optimization

1 Introduction

Nowadays, with the rapid development of wireless communication technology and Internet of Things (IoT) technology, a variety of new network services such as automatic driving and augmented reality are constantly emerging. The demands for IoT devices are becoming increasingly complex and diverse, and the processing of these computation-intensive tasks require powerful data processing capacity [1]. Nevertheless, most of the IoT devices have limited battery and computing capacity, which can not satisfy the processing performance requirements of tasks [2].

H. Gao and X. Wang (Eds.): CollaborateCom 2021, LNICST 407, pp. 144–157, 2021.
https://doi.org/10.1007/978-3-030-92638-0_9

It is recommendable to expand computing and services to near the data generation. As an emerging technology, mobile edge computing (MEC) has received widespread attention from academia, which can reduce delay and energy consumption by deploying edge servers close to IoT devices [3,4]. However, the resources of the edge servers are limited, if all of the computing tasks are offloaded to the edge servers, the service performance and execution efficiency of IoT devices will be reduced [5]. In addition, too many service requests compete with limited computing resources, which will make the system unstable. In order to improve the processing efficiency of IoT devices, considering the edge-cloud collaborative computing framework is an effective resource allocation scheme [6].

The framework of edge-cloud collaboration can provide fast and flexible supply of computing resource for IoT devices, which has sparked interest in market based dynamic resource allocation mechanism. As a fast and effective method of market resource allocation, online auction mechanism has been widely applied. It can dynamically reflect supply-demand relationship of computing resources and offer desirable resource scheduling strategies for edge consumers and auctioneers at the same time [7]. Hence, it is a crucial research issue to devise a truthful online auction mechanism, which can not only make IoT devices compete for computing resources fairly, but also increase the overall revenue of the system.

The problem of server resource allocation in MEC was studied by [8,9], which assigned user requests based on utility function. [10] constructed the optimal power allocation problem for base station to maximize the overall throughput delivered to mobile user. [11] presented an online resource scheduling framework to minimize task delays in MEC system. [12,13] designed a real auction mechanism to get the appropriate allocation policy. Nevertheless, these works gave little insight into the dynamic nature of channel condition and task processing. We study collaborative computing scheme based on auction mechanism, and propose the problem of stochastic optimization.

In this article, we construct the framework of edge-cloud collaboration and investigate the problem of computing resources online auction based on Vickrey-Clarke-Groves (VCG) auction mechanism. In addition, we apply Lyapunov optimization techniques to solve this issue while guaranteeing the queue and system stability. A truthful revenue maximization online auction (RMOA) algorithm is proposed, which considers the randomness of task arrival and channel conditions. The main works and contributions of this article can be summarized as follows,

– The framework of edge-cloud collaboration is constructed for resource allocation based on online auction in radio access network. We apply the Lyapunov optimization technology to solve stochastic optimization problem, which maximizes the long-term revenue in the MEC system.
– We propose the RMOA algorithm and truthful online auction mechanism to obtain effective resource allocation strategy. Dispatcher can balance system revenue and queue length by setting parameter based on RMOA algorithm, and make auction decision dynamically.
– Theoretical analysis shows that the RMOA algorithm can reach to the approximate optimal system revenue while ensuring the stability of MEC system, and simulation experiments prove the effectiveness of RMOA algorithm.

2 System Model and Problem Formulation

We formulate a MEC system in radio access network, where N IoT devices with computation-intensive tasks are offloaded by a MEC server or a cloud data center. Let $\mathcal{I}$ denote the collection of the IoT device. There is a small base station (SBS) with a MEC server in this system, which can be regarded as a dispatcher or auctioneer, and the cloud data center connects to the edge via a wired channel. Owing to the limited processing capacity of edge server, when too many IoT devices arrive at the same time, edge server will offload computing tasks to the cloud. The system operates tasks with a slot length ι, there exist $t \in \{0, 1, ..., T - 1\}$ [14,15].

We assume that all of the IoT devices are heterogeneous, they have different specifications and no prior knowledge. IoT devices submit their own bidding profiles to the dispatcher, which can be denoted by a 3-tuple parameter $\theta_i(t) = <u_i(t), c_i(t), b_i(t)>$, where $\theta_i(t) \in \theta_i, \Phi = \{\theta_1, \theta_2, ..., \theta_\mathcal{I} | i \in \mathcal{I}\}$. $u_i(t)$ represents the profit of completing this calculation task, $c_i(t)$ denotes the CPU cycles required to complete the unit data computation task, $b_i(t)$ represents bid value of IoT device i. Auctioneer will make a computing resource scheduling policy based on the received bidding profiles.

Due to the transmission speed of downlink is much faster than that of uplink, the transmission cost of downlink could be ignored. The transmission rate of device i is given as follows

$$r_i(t) = w_l log_2(1 + \frac{p_i h_i(t)}{w_l \sigma^2}), \qquad (1)$$

where w_l represents channel bandwidth between SBS and terminal equipments, σ^2 denotes the noise power spectral density. p_i and $h_i(t)$ are defined as transmission power and channel gain, respectively. Let $a_i(t)$ (bits) indicate the number of the offloaded computing task requests at time slot t with a time average rate $\lambda_i = \mathbb{E}\{a_i(t)\}$ [16].

We define that $f_e(t)$ is the edge server CPU-cycle frequency, and it has an upper bound denoted by f_e^{max}, which can be written as

$$f_e(t) \leq f_e^{max}. \qquad (2)$$

Let $d_i^s(t)$ is the data execution quantity of edge server for IoT device i. For edge server, given the CPU-cycle frequency $f_e(t)$, the allocated computation tasks have an upper bound, which is

$$\sum_{i \in \mathcal{I}} c_i(t) d_i^s(t) / f_e(t) \leq \iota. \qquad (3)$$

We assume that the winner of the bid is identified as $\mathcal{X}(t) = \{x_i(t) | i \in \mathcal{I}\}$, which can be expressed as

$$x_i(t) = \begin{cases} 1, & \text{if IoT device } i \text{ is winning bid at slot } t, \\ 0, & otherwise. \end{cases} \qquad (4)$$

We assume each IoT device's computing task should be completed in only one time slot, so they can only win a maximum of one bid, the constraint is

$$\sum_{t \in \mathcal{T}} x_i(t) \leq 1, \forall i \in \mathcal{I}. \tag{5}$$

We adopt $Q_i(t)$ to represent the queue length of tasks not being processed in SBS, and $d_i^c(t)$ denotes the number of offloaded data from SBS to cloud server. Then, the queue backlog $Q_i(t)$ is

$$Q_i(t+1) = max\{Q_i(t) - d_i^s(t) - d_i^c(t), 0\} + a_i(t). \tag{6}$$

In order to ensure system stability and reduce queue backlog, we define a limit condition on the average queue backlog. q_i denotes the time average queue backlog, which can be described in

$$q_i = \lim_{T \to \infty} \frac{1}{T} \sum_{t=0}^{T-1} \mathbb{E}\{Q_i(t)\} < \eta, \exists \eta \in \mathbb{R}^+. \tag{7}$$

2.1   Cost Model

In this article, we consider the costs of energy consumption when IoT devices win the bidding, which includes the transmission energy consumption from IoT devices to SBS, the computing energy consumption of MEC server and cloud server. The transmission energy consumption $E_i^{tra}(t)$ is

$$E_i^{tra}(t) = p_i \frac{d_i^s(t) + d_i^c(t)}{r_i(t)}. \tag{8}$$

We define κ as the influence coefficient of relating to capacitor execution, and the computation energy consumption of MEC server is

$$E_i^e(t) = \kappa c_i(t) d_i^s(t) f_e^2(t). \tag{9}$$

Let μ represent the energy consumption coefficient in cloud data center, the computation energy consumption in cloud is defined as

$$E_i^c(t) = \mu d_i^c(t). \tag{10}$$

Since the transmission capacity of wired channels is limited, the constraint should be satisfied when offloading computing tasks from SBS to cloud

$$\sum_{i \in \mathcal{I}} d_i^c(t)/w_c \leq \iota, \tag{11}$$

were w_c is the wired channel bandwidth between SBS and cloud, and w_c has an upper bound, which can be expressed as $w_c \leq w_c^{max}$.

According to the above description, the total cost of energy consumption in the whole system as follows

$$\psi(t) = \sum_{i \in \mathcal{I}} g_i(t) \{E_i^{tra}(t) + E_i^e(t) + E_i^c(t)\}, \tag{12}$$

where $g_i(t)$ is the unit cost of energy consumption for device i, which may vary from different IoT devices. Then, the time average of cost function of the MEC system is

$$\varphi = \lim_{T \to \infty} \frac{1}{T} \sum_{t=0}^{T-1} \mathbb{E}\{\psi(t)\}. \tag{13}$$

2.2   Utility Model

In this model, we introduce the system utility that contains two parts: the utility $U_l(t)$ of IoT devices win the bidding and the revenue $U_e(t)$ of completing the calculation task for MEC system. Hence, the $U_l(t)$ is formulated as

$$U_l(t) = \sum_{i \in \mathcal{I}} [b_i(t) - \pi_i(t)]. \tag{14}$$

Meanwhile, $u_i(t)$ represents the evaluation of the system revenue from the completing the calculation task. Denote the payment to edge server by $\pi_i(t)$. Then, the revenue of edge server is written as

$$U_e(t) = \sum_{i \in \mathcal{I}} [\pi_i(t) + u_i(t)] \tag{15}$$

According to the above formulas, we can get the utility function in this MEC system

$$\begin{aligned} U(t) &= U_l(t) + U_e(t) - \psi(t) \\ &= \sum_{i \in \mathcal{I}} x_i(t) \{[b_i(t) + u_i(t)] - g_i(t)[E_i^{tra}(t) + E_i^e(t) + E_i^c(t)]\}. \end{aligned} \tag{16}$$

2.3   Optimization Problem

In this article, we think about the problem of system revenue maximization (SRM). An optimization problem to maximize the time average revenue in the MEC system with the queue stability constraints is proposed, which is as follows

$$\textbf{(SRM)} \max_{d^s(t), d^c(t)} U = \lim_{T \to \infty} \frac{1}{T} \sum_{t=0}^{T-1} \mathbb{E}\{U(t)\}. \tag{17}$$

$$s.t.\,(2),(3),(4),(5),(7)\,and\,(11).$$

The wireless channel conditions, and information of bidding files are dynamic in our modle. In addition, the MEC system has no prior knowledge and can not obtain future information about IoT devices. An online auction mechanism based on Lyapunov techniques is put forward, which can transform stochastic optimization problem into deterministic optimization problem.

3   Revenue Maximization Online Auction Algorithm Design

To effectively resolve this optimization problem, we propose a truthful online auction mechanism and the revenue maximization online auction (RMOA) algorithm. In the auction, IoT devices could submit real bids through the following pricing strategy to compete computing resource effectively. Then, auctioneer determines the winner and resource allocation strategy.

3.1   Pricing Strategy

Because of the selfishness of IoT device, they might submit bidding information untruthfully in order to maximize own profit. To solve this problem, we have introduced the VCG auction mechanism [17], which can make the system achieve a truthful auction process. The strategy for determining the winner can be effectively solved by Hungarian algorithm [15].

We pay attention to the problem of collaborative computing in IoT after successful bidding of IoT devices with Hungarian algorithm. Then, the task of the IoT device i is performed on the server, where $x_i(t) = 1$. After the winner is determined, the auctioneer needs to determine the payment according to the VCG pricing scheme to ensure the authenticity of the bid. Therefore, the payment charged by auctioneer to IoT device i can be given as

$$\pi_i(t) = [SRM(\Phi) - SRM(\Phi \setminus \theta_i(t))], \tag{18}$$

where $SRM(\Phi)$ is the maximum achievable objective function value, $SRM(\Phi \setminus \theta_i(t))$ denotes the optimal objective function value without IoT device i participation. Due to pricing strategy of VCG auction mechanism contents authenticity of the whole system and the payment $\pi_i(t)$ depends on the bids of other IoT devices, which can encourage the bidders to bid truthfully.

3.2   Evaluation of Computation Tasks

We use Lyapunov optimization technology to transform the problem above. $\Theta(t) = (Q_i(t))$ can be expressed as the queue backlog matrix in MEC system. Then, the *Lyapunov function* is

$$L(\Theta(t)) = \frac{1}{2} \sum_{i \in \mathcal{I}} [Q_i^2(t)] \tag{19}$$

where $L(\Theta(t))$ represents the congestion status of the IoT devices. Then, we set the *conditional Lyapunov drift* $\Delta(\Theta(t))$ is

$$\Delta(\Theta(t)) = \mathbb{E}\{L(\Theta(t+1)) - L(\Theta(t))|\Theta(t)\}. \tag{20}$$

By keeping the Lyapunov function $\Delta(\Theta(t))$ at a small value sate, the revenue function can be maximized. Hence, combining the queue length and scheduling revenue, the *drift plus revenue* is $\Delta(\Theta(t)) - V\mathbb{E}\{U(t)|\Theta(t)\}$, where V is a non-negative number, which is the weight parameters on revenue function and queue length.

Theorem 1. *Under any scheduling algorithm, suppose that the upper bound of* $a_i(t)$ *is* a_i^{max}, *for arbitrary values of* V *and* $\Theta(t)$, *the drift plus revenue will be satisfied the following inequality*

$$\Delta(\Theta(t)) - V\mathbb{E}\{U(t)|\Theta(t)\} = \frac{1}{2}\sum_{i\in\mathcal{I}}[Q_i^2(t+1) - Q_i^2(t)] - V\mathbb{E}\{U(t)|\Theta(t)\}$$

$$\leq C - V\sum_{i\in\mathcal{I}}\mathbb{E}\{b_i(t) + u_i(t) - g_i(t)[E_i^{tra}(t) + E_i^e(t) + E_i^c(t)]|\Theta(t)\}$$

$$+ \sum_{i\in\mathcal{I}}Q_i(t)\mathbb{E}\{a_i(t) - [d_i^s(t) + d_i^c(t)]|\Theta(t)\},$$

(21)

where $C = \frac{1}{2}\sum_{i\in\mathcal{I}}[(a_i^{max})^2 + (\frac{f_e^{max}\iota}{c_i} + w_c^{max}\iota)^2]$ is a constant.

Proof: Combining with the fact $(\max[A - B, 0])^2 \leq A^2 + B^2 - 2AB(A, B \geq 0)$ and taking square on (6), which as follows

$$Q_i^2(t+1) \leq Q_i^2(t) + a_i^2(t) + [d_i^s(t) + d_i^c(t)]^2 - 2Q_i(t)[d_i^s(t) + d_i^c(t)]$$
$$+ 2a_i(t)\max\{Q_i(t) - [d_i^s(t) + d_i^c(t)], 0\}.$$

(22)

Then, we assume $\bar{d}_i(t) = d_i^s(t) + d_i^c(t)$ represents the number of request from IoT device i to edge server, which is

$$\bar{d}_i(t) = \begin{cases} d_i^s(t) + d_i^c(t), & d_i^s(t) + d_i^c(t) \leq Q_i(t), \\ Q_i(t), & otherwise. \end{cases}$$

(23)

Owing to $\max\{Q_i(t) - [d_i^s(t) + d_i^c(t)], 0\} = Q_i(t) - \bar{d}_i(t)$, and according to the formula (22), (23) above, and taking the expectations and summing over all the IoT devices,

$$\Delta(\Theta(t)) \leq \frac{1}{2}\sum_{i\in\mathcal{I}}\mathbb{E}\{a_i^2(t) + [d_i^s(t) + d_i^c(t)]^2|\Theta(t)\}$$

$$+ \sum_{i\in\mathcal{I}}Q_i(t)\mathbb{E}\{a_i(t) - [d_i^s(t) + d_i^c(t)]|\Theta(t)\}.$$

(24)

Due to $f_e(t) \leq f_e^{max}$ and $w_c \leq w_c^{max}$, we can get $d_i^s(t) \leq \frac{f_e^{max}\iota}{c_i}$ and $d_i^c(t) \leq w_c^{max}\iota)$. In addition, according to the fact that $a_i(t) \leq a_i^{max}$, Adding $V\mathbb{E}\{U(t)|\Theta(t)\}$ to inequality (24). Let $C = \frac{1}{2}\sum_{i\in\mathcal{I}}[(a_i^{max})^2 + (\frac{f_e^{max}\iota}{c_i} + w_c^{max}\iota)^2]$, we can get

$$\Delta(\Theta(t)) - V\mathbb{E}\{U(t)|\Theta(t)\}$$
$$\leq C - V\mathbb{E}\{U(t)|\Theta(t)\}$$
$$+ \sum_{i\in\mathcal{I}}Q_i(t)\mathbb{E}\{a_i(t) - [d_i^s(t) + d_i^c(t)]|\Theta(t)\}.$$

(25)

Substituting (12) into (25), therefore, inequality (21) could be obtained.   ∎

3.3   Online Algorithm

Our RMOA algorithm can make the long-term average revenue achieve to the optimal approximately while keeping the whole system stability, through transforming optimization problem SRM into two independent subproblems. The optimization problem can be rewritten as

$$\max_{d^s(t),d^c(t)} VE\{\{u_i(t) + b_i(t) - g_i(t)[E_i^{tra}(t) + E_i^e(t) + E_i^c(t)]\}|\Theta(t)\}$$
$$+ \sum_{i\in\mathcal{I}} Q_i(t)[d_i^s(t) + d_i^c(t)]. \tag{26}$$

$$s.t.\ (2),(3),(7)\ and\ (11).$$

Considering the constraint conditions of formulas (2) and (3), we define the first subproblem **P1** and get the optimal edge computation $d^s(t)$ by solving as

$$\textbf{P1:}\min_{d^s(t)} \sum_{i\in\mathcal{I}}\{V[g_i(t)\frac{p_i}{r_i(t)} + g_i(t)\kappa c_i(t)f_e^2(t)] - Q_i(t)\}d_i^s(t). \tag{27}$$

$$s.t.\ \sum_{i\in\mathcal{I}} c_i(t)d_i^s(t)/f_e^{max} \leq \iota.$$

Since the amount of tasks by computing in edge $d_i^s(t)$ is the decision variable and weighted by $V[g_i(t)\frac{p_i}{r_i(t)} + g_i(t)\kappa c_i(t)f_e^2(t)] - Q_i(t)$, the optimal solution $d_i^s(t)$ is expressed as

$$d_i^s(t) = \begin{cases} \frac{f_e^{max}\iota}{c_i(t)}, & i = i', \\ 0, & otherwise, \end{cases} \tag{28}$$

where $i' = \arg\min_{i\in\mathcal{I}}\{V[g_i(t)\frac{p_i}{r_i(t)} + g_i(t)\kappa c_i(t)f_e^2(t)] - Q_i(t)\}$. Therefore, the optimal resource scheduling strategy according to (28) can be obtained.

Considering the relevant constraint conditions, the second subproblem **P2** can be defined as (29), the optimal resource allocation strategy $d^c(t)$ solves as

$$\textbf{P2:}\min_{d^c(t)} \sum_{i\in\mathcal{I}}\{V[g_i(t)\frac{p_i}{r_i(t)} + g_i(t)\mu] - Q_i(t)\}d_i^c(t) \tag{29}$$

$$s.t.\ \sum_{i\in\mathcal{I}} d_i^c(t)/w_c \leq \iota.$$

We assume that $d_i^s(t)$ is constant, and the decision variable $d_i^c(t)$ is weighted by $V[g_i(t)\frac{p_i}{r_i(t)} + g_i(t)\mu] - Q_i(t)$, which is

$$d_i^c(t) = \begin{cases} w_c\iota, & i = i', \\ 0, & otherwise, \end{cases} \tag{30}$$

Where $i' = \arg\min_{i\in\mathcal{I}}\{V[g_i(t)\frac{p_i}{r_i(t)} + g_i(t)\mu] - Q_i(t)\}$. Hence, the optimal computation allocation $d^s(t)$, $d^c(t)$ can be determined. Furthermore, the queue length $Q_i(t)$ updates according to (6).

Algorithm 1. Revenue Maximization Online Auction Algorithm (RMOA)

1: Get the current queue length $Q_i(t)$ of all the IoT devices
2: **for** all $i \in \mathcal{I}$ **do**
3:    Using Hungarian algorithm to get $x^*(t)$
4:    **if** $x_i^*(t) == 1$ **then**
5:       Compute $\pi_i(t)$ based on (18)
6:    **end if**
7: **end for**
8: **for** all $i \in \mathcal{I}$ **do**
9:    Search for index i_1^* with the minimum value of $V[g_i(t)\frac{p_i}{r_i(t)} + g_i(t)\kappa c_i(t)f_e^2(t)] - Q_i(t)$
10:   Set $d_i^s(t)$ based on (28)
11: **end for**
12: **for** all $i \in \mathcal{I}$ **do**
13:   Search for index i_2^* with the minimum value of $V[g_i(t)\frac{p_i}{r_i(t)} + g_i(t)\mu] - Q_i(t)$
14:   Set $d_i^c(t)$ based on (30)
15: **end for**

Remark: In the MEC system, there is a tradeoff V between resource allocation revenue and queue backlog. The RMOA algorithm can reach the tradeoff with the different times and queue backlog. In time slot t, combining the resource scheduling cost with auction profit, the RMOA algorithm can obtain the optimal resource scheduling policy to maximize the whole system revenue. The details of RMOA is shown in Algorithm 1.

4 Algorithm Analysis

We perform the theoretical analysis of the RMOA algorithm and analysis results indicate that our algorithm can reach the approximate optimal while ensuring the stability of the MEC system. $\bar{Q}$ represents the long-term time average queue backlog, which is

$$\bar{Q} = \lim_{T \to \infty} \frac{1}{T} \sum_{t=0}^{T-1} \sum_{i=1}^{\mathcal{I}} \mathbb{E}\{Q_i(t)\}. \tag{31}$$

Lemma 1. *For arbitrary tasks arrival rate ϑ ($\vartheta > 0$) , there is an optimal randomized policy ρ, which is irrespective of the current queue length and satisfies as follows*

$$\mathbb{E}\{U^{\rho^*}(t)\} = U^*(\vartheta), \tag{32}$$

$$\mathbb{E}\{a_i(t)\} \leq \mathbb{E}\{d_i^{s\rho^*}(t) + d_i^{c\rho^*}(t)\}. \tag{33}$$

Proof: **Lemma 1** can be proved by using Caratheodory's theorem. In order to simplify the paper and enhance the readability, we have omitted the proof. The proof process in detail is just from [18].   ∎

Theorem 2. *If there exists nonnegative ϵ satisfies $\vartheta + \epsilon \in \Omega$, where Ω denotes capacity region of the MEC system. The arbitrary value of V, time average system revenue U^{RMOA} under the assumptions in Lemma 1, which has lower bounded*

$$U^{RMOA} \geq U^* - \frac{C}{V}, \tag{34}$$

C is defined in (21), and U^* is the maximum average system revenue.

Proof: By applying **Lemma** 1, arbitrary tasks arrival rate $\vartheta + \epsilon$, there is an optimal randomized strategy ρ' satisfies

$$\mathbb{E}\{U^{\rho'}(t)\} = U^*(\vartheta + \epsilon), \tag{35}$$

$$\mathbb{E}\{a_i(t)\} \leq \mathbb{E}\{d_i^{s\rho'}(t) + d_i^{c\rho'}(t)\} - \epsilon. \tag{36}$$

According to **Theorem** 1, we can get that the lower bound of *drift plus revenue* could be maximized by our RMOA algorithm. Therefore, applying **Lemma** 1 to formula (25), replacing the random strategy with ρ', and bring (35) and (36) into formula (37), the following inequality holds

$$\Delta(\Theta(t)) - V\mathbb{E}\{U(t)|\Theta(t)\}$$
$$\leq C - VU^*(\vartheta + \epsilon) - \epsilon \sum_{i \in \mathcal{I}} Q_i(t). \tag{37}$$

Taking expectation on both sides in formula (37), considering the over time slot and making use of iterating expectations, there exist formula (38)

$$\mathbb{E}\{L(\Theta(T))\} - \mathbb{E}\{L(\Theta(0))\} - V\sum_{t=0}^{T-1}\mathbb{E}\{U(t)\}$$
$$\leq CT - VTU^*(\vartheta + \epsilon) - \epsilon\sum_{t=0}^{T-1}\sum_{i \in \mathcal{I}}\mathbb{E}\{Q_i(t)\}. \tag{38}$$

Since $L(\Theta(T)) \geq L(\Theta(0))$, ϵ and $Q_i(t)$ are both positive. Dividing both sides of the above formula by VT at the same time, the relaxation method is used for the previous formula, it can be obtained as

$$\frac{1}{T}\sum_{t=0}^{T-1}\mathbb{E}\{U(t)\} \geq U^*(\vartheta + \epsilon) - \frac{C}{V}, \tag{39}$$

according to (39), when $T \to \infty$ and $\epsilon \to 0$, in equation (34) can be proved. ∎

5 Experiments Results

In this paper, we formulate a network model of collaborative computing which is consist of 50 IoT devices. The arrival rate $a_i(t)$ of service request is generated

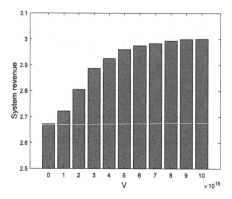

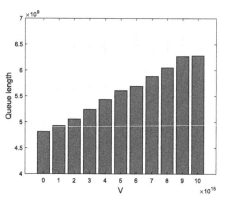

Fig. 1. The system revenue with different values of V.

Fig. 2. The queue length with different values of V.

randomly with [2,6] Mbits. The slot length $\iota = 1$ and the transmit power is $p_i \sim U[1, 10]$ W. Then, w_l is 1 MHz and w_c is 10 MHz. Besides, for each IoT device, CPU cycle required for calculating unit data tasks $c_i(t)$ follows uniform distribution with $U[1200, 1800]$. We assume the channel gain $h_i(t)$ is $h_i(t) \sim E(1)$, which follows an exponential distribution. Then, the noise power spectral density σ^2 is 10^{-7} W/Hz. Furthermore, the price of unit energy consumption cost $g_i(t)$ follows normal distribution $N[0, 3]$.

Figures 1 and 2 depict the impact of parameter V on system revenue and queue length. The system revenue increases with V as shown in Fig. 1, this is because the higher the value of V is, the greater the weight of system revenue will be. The reason is that the RMOA algorithm maximizes the revenue of the system by reducing the scheduling cost. Meanwhile, the stability of the task queue is guaranteed as shown in Fig. 2. From Figs. 1 and 2, system revenue and the queue length grow slower and slower as V augments, which follows **Theorem** 2 that system revenue and the queue length have an definite upper bound. Therefore, it is clear that our RMOA algorithm can adjust queue length and system revenue by changing the V value.

In Fig. 3 and 4, we present the influence of different service request arrival rates $\delta \cdot \vartheta$ on system revenue and queue length. System revenue decreases gradually with the increase of the tasks arrival rate in Fig. 3. The reason is that with the growing of arrival rate, the number of uncalculated tasks will also increase, which leads to system revenue reduce. In Fig. 4, since uncalculated tasks accumulate in the system, queue length increases with arrival rate. From the two figures, we can know that system revenue and task queue length converge eventually with different arrival rates. This indicates that the RMOA algorithm can ensure the stability of the whole system.

In Figs. 5 and 6, we compare the other two auction algorithms with our RMOA algorithm in terms of system revenue and queue length. Random allocation algorithm executes the auction decision in a random way. Queue-weighted makes auction decision according to the weighted the task queue length. From

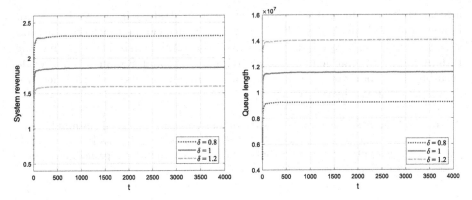

Fig. 3. The system revenue with different arrival rates.

Fig. 4. The queue length with different arrival rates.

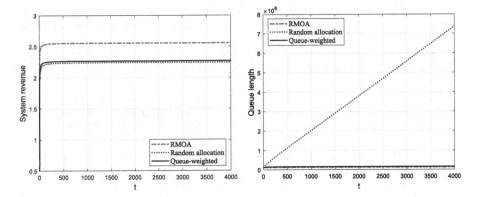

Fig. 5. The system revenue with different algorithms.

Fig. 6. The queue length with different algorithms.

Fig. 5 and 6, it is obvious that our RMOA algorithm could achieve maximum system revenue and the lowest queue length apparently. Although the queue lengths between RMOA and Queue-weight algorithm are approaching, the Queue-weight algorithm does not consider the dynamic of channel state, so that the system revenue is lower than ours. In conclusion, according to Figs. 5 and 6, our RMOA algorithm has good performance and advantage in optimizing system revenue while ensuring system stability.

6   Conclusion

In this paper, we develop a collaborative computing framework for IoT and a dynamic optimization model is formulated to maximize system revenue while providing performance guarantees. Then, we design a truthful online action mechanism to obtain resultful resource allocation strategy in the MEC system. In addition, the RMOA algorithm is proposed, which can make effective auction strategy according to the bidding files. The theoretical analysis shows that the RMOA algorithm can achieve the approximate optimal system revenue while ensuring the stability of queue length, and simulation results verify the effectiveness of the RMOA algorithm.

Acknowledgments. This work is partly supported by the National Natural Science Foundation of China (Nos. 61872044, 61902029), the Excellent Talents Projects of Beijing (No. 9111923401) and Beijing High-level Innovative and Entrepreneurial Talents Project Famous Teacher Program.

References

1. Chen, X., Zhang, Y., Chen, Y.: Cost-efficient request scheduling and resource provisioning in multiclouds for internet of things. IEEE IoT J. **7**(3), 1594–1602 (2020)
2. Zhang, J., Chen, B., Zhao, Y., Cheng, X., Hu, F.: Data security and privacy-preserving in edge computing paradigm: survey and open issues. IEEE Access **6**, 18209–18237 (2018)
3. Gao, Y., Liu, L., Hu, B., Lei, T., Ma, H.: Federated region-learning for environment sensing in edge computing system. IEEE Trans. Netw. Sci. Eng. **7**(4), 2192–2204 (2020)
4. Wu, B., Chen, X., Chen, Y., Lu, Y.: A truthful auction mechanism for resource allocation in mobile edge computing. In: IEEE 22nd International Symposium on a World of Wireless, Mobile and Multimedia Networks (WoWMoM), pp. 21–30 (2021)
5. Lei, Y., Zheng, W., Ma, Y., Xia, Y., Xia, Q.: A novel probabilistic-performance-aware and evolutionary game-theoretic approach to task offloading in the hybrid cloud-edge environment. In: Gao, H., Wang, X., Iqbal, M., Yin, Y., Yin, J., Gu, N. (eds.) CollaborateCom 2020, Part I. LNICST, vol. 349, pp. 255–270. Springer, Cham (2021). https://doi.org/10.1007/978-3-030-67537-0_16
6. Kai, C., Zhou, H., Yi, Y., Huang, H.: Collaborative cloud-edge-end task offloading in mobile-edge computing networks with limited communication capability. IEEE Trans. Cogn. Commun. Netw. **7**(2), 624–634 (2021)
7. Zhang, M., Huang, J.: Mechanism design for network utility maximization with private constraint information. In: IEEE Conference on Computer Communications, INFOCOM, Paris, France, pp. 919–927 (2019)
8. Jiang, W., Li, M., Zhou, X., Qu, W., Qiu, T.: Multi-user cooperative computation offloading in mobile edge computing. In: Yu, D., Dressler, F., Yu, J. (eds.) WASA 2020, Part I. LNCS, vol. 12384, pp. 182–193. Springer, Cham (2020). https://doi.org/10.1007/978-3-030-59016-1_16
9. Mao, Y., Zhang, J., Song, S., Letaief, K.: Stochastic joint radio and computational resource management for multi-user mobile-edge computing systems. IEEE Trans. Wirel. Commun. **16**(9), 5994–6009 (2017)
10. Wu, Y., He, Y., Qian, L., Huang, J., Shen, X.: Optimal resource allocations for mobile data offloading via dual-connectivity. IEEE Trans. Mob. Comput. **17**(10), 2349–2365 (2018)

11. Jiang, F., Wang, K., Dong, L., Pan, C., Yang, K.: Stacked autoencoder-based deep reinforcement learning for online resource scheduling in large-scale MEC networks. IEEE IoT J. **7**(10), 9278–9290 (2020)
12. Zhang, H., Jiang, H., Li, B., Liu, F., Vasilakos, A., Liu, J.: A framework for truthful online auctions in cloud computing with heterogeneous user demands. IEEE Trans. Comput. **65**(3), 805–818 (2016)
13. Zheng, B., Pan, L., Liu, S., Wang, L.: An online mechanism for purchasing Iaas instances and scheduling pleasingly parallel jobs in cloud computing environments. In: IEEE 39th International Conference on Distributed Computing Systems, ICDCS, Dallas, TX, USA, pp. 35–45 (2019)
14. Chen, Y., Zhang, N., Zhang, Y., Chen, X., Wu, W., Shen, X.: Energy efficient dynamic offloading in mobile edge computing for internet of things. IEEE Trans. Cloud Comput. (2019)
15. Zhang, D., et al.: Near-optimal and truthful online auction for computation offloading in green edge-computing systems. IEEE Trans. Mob. Comput. **19**(4), 880–893 (2020)
16. Wang, X., et al.: Dynamic resource scheduling in mobile edge cloud with cloud radio access network. IEEE Trans. Parallel Distrib. Syst. **29**(11), 2429–2445 (2018)
17. Zhang, F., Zhou, X., Sun, X.: Constrained VCG auction with multi-level channel valuations for spatial spectrum reuse in non-symmetric networks. IEEE Trans. Commun. **67**(2), 1182–1196 (2019)
18. Michael, N.: Stochastic Network Optimization with Application to Communication and Queueing Systems. Stochastic Network Optimization with Application to Communication and Queueing Systems. Morgan & Claypool, San Rafael (2010)

A Hashgraph-Based Knowledge Sharing Approach for Mobile Robot Swarm

Xiao Shu[1], Bo Ding[1(✉)], Jie Luo[1], Xiang Fu[1], Min Xie[1], and Zhen Li[2]

[1] College of Computer, National University of Defense Technology, Changsha, China
shuxiao19@nudt.edu.cn, dingbo@aliyun.com
[2] College of Information and Communication, National University of Defense Technology, Wuhan, China

Abstract. Common knowledge in a group of robots, i.e., the knowledge known by everyone or nearly everyone, can significantly promote the efficiency of robot collaboration. In a decentralized environment, it can be achieved through blockchain technology. However, traditional blockchain platforms such as Ethereum are based on Proof of Work (PoW), which requires huge amounts of computation and is not suitable for robots with limited computing resources. And the lack of a stable, fully-connected network will greatly reduce the performance of the traditional blockchain technology as well. To address these challenges, we propose a novel peer-to-peer knowledge sharing approach for mobile robot swarms in this paper. This approach is based on hashgraph, a distributed ledger technology that uses directed acyclic graphs to achieve consensus and does not need huge computational power. We also enhance hashgraph to adapt it to the mobile network environment with a limited communication range for each robot and dynamic network topology in the swarm. With a set of motivated scenarios of collective decision making, we verified the effectiveness of our approach and the results show that our approach helps robot swarm collaborate more efficiently with less computation and waste of resources than the approach based on the traditional blockchain.

Keywords: Robot swarm · Hashgraph · Common knowledge · Consensus algorithm

1 Introduction

A robot swarm is made up of a large group of locally interacting individuals with common goals, and it has been applied in many scenarios, such as site selection [6], and task assignment [4], etc. Common knowledge can be used to form a resultant force on the whole based on the local behavior of the individual to improve the collaborative efficiency, and it has been proved useful in applications such as task allocation in unknown environment [11], synchronization between different swarms [16]. However, it's difficult for swarm robots to support global synthesis of sensory information collected by the swarm without a centralized infrastructure [15].

To solve this problem, the traditional blockchains [20, 24] can be adopted to provide the robot swarm with common knowledge in a decentralized, verifiable, and secure way,

© ICST Institute for Computer Sciences, Social Informatics and Telecommunications Engineering 2021
Published by Springer Nature Switzerland AG 2021. All Rights Reserved
H. Gao and X. Wang (Eds.): CollaborateCom 2021, LNICST 407, pp. 158–172, 2021.
https://doi.org/10.1007/978-3-030-92638-0_10

which has been used in many applications [19,26]. The blockchain, such as Ethereum [29], can act as a peer-to-peer database and computing system in the swarm. Due to the characteristics of PoW [10], the most widely used consensus algorithm of traditional blockchains, robots can mine new blocks locally and store information in them. Despite the environment of limited communication range and dynamic network topology, the blockchains of different robots can be synchronized once robots come into the communication range, and a single point of failure will not affect the synchronization process of blockchains. Besides, the 51% computational power limitation and data verifiability can help the blockchain resist attacks from Byzantine robots efficiently.

Although the approach based on traditional blockchains shows an advantage in achieving common knowledge, it's not suitable for the mobile network environment of robot swarms. PoW requires robots to keep solving puzzles constantly through the reward mechanism to add new blocks to the blockchain [25], which means that electricity will be wasted on extra computations. In Bitcoin [20], PoW takes 10 min to generate a block [9], and most of the time is used for solving the puzzles, which is a huge burden for the robot of onboard computer and limited resources. Besides, the blockchain forks may occur if robots find the solutions to the PoW puzzles at almost the same time, or blocks are not spread through the entire network [26]. Robots in different clusters may take actions based on the forks of blockchains, which may cause unexpected situations. Discarding the forks will result in inefficient use of information and resources.

To address the above-mentioned challenges, we propose a novel peer-to-peer knowledge sharing approach for mobile robot swarms. This approach is based on hashgraph [3], a data structure and consensus algorithm. With no PoW, hashgraph allows the nodes to create many events per second and it doesn't call for high computational power. Besides, hashgraph is 100% efficient in information utilization because no events will be discarded. To adapt to the mobile network environment of the robot swarm, we enhance the gossip rules of hashgraph, that is, each node can only synchronize the local hashgraph with its neighbor nodes. In our hashgraph approach, each robot acts as a node of hashgraph and shares knowledge with neighbors through hashgraph synchronization. As the local hashgraph grows, the robot can achieve common knowledge and take action based on it. In the motivated scenarios of single-feature [27] and multi-feature [7] collective decision making, we test the efficiency of the hashgraph approach in consensus achievement and task allocation respectively. The experimental results show that the mobile robot swarm in the hashgraph approach can collaborate efficiently with less computational power and higher resource utilization than the traditional blockchain approach.

The rest of this paper is organized as follows. We give an overview of robot swarm, consensus algorithms in robot swarms, hashgraph in Sect. 2. We represent the motivated scenarios in Sect. 3 and the hashgraph approach in Sect. 4. Experiments are presented in Sect. 5. We conclude this paper in Sect. 6.

2   Related Work

2.1   Robot Swarm

The robot swarm is a typical distributed system consisting of a large number of simple robots, and the collective behavior of it emerges from numerous local interactions between individuals without any central control [23]. It is increasingly applied to perform dynamic and complex tasks [1, 18]. Ebert et al. [7] propose a decentralized algorithm and a dynamic task allocation strategy that allows the agents to lock in decisions on multiple features in a finite time. Wang et al. [28] propose an adaptive mechanism and design a group-based spatial formation algorithm for swarm robots to adapt to the dynamic environment. But the main focus of these algorithms is still how to manually set the behavior rules of each robot in advance, while how to obtain common knowledge to coordinate swarm behavior is not the point.

The idea of applying blockchain to robot swarms to provide common knowledge is first proposed in [9] and has been applied in some scenarios, such as trust management [14], monitoring quarantine areas [2], etc. A framework for ontology-oriented robots' coalition formation based on blockchain in cyberphysical systems is also proposed [19]. It should be pointed out that due to the high requirements of computational power and the low resource utilization, the blockchain is difficult to be applied to the mobile network environment of robot swarm.

2.2   Consensus Algorithms in Robot Swarms

The robot swarm is similar to the distributed system, and the consensus algorithm can be applied to enable individual units in the robot swarm to reach a common perspective of objectives and state of the world [12]. Many consensus algorithms have emerged in the field of distributed systems, such as Paxos [13], PBFT [5], etc., and some of them have been applied in applications, such as the multi-agent system based on Paxos [17]. But these traditional consensus algorithms often divide the nodes into several different roles, such as leaders, followers, etc., which doesn't meet the requirements of decentralization in a robot swarm. Besides, classical solutions to distributed consensus problems, such as two-phase commit [13], usually require frequent committing, acknowledging, and other interactions among a group of nodes, which is difficult to be applied in an environment of dynamic network topology and limited communication range.

Blockchain technology demonstrates that without a controlling authority, a group of agents can still reach an agreement on a particular state of affairs and record that agreement in a peer-to-peer network [9], and it has been applied in many studies of multi robots [2, 14]. Proof of Work (PoW) is the proof that a certain amount of computational power was consumed to solve a hard puzzle that allows the adding of a block to the blockchain, the process of which is called mining. It is based on SHA256, which inputs a message of arbitrary length smaller than 2^{64} bits and produces as output a 256-bit message digest of the input, resulting in a huge waste of electricity. In Ethereum, the difficulty of mining puzzles can be adjusted to the hash power of the network [25], but the onboard computer of the robot determines that it can only solve less difficult puzzles. Due to the peer-to-peer network and limited communication range, the lower the difficulty of the puzzle, the more likely the robots are to mine new blocks at the same time, leading to the problem of forks. According to the rules of the blockchain, the information in the forks will be discarded, which is a waste of information and resources.

2.3 Hashgraph

In recent years, some new blockchain data structures and consensus algorithms have emerged, one of which is hashgraph [3], a data structure and consensus algorithm that uses Directed Acyclic Graphs(DAG) for time-sequencing transactions. As shown in Fig. 1, hashgraph is made up of several nodes and many events. Each node maintains a local hashgraph. The process of synchronizing their local hashgraph is named gossip about gossip. When Carol randomly tells another node, for example, David, everything she knows, David records the fact by creating a new event "d4", which contains the hash of his most recent event "d3", and the hash of Carol's most recent event "c2". At the same time, David stores a timestamp and some transactions into the event "d4". Thus it can be seen, hashgraph stores information about the history of how nodes have gossiped and all known events. Every node repeatedly chooses another node at random and gives it all the events that it doesn't yet know. As the process of gossip about gossip goes on, based on the local hashgraph, everyone can determine the consensus order of the events according to the virtual voting protocol.

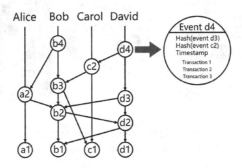

Fig. 1. Hashgraph of four nodes (Alice, Bob, Carol, David). Carol tries to gossip with David, David creates an event "d4" containing hashes of the events "c2" and "d3".

The process of gossip about gossip helps information spread exponentially fast and reliable, which ensures that every node will eventually know every event. Besides, the consensus is determined upon every node's local hashgraph, which greatly reduces the requirements for communication conditions. These characteristics make it possible to combine hashgraph with mobile robot swarms in an environment of dynamic network topology and limited communication range. Compared with blockchain, with no need for PoW, the throughput of hashgraph is high, and there is no problems of computational power and forks with it.

3 Motivated Scenarios

In this paper, we adopt collective decision making scenarios of swarm robots to illustrate our approach. In these scenarios, robots need to reach one or more common decisions among available options, e.g., selecting an escape route or judging the degree of pollution in the cases of nuclear accident emergency rescue, which results in the problems of consensus achievement and task allocation.

The scenario environment is a $1.2\,m \times 1.2\,m^2$ area with a 25 mm thick gray border and contains one or more features (see Fig. 2). The single-feature scenario [27] is characterized by a grid consisting of several black and white tiles. The fill ratio of white tiles to the whole area represents the feature of this scenario. The multi-feature scenario, which is first proposed by Ebert et al. [7], is extended from the single-feature scenario. Several different single-feature layers are combined to form the scenario, and the fill ratio of the light color in each single-feature layer represents one of the features of that scenario. If the fill ratio of the light color is above 0.5, the value of that feature in the scenario is equal to 1, otherwise, it is equal to 0. The value of a feature represents that whether the light color or the black color is more frequent in the environment.

 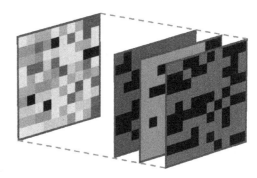

Fig. 2. Left: Robots are exploring the single-feature environment. Right: Generating multi-feature environment by overlaying three different single-feature layers. Colors are combined according to the standard RGB color model.

We adopt the simulator for the Kilobots [22] extended by Ebert et al. [7]. In this simulator, the Kilobot robot is a miniature mobile robot with a circular body of diameter 33 mm, having a linear moving speed of 33 mm/s and a turning speed of $0.2\,\pi$ rad/s. The Kilobot is equipped with different light sensors that can detect different features, but it can only detect one feature at a time. The detection range of its sensors is limited to the point of its location and the communication range is limited to 3 bodylength. To determine the values of features, the robots walk randomly to explore and share knowledge through transmitting messages to neighbors, but the maximum transmission rate is limited to 10 messages/s. The goal of the swarm is to reach a consensus on the value of every feature efficiently.

For the scenarios, Ebert et al. [7] propose a decentralized collective decision-making algorithm and a dynamic task allocation strategy that allow the robots to reach common decisions on features in a finite time. In their approach (classical approach), while keeping walking randomly in the environment, the robots alternatively explore the environment to estimate the features and share the exploration results with local neighbors. Based on the shared knowledge from neighbors, each robot makes decisions on the features. As to the task allocation for different features, the robot judges the difficulty of each feature according to the shared knowledge and dynamically selects an appropriate time to switch to the target feature. The experimental results show that when robots switch to the least certain feature every time before exploring the environment, there is an advantage in decision-making time.

4   Hashgraph-Based Knowledge Sharing Approach

Our hashgraph approach builds on the work of Ebert et al. [7], and the biggest difference is that we use hashgraph as the knowledge sharing medium of the mobile robot swarm. We first prove that the hashgraph consensus can be reached under the condition of a mobile network environment, then describe the hashgraph approach in two cases of single-feature and multi-feature scenarios.

4.1   Enhanced Hashgraph in the Mobile Network Environment

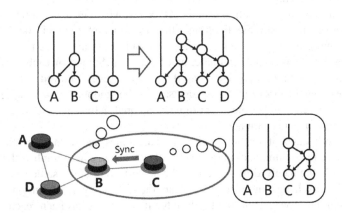

Fig. 3. The red circle represents the communication range of Robot C, while A and D are out of the communication range. Therefore, C can only synchronize the hashgraph with B, and B creates a new event to record this synchronization. (Color figure online)

In common hashgraph, a robot randomly chooses another one to synchronize the hashgraph. But in the mobile network environment of a robot swarm, we stipulate that a robot can only choose its neighbors, as shown in Fig. 3. Therefore, the synchronization process of the hashgraph approach is the same way that an epidemic is propagated throughout a group of individuals. How long it takes for the infection to reach every process has been considered in the "infect forever" model [8,21]:

$$R = log_{f+1}(n) + \frac{1}{f}log(n) + O(1) \tag{1}$$

In the equation, R represents the number of rounds necessary to infect the entire system, f represents the number of other nodes that each infectious node can contaminate in each round, n represents the total number of nodes in the system. Because the value of f and n are both greater than 0, the value of R is finite. Therefore, under such conditions, hashgraph can still be synchronized to each member of the swarm in a finite time. As the hashgraph grows, each node can finally reach the hashgraph consensus.

4.2   Hashgraph Approach in the Single-Feature Scenario

The process of a robot exploring the area is divided into two states: observation and dissemination. The robot first comes into the observation state, the duration of which is 60 s. In this state, the robot walks randomly to explore the feature and calculate the time spent in staying in black (t_b) and light (t_l) color, and receive messages from neighbors. At the end of this state, the robot takes the color corresponding to the larger value in t_b and t_l as its current estimate and updates its current confidence c by calculating the ratio between the time spent in the color of its current estimate and the sum of t_b and t_l. Then the robot turns into the dissemination state.

The duration of dissemination state is $120 \times c$ s, which means that the more confident the robot is in its estimate, the longer the dissemination time will be. In this state, besides receiving messages from others, each robot sends messages to its neighbors. The message contains its ID, estimate, and belief. At the end of each dissemination state, the value of belief b is updated based on the messages received in the past 180 s. In the values of estimates of these messages, the robot adopts the majority as its belief or selects a random belief if the count of each is equal. After this, the robot goes back to the observation state again and so on.

During both states of a robot, once it receives a message from its neighbor, which means they are in communication range, it will synchronize hashgraph with this neighbor and bundle the received message into the newest event at the same time, as shown in Fig. 3. They exchange knowledge and share the same copy of hashgraph in this way. As the hashgraph grows, each robot will judge if consensus has been reached with the virtual voting protocol. Once reaching a consensus on a group of events, each robot will make a decision $d = j$ on the feature if the data of these events satisfies the following two conditions:

$$\begin{cases} |N_1^e - N_0^e| > n \\ N_j^b > 0.5n \end{cases} \tag{2}$$

The variable n means the number of robots in the swarm; the variable N_1^e means the number of estimates of value 1 for the feature, and so on for N_0^e; the variable N_j^b means the number of robots whose newest belief is equal to j (j equals 0 or 1) for the feature. Once the robot makes the decision d, its belief b will be fixed to be d. The two formulas demand that both the number of estimates and that of the beliefs are above the corresponding thresholds respectively.

4.3 Hashgraph Approach in the Multi-feature Scenario

The algorithm in this scenario extends that for the single-feature scenario. Each robot maintains beliefs and makes decisions on each of the features with the same algorithm as in the single-feature scenario. The message it sends also contains the value of all the beliefs. Each robot can explore only one feature at a time and no prior knowledge about the difficulties of features is available, which leads to the problem of feature switching. Intuitively, the more difficult a task is, the more robots are required to perform it. In the multi-feature scenario, with the results of hashgraph consensus, the robot can roughly figure out a variable f_i that measures the difficulties of different features $i(i = 1, 2 \cdots M)$:

$$
f_i = \begin{cases} 0 & d_i = 0 \ or \ 1 \\ \dfrac{N_i^r + 1}{|N_{i1}^e - N_{i0}^e| + 1} & else \end{cases} \tag{3}
$$

As shown in this equation, the variable N_{i1}^e means the number of estimates of value 1 for the feature i, and so on for N_{i0}^e. N_i^r represents the number of robots that are exploring feature i in the recent past. The variable d_i, represents the decision of the robot on feature i and initially equals *null*. If d_i equals 1 or 0, it means the robot has already made a decision on feature i, therefore the corresponding f_i equals 0. A large f_i reflects that the N_i^r robots have no clear distinction in the estimation of the feature i, so feature i requires more robots. A small f_i brings the opposite conclusion. If every f_i equals 0, which means the robot has made decisions on all of the features, there's no need for the robot to switch features; if not, the tasks can be assigned according to the equation below:

$$
A_i = \frac{f_i \times n}{\sum\limits_{k=1}^{M} f_k} \tag{4}
$$

The variable A_i represents that the number of robots that should be assigned to explore feature i. With this equation, the robots numbered 1 through n get to know which features they are assigned to explore: the robots numbered 1 to A_1 explore feature 1, the robots numbered $A_1 + 1$ to $A_1 + A_2$ explore feature 2, and so on, all the way to the last A_M robots are assigned to explore feature M. Even if the robot has made a decision on some feature, it may still be assigned to explore that feature to help others make decisions, which is the embodiment of self-organizing and collaboration among the swarm.

5 Experiments

We first verify whether the robot swarm in the hashgraph approach can effectively realize consensus achievement and task allocation in single-feature and multi-feature scenarios. Then, the effects of the moving speed and communication range of the robot on the consensus time of the hashgraph approach are tested. Finally, we compare the resource consumption of hashgraph and traditional blockchain approaches.

5.1   Single-Feature Experiments

Several simulation experiments are carried out to compare the efficiency of classical and hashgraph approaches under different fill ratios. 30 robots are assigned to explore the single-feature environment. The fill ratio of the color white in the experimental area equals r, which ranges from 0.53 to 0.9, while that of black correspondingly equals $1 - r$, ranging from 0.47 to 0.1. For each r value, we run 10 simulations and take the average (see Fig. 4).

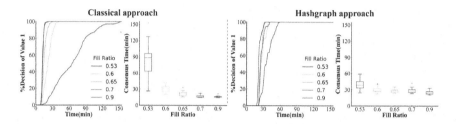

Fig. 4. Single-feature experiments: the percentages of robots that make decisions of value 1 as a function of time, and the time of reaching a consensus on the feature, over different fill ratios. Left: classical approach. Right: hashgraph approach.

In both approaches, the higher the fill ratio, the faster they make decisions, and they reach a consensus on the right decision over all of the fill ratios. In the results of the classical approach, members of the swarm start to make decisions at about 8 min and reach a consensus in 150 min, while the members of the hashgraph approach start to make decisions at about 23 min and reach a consensus in 60 min.

The experiments prove that the robots can reach consensus via hashgraph in the mobile network environment of swarm robots. In the hashgraph approach, because the robots make decisions based on the hashgraph consensus, which is delayed by the processes of gossip about gossip and virtual voting, the robots start to make decisions at a later time, but the curves of decision making rise at a faster slope than that of the classical approach, and finally, converge to the top in 60 min. Compare the box plots of the two approaches, we find that when the fill ratio is less than 0.6, robots of the hashgraph approach can reach a consensus faster than that in the classical approach, while that when the fill ratio is greater than 0.65 comes to the opposite conclusion. On the whole, the consensus time of the hashgraph approach is relatively stable, because its efficiency is more affected by the time to reach a hashgraph consensus, which is relatively fixed, while the consensus time of the classical approach is greatly affected by the fill ratio.

5.2   Multi-feature Experiments

In this subsection, we compare the effectiveness of the robots switching features in the hashgraph approach with that in the classical approach. We set the three features to red, green, and blue, and to distinguish the three features, we set the fill ratios of the features to 0.55, 0.8, and 0.65 respectively, as shown in the right graph of Fig. 2. In the classical approach, the feature switching strategy that robots switch to the least certain feature before each observation state shows an advantage over other strategies, and we compare the hashgraph approach with this strategy. 30 robots are assigned to explore the three features and there are four different initial distributions: equally distributed and all distributed to one of the three features. We run 10 simulations for each of them. The results are shown in Figs. 5 and 6.

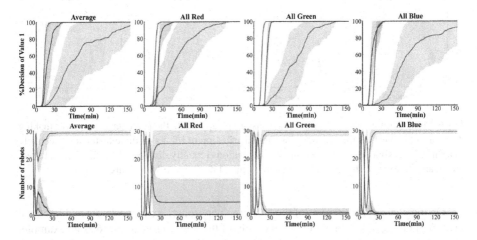

Fig. 5. Multi-feature experiments based on classical approach: the percentages of robots making decisions of value 1 on three features and the distribution of robots on three features respectively as a function of time, over different initial distributions (equally distributed, all distributed to red, green, and blue). The shadow represents the standard deviation (Color figure online).

As we can see in the top row of Fig. 5, in the classical approach, the robots start to make decisions early and reach consensuses quickly on two relatively simple features: green and blue, then all of them switch to explore the hardest feature: red. But their decision making converges slowly, and in some cases, they even can't reach an agreement on the feature of red in 150 min. In the top row of Fig. 6, the robots in the hashgraph approach start to make decisions at a relatively late time, but the curves rise at faster slopes and finally, they reach consensuses on all of the three features in 120 min.

The bottom rows of both Figs. 5 and 6 show the distribution of robots on three features over time. In the classical approach, from the final results, we can see that each robot switches feature efficiently: more robots are assigned to the harder feature. However, there is a problem of over-adaption with the approach. The curves rise and fall frequently and the ranges are large, which means that many robots switch between the three features repeatedly, leading to a waste of time and battery resources in practice. Without a central controller, robots switch features based on their local collected knowledge and follow the local switching strategy, which makes them unable to form a joint force as a whole.

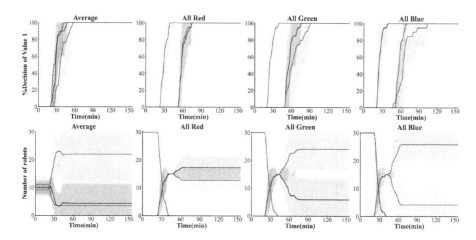

Fig. 6. Multi-feature experiments based on hashgraph approach: the percentages of robots making decisions of value 1 on three features and the distribution of robots on three features respectively as a function of time, over different initial distributions (equally distributed, all distributed to red, green, and blue). The shadow represents the standard deviation (Color figure online).

On the contrary, the curves of the hashgraph approach are much stable and fluctuate in a small range. Take the picture on the right of the bottom row in Fig. 6 as an example, all the robots are initially distributed to blue, after reaching the first round of hashgraph consensus, they switch to the other features. Instead of switching to the same feature, they are assigned equally to two features, then they adjust the tasks according to the results of the next round of hashgraph consensus, realizing efficient task allocation in a fully distributed way. Despite the limited communication range and dynamic network topology, hashgraph can still help robots achieve common knowledge to coordinate their actions well on the overall level.

5.3   Experiments on Consensus Time of Hashgraph Approach

We adopt 30 robots to explore the single-feature scenario to evaluate the performance of the hashgraph approach under different conditions, which is measured by the time of the robot swarm reaching a common decision on the feature. The fill ratio of the color white is fixed at 0.65, the communication range is set to 100, 300, 600, and 1000 mm, while the moving speed is set to 16, 32, and 48 mm/s. We run 10 simulations and take the average (see Fig. 7) for each condition.

As can be seen from Fig. 7, in the case of the same communication range, the greater the moving speed, the shorter the time to reach a consensus, but the difference is relatively small. On the contrary, the communication range has a great impact. When the communication range is limited to 100 mm, the swarm can reach a consensus in more than 20 min. While if the communication range reaches 1000 mm, which means that robots can reach almost every member of the swarm, the time is less than 2 min. The efficiency of the hashgraph approach tested above is also limited by the maximum transmission rate and the observation state during which the robots don't send messages.

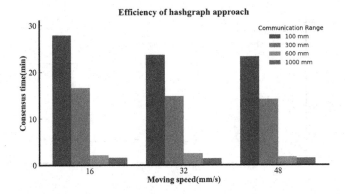

Fig. 7. Experiments on the consensus time of hashgraph approach: time to reach consensus on the feature of the environment under different communication ranges and moving speeds.

By comparison, a wider communication range means a shorter consensus time in the hashgraph approach, while in the traditional blockchain approach, the consensus time depends more on the speed of mining new blocks, and the communication range affects the broadcasting speed of newly mined blocks.

5.4 Experiments of CPU Utilization

In this subsection, we investigate the resource consumption of blockchain and hashgraph approaches by counting CPU utilization. The blockchain approach is derived from Strobel et al.'s work [25], which is based on Ethereum. In this approach, the robots keep mining blocks locally and store the received messages in the newly mined blocks. Blockchains will be synchronized through local interactions, helping the robots achieve common knowledge. The mining difficulty is set to a fixed value of 10^6, which is the same as in [25].

The experiments are carried on a personal computer furnished with an Intel processor of 8 cores, having 3.40 GHz speed and 8 GB RAM. We run 10 simulations and take the average for each approach (see Fig. 8).

As shown in Fig. 8, the blockchain approach consumes more resources than the hashgraph approach. The CPU utilization of the hashgraph approach keeps at about 80% from beginning to end. The CPU utilization of the blockchain approach starts at about 80% and keeps for about 40 min, during which robots start geth processes [25] to register to blockchains, explore the environment, and mine new blocks. After that, the curve rises rapidly and reaches its top, about 350%, which is caused by two factors: mining new blocks and dealing with forks. The mining difficulty is set relatively simple to adapt to the limited computational power of robots, but this leads to the emergence of many forks. Robots have to mine new blocks to restore the information in the forks to the mainchain of blockchains, which requires extra computation.

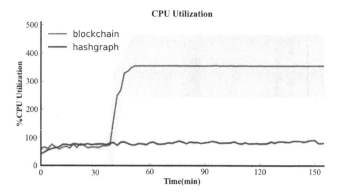

Fig. 8. CPU utilization of 30 robots based on blockchain approach and hashgraph approach as a function of time. The shadow represents the standard deviation.

6   Conclusions and Future Work

To address the shortcomings of the approach based on traditional blockchains in achieving common knowledge among mobile robot swarm, we propose hashgraph as the knowledge sharing medium for the mobile robot swarm in this paper. We describe the hashgraph approach and enhance the gossip rule of hashgraph, and then test the efficiency of the hashgraph approach in the motivated scenarios of single-feature and multifeature collective decision making. With the enhanced consensus algorithms of hashgraph, we demonstrate that the hashgraph approach can efficiently help robot swarms reach consensuses and realize task allocation. The results show that compared with the blockchain approach, the hashgraph approach requires less computational power and has higher resource utilization.

As a private chain, the application scope of hashgraph is limited by its strict access mechanism. In addition, according to the hashgraph consensus algorithm, although it's easy to create events, the process of virtual voting after each round is relatively long, reducing the efficiency of reaching a consensus. In the future, we are going to verify our approach on physical robots, and consider adding Byzantine robots to test whether hashgraph can deal with malicious attacks in robot swarms. Besides, we will investigate the robustness of hashgraph in the case of a large number of failures of robots.

Acknowledgments. This work is partially supported by the major Science and Technology Innovation 2030 "New Generation Artificial Intelligence" project 2020AAA0104803 and Scientific Research Plan of National University of Defense Technology under Grant No. ZK-20-38.

References

1. Alhafnawi, M., Hauert, S., O'Dowd, P.: Self-organised saliency detection and representation in robot swarms. IEEE Robot. Autom. Lett. **6**(2), 1487–1494 (2021). https://doi.org/10.1109/LRA.2021.3057567

2. Alsamhi, S.H., Lee, B.: Blockchain-empowered multi-robot collaboration to fight COVID-19 and future pandemics. IEEE Access **9**, 44173–44197 (2021). https://doi.org/10.1109/ACCESS.2020.3032450
3. Baird, L.: The swirlds hashgraph consensus algorithm: Fair, fast, byzantine fault tolerance
4. Berman, S., Halász, Á., Hsieh, M.: Ant-inspired Allocation: Top-Down Controller Design for Distributing a Robot Swarm Among Multiple Tasks, pp. 243–274. CRC Press, Boca Raton (2016)
5. Castro, M., Liskov, B.: Practical byzantine fault tolerance and proactive recovery. ACM Trans. Comput. Syst. **20**(4), 398–461 (2002). https://doi.org/10.1145/571637.571640
6. Correll, N., Martinoli, A.: Modeling and designing self-organized aggregation in a swarm of miniature robots. Int. J. Robot. Res. **30**(5), 615–626 (2011)
7. Ebert, J.T., Gauci, M., Nagpal, R.: Multi-feature collective decision making in robot swarms. In: AAMAS 2018, International Foundation for Autonomous Agents and Multiagent Systems, Richland, SC, pp. 1711–1719 (2018)
8. Eugster, P.T., Guerraoui, R., Kermarrec, A.M., Massoulie, L.: From epidemics to distributed computing. IEEE Trans. Comput. **37**, 2004 (2004)
9. Castelló Ferrer, E.: The blockchain: a new framework for robotic swarm systems. In: Arai, K., Bhatia, R., Kapoor, S. (eds.) FTC 2018. AISC, vol. 881, pp. 1037–1058. Springer, Cham (2019). https://doi.org/10.1007/978-3-030-02683-7_77
10. Jakobsson, M., Juels, A.: Proofs of work and bread pudding protocols. In: Joint Working Conference on Secure Information Networks: Communications and Multimedia Security (1999)
11. Jamshidpey, A., Afsharchi, M.: Task allocation in robotic swarms: explicit communication based approaches. In: Barbosa, D., Milios, E. (eds.) CANADIAN AI 2015. LNCS (LNAI), vol. 9091, pp. 59–67. Springer, Cham (2015). https://doi.org/10.1007/978-3-319-18356-5_6
12. Lafferriere, G., Williams, A., Caughman, J., Veerman, J.: Decentralized control of vehicle formations. Syst. Control Lett. **54**(9), 899–910 (2005)
13. Lamport, L.: Paxos made simple. In: ACM SIGACT News (Distributed Computing Column) 32, 4 (Whole Number 121, December 2001), pp. 51–58 (2001)
14. Li, J., Wu, J., Li, J., Bashir, A.K., Piran, M.J., Anjum, A.: Blockchain-based trust edge knowledge inference of multi-robot systems for collaborative tasks. IEEE Commun. Mag. **59**(7), 94–100 (2021). https://doi.org/10.1109/MCOM.001.2000419
15. Lumelsky, V., Harinarayan, K.: Decentralized motion planning for multiple mobile robots: the cocktail party model. Auton. Robot. **4**, 121–135 (1997). https://doi.org/10.1023/A:1008815304810
16. Majercik, S.M.: Initial experiments in using communication swarms to improve the performance of swarm systems. In: Kuipers, F.A., Heegaard, P.E. (eds.) IWSOS 2012. LNCS, vol. 7166, pp. 109–114. Springer, Heidelberg (2012). https://doi.org/10.1007/978-3-642-28583-7_12
17. Mocanu, A., Bădică, C.: Bringing Paxos consensus in multi-agent systems. Association for Computing Machinery (2014)
18. Moussa, M., Beltrame, G.: On the robustness of consensus-based behaviors for robot swarms. Swarm Intell. **14**, 205–231 (2020). https://doi.org/10.1007/s11721-020-00183-1
19. Teslya, N., Smirnov, A.: Blockchain-based framework for ontology-oriented robots' coalition formation in cyberphysical systems. MATEC Web Conf. **161**(9), 03018 (2018)
20. Nakamoto, S.: Bitcoin: A peer-to-peer electronic cash system. http://bitcoin.org/bitcoin.pdf
21. Pittel, B.: On spreading a rumor. SIAM J. Appl. Math. **47**(1), 213–223 (1987). https://doi.org/10.1137/0147013
22. Rubenstein, M., Ahler, C., Nagpal, R.: Kilobot: a low cost scalable robot system for collective behaviors. In: 2012 IEEE International Conference on Robotics and Automation, pp. 3293–3298 (2012). https://doi.org/10.1109/ICRA.2012.6224638

23. Schranz, M., Umlauft, M., Sende, M., Elmenreich, W.: Swarm robotic behaviors and current applications. Front. Robot. AI **7**, 36 (2020)

24. Shi, P., Wang, H., Yang, S., Chen, C., Yang, W.: Blockchain-based trusted data sharing among trusted stakeholders in IoT. Soft. Pract. Exp. (2019). https://doi.org/10.1002/spe.2739

25. Strobel, V., Castelló Ferrer, E., Dorigo, M.: Blockchain technology secures robot swarms: a comparison of consensus protocols and their resilience to byzantine robots. Front. Robot. AI **7**, 54 (2020). https://doi.org/10.3389/frobt.2020.00054

26. Strobel, V., Castelló Ferrer, E., Dorigo, M.: Managing byzantine robots via blockchain technology in a swarm robotics collective decision making scenario. In: AAMAS 2018, International Foundation for Autonomous Agents and Multiagent Systems, pp. 541–549 (2018)

27. Valentini, G., Brambilla, D., Hamann, H., Dorigo, M.: Collective perception of environmental features in a robot swarm. In: Dorigo, M., et al. (eds.) ANTS 2016. LNCS, vol. 9882, pp. 65–76. Springer, Cham (2016). https://doi.org/10.1007/978-3-319-44427-7_6

28. Wang, Q., Mao, X., Yang, S., Chen, Y., Liu, X.: Grouping-based adaptive spatial formation of swarm robots in a dynamic environment. Int. J. Adv. Robot. Syst. **15** (2018). https://doi.org/10.1177/1729881418782359

29. Wood, G.: Ethereum: a secure decentralised generalised transaction ledger (2014)

Collaborative Working and Deep Learning and Application

CASE: Predict User Behaviors via Collaborative Assistant Sequence Embedding Model

Fei He[1,2], Canghong Jin[1], and Minghui Wu[1(✉)]

[1] Zhejiang University City College, Hangzhou 310015, China
{jinch,mhwu}@zucc.edu.cn
[2] Zhejiang University, Hangzhou 310027, China
fei.he@zju.edu.cn

Abstract. The order of behaviors implies that sequential patterns play an important role of the user-behavior prediction problem. Traditional behavior-prediction models use large-scale static matrices which ignore sequential information. Moreover, although Markov chains and deep learning methods consider sequential information, they still suffer the problems of the behavior uncertainty and data sparsity in real life scenarios. In this paper, we propose a collaborative-assistant sequence embedding prediction (named CASE) model as a solution to address these shortcomings. The idea is to mine sequential behavior patterns with strong intention-expressing ability based on a collaborative selector, and construct original behavior graph and intent determination graph (IDG), following which we predict user behavior based on graph embedding and recurrent neural networks. The experiments on three public datasets demonstrate that CASE outperforms many advanced methods based on a variety of common evaluation metrics.

Keywords: User behavior prediction · Collaborative selector · Graph pattern mining

1 Introduction

Massive user-behavior data are produced on the Internet, such as video viewing and rating, click and purchase of goods, posts on social networking sites and thumb-up behavior. These data contain rich behavior information, and better understanding them should help solve the problem of "information overload", thereby improving the efficiency of demand matching, and providing better services to users. Behavioral data have huge application prospects in the fields of business scenarios [2], social governance [16], etc., and are currently a topic of significant research interest.

© ICST Institute for Computer Sciences, Social Informatics and Telecommunications Engineering 2021
Published by Springer Nature Switzerland AG 2021. All Rights Reserved
H. Gao and X. Wang (Eds.): CollaborateCom 2021, LNICST 407, pp. 175–189, 2021.
https://doi.org/10.1007/978-3-030-92638-0_11

1.1   Top-N Behavior Prediction

This problem can be summarized as follows: Given a set of users $U = \{u_1, u_2, \ldots, u_{|U|}\}$ and a set of all possible behaviors $A = \{act_1, act_2, \ldots, act_{|A|}\}$. Each user u has a historical behavior sequence $actseq^{(u)} = \langle act_{t_1}^{(u)}, act_{t_2}^{(u)}, \ldots, act_{t_{n-1}}^{(u)}, act_{t_n}^{(u)} \rangle$, where $act_{t_i}^{(u)} \in A$. The index t_i for $act_{t_i}^{(u)}$ denotes the chronological order of each behavior in a sequence. The behavior sequence database $D = \{actseq^{(1)}, actseq^{(2)}, \ldots, actseq^{(|U|)}\}$ contains the behavior sequences of all users. Given all user-behavior sequence $actseq^{(u)}$, the goal is to return a behavior list for each user that contains the user's N most likely future behaviors.

1.2   Limitations of Previous Work

Traditional user-behavior modeling methods focus on the long-term static behavior patterns of users. For example, based on matrix decomposition, the singular value decomposition algorithm [3] considers each behavior record to be independent [1,3,7]. They lost the sequential information in the history behaviors and ignore the dynamic variation in the short-term behavior patterns of users. In fact, user behaviors are mutually influenced and context dependent, and prior behaviors affect subsequent behaviors. Therefore, user behaviors over a certain period should be studied as a sequence structure.

Significant research has focused on behavior-sequence modeling. In terms of machine learning, Liu et al. [10] found explicit association rules through statistics in the mining of sequence behavior patterns, but ignored unobservable behavior patterns. Jarboui et al. [8] used the Markov decision process to predict the behavior of MOOC users. Shi et al. [12] proposed the state-sharing sparse hidden Markov model based on the hidden Markov model to establish a separated transition probability matrix for each user. In recent years, deep learning methods based on neural networks have also been widely used in sequential-behavior modeling. For example, recurrent neural networks (RNNs) have achieved great success in treating sequential data such as speech and text and have been introduced into the study of sequential behavior. The GRU4Rec model proposed by Hidasi et al. [6] used gated recursive units (GRUs) to predict sequential behavior. Yu et al. [17] added a time-aware controller and a content-aware controller to the long short-term memory model, so that contextual information could be fully considered when the status was updated, and the attention mechanism was used to make the model adaptively combine the long- and short-term preferences of users according to specific contextual states. Although they use the sequential information of behaviors, they still ignore the problem of uncertain user behaviors. The behavior sequence of users is not strictly sequential. Behaviors can be inserted or missing from the sequence because they do not necessarily occur to provoke subsequent behaviors. A L-order Markov chain or model containing only RNNs do not explicitly model such behavior patterns because they assume that the previous steps have an influence on the immediate next step. Tang et al. [13]

proposed a Caser model, which models recent behaviors as an "image" in time and latent dimensions and learns sequential patterns using convolutional filters. Based on the horizontal and vertical convolution, Caser can capture additional behaviors patterns that can be skipped, and can solve the behavior uncertainty problem to some extent. However, its ability to learn complex uncertain behavior relationships is affected by the size of the convolution kernel.

To express more complex behavioral relationships, the graph-based neural network method is applied to learn the behavior representation. The global-context-enhanced graph neural networks model proposed by Wang et al. [14] can learn two types of granularity information from local behavior sequence graph and global behavior sequence graph. In the global sequence graph, the session-aware attention mechanism recursively integrates the information of surrounding neighbors, and, in the local graph, the behavior information within the sequence is learned by the graph neural network. However, the graph-based approach ignores the sparsity of user behavior. Since many types of behaviors exist, and the recorded behavior of each user only accounts for a small fraction thereof, the obtained behavior graph is very sparse.

To solve these problems (i.e., behavior uncertainty and sparse behavior data), we proposes a collaborative-assistant sequence embedding prediction (CASE) model. The novelty of the CASE model is that we proposed a collaborative selector to find the effective sequential behavior patterns with strong intention-expressing ability and then construct an intent determination graph (IDG). The IDG encodes new relationships and weights between behaviors from intention-expressing ability and uncertainty perspectives, which helps alleviate the problems. The model contribution is as follows:

i. CASE uses a collaborative selector based on collaborative prediction and information entropy to get the strong intention-expressing sequential behavior patterns, and then constructs the IDG that can alleviates the uncertainty and sparsity involved with predicting user behavior.
ii. CASE proposes a behavior prediction model based on graph embedding and RNNs, which allows the model to learn the relationships between behaviors in graph structure and sequence structure.
iii. CASE outperforms many advanced methods for predicting top-N sequential behavior from real life datasets.

2 Proposed Model

In this section, we introduce the CASE model, which is a method to learn user intent from a temporally ordered sequence of behaviors and predict the future behaviors. The goal of the CASE model is to reduce behavior uncertainty and sparsity problems. Figure 1 shows the network architecture of the CASE model, which can be divided into three components: constructing graphs (original behavior graph and IDG), learning behavior embedding and predicting future behavior. Each component of the model is described in detail below.

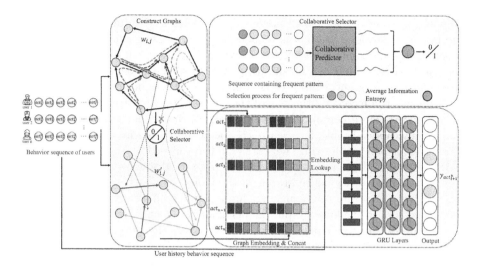

Fig. 1. Network architecture of CASE model. The box on the left contains the original behavior graph, the collaborative selector, and the IDG. The box in the upper-right corner illustrates the process of collaborative selector. The red lines in the box represent the probability distribution of the next behavior predicted by the collaborative predictor. The box in the lower-right corner represents the graph embedding and prediction of future behaviors.

2.1   Constructing Graphs

As shown in the dashed box to the left of Fig. 1, we first build the original behavior graph from the historical behavior sequences of all users. And then frequent sequential pattern mining algorithm is applied to the behavior database D to get the initial sequential behavior patterns. However, not all these sequential behavior patterns are useful because of the behavior uncertainty, and building a behavior graph from these initial patterns will introduces unreliable behavior relationships. Therefore, we propose to use a collaborative selector based on user collaborative prediction and information entropy to further filter these sequential behavior patterns, and then finally construct an intent determination graph (IDG) from the rest.

Original Behavior Graph. According to the behavior-sequence database D, we construct a user original behavior graph $G(V, E)$, where V is the set of nodes in the graph, with every node representing a type of behavior, and E is the set of edges in the graph. For each behavior sequence in D, we add an edge between node i and node j if the user performs behavior i and then behavior j. Refer to previous work [15], the weight $w_{i,j}$ of each edge $e = (i, j) \in E$ is equal to the number of occurrences of the behavior pair in the D.

Because many types of behaviors are possible and users exhibit only a small fraction thereof, the user-behavior co-occurrence matrix is characterized by high dimensionality and sparsity (as shown in Table 1). This prevents the model from learning the relationship between behaviors. Besides, because of behavior uncertainty, the behavior sequences are also not strictly sequential. For example, some intermediate behaviors may be skipped or inserted in sequences, and completely random invalid behaviors may occur in the sequences, which introduce unreliable relationships between behaviors. To alleviate these problems, the IDG is constructed.

Collaborative Selector. The collaborative selector is based on the following idea: the initial sequential behavior patterns obtained by frequent sequential pattern mining algorithm are those that occur frequently in all user behavior sequences, but not all of them are useful. The really effective sequential behavior patterns should have a strong ability to express users' intention. And a concentrated future behavior distribution of sequences containing a sequential behavior pattern indicates that this sequential behavior pattern plays a significant role in determine the sequences' intention. Moreover, the future behavior distribution of a single user may be contingent, so we need to collaborate with all users to conduct a more accurate analysis. We use a modified PrefixSpan algorithm [4] to get the initial sequential behavior patterns on behavior sequence database D. In order to ensure the timeliness of behaviors in sequential behavior patterns, we add a maximum interval limit W between behaviors of frequent sequential patterns in PrefixSpan algorithm. That is to say, during the step of PrefixSpan algorithm which gets a longer sequential pattern $fp = \langle act_1, act_2, \cdots, act_k, act_{k+1} \rangle$ based on the prefix sequential pattern $\langle act_1, act_2, \cdots, act_k \rangle$, where the subscript k represents the order of the behavior act in the pattern, we check that whether the interval between behavior act_{k+1} and acr_k in the behavior sequence is not greater than W. If the condition is met, we take fp as a valid sequential pattern; otherwise, it is discarded. Additional details of the PrefixSpan algorithm are referred to [4].

The dashed box in the upper-right corner of Fig. 1 shows the selection process of the collaborative selector for a three-order sequential behavior pattern. Given a sequential behavior pattern, we first select all behavior sequences containing it from D to form a sub-database D_{sub}. We then regard each sequence in D_{sub} as a query q and input it into the collaborative predictor. The predictor returns the probability distribution P of the ten most likely future behaviors $actset = \{act_i\}_{i=1,\ldots,10}$, and we calculate the information entropy $entropy_q$ of this probability distribution P:

$$entropy_q = - \sum_{act \in actset} P(act) \log(P(act)). \tag{1}$$

The information entropy corresponding to each query in D_{sub} is averaged to obtain the average information entropy $avg\_entropy$,

$$avg\_entropy = \frac{1}{N} \sum_{i=1}^{N} entropy_{q_i} \tag{2}$$

where N is the number of queries. The smaller the $avg\_entropy$ value is, the more centralized is the distribution of future behaviors, and the stronger the ability of the sequential behavior pattern to determine intention is. If $avg\_entropy$ is less than or equal to the threshold λ, it is recognized as an effective behavior pattern, otherwise, it is recognized as an invalid behavior pattern:

$$y = \begin{cases} 1 & avg\_entropy \leq \lambda \\ 0 & otherwise, \end{cases} \tag{3}$$

then we get the filtered sequential behavior patterns with their corresponding $avg\_entropy$.

We implement the collaborative predictor based on the classical collaborative filtering algorithm matrix factorization (MF). MF decomposes the user-behavior co-occurrence matrix $R_{M \times N}$ into a product of two matrices,

$$R_{M \times N} \approx U_{M \times K} \times V_{K \times N} \tag{4}$$

where M is the number of users, and K is the representation dimension of users and behaviors. Each column of the matrix V is a representation of a behavior, which is what we really want. For each query q, we get the representation vector $\{v_i\}_{i=1,...,|q|}$ for each behavior act_i in the query q, where $|q|$ is the behavior number of q. We then calculate the average value of these representation vectors as the query representation. Next, the predictor returns the top ten behaviors $\{act_i\}_{i=1,...,10}$ most similar to that query representation among all the behaviors, and the similarity is defined as cosine similarity. Then we apply an exponential normalization of these cosine similarities $\{sim_i\}_{i=1,...,10}$, get the probability distribution P of the behaviors corresponding to the query q:

$$P(act_i) = \frac{e^{sim_i}}{\sum_j e^{sim_j}} \tag{5}$$

Intent Determination Graph. Based on all sequential behavior patterns that have been filtered by the collaborative selector, we build the IDG graph $G'(V', E')$, where V' is the set of nodes, and E' is the set of edges. For each strong intention-expressing sequential behavior pattern, we add an edge between node i and node j if behavior i appears before behavior j. The weight $w'_{i,j}$ of each edge $e = (i, j) \in E'$ is

$$w'_{i,j} = \frac{1}{|FP|} \sum_{fp \in FP} \frac{1}{avg\_entropy_{fp}} \tag{6}$$

where FP is the set of behavior patterns that contain behavior pair (i, j), $|FP|$ is the number of elements in the FP, $avg\_entropy_{fp}$ is the corresponding $avg\_entropy$ value for each behavior pattern fp in FP. The greater $w'_{i,j}$ is, the stronger the relationship between the behaviors.

First of all, the nodes on the IDG are behaviors with strong intention-expressing ability filtered by collaborative selector, which reduces the interference of uncertain behaviors. Secondly, the weight of the edge designed based on information entropy further describes the degree of uncertainty between the behaviors. Finally, the IDG contains many edges that never appear on the original behavior graph (as show in Table 2), which also alleviates the problem of data sparsity to some extent.

2.2 Learn Behavior Embedding

The goal of the Learn Behavior Embedding component is to learn a low dimensional embedding representation for each behavior and map the relationship that the behavior satisfies on the graph from the original space to a low dimensional space. We learn low dimensional embedding representations of behaviors on both the original behavior graph and the frequent pattern behavior graph, and then concatenate them.

Take the original behavior graph as an example. The edge weight on graph $G(V, E)$ represents the strength of the connection between two behaviors. We first map the edge set E from the original graph space to a probability space. The weight between behavior i and j is $w_{i,j}$, and the sum of weights of graph G is

$$W = \sum_{(i,j) \in E} w_{i,j} \tag{7}$$

The probability of connection for edge (i, j) is

$$p(i,j) = \frac{w_{i,j}}{W} \tag{8}$$

Defining the target space R^d, the low dimensional embedding representations of behaviors i and j are $u_i, u_j \in R^d$. In the target space, the probability of the connection for edge (i, j) is

$$\hat{p}(i,j) = \sigma(\overrightarrow{u}_i^T, \overrightarrow{u}_j) = \frac{1}{1 + exp(-\overrightarrow{u}_i^T \cdot \overrightarrow{u}_j)} \tag{9}$$

When the edge probability distribution in the low dimensional embedding target space tends to be the same as that in the probability source space, the target space retains the behavior relationship in the source space. To learn the effective behavior embedding representation, we minimize the distance between the probability distributions $p(i, j)$ and $\hat{p}(i, j)$. In other words, we minimize the object function,

$$O = d(p(\cdot, \cdot), \hat{p}(\cdot, \cdot)), \tag{10}$$

where $d(\cdot, \cdot)$ is the distance between two probability distributions. This paper uses the KL divergence to represent the distance between probability distributions, and the final objective function is obtained after eliminating the constant term,

$$O = - \sum_{(i,j) \in E} w_{i,j} \log \hat{p}(i,j). \tag{11}$$

By finding the $\{\overrightarrow{u}_i\}_{i=1,...,|V|}$ that minimizes the objective in Eq. (6), we can represent every vertex in the d-dimensional space.

2.3 Predict the Future Behavior

RNNs are devised to model variable-length sequence data. The behaviors of a user over a certain time period can be taken as a sequence and the future behaviors can be predicted by using the recurrent neural network. RNNs have an internal hidden state that encodes the historical information up to time t of the sequence in all units that compose the network. Standard RNNs update their hidden state h by using the following update function:

$$h_t = g(Wx_t + Uh_{t-1}) \tag{12}$$

where g is an activation function, x_t is the input of the unit at time t, and h_{t-1} is the hidden state of the previous time step. In this paper, we get the embedding representations of each behavior in the user's behavior sequence through embedding look-up and take them as input x_t for each time step.

In this paper, we apply GRUs, which constitute a more elaborate model of RNN units. A GRU uses the update gate and reset gate to learn when and by how much to update the hidden state of the unit. The activation of the GRU is

$$h_t = (1 - z_t)h_{t-1} + z_t\hat{h}_t \tag{13}$$

where the update gate z_t is calculated by

$$z_t = \sigma(W_z x_t + U_z h_{t-1}) \tag{14}$$

while the candidate state $\hat{h}_t$ is calculated by

$$\hat{h}_t = \tanh(Wx_t + U(r_t \odot h_{t-1})). \tag{15}$$

Finally, the reset gate r_t is given by

$$r_t = \sigma(W_r x_t + U_r h_{t-1}) \tag{16}$$

Given the hidden state $h_t \in R^d$ of the current time step t, the RNN outputs the probability distribution over the possible future behavior of the sequence of user u:

$$y_{act_{t+1}^u} = \sigma(Wh_t + b), \tag{17}$$

where $b \in R^n$, $W \in R^{n \times d}$ are the bias and weight matrix of the output layer, and $y_{act_{t+1}^u}$ represents the probability distribution of future possible behavior.

The task of predicting the user's future behavior can be regarded as a classification task or a ranking task. Generally, ranking-task training produces better results [6]. Therefore, we use the pairwise-based ranking loss function in this paper to minimize the loss function L by comparing the predicted probabilities of positive samples and negative samples so that the ranking of positive samples keeps coming forward and the ranking of negative samples keeps going back:

$$L = \frac{1}{N} \sum_{j=1}^{N_s} \sigma(\hat{r}_{u,j} - \hat{r}_{u,i}) + \sigma(\hat{r}_{u,j}^2), \qquad (18)$$

where N_s is the number of negative samples, $\hat{r}_{u,i}$ is the probability of positive samples, and $\hat{r}_{u,j}$ is the probability of negative samples.

3   Experiments

3.1   Datasets

We evaluate the proposed model on three real-world representative datasets which vary in domains and sparsity.

MovieLens 1M(**ML**)[1]: This is a popular benchmark dataset for evaluating behavior-prediction algorithms, which contains the user's rating behavior for the movie. In this work, we adopt a well-established versions, MovieLens 1M [5].

RecSys15-Buy[2]: This dataset contains user-purchase data obtained from the RecSys 2015 competition; it aims to predict which items a user intends to purchase. User behavior is divided into purchase behavior and click behavior, and we use the purchase behavior data part of it.

Amazon **Beauty**[3]: This is a series of product review datasets crawled from Amazon.com by McAuley et al. [11]. They split the data into separate datasets according to the top-level product categories on Amazon. In this work, we adopt the "Beauty" category. This dataset is the most sparse of the three.

According to the general practice in the literature [18,19], we converted all numeric ratings to implicit feedbacks of 1. We also removed cold-start users and items of having less than five feedbacks because dealing with cold-start recommendations is usually treated as a separate issue. We use the first 70% of actions in each user' sequence as the training set, and the remaining 30% of actions in each user' sequence serve as the test set for evaluating the model's performance. Table 1 shows the statistical information of the preprocessed dataset. Sparsity refers to the sparsity of the user-behavior matrix.

Table 1. Statistics of the datasets

Dataset	No. users	No. behavior types	Avg seq. length	No. behavior record	Sparsity
ML	6040	3377	165.47	999416	95.10%
RecSys	45520	4519	6.60	300105	99.85%
Beauty	40037	13951	6.52	261205	99.95%

---

[1] https://grouplens.org/datasets/movielens/1m/.
[2] https://2015.recsyschallenge.com/.
[3] http://jmcauley.ucsd.edu/data/amazon/.

3.2 Evaluation Metric

We evaluate a model by Precision@N, Recall@N, and F1@N. Given a list of top-N predicted items for a user, denoted $\hat{R}_{1:N}$, and the last 30% of behaviors in her or his sequence (denoted R for the test set), Precision@N and Recall@N are computed by

$$Prec@N = \frac{\left|R \cap \hat{R}_{1:N}\right|}{N}, \tag{19}$$

$$Recall@N = \frac{\left|R \cap \hat{R}_{1:N}\right|}{|R|}. \tag{20}$$

We report the average of these values of all users. $N \in \{5, 10\}$. The F1@N is defined by

$$F1@N = \frac{2 \times Prec@N \times Recall@N}{Prec@N + Recall@N}. \tag{21}$$

3.3 Experiment Design

In this paper, three different strategies from different perspectives are used to evaluate the effectiveness of the proposed CASE model:

1. We compare the CASE model with other six common and advanced models. The code for the methods involved is publicly available on GitHub.
   i. Random[4]: Randomly select a behavior to predict.
   ii. MostPopular(See Footnote 4): This is the simplest baseline that ranks items according to their popularity as determined by the number of inter-actions.
   iii. ItemKNN (See Footnote 4): Use behavior similar to the current behavior as a prediction result. The similarity between behaviors is defined as the cosine similarity between the behavior vectors in the user-behavior matrix. The num of nearest neighbors k is set to 80.
   iv. BPRMF (See Footnote 4): Uses pairwise ranking loss to optimize the matrix factorization with implicit feedback. And as like in previous work [9], we use the average latent factors of behaviors to represent the sequence. The parameters for this method are set as follows: num of factors is 10, L2 regularization is 0.0025 and learn rate is 0.05.
   v. GRU4Rec[5]: Uses recurrent neural network GRU and ranking loss function to capture the dependencies between user behavior sequences. The parameters for GRU4Rec method are set as follows: latent dimensions is 128, num of negative samples is 10, num of GRU layers is 2, learning rate is 1e-3 and L2 regularization is 1e-6.

---

[4] https://github.com/zenogantner/MyMediaLite .
[5] https://github.com/slientGe/Sequential_Recommendation_Tensorflow.

vi. Caser[6]: This employs CNNs both horizontally and vertically to model high-order MCs for sequential prediction. By following the previous work [9], we also ignore the user latent representations part of Caser when predicting future behaviors. The parameters for Caser method are set as follows: latent dimensions is 128, num of channels produced by horizontal convolution is 16, horizontal convolution kernel size is (i, 128), where i is from $\{1, \cdots, 5\}$, num of channels produced by vertical convolution is 4, vertical convolution kernel size is (5,1), learning rate is 1e-3, L2 regularization is 1e-6 and num of negative samples is 10.

2. We remove the constructing IDG part from the CASE model and keep the total behavior embedding dimension size, obtaining a new model and denoting it as CASE$^-$. We compare these two models to verify the effectiveness of the IDG.

3. Similar to what is done in the literature [13], we study how embedding dimension affects model performance.

The details of the parameters of the CASE model proposed in this paper are as follows: on all datasets, the maximum interval limit W and the minimum frequent pattern length of sequential frequent pattern mining are set to ten and three, respectively. The maximum frequent pattern length is set to three for ML dataset, and no limit for the RecSys and Beauty datasets. The threshold λ used to determine whether a sequential behavior pattern is selected are set to 1.4, 0.8 and 0.7 for ML, RecSys and Beauty, and the K for collaborative selector is set to 100. The total dimension of behavior embedding is 128 and the dimension of behavior embedding learned from original graph and IDG are both set to half of the total dimension.

3.4 Result and Analysis

Table 2 shows the results of the constructing graphs component. No. New edges refers to edges that appear on the IDG $G^{'}$, but not appear on the original behavior graph G. In ML, RecSys and Beauty datasets, the number of newly added edges increased by 18.60%, 7.05% and 3.06% respectively compared with edge numbers on the original behavior graph, which alleviate the problem of data sparsity to a certain extent. There are many strong intention-expressing behaviors on IDG, and the edge weight depicts the uncertain relationship. The model can encode these information in the behavior embedding representation by learning $G^{'}$.

Table 3 summarizes the best results of the six baselines, the CASE model, and the CASE$^-$ model. The best and second best performers on each column are highlighted in bold face and underline, respectively. The CASE model proposed herein performs the best on the RecSys and Beauty datasets according to all evaluation metrics. On ML dataset, CASE achieves the best performance on $Prec@5$, $Prec@10$, as well as on the overall metrics $F1@5$ and $F1@10$. For the

---

[6] https://github.com/graytowne/caser_pytorch.

Table 2. Results of constructed graphs

Dataset	No. nodes	No. edges of G	No. edges of G'	No. new edges
ML	3377	375039	384953	69748
RecSys	4519	92901	18261	6547
Beauty	13951	133135	27265	4084

$F1@10$ metric, the CASE method has the best performance on all datasets, and has improved 1.32%, 6.80% and 16.91% compared with the second best method on ML, RecSys and Beauty datasets, respectively. These three datasets are increasingly sparse, which proves that the more sparse the original dataset is, the effect of the proposed method CASE is more significant. However, we can also find that the precision values of RecSys and Beauty datasets are very small, which may mean that these two datasets are difficult to predict and there is no good algorithm yet for it.

Table 3. Comparison of performance of the three datasets.

	Method	Prec@5	Recall@5	F1@5	Prec@10	Recall@10	F1@10
ML	Random	0.00993	0.00146	0.00255	0.01061	0.00313	0.00483
	MostPopular	0.11129	0.02134	0.03581	0.10109	0.03754	0.05475
	ItemKNN	0.09152	0.02785	0.04271	0.08851	0.05254	0.06594
	BPRMF	0.12543	<u>0.03066</u>	0.04928	0.11334	<u>0.05379</u>	0.07296
	GRU4Rec	<u>0.29106</u>	0.02958	<u>0.05370</u>	<u>0.26023</u>	0.05290	<u>0.08793</u>
	Caser	0.11815	**0.03201**	0.05037	0.12210	**0.06371**	0.08373
	CASE⁻	0.26613	0.02705	0.04911	0.23864	0.048509	0.080629
	CASE	**0.29305**	0.02978	**0.05407**	**0.26369**	0.05360	**0.08909**
RecSys	Random	0.00011	0.00045	0.00018	0.00013	0.00098	0.00023
	MostPopular	0.00308	0.01165	0.00487	0.00298	0.02280	0.00527
	ItemKNN	0.02421	0.09515	0.03860	0.02495	<u>0.19414</u>	0.04422
	BPRMF	0.00323	0.01256	0.00514	0.00327	0.02499	0.00578
	GRU4Rec	0.02086	0.06909	0.03205	0.01666	0.11033	0.02895
	Caser	<u>0.03139</u>	<u>0.10862</u>	<u>0.04871</u>	<u>0.02804</u>	0.19390	<u>0.04899</u>
	CASE⁻	0.02716	0.08995	0.04172	0.01990	0.13182	0.03458
	CASE	**0.04249**	**0.14074**	**0.06528**	**0.03011**	**0.19944**	**0.05232**
Beauty	Random	0.00006	0.00014	0.00008	0.00005	0.00030	0.00009
	MostPopular	0.00207	0.00520	0.00296	0.00182	0.00919	0.00304
	ItemKNN	0.00182	0.00422	0.00254	0.00202	0.00906	0.00330
	BPRMF	0.00205	0.00527	0.00295	0.00174	0.00875	0.00290
	GRU4Rec	0.00338	0.00837	0.00482	0.00312	0.01545	0.00519
	Caser	<u>0.00440</u>	<u>0.00930</u>	<u>0.00597</u>	<u>0.00380</u>	<u>0.01610</u>	<u>0.00615</u>
	CASE⁻	0.00344	0.00852	0.00490	0.00276	0.01366	0.00459
	CASE	**0.00505**	**0.01249**	**0.00719**	**0.00432**	**0.02137**	**0.00719**

The results in Table 3 show that the sequential prediction methods such as GRU4Rec, Caser, CASE, and CASE⁻ perform better than the method without considering sequence characteristics. The results prove the importance of sequential information for predicting behavior.

By comparing the performance of CASE and CASE⁻ on all datasets, we find that constructing the IDG in the CASE model significantly improves the performance of the model. For example, for the RecSys dataset, the performance of the CASE⁻ model is inferior to that of Caser, but the performance of the CASE model clearly exceeds that of the Caser model and produces the best performance according to all evaluation metrics.

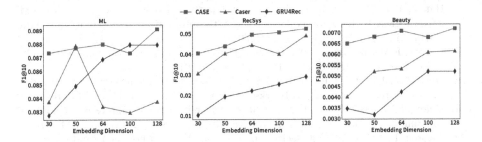

Fig. 2. F1@10 vs. the number of behavior embedding dimensions

Figure 2 shows $F1@10$ for various behavior embedding dimensions while keeping the other optimal hyperparameters unchanged. We can found that the CASE method can provide more stable performance for different behavior representation dimensions. It also works well in smaller representation dimensions, which means the almost good performance can be achieved with less computation.

4   Conclusion

To solve the problems of behavior sparsity and uncertainty in predicting user-behavior sequences, this paper proposes the CASE user-behavior prediction model.

The CASE model is based on frequent-pattern mining with a collaborative selector and graph neural networks to encode user behavior and uses recurrent neural networks to learn the dependencies between behaviors and thereby predict the future behaviors. Experiments show that the proposed CASE model outperforms many advanced methods when applied to various behavioral data sets with different vector dimensions.

In the next step, we can mine the semantic relationship between different behaviors or further study how to find causation as opposed to just correlation between behaviors, and thereby improve the robustness of the model.

Acknowledgements. Our research is supported by the Natural Science Foundation of Zhejiang Province of China under Grant (No. LY21F020003), Zhejiang Provincial Key Research and Development Program of China (NO. 2021C01164, NO.2021C02060).

References

1. Ekstrand, M.D., Riedl, J.T., Konstan, J.A.: Collaborative Filtering Recommender Systems. Now Publishers Inc, Norwell (2011)
2. Feng, X., Zeng, Y.: Joint deep modeling of rating matrix and reviews for recommendation. Chin. J. Comput. **43**(5), 884–900 (2020)
3. Gu, Y., Yang, X., Peng, M., Lin, G.: Robust weighted svd-type latent factor models for rating prediction. Expert Syst. Appl. **141**, 112885 (2020)
4. Han, J., et al.: Prefixspan: mining sequential patterns efficiently by prefix-projected pattern growth. In: Proceedings of the 17th International Conference on Data Engineering, pp. 215–224. Citeseer (2001)
5. Harper, F.M., Konstan, J.A.: The movielens datasets: history and context. ACM Trans. Interact. Intell. Syst. (TIIS) **5**(4), 1–19 (2015)
6. Hidasi, B., Karatzoglou, A., Baltrunas, L., Tikk, D.: Session-based recommendations with recurrent neural networks. arXiv preprint arXiv:1511.06939 (2015)
7. Huang, L., Lin, C., He, J., Liu, H., Du, X.: Diversified mobile app recommendation combining topic model and collaborative filtering. J. Soft. **28**(3), 708–720 (2017)
8. Jarboui, F., et al.: Markov decision process for MOOC users behavioral inference. In: European MOOCs Stakeholders Summit, pp. 70–80. Springer, Cham (2019). https://doi.org/10.1007/978-3-030-19875-6_9
9. Li, J., Ren, P., Chen, Z., Ren, Z., Lian, T., Ma, J.: Neural attentive session-based recommendation. In: Proceedings of the 2017 ACM on Conference on Information and Knowledge Management, pp. 1419–1428 (2017)
10. Liu, D.R., Lai, C.H., Lee, W.J.: A hybrid of sequential rules and collaborative filtering for product recommendation. Inf. Sci. **179**(20), 3505–3519 (2009)
11. McAuley, J., Targett, C., Shi, Q., Van Den Hengel, A.: Image-based recommendations on styles and substitutes. In: Proceedings of the 38th International ACM SIGIR Conference on Research and Development in Information Retrieval, pp. 43–52 (2015)
12. Shi, H., Zhang, C., Yao, Q., Li, Y., Sun, F., Jin, D.: State-sharing sparse hidden markov models for personalized sequences. In: Proceedings of the 25th ACM SIGKDD International Conference on Knowledge Discovery & Data Mining, pp. 1549–1559 (2019)
13. Tang, J., Wang, K.: Personalized top-n sequential recommendation via convolutional sequence embedding. In: Proceedings of the Eleventh ACM International Conference on Web Search and Data Mining, pp. 565–573 (2018)
14. Wang, Z., Wei, W., Cong, G., Li, X.L., Mao, X.L., Qiu, M.: Global context enhanced graph neural networks for session-based recommendation. In: Proceedings of the 43rd International ACM SIGIR Conference on Research and Development in Information Retrieval, pp. 169–178 (2020)
15. Wu, S., Tang, Y., Zhu, Y., Wang, L., Xie, X., Tan, T.: Session-based recommendation with graph neural networks. In: Proceedings of the AAAI Conference on Artificial Intelligence, vol. 33, pp. 346–353 (2019)
16. Yanmin, C., Hao, W., Jianhui, M., Dongfang, D., Hongke, Z.: A hierarchical attention mechanism framework for internet credit evaluation. J. Comput. Res. Dev. **57**(8), 1755 (2020)

17. Yu, Z., Lian, J., Mahmoody, A., Liu, G., Xie, X.: Adaptive user modeling with long and short-term preferences for personalized recommendation. In: IJCAI, pp. 4213–4219 (2019)
18. Yuan, Q., Cong, G., Sun, A.: Graph-based point-of-interest recommendation with geographical and temporal influences. In: Proceedings of the 23rd ACM International Conference on Conference on Information and Knowledge Management, pp. 659–668 (2014)
19. Zhao, S., Zhao, T., Yang, H., Lyu, M.R., King, I.: Stellar: spatial-temporal latent ranking for successive point-of-interest recommendation. In: Thirtieth AAAI Conference on Artificial Intelligence (2016)

A Collaborative Optimization-Guided Entity Extraction Scheme

Qiaojuan Peng[1,2,3], Xiong Luo[1,2,3($\boxtimes$)], Hailun Shen[4], Ziyang Huang[4], and Maojian Chen[1,2,3]

[1] School of Computer and Communication Engineering, University of Science and Technology Beijing, Beijing 100083, China
xluo@ustb.edu.cn
[2] Shunde Graduate School, University of Science and Technology Beijing, Foshan 528399, China
[3] Beijing Key Laboratory of Knowledge Engineering for Materials Science, Beijing 100083, China
[4] Ouyeel Co., Ltd., Shanghai 201999, China

Abstract. Entity extraction as one of the most basic tasks in achieving information extraction and retrieval, has always been an important research area in natural language processing. Considering that most of the traditional entity extraction methods need to manually adjust their hyperparameters, it takes a lot of time and is easy to fall into local optimality. To avoid such limitations, this paper proposes a novel scheme to extract named entities, where the model hyperparameters are automatically adjusted to improve the performance of entity extraction. Here, the proposed scheme is composed of bi-directional encoder representation from transformers (BERT) and conditional random field (CRF). Specifically, through the fusion of collaborative computing paradigm, particle swarm optimization (PSO) algorithm is utilized in this paper to search for the best value of hyperparameters automatically in a cooperative way. The experimental results on two public datasets and a steel inquiry dataset verify that our proposed scheme can effectively improve the performance of entity extraction.

Keywords: Entity extraction · Particle swarm optimization (PSO) · Bi-directional encoder representation from transformers (BERT) · Collaborative optimization

1 Introduction

Currently, the automatic extraction of information from unstructured data has attracted extensive attention. As a basic task in information extraction and retrieval, entity extraction identifies entities with specific meanings, such as location, person, proper noun, and some others from the text [24]. With the development of natural language processing (NLP) technologies, text semantic

H. Gao and X. Wang (Eds.): CollaborateCom 2021, LNICST 407, pp. 190–205, 2021.
https://doi.org/10.1007/978-3-030-92638-0_12

knowledge is becoming more and more important. Recently emerging research fields such as automatic question answering, intelligent search and semantic analysis, require rich semantic knowledge as support. As the most important semantic knowledge in text, entity extraction has always been an important area. However, there are three difficulties in this field. First, the named entity itself has the characteristics of complexity, diversity and randomness, then it is difficult to accurately define and classify its entity type. Second, since it may lack large-scale knowledge databases like Wikipedia in practically industrial applications, it is challenging to obtain a large amount of high-quality annotation data. Third, due to the domain characteristics of different applications, there are many out of vocabulary (OOV) words, i.e., new words, which takes a lot of time and effort to recognize them manually.

In order to cope with the above challenges, some unsupervised and supervised machine learning algorithms are used to label large-scale data automatically [19,25,33,34]. To further improve the performance of achieving this task, we develop a novel scheme through the combination of popular deep learning model and typical evolutionary algorithm. During the implementation process, many important hyperparameters in those algorithms need to be adjusted to guarantee that the satisfactory computing performance of learning model could be achieved. Then, the adjustment that previously were based on painstakingly handcrafted operations, can now be made using intelligent strategies.

Generally, collaborative computing is an efficient paradigm in which different groups can work together for a certain task in a coordinated manner. It indicates that groups in a dispersed state cooperate with each other to achieve a task together, while more effectively promoting the collaboration between social groups and greatly improving the working quality of the group. In this field, particle swarm optimization (PSO) is a typical evolutionary algorithm [16], which aims to address optimization problems with the help of collaboration and information sharing between particles. Through the fusion of it, in our developed scheme PSO algorithm is utilized to intelligently search for the best value of hyperparameters in a cooperative way.

More specifically, we propose a novel scheme to achieve entity extraction using an advanced architecture, which is composed of bi-directional encoder representation from transformers (BERT) and conditional random field (CRF). This scheme is called BERT-CRF-PSO. Among them, BERT uses the encoder architecture in the transformer to obtain the semantic vector and combines with the masked language model (MLM) to achieve contextual prediction [12]. The CRF [17] can effectively use past and future labels to predict the current label, so as to obtain more accurate entity prediction conditional probabilities. Meanwhile, we introduce the PSO to fine-tune the hyperparameters of the BERT model. The probability value of the entity prediction can be obtained finally. In general, the BERT and CRF are responsible for the training data, and the PSO is responsible for fine-tuning the hyperparameters. These three modules share information and collaborate with each other to complete the entity extraction task together. Through this model, it is expected that we can improve the performance of entity extraction.

The contributions of this paper can be summarized as follows.

- Applying collaborative computing to the field of entity extraction, so as to efficiently realize entity extraction in a way of mutual cooperation and information sharing.
- In order to improve the performance of entity extraction, the PSO algorithm is used to automatically fine-tune the hyperparameters of the BERT model, so as to find the global optimal hyperparameters for a specific dataset.

The rest of this paper is organized as follows. In Sect. 2, the related work of entity extraction is simply introduced. In Sect. 3, we present the proposed scheme BERT-CRF-PSO. The relevant experimental results are shown in Sect. 4. Finally, in Sect. 5, our work is summarized.

2   Related Work

The methods of implementing entity extraction can be classified into three categories. In this section, we introduce some related algorithms about entity extraction.

2.1   The Rule and Vocabulary-Based Entity Extraction

Early, the entity extraction was achieved using a rule and vocabulary-based method. The basic idea was to select features, e.g., statistical information, keywords, and punctuation, to construct specific rules manually, and use methods, e.g., pattern and string matching, to perform for entity extraction.

Xie *et al.* proposed a method of combining manually formulated rules with heuristic ideas, and realized the automatic recognition of named entities from unstructured text [32]. Berry *et al.* used a self-training model to conduct entity extraction on the basis of unified medical language system (UMLS) [2], and the optimal result of F_1 reached 85.23%. Farmakiotou *et al.* proposed an entity extraction system based on manual vocabulary resources [14]. The rules were mainly formulated for the Greek language and included hand-made grammar and gazetteers. The system had achieved satisfactory test results for the experiments on a Greek corpus of financial news. Collins *et al.* proposed the DL-CoTrain method [9]. The basic processing of this method could be divided into three steps. Firstly, the seed rule set was pre-defined. Secondly, multiple unsupervised training were performed on the pre-defined rule set to obtain more rules. Finally, the rule set was used to extract named entities. The classification accuracy of this method for three categories of person, location and organization all exceeded 91%.

This class of methods achieved good performance when the extracted rules could accurately reflect the language characteristics in a specific field. However, the feature of those methods had also become their shortcoming. It relied too much on a specific language, domain, and text style, which might lead to poor portability of the model.

2.2   The Traditional Machine Learning-Based Entity Extraction

For those methods using traditional machine learning models, entity extraction were generally regarded as a sequence tagging task. Compared with the classification problem, the predicted label sequences in the sequence tagging task had a very strong interdependence. In other words, the currently predicted label was not only related to the current input feature, but also related to the previous predicted label. Here, in this field, some traditional machine learning were used, and they mainly included CRF, maximum entropy (ME) [28], support vector machine (SVM) [18], and hidden Markov model (HMM) [8].

Among the above four methods, CRF could provide a globally optimal label model for entity extraction. However, it took a long training time and its convergence speed was much slow. ME had the advantages of compact structure and good versatility. Its disadvantage was that explicit normalization calculations were required in the training processing, while leading to relatively large costs. HMM used the viterbi algorithm to address the problem of recognizing entities from sequence. Therefore, its training speed and recognition speed were fast, while it performed worse than ME and SVM in accuracy.

Das *et al.* used the CRF model to achieve entity extraction tasks for Indian languages [11]. The accuracy of this model for entity extraction on Bengali and Hindi were 87% and 79%, respectively. Saha *et al.* used the ME model to extract four types of entities, i.e., person, organization, location, and date, on Hindi, and the value of final F_1 was 81.52% [28]. Lin *et al.* proposed a entity extraction system on the basis of SVM model, and used the system to achieve high accuracy [18]. Chopra *et al.* used HMM for entity extraction tasks on the Treebank corpus with 25 files. In the end, they achieved the result of F_1 is 73.8% on eight types of named entities [8].

2.3   The Deep Learning-Based Entity Extraction

Recently, with the development of deep learning technologies, they were gradually popular in the field of entity extraction [6]. Compared with the above two classes of methods, the deep learning-based methods had three main advantages [30,38]:

- They could learn more complex features and potential knowledge from the original data text through a nonlinear activation function.
- They were end-to-end, which meant that it could avoid error propagation between modules in the pipeline model and could carry more complex internal designs, so as to achieve better experimental results.
- Experiments had verified that the deep learning algorithms were very suitable for processing sequence tagging problems, and did not rely on domain knowledge and feature engineering.

Chiu *et al.* proposed a two-way model combining long short-term memory (LSTM) and convolutional neural network (CNN), which could automatically capture word-level and character-level features [7]. Ma and Hovy proposed a novel neutral network architecture combining bidirectional LSTM (BiLSTM), CNN and CRF, which would automatically benefit from word-level and character-level representations [23]. Zhao *et al.* developed a entity extraction method through the use of CNN. They took word-level embedding, dictionary features, and others as input, and used CNN to automatically extract useful features [36]. Liu *et al.* developed a neural network framework called LM-LSTM-CRF, which merged the character-aware neural language model to extract character-level knowledge. Unlike most transfer learning methods, the framework proposed by Liu *et al.* did not rely on any additional supervision and could identify new entities well [20]. More recently, adding graph neural network, attention mechanism, transfer learning and other technologies to neural network-based models was also a popular direction in the implementation of entity extraction [4,5,27,31].

3   The Proposed Scheme

The overall architecture of our scheme is shown Fig. 1, where [CLS] is a special symbol for classification output, N is the number of characters in the text, Tok_i represents the i-th character, E_i represents the i-th token embedding, T_i represents the final i-th embedding vector, and Tag_i is the final output tag sequence. Here, i is bounded within $[1, N]$.

It can be seen from this figure that, this architecture mainly consists of three modules, including BERT model, CRF layer, and PSO algorithm. Among them, the BERT model effectively achieves the word embedding, transformer encoding and pooling, and it is used to pre-train the language model to obtain the corresponding word vector. The CRF layer adds some constraints to the final predicted label to ensure that it is legal and correct. The CRF layer can automatically learn some rules during the training processing. For example, if a dataset uses the BIO labeling scheme, where "B" represents the beginning of a named entity, "I" represents the middle of a named entity, and "O" represents the non-entity. Meanwhile, the constraints learned by CRF layer are as follows:

- The first word in a sentence always starts with the label "B-" or "O-" instead of "I-".
- A pattern can be learned by "B-label1 I-label2 I-label3 $\cdots$", which means that labels 1, 2, and 3 should be the same entity category. For instance, "B-Location I-Location I-Location" is a legal label sequence. However, "B-Location I-Location I-Person" is an illegal label sequence.
- The label sequence "O I- $\cdots$" is illegal. In other words, the legal label sequence should be "O B- I-".

The PSO algorithm simulates the foraging behavior of a flock of birds. In our model, it iteratively searches for BERT hyperparameters which most suitable for a specific dataset, and continuously adjusts the hyperparameters during the search processing to achieve the best performance of the BERT-CRF model. In short, these three different modules work together to complete a task in a way of

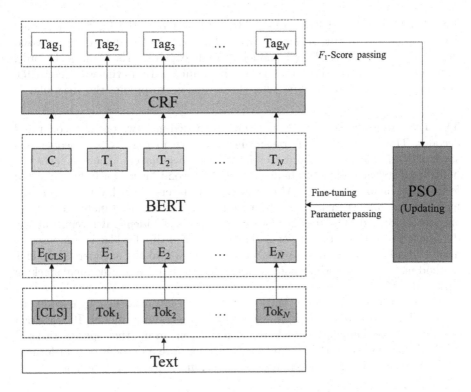

Fig. 1. The architecture of our proposed scheme.

mutual cooperation and information sharing, so as to achieve entity extraction efficiently and accurately.

3.1   The Use of BERT Model

BERT uses a multi-layer two-way transformer as a feature extractor, and uses a self-attention mechanism to make each word have global semantic information, thus capturing long-distance dependencies. In addition, BERT uses the Word-Piece method to build the vocabulary. WordPiece can be understood as splitting a word into subwords. If a word is not in the vocabulary, the tokens are split one by one in the way of subwords. If no token is found, [unknown] is directly assigned. In this way, the information of the root of the word can be effectively captured, the vocabulary capacity can be reduced, and the OOV problem can also be alleviated. BERT contains three important parts: the MLM model, the transformer model, and the next sentence prediction (NSP).

The MLM Model. BERT uses a MLM to overcome the limitation of one-way information. In this scheme, 15% of the words in the dataset are masked randomly, and then the BERT model is used to predict these masked words, which is a bit similar to the cloze task we are familiar with. In this way, the BERT model can rely more on context-related information to predict the vocabulary.

The Transformer Model. Transformer is divided into two parts: encoder and decoder. The architecture of transformer is shown in Fig. 2 [29]. Encoder is a stack of N identical layers, and each layer has two sublayers. The first layer is a multi-head self-attention mechanism, and the second layer is a fully connected feedforward neural network. After the two sub-layers, each layer is connected by residuals, and then layer standardization is performed. Finally, a N-layer encoder is formed. The decoder is also stacked by N identical layers, but the difference from the encoder layer is that the layer in the decoder is composed of a multi-head attention and "Add&Norm" inserted into the encoder layer. This method makes full use of the context and does not require bidirectional stacking such as BiLSTM.

In fact, the BERT model only uses encoder of transformer to encode the input. This is because BERT is essentially a pre-training model. It is carried out through the language model, and it is different from other specific tasks of NLP. Meanwhile, since BERT currently does not have a decoder of transformer, it also reduces a lot of unnecessary operations in its attention function.

Next Sentence Prediction. The role of NSP can be understood that as two sentences in a given text, it is to determine whether the second sentence immediately follows the first one. Some tasks require a model to understand the relationship between two sentences. However, this goal can not be achieved by only training the language model. This is the reason why BERT trains NSP.

Therefore, when BERT pre-trains the data, there is a 50% probability that the model will choose two contextual sentences A and B, and a 50% probability that it will choose two context-independent sentences A and B.

3.2   The Design of CRF Layer

In order to make the classifier perform better, when labeling data, we can consider using the labeling information of adjacent data. It is difficult for general classifiers to do this. However, CRF is particularly good at handling contextual information. Because the typical characteristic of CRF is to use a log-linear model to represent the joint probability of the feature sequence, which is convenient for people to effectively use the context label to predict the current label. CRF is a typical sequence tagging algorithm, that is, given an input sequence $\mathbf{X} = \{x_1, x_2, x_3, \cdots, x_{n-1}, x_n\}$, the target sequence $\mathbf{Y} = \{y_1, y_2, y_3, \cdots, y_{n-1}, y_n\}$ is the output of model. It has been employed in sequence tagging tasks such as word segmentation, part-of-speech tagging and entity extraction [10,15,22]. The structure of CRF is shown in Fig. 3 [17].

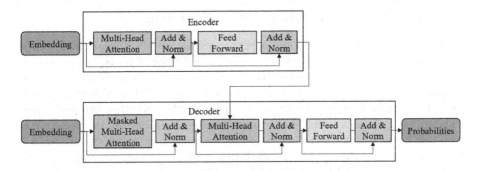

Fig. 2. The architecture of transformer.

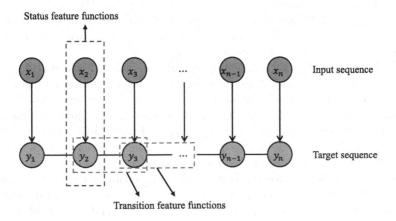

Fig. 3. The structure of CRF.

Let $\mathbf{X} = \{x_1, x_2, x_3, \cdots, x_{n-1}, x_n\}$ be the input sequence of sentence whose length is n, and let $\mathbf{Y} = \{y_1, y_2, y_3, \cdots, y_{n-1}, y_n\}$ be the corresponding output target sequence. Assuming that $P(\mathbf{Y}|\mathbf{X})$ is a linear chain conditional probability, it is shown in (1).

$$P(\mathbf{Y}|\mathbf{X}) = \frac{1}{Z}\exp\left(\sum_{i=1}^{n-1}\sum_{k=1}^{K}\lambda_k t_k\left(y_{i+1}, y_i, \mathbf{X}, i\right) + \sum_{i=1}^{n}\sum_{l=1}^{L}u_l s_l\left(y_i, \mathbf{X}, i\right)\right), \quad (1)$$

where K is the total number of transition feature functions defined at nodes, L is the total number of status feature functions defined at nodes, i is the position of the current node in sequence, λ_k and u_l are weights, and Z is a normalized factor. Moreover, t_k and s_l are transition feature functions and status feature functions, respectively.

3.3   The PSO-Based Collaborative Optimization

PSO is a population-based random optimization algorithm. The core idea of this algorithm is to simulate the foraging behavior of a flock of birds. In the process of foraging, the birds continuously communicate and share their positions and information with each other, so that other birds know their positions. Through the collaboration between the group, each bird judges whether the position it finds is the optimal solution (the closest food source), and at the same time, they also transmit the information of the optimal solution to the entire bird group. In each iteration process, each bird adjusts its position according to the optimal solution found by itself and the optimal solution of the population to ensure that the entire flock of birds can finally gather around the food source, that is, the optimal solution is found. The advantage of PSO is that it is easy to implement, fast to converge, and does not need to adjust a large number of parameters. At present, it has been widely used in neural networks, data mining, image processing and other fields [1,3,26,37].

The best value of BERT model hyperparameters will help the model perform better on a specific dataset, which is essentially an optimization problem. Here, PSO is particularly suitable for dealing with optimization problems. In PSO, the position of birds in the searching space represents the solution space of the problem, and these birds are also as "particles". Every particle has three basic attributes, including position, speed, and fitness. The position and speed determine the direction and distance of the particles, and the fitness is determined by an optimization function. In this paper, the position refers to the hyperparameters of the BERT model, the speed represents the direction of the change of hyperparameters, the optimization function is the BERT-CRF model, and the fitness can be measured by F_1-Score. Actually, the metrics used for evaluating the effectiveness of model usually include precision, recall, and F_1-score. However, precision and recall are a pair of contradictory measures. Generally, when the precision is high, the recall tends to be low, and when the precision is low, the recall tends to be high. Since F_1-score is a weighted average of precision and recall, it can take into account the precision and recall of classification model at the same time. Hence, we choose F_1-score to measure fitness in our scheme. Each particle has a memory function, which can save all historical solutions. While searching, they can follow the best optimal particle in a certain iteration in the population, and find the next solution in accordance with the solution of the best optimal particle.

PSO initializes a group of particles, so that they have random initial positions and speeds. In the iterative process, each particle updates its attributes by tracking two "extreme", i.e., the historically optimal solution of particle itself, called the individual extreme point (using pbest to represent its position), the historically optimal solution of entire population, called the global extreme point (using gbest to represent its position). In fact, pbest can be regarded as the flying experience of the particle itself (individual cognition), and gbest can be regarded as the flying experience of the particle's companion (social behavior). By finding these two optimal solutions, the particles update their speeds and positions according to (2) and (3). Assuming that the information of the i-th particle is represented by a D-dimensional vector, where D is the number of hyperparameters required to adjust, the position can be expressed as $\mathbf{X}_i = (x_{i1}, x_{i2}, \cdots, x_{id}, \cdots, x_{iD})^{\top}$, and the speed can be expressed as $\mathbf{V}_i = (v_{i1}, v_{i2}, \cdots, v_{id}, \cdots, v_{iD})^{\top}$. Then, we have:

$$v_{id}^{k+1} = w \times v_{id}^k + c_1 \times \text{rand}_1^k \times (\overline{\text{pbest}}_{id}^k - x_{id}^k) + c_2 \times \text{rand}_2^k \times (\overline{\text{gbest}}_d^k - x_{id}^k), \quad (2)$$

$$x_{id}^{k+1} = x_{id}^k + v_{id}^{k+1}, \quad (3)$$

where v_{id}^k $(1 \leqslant d \leqslant D)$ represents the velocity of the d-th hyperparameter of the i-th particle during the k-th iteration. The larger the inertia factor w, the stronger its global search ability, and the smaller the inertia factor w, the stronger its local search ability. So the introduction of inertia factor w can adjust the global and local searching capabilities of algorithm. Moreover, c_1 and c_2 are learning factors used to adjust the maximum step length during the particle flight. Appropriate c_1 and c_2 can speed up the convergence of algorithm and make the results avoid local minimum. Moreover, rand_1 and $\text{rand}_2 \in [0, 1]$ are random values. In addition, x_{id}^k represents the position of the d-th dimension of the i-th particle during the k-th iteration. Finally, $\overline{\text{pbest}}_{id}$ is the position of the individual extreme point of the i-th particle during the d-th dimension, and $\overline{\text{gbest}}_d$ is the position of the global extreme point of entire population during the d-th dimension. In addition, in order to prevent the particles from gradually moving away from the searching space, the position and velocity of each dimension of the particles will be limited to an interval [13].

Then, the parameters optimization via PSO is shown in Algorithm 1.

4 Experiments

4.1 Experimental Dataset

The experiment in this paper uses a total of three datasets. The first type is the boson dataset[1], which includes six types of entities: time, location, person, organization, company, and product. The second type is the People's Daily dataset[2], including three named entities of organization, institution and person. The last type is the inquiry data of steel industry. It possesses 744 data including eight entity categories, such as grade, variety, specification, place of production, thickness, weight, surface structure, and surface treatment. It is noted that both the boson and the People's Daily datasets can be obtained on the Internet. The steel dataset is the historical inquiry information of customers on the steel e-commerce platform. Considering the consistency of different datasets, we select 1,000 corpora from the boson dataset and 1,000 corpora from the People's Daily dataset in the experiment.

---

[1] http://static.bosonnlp.com/dev/resource.
[2] http://www.ling.lancs.ac.uk/corplang/pdcorpus/pdcorpus.html.

Algorithm 1. The implementation process of PSO

1: Set the fitness: F_1-Score;
2: Set the position vector (BERT model hyperparameters): $[x_1, x_2, \cdots, x_D]$;
3: Set the maximum number of iterations: $k_{\max}$;
4: Initialize the number of particles n, and use a random function to initialize the position and speed of each particle;
5: Calculate the F_1-Score of each particle;
6: Initialize the optimal parameter $\overline{\text{pbest}}$ of each particle, and the optimal parameter $\overline{\text{gbest}}$ of the population according to F_1-Score;
7: Initialize the iteration number $k = 1$;
8: Use (2) and (3) to update the position and speed of each particle;
9: Update the value of F_1-Score;
10: Update the historically optimal parameters of each particle;
11: Update the globally optimal parameters of the population;
12: $k = k + 1$
13: **if** $k > k_{\max}$ **then**
14:     Output the optimal position vector and the corresponding F_1-Score value;
15: **else**
16:     Go back to Step 8;
17: **end if**

4.2 Metric

This paper uses three metrics, i.e., precision, recall and F_1-Score, to evaluate the performance of our proposed scheme.

Here, according to the correct and wrong results of classifier's prediction on the test dataset, it can be divided into three situations:

- TP (True Positive): the entities in test dataset and they are recognized by model.
- FP (False Positive): the entities recognized by model while they are not existing in test dataset.
- FN (False Negative): the entities existing in datasets but they are not recognized by model.

Then, we can get the definition of three metrics as follows:

- Precision (P): the proportion of positive predictions that are correct in all predictions.
- Recall (R): the proportion of all positive samples that are correctly predicted to be positive.
- F_1-Score (F): Harmonized average of Precision and Recall.

Furthermore, they are shown as:

$$P = \frac{\text{TP}}{\text{TP} + \text{FP}}, \tag{4}$$

$$R = \frac{\text{TP}}{\text{TP} + \text{FN}}, \tag{5}$$

$$F = \frac{2 \times P \times R}{P + R}. \tag{6}$$

4.3   Experimental Comparison

We use BERT-CRF [21], BERT-BiLSTM-CRF [35] and our BERT-CRF-PSO to conduct experiments on three datasets described in Sect. 4.1. By consulting the literature, we found that for fine-tuning, except for batch_size, training_epoch and learning_rate, most model hyperparameters are the same as in pre-training [12]. Where batch_size is the number of samples sent to the network for training each time, training_epoch refers to the process of sending all data to the network to complete a forward calculation and back propagation, and learning_rate controls the learning speed of the model. Therefore, in the experiment, we choose the above three hyperparameters as the objects to be automatically fine-tuned by the PSO algorithm. In addition, in order to prove the effectiveness of the proposed method, we designed a comparative experiment of fine-tuning two hyperparameters (batch_size, training_epoch) and fine-tuning three hyperparameters (batch_size, training_epoch and learning_rate). On the basis of experience and many experiments, w is set to 0.4, c_1 and c_2 are both set to 2. Meanwhile, batch_size $\in [8, 32]$, training_epoch $\in [10, 30]$ and learning_rate $\in [1e-5, 1e-4]$ are three hyperparameters of BERT model, and they need to be adjusted with PSO algorithm.

Table 1 shows the comparison results of different methods on different datasets. Compared with other two models, our proposed scheme employs PSO to automatically search for the optimal value of hyperparameters in a given searching space, so that the effect of the model for a specific dataset reaches the global optimal. During the experiment, the hyperparameters of other two models are manually set by us in consideration of experience and the results of multiple experiments. The experimental results show that the model that requires manual adjustment of hyperparameters is not only time-consuming and labor-intensive, but also easy to fall into the local optimum. The proposed scheme can find the global optimal solution through collaboration and information sharing between individuals in the group. The results in Table 1 confirm the superiority of our scheme. Additionally, if we increase the dimensional number of position vectors, i.e., model hyperparameters in Algorithm 1, the improved performance of our scheme will be more obvious. The comparative experimental results of fine-tuning two hyperparameters and fine-tuning three hyperparameters in Table 1 prove this statement.

Specifically, in Table 2 we provide the optimal hyperparameters found by PSO in our scheme on the three datasets. Obviously, for different dataset, the optimal values of model hyperparameters are different. The experimental results show that the model we propose can help us automatically find the global optimal hyperparameters for a specific dataset, which is a very efficient method.

Table 1. Comparison results of different methods on different datasets.

Dataset	Method	Precision	Recall	F_1-Score
Boson	BERT-CRF	82.45%	85.14%	83.78%
	BERT-BiLSTM-CRF	82.69 %	85.42%	84.03%
	BERT-CRF-PSO(a)	**82.97%**	**85.98%**	**84.45%**
	BERT-CRF-PSO(b)	**83.78%**	**85.37%**	**84.57%**
People's daily	BERT-CRF	93.50%	95.63%	94.55%
	BERT-BiLSTM-CRF	92.29%	94.59%	93.43%
	BERT-CRF-PSO(a)	**93.27%**	**97.86%**	**95.51%**
	BERT-CRF-PSO(b)	**95.43%**	**98.29%**	**96.84%**
Inquiry data of the steel industry	BERT-CRF	91.39%	93.40%	92.39%
	BERT-BiLSTM-CRF	92.14%	94.57%	93.34%
	BERT-CRF-PSO(a)	**93.21%**	**94.57%**	**93.89%**
	BERT-CRF-PSO(b)	**92.84%**	**95.01%**	**93.91%**

Note: (a) represents fine-tuning two hyperparameters, (b) represents fine-tuning three hyperparameters.

Table 2. Comparison of optimal model hyperparameters of different datasets.

Dataset	batch_size	training_epoch	learning_rate
Boson	21	20	–
	12	24	3e−5
People's daily	24	22	–
	19	17	4e−5
Inquiry data of the steel industry	22	29	–
	24	24	2e−5

5 Conclusion

Through the combination of collaborative optimization mechanism, we design a novel scheme BERT-CRF-PSO to achieve entity extraction task in this paper. Then, three modules, including BERT, CRF and PSO algorithm, are incorporated into our scheme. Here, the BERT model is utilized to pre-train data, the CRF adds constraints to the predicted label to ensure its legitimacy, and the PSO fine-tunes the hyperparameters of the BERT module, which can automatically find the optimal value of the hyperparameters for a specific dataset in a cooperative way. These three modules cooperate with each other and share information to complete the entity extraction task. Hence, the training results within entire architecture can achieve the global optimum. The experimental results on two public datasets and a steel inquiry dataset confirm the effectiveness of our scheme, while improving the performance of entity extraction.

Acknowledgment. This work was supported in part by the National Natural Science Foundation of China under Grant U1836106, in part by the Beijing Natural Science Foundation under Grants 19L2029 and M21032, in part by the Scientific and

Technological Innovation Foundation of Shunde Graduate School, USTB, under Grants BK19BF006 and BK20BF010, and in part by the Fundamental Research Funds for the University of Science and Technology Beijing under Grant FRF-BD-19-012A.

References

1. Bashir, Z., El-Hawary, M.: Applying wavelets to short-term load forecasting using PSO-based neural networks. IEEE Trans. Power Syst. **24**(1), 20–27 (2009)
2. de Bruijn, B., Cherry, C., Kiritchenko, S., Martin, J., Zhu, X.: Machine-learned solutions for three stages of clinical information extraction: the state of the art at i2b2 2010. J. Am. Med. Inform. Assoc. **18**(5), 557–562 (2011)
3. Cai, J., Wei, H., Yang, H., Zhao, X.: A novel clustering algorithm based on DPC and PSO. IEEE Access **8**, 88200–88214 (2020)
4. Cao, P., Chen, Y., Liu, K., Zhao, J., Liu, S.: Adversarial transfer learning for Chinese named entity recognition with self-attention mechanism. In: Proceedings of the 2018 Conference on Empirical Methods in Natural Language Processing, pp. 182–192. Association for Computational Linguistics, Brussels, Belgium (2018)
5. Carbonell, M., Riba, P., Villegas, M., Fornés, A., Lladós, J.: Named entity recognition and relation extraction with graph neural networks in semi structured documents. In: Proceedings of the 25th International Conference on Pattern Recognition, pp. 9622–9627. IEEE, Milan, Italy (2020)
6. Chen, M., Shen, H., Huang, Z., Luo, X., Yin, J.: Towards accurate search for e-commerce in steel industry: a knowledge-graph-based approach. In: Gao, H., Wang, X., Iqbal, M., Yin, Y., Yin, J., Gu, N. (eds.) CollaborateCom 2020. LNICST, vol. 349, pp. 3–18. Springer, Cham (2021). https://doi.org/10.1007/978-3-030-67537-0_1
7. Chiu, J., Nichols, E.: Named entity recognition with bidirectional LSTM-CNNs. Trans. Assoc. Comput. Linguist. **4**, 357–370 (2016)
8. Chopra, D., Joshi, N., Mathur, I.: Named entity recognition in Hindi using hidden Markov model. In: Proceedings of the Second International Conference on Computational Intelligence & Communication Technology, pp. 581–586. IEEE, Ghaziabad, India (2016)
9. Collins, M., Singer, Y.: Unsupervised models for named entity classification. In: Proceedings of the Joint SIGDAT Conference on Empirical Methods in Natural Language Processing and Very Large Corpora, pp. 100–110. Association for Computational Linguistics, MD, USA (1999)
10. Constant, M., Sigogne, A.: MWU-aware part-of-speech tagging with a CRF model and lexical resources. In: Proceedings of the Workshop on Multiword Expressions: from Parsing and Generation to the Real World, pp. 49–56. Association for Computational Linguistics, Oregon, USA (2011)
11. Das, A., Garain, U.: CRF-based named entity recognition @icon 2013. arXiv:1409.8008 (2014)
12. Devlin, J., Chang, M.W., Lee, K., Toutanova, K.: BERT: pre-training of deep bidirectional transformers for language understanding. In: Proceedings of the Conference of the North American Chapter of the Association for Computational Linguistics: Human Language Technologies, pp. 4171–4186. Association for Computational Linguistics, Minneapolis, Minnesota (2019)
13. Eberhart, R.C., Shi, Y.: Particle swarm optimization: developments, applications and resources. In: Proceedings of the Congress on Evolutionary Computation, vol. 1, pp. 81–86. IEEE, COEX, Seoul, Korea (2001)

14. Farmakiotou, D., Karkaletsis, V., Koutsias, J., Sigletos, G., Spyropoulos, C.D., Stamatopoulos, P.: Rule-based named entity recognition for greek financial texts. In: Proceedings of the Workshop on Computational lexicography and Multimedia Dictionaries, pp. 75–78. Citeseer (2000)
15. Khabsa, M., Giles, C.L.: Chemical entity extraction using CRF and an ensemble of extractors. J. Cheminformatics **7**(1), 1–9 (2015)
16. Khalifa, M.H., Ammar, M., Ouarda, W., Alimi, A.M.: Particle swarm optimization for deep learning of convolution neural network. In: Proceedings of the Sudan Conference on Computer Science and Information Technology, pp. 1–5. IEEE, Elnihood, Sudan (2017)
17. Lafferty, J., McCallum, A., Pereira, F.C.: Conditional random fields: probabilistic models for segmenting and labeling sequence data. In: Proceedings of the 18th International Conference on Machine Learning, pp. 282–289. Morgan Kaufmann, San Francisco, CA, USA (2001)
18. Lin, X., Peng, H., Liu, B.: Chinese named entity recognition using support vector machines. In: Proceedings of the International Conference on Machine Learning and Cybernetics, pp. 4216–4220. IEEE, Guangzhou, China (2006)
19. Lison, P., Barnes, J., Hubin, A., Touileb, S.: Named entity recognition without labelled data: a weak supervision approach. In: Proceedings of the 58th Annual Meeting of the Association for Computational Linguistics, pp. 1518–1533. Association for Computational Linguistics (2020)
20. Liu, L., et al.: Empower sequence labeling with task-aware neural language model. In: Proceedings of the 32th AAAI Conference on Artificial Intelligence, vol. 32. AAAI Press, Hilton New Orleans Riverside, New Orleans, Louisiana, USA (2018)
21. Liu, M., Tu, Z., Wang, Z., Xu, X.: LTP: a new active learning strategy for BERT-CRF based named entity recognition. arXiv:2001.02524 (2020)
22. Liu, Y., Zhang, Y., Che, W., Liu, T., Wu, F.: Domain adaptation for CRF-based Chinese word segmentation using free annotations. In: Proceedings of the 2014 Conference on Empirical Methods in Natural Language Processing, pp. 864–874. ACL, Doha, Qatar (2014)
23. Ma, X., Hovy, E.: End-to-end sequence labeling via bi-directional LSTM-CNNs-CRF. In: Proceedings of the 54th Annual Meeting of the Association for Computational Linguistics, pp. 1064–1074. Association for Computational Linguistics, Berlin, Germany (2016)
24. Nadeau, D., Sekine, S.: A survey of named entity recognition and classification. Lingvisticae Investigationes **30**(24), 3–26 (2007)
25. Nadeau, D., Turney, P.D., Matwin, S.: Unsupervised named-entity recognition: generating gazetteers and resolving ambiguity. In: Lamontagne, L., Marchand, M. (eds.) AI 2006. LNCS (LNAI), vol. 4013, pp. 266–277. Springer, Heidelberg (2006). https://doi.org/10.1007/11766247_23
26. Omran, M.G.H., Engelbrecht, A.P., Salman, A.A.: Particle swarm optimization for pattern recognition and image processing. In: Abraham, A., Grosan, C., Ramos, V. (eds.) Swarm Intelligence in Data Mining. Studies in Computational Intelligence, vol. 34. Springer, Heidelberg (2006). https://doi.org/10.1007/978-3-540-34956-3_6
27. Qu, L., Ferraro, G., Zhou, L., Hou, W., Baldwin, T.: Named entity recognition for novel types by transfer learning. In: Proceedings of the Conference on Empirical Methods in Natural Language Processing, pp. 899–905. The Association for Computational Linguistics, Texas, USA (2016)
28. Saha, S.K., Sarkar, S., Mitra, P.: Feature selection techniques for maximum entropy based biomedical named entity recognition. J. Biomed. Inform. **42**(5), 905–911 (2009)

29. Vaswani, A., et al.: Attention is all you need. In: Proceedings of the 31st Annual Conference on Neural Information Processing Systems, pp. 5999–6009. Neural information processing systems foundation, Long Beach, CA, USA (2017)

30. Wang, Q., Iwaihara, M.: Deep neural architectures for joint named entity recognition and disambiguation. In: Proceedings of the IEEE International Conference on Big Data and Smart Computing, pp. 1–4. IEEE, Kyoto, Japan (2019)

31. Wang, X., et al.: Cross-type biomedical named entity recognition with deep multi-task learning. Bioinformatics 35(10), 1745–1752 (2019)

32. Xie, R., Liu, Z., Jia, J., Luan, H., Sun, M.: Representation learning of knowledge graphs with entity descriptions. In: Proceedings of the Thirtieth AAAI Conference on Artificial Intelligence, vol. 30, pp. 2659–2665. AAAI Press, Phoenix, Arizona USA (2016)

33. Zhang, D., et al.: Improving distantly-supervised named entity recognition for traditional Chinese medicine text via a novel back-labeling approach. IEEE Access 8, 145413–145421 (2020)

34. Zhang, S., Elhadad, N.: Unsupervised biomedical named entity recognition: experiments with clinical and biological texts. J. Biomed. Inform. 46(6), 1088–1098 (2013)

35. Zhang, W., Jiang, S., Zhao, S., Hou, K., Liu, Y., Zhang, L.: A BERT-BILSTM-CRF model for Chinese electronic medical records named entity recognition. In: Proceedings of the 12th International Conference on Intelligent Computation Technology and Automation, pp. 166–169. IEEE, Xiangtan, China (2019)

36. Zhao, Z., et al.: ML-CNN: a novel deep learning based disease named entity recognition architecture. In: Proceedings of the IEEE International Conference on Bioinformatics and Biomedicine, pp. 794–794. IEEE, Shenzhen, China (2016)

37. Zhou, H., Sun, G., Fu, S., Liu, J., Zhou, X., Zhou, J.: A big data mining approach of PSO-based BP neural network for financial risk management with IoT. IEEE Access 7, 154035–154043 (2019)

38. Žukov-Gregorič, A., Bachrach, Y., Coope, S.: Named entity recognition with parallel recurrent neural networks. In: Proceedings of the 56th Annual Meeting of the Association for Computational Linguistics, pp. 69–74. Association for Computational Linguistics, Melbourne, Australia (2018)

A Safe Topological Waypoints Searching-Based Conservative Adaptive Motion Planner in Unknown Cluttered Environment

Jiachi Xu[1], Jiefu Tan[1], Chao Xue[2], Yaqianwen Su[2,3], Xionghui He[1], and Yongjun Zhang[2(✉)]

[1] College of Computer, National University of Defense Technology, Changsha 410073, China
jcxu@nudt.edu.cn
[2] Artificial Intelligence Research Center (AIRC), National Innovation Institute of Defense Technology (NIIDT), Beijing 100071, China
yjzhang@nudt.edu.cn
[3] Tianjin Artificial Intelligence Innovation Center, Tianjing 300457, China

Abstract. Autonomous navigation of unmanned aerial vehicles (UAVs) in unknown and complex environments is still a challenge. Because the environment is partially observable to the drone, it is hard to consider trajectory safety and exploration efficiency simultaneously in autonomous navigation. In this paper, we present a motion planning method composed of a geometrically topological waypoints searching method and an adaptive trajectory replanning framework, which improves trajectory safety without sacrificing navigation efficiency. Our waypoint searching approach considers the safety distance and reduces pathfinding's search space by extracting some feasible path points on both sides of the obstacle. And this is based on the ESDF gradient and geometry information of a given obstacle. Besides, the found waypoints keep a safe distance from the obstacles, making the method work well in a scene that contains large obstacles. Based on the waypoint searching method, we proposed an adaptive trajectory replanning framework to improve trajectory safety and navigation efficiency further. The replanning procedure is event-triggered. When the planned trajectory is too close to an obstacle according to our safe condition, the trajectory will be re-planned. The proposed method is tested extensively in various simulation environments. Results show that the trajectory safety of our method is improved by 27.8%, and the computing time for replanning is reduced by 90.8% compared to the state-of-the-art method.

Keywords: Autonomous systems · Unmanned aerial vehicle · Motion planning

H. Gao and X. Wang (Eds.): CollaborateCom 2021, LNICST 407, pp. 206–224, 2021.
https://doi.org/10.1007/978-3-030-92638-0_13

1   Introduction

Recently, unmanned aerial vehicles (UAVs) have been widely used in many practical applications such as flying film, search-and-rescue, autonomous inspection. The flexible feature and small size allow them to carry out missions in dangerous or unfavorable areas for humans. In these application scenarios, environmental information is usually unknown and complex. The drones need to frequently re-plan safe and smooth trajectories to pass by unpredicted obstacles, and the motion planning module plays a vitally important role in an autonomous navigation system.

The motion planning module can be decomposed into front-end pathfinding and back-end trajectory optimization [5,13]. The pathfinding part is responsible for searching an obstacle-free path in the low-dimensional discrete space. After that, the path is time parameterized to an executable trajectory in high-dimensional continuous space by the trajectory optimization part. There are many classic methods can generate a high-quality trajectory in seconds [1–4,11,12,15].

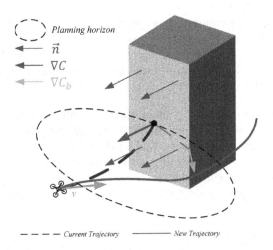

Fig. 1. Illustration of topological waypoints searching. When an impending collision is detected on the current trajectory of the UAV, a new safe trajectory located in the planning horizon is generated.

Plenty of above works are based on optimistic assumptions and use standard pathfinding algorithms, which will bring about the trajectory safety problem. As is well-known, the onboard sensor has a limited field-of-view (FOV) and can only gain information about the nearby environment. In an optimistic motion planning system, the unknown environment is treated as collision-free. This speeds up the trajectory optimization process but may not guarantee the safety of the planned trajectory. On the other hand, the standard pathfinding algorithms, such as A* and RRT*, search for the shortest optimal path. However, the points on this path are close to obstacles, making the optimized trajectory low safety clearance. Besides, when there are large obstacles in the environment, such methods usually crash and cannot navigate to the target.

In this paper, we proposed a safe motion planning method composed of a geometrically topological waypoints searching method and an adaptive conservative trajectory replanning strategy, which improves trajectory safety and navigation efficiency (displayed in Fig. 1). To guarantee the safety of UAVs, we treat the environment in a conservative way. The unknown environment is regarded as obstacles occupied, and we only allow motions in known-free space. Firstly, instead of using the standard pathfinding algorithm, we propose to combine the Euclidean signed distance field (ESDF) gradient and geometric information of obstacles to search for feasible topological points, which can significantly reduce the search space and improve the exploration efficiency. Secondly, we generate polynomial trajectories from the current state of the UAV to each found topological point parallelly. After that, the one with the least transfer cost is selected as the new global guiding trajectory. Finally, the part of the new trajectory located in known-free space is reparameterized to a smooth, safe, and dynamically feasible B-spline trajectory.

We conduct a lot of comparison experiments in the simulation environment to verify the performance of our proposed motion planning method, and the results show that the trajectory safety and replanning cost of our method is significantly better than the state-of-the-art method. The contributions of this paper are summarized as follows:

– A fast and safe geometrically topological waypoints searching method is proposed to improve the efficiency of searching safe waypoint by combining the geometric properties of obstacles and ESDF map to reduce the search space.
– An adaptive trajectory replanning method based on the conservative estimation is proposed to reduce the computation cost for replanning and further guarantee the trajectory's safety.

2   Related Works

2.1   Standard Pathfinding Algorithm

Pathfinding is the front-end part of the motion planning module, aiming at finding an obstacle-free geometric path in low-dimensional discrete space. The standard pathfinding algorithms can be divided into sampling-based and searching-based. For sampling-based pathfinding algorithms, one of the most representative methods is Rapidly-Exploring Random Tree (RRT) [8]. RRT* [7] is an asymptotically optimal sampling-based method. The solution found by RRT* will converge to the global optimality as the samples increase. However, this method requires prior knowledge of the global map. For searching-based algorithms which usually convert the pathfinding to graph searching problem, the A* [6] is the most widely used method. Many works use standard A* or the derivative of A* algorithms to search for a safe path to bypass the new-emerged obstacles in case of collision. [1] initializes an obstacle-free flight corridor by A* algorithm and then generated a feasible trajectory within the flight corridor through hard-based optimization method. [20] adopts the hybrid A* algorithm to find a rough time-parameterized path and optimizes it to a refined trajectory in the back-end.

However, the limited sensor FOVs make the environment locally observable, and the path obtained by front-end methods may not be globally optimal. To ensure the safety of the trajectory, frequent search is required, which increases the computational overhead.

2.2 Trajectory Replanning

Local trajectory planning is a mechanism to generate a new safe trajectory when the current trajectory collides with an unpredicted obstacle. Existing methods can be categorized into optimistic and conservative methods. Plenty of methods are based on the optimistic assumption. PGO [19], and TGK-Planner [18] initialize a global trajectory that does not consider collisions as a guideline, and then get the position where the global trajectory goes in and out of obstacles. After that, a new local trajectory that guides the drone to bypass the obstacle is generated. Interest in using B-spline to represent the trajectory was revived by [17], which utilizes the local modification scheme of B-spline curve to achieve real-time local trajectory re-planning.

Another category is conservative local trajectory planning methods, which consider the unknown space as obstacle occupied. [9,10] discretizes the control space and only allows the motion primitives in known-free space. FASTER [16] proposes a local planner to generate a committed trajectory in both known-free and unknown space and a safe back-up trajectory in known-free space. Nevertheless, the former does slow control space discretization and may cause infeasibility, while the latter decomposes the free space to a set of overleaping polyhedral, which is computationally expensive.

Optimistic assumption-based methods simplify the replanning process and improve the chance of reaching target. However, it may not ensure the safety of trajectory, especially in a scene with large obstacles. In contrast, conservative planning methods often require tremendous computation to ensure the trajectory's safety, leading to a decrease in navigation efficiency.

3   Geometrically Topological Waypoints Searching

The standard pathfinding methods search for the shortest optimal path in a large space, which is inefficient. Since the environment is only locally observable, the shortest path is not necessarily optimal. Besides, points on the shortest path are usually too close to the obstacle, which makes the generated trajectory a low clearance and safety, especially in scenarios with large obstacles. We proposed a geometrically topological waypoints searching method to extract some feasible path points on both sides of the obstacle, which considers the safety distance and reduces searching space.

3.1   Topological Points Searching

Algorithm 1. Topological points searching

1: **function** GETTOPOPOINT(cur_{traj})
2:     $P_{in} \leftarrow$ FINDCOLLISION(cur_{traj})
3:     Let($\nabla c, \vec{n}$) be the ESDF gradient
4:          and normal vector in P_{in}
5:     **if** $\nabla c \parallel \vec{n}$ **then**
6:          $P_{topo} \leftarrow$ FINDCORNERPTS($P_{in}, \nabla c$)
7:     **else**
8:          $P_{topo} \leftarrow grad \times d_{thr}$
9:     **if** no topoPoint were found before **then**
10:         $P_{topo} \leftarrow$ PUSHAWAYFROMOBS($P_{in}, \nabla c, d_{thr}$)
11:     **return** P_{topo}
12: **function** FINDCOLLISION(cur_{traj})
13:     **for** P_c inside the planning horizon **do**
14:         Let $safe$ be whether P_c in the obstacle
15:         **if** $last_{safe}$ and $!safe$ **then**
16:             $P_{in} \leftarrow P_c$
17:             **return** P_{in}
18: **function** FINDCORNERPTS($P_{in}, \nabla c$)
19:     Let $\vec{d}$ be the vectors perpendicular to ∇c
20:          and pointing to the sides of obstacle
21:     topoPoint $\leftarrow$ RAYTRACING($P_{in}, \vec{d}$)
22: **function** PUSHAWAYFROMOBS($P_{in}, \nabla c, d_{thr}$)
23:     Let $\vec{d}$ be the vector perpendicular to ∇c
24:          and at an acute angel to d_{thr}
25:     $P_b \leftarrow$ RAYTRACING($P_{in}, \vec{d}$)
26:     $grad \leftarrow$ the ESDF gradient in P_b
27:     $P_{topo} \leftarrow grad \times d_{thr}$
28: **function** RAYTRACING(P_{in}, dir)
29:     scan from P_{in} in direction $\vec{d}$
30:     **if** ray touches the planning horizon boundary **then**
31:         **return** the intersection P_b
32:     **else**
33:         $P_s \leftarrow$ first point satisfying safe distance

---

Pseudocode implementing of the method is presented in Algorithm 1. We periodically check whether the local trajectory in the planning horizon ahead of the UAV collides with obstacles. If a collision is detected, the topological points searching process is triggered (line 1). Firstly, the intersection P_{in} between the trajectory and the obstacle surface is obtained (line 2). Then the algorithm calculates the Euclidean signed distance field (ESDF) gradient and the normal vector of the obstacle surface at P_{in} through the local ESDF map (line 3 to 4).

Once we get the gradient and normal vector, the search direction of the topological points is determined according to the relationship between the direction of the two vectors. The geometric relationship between the ESDF gradient and the normal vector at the collision point is as follows:

$$\xi = \|\nabla c \times \vec{n}\| \tag{1}$$

If the ESDF gradient and the normal vector are collinear, then $\xi = 0$, otherwise, $\xi \neq 0$. After calculating ξ, the search direction vector $\vec{d}$ can be calculated as:

$$\vec{d} = \begin{cases} \nabla c & \xi \neq 0 \\ \vec{v} + \frac{\langle -\nabla c, \vec{v} \rangle}{\|\nabla c\|} \cdot \nabla c & \xi = 0 \end{cases} \tag{2}$$

At this time, the search direction vector $\vec{d}$ is related to the UAV's motion property. We can simply rotate $\vec{d}$ by 180° to obtain the topological search direction $\vec{d'}$ with symmetric characteristics.

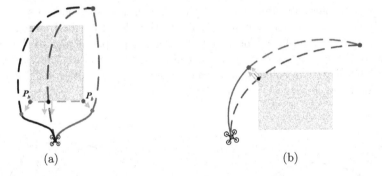

Fig. 2. The proposed waypoint searching method. (a) The ESDF gradient at the collision point (black point) is collinear with the normal vector. (b) Push the collision point away from the obstacle along the ESDF gradient at the collision point.

If the gradient is collinear with the normal vector, the search direction $\vec{d}$ is set perpendicular to both of them and points to the sides of the obstacle (line 6, illustrated as Fig. 2(a)). We do ray tracing from the collision point P_{in} along the search direction $\vec{d}$. The tracing stops when finding the corner point of obstacles or the projection exceeds the planning horizon, and the boundary point P_b is obtained. Then the topological waypoint can be calculated by Eq. 3, and the calculated point will be added to the topological waypoint set (line 24 to 28).

$$P_{topo} = P_b + \nabla c \cdot d_{thr} \tag{3}$$

where d_{thr} is the preset safety distance threshold, which make the generated trajectory maintain a certain buffer distance between obstacles. In actual mission scenarios, the UAV cannot accurately move along the trajectory. If the trajectory is too close to the obstacle, it may cause the UAV to hit the obstacle due to deviation. Another situation is that the trajectory collides with an obstacle's corner, as shown in Fig. 2(b). At this time, the ESDF gradient and the normal vector at the collision point are no longer collinear. And the search direction $\vec{d}$ is set to be collinear with the gradient direction to guide the drone away from obstacles (line 8).

If no topological points are found in the previous step, it means the discovered obstacle is too large, and the ray tracing exceeds the planning horizon of the UAV. By this time, we need to reset the search direction. An UAV's motion has high-order dynamic properties (velocity, acceleration, etc.), which cannot be mutated. Therefore, we tend to search in the direction that can reflect the motion properties of the UAV. The motion orientation is a critical property, which can be calculated by the coordinates of the trajectory points near the current position. After selecting a new search direction, the consistency of the search direction should be ensured. This is because the environment for the UAV is only partially observable. If the UAV is not specified to search along one direction all the time, it may fall into the "local optimal trap", spinning around in the same place. The search direction is perpendicular to the gradient at the collision point and is acute to the motion orientation. Similarly, we do ray tracing from the collision point along the search direction until getting P_b at the planning horizon boundary.

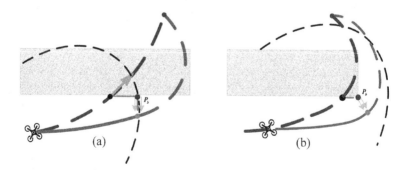

Fig. 3. A scenario with the large obstacle. (a) The obstacle exceeds the planning horizon, and the waypoint satisfying safe distance is obtained at the boundary. (b) Bypass the large obstacle by searching for a safe waypoint progressively.

This point is then pushed away from obstacles toward the ESDF gradient descent direction, after which the next waypoint is obtained. Repeat the above searching process until the drone bypasses the obstacle. (depicted in Fig. 3).

3.2 Optimal State Transition Waypoint

When there are multiple topological points, we need to choose one of them as the next key waypoint. Given the drone's high-order dynamic properties, the best choice may not be the point that guides a shorter path to the end. As shown in Fig. 4, the trajectory generated by the shorter path takes a sharp turn, which is dynamic infeasibility and leads to a high control cost. Actually, it is challenging to rely on geometrically topological points alone to make decisions due to the lack of high-order dynamic information and the UAV's true motion at the current moment. We propose generating multiple jerk-controlled polynomial trajectories from the UAV's current state to the points obtained by the geometrically topologic points finding method. After that, we choose the one with the minimum transition cost as the waypoint according to the control cost of the polynomial trajectories.

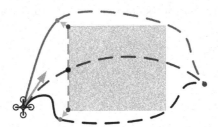

Fig. 4. Dynamic infeasibility led by the shortest path. The blue dash solid line is the current trajectory. The black line is the trajectory generated by a shorter path. The arrow is the velocity direction at the current moment, and the red line is the trajectory that conforms to the dynamic feasibility. (Color figure online)

For each topological point, we consider to generate a m-segment, n-th order polynomial trajectory through it to the target point, and the i-th segment is parameterized as:

$$p_i(t) = c_n t^n + c_{n-1} t^{n-1} + \cdots + c_1 t + c_0 \tag{4}$$

where $\{c_0, c_1, \cdots, c_n\}$ is the coefficient of the i-th segment.

To find the optimal state transition point, we need to calculate the control cost of each trajectory:

$$J = \sum_{k \in \{x,y,z\}} \sum_{i \in \{0,1,\cdots,m\}} \int_0^T [p_{k,i}^{(3)}(t)]^2 dt \tag{5}$$

where T is the total transition time of m trajectory segments. Then the one with the least control overhead J is chosen as the new global guiding trajectory and input to the back-end trajectory optimization. In the following section, we introduce the process of generating an executable B-spline local trajectory, which will make the drone flight safer and smoother.

4   Conservative Trajectory Replanning

In an optimistic trajectory replanning method, it is usually assumed that the generated local trajectory can bypass obstacles and rejoin the global trajectory. However, in an environment with dense or large obstacles, such a hypothesis may lead to unsafe trajectories and frequent replanning in a high probability. We propose an adaptive conservative trajectory replanning framework for ensuring trajectory safety and reducing replanning frequency. Moreover, we parameterize the trajectory by B-spline to improve the efficiency of trajectory optimization. The proposed method adopts a hierarchical structure of global trajectory guiding motion and local trajectory avoiding unpredicted obstacles. The monomial polynomial represents the global trajectory without considering whether it passes through obstacles. In contrast, the local trajectory is represented by a B-spline and is only located in the drone's currently known-free space.

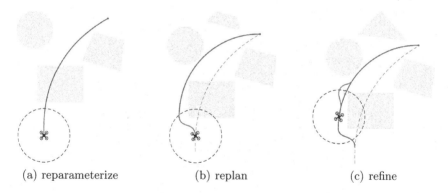

(a) reparameterize   (b) replan   (c) refine

Fig. 5. The trajectory replanning method. (a) A segment of the current global trajectory (blue solid line) within the planning horizon (black dotted circle) is reparameterized as a B-spline local trajectory (red solid line). (b) The replanning process is triggered when detecting a collision on the current trajectory. A new global guiding trajectory is generated by the geometrically topological waypoint searching. Meanwhile, a local trajectory is also generated to avoid the obstacle. (c) When the local trajectory is detected with low clearance, it is refined to a safer trajectory by the B-spline's local modification scheme. (Color figure online)

4.1 Adaptive Trajectory Replanning

The replanning module is responsible for adjusting the flight trajectory in time to avoid unpredicted obstacles and guarantee the drone's safety. In our method, the global guiding trajectory is represented as the monomial polynomial, which does not take the obstacles in the environment into account. Moreover, the UAV has a limited sensing range, making it necessary to replan the trajectory to avoid unpredicted obstacles frequently. We assume that the replanned local trajectory cannot return to the original global trajectory, which is reasonable for conservative considerations. Therefore, when detecting a collision between the current trajectory and an obstacle in the environment, a new globalguiding trajectory is generated through the geometrical topological waypoint searching. Afterward, the segment of the new global trajectory located in the planning horizon is optimized to a local trajectory parameterized by the B-spline curve (depicted in Fig. 5(b)). In addition, the current local trajectory may be too close to the newly discovered obstacle. In this case, we need to use the ESDF gradient information to push this part of the trajectory segment away from the obstacle. The obtained trajectory is called refined trajectory (displayed in Fig. 5(c)).

Algorithm 2. Conservative trajectory replanning

1: **function** TRAJREPLAN(cur_{traj})
2:     **if** a collision is detected on cur_{traj} **then**
3:         $P_{topo} \leftarrow$ GETTOPOPOINT(cur_{traj})
4:         update the global guiding trajectory gl_{traj}
5:         $local_{new} \leftarrow$ REPARAMLOCALTRAJ(gl_{traj})
6:     **else if** cur_{traj} is close to the obstacle **then**
7:         refine the cur_{traj} by the local modification
8:         scheme of B-spline
9:     **else**
10:         $local_{new} \leftarrow$ REPARAMLOCALTRAJ(gl_{traj})

4.2 B-Spline Trajectory Representation

The monomial polynomial is elementary in form and easy to calculate, but it is pure numerical formula and does not contain any spatial geometric information. Therefore, it is necessary to iteratively detect the extreme value in optimization to ensure that the trajectory meets the safety and dynamic constraints, which will bring about numerical instability [17] and increase the calculation time. On the contrary, the B-spline curve has appropriate geometric properties, which can be well combined with the ESDF gradient information to reduce the complexity of optimization.

We use B-spline to parameterize the local trajectory. Given $n + 1$ control points $\{P_0, P_1, \cdots, P_n\}$ and a knot vector $U = \{u_0, u_1, \cdots, u_m\}$, the B-spline of degree p can be uniquely defined as:

$$C(t) = \sum_{i=0}^{n} N_{i,p}(t) P_i \tag{6}$$

where $N_{i,p}(u)$ are the basis functions of B-spline which can be computed by De Boor-Cox recursive formula and t is the normalized parameter which can be computed according to $t = (u - u_i)/\Delta u$, for $u \in [u_i, u_{i+1}]$. In proposed method, the degree p is set to 3, and n, m, p must satisfy $m = n + p + 1$.

4.3 Problem Formulation

In our proposed method, to ensure the smoothness, safety and dynamic feasibility of the final executable trajectory, the local trajectory planning problem is formalized as an optimization problem of the cost function:

$$f_{total} = \lambda_s f_s + \lambda_c f_c + \lambda_d (f_v + f_a) \tag{7}$$

where f_s is the smoothness cost that is designed as an elastic band cost function; f_c is the collision cost that penalizes the point on trajectory which are less than the given threshold distance d to the nearest obstacles; f_v *and* f_a are dynamic feasibility cost that penalize infeasible high-order motion properties (velocity and acceleration).

The purpose of the smoothness cost function is to make the generated trajectory smoother so that the control overhead for UAV moving along the trajectory is as slight as possible. For the consideration of being able to adjust the time allocation in optimization, rather than the integral over squared snap or jerk, we adopt the elastic band cost function as [14]:

$$f_s = \sum_{i=p+1}^{n-p+1} \left\| (P_{i+1} - P_i) + (P_{i-1} - P_i) \right\|^2 \tag{8}$$

To ensure that the generated trajectory is far from the obstacle and meets the dynamic constraints, we use the piecewise quadratic functions to punish collisions and feasibility costs:

$$F_c(d) = \begin{cases} (d - d_{thr})^2 & d \leq d_{thr} \\ 0 & d > d_{thr} \end{cases} \tag{9}$$

$$F_d(v) = \begin{cases} (v^2 - v_{max}^2)^2 & v^2 \geq v_{max}^2 \\ 0 & v^2 < v_{max}^2 \end{cases} \tag{10}$$

5 Experiments

In this section, we present the experimental result of the proposed method. First, we evaluate the searching part with the baseline method that uses a standard front-end pathfinding algorithm. Second, we evaluate the proposed adaptive conservative trajectory planning approach with the state-of-the-art method.

5.1   Implementation Details

The motion planning method proposed in this letter is implemented in C++11 with a non-linear optimization solver NLopt. We built a $40 \times 20 \times 5$ m random forest environment with 100 deployed pillar and circle obstacles for simulation experimental (as is shown in Fig. 6). All computations are done in a 3.0 GHz Intel i7-9700 processor. In the topological points finding part, we set the safety distance threshold to obstacles $d_{thr} = 1.0$ m. For the trajectory optimization part, we set the $\lambda_s = 10$, $\lambda_c = 8, \lambda_d = 0.01$. Finally, to simulate the autonomous flight experiment of the UAV under an unknown environment, we set the sensing radius to be 6m, and the UAV maintains only a $6 \times 6 \times 3$ m local map.

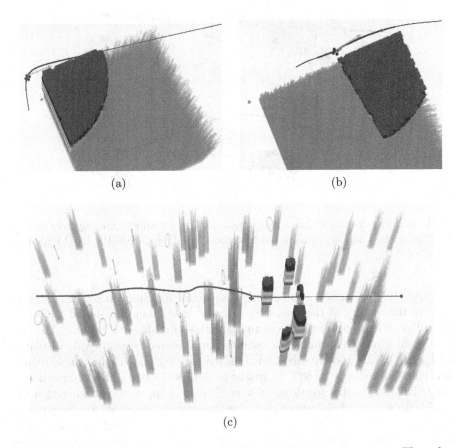

(a)   (b)

(c)

Fig. 6. Autonomous flight experiments in Rviz simulation environments. The colorful voxels represent the mapped obstacles in the UAV's FOV, while the grey voxels represent the unknown obstacles.

5.2 Topological Waypoints Searching

We compare the proposed geometrically topological waypoints searching method with PGO [19], which use the standard sampling-based pathfinding algorithms. Since the proposed approach returns a set of feasible topological points rather than a path, we mainly compare the searching time of each method. We conduct 10 random maps with different obstacle size and density and run both methods in each map 10 times from the same start point to endpoint.

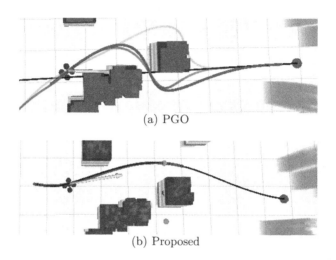

(a) PGO

(b) Proposed

Fig. 7. Benchmark comparison of the proposed method with PGO in waypoint searching. Our method find two topological waypoints in 1.12 ms, while the PGO find three in 6.92 ms.

PGO [19] proposes to find multiple safe and feasible topological paths to improve the quality of the final trajectory. It uses a sampling-based PRM-like algorithm and integrates time-consuming path shortening and pruning. For better visualization, we optimize the path to the displayed trajectory. As displayed in Fig. 7 and Table 1, our method finds a fewer topological path, but the searching time has been reduced by 80% compared to the PRM-like pathfinding method in PGO. This is expected for three reasons. First, our approach considers that the UAV lacks a view of the upper and lower fuselage areas, so it avoids exploring the path in the z-axis direction. Second, our method is based on conservative estimates of the environment and only searches for topological path points in the known-free space. Third, we reduce the search space of pathfinding by taking the geometric and gradient information of the obstacle into account and extracting several feasible waypoints on both sides of the obstacles.

Table 1. Comparisons of waypoint searching

Obstacle size	Method	Average time (ms)	Max time (ms)
<1 m	Proposed	**1.2**	**1.7**
	PGO	7.1	8.7
1–4 m	Proposed	**1.2**	**1.2**
	PGO	7.2	7.9
>4 m	Proposed	**1.3**	**1.8**
	PGO	–	–

5.3 Conservative Trajectory Replanning

Moreover, our method considers the safety distance when searching for way-points. The found waypoints keep a safe distance from the obstacle, which gives the drone sufficient reaction time and braking distance when encountering unpredicted obstacles. This is meaningful for drones navigating autonomously in environments containing large obstacles. As is shown in Table 1, our method is still stable when there are obstacles with a diameter of more than 4 m in the environment. However, the baseline method rarely successes, even if we increase the sampling range to 10 × 10 m and set the maximum number of iterations to 2000.

In the following, we compare the performance of our conservative trajectory planning framework with the baseline method. We set the maximum velocity and acceleration constraints are 3 m/s and 4 m/s^2, respectively. The UAV is initialized with a global trajectory generated by [15] and does not consider collision. For a fair comparison, we use the open-source implementation of PGO [19] and the default parameter settings. We check for the re-planning frequency and time, as well as the safety and quality of trajectories generated by different methods.

Re-planning Frequency and Time: Our proposed trajectory replanning method is adaptive and event-triggered. When an unsafe event in the current trajectory is detected, such as collisions or being too close to an obstacle according to our safe condition, the trajectory will be re-planned. We compare the replanning frequency and average planning time in random maps with different obstacle densities. As shown in Table 2, the replanning frequency of the proposed strategy is significantly less compared to the baseline method, no matter in high-density or low-density environments, and it has a considerable average planning time. Our method is based on the conservative estimation of the environment and only generates a new local trajectory in known-free space, which can naturally ensure trajectory safety. In contrast, the approach based on optimistic assumptions requires frequent replanning to ensure safety.

Safety: For autonomous navigation in the unknown and complex environment, we hope that the drone can always maintain a safe distance from the surrounding

Table 2. Comparisons of the trajectory planning.

Obstacle density and size	Method	Replan number	Average replan time (ms)
High and Small	Proposed	**5.6**	**11.2**
	PGO	28.5	13.4
Medium	Proposed	**3.5**	**9**
	PGO	69.1	9.3
Low and Large	Proposed	**5.0**	**5.1**
	PGO	–	–

obstacles. To evaluate the safety performance of the generated trajectory, we propose a new evaluation indicator: the length of the trajectory segment on which the distance to obstacles is less than the given safety threshold. The safe distance threshold is set as the braking distance that the drone decelerates from the maximum speed to stop state using the maximum acceleration and can be calculated by:

$$d_{safe} = \frac{V_{max}^2}{2A_{max}} \tag{11}$$

If the distance between the UAV and obstacles in the environment is greater than the safety threshold d_{safe}, no matter how fast the UAV is when it observes an imminent danger of collision (less than the maximum speed of the UAV), it can successfully stop in front of the obstacle without hitting the obstacle. Conversely, if the distance between the UAV and the obstacle is less than the safety threshold d_{safe}, the UAV may hit the obstacle due to the long braking distance. The more segments on a trajectory whose distance to the obstacle in the environment is greater than the safety threshold, the smaller the probability of collision when the UAV flying along such trajectory, that is, the safer the trajectory. Therefore, our proposed trajectory safety evaluation indicator is reasonable and feasible.

According to the parameter setting, the safe distance in our simulation experiment is 1.15 m. As displayed in Fig. 8, our method always have a safer trajectory compared with the baseline. In the scene with large obstacles, only 18.86% of the trajectory segments in our method are less than the safe distance, while the unsafe trajectory segments in baseline method account for 34.16% (depicted in Fig. 8(c)). In other words, the safety of our trajectory has improved by 44.8%. Furthermore, when the diameter of the obstacle in the environment is greater than 10 m, our method can navigate to the target point while maintaining an absolute safe distance between the UAV and the obstacle, while the baseline method cannot complete the autonomous navigation task (as is shown in Fig. 8(d)). With the increase of obstacle density, the proportion of unsafe trajectory segments also increases. However, our method is still better than the baseline method, and the safety is improved by 21.1% and 17.5% respectively (displayed in Fig. 8(b) and 8(a)).

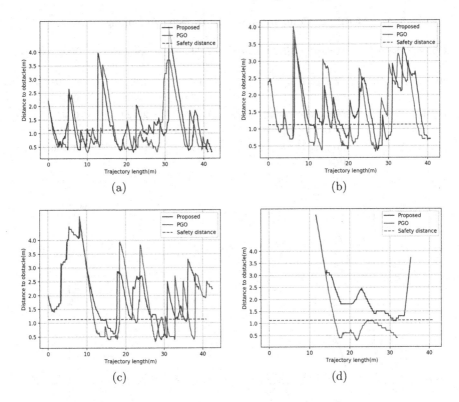

Fig. 8. Comparisons of the trajectory safety in different maps.

Trajectory Quality: The UAV is a motion system with high-order properties (velocity, acceleration, etc.). Therefore, the generated trajectory should satisfy the kinodynamic constraints. We evaluate the trajectory quality by comparing the flight time, flight distance, and the average flight speed. As is shown in Table 3, the proposed method does not perform as well as the baseline method in flight distance and the variance of velocity. This can be explained that the drone in our method tends to take long detours for guaranteeing the safety due to the conservative consideration. However, our method outperforms the baseline method in aspects of flight time, and average flight speed, especially in an environment containing obstacles whose diameter is more than $4m$. For the partially observable environment, the baseline method, which adopts a standard pathfinding algorithm and optimistic assumption, may fall into the local optimal trap when encountering a large obstacle. In contrast, the drone can maintain high speed when flying along the trajectory generated by our method, even in the environment containing large obstacles (displayed in Fig. 9).

Table 3. Comparisons of the trajectory planning.

Obstacle density and size	Method	Filght time(s)	Flight distance(m)	Average speed(m/s)	Var. velocity
High and Small	Proposed	**21.467**	41.935	**1.938**	0.797
	PGO	21.833	**35.334**	1.613	**0.654**
Medium	Proposed	**18.74**	39.843	**2.124**	0.859
	PGO	22.302	**34.113**	1.512	**0.736**
Low and Large	Proposed	**13.454**	**25.347**	1.86	**0.866**
	PGO	–	–	–	–

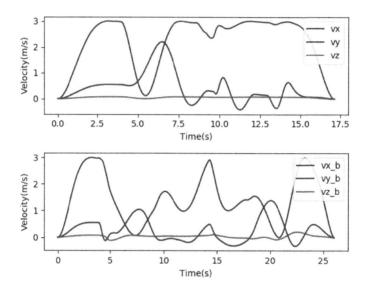

Fig. 9. Velocity curve of simulating flight in environment with large obstacles. The top half is the velocity curve of our method, and the bottom half is the baseline method.

5.4   Comparisons of Planning Efficiency

An efficient trajectory planning method should reduce the computational cost of replanning while ensuring the safety of the trajectory. We propose to use the calculation time of the drone for replanning to evaluate the overall efficiency of the motion planning system, and it can be computed by:

$$E(t) = E(n)E(t_r) \qquad (12)$$

where t is the total computing time for replanning, n is the replanning frequency, and t_r is the replanning time.

Replanning time includes the time for waypoint searching, and the quality of found waypoints can influence the replanning frequency. In our proposed method, the front-end geometrically topological waypoint searching method considers the safe distance and finds a safe enough waypoint rather than the shortest path, which is close to the obstacle. This allows the drone to observes more and plan a long safe trajectory. Thereby, the replanning frequency is decreased. For fairness, we only compare the planning efficiency of two methods in scenarios where the baseline method can work. As shown in Table 2, the expected planning time of our method in different environment can be computed by Eq. 12 as 47.11 ms, while 512.27 ms in the baseline method.

6   Conclusions

In this paper, we present a safe and efficient motion planning method based on conservative estimation for autonomous navigation. The geometrically topological waypoints searching and adaptive trajectory re-planning are devised to improving trajectory safety without sacrificing navigation efficiency. Extensive benchmark comparisons in the simulation environment are conducted to validate the performance of our method. The results show that the trajectory safety of our method is improved by 27.8%, and the replanning frequency is significantly reduced, while the average replanning time is not increased. Currently, this method does not consider active environmental perception and is only suitable for quadrotors. In the future, we will introduce the active planning of yaw angle. Besides, we will extend this method to adapt to other types of UAVs, such as fixed-wing.

Acknowledgment. This work was supported by the National Key Research and Development Program of China under Grant No.2017YFB1001901.

References

1. Chen, J., Liu, T., Shen, S.: Online generation of collision-free trajectories for quadrotor flight in unknown cluttered environments. In: 2016 IEEE International Conference on Robotics and Automation (ICRA), pp. 1476–1483. IEEE (2016)
2. Ding, W., Gao, W., Wang, K., Shen, S.: An efficient B-spline-based Kinodynamic replanning framework for quadrotors. IEEE Trans. Rob. **35**(6), 1287–1306 (2019)
3. Gao, F., Lin, Y., Shen, S.: Gradient-based online safe trajectory generation for quadrotor flight in complex environments. In: 2017 IEEE/RSJ International Conference on Intelligent Robots and Systems (IROS), pp. 3681–3688. IEEE (2017)
4. Gao, F., Shen, S.: Online quadrotor trajectory generation and autonomous navigation on point clouds. In: 2016 IEEE International Symposium on Safety, Security, and Rescue Robotics (SSRR), pp. 139–146. IEEE (2016)
5. Gao, F., Wu, W., Lin, Y., Shen, S.: Online safe trajectory generation for quadrotors using fast marching method and Bernstein basis polynomial. In: 2018 IEEE International Conference on Robotics and Automation (ICRA), pp. 344–351. IEEE (2018)
6. Hart, P.E., Nilsson, N.J., Raphael, B.: A formal basis for the heuristic determination of minimum cost paths. IEEE Trans. Syst. Sci. Cybern. **4**(2), 100–107 (1968)
7. Karaman, S., Frazzoli, E.: Sampling-based algorithms for optimal motion planning. Int. J. Robot. Res. **30**(7), 846–894 (2011)

8. LaValle, S.M., Kuffner, J.J.: Rapidly-exploring random trees: progress and prospects. Algorithmic Comput. Robot. New Dir. **5**, 293–308 (2001)

9. Liu, S., Atanasov, N., Mohta, K., Kumar, V.: Search-based motion planning for quadrotors using linear quadratic minimum time control. In: 2017 IEEE/RSJ International Conference on Intelligent Robots and Systems (IROS), pp. 2872–2879. IEEE (2017)

10. Liu, S., et al.: Planning dynamically feasible trajectories for quadrotors using safe flight corridors in 3-D complex environments. IEEE Robot. Autom. Lett. **2**(3), 1688–1695 (2017)

11. Mellinger, D., Kumar, V.: Minimum snap trajectory generation and control for quadrotors. In: 2011 IEEE International Conference on Robotics and Automation, pp. 2520–2525. IEEE (2011)

12. Oleynikova, H., Burri, M., Taylor, Z., Nieto, J., Siegwart, R., Galceran, E.: Continuous-time trajectory optimization for online UAV replanning. In: 2016 IEEE/RSJ International Conference on Intelligent Robots and Systems (IROS), pp. 5332–5339. IEEE (2016)

13. Quan, L., Han, L., Zhou, B., Shen, S., Gao, F.: Survey of UAV motion planning. IET Cyber-Systems Robot. **2**(1), 14–21 (2020)

14. Quinlan, S., Khatib, O.: Elastic bands: connecting path planning and control. In: Proceedings IEEE International Conference on Robotics and Automation, pp. 802–807. IEEE (1993)

15. Richter, C., Bry, A., Roy, N.: Polynomial trajectory planning for aggressive quadrotor flight in dense indoor environments. In: Inaba, M., Corke, P. (eds.) Robotics Research. STAR, vol. 114, pp. 649–666. Springer, Cham (2016). https://doi.org/10.1007/978-3-319-28872-7_37

16. Tordesillas, J., Lopez, B.T., How, J.P.: Faster: fast and safe trajectory planner for flights in unknown environments. In: 2019 IEEE/RSJ International Conference on Intelligent Robots and Systems (IROS), pp. 1934–1940. IEEE (2019)

17. Usenko, V., von Stumberg, L., Pangercic, A., Cremers, D.: Real-time trajectory replanning for MAVs using uniform B-splines and a 3D circular buffer. In: 2017 IEEE/RSJ International Conference on Intelligent Robots and Systems (IROS), pp. 215–222. IEEE (2017)

18. Ye, H., Zhou, X., Wang, Z., Xu, C., Chu, J., Gao, F.: TGK-planner: an efficient topology guided kinodynamic planner for autonomous quadrotors. IEEE Robot. Autom. Lett. **6**(2), 494–501 (2020)

19. Zhou, B., Gao, F., Pan, J., Shen, S.: Robust real-time UAV replanning using guided gradient-based optimization and topological paths. In: 2020 IEEE International Conference on Robotics and Automation (ICRA), pp. 1208–1214. IEEE (2020)

20. Zhou, B., Gao, F., Wang, L., Liu, C., Shen, S.: Robust and efficient quadrotor trajectory generation for fast autonomous flight. IEEE Robot. Autom. Lett. **4**(4), 3529–3536 (2019)

Multi-D3QN: A Multi-strategy Deep Reinforcement Learning for Service Composition in Cloud Manufacturing

Jun Zeng$^{(\boxtimes)}$, Juan Yao, Yang Yu, and Yingbo Wu

School of Big Data and Software Engineering, Chongqing University,
Chongqing, China
{zengjun,yaojuan,yuyang96,wyb}@cqu.edu.cn

Abstract. Service composition is an indispensable technology in the cloud manufacturing process to ensure the smooth execution of tasks. To implement effective and accurate service composition strategies, many researchers choose to use Meta-heuristics algorithms with strong optimization capabilities. However, as users' demand of personalized products increasing, dynamic service composition is essential. Meta-heuristics algorithms lack dynamic adaptability, so they are not suitable for solving complex and dynamic service composition problems. Deep Reinforcement Learning (DRL) algorithm is difficult to reach a stable state, when the hyper-parameters and rewards in the algorithm are not properly designed. To solve these problems, we propose a Multi-strategy Deep Reinforcement Learning (DRL) algorithm, named Multi-D3QN, which combines the basic DQN algorithm, the dueling architecture, the double estimator and the prioritized replay mechanism. Meanwhile, we add some strategies such as instant reward, the ε-greedy policy and a heuristic strategy to ensure better performance of the algorithm in dynamic environment. Experiments show that our proposed method not only adapt to the dynamic environment, but also obtain a better solution.

Keywords: Cloud manufacturing · Dynamic service composition · Quality of service · Deep reinforcement learning

1 Introduction

Today, the quality of life is constantly improving, and the demand of users for personalized products is also increasing [1]. However, due to resource constraints, the manufacturing resources and capabilities of a single enterprise have been unable to meet user's needs. In order to solve this problem, enterprises need to collaborate effectively by sharing manufacturing resources and capabilities [2]. A new service-oriented intelligent manufacturing model known as Cloud manufacturing (CMfg) has been proposed [3]. In the CMfg platform, the shared manufacturing resources and capabilities by enterprises are encapsulated into services and provided to users through the internet for selection. Service composition and optimization selection (SCOS) [4, 5] is considered to be the critical technology to realize the sharing function of resources and capabilities in the CMfg platform [6, 7]. Based on different composition structures,

H. Gao and X. Wang (Eds.): CollaborateCom 2021, LNICST 407, pp. 225–240, 2021.
https://doi.org/10.1007/978-3-030-92638-0_14

SCOS integrates various fine-grained services with different functions into coarse-grained services with comprehensive functions to deal with complex manufacturing tasks, and then meets the needs of users. Widespread attention has been received dealing with the quickly and effectively optimal combination strategy problem.

So far, many researchers have proposed a lot of heuristic methods for the SCOS problem [8, 9]. Although these methods have promoted the research work of SCOS, they lack adaptability to dynamic environments. For instance, when the environments change, the algorithms may need to be redesigned. Therefore, SCOS problems require new and innovative methods. Some researchers considered that Reinforcement Learning (RL) is adaptable to dynamic environments, and tried to use RL to solve the SCOS environment change problems [10–12]. Wang et al. [10] used Deep Reinforcement Learning (DRL) to solve the SCOS problems, in which the state set is divided into two state subsets, and behavior strategies are selected in different types of states. These methods can re-adjust the system to reach a stable state through adaptability when the environment changes suddenly. And there is still a key issue that needs to be addressed: If the hyper-parameters and rewards in the algorithm are not properly designed, it is difficult to return to a stable state. Therefore, some strategies need to be adopted to avoid this problem.

To solve the problems above, a Multi-strategy DRL algorithm, named Multi-D3QN, that combines the basic DQN algorithm, the dueling architecture, the double estimator and the prioritized replay mechanism is proposed. Specifically, the dueling architecture can improve the convergence speed of the algorithm. The double estimator can overcome the estimation problem, and the Prioritized replay mechanism can accelerate the learning speed of the algorithm. Moreover, three different strategies are added to the model, which leads the algorithm to return to a stable state and get better solutions in a dynamic environment. Based on Multi-D3QN, the dynamic SCOS problem in cloud manufacturing is studied. Experimental results reveal that the Multi-D3QN method can achieve better performance in cases with hyper-parameters and rewards that are inappropriate.

In summary, our contributions in this paper are as follows:

- Aiming at the problem that the meta-heuristic methods have complex design flow in the dynamic environment, we proposed Multi-D3QN, which combines DQN, the dueling architecture, the double estimator and the prioritized replay mechanism, and generates an algorithm with a better solution in the dynamic environment by integrating their advantages.
- Aiming at the shortcoming that DRL is difficult to return to a stable state when the service is unavailable, due to the values of the parameters are not appropriate. We developed a strategy, which according to heuristic rules, to shield unavailable services.
- To get the best performance of our algorithm, we compared different strategies in experiments to determine the final algorithm.

The remainder of this paper is organized as follows: Sect. 2 introduced the related work. The problem description and MDP-based CMfg service composition are presented in Sect. 3. The detailed description of framework is given in Sect. 4. In Sect. 5, the comparative experiment and analysis are performed to verify the proposed approach. Finally, the conclusion is provided in Sect. 6.

2 Related Work

As a key issue for sharing and collaborating of manufacturing resources and capabilities among enterprises on the CMfg platform, SCOS is gaining ever-increasing significance. In previous work, there have been many studies on SCOS.

2.1 Meta-heuristics-based Service Composition

Cloud manufacturing SCOS problem is an NP-hard problem, and it is difficult to find the optimal solution in a limited time. Many researchers attention to the strong optimization ability of the Meta-heuristics algorithms, which can find the optimal or nearly optimal solution [7]. Yang et al. [5] proposed an improved gray wolf optimizer algorithm (IGWO) by improving the control factor and location update method in the gray wolf optimizer algorithm, which improved the search ability of the algorithm and ensured the accuracy of the scheme. On this basis, they also proposed an enhanced gray wolf optimization algorithm (EMOGWO) [4] for multi-objective SCOS problems, which made three improvements to the basic multi-objective GWO and overcame the shortcoming of local optimum and less diversity in multi-objective CMfg SCOS problems. In Zhou et al. [13], according to the high flexibility and complexity characteristics of CMfg, a hybrid artificial colony method (HABC) is designed to solve the large-scale service composition solution space problem by introducing archimedean copula estimation of distribution algorithm (ACEDA) probability model and the chaos operators of global best-guided artificial bee colony, which has the advantages of high performance and high stability. Fazeli et al. [14] combined genetic algorithm (GA), particle swarm optimization (POS) and social spider algorithm (SSO), an ensemble optimization approach (EOA) is proposed. In this approach, the algorithm combination process is regarded as a black box and used a new operator to summarize the results. The algorithm has the characteristics of flexible expansion and easy composition, which improved the QoS value of the service composition.

2.2 RL/DRL-Based Service Composition

Lei et al. [15] proposed a reinforcement learning of Time-based Learning method, named TL, which can effectively control exploration and exploitation, so the service composition success rate is improved. Li et al. [12] based on Q-Learning algorithm, a multi-task oriented algorithm named multi-Q learning is proposed to realize subtask-assistance strategy for large-scale and adaptive service composition. It has faster learning speed and convergence compared with other methods. In Wang et al. [16] the model combines on-policy reinforcement learning and game theory, a new model for large-scale and adaptive service composition based on multi-agent reinforcement learning is proposed, which can make the algorithm highly adapt to the dynamic environment, and multi-agent cooperation can quickly find the optimal solution. In Wang et al. [17] the service composition process is modeled as a Markov Decision Process (MDP) and trained with the LSTM-based deep Q-network method to find the optimal service composition. Liang et al. [11] established a cloud manufacturing service composition model based on deep reinforcement learning, the service composition process is modeled as a Markov Decision Process (MDP), and the reward function with the consideration of logistics is designed.

So far, the existing studies have not achieved satisfactory results whether using meta-heuristics algorithms or using reinforcement learning methods to solve SCOS problems. Especially when the hyper-parameters and rewards design in reinforcement learning are inappropriate, it is difficult to reach a stable state again when the environment changes. We are trying to find some strategies to change this situation. Therefore, a Multi-strategy DRL algorithm is developed in this paper.

3   Service Composition Problem Description and MDP-Based CMfg Service Composition

3.1   Problem Description

The process of SCOS can be divided into the following steps [5]: (1) Task decomposition, (2) Service discovery and matching, (3) Service composition and optimization selection. The detailed description of the SCOS process can be seen in the existing study [18]. This paper focuses mainly on the third step. In the process of performing tasks, due to the influence of many factors such as the change of tasks or users' requirements and unavailability services, the service composition process is highly dynamic. It is necessary to study these factors. The impacts of service unavailability are studied in this paper. In cloud manufacturing, there are many reasons for service unavailability, such as machine failures, enterprise departure, and service shutdown, etc. Hence, when there are unavailable services in the service chains, the SCOS algorithms need to quickly and effectively find the optimal service again from the service sets to replace the unavailable service, which can ensure the smooth completion of the task. As shown in Fig. 1.

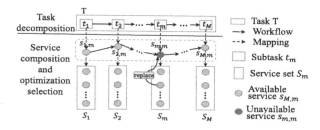

Fig. 1. Dynamic service composition flowchart

3.2   MDP-Based CMfg Service Composition

In the cloud manufacturing environment, a task T is usually decomposed into several subtasks t, $T = \{t_1, t_2, ..., t_i, ..., t_n\}$, where N is the number of subtasks of T, t_i is the i-th subtask of T. The service composition process for T can be modeled as a MDP.

State. In MDP an optimal(or near-optimal) service is selected for each subtask t_i, $i = 1$, $2, ..., N$. There are two states for t_i and as the service composition progresses, the states of the subtasks and the services will change. The detailed description of the states is comprehensively explained in the existing study [11].

Action. There is an action set for each t_i. An action corresponds the selection of a service from a service set for t_i, and the result of an action is that a service is selected. In the whole system, the number of action sets is equal to the number of service sets, and the size of the action set for each subtask is equal to the size of the service set corresponding to the subtask.

Reward Function. The reward function plays an important role in SCOS by guiding the DRL agent to find the optimal service composition solution. When a service is selected from the service set in the current state, we get a reward r from the environment after performing the action. Because the measurement standards and units of each QoS attribute are different. Before calculating the reward, it is necessary to normalize the QoS value of each indicator. The reward is calculated based on the normalized QoS values:

$$Q_i^+ = \begin{cases} \frac{q_i - q_{min}^i}{q_{max}^i - q_{min}^i}, & q_{min}^i \neq q_{max}^i \\ 1, & q_{min}^i = q_{max}^i \end{cases} \tag{1}$$

$$Q_i^- = \begin{cases} \frac{q_{max}^i - q_i}{q_{max}^i - q_{min}^i}, & q_{min}^i \neq q_{max}^i \\ 1, & q_{min}^i = q_{max}^i \end{cases} \tag{2}$$

In Eqs. (1) and (2) q_{min}^i and q_{max}^i indicate the minimum and maximum aggregated values of the i-th QoS attribute for all possible composition paths, q_i is the aggregated values of the i-th QoS attribute. The aggregation functions of QoS attributes are shown in [19]. For positive indices (Q_i^+), the bigger value of QoS is, the better quality is, like reliability, security and availability, and the others are just opposite (Q_i^-), such as time and cost. In this paper, a bigger value means the performance is better for all indices through normalization. The QoS value of the normalized attribute can be integrated into an overall QoS value through a simple weighting method [20].

4 Proposed Algorithm Framework

In this paper, we propose a Multi-strategy DRL algorithm (Multi-D3QN), which combines the basic DQN algorithm, the dueling architecture, the double estimator and the prioritized replay mechanism. Specifically, the dueling architecture can shield some actions that have little influence on the optimal value function, so that the algorithm can quickly obtain the optimal value function and improve the convergence speed of the algorithm. However, the actions found by the dueling architecture may have overestimation, which can be avoided by the double estimator. The prioritized replay mechanism is used to find the sample data effectively that needs to be learned, which can promote faster learning of the algorithm. In addition, a heuristic strategy is added in the algorithm to shield unavailable services to adapt to the dynamic environment. The overall framework of our method is shown in Fig. 2, and the specific operations are indicated in Algorithm 1. Then, we will introduce more details of the framework.

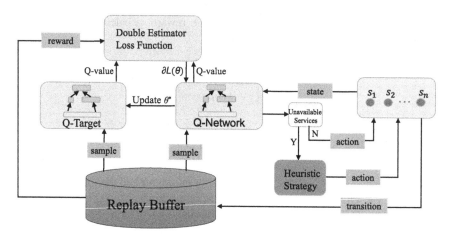

Fig. 2. Framework of the Multi-D3QN

Algorithm 1. Multi-D3QN Algorithm

Input: initial exploration and final exploration ε; learning rate α; mini-batch size b; sampling weights β; discounted rate γ.
Output: reward r.

    // Initialization
1: Initialize replay memory D with capacity N and initial priority $p_1=1$;
2: Initialize action-value function Q with Q-network parameters θ;
3: Initialize action-value function Q* with Q-target parameters θ^*;
4: **for** each episode **do**;
5:    **for** each t **do**;
        // The Dueling Architecture and The Strategy for Adaptability
7:       **if** services unavailability **then**
8:          Into The shielding algorithm:
9:          With probability ε select a random action a_t;
10:            **if** $a_t(o)<0$ **then**   *// $a_t(o)$ is the Qos value of the corresponding service*
11:              Shield unavailability services;
12:              Select a random action a_t;
13:            **end if**
14:          Otherwise select $a_t = \arg max_a\, Q(s_t, a, \theta)$;
15:            **if** $a_t(o)<0$ **then**
16:              Shield unavailability services;
17:              Select a random action a_t;
18:            **end if**
19:       **else**
20:          With probability ε select a random action a_t;
21:          Otherwise select $a_t = \arg max_a\, Q(s_t, a, \theta)$;
22:       **end if**
        // The Prioritized Replay Mechanism
23:       Execute action a_t, observe reward r_t and next state s_{t+1}, $s_t = s_{t+1}$;
24:       Store transition (s_t, a_t, r_t, s_{t+1}) in D with maximal priority $p_1 = max_{i<t}\, p_i$;
25:       Sample mini-batch of transition (s_j, a_j, r_j, s_{j+1}), for each sample $j\sim p(\mathrm{j}) = p_j/\sum_j p_i$;
26:       Compute importance-sampling weight $w_j = \left(N * p(\mathrm{j})\right)^{-\beta}/\max_i(w_i)$
        // The Double Estimator
27:       **if** episode terminates at step $j + 1$ **then**
28:          set $y_j = r_j$;
29:       **else**
30:          $y_j = r_j + \gamma Q(s_{t+1}, \arg max_a\, Q(s_{t+1}, a, \theta), \theta^*)$
31:       **end if**
32:       Update Q-network parameters θ with a loss function of $\frac{1}{b}\sum_{j=1}^b w_j(y_j - Q(s_t, a_t, \theta))^2$;
        // The Prioritized Replay Mechanism
33:       Compute TD-error $\delta_j = y_j - Q(s_t, a_t, \theta)$;
34:       Update transition priority $p_j \leftarrow |\delta_j|$;
35:       Every c steps reset $\theta^* \leftarrow \theta$;
36:      **end for**
37:    Continue to iterate until the convergence condition is satisfied
38: **end for**

4.1 DQN Algorithm

DQN, in addition to Q-Learning, is the basic algorithm in Reinforcement Learning (RL). It uses deep neural network to approximate a value function instead of Q-table in Q-Learning, which overcomes the shortcoming that Q-Learning can't deal with a large amount of data. In DQN, two deep neural networks are constructed: Q-network and Q-target. It uses Q-network to estimate the current value function, and Q-target to generate the target Q-value. During learning, DQN uses random sampling to extract samples from the Replay Buffer, then update the parameters in Q-network according to the loss function, and finally get the maximum future rewards [11]. The methods used in Sects. 4.2, 4.3, 4.4 and 4.5 are all improvements to improve the DQN framework.

4.2   The Dueling Architecture

The dueling architecture is an improvement of the deep learning network structure in DQN, so that the algorithm can learn something faster. The core idea is that the last layer of the network is generated with two quantities: the value of the state $V(s)$ and the advantage of actions in this state $A(s, a)$, i.e.

$$Q(s, a) = V(s) + A(s, a) \tag{3}$$

This means that $A(s, a)$ is a gain that implies how much Q-value exceeds the expected value when action a is selected [21]. Advantage $A(s, a)$ could be positive or negative. The division of the value and the advantage in the network architecture improves the stability and convergence speed of the algorithm.

4.3   The Double Estimator

The traditional RL such as DQN and Q-leaning use the single estimator to update parameters, which will lead to overestimation. This means that the algorithm will suffer a lot of negative effects. In order to solve this problem, Hasselt et al. [22] proposed a double estimation method. Its core idea can be briefly summarized as: In the learning phase, two different network parameters are used to estimate the value function, in form:

$$y_j = r_j + \gamma Q(s_{t+1}, argmax_a Q(s_{t+1}, a, \theta), \theta^*) \tag{4}$$

Where r_j is the j-th reward take from replay buffer D; s_{t+1} is the next state at iteration $t+1$. θ^* and θ represent the parameters of the Q-network and the Q-target, respectively. γ is discount rate.

The calculation formula of the loss function is as follows:

$$L(\theta) = \frac{1}{b} \sum_{j=1}^{b} w_j \left(y_j - Q(s_t, a_t, \theta) \right)^2 \tag{5}$$

where $Q(s_t, a_t, \theta)$ is the output of the Q-network, s_t, a_t represent the state and action at iteration t, respectively. b is sample mini-batch from replay buffer D, w_j is the sample weight.

4.4 The Prioritized Replay Mechanism

DQN uses a random sampling strategy to learn, that is, samples are randomly selected from the experience replay buffer, which ignores the importance of conversion. Some scholars have proposed priority methods to make experience playback more efficient [23]. The core idea is that RL agent can learn more efficiently from experiences. Specifically, more samples of experience with high expectations are measured by TD error.

$$\delta_j = y_j - Q(s_t, a_t, \theta) \tag{6}$$

Where y_j is the Q-value in the double estimator at iteration $t + 1$.

4.5 The Strategy for Adaptability

In this subsection, a heuristic strategy is developed for the dynamic SCOS problems. It is well-known that when an agent interacts with the environment, given a state, an agent possibly gets an action set, which has different values. In this paper, the value of an action is the QoS value of service from the service set.

According to the existing research [10, 11], when services are unavailability, the QoS value of the whole service chain will become smaller, so we give the following definition:

Unavailability service: In a state, when the QoS values of some actions become anomaly (according to many experiments we performed, in this paper, we have observed that the abnormal value of an action has a negative QoS value), it can be judged that the service corresponding to the action is an unavailability service.

If a service chain contains unavailability services, then the service chain will be greatly affected. Not only the overall QoS value is reduced, but also the execution of the task will be affected. However, for the most part, the DRL method to return to a stable state within a limited time is very hard, due to the fact that the appropriate values of hyper-parameters and rewards have not been found. Therefore, in order to ensure the smooth progress of the task, these unavailability services need to be shielded by heuristic strategies.

The heuristic strategy will be elaborated in this section. As the program starts, the average QoS value m_1 will be calculated. If the action values are less than zero, the services will be judged unavailable. At the same time, the average QoS value m_2 will also be calculated. When it comes to the condition that m_2 is less than m_1, which means the model is not adaptive to a stable state, the heuristic strategy will start. The pseudo code is as Algorithm 2.

Algorithm 2: The Shielding Algorithm
Input: action sets
Output: optimal action
1: **for** each episode **do**
2:   **for** each t **do**;
3:     Calculate the average QoS value m_1
4:     **if** the action values <0 **then**
5:       Calculate the average QoS value m_2
6:     **end if**
7:     **if** $m_2 < m_1$ after a period of time **then**
8:       Find out actions with QoS value less than zero
9:       Shield all actions with values less than zero
10:      Randomly select an action as the optimal action
11:    **end if**
12:    Continue to iterate until the convergence condition is satisfied
13: **end for**
14: **end for**

5 Experiments

We conduct the experiments to assess the proposed Multi-strategy Deep Reinforcement Learning algorithm (Multi-D3QN) on three aspects: effectiveness, adaptability and robustness. Experiment results obtained with Multi-D3QN are compared with those results with other three competitive methods DQN, dueling-DQN and double-DQN.

5.1 Experiment Setting

- **Dataset.** In the experiment, we mainly consider five QoS attributes, including reliability, security, availability, time and cost. Since there is no publicly available dataset for cloud manufacturing services, without loss of generality, all QoS attributes values are randomly generated between [0.7, 0.95] [13, 14]. Due to the QoS value of the data from the dataset calculated by Eqs. (1) and (2) are too small, the comparison of results between the algorithms is not obvious. Therefore, the weights of QoS attributes are equal to 1 instead of decimals which usually used. Besides, each task is decomposed into 30 subtasks, each subtask corresponds to 30 candidate services.

- **Network Structure.** The neural network for Multi-D3QN model has an input layer, a LSTM layer and two fully connected hidden layer with LSTM layer having 64 neurons and the other layers having 30 neurons. The hyper-parameters used for Multi-D3QN training are shown in Table 1.

Table 1. Hyper-parameters for the training of Multi-D3QN

Parameters	Value	Description
N	10000	The capacity of experience replay buffer
c	500	Target network update step
b	32	Mini-batch size
α	0.01	Initial learning rate used by Adam
lp	1000	Decay step used by exponential decay
lr	0.96	Decay rate used by exponential decay
γ	0.9	Discount factor
ε_{min}	0.01	Probability of initial exploration
ε_{end}	0.9	Probability of final exploration
β	0.4	Sampling weights

The ε-greedy policy is used with ε annealed linearly from 0.9 to 0.01

5.2 Result Analysis

(1) Learning Rate

Learning rate plays a very important role in algorithm performance. If the learning rate is too high, the model will not converge. However, if the learning rate is too low, the model will converge too slowly or fail to learn. So it is very important to choose a suitable learning rate. The experimental results are shown in Fig. 3. It can be observed that D3QN with $\alpha = 0.01$ performs best than that for $\alpha = 0.001$ and $\alpha = 0.1$, because the result of $\alpha = 0.01$ obtains a higher QoS value and a quicker convergence speed. Specifically, the D3QN algorithm with $\alpha = 0.01$ converged at about 46000th, but at about 50000th and 65000th, respectively, for $\alpha = 0.001$ and $\alpha = 0.1$; with $\alpha = 0.01$, the D3QN algorithm can achieve a higher QoS values than that for $\alpha = 0.1$ and $\alpha = 0.001$. It can also be seen that D3QN with $\alpha = 0.01$ and $\alpha = 0.001$ have almost the same the range of fluctuations, while $\alpha = 0.01$ has a higher Qos value. This is because the

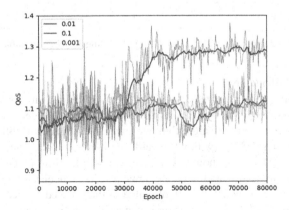

Fig. 3. Different learning rate for D3QN

learning rate is too small, which leads to the slower learning of the algorithm. However, the D3QN with $\alpha = 0.1$ the range of fluctuations is larger than the other two learning rates, which is because the large learning rate leads to the difficulty of model convergence. Therefore, $\alpha = 0.1$ is selected for the following experiments.

(2) Effectiveness and Efficiency

In order to verify the effectiveness of our proposed method. The D3QN is compared with DQN, dueling DQN and Double DQN. Experimental results are obtained with four different algorithms, as shown in Fig. 4. According to the results, there is little difference between the results of the algorithms in the initial stage, but with the number of iterations increasing, D3QN obtains a larger QoS value than DQN, dueling DQN and double DQN. For the convergence of the algorithms, DQN converges at the 55000th, and double DQN converges at around the 48000th. Dueling DQN and D3QN converge at around the 45000th and 46000th, respectively, which indicates that D3QN has the advantage of faster convergence speed of dueling DQN. Compared with other algorithms, D3QN not only has the advantage of faster convergence, but also can get better solutions. The reason is that the dueling architecture enables to boost the convergence of the algorithm faster, the double estimator can overcome the shortcomings of overestimation and the prioritized replay mechanism can improve the learning speed of the sample to promote faster learning of the algorithm.

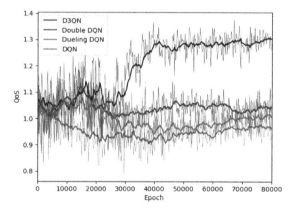

Fig. 4. Training curves for D3QN, DQN, dueling DQN and double DQN

(3) Influence of Strategies

To verify that our proposed algorithm is suitable for dynamic environments, we simulate a dynamic environment by randomly disabling the percentage of services. And to get the best performance of the algorithm, we study the influence of different strategies on the algorithm, i.e. D3QN (without reward, the ε-greedy policy and heuristic strategy), NS-D3QN (D3QN without the ε-greedy policy), Multi-D3QN (D3QN with reward, the ε-greedy policy and heuristic strategy). In particular, D3QN with reward means that the reward is equal to the QoS value of the selected service, after an action is executed. While D3QN without reward, it means that the reward is equal to zero.

These strategies start to change when the service is disabled. The detailed process is as follows: When the algorithm reaches a stable state, randomly disable 10% of the services at a certain episode, the episode is applied to the algorithm at 60000th episode, in this paper.

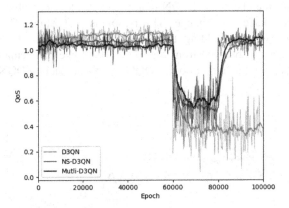

Fig. 5. The influence of different strategies

Figure 5 shows the experimental result. According to the results, the Multi-D3QN has the best results in this experiment. Similarly, NS-D3QN and D3QN provide the second and the worst results, respectively. Careful observation reveals that when the services are unavailable, the QoS values of the optimal solution are reduced. However, at 80000th, the Multi-D3QN and NS-D3QN return to a stable state, while this does not happen to the D3QN. This proves that unavailable services are shielded by the heuristic strategies in the Multi-D3QN and NS-D3QN, so that there are no unavailable services in the service compositions, thereby improving the QoS values. It can be observed that Multi-D3QN obtains a higher QoS value than NS-D3QN after 60000th, because the algorithm has a chance to jump out of the local optimal through the policy. In terms of reward, the algorithms with reward can find a higher solution than the algorithm without reward, the reason is that DRL can effectively adjust the parameters according to the real reward value. Through experiments, it can be concluded that Multi-D3QN with multiple strategies is better in terms of performance.

(4) Adaptability and Robustness
To verify the adaptability and robustness of the proposed algorithm, the Multi-D3QN is compared with other algorithms. In this experiment, the experiment setting is the same as 3. Figure 6 shows the experimental result of the Multi-D3QN, double DQN, DQN and dueling DQN, respectively. It can be observed that the DQN has the best QoS values when the environment is static (before 60000th episode). Multi-D3QN, double DQN, and dueling DQN get the second, third, and the worst QoS values, respectively. However, when the services are unavailable (between 60000th episode and 80000th episode). The Multi-D3QN has higher QoS values than other algorithms, this is because the reward strategy and the ε-greedy policy in the Multi-D3QN enable the

algorithm to find a better solution. The dueling DQN gets the worst QoS values during the whole process, which indicates that the dueling DQN has an overestimation problem. While, the double DQN obtains the second QoS values, due to the double estimator can overcome the overestimation problem. The QoS values of DQN reduces the most, which shows that the DQN is very unstable when the environment change. After a period of time, the Multi-D3QN returns to a stable state, while the other three algorithms do not have this change. The reason is that Multi-D3QN triggers the heuristic strategy, which shielding the unavailable services in the service chains. Furthermore, it can be observed from Fig. 6 that the range of fluctuations for Multi-D3QN is also smaller than that for double DQN, DQN and dueling DQN, which proves that our method is robust.

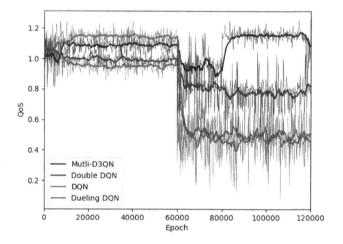

Fig. 6. Adaptability for Multi-D3QN, double DQN, DQN and dueling DQN

6 Conclusions

In this paper, we proposed the Multi-D3QN method by combining the basic DQN algorithm, the dueling architecture, the double estimator and the prioritized replay mechanism. Most importantly, some strategies, i.e. a heuristic strategy, instant reward and the ε-greedy policy, are added to our method to improve the performance of the algorithm. Specifically, the heuristic strategy can shield some unavailable services, and overcome the shortcomings of the algorithm that cannot be restored to a stable state due to the improper design of hyper-parameters and rewards. Instant reward allows DRL to effectively adjust parameters according to the real reward value, and the ε-greedy policy allows the algorithm to have a chance to jump out of the local optimum. The experiment shows that our proposed method not only has the advantage of strong adaptability in the dynamic environment, but also can find a better solution than other deep reinforcement learning such as DQN, dueling DQN and double DQN.

Acknowledgments. This work was supported in part by the National Key Research and Development Project under grant 2019YFB1706101, the Natural Science Foundation of Chongqing, China (No. cstc2020jcyj-msxmX0900).

References

1. Mourad, M.H., Nassehi, A., Schaefer, D., Newman, S.T.: Assessment of interoperability in cloud manufacturing. Robotics and Computer-Integrated Manufacturing 61, (2020)
2. Bouzary, H., Chen, F.F.: A classification-based approach for integrated service matching and composition in cloud manufacturing. Robotics and Computer-Integrated Manufacturing 66, (2020)
3. Zhang, L., et al.: Cloud manufacturing: a new manufacturing paradigm. Enterprise Information Systems **8**, 167–187 (2014)
4. Yang, Y., Yang, B., Wang, S., Jin, T., Li, S.: An enhanced multi-objective grey wolf optimizer for service composition in cloud manufacturing. Applied Soft Computing 87, (2020)
5. Yang, Y., Yang, B., Wang, S., Liu, W., Jin, T.: An Improved Grey Wolf Optimizer Algorithm for Energy-Aware Service Composition in Cloud Manufacturing. The International Journal of Advanced Manufacturing Technology **105**(7–8), 3079–3091 (2019). https://doi.org/10.1007/s00170-019-04449-9
6. Akbaripour, H., Houshmand, M., van Woensel, T., Mutlu, N.: Cloud manufacturing service selection optimization and scheduling with transportation considerations: mixed-integer programming models. The International Journal of Advanced Manufacturing Technology **95**(1–4), 43–70 (2017). https://doi.org/10.1007/s00170-017-1167-3
7. Liu, Y., Wang, L., Wang, X.V., Xu, X., Zhang, L.: Scheduling in cloud manufacturing: state-of-the-art and research challenges. Int. J. Prod. Res. **57**, 4854–4879 (2019)
8. Lartigau, J., Xu, X., Nie, L., Zhan, D.: Cloud manufacturing service composition based on QoS with geo-perspective transportation using an improved Artificial Bee Colony optimisation algorithm. Int. J. Prod. Res. **53**, 4380–4404 (2015)
9. Que, Y., Zhong, W., Chen, H., Chen, X., Ji, X.: Improved adaptive immune genetic algorithm for optimal QoS-aware service composition selection in cloud manufacturing. Int. J. Adv. Manuf. Technol. **96**(9–12), 4455–4465 (2018). https://doi.org/10.1007/s00170-018-1925-x
10. Wang, H., et al.: Adaptive and large-scale service composition based on deep reinforcement learning. Knowl.-Based Syst. **180**, 75–90 (2019)
11. Liang, H., Wen, X., Liu, Y., Zhang, H., Zhang, L., Wang, L.: Logistics-involved QoS-aware service composition in cloud manufacturing with deep reinforcement learning. Robot. Comput. Integr. Manuf. **67**, 101991 (2021)
12. Quan, L., Wang, Z.-L., Liu, X.: A real-time subtask-assistance strategy for adaptive services composition. IEICE Trans. Inf. Syst. **E101D**, 1361–1369 (2018)
13. Zhou, J., Yao, X.: A hybrid artificial bee colony algorithm for optimal selection of QoS-based cloud manufacturing service composition. Int. J. Adv. Manuf. Technol. **88**(9–12), 3371–3387 (2016). https://doi.org/10.1007/s00170-016-9034-1
14. Fazeli, M.M., Farjami, Y., Nickray, M.: An ensemble optimisation approach to service composition in cloud manufacturing. Int. J. Comput. Integr. Manuf. **32**, 83–91 (2018)
15. Yu, L., Zhou, J., Wei, F., Gao, Y., Yang, B., Zhu, H.: Web Service Composition Based on Reinforcement Learning (2015)

16. Wang, H., Chen, X., Wu, Q., Yu, Q., Zheng, Z., Bouguettaya, A.: Integrating on-policy reinforcement learning with multi-agent techniques for adaptive service composition. In: Franch, X., Ghose, A.K., Lewis, G.A., Bhiri, S. (eds.) ICSOC 2014. LNCS, vol. 8831, pp. 154–168. Springer, Heidelberg (2014). https://doi.org/10.1007/978-3-662-45391-9_11

17. Wang, H., Gu, M., Yu, Q., Fei, H., Li, J., Tao, Y.: Large-scale and adaptive service composition using deep reinforcement learning. In: Maximilien, M., Vallecillo, A., Wang, J., Oriol, M. (eds.) ICSOC 2017. LNCS, vol. 10601, pp. 383–391. Springer, Cham (2017). https://doi.org/10.1007/978-3-319-69035-3_27

18. Yuan, M., Zhou, Z., Cai, X., Sun, C., Gu, W.: Service composition model and method in cloud manufacturing. Robot. Comput. Integr. Manuf. 61, 101840 (2020)

19. Liu, Z.Z., Song, C., Chu, D.H., Hou, Z.W., Peng, W.P.: An approach for multipath cloud manufacturing services dynamic composition. Int. J. Intell. Syst. 32, 371–393 (2017)

20. Zhou, J., Yao, X.: Multi-population parallel self-adaptive differential artificial bee colony algorithm with application in large-scale service composition for cloud manufacturing. Appl. Soft Comput. 56, 379–397 (2017)

21. Wang, Z., Schaul, T., Hessel, M., Hasselt, H., Lanctot, M., Freitas, N.: Dueling network architectures for deep reinforcement learning. In: Maria Florina, B., Kilian, Q.W. (eds.) Proceedings of The 33rd International Conference on Machine Learning, vol. 48, pp. 1995–2003. PMLR, Proceedings of Machine Learning Research (2016)

22. van Hasselt, H., Guez, A., Silver, D.: Deep reinforcement learning with double Q-learning. In: AAAI (2016)

23. Schaul, T., Quan, J., Antonoglou, I.: Prioritized experience replay, arXiv preprint arXiv: 1511.05952 (2015)

Transfer Knowledge Between Cities by Incremental Few-Shot Learning

Jiahao Wang[1,2], Wenxiong Li[1], Xiuxiu Qi[1(✉)], and Yuheng Ren[3]

[1] School of Information and Software Engineering, University of Electronic
Science and Technology of China, Chengdu, China
[2] Yangtze River Delta Research Institute, University of Electronic Science
and Technology of China, Huzhou, China
[3] Xiamen Construction and Climb Corporation Limited, Xiamen, China

Abstract. The objective of cross-city transfer learning methods focuses on how to effectively transfer knowledge from data-rich cities to help data-scarce cities, and solve the problem that city development levels are quite unbalanced. However, transfer-learning and meta-learning-based spatial-temporal approaches can quickly learn and adapt to (novel-) source cities, but the prior experience in base-source cities will be largely forgotten, i.e., the models may lead to catastrophic forgetting problem on base attributes. In this paper, we proposed an incremental few-shot learning based spatial-temporal model (IFS-STP), which utilized an incremental few-shot learner strives to build a generalized model that can not only transfer learned knowledge from source cities to improve the performance of spatial-temporal prediction in a target city with limited data but also prevent the catastrophic forgetting problem of source cities. We evaluate IFS-STP on traffic prediction tasks and the experience results show that our approach significantly outperforms competitive baseline models.

Keywords: Spatial-temporal prediction · Incremental few-shot learning · Meta-learning · Traffic prediction

1 Introduction

Recently, the construction of smart cities has been promoted with the application of deep learning [1, 2]. In smart urban computing, the spatial-temporal prediction problem is a fundamental problem, e.g., traffic flow, water quality, and air quality, which is the key technique in building a smart city. Traffic prediction system has drawn increasing attention due to its impacts in real-world applications such as deploy transportation resources and control traffic signal intelligently.

Previous works achieve impressive breakthroughs in the spatial-temporal prediction problem. To get around spatial-temporal prediction, basic time series models [3, 4], regression models with spatial-temporal regularizations [5], and external context features [6] are used for spatial-temporal prediction. Moreover, deep neural network models significantly improve the performance of spatial-temporal prediction [6–8] by characterizing nonlinear spatial-temporal correlations more exactly.

© ICST Institute for Computer Sciences, Social Informatics and Telecommunications Engineering 2021
Published by Springer Nature Switzerland AG 2021. All Rights Reserved
H. Gao and X. Wang (Eds.): CollaborateCom 2021, LNICST 407, pp. 241–257, 2021.
https://doi.org/10.1007/978-3-030-92638-0_15

However, the superior performance of these methods is conditioned on large-scale training data which are probably inaccessible in real-world applications. Data collection with unbalanced spatial distributions is the most common way to spatial-temporal prediction problems. As an example, some regions may have abundant traffic data whereas some regions may exist only a few days of traffic data for prediction.

The similarity of distributions between different cities verifies the spatial functionality is globally shared [9]. Transfer learning [10] has been studied as an effective solution to address the data insufficiency problem, by leveraging knowledge from those cities with abundant data. While previous works achieve impressive breakthroughs in the spatial-temporal prediction problem, there are at least three challenges in the existing approaches: (i) The earlier methods transferring the knowledge from only a single source city, would cause unstable results and the risk of negative transfer. (ii) Existing approaches are difficult to learn effectively with limited data due to missing values or the effects of special events (e.g., holidays). (iii) [9] using meta-learning methods with a rapid adaptation according to new information, e.g. MAML [11], but old knowledge is forgotten equally quickly. This greatly reduces the generalization ability of the model. To tackle the aforementioned practice problems, we proposed an incremental few-shot learning algorithm that enables the backbone network to transfer knowledge from multiple cities. Build on the insights of incremental learning, our motivation is to pursue novel knowledge from new-source cities and merge it with prior knowledge learned from previous experience (base-source cities) to prevent catastrophic forgetting [12]. Different from previous studies [9, 13], we aim to utilize incremental few-shot learner strives to build a generalized model that can not only transfer learned knowledge from source cities to improve the performance of spatial-temporal prediction in a target city with limited data, but also prevent the catastrophic forgetting problem of source cities. We summarize our contributions as follows.

- To the best of our knowledge, we are the first to utilize incremental few-shot learning algorithm to solve the traffic flow prediction problem.
- We propose a novel IFS-STP framework to solve the problem by combining a spatial-temporal network with the meta-learning paradigm. Moreover, we optimize a memory regularizer, describing and storing long-term spatial-temporal patterns, that reduces catastrophic forgetting from the incremental few-shot learning.
- We empirically demonstrate that IFS-STP compares favorably to state-of-art conventional methods.

The remainder of this paper is organized as follows: Sect. 2 reviews the related work. Section 3 defines some notations and formulate the problem. Section 4 introduces the details of our proposed framework of IFS-STP. Then we apply our model on five real-world datasets and conduct extensive experiments in Sect. 5. Finally, we conclude our paper in Sect. 6.

2 Related Work

In this section, we present recent researches related to our work, which mainly contains some representative works for spatial-temporal prediction and knowledge transferring. All these observations indeed motivate the work of this paper.

2.1 Spatial-Temporal Prediction

The earliest studies on spatial-temporal prediction problems almost only utilizes the basic time series data (e.g., ARIMA). Recent work further utilize some context data to make model more effective [14–16]. Wang et al. [14] propose to capture city dynamics via venue information of POI data. Wu et al. [15] study shows that external datasets (e.g., geotagged tweets, holiday and weather conditions) can be helpful. Tong et al. [16] adopt a simple linear model with very high-dimensional features in predicting the Unit Original Taxi Demand.

Recently, various deep learning methods have attracted much attention from many researchers and have been applied to deal with the problem of spatial-temporal prediction. Yi et al. [6] proposed a DNN-based distributed fusion network to fuse heterogeneous urban data. Yu et al. [17] build a deep neural network based on LSTM units to forecast urban traffic. Yao et al. [18] propose a novel Spatial-Temporal Dynamic Network to model both spatial and temporal information with CNN and RNN.

2.2 Transfer Learning

Different from the traditional spatial-temporal prediction tasks which all rely on large-scale training data, we aim to utilize meta-learning paradigm to transfer learned knowledge from source cities to a target city with limited data samples to improve the performance of spatial-temporal prediction of the target city.

Recently, few-shot learning methods have caught the attention of researchers. These methods aim to transfer shared knowledge from multiple training tasks to a new task for quick adaptation. [19] proposed a novel few-shot learning method to especially adopt a deep neural network—meta-transfer learning. Jiang et al. [20] proposed to extract multi-scale features and learns the relations between samples to achieve classification. In addition, this study also proposed a new loss function to optimize the model. But a key challenge for meta-learning methods is catastrophic forgetting [12], i.e., the model forgets the learned knowledge. Incremental Few-Shot (IFS) learning is also known as few-shot learning. Different from previous meta-learning methods, IFS will add basic tasks to the query set during the evaluation stage, and the classifier will be augmented to include all tasks. Ren et al. [21] propose to add a learned regularizer to help identify new classes while remembering old classes without having to review the original training data.

However, only a few attempts have been made on transferring knowledge of space. Wei et al. [22] propose to construct a regularization that can transfer the knowledge between cities. For predicting traffic flow, Yao et al. [9] propose a framework to solve spatial-temporal prediction by constructing a memory regularizer, which can learn a global memory from all source cities. But this method is still based on MAML.

3 Preliminaries

In this section, we first briefly and formally define the spatial-temporal prediction problem. We following previous works [9, 13], and propose cross-city transfer learning methods for spatial-temporal prediction, which solve the problem of the city development levels are quite unbalanced. The objective of cross-city transfer learning methods is to predict a certain type of service data (e.g., crowd flow) in a data-scarce city (target cities) by transferring knowledge learned from a data-rich city (source cities).

Definition 1. Region. For consistency to prior works [7–9, 23], we partition a city c into the $W_c \times H_c$ size (e.g., 1 km × 1 km) grid map with M regions in total ($M = W_c \times H_c$). We take each grid as a region r and r_{ij} denotes a city region with coordinates of (i, j). The whole set of regions in the city c is denoted as $\mathbb{G}_c$.

Definition 2. Time Series. In a city c, we split the time period (e.g., 1 year) into equal-length continuous time intervals. To be more specific, we denote the current/last time-stamp as d_c and the set of data time-stamps of c can be defined as:

$$\mathbb{D}_c = [d_c - |\mathcal{D}_c| + 1, d_c] \tag{1}$$

Where $|\mathcal{D}_c|$ is the number of time-stamps and $\mathbb{D}_c$ is consist of $|\mathcal{D}_c|$ equal-length time intervals (e.g., 1 h). At a specific time-stamp d_c, we define the spatial-temporal series in city c as follows:

$$\mathcal{Y}_c = \{y_{r_c,d_c} | r_c \in \mathbb{G}_c, d_c \in \mathbb{D}_c\} \tag{2}$$

Where y_{r_c,d_c} is the spatial-temporal information. It's a most common way to model a variety of urban data in reality, e.g., traffic demand and air quality.

Definition 3. Spatial-Temporal Data. Given a set of source cities $\mathcal{C}_S = \{c_1, c_2, \ldots, c_o\}$ with rich data and a target city c_k with limited data, i.e., $|\mathbb{D}_{\mathcal{C}_S}| \gg |\mathbb{D}_{\mathcal{C}_K}|$. In this aforementioned case, we formalize the problem.

Definition 4. Problem Definition. Our goal is to learn a spatial-temporal network $\mathcal{F}_\theta(\cdot)$ with parameters θ to predict the spatial-temporal data in target city c_k at the next time-stamp $d_{c_k} + 1$. Thereby, the problem can be calculated as predicting the spatial-temporal information that maximizes the conditional probability:

$$\tilde{y}_{r_{c_k},d_{c_k}+1} = \arg\max_{y_{r_{c_k},d_{c_k}+1}} p(y_{r_{c_k},d_{c_k}+1} | \mathcal{Y}_{c_k}, \mathcal{F}_\theta) \tag{3}$$

Then, we can formulate the error function of base-learner for each city c as:

$$\min_{\mathcal{F}_\theta} error(\tilde{y}_{r_{c_k},d_{c_k}+1}, y_{r_{c_k},d_{c_k}+1}),$$
$$where\ \tilde{y}_{r_{c_k},d_{c_k}+1} = \mathcal{F}_\theta(c_k, c_s),\ |\mathbb{D}_{c_s}| \gg |\mathbb{D}_{c_k}|, \tag{4}$$

According to the real application requirement, the error metric can be mean absolute error, root mean squared error (RMSE), etc.

Definition 5. Application. In this paper, we use traffic prediction tasks to illustrate the aforementioned problem concretely. Similar as the previous traffic volume prediction studies in [8, 9, 23], each individual trip as the important part of the whole city traffic is always departs from a region, and then arrives at the destination region after a period of time. The start/end traffic volume in a region as the number of trips departing/arriving from/in the region at a fixed time interval. Therefore, our work is aim to predict the start and end volume of taxi at time interval $d_{c_k} + 1$.

4 Methodology

4.1 The Spatial-Temporal Network Architecture (ST-Net)

Recent researches [7, 9, 13, 23, 24] utilize convolution neural networks (CNN) and long short-term memory (LSTM) as the basic components of the neural network to learn spatial-temporal patterns and have achieved superior results. Thus, we follow previous works [7, 9] that use CNN to capture the spatial interactions between regions and an LSTM to learn sequential dependency, as shown in Fig. 1.

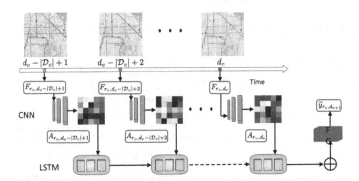

Fig. 1. The architecture of the backbone network.

Convolution: Intuitively, the traffic volume in nearby regions may affect each other, and the CNN can be effectively handled this situation. Specifically, in city c at each time interval d_c, we treat the spatial-temporal value of region r_c and its surrounding neighbors as a $S \times S$ image with v channels $F_{r_c,d_c} \in \mathbb{R}^{S \times S \times v}$. In our work, we set $v = 2$, i.e., we jointly predict taxi volume, one channel contains the start volume information, another one contains end volume information. The CNN takes F_{r_c,d_c} as input $F^0_{r_c,d_c}$, and feeds it into L convolutional layers. The formulation of each convolutional layer l is defined as follows:

$$F_{r_c,d_c}^l = \sigma\left(\mathbf{W}_r^l * F_{r_c,d_c}^{l-1} + \mathbf{b}_r^l\right),\tag{5}$$

$\sigma = RELU(\cdot)$ is an activation function and $*$ denotes the convolutional operation. $\mathbf{W}_r^l$ and $\mathbf{b}_r^l$ are two learnable parameters in the l-th convolution layer. After stacking L convolutional layers, a fully connected layer following a flatten layer is used to infer the spatial representation A_{r_c,d_c} for region r_c.

Temporal: In the sequel, we use LSTM to capture the temporal sequential dependency and model sequential relations in the time series. The memory cell $\mathbf{c}_d$ at time interval d in LSTM is an accumulator of the state information. To be more specific, in each time interval d_c, we take A_{r_c,d_c} as LSTM input, Ultimately, $\mathbf{h}_{r_c,d_c}$ from LSTM represents the spatial and temporal representations of region r_c. At last $\tilde{y}_{r_c,d_c+1}$ can be accessed by:

$$\tilde{y}_{r_c,d_c+1} = \tanh\left(\mathbf{W}_a \mathbf{h}_{r_c,d_c} + \mathbf{b}_a\right)\tag{6}$$

Where $\mathbf{W}_a$ and $\mathbf{b}_a$ are learnable parameters. The output of our backbone framework is scaled to $(-1, 1)$ via a $\tanh(\cdot)$ function since we normalize the value of start and end volume. We later demoralize the prediction to get the actual demand values. Moreover, the loss function for each city c we used is defined as:

$$\mathcal{L}_c = \sum_{r_c} \sum_{k_c} \left(\mathcal{F}_\theta\left(f_{r_c,d_c}\right) - y_{r_c,d_c+1}\right)^2\tag{7}$$

where θ is the learnable parameters in the spatial-temporal network.

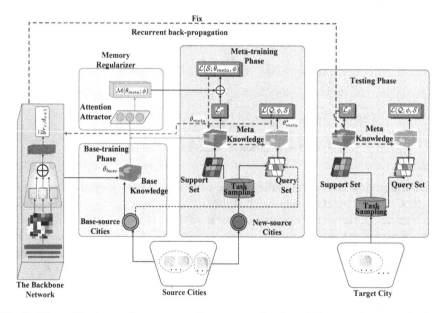

Fig. 2. The architecture and parameter update process (i.e., knowledge transfer process) of our proposed model

4.2   Incremental Few-Shot Learning

In this subsection, we proposed an incremental few-shot learning algorithm that enables ST-Net to transfer knowledge from multiple cities. Albeit used meta-learning methods with a rapid adaptation according to new information, such as MAML [11], Yao used a meta-learning approach for spatial-temporal prediction [9], but old knowledge is forgotten equally quickly. The main issue of incremental learning [21, 25, 26] is to overcome catastrophic forgetting [12], after learning the new tasks, the information of the old task is missed, resulting in the poor performance of the model. Build on the insights of incremental learning, our motivation is to pursue novel knowledge from new-source cities and merge it with prior knowledge learned from previous experience (base-source cities) to prevent catastrophic forgetting of the base-source cities. Thus, we detail our meta-learning approach to incremental few-shot learning in three parts: (i) Base-training phase, pre-training a backbone network (ST-Net) on a set of basic cities; (ii) Incremental Few-Shot task, built upon the pre-trained model, meta-training is done with episodes(tasks) form of training with our meta-learnd memory loader; (iii) Meta-training phase, leverage memory regularizer to extract the mixture of the base and novel knowledge. For better illustration, the incremental few-shot attribute learning process of the proposed model is shown in Fig. 2. Details of these stages follow.

Base-Training Phase: C_S denotes the set of source cities $C_S = \{c_1, c_2, \ldots, c_o\}$. It is split into base-source cities C_S^a and new-source cities C_S^b for base-training and meta training, i.e., $C_S = C_S^a \cup C_S^b$. We learn the backbone network (ST-Net) $\mathcal{F}_\theta(\cdot)$ on C_S^a. The purpose of this stage is to learn both a good base learner and a good representation. The parameters of the backbone network θ_{base} are learned in this stage and will be fixed after base-training.

Incremental Few-Shot Task: We define the task training strategy widely used by existing meta-learning based few-shot learning models [9, 11, 27]. Meta-learning leverage the shared structure across different tasks from the task distribution $p(\mathcal{T})$, learning prior knowledge for new tasks. Each task $\mathcal{T}_i$ splits the sampled data-points into support set $\mathcal{S}$ used for training the model with a memory loader and the query sets $\mathcal{Q}$ for measuring whether or not training was effective.

Concretely, under the few-shot setting, we give a sample set from a set of new-source cities C_S^b. For each $|C_S^b|$-way η-shot task, there are $|C_S^b|$ novel source cities disjoint from the base-source cities. Each new-source city has η and ν datapoints to form the support set $\mathcal{S}^b$ and novel-query set $\mathcal{Q}^b$ respectively. Therefore, we have subtask $(\mathcal{S}^b, \mathcal{Q}^b)$, in which we learn on $\mathcal{S}^b$ whose learnable parameters θ_{meta} are called the fast weights as they are only used during this task. The query set $\mathcal{Q}$ consists of samples not only from the novel but also base source cities, i.e., a $(|C_S^a| + |C_S^b|)$-way. Formally, we sampled ν datapoints from C_S^a to form the base-query set $\mathcal{Q}^a$ and added to $\mathcal{Q}^b$ to form the query set $\mathcal{Q} = \mathcal{Q}^a \cup \mathcal{Q}^b$. For each task, learnable parameters are updated by computing loss during training on $\mathcal{Q}_i$. As indicated aforementioned, we use the following steps to iteratively sample tasks $\mathcal{T} = \mathcal{S}^b \cup \mathcal{Q}$ and use them to train the model:

- For each new-source city $c \in C_S^b$, randomly sample η datapoints to form a support set S_i^b;
- υ data-points ($\notin S_i^b$) were extracted from base-source cities C_S^a and new-source cities C_S^b respectively to form Q_i^a and Q_i^b, where $Q_i = Q_i^a \cup Q_i^b$.
- Repeat step (1) and (2) for $|T| = \mathcal{I}$ times.

Meta-training Phase: In the meta-training phase, we learn the meta-parameters in order to minimize the joint prediction loss on $Q_i = Q_i^a \cup Q_i^b$. Here, we design a memory regularizer $\mathcal{M}(\cdot, \phi)$ such that the fast weights are learned via minimizing the loss $\mathcal{L}(\theta_{meta}, S) + \mathcal{M}(\theta_{meta}, \phi)$ where $\mathcal{L}(\theta_{meta}, S)$ is root mean square error for traffic volume prediction. For the meta-learning stage, the meta-parameters of meta-learner ϕ are optimized by iterative updating on $S(\theta_{meta} \to \theta_{meta}^*)$, which are exactly the knowledge that encrypts spatial-temporal correlations. In our model, meta-parameters are encapsulated via the attention-attractor network, which produces regularizers for the fast weights in the few-shot learning objective.

4.3   Memory Regularizer Combine Base and Novel Knowledge

The similarity of distributions between different cities verifies the spatial functionality is globally shared [9]. However, a target city still suffers from certain constraints.

To this end, we proposed a spatial-temporal memory regularizer to load the mixture weight vectors θ_{base} and θ_{meta}. We start with an attention mechanism to encode base information (knowledge) θ_{base}. Here we taken the learned vector ($\mathcal{U}_w = \theta_{base,\omega}$) of each base class stored in the memory matrix $\mathcal{U} = \{\mathcal{U}_1, \mathcal{U}_2, ..., \mathcal{U}_{|C_S^a|}\}$. The attention mechanism assigns the attention weight $\mathcal{V}_{\omega',\omega}$ to base weight vectors as follows ($\omega \in C_S^a$):

$$\alpha_\omega = \tau \mathcal{A}\left(\frac{1}{\eta}\sum_{j \in S_i} \mathbf{h}_j, \theta_{base,\omega}\right),$$

$$\mathcal{V}_{\omega',\omega} = \frac{\exp(\alpha_\omega)}{\sum_{\omega' \in C_S^b} \exp(\alpha_{\omega'})}, \tag{8}$$

$$\mathcal{U}_{\omega'} = \sum_{\omega \in C_S^a} \mathcal{V}_{\omega',\omega} \theta_{base,\omega} + U_0,$$

where $\mathcal{A}$ is the cosine similarity function, $\mathbf{h}_j$ represents the spatial-temporal representations of inputs in the support set S and τ is a learnable temperature scalar. Thus, the attention vector is used to compute the memory matrix, which stored a learned attractor vector of each base-source city, where $\mathcal{U}_0$ is an embedding vector and serves as a bias for the attractor. Thus we can derive the memory regularizer. The key feature of memory regularizer is the regularization term $\mathcal{M}(\theta_{meta}, \phi)$:

$$\mathcal{M} = \sum\nolimits_{\omega' \in |\mathcal{C}_S^b|} \left(\theta_{meta,\omega'} - u_{\omega'}\right)^{\mathrm{T}} \mathrm{diag}(\exp(\gamma)) \left(\theta_{meta,\omega'} - u_{\omega'}\right) \qquad (9)$$

where $u_{\omega'}$ is the so-called attractor and $\theta_{meta,\omega'}$ is the ω'-th column of θ_{meta}. This sum of squared Mahalanobis distances from the attractors adds a bias to the learning signal arriving solely from novel-source cities. To conclude, the meta-parameters ϕ include $\mathcal{U}_0$, γ, and τ, which have the same dimension as base parameters θ_{base}. In meta-training phase, we can formulate the task objective as:

$$\mathcal{L}(\mathcal{S}_i; \theta_{meta}, \phi) = -\frac{1}{|\mathcal{C}_S^b|\eta} \sum\nolimits_{j \in \mathcal{S}_i} y_{i,j}^S \log \tilde{y}_{i,j}^S + \mathcal{M}(\theta_{meta}, \phi) \qquad (10)$$

Once the support set is processed, θ_{meta}^* is the optimal parameters that minimize the regularized objective in Eq. 10. During testing on the joint prediction of both base and novel source cities in query set $\mathcal{Q}$, $\tilde{y}_v^S = \mathcal{F}(F_v; \theta_{meta}^*)$.

During meta-learning, for each task, ϕ are updated to minimize an expected loss of the query set $\mathcal{Q}$ which contains both base and novel classes:

$$\mathcal{L}(\mathcal{Q}_i; \phi, \mathcal{S}_i) = \mathrm{argmin} - \log p\left(\mathcal{Q}_i | \theta_{meta}^*(\phi, \mathcal{S}_i)\right) \qquad (11)$$

The pseudo-codes for meta-training phase is outlined in Algorithm 1.

4.4 Parameter Optimization (Knowledge Transfer)

In each task, we need to minimize $\mathcal{L}(\mathcal{S}_i)$ to obtain θ_{meta}^* through an iterative optimizer. More importantly, need to transfer all learned knowledge to model and optimize it to improve the prediction of the target cities. For this reason, the question is how to efficiently compute $\frac{\partial \theta_{meta}^*}{\partial \phi}$, i.e., back-propagating through the optimization. In our work, we use the recurrent back-propagation (RBP) algorithm [28, 29] to efficiently back-propagate through the fixed point. The fast weight updating via a fixed number of gradient descent can be formulate as:

$$\theta_{meta}^{\epsilon+1} = \theta_{meta}^{\epsilon} - \beta \nabla \mathcal{L}(\mathcal{S}_i, \theta_{meta}^{\epsilon}) \qquad (12)$$

Algorithm 1: IFS-STP Training Algorithm.

Input: The set of source cities $\mathcal{C}_S = \mathcal{C}_S^a \cup \mathcal{C}_S^b$, the set of target cities $\mathcal{C}_\mathcal{k}$.

Output: Traffic volume prediction of each target city.

/* Base-Training Phase. */

1 Learn the parameters of backbone network θ_{base} on $\mathcal{C}_S^a$

/* Meta-Training Phase. */

2 **for** $i = 1, \cdots, \mathcal{J}$ **do**

3    $\{\mathcal{S}_i^b, \mathcal{Q}_i^b\} \leftarrow$ Sample support/novel-query set $(\mathcal{C}_S^b)$;

4    $\mathcal{Q}_i^{a+b} \leftarrow$ Sample base-query set $(\mathcal{C}_S^a) \cup \mathcal{Q}_i^b$

5   Get the task $\mathcal{T}_i = \{\mathcal{S}_i^b, \mathcal{Q}_i\}$

6   **while** θ_{meta} not converged **do**

7   Compute memory knowledge $\mathcal{M}$ by Eq 8 and 9 using θ_{base} and θ_{meta};

8   Compute $\mathcal{L}(\mathcal{S}_i; \theta_{meta}, \phi)$ by Eq 10 using $\mathcal{S}_i$ and $\mathcal{M}(\theta_{meta}, \phi)$;

9   Update θ_{meta} through optimization step: $\theta_{meta} \leftarrow \nabla_{\theta_{meta}} \mathcal{L}(\mathcal{S}_i)$

10   **end**

11   Evaluate task loss $\mathcal{L}(\mathcal{Q}_i; \phi; \mathcal{S}_i)$ on query set $\mathcal{Q}_i$ by Eq 11;

     /* Backprop through the above optimization via RBP */

     /* A dummy gradient descent step */

12   $\theta_{meta}' \leftarrow \theta_{meta} - \beta \nabla_{\theta_{meta}} \mathcal{L}(\mathcal{S}_i)$

13   $\mathcal{J} \leftarrow \dfrac{\partial \theta_{meta}'}{\partial \theta_{meta}}$; $\rho \leftarrow \dfrac{\partial \mathcal{L}(\mathcal{Q}_i)}{\partial \theta_{meta}}$;

14   Initialization $g \leftarrow \rho$;

15   **while** g not converged **do**

16     $\tilde{\rho} = \mathcal{J}^T \rho - \delta \rho$

17     $g \leftarrow g + \tilde{\rho}$;

18   **end**

19   Update the network parameters: $\phi^* \leftarrow g^T \dfrac{\partial \theta_{meta}'}{\partial \phi}$

20 **end**

   /* Evaluating IFS-STP on target cities. */

21 **for** each target city $c_\mathcal{k} \in \mathcal{C}_\mathcal{K}$ **do**

22   $\mathcal{S} \leftarrow$ Sample a support set $(c_\mathcal{k})$;

23   Compute $\mathcal{L}(\mathcal{S}; \theta_{meta}, \phi^*)$ by Eq 12 and adapt parameters θ_{meta} through optimization step: $\theta_{meta} \leftarrow \nabla_{\theta_{meta}} \mathcal{L}(\mathcal{S})$

24   Sample new series to form a query set $\mathcal{Q}$ and predict.

25 **end**

---

where β is the step size. We update θ_{meta} by a vanilla gradient descent process with step size β. The difference between two steps ψ can be written as:

$$\psi(\theta_{meta}^\epsilon) = (\theta_{meta}^\epsilon) - \mathcal{Z}(\theta_{meta}^\epsilon) \tag{13}$$

where $\mathcal{Z}(\theta_{meta}^\epsilon) = \theta_{meta}^{\epsilon+1}$ is the update function parameterized by θ_{meta}. At the fixed point, $\psi(\theta_{meta}^*) = 0$, using the total derivative and the dependence of θ_{meta}^* on ϕ we can get:

$$\frac{\partial \psi(\theta^*_{meta})}{\partial \phi} = \left(\mathcal{I} - \mathcal{J}^T_{\mathcal{Z},\theta^*_{meta}}\right)^{-1} \frac{\partial \theta^*_{meta}}{\partial \phi} - \frac{\partial \mathcal{Z}}{\partial \phi} = 0 \tag{14}$$

where $\mathcal{J}_{\mathcal{Z},\theta^*_{meta}}$ is the Jacobian matrix of $\mathcal{Z}$wvaluated at θ^*_{meta}. Since $\mathcal{I} - \mathcal{J}^T_{\mathcal{Z},\theta^*_{meta}}$ is invertible, we reformulate Eq. 14 as:

$$\frac{\partial \theta^*_{meta}}{\partial \phi} = \left(\mathcal{I} - \mathcal{J}^T_{\mathcal{Z},\theta^*_{meta}}\right)^{-1} \frac{\partial \mathcal{Z}}{\partial \phi} \tag{15}$$

It is worth noting that, Eq. 13, Eq. 14, and Eq. 15 apply the Implicit Function Theorem, which guarantees the existence and uniqueness of an implicit function. Similar to previous work [9, 28], we use the Neumann series $(\mathcal{I} - \mathcal{J}^T)^{-1}\rho = \sum_{n=0}^{\infty}(\mathcal{J}^T)^n \rho \equiv$ to compute the matrix-inverse vector product $(\mathcal{I} - \mathcal{J}^T)^{-1}\rho$. To avert numerical instability caused by directly applying the Neumann RBP algorithm, it proposed to add a damping term δ to $(\mathcal{I} - \mathcal{J}^T)$. The results is update by: $\tilde{\rho}^{(n)} = (\mathcal{J}^T - \delta\mathcal{I})^n \rho$, where $\delta = 0.1$.

5 Experiment

In this Section, we use traffic volume prediction (i.e., taxi volume prediction), an important type of spatial-temporal prediction task in urban computing. Following previous studies on traffic prediction [8, 9, 23], we aim to predict the start and end volume of taxi at each time interval for each region to tackle the following issues:

- **Q1**: How does IFS-STP perform compared with the traditional traffic volume prediction models, transfer-learning based models and meta-learning based approaches?
- **Q2**: How do different parts in IFS-STP affect predictive performance?
- **Q3**: How do the optimization method affect the performance of IFS-STP?

5.1 Datasets

We use the datasets and experimental setup in [9]. We conduct experiments for the domain application of taxi volume prediction, and collect datasets from five different cities, i.e., New York City (NYC), Washington (D.C.), Chicago (CHI), Porto and Boston (BOS).

Table 1. Descriptive statistics of all datasets.

Task	City	Trip records	Map size	Time span
Taxi	NYC	6,748,857	10 × 20	1/1/15–7/1/15
	D.C.	8,151,077	16 × 16	5/1/15–1/1/16
	Porto	1,710,671	20 × 10	7/1/13–6/30/14
	CHI	124,820	15 × 18	9/1/13–11/1/14
	BOS	839,897	18 × 15	10/1/12–10/31/12

Taxi Volume Prediction: For the task, we evaluate our proposed method on five real-world mobility datasets, which collecting from five different cities, i.e., NYC, D.C., CHI, Porto, and BOS. Remarkably, we use $\mathcal{C}_\mathcal{S} = \{\text{NYC}, \text{D.C.}, \text{Porto}\}$ as the source cities (where $\mathcal{C}_\mathcal{S}^a = \{\text{NYC}\}, \mathcal{C}_\mathcal{S}^b = \{\text{D.C.}, \text{Porto}\}$) and $\mathcal{C}_\mathcal{K} = \{\text{CHI}, \text{BOS}\}$ (we only predict start volume in BOS) as target cities.

5.2 Data Preprocessing

Table 1 details the statistics of all datasets. We spatially partition a city into a grid map (regions). For example, in taxi volume prediction, the grid map size of NYC, D.C., CHI, BOS, Porto are 10×20, 16×16, 15×18, 18×15, 20×10, respectively. In addition, for each source city, we select 80% data for training/validation, and the rest for testing. For each target city, we select the 1-day, 3-day and 7-day data for training, and the rest for testing. And the time intervals of the traffic prediction task is 1 h.

5.3 Baselines

We compare our model IFS-STP with the following three group benchmark baselines.
Traditional traffic prediction methods:

- **Historical average (HA):** Historical average is the traditional time-series prediction method, which predicts spatial-temporal value based on the average value of the previous relative time interval.
- **Autoregressive integrated moving average (ARIMA)** [30]: ARIMA is a widely used time-series prediction method in statistics.
- **ST-Net*:** ST-Net is a deep learning based method for traffic prediction.

Transfer-learning based traffic models:

- **Fine-tuning Methods (FT):** FT method is a transfer baseline. Following [13], we use single-source fine-tune (Single-FT) and multi-source fine-tune (Multi-FT) methods.
- **RegionTrans** [31]: RegionTrans proposed a novel deep spatial-temporal transfer learning framework for traffic flow prediction.

Meta-learning based traffic approaches:

- **MAML** [11]: MAML proposed a meta-learning method based on learning easily adaptable model parameters through gradient descent.
- **MetaST** [9]: MetaST leverages learned knowledge from multiple source cities to help the prediction in target data-scarce cities for spatial-temporal prediction.

5.4 Evaluation Metric

We evaluate our model using the widely used metrics: Root Mean Squared Error (RMSE), which is defined as follows:

$$\text{RMSE} = \frac{1}{|N|} \sqrt{\Sigma_{r_{c_k}} \Sigma_{d_{c_k}} \left(\tilde{y}_{r_{c_k},d_{c_k}+1} - y_{r_{c_k},d_{c_k}+1} \right)^2} \tag{16}$$

where $\tilde{y}_{r_{c_k},d_{c_k}+1}$ and $y_{r_{c_k},d_{c_k}+1}$ mean the prediction value and ground truth of region at time interval $d + 1$, respectively. $|N|$ is the total number of samples in target city c_k.

5.5 Experimental Settings

In the backbone network, we set all convolution kernel size to 3×3 with 64 filters, the size of each neighborhood as 7×7 for convolution component and IFS-STP does not use other external features; we set the number of steps in LSTM as 8, and the dimension of hidden representation of LSTM as 128 in temporal component. In meta-training phase of taxi volume prediction, we use Adam optimizer with a learning rate of 1e–5. Moreover, in order to alleviate overfitting, we use early-stop in our experiments.

Table 2. Evaluation result compared to baseline.

Models		Chicago(CHI)						Boston(BOS)		
		Start			End			Start		
		1-day	3-day	7-day	1-day	3-day	7-day	1-day	3-day	7-day
HA		2.83	2.36	2.18	2.67	2.28	2.13	11.07	9.13	7.71
ARIMA		3.19	2.76	2.71	2.93	2.43	2.41	2.93	2.43	2.41
ST-Net		10.51	6.04	3.89	10.51	6.04	3.89	10.51	6.04	3.89
Single-FT	NYC CHI	2.72	2.06	1.76	2.57	1.87	1.60	12.86	9.50	8.11
	D.C. CHI	3.90	2.62	2.05	4.17	2.19	2.15	15.88	10.07	10.16
	Porto CHI	2.57	1.87	1.60	2.87	2.03	1.74	12.91	8.54	8.08
Multi-FT		2.18	1.89	1.60	2.20	2.08	1.69	8.50	8.22	8.01
Region Trans	NYC CHI	2.53	2.01	1.69	2.83	2.56	1.72	11.98	9.46	7.95
	D.C. CHI	3.87	2.51	2.04	3.95	2.16	2.03	14.76	9.23	10.12
	Porto CHI	2.45	1.83	1.60	2.85	1.98	1.73	8.43	8.09	8.07
MAML		2.01	1.78	1.52	2.10	1.92	1.66	8.18	7.60	7.25
MetaML		1.95	1.70	1.48	2.04	1.79	1.65	7.81	6.97	6.58
IFS-STP		1.91	1.65	1.46	1.99	1.70	1.65	7.67	6.71	6.37

5.6   Experimental Result

We evaluate IFS-STP on taxi volume prediction. To ensure a fair comparison, we compare the baseline results obtained in [9] and use the experimental settings in [9]. We average the results of the 10 test times. Thus Table 2 shows the performance of our proposed method as compared to all other competing methods in the taxi datasets, respectively. According to Table 2, our proposed IFS-STP model implements the lowest RMSE on test datasets, which significantly outperforms all baselines. To validate, we evaluate our IFS-STP model on the standard traffic prediction methods and meta-learning benchmark.

The traditional traffic volume prediction methods, e.g., HA and ARIMA, are perform ineffective, because these methods only rely on the historical records of predicted value and overlook the spatial and temporal features. Nonetheless, in some situations (1-day data for training), the traditional traffic volume prediction methods still have competitive results when compared with ST-Net and some Single-FT, Region Trans models, the reason lies in the traffic data is periodicity, so that we could predict traffic start/end volume from limited data.

For transfer-learning based methods, e.g., Single-FT, Multi-FT and Region Trans models, construct the deep spatial-temporal transfer-learning framework, which can predict future traffic volume in target cities by transferring knowledge from source cities. The experiment results in Table 2 show that comparing with ST-Net the knowledge transfer between cities is effective for prediction. To be more specific, in contrast to Single-FT and RegionTrans, Multi-FT is preferable in most cases, the possible reason is that training on multiple source cities can obtain the diversity information from the source domain.

Comparing with traditional and transfer-learning based models, all meta-learning methods, e.g., MAML, MetaST, and IFS-STP achieve better performance. This is because meta-learning methods learn the initialization of multiple cities based on multiple cities, which can learn the common representation of spatial-temporal tasks in different cities and quickly adapt to new tasks. In particular, our proposed model IFS-STP achieves the best performance in all experimental settings. For every learning model, the performance improves with more training data (e.g., 3-day, 7-day). On all benchmarks, our model still shows a significant margin over the prior works, which signifies that our iterative model can solve the few-shot objective till convergence is better than baselines and that recurrent back-propagation is an effective and modular tool for learning in a general meta-learning setting.

5.7   Parameter Sensitivity

We conduct a sensitivity analysis to investigate the influence of two important parameters of IFS-STP. In this work, we report the results on Chicago dataset, but note that the results are similar on other datasets. Figure 3 illustrates the impact of the optimization method RBP on RMSE. We use the scenario of 3-day data for sensitivity analysis.

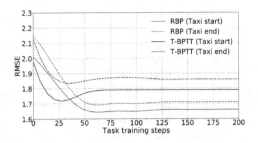

Fig. 3. Using T-BPTT and RBP to learn the proposed model.

In this study, we use the truncated BPTT [32] (T-BPTT) as the contrast experiment, which is a commonly used algorithm in many recent meta-learning approaches [11, 33]. TBPTT is optimized for gradient-based T-step optimization, when T is small, the training objective may have significant deviation. Remarkable, the RBP algorithm has the same time complexity compared to truncated BPTT given the same number of unrolled steps, but RBP does not have to store intermediate activations. From Fig. 3, the performance of TBPTT learned models are comparable to RBP. However, when solved to convergence at test time, the performance of T-BPTT models drops significantly. The reason may be they are only guaranteed to work well for a certain number of steps and failed to learn a good regularizer.

6 Conclusions

In this paper, we show that our model trained with an incremental few-shot learning curriculum achieves the top performance for tackling traffic prediction problems. We start with the spatial-temporal network architecture with learnable parameters, and then define the setup of incremental few-shot learning. In addition, we proposed a memory regularizer to store the prior knowledge about source cities and extend it to the target city, so as to improve the prediction accuracy of the target city.

For future work, we plan to investigate from three directions: (1) we plan to organize the hierarchical memory to improve the long-term spatial-temporal characteristics of the model. (2) We plan to further consider basic network structure and combine Graph Neural Network with our model. (3) We plan to perform an interpretative analysis of our model and analyze how the information is transferred.

Acknowledgement. This work is supported by UESTC-ZHIXIAOJING Joint Research Center of Smart Home (No. H04W210180), Neijiang technology incubation and transformation Funds (No. 2021KJFH004).

References

1. Liu, Y., Zhao, K., Cong, G.: Efficient similar region search with deep metric learning. In: Proceedings of the 24th ACM SIGKDD International Conference on Knowledge Discovery & Data Mining, pp. 1850–1859 (2018)
2. Wei, H., Zheng, G., Yao, H., Li, Z.: Intellilight: A reinforcement learning approach for intelligent traffic light control. In: The 24th ACM SIGKDD, pp. 2496–2505 (2018)
3. Lippi, M., Bertini, M., Frasconi, P.: Short-term traffic flow forecasting: an experimental comparison of time-series analysis and supervised learning. IEEE Trans. Intell. Trans. Syst. **14**(2), 871–882 (2013)
4. Moreira-Matias, L., Gama, J., Ferreira, M., Mendes-Moreira, J., Damas, L.: Predicting taxi–passenger demand using streaming data. IEEE Trans. Intell. Trans. Syst. **14**(3), 1393–1402 (2013)
5. Zheng, J., Ni, L.M.: Time-dependent trajectory regression on road networks via multi-task learning. In: Proceedings of the AAAI Conference on Artificial Intelligence, 27(1), (2013)
6. Yi, X., Zhang, J., Wang, Z., Li, T., Zheng, Y.: Deep distributed fusion network for air quality prediction. In: Proceedings of the 24th ACM SIGKDD, pp. 965–973 (2018)
7. Yao, H., et al.: Deep multi-view spatial-temporal network for taxi demand prediction, In: AAAI, vol. 32(1), pp. 2588–2595 (2018)
8. Zhang, J., Zheng, Y., Qi, D.: Deep spatio-temporal residual networks for citywide crowd flows prediction. In: Thirty-first AAAI Conference, vol. 31(1), pp. 1655–1661 (2017)
9. Yao, H., Liu, Y., Wei, Y., Tang, X., Li, Z.: Learning from multiple cities: a meta-learning approach for spatial-temporal prediction. In: WWW Conference, pp. 2181–2191 (2019)
10. Pan, S.J., Tsang, I.W., Kwok, J.T., Yang, Q.: Domain adaptation via transfer component analysis. IEEE Trans. Neural Networks **22**(2), 199–210 (2011)
11. Finn, C., Abbeel, P., Levine, S.: Model-agnostic meta-learning for fast adaptation of deep networks. In: International Conference on Machine Learning, pp. 1126–1135 (2017)
12. Goodfellow, I.J., Mirza, M., Courville, A., Bengio, Y.: An empirical investigation of catastrophic forgetting in gradient-based neural networks. Stat. **6**, 1050 (2014)
13. Wang, L., Geng, X., Ma, X., Liu, F., Yang, Q.: Cross-city transfer learning for deep spatio-temporal prediction. In: Proceedings of the 28th IJCAI, pp. 1893–1899 (2019)
14. Wang, H., Yao, H., Kifer, D., Graif, C., Li, Z.: Non-Stationary model for crime rate inference using modern urban data. IEEE Trans, Big Data **5**(2), 180–194 (2017)
15. Fei, W., Wang, H., Li, Z.: Interpreting traffic dynamics using ubiquitous urban data. In: Proceedings of the 24th ACM SIGSPATIAL, pp.1–4 (2016)
16. Tong, Y., Chen, Y., Zhou, Z., Lei, C., Lv, W.: The simpler the better: a unified approach to predicting original taxi demands based on large-scale online platforms. In: ACM SIGKDD, pp. 1653–1662 (2017)
17. Rose, Y., Li, Y., Shahabi, C., Demiryurek, U., Liu, Y.: Deep learning: a generic approach for extreme condition traffic forecasting. In: Chawla, N., Wang, W. (eds.) Proceedings of the 2017 SIAM International Conference on Data Mining, pp. 777–785. Society for industrial and applied mathematics, Philadelphia, PA (2017). https://doi.org/10.1137/1.9781611974973.87
18. Yao, H., et al.: Deep multi-view spatial-temporal network for taxi demand prediction. In: Proceedings of the AAAI, 32 (1) (2018)
19. Sun, Q., Liu, Y., Chua, T.S., Schiele, B.: Meta-transfer learning for few-shot learning. In: Proceedings of the IEEE/CVF Conference on Computer Vision and Pattern Recognition, pp. 403–412 (2019)

20. Jiang, W., Huang, K., Geng, J., Deng, X.: Multi-Scale metric learning for few-shot learning. IEEE Trans, Circuits Syst. Video Technol. **31**(3), 1091–1102 (2021)
21. Ren, M., Liao, R., Fetaya, E., Zemel, R.: Incremental few-shot learning with attention attractor networks. Adv. NeurIPS **32**, 5275–5285 (2019)
22. Wei, Y., Zheng, Y., Yang, Q.: Transfer knowledge between cities. In: Proceedings of the 22nd ACM SIGKDD, pp. 1905–1914 (2016)
23. Yao, H., Tang, X., Wei, H., Zheng, G.: mRevisiting spatial-temporal similarity: a deep learning framework for traffic prediction, In: The 33rd AAAI Conference, pp. 5668–5675 (2019)
24. Shi, X., Chen, Z., Wang, H., Yeung, D., Wong, W.: Convolutional LSTM network: a machine learning approach for precipitation nowcasting. In: NeurIPS, pp. 802–810 (2015)
25. Yoon, S.W., Kim, D.Y., Seo, J., Moon, J.: Xtarnet: Learning to extract task-adaptive representation for incremental few-shot learning. In: ICML, pp. 10852–10860 (2020)
26. Xiang, L., Jin, X., Ding, G., Han, J., Li, L.: Incremental few-shot learning for pedestrian attribute recognition, In Proceedings of the 28th IJCAI 2019, pp. 3912–3918 (2019)
27. LIU, L., Zhou, T., Long, G., Jiang, J., Zhang, C.: Learning to Propagate for Graph Meta-Learning. In: Advances in Neural Information Processing Systems, 32, 1039–1050 (2019)
28. Liao, R., et al.: Reviving and improving recurrent back-propagation. In Proceedings of the 35th ICML 2018, Stockholmsmassan, Stockholm, Sweden, pp. 3088–3097 (2018)
29. Pineda, F.J.: Generalization of back propagation to recurrent and higher order neural networks. In: Anderson, D.Z., (ed.) Neural Information Processing Systems, Denver, Colorado, USA, American Institue of Physics, pp. 602–611 (1987)
30. Hyndman, R.J., Athanasopoulos, G. Forecasting: principles and practice. OTexts (2018)
31. Wang, L., Geng, X., Ma, X., Liu, F., Yang, Q.: Crowd flow prediction by deep spatio-temporal transfer learning. arXiv preprint arXiv:1802.00386 (2018)
32. Williams, R.J., Peng, J.: An efficient gradient-based algorithm for on-line training of recurrent network trajectories. Neural Comput. **2**(4), 490–501 (1990)
33. Sprechmann, P., Jayakumar, S.M., Rae, J.W., Pritzel.: Memory-based parameter adaptation. In: The 6th International Conference on Learning Representations, ICLR (2018)

Deep Learning and Application

Multi-view Representation Learning with Deep Features for Offline Signature Verification

Xingbiao Zhao, Changzheng Liu, Benzhuang Zhang, Limengzi Yuan, and Yuchen Zheng[✉]

College of Information Science and Technology, Shihezi University, Shihezi, China
{zxb,benzhuangzhang}@stu.shzu.edu.cn, {liucz,ylmz}@shzu.edu.cn,
ouczyc@outlook.com

Abstract. Feature learning is one of the most crucial steps in offline signature verification systems. In this paper, to improve the performance of deep learning-based features for the offline signature verification task, we propose a novel framework to learn the new representations from two views of deep features by Canonical Correlation Analysis-based (CCA-based) multi-view representation learning approaches. Specifically, the features from one view can be extracted from deep learning-based feature extractors and the other view can be generated from the extracted view by adding the noise to another homologous sample. Then, the different CCA-based multi-view representation learning methods are evaluated on these two-view deep features to generate the joint features as the final features for the next verification step. Extensive experiments and discussions on three benchmark offline handwritten signature datasets demonstrate that the proposed framework improves the deep learning-based features and achieves the state-of-the-art results compared with other verification systems.

Keywords: Offline signature verification · Feature learning · Multi-view representation learning · Deep learning · Canonical correlation analysis

1 Introduction

The handwritten signature verification system is a typical human-computer interface system which automatically verifies whether a query signature is genuine or forged. Generally, according to the collection process, the signature verification systems are divided into two types: online and offline. The online systems collect the signatures as a series of dynamic sequences which include the speed, the pressure coordinate sequence, the pen-ups trajectory, etc. Different from the online verification systems, the offline verification systems collect the signatures as static digit images. Since the dynamic information can not be accessed during the training process and the skilled forgeries are very similar to the genuine

H. Gao and X. Wang (Eds.): CollaborateCom 2021, LNICST 407, pp. 261–275, 2021.
https://doi.org/10.1007/978-3-030-92638-0_16

signatures (the imitators can access the genuine signatures and imitate many times), the offline signature verification task is relatively challenging compared with the online signature verification task. Therefore, discriminating the genuine signatures and skilled forgeries is a crucial task in verification systems.

The verification task is often composed of preprocessing, feature extraction, and building Writer-Dependent (WD) or Writer-Independent (WI) classifiers [7]. Among them, feature extraction is one of the most crucial processes and determines the success or failure of the whole task. The handcrafted and deep learning-based features are typically applied to various verification systems. Comparing with traditionally handcrafted features, such as Local Binary Pattern (LBP) [8], Histogram of Oriented Gradient (HOG) [38], and Scale Invariant Feature Transform (SIFT) [28], deep learning-based features [9,12,35] are more popular in recent years.

The deep learning-based feature extractors often train the deep neural networks (DNNs) with different strategies to capture the discriminative information between different signatures. However, to achieve good performances, a large-scale training set is needed, which makes it hard to transfer to different datasets and implement in real-world applications. In addition, the problem of signature diversity that only several signatures could be accessed from the target signer also limits the learning ability of deep learning-based feature extractors.

To improve the learning ability of deep learning-based features for the offline signature verification task, in this paper, we propose a novel CCA-based multi-view representation learning framework which generates a new joint feature from different views of deep features. Detailedly, for the feature extraction process, we extract one view of deep features from a fully connected layer in a convolutional neural network (CNN). Then, the features from another view could be generated by adding random noise to another sample from the same class. Based on these two-view features, we evaluate several CCA-based multi-view representation learning approaches and generate the final learned features from one of them. After the feature learning process, we train the Support Vector Machine (SVM) as the WD classifiers for each user to build the completed verification system. The main contributions of this paper are listed as follows.

- We propose a novel framework to apply and explore the learning ability of multi-view representation learning approaches for the offline signature verification task.
- The different CCA-based multi-view representation learning approaches are evaluated and discussed on deep learning-based features, which improves the learning ability of deep features and demonstrates a novel view for the feature extraction process.
- Extensive experimental results and evaluations on three benchmark offline handwritten signature datasets demonstrate that the proposed framework achieves the state-of-the-art performance in most cases.

The rest of the paper is organized as follows. We review related work of traditional and deep learning-based feature extractors in offline signature verification systems and multi-view representation learning approaches in Sect. 2. In Sect. 3, the proposed framework is described in detail. Experimental results performed on three benchmark datasets are presented in Sect. 4. Section 5 concludes this paper with remarks and future work.

2 Related Work

2.1 Feature Extraction in Offline Signature Verification Systems

To capture the discriminative information between different signatures, many traditionally handcrafted [16,17,40] and deep learning-based [9,12,35] feature extractors are proposed in recent years. For traditionally handcrafted feature extractors, they aim to design different descriptors to capture the local or global information of signatures. In [16], it extracted parametric LBP features from the signatures, and then applied fusion using CCA to improve the discriminative features. In [17], two global (the number of connected components and the number of active pixels) and eight local (coordinates of effective mass, number of active pixels, isolated points, etc.) features were extracted from each signature, and then they were concatenated to create a final feature vector for feature learning. More recently, Zhou et al. extracted Gray-Level Co-Occurrence Matrix (GLCM) and HOG features from the static signature images and then fused them with dynamic information from online data to build the feature extraction procedure [40]. Although the handcrafted feature extractors achieve good performance in many scenarios, they are hard to capture the micro differences between the genuine signatures and their corresponding skilled forgeries.

Since the deep learning-based approaches have obtained excellent achievement in various areas, such as edge computing [4,21], Internet of Things (IoT) [25,36], document recognition and analysis [5,23], etc. [2,20], the deep learning-based feature extractors are more and more popular in modern signature verification systems [12,26,35]. In [12], a CNN-based architecture was applied to capture the difference not only between different signers but also between genuine signatures and skilled forgeries. In [26], Masoudnia et al. proposed Multi-Loss Snapshot Ensemble (MLSE) that combines a dynamic multiloss function and a novel ensemble framework for simultaneously learning the features between different signatures. Similarly, Wan and Zou [35] used a dual triplet loss to train the model for feature learning, where two different triplets are constructed for random and skilled forgeries, respectively. On the whole, the deep learning-based feature extractors are designed to capture the discriminative information between genuine signatures and forgeries. However, only several signatures could access from the target signer, which limits the learning ability and makes it hard to train.

2.2 Multi-view Representation Learning

Multi-view representation learning is an emerging research area in machine learning which aims to learn a projection to model each view and jointly optimizes all the functions to improve the generalization performance [39]. In recent year, many multi-view learning approaches are proposed to handle different applications [1,22,29]. In [29], Nie et al. proposed a novel multi-view learning model which learns local structure and performs clustering or semi-supervised classification tasks simultaneously. In [22], the Gaussian Process Latent Variable Model (GPVLM) was applied to represent multiple views in a common subspace for visual classification. In [1], Deep Canonical Correlation Analysis (DCCA) was proposed to learn complex nonlinear transformations of two views of data. Unlike Kernel Canonical Correlation Analysis (KCCA) [27], DCCA does not require to compute inner product of original representations, which is more efficient than KCCA.

To improve the learning ability of deep learning-based feature extractors in offline signature verification systems, applying multi-view representation learning to automatically learn a new representation from multiple views of signatures is very natural. To the best of our knowledge, only several studies like [16,19] used CCA to learn the new representation from the views of traditionally hand-crafted and dynamic features. It is better to use the multiple views of deep learning-based features to further improve the performance of offline signature verification systems.

3   Multi-view Representation Learning for Offline Signature Verification Systems

In this section, we first introduce how to generate the second view from the original view of deep features. Then, we introduce several CCA-based multi-view representation learning approaches. Finally, we introduce how to train SVMs as the WD classifiers for building the completed verification system.

3.1   Generating the Second View from Deep Features

After feature extraction, we obtain the deep features from a fully connected layer in a deep CNN and take them as the first view for multi-view representation learning. Based on the deep features, we first rescale the feature values to $[0, 1]$ by Min-Max normalization. The rescaled element can be described as,

$$X_{ij}^* = \frac{X_{ij} - \min\{X_{ij}\}}{\max\{X_{ij}\} - \min\{X_{ij}\}}. \tag{1}$$

For each feature from the first view, we randomly select a feature from the same class with the feature of the first view in the same specific signer and rescale the feature to $[0, 1]$. Then, we add the independently random noise uniformly sampled from $[0, 1]$ to each value of a feature. Finally, we also rescale the values to $[0, 1]$ by Min-Max normalization and take the final features as the second view features. For a robust multi-view representation learning method, it should learn an effective representation from two views of features by ignoring the noise. The next section will introduce several CCA-based multi-view representation learning approaches for further learning the features for the verification system.

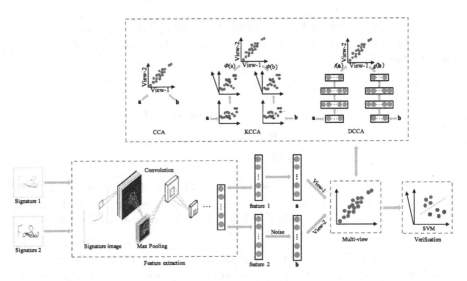

Fig. 1. The proposed framework for offline signature verification.

3.2 CCA-based Multi-view Representation Learning Approaches

In this part, we introduce three CCA-based representation learning approaches, CCA, KCCA, and DCCA which are used in our experiments. **Canonical Correlation Analysis (CCA)** [15] analyzes the linear relationship between the characteristics of two views. Let $\mathbf{A} = \{\mathbf{a}_1, ..., \mathbf{a}_n\}$ and $\mathbf{B} = \{\mathbf{b}_1, ..., \mathbf{b}_n\}$ denote the data from two views, $\mathbf{U} = \{\mathbf{u}_1, ..., \mathbf{u}_d\}$ and $\mathbf{V} = \{\mathbf{v}_1, ..., \mathbf{v}_d\}$ denote the CCA directions that project the data from two views, the objective function can be described as,

$$
\begin{aligned}
\max_{\mathbf{u}_i, \mathbf{v}_i} \quad & \mathbf{u}_i^\top \mathbf{A}\mathbf{B}^\top \mathbf{v}_i \\
\text{s.t.} \quad & \mathbf{u}_i^\top (\frac{1}{N}\mathbf{A}\mathbf{A}^\top + r_a\mathbf{I})\mathbf{u}_i = 1, \\
& \mathbf{v}_i^\top (\frac{1}{N}\mathbf{B}\mathbf{B}^\top + r_b\mathbf{I})\mathbf{v}_i = 1, \\
& \mathbf{u}_i^\top \mathbf{A}\mathbf{B}^\top \mathbf{v}_j = 0, \quad i \neq j,
\end{aligned}
\tag{2}
$$

where, r_a, $r_b > 0$ are regularization parameters which are used to handle the overfitting problem. This objective function can be solved by several approaches, such as Singular Value Decomposition (SVD). CCA tries to find linear projections of two random vectors that are maximally correlated. In CCA, the final projection mapping of a test sample $\mathbf{x}_{test}$ is $\mathbf{U}^\top \mathbf{x}_{test}$. The learned dimensions in each view should be uncorrelated and provide different information from their own perspectives.

Kernel CCA (KCCA) [14] is an extension of CCA, which tries to find non-linear projection mappings from two views of data. The objective function of KCCA is "max $\mathbf{u}_i^\top \Phi(\mathbf{A})\Phi(\mathbf{B})^\top \mathbf{v}_i$", where, $\Phi(\mathbf{A})$ and $\Phi(\mathbf{B})$ are the projections of two views of data in a kernel space. We replace $\Phi(\mathbf{a}) = \boldsymbol{\alpha}_i^\top \kappa_a(\mathbf{a}, \cdot)$, where $\kappa_a(\mathbf{a}, \cdot)$ is a vector whose i-th element is $\kappa_a(\mathbf{a}, \mathbf{a}_i)$. Then, the objective function can be replaced as,

$$
\begin{aligned}
\max_{\boldsymbol{\alpha}_i, \boldsymbol{\beta}_i} \quad & \boldsymbol{\alpha}_i^\top \mathbf{K}_a \mathbf{K}_b \boldsymbol{\beta}_i \\
\text{s.t.} \quad & \boldsymbol{\alpha}_i^\top \mathbf{K}_a^2 \boldsymbol{\alpha}_i + r_a \boldsymbol{\alpha}_i^\top \mathbf{K}_a \boldsymbol{\alpha}_i = 1, \\
& \boldsymbol{\beta}_i^\top \mathbf{K}_b^2 \boldsymbol{\beta}_i + r_b \boldsymbol{\beta}_i^\top \mathbf{K}_b \boldsymbol{\beta}_i = 1, \\
& \boldsymbol{\alpha}_i^\top \mathbf{K}_a \mathbf{K}_b \boldsymbol{\beta}_j = 0, \quad i \neq j,
\end{aligned}
\tag{3}
$$

where, $\mathbf{K}_a \in \mathbb{R}^{n \times n}$, $\mathbf{K}_a = \mathbf{K} - \mathbf{K1} - \mathbf{1K} + \mathbf{1K1}$, and $K_{ij} = \kappa_a(\mathbf{a}_i, \mathbf{a}_j)$. For regularization, the $\mathbf{K}_a^2$ is replaced by $\mathbf{K}_a^2 + r_a \mathbf{K}_a$ here. The size of kernel matrices is $n \times n$. If n is very large, this problem is hard to solve and time consuming, which is not friendly for large-scale applications.

Deep Canonical Correlation Analysis (DCCA) [1]. Different from KCCA, DCCA learns the nonlinear representation of two views of data by building two DNNs. The features extracted from two DNNs from two views are $f(\mathbf{A})$ and $g(\mathbf{B})$. Then, the canonical correlation between the two views of deep features is maximized,

$$
\begin{aligned}
\max_{\mathbf{u}_i, \mathbf{v}_i, \boldsymbol{\Theta}_f, \boldsymbol{\Theta}_g} \quad & \mathbf{u}_i^\top f(\mathbf{A}) g(\mathbf{B})^\top \mathbf{v}_i \\
\text{s.t.} \quad & \mathbf{u}_i^\top \left(\frac{1}{N} f(\mathbf{A}) f(\mathbf{A})^\top + r_a \mathbf{I} \right) \mathbf{u}_i = 1, \\
& \mathbf{v}_i^\top \left(\frac{1}{N} g(\mathbf{B}) g(\mathbf{B})^\top + r_b \mathbf{I} \right) \mathbf{v}_i = 1, \\
& \mathbf{u}_i^\top f(\mathbf{A}) g(\mathbf{B})^\top \mathbf{v}_j = 0, \quad i \neq j,
\end{aligned}
\tag{4}
$$

where, $\boldsymbol{\Theta}_f$ and $\boldsymbol{\Theta}_g$ are the weight parameters of two DNNs. The parameters of CCA and DNNs can be optimized by Limited-memory Broyden Fletcher Goldfarb Shanno (L-BFGS) [24] method with large mini-batches. Then, the final features for a test sample $\mathbf{x}_{test}$ can be represented as $\mathbf{U}^\top f(\mathbf{x}_{test})$. In addition, DCCA does not need to compute the inner product between two samples to obtain the nonlinear representation. However, designing suitable architectures for two DNNs is very important and decides the learning performance of DCCA.

3.3   Training the Writer-Dependent Classifiers

After feature extraction and multi-view feature learning processes, the final features are learned from two views of deep features. Then, we choose SVMs as the WD classifiers for building the completed verification system. For each signer, we take the genuine signatures from a target signer as the positive samples, and the genuine signatures from other signers as the negative samples since the skilled forgeries can not be accessed during the training process. In this scenario, the negative samples are much more than the positive samples. To solve the imbalance problem in a fair way, the different weights C to balance the relationship between the positive and negative classes,

$$C_N = \frac{N}{P} C_p, \tag{5}$$

where, N and P represent the numbers of negative and positive samples. Then, the objective function of SVM is described as,

$$\min_{\mathbf{w}, \xi} \frac{1}{2} \mathbf{w}^\top \mathbf{w} + C_P \left(\sum_{i:y_i=+1} \xi_i \right) + C_N \left(\sum_{i:y_i=-1} \xi_i \right), \tag{6}$$

$$\text{s.t.} \quad y_i \left(\mathbf{w}^\top \mathbf{x}_i + b \right) \geq 1 - \xi_i, \quad \xi_i \geq 0,$$

where, $\mathbf{x}_i$ is a training sample with target label y_i, and ξ_i is the slack variables.

The whole framework is illustrated in Fig. 1. First, we apply a CNN-based feature extractor to extract the features for different signatures. Then, based on one view of features from a signature, we generate the second view of features from another homologous sample. Next, the multi-view representation learning approaches are used to further generate the final features for the verification process. Finally, the SVMs are trained for each user as the WD classifiers for building the completed verification system.

4   Experiment

In this section, we first introduce the datasets used in the experiments. Then, we introduce the experimental settings in detail. Finally, We demonstrate the experimental results and discussion.

4.1   Dataset

We conduct the experiments by extracting the deep features from two CNN-based architectures, named 'SigNet' and 'SigNet-F' [12], on GPDS-960 [34], CEDAR [18], and Brazilian PUC-PR [6] datasets. The SigNet aims to capture the differences only between different users. The SigNet-F aims to capture the differences not only between different users but also between genuine signatures and skilled forgeries. The SigNet and SigNet-F are trained on the development set (signatures of the final 531 users) of the GPDS-960 dataset.

For the GPDS-960 dataset, it contains 881 users. Each user has 24 genuine signatures and 30 skilled forged signatures, with a total of 47,574 signatures. GPDS-160 and GPDS-300 datasets are the subsets of the GPDS-960 dataset. They contain the signatures of the first 160 and 300 users of the GPDS-960 dataset. For the CEDAR dataset, it contains 55 users and each user has 24 genuine signatures and 24 forged signatures, with a total of 2,640 signatures. The Brazilian PUC-PR dataset contains 168 users. For the first 60 users, each user has 40 genuine signatures, 10 simple forged signatures, and 10 skilled forged signatures. For the last 108 users, each user only has 40 genuine signatures and with a total of 7,920 signatures.

4.2 Experimental Settings

For the feature extraction, we extract features from the output of the second fully connected layer from SigNet and SignNet-F. The dimension size of extracted features is 2,048. After the feature extraction, we generate the second view of extracted features and apply the CCA-based multi-view representation learning approaches for feature learning. For KCCA, we use Radial Basis Function (RBF) as the kernel function, and set $\gamma = 0.001$. Since the KCCA is hard to train when the number of training samples is too large, we use 50% samples for each user to build the training set in our experiments to reduce the memory requirement. For DCCA, we use two DNN networks with the same structure of $2048 - 1024 - 2048 - 4096 - 2048$. The epoch is set to 10, batch size = 2000 (because the training process needs a relatively big batch size for observing the behavior on different views of signatures), and learning rate = 0.001.

After feature extraction and feature learning processes, we train SVMs as the WD classifiers for establishing a completed signature verification system. We follow the data partition scheme in [12] to build the training set. For the GPDS-160 dataset, we randomly select $n \in \{1, ..., 14\}$ genuine signatures from the target user as the positive samples, and 10 genuine signatures of each user from the last 721 users in the GPDS-960 dataset as the negative samples. For the GPDS-300 dataset, we also randomly select $n \in \{1, ..., 14\}$ genuine signatures from the target user as the positive samples, and 10 genuine signatures of each user from the last 581 users in the GPDS-960 dataset as the negative samples. For the CEDAR dataset, we randomly select $n \in \{1, ..., 12\}$ genuine signatures from the target user as the positive samples, and 10 genuine signatures of each user from the remaining 54 users. For the Brazilian PUC-PR dataset, we randomly select $n \in \{1, ..., 30\})$ genuine signatures from the target user in the first 60 users as the positive samples, and 10 genuine signatures of each user from the last 108 users as the negative samples. For parameters in linear SVM, the C_N is set to 1 and C_P is calculated by Eq. 5.

For the test process, we randomly select 10 genuine signatures and 10 skilled forgeries from the target user, 10 genuine signatures from the development set as random forgeries for each user on GPDS-160 and GPDS-300 datasets. For the CEDAR dataset, we randomly select 10 genuine signatures and 10 skilled forgeries for each user as the test set. For the Brazilian PUC-PR dataset, we randomly select 10 genuine signatures, 10 skilled forgeries from the target user, and 10 genuine signatures from the last 108 users in the Brazilian PUC-PR dataset as random forgeries. Finally, the experimental results are the averages with 10 trials.

Table 1. Comparing with different evaluation measurements on CCA, KCCA, and DCCA-based multi-view representation learning approaches on GPDS-160 and GPDS-300 datasets. Here, the feature that we use is SigNet-F, the number of reference samples is 12 (the number of training samples in SVM). The red and green values represent the improvement and deterioration compared with the original features, respectively.

Method	Dataset	FRR	FAR_random	FAR_skilled	EER_global	EER_user
-	160	6.39 (±0.67)	0.01 (±0.02)	3.96 (±0.18)	5.15 (±0.28)	2.60 (±0.39)
CCA	160	5.34 (±0.33)	0.01 (±0.00)	3.22 (±0.24)	4.21 (±0.13)	1.93 (±0.22)
KCCA	160	3.24 (±0.21)	0.02 (±0.00)	5.42 (±0.21)	4.25 (±0.20)	1.98 (±0.13)
DCCA	160	19.48 (±1.10)	0.48 (±0.02)	5.06 (±0.25)	9.78 (±0.20)	7.60 (±0.27)
-	300	6.80 (±0.31)	0.00 (±0.01)	6.16 (±0.17)	6.44 (±0.17)	3.56 (±0.18)
CCA	300	5.70 (±0.36)	0.01 (±0.00)	3.53 (±0.14)	4.49 (±0.15)	2.35 (±0.17)
KCCA	300	3.60 (±0.36)	0.01 (±0.00)	5.82 (±0.17)	4.63 (±0.18)	2.43 (±0.21)
DCCA	300	20.35 (±0.89)	0.53 (±0.02)	5.05 (±0.25)	9.63 (±0.28)	7.39 (±0.29)

Table 2. Comparison with the state-of-the-art verification systems on the GPDS-160 dataset. Here, "#Refs" represents the number of reference samples during the training process.

Feature	#Refs	EER (%)
Curvelet transform [10]	12	15.07
LBP, HOG, SIFT [37]	5	7.98
LBP, HOG, SIFT [37]	12	6.97
AlexNet [11]	14	2.74 (±0.18)
SigNet-F [12]	5	3.52 (±0.28)
SigNet-F [12]	12	2.60 (±0.39)
CCA-SigNet-F	12	**1.93 (±0.22)**
KCCA-SigNet-F	12	1.98 (±0.13)
DCCA-SigNet-F	12	7.60 (±0.27)

4.3 Evaluation Measurements

We use the following evaluation measurements to measure the performance of different approaches. False Rejection Rate (FRR): the rate of the genuine signatures that are rejected as forgeries; False Acceptance Rate for random forgeries (FAR_random): the rate of the random forgeries that are accepted as genuine signatures; False Acceptance Rate for skilled forgeries (FAR_skilled): the rate of the skilled forgeries that are accepted as genuine signatures; Equal Error Rate (EER): the error when FAR = FRR. Here, the EER includes two forms, i.e. EER_user: using user-specific decision thresholds and EER_global: using a global decision threshold.

4.4   Experiments on the GPDS Dataset

Table 1 shows the performance of CCA, KCCA, and DCCA-based multi-view representation learning methods with several evaluation measurements on the GPDS-160 and GPDS-300 datasets. We can see that the KCCA-based approach achieves the lowest FRR both in the GPDS-160 and GPDS-300 datasets, and the CCA-based method also improves FRR. For the $FAR_{skilled}$, only the CCA-based method improves it on the GPDS-160 dataset and all multi-view representation learning methods improve it and the CCA-based method achieves the best $FAR_{skilled}$ on the GPDS-300 dataset. For the EER_{global} and EER_{user}, the CCA and KCCA-based methods improve them on the GPDS-160 and GPDS-300 datasets. In addition, the DCCA-based method does not perform well. The reason might be that the deep features extracted from the SigNet-F have already included the major information of the signatures. The DNNs in DCCA-based methods may destroy this information and are hard to train from the features learned from the other deep architectures.

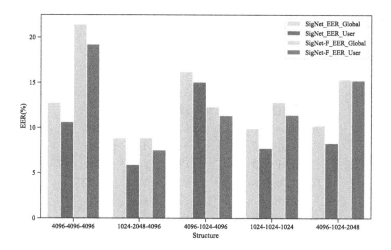

Fig. 2. The performance of the DCCA with different structures on the validation set (the users from No. 352 to No. 402) of the GPDS-960 dataset. Here, the input and output are all 2048. Therefore, we only show the middle three layers in the figure.

Tables 2 and 3 demonstrate the results that compares with the state-of-the-art verification systems on the GPDS-160 and GPDS-300 datasets. According to the tables, we can see that the CCA and KCCA-based methods improve the performance of the SigNet-F feature. The CCA-based method achieves 1.93% and 2.35% EERs which are the best results on the GPDS-160 and GPDS-300 datasets compared with the other state-of-the-art verification systems. In addition, the DCCA-based method also degrades the performance compared with CCA and KCCA-based methods, the reason might be similar to before.

Table 3. Comparison with the state-of-the-art verification systems on the GPDS-300 dataset.

Feature	#Refs	EER (%)
LBP [33]	10	20.94
Grid Feat [41]	12	3.24
GLBP [31]	12	2.84
Quad-tree [32]	10	9.30
SigNet-F [12]	5	4.84 (±0.26)
SigNet-F [12]	12	3.56 (±0.18)
CCA-SigNet-F	12	**2.35 (±0.17)**
KCCA-SigNet-F	12	2.43 (±0.21)
DCCA-SigNet-F	12	7.39 (±0.29)

Table 4. Comparison with the state-of-the-art verification systems on the CEDAR dataset.

Feature	#Refs	EER (%)
Quad-tree [32]	10	18.15
Grid Feat [41]	10	3.02
GLBP [31]	12	7.94
SigNet [12]	8	5.03 (±0.75)
SigNet [12]	12	4.76 (±0.36)
SigNet-F [12]	8	4.77 (±0.76)
SigNet-F [12]	12	4.63 (±0.42)
CCA-SigNet-F	8	2.79 (±0.53)
CCA-SigNet-F	12	**2.55 (±0.41)**
KCCA-SigNet-F	8	4.41 (±0.80)
KCCA-SigNet-F	12	3.93 (±0.41)
DCCA-SigNet-F	8	11.49 (±0.84)
DCCA-SigNet-F	12	10.90 (±0.70)

Since the DCCA-based method does not work well in most cases, we evaluate different structures of DCCA on the validation set of the GPDS-960 dataset. Figure 2 shows the performance of different structures of DCCA with the EER measurements on the features of SigNet and SigNet-F. From the figure, we can see that the structure $1024-2048-4096$ achieves the best performance compared with the other structures. That is the reason why we choose this structure in our experiments. In addition, if the structure is $4096-4096-4096$, the performance becomes much worse, which means the completed architectures will degrade the learning ability of the DCCA-based method.

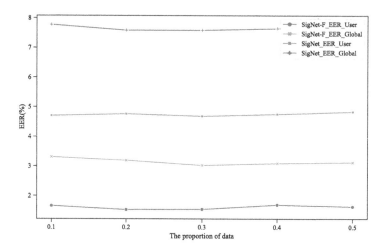

Fig. 3. The performance of the KCCA with different proportions of data on the validation set.

To evaluate the influence of the proportion of data on the KCCA-based method, we design an experiment using the different proportions of signatures from each user to train the KCCA. Figure 3 demonstrates the results with the EER measurements on the features of SigNet and SigNet-F on the validation set of the GPDS-960 dataset. We can see that the performance is not very sensitive to the change of proportions. It means that we can use a small amount of data to train the KCCA in our experiments.

4.5 Experiments on the CEDAR and Brazilian PUC-PR Datasets

To evaluate the generalization ability of the proposed framework, we test it on the CEDAR and Brazilian PUC-PR datasets. Here, the features are also extracted from the SigNet or SigNet-F which are trained on the GPDS dataset. Especially, due to the simple forgeries that are existed in the Brazilian PUC-PR dataset, some systems report the Average Error Rate (AER) that is calculated as $AER = (FRR + FAR_{random} + FAR_{simple} + FAR_{skilled})/4$, where, the FAR_{simple} is the rate of the simple forgeries that are accepted as genuine signatures. The experimental results are shown in Tables 4 and 5.

It can be seen from the tables that the proposed framework also obtains the best performance compared with the other state-of-the-art verification systems on the CEDAR and Brazilian PUC-PR datasets. The CCA and KCCA-based methods improve the performance of features that are extracted from the SigNet or SigNet-F. The CCA-based method achieves 2.65% and 2.55% EERs on the CEDAR and Brazilian PUC-PR datasets when the number of reference samples is 12, respectively, which is better than the KCCA and DCCA-based methods.

Table 5. Comparison with the state-of-the-art verification systems on the Brazilian PUC-PR datasets.

Feature	#Refs	AER/EER (%)
Deep CNN features [30]	30	4.17
Graphometric [3]	15	5.65
MAML [13]	15	5.74 (±0.84)
SigNet [12]	15	2.07 (±0.63)
SigNet [12]	30	2.01 (±0.43)
SigNet-F [12]	15	4.03 (±0.59)
SigNet-F [12]	30	3.44 (±0.37)
CCA-SigNet	15	1.06 (±0.37)
CCA-SigNet-F	15	1.42 (±0.50)
CCA-SigNet	30	**0.92 (±0.24)**
CCA-SigNet-F	30	1.08 (±0.34)
KCCA-SigNet	15	2.38 (±0.38)
KCCA-SigNet-F	15	2.29 (±0.51)
KCCA-SigNet	30	2.11 (±0.37)
KCCA-SigNet-F	30	1.98 (±0.47)
DCCA-SigNet	15	3.83 (±0.48)
DCCA-SigNet-F	15	5.40 (±0.62)
DCCA-SigNet	30	3.57 (±0.69)
DCCA-SigNet-F	30	5.20 (±0.76)

5   Conclusion

In this paper, we propose that applying multi-view representation learning approaches to build a framework to further improve the performance of the features learned from the deep learning-based architectures for offline signature verification tasks. Extensive experimental results on three benchmark datasets prove that the CCA and KCCA-based multi-view representation learning methods improve the learning ability of deep learning-based feature extractors and achieve state-of-the-art or competitive performance in most cases. In future work, since the DCCA-based method can not work well, we plan to explore different strategies on this method and evaluate more multi-view representation learning-based methods for combining dynamic information for verification systems.

Acknowledgement. This work was supported by Innovation and Cultivation Project for Youth Talents of Shihezi University (Grant Number CXPY201905), Financial and Science Technology Plan Project of Xinjiang Production and Construction Corps (Grant Number 2017DB005), Key Industry Innovation and Development Support Plan in Southern Xinjiang (Grant Number 2017DB005), Fund Project of XJPCC (2019AB001, 2017CD010, and 2017CA018), and Shihezi University Scientific Research Project for High-level Talents (RCZK202028).

References

1. Andrew, G., Arora, R., Bilmes, J., Livescu, K.: Deep canonical correlation analysis. In: ICML, pp. 1247–1255 (2013)
2. Bengio, Y., Lecun, Y., Hinton, G.: Deep learning for AI. Commun. ACM **64**(7), 58–65 (2021)
3. Bertolini, D., Oliveira, L.S., Justino, E., Sabourin, R.: Reducing forgeries in writer-independent off-line signature verification through ensemble of classifiers. Pattern Recogn. **43**(1), 387–396 (2010)
4. Chen, J., Ran, X.: Deep learning with edge computing: a review. Proc. IEEE **107**(8), 1655–1674 (2019)
5. Chen, X., Jin, L., Zhu, Y., Luo, C., Wang, T.: Text recognition in the wild: a survey. ACM Comput. Surv. **54**(2), 1–35 (2021)
6. de Freitas, C.O.A., et al.: Bases de dados de cheques bancários brasileiros
7. Diaz, M., Ferrer, M.A., Impedovo, D., Malik, M.I., Pirlo, G., Plamondon, R.: A perspective analysis of handwritten signature technology. ACM Comput. Surv. **51**(6), 1–39 (2019)
8. Ferrer, M.A., Vargas, J.F., Morales, A., Ordonez, A.: Robustness of offline signature verification based on gray level features. IEEE Trans. Inf. Forensics Secur. **7**(3), 966–977 (2012)
9. Ghosh, R.: A recurrent neural network based deep learning model for offline signature verification and recognition system. Expert Syst. Appl. **168**, 114249 (2021)
10. Guerbai, Y., Chibani, Y., Hadjadji, B.: The effective use of the one-class SVM classifier for handwritten signature verification based on writer-independent parameters. Pattern Recogn. **48**(1), 103–113 (2015)
11. Hafemann, L.G., Sabourin, R., Oliveira, L.S.: Analyzing features learned for offline signature verification using deep CNNs. In: ICPR, pp. 2989–2994 (2016)
12. Hafemann, L.G., Sabourin, R., Oliveira, L.S.: Learning features for offline handwritten signature verification using deep convolutional neural networks. Pattern Recogn. **70**, 163–176 (2017)
13. Hafemann, L.G., Sabourin, R., Oliveira, L.S.: Meta-learning for fast classifier adaptation to new users of signature verification systems. IEEE Trans. Inf. Forensics Secur. **15**, 1735–1745 (2019)
14. Hardoon, D.R., Szedmak, S., Shawe-Taylor, J.: Canonical correlation analysis: an overview with application to learning methods. Neural Comput. **16**(12), 2639–2664 (2004)
15. Hotelling, H.: Relations between two sets of variates*. Biometrika **28**(3–4), 321–377 (1936)
16. Houtinezhad, M., Ghaffary, H.R.: Writer-independent signature verification based on feature extraction fusion. Multimedia Tools Appl. **79**, 6759–6779 (2019). https://doi.org/10.1007/s11042-019-08447-7
17. Jain, A., Singh, S.K., Singh, K.P.: Signature verification using geometrical features and artificial neural network classifier. Neural Comput. Appl. **33**(12), 6999–7010 (2020). https://doi.org/10.1007/s00521-020-05473-7
18. Kalera, M.K., Srihari, S., Xu, A.: Offline signature verification and identification using distance statistics. Int. J. Pattern Recognit Artif Intell. **18**(07), 1339–1360 (2004)
19. Khan, S.H., Khan, Z., Shafait, F.: Can signature biometrics address both identification and verification problems? In: ICDAR, pp. 981–985 (2004)

20. LeCun, Y., Bengio, Y., Hinton, G.: Deep learning. Nature **521**(7553), 436–444 (2015)
21. Li, H., Ota, K., Dong, M.: Learning IoT in edge: deep learning for the internet of things with edge computing. IEEE Netw. **32**(1), 96–101 (2018)
22. Li, J., Li, Z., Lu, G., Xu, Y., Zhang, B., Zhang, D.: Asymmetric Gaussian process multi-view learning for visual classification. Inf. Fusion **65**, 108–118 (2021)
23. Lin, Q., Luo, C., Jin, L., Lai, S.: STAN: a sequential transformation attention-based network for scene text recognition. Pattern Recogn. **111**, 107692 (2021)
24. Liu, D.C., Nocedal, J.: On the limited memory BFGS method for large scale optimization. Math. Program. **45**(1), 503–528 (1989)
25. Lv, Z., Qiao, L., Li, J., Song, H.: Deep-learning-enabled security issues in the internet of things. IEEE Internet Things J. **8**(12), 9531–9538 (2020)
26. Masoudnia, S., Mersa, O., Araabi, B.N., Vahabie, A.H., Sadeghi, M.A., Ahmadabadi, M.N.: Multi-representational learning for offline signature verification using multi-loss snapshot ensemble of CNNs. Expert Syst. Appl. **133**, 317–330 (2019)
27. Melzer, T., Reiter, M., Bischof, H.: Kernel canonical correlation analysis. In: ICANN, pp. 353–360 (2001)
28. Nasser, A.T., Dogru, N.: Signature recognition by using sift and surf with SVM basic on RBF for voting online. In: ICET, pp. 1–5 (2017)
29. Nie, F., Cai, G., Li, J., Li, X.: Auto-weighted multi-view learning for image clustering and semi-supervised classification. IEEE Trans. Image Process. **27**(3), 1501–1511 (2017)
30. Rantzsch, H., Yang, H., Meinel, C.: Signature embedding: writer independent offline signature verification with deep metric learning. In: Bebis, G., et al. (eds.) ISVC 2016. LNCS, vol. 10073, pp. 616–625. Springer, Cham (2016). https://doi.org/10.1007/978-3-319-50832-0_60
31. Serdouk, Y., Nemmour, H., Chibani, Y.: New gradient features for off-line handwritten signature verification. In: INISTA, pp. 1–4 (2015)
32. Serdouk, Y., Nemmour, H., Chibani, Y.: Handwritten signature verification using the quad-tree histogram of templates and a support vector-based artificial immune classification. Image Vis. Comput. **66**, 26–35 (2017)
33. Soleimani, A., Araabi, B.N., Fouladi, K.: Deep multitask metric learning for offline signature verification. Pattern Recogn. Lett. **80**, 84–90 (2016)
34. Vargas, F., Ferrer, M., Travieso, C., Alonso, J.: Off-line handwritten signature GPDS-960 corpus. In: ICDAR, vol. 2, pp. 764–768 (2007)
35. Wan, Q., Zou, Q.: Learning metric features for writer-independent signature verification using dual triplet loss. In: ICPR, pp. 3853–3859 (2021)
36. Yao, S., Zhao, Y., Zhang, A., Hu, S., Shao, H., Zhang, C., Su, L., Abdelzaher, T.: Deep learning for the internet of things. Computer **51**(5), 32–41 (2018)
37. Yılmaz, M.B., Yanıkouglu, B.: Score level fusion of classifiers in off-line signature verification. Inf. Fusion **32**, 109–119 (2016)
38. Yilmaz, M.B., Yanikoglu, B., Tirkaz, C., Kholmatov, A.: Offline signature verification using classifier combination of hog and LBP features. In: IJCB, pp. 1–7 (2011)
39. Zhao, J., Xie, X., Xu, X., Sun, S.: Multi-view learning overview: recent progress and new challenges. Inf. Fusion **38**, 43–54 (2017)
40. Zhou, Y., Zheng, J., Hu, H., Wang, Y.: Handwritten signature verification method based on improved combined features. Appl. Sci. **11**(13), 5867 (2021)
41. Zois, E.N., Alewijnse, L., Economou, G.: Offline signature verification and quality characterization using poset-oriented grid features. Pattern Recogn. **54**, 162–177 (2016)

Backdoor Attack of Graph Neural Networks Based on Subgraph Trigger

Yu Sheng, Rong Chen, Guanyu Cai, and Li Kuang[(⊠)]

School of Computer Science and Engineering, Central South University,
Changsha Hunan 410075, China
kuangli@csu.edu.com

Abstract. Graph Neural Networks (GNN) is a kind of deep learning model to process structural and semantic features of graph data. They are widely used in node classification, graph classification, and link prediction. However, deep learning models require a lot of training data and computational costs, and users usually choose the models provided by third-party platforms. Attackers make full use of their insecurity, subtly modify the training data, and affect the model accuracy. To ensure the service quality and the model robustness, researches on model attacks and defenses are launched. As a new type of attack, backdoor attacks have also been verified on the GNN model. However, existing research still has the following problems: 1) the design of triggers is single; 2) the selection of attack nodes is random; 3) the attack is only effective for some specific GNN models. To address these problems, we study the GNN backdoor attack based on the subgraph trigger. We design the trigger based on the features of the sample data and use the random graph generation algorithm to obtain the subgraph trigger. We propose to select the attack nodes by fusing the local and global structural features and fine-tuned edges when inserted into datasets. We apply it to multiple GNN models. Finally, we use fewer nodes, smaller densities and randomly fine-tune the trigger structure, the experimental results show that the attack we propose has a significant effect on the real datasets, in which clean accuracy drop is less than 0.07 and the attack success rate increases more than 75%.

Keywords: Backdoor attack · Graph classification · GNN

1 Introduction

In the real world, graph data has wide applications. Nodes and edges can represent individuals and relationships in different scenarios, respectively. For example, in social networks, a graph illustrates the attributes of each person and the relationships among them. In transportation areas, a graph can represent the changes in traffic flow between different regions. Due to the powerful expression of graphs, deep learning models which analyze and capture information in graphs have also attracted more attention. The graph neural network model learns the structural features of the graph by aggregating the information of nodes and their neighbors, which has achieved excellent performance in various graph analysis tasks such as node classification, graph classification and link prediction. With the promotion of deep learning, the computing costs

© ICST Institute for Computer Sciences, Social Informatics and Telecommunications Engineering 2021
Published by Springer Nature Switzerland AG 2021. All Rights Reserved
H. Gao and X. Wang (Eds.): CollaborateCom 2021, LNICST 407, pp. 276–296, 2021.
https://doi.org/10.1007/978-3-030-92638-0_17

for dealing with large amounts of data and huge models are increased. Service providers upload trained models to third-party platforms, and users use them to obtain services. Due to the incredible providers, malicious attackers have the opportunity to attack models. Previous studies have shown that deep learning models have some inherent weaknesses, there is uncertainty with some subtle disturbances. If a malicious attacker makes a simple modification to the training dataset, the accuracy will be affected. The attacker operates samples during the training and testing phases, reducing the model's accuracy to affect the quality of services, or to achieve some illegal intrusion purposes, such as releasing malicious advertisement.

Common model attacks include poisoning attacks [1–5], model inversion attacks [6–9], and model extraction attacks [10–13]. The poisoning attack occurs at the model training stage, aiming at reducing the model performance. The attacker mixes well-designed samples into the training dataset to mislead the model. For example, a panda picture is mixed with noise in the image data, and the picture is identified as Gibbon [14]. In the network graph, edges are added or deleted to modify the graph structure or to change the features of the nodes. Thereby the accuracy of the classification task is affected. Model inversion attack uses the memory information in the training process of the neural network to infer the statistical information of the dataset from the model. The attacker can use the inferred information to synthesize the datasets, and the users' private information will also be leaked during the iterative inference. The model extraction attack aims to infer the model's parameters, hyper-parameters, architectures, and functions. The attackers continuously submit input samples to query the corresponding prediction of the model. As a result, the confidential information of the model can be extracted from many inputs and outputs, and the entire model can even be inferred, which leads to an approximate replacement model constructed for further attacks.

The backdoor attack is a new type of poisoning attack. The attacker inserts well-designed triggers into datasets, the backdoor model normally shows in clean samples. When the samples contain triggers, they will be misclassified as the label which the attacker specifies. Deep neural network (DNN) models have been demonstrated that they were easily attacked, such as image recognition [15, 16] and text prediction [17, 18]. For example, an attacker uses triggers to forge a legitimate user's identity to deceive the access control system. Due to the system's misjudgment, the user's life and property safety are threatened [19]. As a type of deep learning model, GNN is also vulnerable to backdoor attacks. In a recommendation system or social network, the attacker generates a specific subgraph trigger and modifies the relationship between users according to the trigger. The relationship between two users will be added or deleted, and the target labels are changed to the ones specified by the attacker. Users may be exposed to malicious advertisements, reducing the recommendation system's service quality and user experience. Our original intention of studying the graph neural network backdoor attack is to guess and simulate the various ideas and methods of the attacker as much as possible, and once the weakness of model is found, the subsequent research can pay attention to designing a better model defense plan.

The dataset used by the GNN model is a graph composed of nodes and edges. Inspired by the backdoor attack in the image domain, we use a specific subgraph structure, which is composed of a small number of nodes and edges, as the backdoor trigger for the graph data. The existing research on backdoor attacks to GNN still has the following problems:

- The generated trigger is single. Most of the existing researches design a specific subgraph structure as the trigger, and then insert it for all target samples uniformly, while the diversity of the triggers is not investigated thoroughly.
- The selection of attack nodes is random. The attack nodes are usually selected by randomly sampling from the graph structure. The importance of nodes in the entire graph and the influence of nodes on the attack success rate are not investigated in detail.
- The backdoor attack method cannot adapt to various kinds of GNN models. Existing researches only show the effectiveness of attack to some specific models of GNN for some particular tasks, lacking verification on multiple variant models of GNN.

To address the problems, we start the research on backdoor attacks to GNN models and focus on three points, i.e., the generation of trigger, the selection of attack nodes, and the injection of trigger. We insert the backdoor triggers into the dataset of the GNN graphs for classification task and evaluate the effect of backdoor attacks. Our main contributions can be summarized as follows:

- We make statistical analysis of the dataset and generate triggers with specific labels according to the statistical features, and when inserting triggers, we reserve the structure of the trigger for a certain proportion of samples randomly while making minor adjustments of the trigger for the rest of samples.
- We propose a method to select attack nodes based on the structural features of the nodes, which combines the local and global structural features of the nodes in the entire graph to evaluate the importance of the nodes, and then select the most important nodes to attack.
- We use real datasets with node features to verify the effect of attack on multiple GNN models, and prove that the proposed method can achieve a relatively high attack success rate.

The rest of this paper is organized as follows. Section 2 introduces the related research in the attack of deep learning models, especially the backdoor attack to GNN models. Section 3 shows the preliminary concepts. Section 4 presents our motivation and our proposed method of backdoor attack to GNN model. Section 5 gives the experimental details and result analysis. Finally, Sect. 6 provides the conclusions and future work.

2   Related Works

Deep learning models convenient for users but expose some weaknesses. For example, the model suffers severe losses caused by some subtle modifications related to the safety of the model and the quality of service, and the modifications even violate users' privacy and legal rights. Many researchers explore the attacks and defenses to improve the stability of the model in the face of uncertain factors. In this chapter, we will introduce the related work of attacks on deep learning model.

Attacks on Deep Learning Models. Szegedy et al. [20] found that the attacker perturbed the input data in the neural network model, which eventually led to the wrong output of the model. This discovery laid the foundation for the research on neural network model attacks. The researches on model attacks and defenses are essential in artificial intelligence and security. In deep learning, a lot of studies have been launched from the attack of deep learning models in different fields, such as image recognition [21–24]. The attacker added one or more pixels to the image, and these special pixels act as triggers to make the image with these pixels be misclassified into other classes. In natural language processing [25–27], the attacker modified words without changing the flow of the sentence. It changed the sentiment or meaning of the entire sentence. And in the GNN model with graph data [28–30], attackers inserted samples of specific subgraph structure triggers, misclassifying the samples into the class specified by them. Attackers have different data manipulation permissions. In most cases, they only need to manipulate a few data, causing model errors.

Backdoor Attacks. Gu et al. [31] first proposed this concept. From this work, we can learn that the goal of a backdoor attacker is to insert a hidden backdoor, that is, a trigger, into the model. They applied the backdoor trigger to the field of traffic sign recognition. The "stop" traffic sign with a trigger will be misidentified as "deceleration". When the backdoor is not activated, the infected model can recognize benign samples normally. Once the input sample has an activated backdoor trigger, the model will modify the predicted label to the target label specified by the attacker, which is a misclassification. Users often input their data to train the models provided by third-party platforms, they cannot guarantee the security of third-party platform, It is challenging to discover the backdoor, and it is harmful to users' privacy and security. Most of the existing works on backdoor attacks are oriented to the image data, and attackers often manipulate images by designing pixel triggers [32]. Chen et al. [19] applied backdoor attacks to face recognition, and inserted triggers, such as "red glasses" into the access control system. When a malicious user wears the same glasses as the trigger, it can impersonate a legitimate user. In federal learning, similar backdoor attacks will also occur [33–35]. Backdoor attacks threaten the security of the model and can cause huge losses to users. Therefore, research on them is very important and developing.

Attack on GNN Models. Many studies have shown that operating node features or modifying structure in the graph can affect the learning performance of the GNN model. Zügner et al. [36] first studied the adversarial attack on the attribute graph. They modified the node features and graph structure in the attribute graph, which significantly reduced the accuracy of the node classification model. Dai [30], Ma [37] used reinforcement learning to explore strategies for modifying the graph structure, achieving remarkable results. For the GNN model, the backdoor attack based on the adversarial attack, Zhang et al. [38] studied the backdoor attack of random inserted triggers. To select the attack nodes randomly under a designed subgraph trigger structure, they proposed a random smoothing method to defend backdoor attacks effectively. At the same time, Xi et al. [39] also studied graph neural network backdoor attacks. This study focused on trigger generation. They used the attention mechanism to generate customized triggers, which thoroughly combined the characteristics of different graph structures to achieve better attack effects. There are still several problems in the research of GNN backdoor attacks. First, the trigger is too simple. In most cases, the shape of the triggers is fixed. A graph structure is obtained through the random graph generation algorithm to be used as a single trigger. Second, the impact of the importance of nodes on the attack effect is not considered. The third is that backdoor attack has not been verified on various GNN models, and the attack effect lacks universality. In our work, we have carried out corresponding research and have made improvements on the above three problems. See Sect. 4 for details.

Attack Nodes Selection. In the social networks, the analysis of key nodes is an important research work, because key nodes are responsible for the critical role of information transmission in the graph structure. At present, this research has a complete theory in recommendation systems and traffic road networks. Using this intuition, attackers find the key nodes in the network graph to attack when the GNN model aggregates the information of the nodes and their neighbors. The attacked nodes transmit the wrong information to the neighbors and the model. Attackers only need to operate with a small amount of data and get a better attack effect. Ma et al. [40] proposed a node importance measurement method based on random walks, attacking nodes with higher importance scores, and verified that attacking important nodes can effectively reduce the model's accuracy. Takahashi et al. [41] considered the relationship between the classification result of a node and the neighbor nodes, modeling the neighbor nodes of the graph as a neighbor tree. They selected the most influential node from the 2-hop neighbors as the attack target. Mo et al. [42] proposed measuring the local structural characteristics and global structural characteristics of the nodes, and Ma et al. [43] proposed a three-layer comprehensive impact evaluation index to measure the influence of the nodes. In [44], they took advantage of a GNN interpreter to identify the importance of nodes, then selected key nodes to insert backdoor triggers. Currently, the existing works on GNN backdoor attacks do not measure the nodes from the structural features. Our work solves this problem and measures the importance of nodes based on nodes' features.

3 Preliminaries

This section mainly introduces the basic concepts involved in the paper, laying a theoretical foundation for further research.

3.1 Concepts

Graph. Undirected graphs are used in our work. We define them as $G = (V, E)$, where $V = (v_1, v_2, \ldots, v_N)$, which means there are N nodes in the graph, and E means the set of edges $e_{i,j}$ existing between any two nodes v_i and v_j. $A \in \{0, 1\}^{N \times N}$ represents the adjacency matrix of the graph. There is an edge e_{ij} between node v_i and v_j, then $A_{i,j} = 1$, otherwise 0. At the same time, we also have a feature matrix $X \in \mathbb{R}^{N \times D}$, where x_i represents the l-dimensional features of node v_i.

GNN Graph Classification. We regard the GNN model for the graph classification task as a function $f_G : G \rightarrow y$, where f_G is the graph classifier, $y = \{y_1, y_2, \ldots, y_K\}$ indicates that the graph has K classes. The input data is represented as M samples of Graphs G and their corresponding label y, namely $D_G = \{(G_1, y_1), (G_2, y_2), \ldots, (G_M, y_M)\}$. By learning the embedding of the nodes, aggregating the features of the node and its neighbors, the model predicts graph labels as $\widehat{y}$. The graph classification by GNN is shown in Fig. 1.

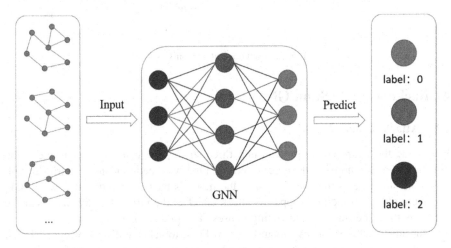

Fig. 1. GNN graph classification task

GNN Backdoor. Inspired by the poisoning attack of the GNN model, we design the backdoor attack by adding or deleting the edges of the graph to disturb the structure, as shown in Fig. 2. Unlike the poisoning attack, this modification does not happen randomly. Then, the attacked nodes in the graph are replaced one by one according to the trigger's structure. The selected attacked nodes are the same as the number of nodes in the subgraph trigger. And we will modify their original links between the attacked nodes according to the structure of the trigger.

3.2 Attack Model

Our attack model is like the work of [38, 39]. The backdoor is inserted into the graph data by well-designed subgraph triggers. In this process, we do not change the architectures and parameters of the model. A specific wrong label is assigned to the trigger. We assume that the learning model comes from a third-party platform, users input their data to obtain services. Therefore, the attacker can operate the training and test data, design and insert samples with triggers, and attack a clean model. Once the model is successfully backdoored, the clean sample input by the user can get similar results to the clean model, which is difficult to detect the backdoor triggers. While inputting the samples with triggers, the attacker's target output will be predicted by the backdoored model, and the classification accuracy will decrease significantly.

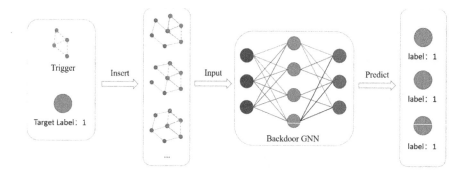

Fig. 2. Backdoor attack on GNN

4   Backdoor Attack on GNN

4.1   Attack Overview

We divide the entire attack process into three stages, the generation of triggers, the selection of attack nodes and trigger insertion. First, we need to generate a trigger with a specific structure as the "key" to open the model's backdoor. After that, we should find the nodes with the most apparent attack effect as the target. Finally, we insert the trigger both in the training and testing phases. The process is shown in Fig. 3.

Our attack scheme has two main features. First, to achieve diverse trigger attacks, we make minor adjustments based on the basic structure of the trigger for a certain proportion of samples, that is, randomly delete a small part of the edges in the trigger and maintain most of the trigger structure. Second, we measure the importance of nodes based on their global and local structural features and select the nodes with higher importance as attack nodes. The attack's goal is to classify the samples with the specific triggers to the target label specified by the attack while keeping the classification of clean samples as much as possible.

4.2   Generation of Trigger

The generation of the trigger is composed of three steps: First, we analyze the statistical information of each dataset so that we can design triggers for different datasets and different categories. Second, we use a random graph generation algorithm to generate the structure of the trigger based on the statistical information achieved in the previous step. Third, we use the nodes' label in graph samples to generate nodes' feature of the trigger, and the attacker will modify the graph labels.

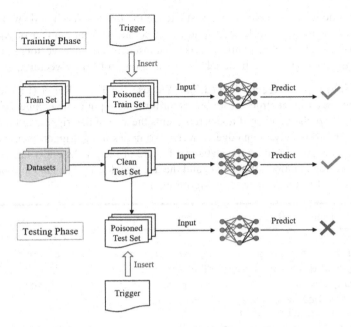

Fig. 3. The process of backdoor attack

Statistical Analysis of Dataset. We believe that there are many similarities between the graphs of the same label and differences among the graphs of different labels. We use the similarities and differences as a breakthrough in the design of backdoor triggers. Therefore, we associate the trigger with target label graphs and insert them into other labels. In the same way, we can also generate triggers corresponding to each class based on the samples of other classes.

Assuming that the attacker can only manipulate a small part of the training dataset, we randomly select 5% of the samples from the clean training dataset. Specifically, we define the target label of the attack as y_t and $y_t \in y$. In 5% of the attack samples, we calculate the average nodes $\overline{n_t}$ and average density $\overline{\rho_t}$ of samples y_t (shown in the Eq. 1 and Eq. 2), and node features x_t.

$$\overline{n_t} = \frac{\sum_{i=1}^{M_{train} \times 5\%} n_i}{M_{train} \times 5\%} \tag{1}$$

where M_{train} represents the total number of samples in the training set, n_i represents the number of nodes in sample i, the same as Eq. 2.

$$\overline{\rho_t} = \sum_{i=1}^{M_{train} \times 5\%} \frac{2e_i}{n_i(n_i - 1)} / (M_{train} \times 5\%) \tag{2}$$

where e_i represents the number of edges in sample i, and $n_i(n_i - 1)/2$ represents the edges of the fully connected graph obtained by connecting all nodes in sample i.

For the node features vector x_t, we first encode the labels of each node with one-hot to obtain the vector x_i of each node i, and then count the total number of each label. Then we sum each column of the matrix composed of all node vectors, and finally normalize them to obtain the node labels distribution probability vector x_t.

Random Subgraph Trigger Generation. We use the Erdős-Rényi (ER) algorithm [45] to generate a trigger structure. In this algorithm, the input is the number of nodes m and the density ρ, the number of nodes represents the size of the trigger, and the density represents the probability of an edge between two nodes in the trigger, then output is a random graph g. According to the statistical feature of the graphs under target label y_t, we use the average number of nodes $\overline{n_t}$ and the average density $\overline{\rho_t}$ as input to obtain the trigger g_t related to the label y_t, see Algorithm 1.

Algorithm 1: ER random graph generation

```
Input: m-nodes of trigger; ρ-density of trigger;
y_k-target label of trigger
Output: g_k-a random subgraph trigger with specif-
ic label y_k
// initialization
1 specify a topological order v_0, v_1, ..., v_m for nodes
2 foreach node v_i in nodes do
3     add node v_i to g_k
4     select node v_j in nodes randomly
5     generate r ∈ [0,1] randomly
6     if r < ρ then
7         add edge (v_i, v_j) to g_k
8 return g_k, y_k
```

Trigger Features Design. First, we use the node label distribution to generate the node characteristics of the trigger. Specially, we use one-hot encoding to obtain a vector s_i of length l for all node labels, representing the label vector of node i. The vector of n nodes can form a matrix with $n \times l$. Since a node has only one label, this matrix is very sparse. We sum up each column and finally get the label distribution of the nodes in the samples. After normalization, we get the probability of node feature distribution, and generate trigger node features based on it. Figure 4 shows the process of trigger generation.

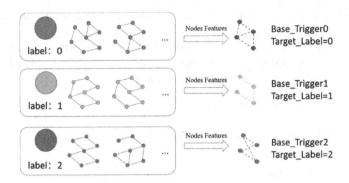

Fig. 4. Trigger generation with structural and node features

4.3 Selection of Attack Nodes

Since the GNN model aggregates information by learning the characteristics of nodes and neighbors, key nodes are essential in information transmission in the graph structure. We believe that selecting the most significant nodes to attack will increase the attack success rate. We use the degree centrality (DC) and closeness centrality (CC) of the node as the nodes' local structural feature and the global structural feature, respectively. Their definitions are as follows.

Degree Centrality. In an undirected graph, the degree centrality of node i is expressed as the number of nodes directly connected to node i, the larger the number of 1-hop neighbors of a node is, the bigger the degree centrality of the node is, the more important the node in the graph network. The degree centrality of node i is expressed as Eq. 3:

$$DC(i) = \sum_{j \neq i}^{N} (e_{i,j} \in E) \tag{3}$$

Closeness Centrality. Indicates the closeness of the distances between the current node and other nodes. If the sum of the distances between this node and other nodes is shorter, the closeness centrality is higher, and the relationship with other nodes is closer. Suppose there are multiple disconnected components in the dataset, the nodes between different connected components have no paths to communicate with others. The nodes' number of different connected components will also be different, so the closeness centrality of node i can be calculated by the following Eq. 4:

$$CC(i) = \frac{n-1}{N-1} \left(\frac{n-1}{\sum_{j}^{n-1} d_{i,j}} \right) \tag{4}$$

We use Eq. 4 to calculate the closeness centrality of multiple unconnected sub-graphs, where N represents the number of all nodes in the sample graph, n represents the number of nodes in the connected component where node i is located, and the result is the ratio of the average distance between the middle node to reachable nodes in the connected component.

Subsequently, we normalize the obtained DC and CC to map the two indicators into the same interval, and the normalized indicators are respectively marked as DC_{norm} and CC_{norm}, the two indicators are fused as shown in Eq. 5.

$$DCC = \lambda DC_{norm} + (1 - \lambda)CC_{norm} \tag{5}$$

where λ is the fusion factor used to control the ratio of two indicators.

4.4   Backdoor Insertion

After identifying the attacking nodes, we insert triggers into the graphs. In this process, the edges between the attack nodes and the normal nodes will not change, and the attack nodes are replaced with the trigger nodes one by one, including the structural information between the nodes and the features of the nodes.

We divide the trigger insertion into two phases: training and testing phase. The attacker's goal is not to affect the accuracy but ensure the attack is hidden in the training phase. We only select a small part of the training data to insert triggers. Since the generated triggers are related to a specific class of graphs, labels of samples with triggers are all modified to the target label in the training set. In the testing phase, the attacker hopes to increase the attack effect and ensure the effectiveness of the attack. In a word, the accuracy does not change significantly on the clean samples but drops significantly on the poisoned test set with inserted triggers. We insert triggers into all samples in the test set and evaluate the effect of the attack based on the results predicted by the model.

5   Experiment and Evaluation

5.1   Datasets

We use three public datasets DD[1], Mutagenicity[2] and Proteins-full[3] with graph labels and node labels in experiments. The statistical information is shown in Table 1. The three datasets are all binary classification tasks, and the part in brackets represents the data situation of the two labels. According to statistical information, we conclude that samples with different labels have different structural features such as node distribution and density in the same dataset. We generate the trigger by selecting the information of the target label, so that our trigger is associated with the sample data, and the attack target is not blind, this label can be used as the attacker's set tag during attack.

---

[1] https://networkrepository.com/DD.php.

[2] https://networkrepository.com/Mutagenicity.php.

[3] https://networkrepository.com/PROTEINS-full.php.

Table 1. Statistical information of datasets

Datasets	DD	Mutagenicity	Proteins-full
Graphs	1178	4337	1113
Classes	2(690|486)	2(2400|1935)	2(662|449)
Avg_Nodes	284(355|183)	30(29|31)	39(50|23)
Max_Nodes	5748	417	620
Min_Nodes	30	4	4
Node_Labels	89	14	3
Avg_Edges	715.66(903.3|449.25)	30.77(30.29|31.35)	72.82(94.08|41.47)
Avg_Desity	0.0278(0.02|0.04)	0.0913(0.09|0.09)	0.2122(0.14|0.32)
Avg_Degree	5.03	2.03	3.73
Max_Degree	19	4	25
Min_Degree	1	0	0

5.2 Evaluation Metrics

We set up three evaluation indicators to comprehensively evaluate our attack, including model accuracy, attack success rate, and clean test set accuracy drop. The detailed explanation is as follows.

Model Accuracy. We denote the label of the graph i as y_i, and the predicted result of the model is $\widehat{y}_i$. The accuracy represents the proportion of correctly classified samples in the total samples, which is expressed as Eq. 6:

$$ACC = \frac{\sum_i^N \mathbb{I}(\widehat{y}_i = y_i)}{N} \qquad (6)$$

Attack Success Rate. The attack success rate is used to measure the effectiveness of the attack. We mark the attacker's expected error label as y, and attack success rate is expressed as the misclassified samples among all the samples classified as y. The attack success rate can be expressed as Eq. 7:

$$ASR = \frac{\sum_i^N \mathbb{I}(\widehat{y}_i = y | y_i \neq y)}{\sum_i^N \mathbb{I}(y_i \neq y)} \qquad (7)$$

Clean Accuracy Drop. This indicator is used to calculate the difference between the accuracy of the clean test set and the baseline test set when triggers are inserted into the training set but not in test set. The accuracy of the baseline test set comes from the test accuracy of the clean dataset when the backdoor triggers are not inserted. It is defined as Eq. 8:

$$CAD = ACC_{baseline\_test} - ACC_{backdoor\_clean\_test} \tag{8}$$

According to the above indicators, our goal is to only insert triggers into the training set without affecting the model's accuracy. After triggers are inserted into both the training set and test set, the accuracy will drop significantly, ensuring that the attack success rate is high, and the accuracy drop of the clean test set is as small as possible.

5.3   Experimental Setup

According to node features distribution and target label of the trigger, we use the ER algorithm to generate a trigger with m nodes and density of ρ. If there are no special instructions, we default m = 4, ρ is from the average density of the sample with the label of 0 in the attacked graph, and the target label is 0. The training set and the test set are divided based on the ratio of 9:1. In the first stage of the attack, we randomly select 5% of the samples from the training set, according to the DCC ranking, select the m nodes with the highest scores as the attack nodes, and modify the graphs' labels. In the second stage of the attack, we insert triggers in the same way for all test samples, and keep a clean test set as a reference without modifying the graph labels. Table 2 summarizes the default parameter settings of the model.

Table 2. Default parameter settings

Type	Parameters	Setting
GCN	Layer	2
GraphSAGE	Layer	2
	Aggregate	Mean
GIN	Layer	5
	Aggregate	Sum
Training	Optimizer	Adam
	Learning rate	0.01
	Dropout	0.5
	Epochs	350
Trigger	Size	4
	Density	Sample
	Intensity	5%(train_set),100%(test_set)
	Nodes features	Sample, Reverse
	Tuning parameter	0.8

Note: Layer in the table refers to the number of layers of the GNN model. Aggregate is an aggregation function. Sample means it is generated according to the statistical features of the corresponding dataset, and reverse sorts the probability values in the distribution vector of the node features based on Sample. Then we reverse the result of the sorting, exchanging the largest and smallest values one by one. Finally, we obtain a new probability value distribution and generate node features according to the new distribution vector

5.4   Result and Analysis

We evaluate the basic classification accuracy of different models on three datasets as a baseline for subsequent reference and comparison. The results are shown in Table 3.

Table 3. Baseline accuracy

Model	Accuracy	DD	Mutagenicity	Proteins-full
GIN	TrainAcc_Baseline	0.9903	0.9024	0.7445
	TestAcc_Baseline	0.7421	0.8078	0.7398
GraphSAGE	TrainAcc_Baseline	0.9961	0.8682	0.7901
	TestAcc_Baseline	0.7419	0.8295	0.7190
GCN	TrainAcc_Baseline	0.9519	0.8443	0.7690
	TestAcc_Baseline	0.7266	0.7717	0.7473

Influence of Trigger Size and Density. In this experiment, we inserted triggers into the training and test sets on the GIN model. We used the comprehensive indicators of CAD and ASR to choose the most negligible impact on the dataset (the CAD is smaller), the better attack effect (the ASR is large), and triggers with fewer nodes. The results are shown in Fig. 5, where (a) shows the influence of the number and density of trigger nodes on CAD; (b) is the influence of the number and density of trigger nodes on ASR.

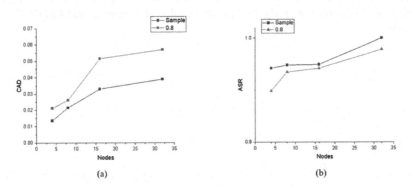

(a)   (b)

Fig. 5. Influence of trigger parameters

From Fig. 5(a), we can find that the smaller the number of trigger nodes, the smaller the CAD, and the smaller the impact on the clean dataset. At the same time, the sample density is much less than 0.8, and the higher the trigger density, the larger the CAD, the greater the impact on the clean dataset. Figure 5(b) shows the relationship between the attack success rate and the number of nodes and density. We found that the larger the number of nodes, the higher the attack success rate, and the sample density of the dataset can be used simultaneously to get better results.

Through the above results, we prefer to select triggers with a smaller number of nodes and a density closer to the dataset to ensure a higher attack success rate and better interference to the dataset, making the attack effective and hidden. Finally, we set the number of trigger nodes to 4 nodes, and the trigger density is the average density of the target category of each dataset. On the one hand, four nodes have achieved a higher attack success rate and a lower clean dataset error. On the other hand, four nodes can have more connection methods than other nodes, which is convenient to operate the structure of the trigger.

Influence of Trigger Node Features. We use two ways to add node features to the trigger subgraph. We count the node features of the attacked sample graphs, mapping them into a one-dimensional vector, and then normalize them to get the node features' distribution probability vector. The Sample method generates similar node features based on the distribution vector. In contrast, the Reverse uses reverse sorting based on Sample to get opposite node features distributions to generate opposite node features. By comparing the attack success rate of the two methods, we find that the latter's attack effect is more obvious, as shown in Fig. 6. Therefore, the node features generation of our trigger is implemented according to the Reverse method, and we use the generated trigger with node features as the default trigger for subsequent comparison experiments.

Influence of Attack Nodes Selection. In response to the selection of attacking nodes based on the importance of the nodes proposed in our work, we compare the DCC and randomly select nodes, the most important nodes and the least important nodes based on the DCC metric. The experimental results are shown in Table 4, where MaxDCC indicates that the nodes with the highest DCC value are selected, and MinDCC is the opposite.

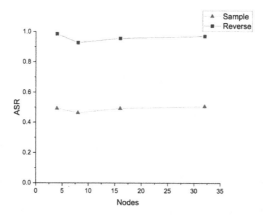

Fig. 6. Influence of node features

Table 4. Influence of attack nodes selection

Method	TrainAcc	CleanTestAcc	BackdoorTestAcc	ASR
RandomSample	0.9742	0.6772	0.3580	0.9420
MaxDCC	0.9852	0.6821	0.3611	0.9710
MinDCC	0.9814	0.6684	0.5377	0.8841

According to the results in Table 4, it is better to select attack nodes based on the importance of nodes than random selection, and the more important nodes are attacked, the higher the attack success rate is. The DCC that we propose achieves a 97.1% success rate, which is better than random selection. The method is about 3% higher than the random sample, and about 9% higher than MinDCC.

Fine-Tuning of Trigger. This experiment learns the attack effect of inserting triggers with different shapes into the same dataset. We adjust the structure of the trigger with a fine-tuning parameter of 0.8 on the basic trigger structure. The fine-tuning parameter guides us to retain the edges of the trigger, and we obtain triggers with different structures. The structure of the trigger subgraph is not fixed, which is more difficult to detect the backdoor by analyzing the graph structure. The experimental results are presented in Table 5. The first row of each dataset corresponds to the result of using the basic trigger, and the second row is the fine-tuning of the base trigger. We also use three other triggers to compare the fine-tuning experiments and then visualize the maximum attack success rate and the average attack success rate. Results are shown in Fig. 7.

Table 5. Results of fine-tuning trigger

Datasets	TrainAcc	CleanTestAcc	BackdoorTestAcc	ASR
DD	0.9852	0.6821	0.3611	0.9710
	0.9856	0.7542	0.3808	0.9855
Mutagenicity	0.8833	0.7868	0.3038	1
	0.8871	0.7845	0.3070	1
Proteins-full	0.7246	0.6988	0.6050	0.7679
	0.7184	0.6810	0.5708	0.8214

From Table 5, we find that the fine-tuning of the trigger has an unnoticeable impact on the attack success rate of the DD dataset and the Mutagenicity dataset. We think it is because the trigger densities of these two datasets are small, and the number of nodes is minimal. In the case of a small trigger size, it does not have too many edges to satisfy our fine-tuning strategy, and the Proteins-full dataset density is slightly larger, so the fine-tuning strategy has an impact.

From Fig. 7, we can find that even if the number and density of nodes increase, the fine-tuning of the trigger does not affect the attack effect. In summary, we can conclude that even if the attacker makes a slight modification to the trigger, attack also has a good effect.

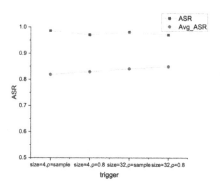

Fig. 7. Results of fine-tuning trigger

Attack on Different GNN Models. To better explore the universal applicability of backdoor attacks to the GNN model, we use the other two classic GNN models (GraphSAGE and GCN). In this part, our attack strategy is to use the base trigger of each dataset, according to DCC metric, to select the node with the largest value for trigger insertion. Table 6 presents the final experimental results.

Table 6. Attack on GNN models

ASR	DD	Mutagenicity	Proteins-full
(a) Attack on GIN			
Max_ASR	0.971	1	0.7857
Avg_ASR	0.859	1	0.6219
(b) Attack on GraphSAGE			
Max_ASR	1	1	0.8571
Avg_ASR	0.986	1	0.6721
(c) Attack on GCN			
Max_ASR	1	1	0.875
Avg_ASR	0.974	1	0.6604

In these three models, GIN pays more attention to the structure information of the sample, GraphSAGE and GCN pay more attention to the node's features. From the results, our trigger modifies the sample structure while also modifying the node features of the sample. In different GNN models, our attack methods have shown promising results. A 100% attack success rate has been achieved on the Mutagenicity dataset.

We compare the number and density of nodes in the three datasets and find that this dataset has fewer nodes and a lower density. The number of nodes in the same trigger. The ratio of attacked nodes and modified edges in this dataset is larger in the whole graph, and the effect will be more significant than other datasets. The Proteins_full dataset has fewer nodes but a slightly larger density. Compared with the Mutagenicity dataset, its edges are more abundant, and the proportion of its edges modified during backdoor attacks is relatively small, so the effect is slightly worse than other datasets. Overall, our attack scheme uses fewer attack nodes and the same density as the dataset. Whether there are more nodes or fewer datasets, we can obtain a higher attack success rate and attack different GNN models.

6   Conclusions and Future Work

In this work, we study the backdoor attack of the GNN model based on subgraph triggers, and use sample statistics to generate specific triggers. We also design a fine-tuning strategy to study the impact of diversified triggers on attack success rate. At the same time, we propose measuring the importance of nodes based on the node structural features and selecting attacking nodes according to the metrics. Our method has been validated on GNN models and multiple real datasets. The experimental results show that designing diversified triggers to implement GNN backdoor attacks is effective. To achieve a higher attack success rate, using node importance to select attack nodes is better than randomly selecting attack nodes.

There are still many issues worthy of researching in our work, the most important of which is to design an effective defense strategy to actively respond to different backdoor attacks and maintain the model's security and stability. In general, it can be divided into the following two aspects.

- Detection of backdoor attacks. Through the research of the attacks, we can find the attacker's similar destructive behaviors, such as the strategy of modifying the dataset. We can start from the anomaly detection of the dataset, detecting whether there is a backdoor trigger in the dataset, or analyzing the similarity of nodes and edges. It can detect abnormal nodes and edges to troubleshoot backdoor triggers.
- Defense against backdoor attacks. Attack and defense are like two parties in a game. Both parties need to constantly explore new strategies to interfere with the opponent's operations. We hope future work will explore the defense against model backdoor attacks from two aspects, pre-training before attack and cleaning the backdoor after attack.

Acknowledgement. This work was supported by the National Natural Science Foundation of China (grant no.61772560).

References

1. Jagielski, M., Oprea, A., Biggio, B., et al.: Manipulating machine learning: Poisoning attacks and countermeasures for regression learning. In: 2018 IEEE Symposium on Security and Privacy (SP). IEEE, 19–35 (2018)
2. Shafahi, A., Huang, W.R., Najibi, M., et al.: Poison frogs! targeted clean-label poisoning attacks on neural networks. arXiv preprint arXiv:1804.00792 (2018)
3. Demontis, A., Melis, M., Pintor, M., et al.: Why do adversarial attacks transfer? Explaining transferability of evasion and poisoning attacks. In: 28th {USENIX} Security Symposium ({USENIX} Security 19), pp. 321–338 (2019)
4. Wang, Y., Chaudhuri, K.: Data poisoning attacks against online learning. arXiv preprint arXiv:1808.08994 (2018)
5. Steinhardt, J., Koh, P.W., Liang, P.: Certified defenses for data poisoning attacks. arXiv preprint arXiv:1706.03691 (2017)
6. Basu, S., Izmailov, R., Mesterharm, C.: Membership model inversion attacks for deep networks. arXiv preprint arXiv:1910.04257 (2019)
7. Song, C., Ristenpart, T., Shmatikov, V.: Machine learning models that remember too much. In: Proceedings of the 2017 ACM SIGSAC Conference on Computer and Communications Security, pp. 587–601 (2017)
8. Veale, M., Binns, R., Edwards, L.: Algorithms that remember: model inversion attacks and data protection law. Philos. Trans. Royal Soc. Math. Phys. Eng. Sci. **376**(2133), 20180083 (2018)
9. Romagnoli, R., Weerakkody, S., Sinopoli, B.: A model inversion based watermark for replay attack detection with output tracking. In: 2019 American Control Conference (ACC). IEEE, pp. 384–390 (2019)
10. Wang, B., Gong, N.Z.: Stealing hyperparameters in machine learning. In: 2018 IEEE Symposium on Security and Privacy (SP). IEEE, pp. 36–52 (2018)
11. Papernot, N., McDaniel, P., Goodfellow, I., et al.: Practical black-box attacks against machine learning. In: Proceedings of the 2017 ACM on Asia Conference on Computer and Communications Security, pp. 506–519 (2017)
12. Orekondy, T., Schiele, B., Fritz, M.: Knockoff nets: Stealing functionality of black-box models. In: Proceedings of the IEEE/CVF Conference on Computer Vision and Pattern Recognition, pp. 4954–4963 (2019)
13. Correia-Silva, J.R., Berriel, R.F, Badue, C., et al.: Copycat cnn: Stealing knowledge by persuading confession with random non-labeled data. In: 2018 International Joint Conference on Neural Networks (IJCNN). IEEE, pp. 1–8 (2018)
14. Launchbury, J.: A DARPA Perspective on Artificial Intelligence. 11 (2019). Accessed November 2017
15. Li, H., Wang, Y., Xie, X., et al.: Light can hack your face! black-box backdoor attack on face recognition systems. arXiv preprint arXiv:2009.06996 (2020)
16. Zhao, S., Ma, X., Zheng, X., et al.: Clean-label backdoor attacks on video recognition models. In: Proceedings of the IEEE/CVF Conference on Computer Vision and Pattern Recognition, pp. 14443–14452 (2020)
17. Sun, L.: Natural backdoor attack on text data. arXiv preprint arXiv:2006.16176 (2020)
18. Dai, J., Chen, C., Li, Y.: A backdoor attack against LSTM-based text classification systems. IEEE Access **7**, 138872–138878 (2019)
19. Chen, X., Liu, C., Li, B., et al.: Targeted backdoor attacks on deep learning systems using data poisoning. arXiv preprint arXiv:1712.05526 (2017)

20. Szegedy, C., Zaremba, W., Sutskever, I., et al.: Intriguing properties of neural networks. arXiv preprint arXiv:1312.6199 (2013)
21. Lin, Y., Zhao, H., Tu, Y., et al.: Threats of adversarial attacks in DNN-based modulation recognition. In: IEEE INFOCOM 2020-IEEE Conference on Computer Communications. IEEE, pp. 2469–2478 (2020)
22. Goswami, G., Ratha, N., Agarwal, A., et al.: Unravelling robustness of deep learning based face recognition against adversarial attacks. In: Proceedings of the AAAI Conference on Artificial Intelligence, 32(1) (2018)
23. Dong, Y., Su, H., Wu, B., et al.: Efficient decision-based black-box adversarial attacks on face recognition. In: Proceedings of the IEEE/CVF Conference on Computer Vision and Pattern Recognition, pp. 7714–7722 (2019)
24. Akhtar, N., Mian, A.: Threat of adversarial attacks on deep learning in computer vision: a survey. IEEE Access 6, 14410–14430 (2018)
25. Zhang, W.E., Sheng, Q.Z., Alhazmi, A., et al.: Adversarial attacks on deep-learning models in natural language processing: a survey. ACM Trans. Intell. Syst. Technol. (TIST) 11(3), 1–41 (2020)
26. Morris, J., Lifland, E., Yoo, J.Y., et al.: TextAttack: a framework for adversarial attacks, data augmentation, and adversarial training in NLP. In: Proceedings of the 2020 Conference on Empirical Methods in Natural Language Processing: System Demonstrations, pp. 119–126 (2020)
27. Behjati, M., Moosavi-Dezfooli, S.M., Baghshah, M.S., et al.: Universal adversarial attacks on text classifiers. In: ICASSP 2019–2019 IEEE International Conference on Acoustics, Speech and Signal Processing (ICASSP). IEEE, pp. 7345–7349 (2019)
28. Sun, L., Dou, Y., Yang, C., et al.: Adversarial attack and defense on graph data: a survey. arXiv preprint arXiv:1812.10528 (2018)
29. Chen, L., Li, J., Peng, J., et al.: A survey of adversarial learning on graphs. arXiv preprint arXiv:2003.05730 (2020)
30. Dai, H., Li, H., Tian, T., et al.: Adversarial attack on graph structured data. In: International Conference on Machine Learning, PMLR, pp. 1115–1124 (2018)
31. Gu, T., Liu, K., Dolan-Gavitt, B., et al.: Badnets: evaluating backdooring attacks on deep neural networks. IEEE Access 7, 47230–47244 (2019)
32. Li, Y., Wu, B., Jiang, Y., et al.: Backdoor learning: a survey. arXiv preprint arXiv:2007.08745 (2020)
33. Bagdasaryan, E., Veit, A., Hua, Y., et al.: How to backdoor federated learning. In: International Conference on Artificial Intelligence and Statistics. PMLR, 2938–2948 (2020)
34. Sun, Z., Kairouz, P., Suresh, A.T., et al.: Can you really backdoor federated learning?. arXiv preprint arXiv:1911.07963 (2019)
35. Wang, H., Sreenivasan, K., Rajput, S., et al.: Attack of the tails: yes, you really can backdoor federated learning. arXiv preprint arXiv:2007.05084 (2020)
36. Zügner, D., Akbarnejad, A., Günnemann, S.: Adversarial attacks on neural networks for graph data. In: Proceedings of the 24th ACM SIGKDD International Conference on Knowledge Discovery & Data Mining, pp. 2847–2856 (2018)
37. Ma, Y., Wang, S., Derr, T., et al.: Attacking graph convolutional networks via rewiring. arXiv preprint arXiv:1906.03750 (2019)
38. Zhang, Z., Jia, J., Wang, B., et al.: Backdoor attacks to graph neural networks. arXiv preprint arXiv:2006.11165 (2020)
39. Xi, Z., Pang, R., Ji, S., et al.: Graph backdoor. In: 30th {USENIX} Security Symposium ({USENIX} Security 21) (2021)
40. Ma, J., Ding, S., Mei, Q.: Towards more practical adversarial attacks on graph neural networks. arXiv preprint arXiv:2006.05057 (2020)

41. Takahashi, T.: Indirect adversarial attacks via poisoning neighbors for graph convolutional networks. In: 2019 IEEE International Conference on Big Data (Big Data). IEEE, 1395–1400 (2019)

42. Mo, H., Deng, Y.: Identifying node importance based on evidence theory in complex networks. Physica A: Stat. Mech. Appl. **529**, 121538 (2019)

43. Ma, L., Liu, Y.: Maximizing three-hop influence spread in social networks using discrete comprehensive learning artificial bee colony optimizer. Appl. Soft Comput. **83**, 105606 (2019)

44. Xu, J., Picek, S.: Explainability-based backdoor attacks against graph neural networks. arXiv preprint arXiv:2104.03674 (2021)

45. Gilbert, E.N.: Random graphs. Ann. Math. Stat. **30**(4), 1141–1144 (1959)

A UniverApproCNN with Universal Approximation and Explicit Training Strategy

Yin Yang, Yifeng Wang[(✉)], and Senqiao Yang

Harbin Institute of Technology, Shenzhen Graduate School,
Shenzhen, Guangdong Province, China

Abstract. Approximation theory has achieved many results in the field of deep learning. However, these results and conclusions can rarely be directly applied to the solution of practical problems or directly guide the training and optimization of deep learning models in the actual context. To address this issue, we construct a CNN structure with universal approximation, which is called UniverApproCNN. It is ensured that the approximation error of such CNN is bounded by an explicit approximation upper bound that relies on the hyper parameters of this model. Moreover, a general case of multidimensional is considered by generalizing the conclusion of the universality property of CNN. A practical problem in the field of inertial guidance is used as a background to conduct experiments, so that the theory can give an explicit training strategy and break the barrier between the theory and its application. We use the curve similarity index defined by Fréchet distance to prove that the experimental results are highly consistent with the functional relationship given by the theory. On this basis, we define the 'approximation coefficient' of UniverApproCNN, which can give the stop time of model training and related training strategies. Specifically, taking the operation of normalization as a widely used technique into consideration, we then show that this operation does not take effect on the approximation performance of the CNN and UniverApproCNN.

Keywords: Approximation theory · Universality of CNN · Normalization · Inertial guidance · Fréchet distance

1 Introduction

In the 1980s, the neural network model received people's attention again because of the successful applications such as on signal processing and control. The dense problem naturally arises from these applications [1], that is, for such a set

$$\mathcal{M}(\sigma) = span\{\sigma(\mathbf{w} \cdot \mathbf{x} - \theta) : \theta \in \mathbb{R}, \mathbf{w} \in \mathbb{R}^n\},$$

Supported by special fund for scientific and technological innovation strategy of Guangdong Province.
Y. Yang, Y. Wang and S. Yang—These authors contributed equally.

H. Gao and X. Wang (Eds.): CollaborateCom 2021, LNICST 407, pp. 297–315, 2021.
https://doi.org/10.1007/978-3-030-92638-0_18

what properties does the activation function need to make it dense in the corresponding function space? This denseness is considered to be fundamental important in neural network theory as the t heoretical ability of approximation [2,3]. For the single hidden layer perceptron model

$$\mathcal{M}_r(\sigma) = \left\{ \sum_{i=1}^{r} c_i \sigma(\mathbf{w}^i \mathbf{x} - \theta_i) : c_i, \theta_i \in \mathbb{R}, \mathbf{w}^i \in \mathbb{R}^n \right\},$$

which is one of the more simpler neural networks models mathematically, Pinkus [2] has made a detailed summary, including the approximation bound with different activation functions and under different norms [4–8]. For networks with a certain depth and special connection structure with sparsity

$$h^{(j)}(x) = \left(\sigma\left(w_i^{(j)} h^{(j-1)}(x) - b_i^{(j)} \right) \right)_{i=1}^{d_j},$$

compared with their success in practical applications, there is relatively little research on their theoretical approximation capabilities [9], although there are some theoretical interpretations for superior behavior due to their depth and special connection structure [10–13]. Recently, Zhou Dingxuan proved that the deep convolutional neural network is universally approximated in the continuous function space, and given the upper bound of the approximation under certain conditions [14].

Following Zhou Dingxuan's work, we propose the construction of a generic convolutional neural network with explicit approximation bound, which is called the UniverApproCNN model. Based on the inertial guidance data, an experimental design was made to verify the approximation bound, as well as some necessary theoretical expansions. Since Zhou's proof method is constructive, we find it is easy to prove that the approximation performance of the network with layer normalization operation [15,16] is unchanged using his method.

In the second chapter, some preliminary knowledge is given. In the third chapter, we will conduct in-depth analysis and model design of the CNN with known approximation bound introduced in Zhou Dingxuan's article. Based on the data of inertial guidance, we need to prove the universality of approximation and model design of CNN suitable for two-dimensional input, these works will be presented in Sect. 4. At the same time, we construct UniverApproCNN with universal approximation, and design an object motion tracking problem based on inertial guidance theory to further explore and analyze the performance of UniverApproCNN in Sect. 5. In Sect. 6, we use the interpretability advantage of UniverApproCNN to guide the model design and training strategy by defining "approximation coefficient".

2   Preliminaries

Before introducing the main work of this article, we first give the symbols that will be used in the article and some results in the approximation theory.

Consider the activation function defined as $\sigma(u) = max\{u, 0\}, u \in \mathbb{R}$, called ReLU (rectified linear unit), and a sequence of convolutional filter masks $\{w^{(j)}\}_j$ with finite support, that is, $w_k^{(j)} \neq 0$ if and only if $0 \leq k \leq s$ Convolution of two sequences can be written as the product of a matrix and a vector. The convolution kernel represented by the mask slides on the input of length $D(s \leq D)$, that is, the process of convolution, which can induce the following Toeplitz type matrix T of size $(D + s) \times D$:

$$T = \begin{pmatrix} w_0 & 0 & \cdots & \cdots & \cdots & \cdots & 0 \\ w_1 & w_0 & 0 & \cdots & \cdots & & 0 \\ \vdots & \ddots & \ddots & \ddots & \cdots & \cdots & \vdots \\ w_s & w_{s-1} & \cdots & w_0 & 0 & \cdots & 0 \\ 0 & w_s & w_{s-1} & \cdots & w_0 & 0 \cdots & 0 \\ \vdots & \ddots & \ddots & \ddots & \cdots & \ddots & 0 \\ 0 & \cdots & 0 & w_s & w_{s-1} & \cdots & w_0 \\ 0 & \cdots & \cdots & 0 & w_s & w_{s-1} & w_1 \\ 0 & \cdots & \cdots & \cdots & 0 & \ddots & \vdots \\ 0 & \cdots & \cdots & \cdots & \cdots & 0 & w_s \end{pmatrix}$$

Definition 1. *Consider the input vector $x \in \mathbb{R}^d$, a convolutional neural network with depth J and width $d_j = d + js$ can be induced by a sequence $\{w^{(j)}\}_{j=1}^J$, whose hidden layer can be defined a vector-valued function column*

$$\{h^{(j)}(x)\}_{j=1}^J,$$

generated by iteration:

$$h^{(0)}(x) = x,$$

$$h^{(j)}(x) = \sigma(T^{w^{(j)}} h^{(j-1)}(x) - b^{(j)}), \quad j = 1, 2, \cdots, J.$$

where $T^{w^{(j)}} = (w_{i-k}^{(j)})_{d_j \times d_{j-1}}$ is the Toeplitz type convolutional matrix induced by $w^{(j)}$, σ acts on vectors by component, and $b^{(j)}$ is the bias vector.

Definition 2. *The hypothesis space of the convolutional neural network model defined above is the following function set:*

$$\mathcal{H}_J^{\mathbf{w},\mathbf{b}} = \left\{ \sum_{k=1}^{d_J} c_k h_k^{(J)}(x) : c \in \mathbb{R}^{d_J} \right\},$$

where $\mathbf{w} = \{w^{(j)}\}_{j=1}^J$, $\mathbf{b} = \{b^{(j)}\}_{j=1}^J$.

Zhou proved the universal approximation of the network to the continuous function space $C(\Omega)$:

Theorem 1. *Let $2 \leq s \leq d$ and $\Omega \subseteq [-1,1]^d$. If $J \geq 2d/(s-1)$ and $f = F|_\Omega$, with $F \in H^r(\mathbb{R}^d)$ and an integer index $r > 2 + d/2$, then there exist $\mathbf{w}, \mathbf{b}$ and $f_J^{\mathbf{w},\mathbf{b}} \in \mathcal{H}_J^{\mathbf{w},\mathbf{b}}$ such that*

$$\|f - f_J^{\mathbf{w},\mathbf{b}}\|_{C(\Omega)} \leq c\|F\|\sqrt{\log J}(1/J)^{\frac{1}{2}+\frac{1}{d}},$$

where c is an absolute constant and $\|F\|$ denotes the Soblev norm of $F \in H^r(\mathbb{R}^d)$.

The theorem above is based on a result on ridge approximation to $F|_{[-1,1]^d}$ shown as follows:

Theorem 2. *Let $D = [-1,1]^d$. Suppose f admits a Fourier representation $f(x) = \int_{\mathbb{R}^d} e^{ix\cdot\omega}\tilde{f}(\omega)d\omega$ and*

$$v_{f,2} = \int_{\mathbb{R}^d} \|\omega\|_1^2|\tilde{f}(\omega)|d\omega < \infty.$$

There exists a linear combination of ramp ridge functions of the form

$$f_m(x) = \beta_0 + x\cdot\alpha_0 + \frac{v}{m}\sum_{k=1}^{m}\beta_k(x\cdot\alpha_k - t_k)_+$$

with $\beta \in [-1,1]$, $\|\alpha_k\|_1 = 1$, $0 \leq t_k \leq 1$, $\beta_0 = f(0)$, $\alpha_0 = \nabla f(0)$, and $v \leq 2v_{f,2}$ such that

$$\|f - f_m\|_{C(\Omega)} \leq cv_{f,2}\max\{\sqrt{\log m}, \sqrt{d}\}m^{-1/2-1/d}.$$

3   A CNN Structure with Universal Approximation: UniverApproCNN

3.1   Model Design

In the proof of Zhou's article, they tried to decompose the coefficients $W = [W_{(m+1)d-1} \cdots W_1\ W_0] = [\alpha_m^T \cdots \alpha_1^T\ \alpha_0^T]$ in the ramp ridge function into the weight parameters of each layer. With the help of the generating function of a sequence, they decompose W into the convolution of multiple sequences $W = w^{(J)} * \cdots * w^{(1)}$, that is, decompose $\widetilde{W}$ into $\widetilde{W}(z) = \widetilde{w}^{(J)}(z)\widetilde{w}^{(J-1)}(z)\cdots\widetilde{w}^{(1)}(z)$. Note that $\widetilde{W}(z)$ can be factored into

$$\widetilde{W}(z) = W_M \prod_{k=1}^{K}[z^2 - 2x_kz + (x_k^2 + y_k^2)] \prod_{k=2K+1}^{M}(x - z_k),$$

where $M = (m+1)d - 1$. Next, we decide the hyper parameters of the network according to the above decomposition formula.

Zhou's decomposition emphasizes the existence of $\{s_j\}_{j=1}^{J}$, where $s_j \leq s$, satisfying $deg(\widetilde{w}^{(j)}(z)) = s_j$ and $s_1 + s_2 + \cdots + s_J = M$. Since K is unknown, the size of s_j is ambiguous. In order to determine the number of nodes in each hidden layer, we use an even-numbered mask length s_j. Further, in order to make an explicit relationship between depth J and M, we use a fixed $s_j = s$, then J, s and M satisfy the following relationship:

$$M = (J-1)s + t,$$

that is,

$$(m+1)d - 1 = (J-1)s + t, \quad J, t \in \mathbb{N}^*, 0 < t \le s,$$

where

$$deg(\widetilde{w}^{(J)}(z)) = t, deg(\widetilde{w}^{(j)}(z)) = s, j = 1, \cdots, J-1,$$

the corresponding sequences are

$$w^{(J)} = \{w_0^{(J)}, \cdots, w_t^{(J)}\}, \quad w^{(j)} = \{w_0^{(j)}, \cdots, w_s^{(j)}\}$$

satisfying $W = w^{(J)} * \cdots * w^{(1)}$. Let

$$d_j = d + (j-1)s, \quad j = 1, \cdots, J-1,$$

$$d_J = d_{J-1} + t,$$

then $T^{w^{(j)}} \in \mathbb{R}^{d_j \times d_{j-1}}, j = 1, \cdots, J, T^{w^{(j)}}$ represents the Toeplitz type matrix generated by the sequence $w^{(j)}$.

Now we have $T^W = T^{w^{(J)}} \cdots T^{w^{(1)}}$. Let $w^{(J+1)} = \{w_0^{(J+1)}\} = \{0\}$, the Toeplitz matrix induced by $w^{(J+1)}$ is identity matrix, that is, $T_{d_{J+1} \times d_J}^{w^{(J+1)}} = I$, where $d_{J+1} = d_J$, the corresponding physical meaning is not to do zero padding to the output of the J-th hidden layer.

In order to get the desired term, we construct the bias as follows. Denote

$$\|w\|_1 = \sum_{k=-\infty}^{\infty} |w_k|, \quad B^{(0)} = max_{x \in \Omega} max_{k=1,\cdots,d} |x_k|,$$

$$B^{(j)} = \|w^{(j)}\|_1 \cdots \|w^{(1)}\|_1 B^{(0)}, j \ge 1.$$

If nonlinear activation is considered only in the J-th layer, let

$$b_l^{(J)} = \begin{cases} -B^{(J)}, & l = d \\ t_k, & l = (k+1)d, 1 \le k \le m \\ B^{(J)}, & \text{otherwise} \end{cases},$$

then

$$h_l^{(J)} = \sigma\left((T^W x)_l - b_l^{(J)}\right)$$

$$= \begin{cases} \alpha_0 \cdot x + B^{(J)}, & l = d \\ (\alpha_k \cdot x - t_k)_+, & l = (k+1)d, 1 \le k \le m \\ 0, & \text{otherwise} \end{cases}.$$

Let

$$b_l^{(J+1)} = \begin{cases} -B^{(J)}, l = 1 \\ 0, \qquad \text{otherwise} \end{cases},$$

then $h^{(J+1)}(x) = \sigma\left(T^{w^{(J+1)}} h^{(J)}(x) - b^{(J+1)}\right)$, expressed by component as

$$h_l^{(J+1)} = \begin{cases} \alpha_0 \cdot x + B^{(J)}, & l = d \\ (\alpha_k \cdot x - t_k)_+, l = (k+1)d, 1 \leq k \leq m \\ B^{(J)}, & l = 1 \\ 0, & \text{otherwise} \end{cases}.$$

For the above $\mathbf{w}, \mathbf{b}$, we can take

$$f_{J+1}^{\mathbf{w},\mathbf{b}} = F_m|_\Omega \in span\{h_k^{J+1}(x)\}_{k=1}^{d_{J+1}},$$

satisfying

$$\|f - f_J^{\mathbf{w},\mathbf{b}}\|_{C(\Omega)} \leq \|F - F_m\|_{C([-1,1]^d)}$$
$$\leq c_0 v_{F,2} max\{\sqrt{\log m}, \sqrt{d}\} m^{-1/2 - 1/d}.$$

Remark 1. When $t = 0$, we only get $J - 1$ sequences from the decomposition, and then let $w^{(J)} = \{W_0^{(J)}\} = \{1\}$ and assign the value of $b^{(J)}$ to $b^{(J-1)}$, $b^{(J+1)}$ to $b^{(J)}$.

It is worth noting that the UniverApproCNN model not only has strong interpretability, but its backpropagation process is compatible with almost all optimization algorithms. This advantage brings a broad application prospect for UniverApproCNN. The back propagation process is shown in the appendix.

3.2   UniverApproCNN for Multiple Outputs

The method in the Theorem 1 can be extended to multi-dimensional output, that is, the UniverApproCNN also has universal approximation to the vector-valued function space. For a l-dimensional continuous vector-valued function $f(x) = (f_1(x), \cdots, f_l(x))$, there exist ramp ridge functions

$$F_m^i = \beta_0^i + \alpha_0^i x + \frac{v^i}{m} \sum_{k=1}^m \beta_k^i (\alpha_k^i x - t_k^i)_+, \quad i = 1, \cdots, l,$$

such that

$$\|f_i - F_m^i\|_{C(\Omega)} \leq c_0^i v_{F^1,2} max\{\sqrt{\log m}, \sqrt{d}\}^{-\frac{1}{2} - \frac{1}{d}}.$$

We stack all the coefficients $\alpha_k^i, i = 1, \cdots, l, k = 0, \cdots, m$ into a row vector, let

$$W^i = \left(W_{(m+1)d-1}^i, \cdots, W_0^i\right) = \left((\alpha_m^i)^T, \cdots, (\alpha_0^i)^T\right)$$

$$W = \left(W_{l(m+1)d-1}, \cdots, W_0\right) = \left(W^l, \cdots, W^1\right),$$

it is easy to find by definition that

$$T^W_{(i-1)(m+1)d+(k+1)d;:} = (\alpha^i_k)^T,$$

which means the term $(\alpha^i_k)^T$ can be represented by the node with order $(i-1)(m+1)d + (k+1)d$ of the last convolutional layer. Using the decomposition strategy mentioned in the first section in this chapter, we can decompose W into the weight parameters of the CNN with depth $J+1$, satisfying

$$l(m+1)d - 1 = (J-1)s + t, \quad J, t \in \mathbb{N}^*, 0 < t \le s.$$

3.3   Normalized CNN and UniverApproCNN

In this section, we try to show that the approximation performance of CNN and UniverApproCNN with batch normalization operation will not be weakened at least. Because UniverApproCNN is a special form of CNN, the universal approximation condition of normalized CNN is more stringent, and its establishment can guarantee the universal approximation of normalized UniverApproCNN. Therefore, we verify the universal approximation of the normalized CNN.

Consider N input vectors of length d, and define $a^{k,j} = T^{w^{(j)}} \cdot h^{(j-1)}(x_k), j = 1, 2, \cdots, J$ as the summed input of the j-th hidden layer of the k-th input vector. The batch normalization method normalizes the summed input of each unit in the same layer, that is, scales the summed input according to the batch normalization statistics defined below:

$$\mu = \frac{1}{Nd_j} \sum_{k=1}^{N} \sum_{i=1}^{d_j} a^{k,j}_i, \quad \sigma_j = \sqrt{\frac{1}{Nd_j} \sum_{k=1}^{N} \sum_{i=1}^{d_j} (a^{k,j}_i - \mu_j)^2},$$

then, the input of the hidden layer after batch normalization can be defined as

$$\overline{a^{k,j}_i} = \frac{g^j_i}{\sigma_j} \cdot (a^{k,j}_i - \mu_j),$$

where $g^j_i, j = 1, 2, \cdots, J, i = 1, 2, \cdots, d_j$ are gain parameters, further, the output of the hidden layer can be defined as

$$\overline{h^j} = \sigma(\overline{a^{k,j}} - b^{(j)}) = \sigma\left(\frac{g^j}{\sigma_j} \odot (a^{k,j} - \mu_j \mathbf{1}_{d_j}) - b^{(j)}\right),$$

where $\odot$ means product by component between two vectors, $\mathbf{1}_{d_j} = (1, 1, \cdots, 1)^T$ with length d_j, $b^{(j)}$ is the bias parameter.

Only consider batch normalization operations on the first layer, when $g^1_i : \Omega \to \mathbb{R}, i = 1, 2, \cdots, d_1$ are continuous, consider the influence of the activation function σ, since there exists a similar bound for the normalized summed input, that is, for any $x \in \Omega$, we have

$$\left| \frac{g^1_i}{\sqrt{\frac{1}{Nd_j} \sum_{k=1}^{N} \sum_{i=1}^{d_j} (a^{k,1}_i - \mu_j)^2}} \cdot (a^{k,1}_i - \mu_1) \right|^2 \le MNd_1,$$

Therefore, by reconstructing the bias parameters $\beta^{(1)}$ of the first hidden layer, the weight parameter $T^{(2)}$ and bias parameter $\beta^{(2)}$ of the second hidden layer, the regularized network output $f_J^{\mathbf{w}',\mathbf{b}'}$ can be restored to the output $f_J^{\mathbf{w},\mathbf{b}}$ of the original network, where $\mathbf{w}' = \{w^{(1)}, T^{(2)}, w^{(3)}, \cdots, w^{(J)}\}, \mathbf{b}' = \{\beta^{(1)}, \beta^{(2)}, b^{(3)}, \cdots b^{(J)}\}$, which means the approximation performance of the normalized CNN does not changed compared with the original network.

4   UniverApproCNN for Two-Dimensional Input

4.1   Proof of the Approximation of the CNN Suitable for Two-dimensional Input

Consider a two-dimensional input I of size $d \times n$, the size of the first layer of convolution kernel is $d \times (s+1)$, with s column zero padding on both sides of the input, the first layer convolution is regarded as a matrix form, which is expressed as follows:

First, expand the input matrix by rows, namely

$$x\big((i-1)n + k\big) = I(i,k), 1 \le i \le d, 1 \le k \le n,$$

Denote the output of the first layer as

$$h^{(1)}(x) = \sigma\big(T^{(1)} h^{(0)}(x) - b^{(1)}\big),$$

where $h^{(0)} = x$, $T^{(1)} = \big(T^{w^{(1),1}}, \cdots, T^{w^{(1),d}}\big)$ is a matrix of size $n_1 \times dn$, every block of which is a Toeplitz matrix generated by the corresponding row vector of the first convolution kernel.

Next we can define a CNN with depth J generated by a sequence of finitely supported convolutional filter masks $\{w^{(j)}\}_{j=1}^{J}$ as a sequence of vector-valued functions $\{h^{(j)}\}_{j=1}^{J}$, and $h^{(j)}(x) = \sigma\big(T^{(j)} h^{(j-1)}(x) - b^{(j)}\big), j = 1, 2, \cdots, J$, where $T^{w^{(j)}} = (w_{i-k}^{(j)})$ is a Toeplitz type matrix of size $n_j \times n_{j-1}$. The hypothesis space of such network can be expressed as

$$\mathcal{H}_J^{\mathbf{w},\mathbf{b}} = \left\{ \sum_{k=1}^{d_J} c_k h_k^{(J)}(x) : c \in \mathbb{R}^{d_J} \right\}.$$

The following theorem about universality of the CNN above is the extension of Zhou's work. We give the proof in the appendix.

Theorem 3. *For any compact subset Ω of $[-1,1]^{nd}$ and any $f \in C(\Omega)$, there exist $\mathbf{w}, \mathbf{b}$ and $f_{J+1}^{\mathbf{w},\mathbf{b}}$ such that*

$$\|f - f_{J+1}^{\mathbf{w},\mathbf{b}}\|_{C(\Omega)} \le c_0 v_{F,2} \max\{\sqrt{\log m}, \sqrt{nd}\} m^{-\frac{1}{2} - \frac{1}{nd}}.$$

4.2   Model Design

Since the objective function is unknown, we cannot find non-trivial common factors. We only verify the model with the following settings:

- For a two-dimensional input vector $I \in \Omega$, $\Omega \subseteq [-1, 1]^{d \times n}$, consider two layers of convolution.
- The size of the convolutional kernel of the first layer is $d \times (m+1)n$, perform $(m+n)n - 1$ columns of zero padding on both sides of the input, set the stride equal to 1.
- In the first hidden layer, first reduce the bias and then activate by the non-linear function, where

$$b_l^{(1)} = \begin{cases} -B^{(1)}, & l = n \\ t_k, & l = (k+1)n, 1 \le k \le m \\ B^{(1)}, & \text{otherwise} \end{cases},$$

and $B^{(1)} = \|w^{(1),1}\|_1 + \cdots + \|w^{(1),d}\|_1$.
- The convolutional filter mask of the second is $w^{(2)} = \{w_0^{(2)}\} = \{1\}$, then reduce the bias and activate, where

$$b_l^{(2)} = \begin{cases} -B^{(1)}, & l = 1 \\ 0, & \text{otherwise} \end{cases}.$$

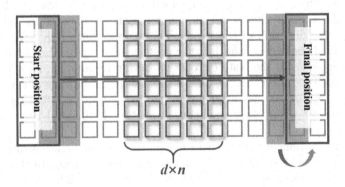

Fig. 1. The structure of UniverApproCNN model.

Figure 1 shows the structure of UniverApproCNN model and the sliding mode of convolution kernel. Since the structure of the model completely conforms to the universality theorem, under the condition of sufficient training, theoretically, when the hyper parameters of the model change, in addition to the structure of the model itself, its corresponding approximation upper bound also changes accordingly, the corresponding relationship between these two changes can guide us to get the ideal training strategy in the experiment.

5   Performance Experiment of UniverApproCNN for Inertial Guidance

In order to verify the relationship between the approximation bound of UniverApproCNN and related parameters, we designed an experiment oriented to inertial guidance theory. We will use the UniverApproCNN model to approximate a complex model in this theory. The model is composed of many highly nonlinear functions, involving coordinate system transformation, normalization, multiple integration, cosine matrix calculation, quaternion calculation, and other operations. The complex coupling relationship of these operations is very suitable for testing the approximation effect of the UniverApproCNN model. Moreover, since our verification is based on actual problems, the experimental process can be directly guided by theory, and the experimental results can directly echo the theory. Therefore, our experiment actually breaks through the barrier between theory and application, which is of great help to the development and application of the theory.

Our experimental object is a trajectory restoration model based on inertial sensors. The input is six-axis inertial sensor data: three-axis acceleration, three-axis angular velocity, and the output is the spatial position of the object's movement. Regarding the model as a mapping from input to output, the mapping relationship f is the object we want to approximate with UniverApproCNN. The form of f is closely related to the way of movement of the object. We define the form of movement as follows:

Suppose an object with a mass of m makes horizontal projectile motion in three-dimensional space at an initial velocity v_0, and its direction is the positive direction of the x-axis; the acceleration of gravity is $g = 9.8\,\mathrm{m/s^2}$, whose direction is the negative direction of the z-axis; The air resistance is $F = kv^2$, where v is the speed of the object, and k is the coefficient of air resistance; at the same time, the object is in the state of rotation during the motion, and the rotation angular velocity around the x, y, and z axes at the initial time of the horizontal throwing is ω_x, ω_y, ω_z, its attenuation law is $\omega_{t_1} = \omega_{t_0} e^{-Kt}$, where K is the angular velocity attenuation coefficient, and t is the interval time between t_0 and t_1.

After the movement mode is determined, the mapping relationship f between the input data and the output data is determined accordingly. In this horizontal throwing movement, since the object is always in a weightless state, inertial sensors can only measure the acceleration of an object due to air resistance from all directions. The acceleration and angular velocity measured by the inertial sensor are all based on its own coordinate system (Object Coordinate System), but the calculation of its trajectory is based on the spatial absolute coordinate system (World Coordinate System). At the same time, the spatial posture of the object changes all the time, so the transformation relationship between the two coordinate systems is constantly changing. In addition, the effect of the decomposition of the gravitational acceleration in the object coordinate system must also be considered. The entire complex system is included in the mapping relationship f, so it is difficult to train UniverApproCNN to approximate it.

At this time, we need to generate a data set based on a large number of variable parameters during the movement for training, verification and testing of the UniverApproCNN model. In the motion process we define, the variable parameters include: mass m, initial horizontal throwing velocity v_0, air resistance coefficient k, initial angular velocity of the object rotation ω_x, ω_y, ω_z, and rotation attenuation coefficient K. We use a grid method to set 2 specific values for the parameter $\theta : \pi/3, \pi/6$, and 10 values for each of the remaining 7 parameters. A total of 2×10^7 sets of parameter combinations are generated for 8 parameters. Combining each set of parameters with f can determine the specific motion details, such as the acceleration, angular velocity at each moment, and the spatial coordinates of the object at each moment. For each set of parameters, we start from the initial moment of motion, generate 100 frames of object motion acceleration and angular velocity information as inertial data, that is, the input data of the UniverApproCNN model, and generate the position information of the 101st frame of object motion as the data to be predicted, which is the output data of UniverApproCNN. In the end, a total of 2×10^7 training samples were generated. We randomly divide 2×10^7 training samples into training set, validation set, and test set according to the ratio of 98 : 1 : 1. In order to enhance the credibility of the experimental results, we independently predict the motion trajectories of objects in different directions, that is, use the parallel experimental method to predict the motion trajectories of x, y, and z axes. The final experimental result of x axis is shown as Fig. 2, and the results of y, z axes are shown in the appendix. Figure 4 and Fig. 5:

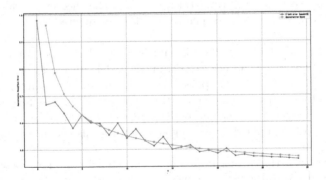

Fig. 2. The experiment on x-axis.

It can be seen that the experimental results are highly consistent with the functional relationship given by the theory. In order to measure the degree of agreement, we use Fréchet distance to define the similarity index between the experimental result curve and the theoretical curve: assuming that the experimental result curve and the theoretical curve can be respectively expressed as a sequence: $P = [u_1, u_2, u_3, \cdots, u_p]$ and $Q = [v_1, v_2, v_3, \cdots, v_q]$, we can obtain the following sequence pairs L:

$$(u_{a_1}, v_{b_1}), (u_{a_2}, v_{b_2}), \cdots, (u_{a_m}, v_{b_m})$$

where $a_1 = 1, b_1 = 1$ and $a_m = p, b_m = q$ for any $i = 1, 2, \cdots, q$, let $a_{i+1} = a_i$ or $a_{i+1} = a_i + 1$ and $b_{i+1} = b_i$ or $b_{i+1} = b_i + 1$. For any point $m = (x_m, y_m, z_m)$ and $n = (x_n, y_n, z_n)$, the Euclidean distance between the two points can be defined as

$$D(m, n) = \sqrt{(x_m - x_n)^2 + (y_m - y_n)^2 + (z_m - z_n)^2}.$$

The length $\|L\|$ between two sequences P and Q is defined as the maximum Euclidean distance in each sequence pair. The expression is as follows:

$$\|L\| = \max_{i=1,2,\cdots,m} D(u_{a_i}, v_{a_i}).$$

Then the Fréchet distance between sequence P and Q is defined as

$$Fd(P, Q) = min\|L\|.$$

Calculate the module of P and Q as $R_P = \sum_{i=1}^{p-1} D(u_i, u_{i+1})$ and $R_Q = \sum_{i=1}^{q-1} D(v_i, v_{i+1})$ respectively. Then we define the similarity between the P and Q curves as

$$Accuracy = max\left\{0, 100 - \frac{100 \times Fd(P, Q)}{\sqrt{2}(R_P + R_Q)}\right\}.$$

After checking the similarity of the result curves of the three experiments, the agreement between the experimental results and the theoretical values reached 96.45%, 95.76%, and 98.31% respectively, which completed the theoretical verification.

Only when the amount of data is sufficient, the data types are rich, and the training strategy is appropriate, the trained model can meet the upper bound of the error given above. This puts high demands on our training process. In addition, as the model parameter m (this m is not the mass, pay attention to distinguish) changes, the scale and performance of the whole model are changing accordingly, so the applicable training strategy will also continue to change, as shown in Fig. 3.

It can be seen that when m is small, the model converges slowly. At this time, we need more iterations. However, as m increases, the model converges faster and faster. At this time, if the number of iterations is not appropriately reduced, there will be overfitting.

The change of m causes the number of training iterations (epoch) to also change instantly. Although this brings inconvenience to the experiment, this feature also reveals the relationship between m and many hyper parameters in the training strategy such as epoch, batchsize, and learning rate. If we can analyze the relationship through some methods, then we can formulate a rigorous and effective training strategy for the hyper parameter adjustment of the model, so we designed follow-up related experiments.

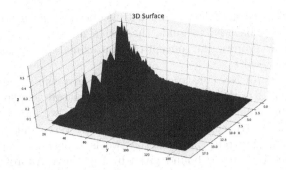

Fig. 3. Convergence rate of model cahanging with parameter m during training.

6   Approximation Coefficients of UniverApproCNN

Although deep learning model has achieved very good results in many fields, it lacks relevant explanatory power, which is also one of its most criticized defects. As a function, the essence of deep learning model is to approximate the function behind the real problem. The approximation theory ensures its approximation effect, and demonstrates the approximation potential of specific deep learning model from the perspective of function space.

However, although the approximation theory gives the approximation potential of deep learning model, the research on the approximation potential can only play a certain effect in theory. Although the research results in this aspect can give a theoretical upper bound of the error of deep learning model, there are two major problems in the application of the upper bound:

1. The upper bound of the error is only theoretical, that is, the default deep learning model has been trained to the optimal state. However, in fact, due to the data quantity, data richness, data error [17], optimization theory and other related limitations, deep learning model is almost impossible to achieve its theoretical maximum approximation potential, especially for some complex problems, as well as the corresponding more complex deep learning model. The complex network structure, complex combination of hyper parameters, the limitation of computing resources and the possible over fitting phenomenon all make it difficult for deep learning model to reach the limit of its approximation potential.
2. The theory can only give the upper bound of the approximation error of the model. In fact, the upper bound is much larger than the error of the model in the training set, verification set and test set, and they are not even in the same order of magnitude. Therefore, the theory can not play a guiding role in our modeling and training process.

These two problems make the gap between approximation theory and deep learning model application appear. In order to fill the gap between theory and application, and make the relevant conclusions obtained in the study of approximation theory can be used to guide the design and training process of deep learning model, we propose the concept of "approximation coefficient" based on the experimental results.

The UniverApproCNN constructed by us can give the upper bound of the approximation error of the model under specific structure and specific problem, that is, the approximation rate. As like as two peas, we found that the error patterns of different structural models on test set are very similar to the approximation rate, and the trend between the two is almost the same. Therefore, we multiply the error upper bound given by the UniverApproCNN model by a coefficient, which is named "approximation coefficient". When the coefficient is in a certain range, the two curves almost coincide. In order to measure the similarity between the error upper bound curve and the test error curve, we use the curve similarity measurement index defined by Fréchet distance i.e. the similarity between P and Q curves

$$Accuracy = max\left\{0, 100 - \frac{100 \times Fd(P,Q)}{\sqrt{2}(R_P + R_Q)}\right\}.$$

This index can help us to find the value of approximation coefficient under different problem background and different model structure.

As a matter of fact, for a fixed problem and a fixed data set, we will choose to train several times on the model with a relatively simple structure, and explore a relatively reasonable training strategy for the simple structure. Under the condition of sufficient training, the trained model is tested on the test set, and some test errors are obtained. Through these simple structure test errors, combined with the curve similarity measure we defined, we can determine the value range of the approximation coefficient, and then predict the possible errors of the complex structure deep learning model in the test set.

At this time, we train the deep learning model with complex structure, and constantly test it on the test set during the training process, but the error calculation results on the test set do not participate in the process of back propagation and parameter adjustment. This operation can be regarded as a "monitor" in the process of model training. Since we have obtained the approximate error of the model in the test set in advance, if the test error of the model is always significantly larger than the error range predicted by us during training, it means that the training is not sufficient, and we need to increase the number of iterations, on the contrary, it shows that the training effect has reached a good level, and the training should be stopped at this time, otherwise the situation of over fitting may appear.

To sum up, we build a bridge between approximation theory and model design, model implementation, model training by defining "approximation coefficient", so that the relevant conclusions of approximation theory can be applied to specific experiments. In the future, it can also be extended to more research on models and approximation theory, so it has high application value.

7   Conclusion

This paper proposed a CNN model supported by related approximation theory: UniverApproCNN. We successfully applied it to the object motion tracking problem in inertial guidance theory, and successfully verified the relevant conclusions in the approximation theory. In the process of verifying the relationship between the approximation bound and the network structure parameters, we discovered the relationship between the training strategy and the network structure, and we successfully used this relationship to guide the training of the model. As a deep learning network, although it has sacrificed performance, it has made significant progress in interpretability, and this interpretability can guide the formulation of model training strategies very well. In the future, we can use this as a basis to optimize performance to enhance its interpretability while ensuring performance, or use this solution as a basis to find a balance between the performance and interpretability of more deep learning models.

A   Appendix

A.1   Proof of the Theorem 3

Proof. Because of the density of $H^r(\Omega)$ in $C(\Omega)$ when $r \geq \frac{nd}{2} + 2$, without loss of generality, we assume $f \in H^r(\Omega)$. When the activation function $\sigma(u) = max\{u, 0\}, u \in \mathbb{R}$ is not considered, the input-related coefficients in the network are all included in the convolution matrix

$$\left(T^{w^{(J)}} \cdots T^{w^{(2)}} T^{w^{(1),1}}, \cdots\cdots, T^{w^{(J)}} \cdots T^{w^{(2)}} T^{w^{(1),d}}\right),$$

given the following notation:

$$\left(T^{w^{(J)}} \cdots T^{w^{(2)}} T^{w^{(1),1}}, \cdots\cdots, T^{w^{(J)}} \cdots T^{w^{(2)}} T^{w^{(1),d}}\right)$$

$$\triangleq \left(T^{W^1}, \cdots\cdots, T^{W^d}\right) \triangleq T$$

where $W^i = w^{(J)} * \cdots * w^{(2)} * w^{(1),i}$ and T^{W^i} is the Toeplitz type matrix induced by W^i.

Note that in the ramp ridge function, the coefficients associated with the first sub-block $x(1:n)$ of length n of input x are

$$\{\alpha_m^1, \cdots, \alpha_m^n, \cdots\cdots, \alpha_1^1, \cdots, \alpha_1^n, \alpha_0^1, \cdots, \alpha_0^n\},$$

the coefficients related to $x(1:n)$ in the network are included in T^{W^1}.

Let $\left(W_{(m+1)n-1}^1, \cdots, W_1^1, W_0^1\right)$

$$= (\alpha_m^1, \cdots, \alpha_m^n, \cdots\cdots, \alpha_1^1, \cdots, \alpha_1^n, \alpha_0^1, \cdots, \alpha_0^n),$$

We have

$$T_{(k+1)n;:}^{W^1} = \left(\alpha(1:n)\right)^T.$$

Similarly, let $\left(W^i_{(m+1)n-1}, \cdots, W^i_1, W^i_0\right)$

$$= \left(\alpha^{(i-1)n+1}_m, \cdots, \alpha^{in}_m, \cdots\cdots, \alpha^{(i-1)n+1}_0, \cdots, \alpha^{in}_0\right),$$

we can get

$$T^{W^i}_{(k+1)n;:} = \left(\alpha_k\big((i-1)n+1 : in\big)\right)^T$$

and

$$T_{(k+1)n;:} = \left(T^{W^1}_{(k+1)n;:}, \cdots, T^{W^d}_{(k+1)n;:}\right) = (\alpha_k)^T,$$

$$k = 0, 1, 2, \cdots, m.$$

Since $W^i = w^{(J)} * \cdots w^{(2)} * w^{(1),i}$, using the generating function of a sequence and the basic theorem of algebra, we can decompose $W^{(i)}$ into a finitely supported sequence $\{w^{(j)}\}_{j=1}^J$. So far, we have decomposed the coefficients $\{\alpha_0, \alpha_1, \cdots, \alpha_m\}$ in the ramp ridge function $F_m(x)$ into the weight parameters of each layer of this particular network.

Note that when we decompose

$$W^i = w^{(J)} * \cdots w^{(2)} * w^{(1),i}, i = 1, 2, \cdots, d$$

a common factor of $\widetilde{w^{(J)}}(z) \cdots \widetilde{w^{(2)}}(z)$ is required. When a untrivial common factor exists, we can decompose it into a sequence $\{w^{(j)}\}_{j=2}^J$ with finite support.

If nonlinear activation is considered only in the J-th layer, let

$$b^{(J)}_l = \begin{cases} -B^{(J)}, & l = n \\ t_k, & l = (k+1)n, 1 \le k \le m \\ B^{(J)}, & \text{otherwise} \end{cases},$$

what is different from the case in one-dimensional input is

$$B^{(0)} = \max_{x \in \Omega} \max_{k=1,2,\cdots,dn} |x_k|, \Omega \in [-1,1]^{d\times n},$$

$$B^{(1)} = \left(\|w^{(1),1}\|_1, + \cdots + \|w^{(1),d}\|_1\right) B^{(0)}.$$

We have

$$h^{(J)}_l = \sigma(T \cdot x - b^{(J)})_l$$

$$= \begin{cases} \alpha_0 x + B^{(J)}, & l = n \\ (\alpha_k - t_k)_+, & l = (k+1)n, 1 \le k \le m \\ 0, & \text{otherwise} \end{cases},$$

let $w^{(J+1)} = \{w^{J+1}_0\} = \{1\}$ and

$$b^{(J+1)}_l = \begin{cases} -B^{(J)}, & l = 1 \\ 0, & \text{otherwise} \end{cases},$$

then $T^{w^{(J+1)}} = I_{d_J}$ and

$$h_l^{(J+1)} = \sigma(I \cdot h^{(J)} - b^{(J+1)})_l$$
$$= \begin{cases} B^{(1)}, & l = 1 \\ \alpha_0 x + B^{(J)}, & l = n \\ (\alpha_k - t_k)_+, & l = (k+1)n, 1 \le k \le m \\ 0, & \text{otherwise} \end{cases}.$$

For a set of $\mathbf{w}$, $\mathbf{b}$ constructed above, there exists $f_{J+1}^{\mathbf{w},\mathbf{b}} \in \mathcal{H}_{J+1}^{\mathbf{w},\mathbf{b}}$, such that

$$\| f - f_{J+1}^{\mathbf{w},\mathbf{b}} \|_{C(\Omega)} \le c_0 v_{f,2} max\{\sqrt{\log m}, \sqrt{nd}\} m^{-\frac{1}{2}-\frac{1}{nd}}.$$

If there is no untrivial common factor, we consider single convolutional layer, at this time, $w^{(1),i} = W^i$ is a sequence of length $(m+1)d$, then $s = (m+1)n - 1$. In other words, this is a special case when $J = 1$, that is, there exists $f_2^{\mathbf{w},\mathbf{b}} \in \mathcal{H}_2^{\mathbf{w},\mathbf{b}}$, such that

$$\| f - f_2^{\mathbf{w},\mathbf{b}} \|_{C(\Omega)} \le c_0 v_{f,2} max\{\sqrt{\log m}, \sqrt{nd}\} m^{-\frac{1}{2}-\frac{1}{nd}}.$$

A.2 Model Training Results in the Trajectory Prediction Experiments

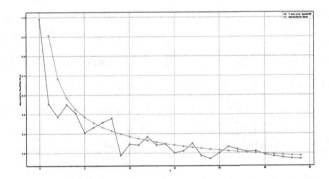

Fig. 4. The experiment on y-axis.

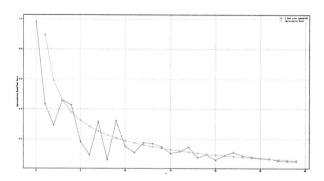

Fig. 5. The experiment on z-axis.

A.3   Back Propagation Process of UniverApproCNN

Take the single-output CNN with two convolutional layers and a full connected layer considered above as an example, find the derivative of the loss function L with respect to $w_k^{(1)}$, where $L = (Y - y)^2$, and $y = \sum_{l=1}^{d_2} c_l h_l^{(2)}$. The derivative of loss function $L = (Y - y)^2$ with respect to $w_k^{(1)}$ is

$$\frac{\partial L}{\partial w_k^{(1)}} = \frac{\partial L}{\partial y} \cdot \sum_{l=1}^{d_2} \frac{\partial y}{\partial h_l^{(2)}} \cdot \frac{\partial h_l^{(2)}}{\partial w_k^{(1)}},$$

For fixed $0 \leq k \leq s$,

Define $a^{(j)} = T^{w^{(j)}} \cdots T^{w^{(1)}} x$, then essentially we find $\frac{\partial a_l^{(2)}}{w_k^{(1)}}$ and $\frac{\partial B^{(2)}}{\partial w_k^{(1)}}$. For fixed $0 \leq k \leq s$, observe that when $k+1 \leq i \leq k+d$, $a_i^{(1)}$ contains items related to $w_k^{(1)}$, and $\frac{\partial a_i^{(1)}}{\partial w_k^{(1)}} = x_{i-k}$.

Further, when $k+1 \leq l \leq k+d+s$, $a_l^{(2)}$ contains items related to $w_k^{(1)}$, and we only need to consider $\sum_{i=k+1}^{k+d} w_{l-i}^{(2)} a_i^{(1)}$ in $a_l^{(2)}$. Since $w^{(2)}$ is finite supported, we only consider $\sum_{i=max\{k+1,l-s\}}^{min\{k+d,l\}} w_{l-i}^{(2)} a_i^{(1)}$, then $\frac{\partial a_l^{(2)}}{\partial a_i^{(1)}} = w_{l-i}^{(2)}$ and

$$\frac{\partial a_l^{(2)}}{w_k^{(1)}} = \sum_{i=max\{k+1,l-s\}}^{min\{k+d,l\}} \frac{\partial a_l^{(2)}}{\partial a_i^{(1)}} \cdot \frac{\partial a_i^{(1)}}{\partial w_k^{(1)}}$$

$$= \sum_{i=max\{k+1,l-s\}}^{min\{k+d,l\}} w_{l-i}^{(2)} \cdot x_{i-k}.$$

It is easy to find that

$$\frac{\partial B^{(2)}}{\partial w_k^{(1)}} = \sum_{l=1}^{d_2} c_l \cdot \|w^{(2)}\|_1 \cdot (|w_k^{(1)}|)' \cdot B^{(0)}$$

Similar conclusions can be obtained for the CNN with depth $J+1$ and single output.

References

1. Cybenko, G.: Approximation by superpositions of a sigmoidal function. Math. Control Signals Systems **2**(4), 303–314 (1989)
2. Pinkus, A.: Approximation theory of the MLP model in neural networks. Acta Numer. **8**, 143–195 (1999)
3. Zhou, D.X., Jetter, K.: Approximation with polynomial kernels and SVM classifiers. Adv. Comput. Math. **25**(1–3), 323–344 (2006)
4. Breiman, L.: Hinging hyperplanes for regression, classification, and function approximation. IEEE Trans. Inf. Theory **39**(3), 999–1013 (1993)
5. Klusowski, J.M., Barron, A.R.: Approximation by combinations of ReLU and squared ReLU ridge functions with l^1 and l^0 controls (2016)
6. Barron, A.R.: Universal approximation bounds for superpositions of a sigmoidal function. IEEE Trans. Inf. Theory **39**(3), 930–945 (1993)
7. Klusowski, J.M., Barron, A.R.: Uniform approximation by neural networks activated by first and second order ridge splines. IEEE Trans. Inf. Theory (2016)
8. Hornik, K.M., Stinchcomb, M., White, H.: Multilayer feedforward networks are universal approximator. IEEE Trans. Neural Networks **2**, 01 (1989)
9. Zhou, D.-X.: Deep distributed convolutional neural networks: Universality. Anal. Appl. **16**(92), 895–919 (2018)
10. Mhaskar, H.N., Poggio, T.: Deep vs. shallow networks: an approximation theory perspective. Anal. Appl. **14**(06), 829–848 (2016)
11. Mallat, S.: Understanding deep convolutional networks. Phil. Trans. R. Soc. A **374**(2065), 20150203–20150203 (2016)
12. Steinwart, I., Thomann, P., Schmid, N.: Learning with hierarchical gaussian kernels. arXiv Machine Learning (2016)
13. Bruna, J., Mallat, S.: Invariant scattering convolution networks. IEEE Trans. Pattern Anal. Mach. Intell. **35**(8), 1872–1886 (2013)
14. Zhou, D.: Universality of deep convolutional neural networks. Appl. Comput. Harmon. Anal. **48**(2), 787–794 (2020)
15. Santurkar, S., Tsipras, D., Ilyas, A., Mądry, A.: How does batch normalization help optimization? In: Proceedings of the 32nd International Conference on Neural Information Processing Systems, pp. 2488–2498 (2018)
16. Wang, Y., Wang, Y., Hu, G., Liu, Y., Zhao, Y.: Adaptive skewness kurtosis neural network: enabling communication between neural nodes within a layer, pp. 498–507 (2020)
17. Burger, M., Engl, H.W.: Training neural networks with noisy data as an Ill-posed problem. Adv. Comput. Math. **13**(4), 335–354 (2000)

MS-BERT: A Multi-layer Self-distillation Approach for BERT Compression Based on Earth Mover's Distance

Jiahui Huang, Bin Cao[✉], Jiaxing Wang, and Jing Fan

College of Computer Science and Technology, Zhejiang University of Technology, Hangzhou, China
{huangjh,bincao,wjx,fanjing}@zjut.edu.cn

Abstract. In the past three years, the pre-trained language model is widely used in various natural language processing tasks, which has achieved significant progress. However, the high computational cost has seriously affected the efficiency of the pre-trained language model, which severely impairs the application of the pre-trained language model in resource-limited industries. To improve the efficiency of the model while ensuring the model's accuracy, we propose MS-BERT, a multi-layer self-distillation approach for BERT compression based on Earth Mover's Distance (EMD), which has the following features: (1) MS-BERT allows the lightweight network (student) to learn from all layers of the large model (teacher). In this way, students can learn different levels of knowledge from the teacher, which can enhance students' performance. (2) Earth Mover's Distance (EMD) is introduced to calculate the distance between the teacher layers and the student layers to achieve multi-layer knowledge transfer from teacher to students. (3) Two design strategies of student layers and the top-K uncertainty calculation method are proposed to improve MS-BERT's performance. Extensive experiments conducted on different datasets have proved that our model can be 2 to 12 times faster than BERT under different accuracy losses.

Keywords: Pre-trained language model · BERT · Self-distillation · Multi-layer · EMD

1 Introduction

Nowadays, there are many collaborative management systems, which can realize the assignment and management of tasks by managers. Improving the performance of the system can improve the system's quality of service. For example, the telecommunications complaint system is an agent collaboration system. During the complaint dialogue between the user and the agent, a large number of customer complaints are recorded as the text will be generated. The agent can assign the complaint task to the corresponding business staff for handling. The task allocation process can be regarded as a text classification task in natural

H. Gao and X. Wang (Eds.): CollaborateCom 2021, LNICST 407, pp. 316–334, 2021.
https://doi.org/10.1007/978-3-030-92638-0_19

language processing (NLP). With the proposal of Transformer-based language models, such as BERT [1], GPT-2 [17], and XLNet [27], NLP has entered a new era. These transformer-based language models have achieved great success through pre-training on large-scale corpus and fine-tuning on downstream NLP tasks. Applying these models to collaborative systems can greatly improve the performance of the models. However, these transformer-based language models suffer from the following problems: (1) Due to the continuous increase of model parameters, the amount of calculation of inference also increases, which will cause the model's inference speed to be very slow. (2) In the service industry, time and resources are often limited, where makes these language models hard to come into service. Therefore, how to reduce the computational cost and accelerate inference speed has become a widespread concern. Only in this way can the pre-trained language model be better put into use in the industry.

Based on the above questions, many existing studies of Transformer-based language models have tried to accelerate inference speed and reduce the amount of calculation in various aspects, such as weight pruning [2,14], parameter sharing [5,24], low-rank decomposition [10], and knowledge distillation (KD) [6]. Among them, KD is considered the most popular and practical method at present [3]. It is the process of inducing small models (student models) to train through a well-trained large model (teacher model). However, KD also has some problems: (1) KD requires an additional pre-training language model structure, which will put more pressure on deploying these models. (2) The pre-trained language model has been proven to contain a lot of redundant calculations. In industry, the demand for services varies significantly over time. For example, during holidays, the number of complaints may be several times more than on workdays. The pre-trained language model, which after knowledge distillation, cannot cope with the rapid changes in demand due to redundant calculations.

Aiming at the problems of KD, self-distillation can solve them well. Self-distillation [12] does not require additional external resources where the output of teachers and students are in the same model. Moreover, its unique sample-wise adaptive mechanism [12] can well solve the problem of demand changes. Although the previous self-distillation method [12,25] is effective, there are still some limitations: (1) The existing self-distillation method only uses a specific teacher layer to guide the student layers. For example, FastBERT [12] only uses the last teacher layer to guide all student classifiers. However, this method of knowledge transfer is only based on experience without a theoretical basis. The research of Jawahar [7] has proved that different layers of BERT learn different levels of knowledge. The surface information features are in the bottom networks, the syntactic information features are in the middle layer networks, and the semantic information features are in the upper networks. Different NLP tasks require different levels of knowledge contained in different layers of BERT. Therefore, only learning from the specific layer will lead to the lack of partial knowledge and reduce the performance of the models. (2) Previous research directly spliced a student classifier behind each Transformer layer without considering the complexity of different task samples [23]. Some samples with higher complexity may be considered correct in the low-level student classifiers and output early, which results in a decrease in the models' performance. (3) The information entropy [20] of the complex dataset that contains hundreds of classes is very large, which makes the sample-wise adaptive mechanism [12] useless.

To solve the issues mentioned above, we propose a multi-layer self-distillation BERT based on Earth Mover's Distance (EMD) [16]. First, we design a hierarchical mapping relationship based on EMD where each student classifier can learn knowledge from multiple teacher layers. And the transfer of knowledge is no longer subject to a specific teacher layer. In this way, the students can adaptively learn from various teachers regarding different data sets or NLP tasks. Then, to further improve the performance of our model, we propose two splicing methods of student classifiers, which divide into splicing student classifiers after every k Transformer layer and splicing student classifiers after the last k Transformer layers. It can reduce the error output of samples with higher complexity in the low-level classifiers. Finally, we propose a calculation method of top-K uncertainty, where K refers to the max top K values in the sample output distribution. This calculation method solves the problem that the samples' uncertainty is very high when the sample information is too large and can effectively reduce the samples' uncertainty.

The main contributions of this paper are summarized as follows:

- A multi-layer self-distillation approach is proposed, which can learn the rich linguistic knowledge in the different layers of BERT. In addition, MS-BERT can apply to various BERT-like models, and the best-performing model can be selected for different services to improve the quality of service.
- We use EMD to design a new method of calculating the difference between teachers and students and then find the best way of knowledge transfer.
- We propose two student classifier splicing methods which divide into every k-layers splicing and last k-layers splicing. They can further improve the accuracy of the model. For different data sets, we can choose different splicing strategies.
- We use the top-K strategy to calculate the uncertainty of samples. It can effectively reduce the complexity of the sample so that the model can apply to various data sets.
- We have conducted extensive experiments on public data sets and real data sets. Experiment results prove that our method is effective.

The rest of this paper is organized as follows. In Sect. 2, we will summarize the preliminaries. Section 3 gives a detailed introduction to our method. Section 4 analyzes the validity of the experimental results. In Sect. 5, we will introduce related work of knowledge distillation. Finally, we conclude this paper in Sect. 6.

2   Preliminaries

In this section, we will introduce some preliminary content, which is very important to understand MS-BERT. We first introduce the self-distillation method and then introduce the sample-wise adaptive mechanism.

2.1 Self-distillation

Knowledge distillation refers to transferring the knowledge of the pre-trained teacher model to the student model through distillation. Self-distillation means the transfer of knowledge to oneself.

There are currently two ways of self-distillation: distilling knowledge from the past model to the present (BERT$_{SDV}$) [25] and distilling knowledge from the high-layer to the low-layer (FastBERT) [12]. Because the self-distillation method in BERT$_{SDV}$ has nothing to do with inference acceleration, and our method aims at inference acceleration. So, we mainly describe the self-distillation in FastBERT. FastBERT is divided into two parts: backbone and branches. The backbone is a well-trained BERT model, and the branches are the student classifiers spliced behind each Transformer layer. The model takes the output of the backbone as a high-quality soft target and extracts it to train the student classifiers. And it uses Kullback-Leibler (KL) divergence to measure the difference between student S and teacher's soft target T as $D_{KL}(S,T)$. The formula is as follows:

$$D_{KL}(S,T) = \sum_{i=1}^{L} S(i) \cdot \log \frac{S(i)}{T(i)} \tag{1}$$

where L is the number of data set categories.

Except for the last layer, there is a student classifier after each Transformer block. FastBERT defines the number of student classifiers as $N-1$, where N is the number of Transformer blocks. It uses the sum of KL divergence to calculate the overall loss of the model as in:

$$Loss = \sum_{i=1}^{N-1} D_{KL}(S_i, T) \tag{2}$$

where S_i refers to the output distribution of the i-th student classifier.

According to the above method, FastBERT can distill knowledge from the high-layer Transformer block to the low-layer student classifiers. Furthermore, it has no additional pre-training structure. The input and output of the teacher and the student are in the same model, so it is called self-distillation.

2.2 Sample-wise Adaptive Inference

The adaptive inference is to control the output depth of samples in the deep network through adaptive calculation [4], and it can even control the complexity of the model. Specifically, given a sample sequence, each level of student classifier will have an output distribution for the sequence. The uncertainty of the sample output distribution is calculated by normalized entropy. The calculation formula is as follows:

$$Uncertainty = \frac{\sum_{i=1}^{L} S(i) \log S(i)}{-\log L} \tag{3}$$

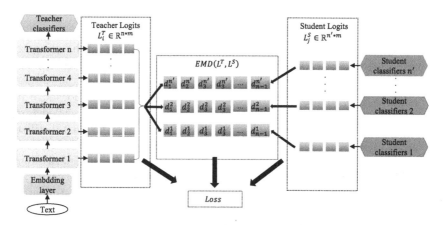

Fig. 1. An ensemble of MS-BERT, which distills knowledge from the N-layer Transformer blocks to each student classifier. The stitching method of the student classifier is stitching every k layer. L^T and L^S are the output distributions of teachers and students, respectively. Calculate the distance between them by EMD and d_i^j represents the output distance between the i-th Transformer layer and the j-th student classifier. n and n' are the number of Transformer layers and student classifiers, respectively. m is the number of categories in the dataset.

where $S(i)$ refers to the value of the i-th label in the sample output distribution. The higher the uncertainty, the greater the amount of information contained in the sample, and the more incorrect the sample.

Subsequently, FastBERT sets a threshold *speed* between 0 and 1 to compare with the uncertainty. Once samples' uncertainty is lower than *speed*, they are considered to be correct enough and will be output in the current student classifier in advance. Otherwise, the samples will go to higher layers for calculation. As the *speed* increases, there will be fewer and fewer samples output in the high-layer classifiers. The comparison method of uncertainty and *speed* avoids that all samples are output in the last layer, and samples can be adaptively output in different layers. It dramatically reduces the inference computation. The above process is the specific process of adaptive inference.

3   Methodology

In this section, we propose a self-distillation BERT based on multi-layer knowledge transfer. In addition, we present two splicing strategies for student layers and a calculation method for top-K uncertainty. Next, we first give an overall overview of our model and approach. Then, we provide a detailed description of the three proposed methods.

3.1   Overview of MS-BERT

The main idea of MS-BERT is to transfer knowledge from different layers of BERT to the student classifier. Like FastBERT [12], our model also contains two parts: backbone and branch, as shown in Fig. 1. The backbone is the BERT-base[1] model officially released by Google. The branch part is mainly some student classifiers spliced behind Transformers, which is mainly used to balance the prediction speed and performance of the model.

Unlike FastBERT, we propose a self-distillation method that utilizes the knowledge contained in all Transformer blocks. Each student classifier in the branch learns from different layers of BERT. In this way, the rich knowledge learned by the 12 layers BERT model can fully transfer to student classifiers, and the performance of all student classifiers can further enhance. In addition, we no longer simply set a classifier after each Transformer, which will cause some high-complexity samples [23] to be output incorrectly in the lower layer. We designed two classifier design strategies to further improve the model's performance by reducing the number of student classifiers. Moreover, we propose a calculation method of top-K uncertainty to reduce the information entropy [20] of the sample. Next, we first introduce the multi-layer self-distillation method based on EMD and then introduce two student classifier splicing strategies. Finally, we will introduce the calculation method of top-K uncertainty.

3.2   Self-distillation with Earth Mover's Distance

BERT encodes a wealth of hierarchical linguistic information. The study of [7] shows that different layers of BERT encode various levels of knowledge. Specifically, the lower layer encodes phrase information and special symbols. In addition, the lower layer still encodes the token's position adequately, while the upper layer has lost the position information. At the same time, the high-layer semantic knowledge will have a feedback effect on the intermediate layer syntactic knowledge, and the intermediate layer syntactic features will be corrected through the high-layer semantic guidance. Therefore, we designed a multi-layer knowledge extraction method based on Earth Mover's Distance (EMD) [16].

EMD is a histogram similarity measure based on the efficiency of the transportation problem, and it is a linear programming problem that has been well solved. It extends the distance between individual elements to the distance between distributions, which can measure the difference between distributions. Our self-distillation method calculates the difference between the output distribution of all Transformer blocks and the student classifiers. Then we use it as the sum of transfer knowledge. Our goal is to reduce this difference to make the student more powerful. The specific process is as follows:

First, in the model training stage, given a text t of length n, we use WordPiece embedding [1] in the embedding layer and encode it as a vector $v = [x_1, x_2, ...x_n]$,

---

[1] https://github.com/google-research/bert.

where each x_i is constructed by summing the token, segment and position embeddings. We can see how it is calculated as:

$$v = Token\_emd(t) + Seg\_emd(t) + Pos\_emb(t) \tag{4}$$

where $Token\_emd()$ is the token embedding of t, $Seg\_emd()$ is the segment embedding of t, $Pos\_emb()$ is the position embedding of t.

After the embedding is complete, layer-by-layer feature extraction will perform in the multi-layer Transformer blocks, and there will be a probability output in each layer. We use $Logits^T = [Logits_1^T, Logits_2^T, ...Logits_N^T]$ as the output of all Transformer layers, where N represents the number of Transformer, and $Logits_i^T$ represents the output of the i-th layer of Transformer. Similarly, we define the output of each layer of the student classifier as $Logits_j^S$, where j represents the j-th student classifier. We use EMD to calculate the distance between the distribution of students and teachers as:

$$Distance_i^j = Emd\_samples(Logits_i^T, Logits_j^S) \tag{5}$$

where $Distance_i^j$ represents the distance between the output of the i-th layer of Transformer and the output of the j-th layer of student classifier.

Then, we try to get the difference between the j-th student classifier and the overall teacher as $Difference_j$, which makes no knowledge loss in the self-distillation process. Student classifiers can learn different levels of knowledge. The calculation formula is as follows:

$$Difference_j = \sum_{i=1}^{N-1} Distance_i^j \cdot Logits_i^T \tag{6}$$

Next, we use softmax to normalize the overall difference and use it as the teacher's knowledge carrier p_t. We defined it as:

$$p_t = softmax(Difference_j + \lambda Logits_N^T) \tag{7}$$

Similarly, the knowledge carrier p_s of each layer of students is normalized as:

$$p_{s_j} = softmax(Logits_j^S) \tag{8}$$

After that, we use KL divergence to measure the learning goal of each student classifier:

$$Loss_{KL}(p_{s_j}, p_t) = \sum_{i=1}^{M} p_{s_j}(i) \cdot \log \frac{p_{s_j}(i)}{p_t(i)} \tag{9}$$

where M is the number of data set categories.

Finally, we use the sum of the losses of all student classifiers as the overall loss of self-distillation:

$$Total\_loss = \sum_{j=1}^{N'} Loss_{KL}(p_{s_j}, p_t) \tag{10}$$

where N' is the number of student classifiers.

After the above steps, we successfully transferred all the knowledge in Transformers to each layer of the student classifier. Each student classifier can adaptively learn the knowledge contained in different layers of BERT through EMD. Therefore, we have completed the multi-layer mapping strategy. And then, we only need to reduce the *Total_loss* to narrow the difference between teachers and students.

3.3   Student Classifiers Splicing Strategy

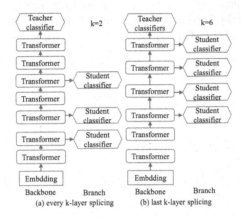

Fig. 2. The model structure of the two splicing strategies. (a) is to splice a classifier every 2 layers; (b) is to splice a classifier in the last 6 layers.

In the process of adaptive inference, the model can exchange for higher efficiency by reducing the accuracy. However, in some experiments, the loss of accuracy is too large. In the service industry, we may not tolerate such a significant loss of accuracy. A reasonable explanation is that different samples have different levels of difficulty [23], and the more difficult samples require a higher-level Transformer to be inferred correctly. The sample-wise adaptive inference mechanism will cause some complex samples to be considered correct in advance and output prematurely, which leads to a decrease in overall performance.

To alleviate this problem, we propose two splicing strategies for student classifiers, as shown in Fig. 2: splicing classifiers every k layers (a); splicing classifiers in the last k layers (b). These two strategies allow the samples to pass through more Transformers before output to determine whether they are correct. In this way, the sample can be more accurate before output. We will verify our strategies in Sect. 4.

3.4 Top-K Uncertainty

For an event or a piece of information, its uncertainty closely relates to the amount of information. For example, we need a lot of information to understand things that are unfamiliar to us. On the contrary, we only need a small amount of information for things we are familiar with. We can use Shannon entropy [20] as a quantitative indicator of information content:

$$H(X) = -\sum_{i=1}^{n} p(x_i) \log p(x_i) \tag{11}$$

where $p(x_i)$ is the distribution of variable X, and n is the length of the distribution. Uncertainty is the normalized information entropy, as shown in (3). We can calculate the uncertainty of distribution through (3), so as to realize adaptive inference.

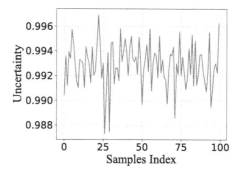

Fig. 3. The uncertainty distribution of the samples. We randomly select 100 texts from the data set and calculate their uncertainty. We can see that the uncertainty of almost all texts is close to 1.

However, complex multi-category data sets, such as the sample of a complaint ticket in the telecommunications industry, contain dozens of categories. Through the calculation of (3), the uncertainty of almost every sample is above 0.99. An intuitive example is shown in Fig. 3. In this way, it is difficult to find a suitable threshold to compare with the uncertainty, which causes the model to lose the ability of adaptive inference. To solve this problem, we propose the calculation method of top-K uncertainty:

$$TopK - uncertainty = \frac{\sum_{i=1}^{K} max_K(p_{s_i} \log p_{s_i})}{-\log K} \tag{12}$$

where K is the top K number in the distribution. In this way, we effectively reduce the uncertainty of the samples, thereby realizing sample-wise adaptive inference for complex data sets. We will verify the effectiveness of our method in Sect. 4.

4   Experiments

In this section, we validate MS-BERT on 4 NLP datasets collected from real-world environments. And we compare MS-BERT with several well-known baselines. A brief introduction of the baselines is as follows.

- **BERT** [1]. We use the BERT-base version, which is pre-trained on a large-scale general corpus.
- **BERT-EMD** [11]. A knowledge distillation method based on multi-layer knowledge transfer surpasses most of the current knowledge distillation methods in accuracy.
- **FastBERT** [12]. The first distillation model combines self-distillation and adaptive inference in NLP tasks.

All experiments are done on a computer with Intel Core(TM) i9-9940X 3.30 GHz CPU and 4 RTX 2080Ti graphics. In the following content, we will first introduce data sets, measurement standards. Then, we compared and analyzed the experimental results. Finally, we conduct an ablation study to analyze the effectiveness of MS-BERT.

4.1   Datasets

We conducted a lot of experiments on public data sets and real-world datasets. These datasets contain three text classification tasks: sentiment analysis, question matching, and complaint service text classification.

(1) *Sentiment analysis.* For the sentiment analysis task, we chose two different datasets. The first one is ChnSentiCorp, a two-category Chinese hotel review dataset with 12,000 texts. The second is the book review [22] dataset, which contains more than 40,000 texts.
(2) *Question matching.* Question matching is a basic task of question answering technology, which is usually regarded as a semantic matching task, and sometimes a paraphrase recognition task. This task aims to search for questions with similar intent to the input questions in the existing database. LCQMC is a large-scale Chinese question matching corpus [13], which contains more than 260,000 question pairs manually labeled and divided into the training set, validation set, and test set.
(3) *Complaint classification.* Telecom complaints service text (TCST) dataset is a real-world complaint text collected from China Telecom. It contains information about users' complaints about telecommunications services. This dataset has a total of 580 categories and a total of 500,000 texts. However, due to data imbalance, the number of texts in many categories is too small, which greatly impacts the overall experimental results. Therefore, we choose 166 categories with a large number of texts for the experiment. We divide the data set into three parts. The training set contains about 280,000 pieces of data, and the validation set and test set each have about 90,000 pieces of data.

To make the experiment fair and reduce the search space of hyperparameters, except for the TCST dataset, the max length of the input sequence of all experiments is 128, the learning rate is 2e−5, and the batch size is 16. For the TCST dataset, the max length of the input sequence is 256, the learning rate is 2e−5, and the batch size is 16. Because there are more than 50% of the texts of telecommunications complaints are longer than 128. Next, we fine-tune all models with three epochs and save the results. Then, we use five epochs for self-distillation.

4.2 Evaluation Metrics

The experiments in this paper mainly have two evaluation indicators: accuracy [19] and Floating-point operations (FLOPs) [12]. Next, we will make a detailed introduction.

(1) **Accuracy.** Accuracy is an evaluation of the overall model, which is widely used in the fields of information retrieval and statistical classification. It can intuitively evaluate the quality of a model. For the binary datasets, the calculation method of accuracy is shown as follows:

$$Accuracy = \frac{TP + TN}{TP + TN + FN + FP} \tag{13}$$

where TP refers to the number of positive samples predicted to be positive samples. FP refers to the number of positive samples predicted to be negative samples. TN refers to the number of negative samples predicted to be negative samples. FN refers to the number of negative samples predicted to be positive samples. For a multi-class dataset, the calculation method of accuracy is shown as follows:

$$Accuracy = \frac{\sum TP}{TP + TN + FN + FP} \tag{14}$$

When calculating one of the classes at this time, we treat all other classes as negative classes.

(2) **FLOPs.** FLOPs can use to measure the complexity of an algorithm or model. It represents the amount of model calculation. The smaller the FLOPs of the model, the smaller the amount of calculation required for the model, and the faster the model speed.

4.3 Experimental Result

In this section, we conducted three types of experiments. First, we analyzed the overall performance of the model compared with the baselines. Secondly, we analyzed the effectiveness of the two splicing strategies proposed in this paper. Finally, we analyzed the K value in the uncertainty calculation method. In the following parts, we will analyze the three experiments in detail.

4.3.1   Overall Performance Study

We summarize the overall experimental results on the 4 datasets in Table 1. Compared with BERT-base, MS-BERT can speed up 2 to 12 times under different accuracy losses. We can adjust the speed of the model according to the tolerance for accuracy loss. Compared with BERT-EMD, MS-BERT is slightly insufficient in accuracy. However, MS-BERT far surpasses BERT-EMD in speed when the accuracy is not much different. Moreover, due to the fixed model structure of BERT-EMD, there are a lot of redundant calculations. Redundant calculations make it unable to respond to changes in industrial demand. On the contrary, MS-BERT can effectively reduce redundant calculations due to its adjustable speed. Therefore, our model is more attractive in the industry. Compared with FastBERT, MS-BERT has improved accuracy on all datasets except the TCST dataset. Especially when the *speed* = 0.8, the accuracy rate increases significantly. It increased by 1.16% on ChnSentiCorp, 0.61% on Book review, and 1.57% on LCQMC. Except for the Book review dataset, compared to the increase in accuracy, the increase in FLOPs is not apparent. The reason is that through the multi-layered self-distillation method, the knowledge obtained by each student classifier from the backbone network is more accurate and complete, which makes the output distribution of the student classifier for each sample more accurate. At the same time, the splicing strategy we proposed reduces the error output of samples.

Table 1. Experimental results

Dataset	ChnSentiCorp 12k		Book review 40k		LCQMC 260k		TCST 460k	
Model	Acc	FLOPs speedup	Acc	FLOPs speedup	Acc	FLOPs speedup	Acc	FLOPs speedup
BERT	94.75	10892M 1.00×	88.38	10892M 1.00×	87.19	10892M 1.00×	57.51	21785M 1.00×
BERT-EMD	92.50	5436M 2.00×	86.11	5436M 2.00×	85.71	5436M 2.00×	55.13	10872M 2.00×
FastBERT (speed = 0.5)	91.25	1696M 6.42×	87.92	3270M 3.33×	84.81	3374M 3.22×	–	–
MS-BERT* (speed = 0.5)	91.83	1817M 6.00×	88.13	3793M 2.87×	85.38	3459M 3.15×	54.93	12151M 1.79×
FastBERT (speed = 0.8)	88.92	1153M 9.44×	85.80	1726M 6.3×	78.98	1736M 6.27×	–	–
MS-BERT (speed = 0.8)	90.08	1204M 9.04×	86.41	1937M 5.63×	80.55	1784M 6.11×	50.48	1854M 11.75×

* For TCST dataset, K is set to 18.

* The student classifiers adopt the way of splicing every two layers of Transformer.

With regard to the Book review dataset, regardless of the speed, the model's accuracy is very close in FastBERT. It shows that the samples' complexity of this dataset is low, and most can predict correctly in the low-level networks. Therefore, as the speed increases, the model's accuracy does not change much, but the acceleration continues to increase. For MS-BERT, due to its low complexity, the student classifier splicing strategy will increase some redundant calculations, which leads to an increase in FLOPs. However, MS-BERT can increase the speed by 2.8 times with almost no loss of accuracy when the *speed* is equal to 0.5. Because the knowledge transfer method of multi-layer self-distillation makes the student classifier's classification performance more robust. Therefore, when the *speed* is not high, the model accuracy loss is small, which is very attractive.

For the TCST dataset, FastBERT loses the ability of adaptive inference because the uncertainty of each sample is too high (see in Fig. 3). Therefore, it cannot achieve inference acceleration, and its experimental results are equivalent to BERT-base. We use '–' to indicate the result. However, based on our method, it can speed up 2 to 12 times under different accuracy losses compared with BERT because the calculation method of top-K uncertainty can greatly reduce the uncertainty of the sample.

4.3.2   Analysis of Different Splicing Strategies

We further studied the performance of two different student classifier splicing strategies. Table 2 summarizes the accuracy and FLOPs of the two strategies under the same speed constraint (*speed* = 0.8). We researched two data sets (ChnSentiCorp and LCQMC). The accuracy of the two strategies improves to different degrees compared with FastBERT. However, the last k-layers splicing strategy will significantly increase the calculation amount of the model, while the increase in the calculation amount of every k-layers splicing strategy can be ignored. A reasonable explanation is that the last k-layer splicing strategy completely eliminates the possibility of samples being output in the lower layers so that samples classified correctly in the lower layers can only be output in the upper layers. The strategy of splicing every k-layer is to prevent samples from being output in each layer so that samples that were initially classified incorrectly can obtain higher correctness, and samples that were initially correct can be output in lower layers.

Table 2. Experimental results of different splicing strategies

Dataset	ChnSentiCorp		LCQMC	
Strategy	*Accuracy*	*FLOPs* speedup	*Accuracy*	*FLOPs* speedup
Every k-layer splicing	90.08	1204M 9.04×	80.55	1784M 6.11×
Last k-layer splicing	**93.83**	5688M 1.9×	**87.20**	5803M 1.87×

In summary, we can choose different splicing strategies according to the actual situation of the industry. If the accuracy is more critical, we can choose the stitching strategy of the last k layers. Otherwise, we can choose the stitching strategy of every k layer.

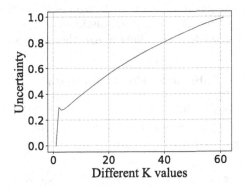

Fig. 4. The relationship curve between K and uncertainty in the TCST dataset.

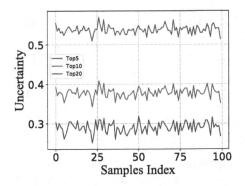

Fig. 5. The uncertainty of different texts in the TCST data set when K is different. We randomly selected 100 pieces of text and set K values to 5, 10, and 20 respectively.

4.3.3 K Value Analysis

For different K values, the uncertainty of the samples is different. We randomly select a sample and calculate its uncertainty as K increases. It can be seen from Fig. 4 that the larger the K values, the higher the uncertainty of the sample. In order to avoid the contingency of a sample, we randomly selected 100 samples and calculated their uncertainty under different K values (5, 10, and 20). Figure 5 shows three different uncertainty curves. It can be proved that when the value of K decreases, the uncertainty decreases. When the data set has a particularly large number of categories, we can realize the adaptive inference of the samples by choosing the appropriate K value. Otherwise, we can make K equal to the number of categories in the data set.

4.4   Ablation Study

To verify the effectiveness of the multi-layer self-distillation method and the student classifier splicing strategy, we conducted ablation experiments on the ChnSentiCorp dataset and the LCQMC dataset. The experimental results are summarized in Table 3, where "w/o multi-layer self-distillation" means only using the last layer of the BERT for self-distillation, and "w/o splicing strategy" refers to splicing student classifiers in each layer of the Transformer.

Table 3. Results of ablation studies

Dataset	Speed	ChnSentiCorp		LCQMC	
Method		Accuracy	FLOPs speedup	Accuracy	FLOPs speedup
MS-BERT	0.4	92.83	2139M 5.09×	86.14	4051M 2.68×
	0.7	90.67	1446M 7.53×	82.60	2209M 4.93×
W/o multi-layer	0.4	93.58	2302M 4.73×	86.46	4437M 2.45×
Self-distillation	0.7	90.75	1488M 7.3×	83.22	2608M 4.17×
W/o	0.4	92.58	1861M 5.85×	85.76	3658M 2.98M
Splicing strategy	0.7	90.33	1268M 8.58×	81.14	1879M 5.60×

As can be seen from Table 1, MS-BERT has a significant improvement in the model's accuracy. It proves that the multi-layer self-distillation method using EMD and the student classifier splicing strategy is effective. From Table 3, we can find that after removing the multi-layer self-distillation, the model's accuracy rises slightly, and the calculation amount of the model increases significantly. Hence, the overall performance of the model decreases. It shows that it is necessary to use EMD to measure the overall difference between teachers and students, and it plays a key role in reducing the amount of calculation of the model. Because EMD regards the distance between the backbone and the branches as the optimal transmission problem, it learns the optimal multi-layer knowledge transfer method instead of just learning knowledge from a specific layer. The more complete the knowledge learned by the branches, the smaller the amount of calculation they need to process samples. After removing the splicing strategy, the model's accuracy decreases. Because the low-level student classifier has output many errors in advance due to insufficient training depth. Therefore, when adaptive reasoning, we cannot treat all samples equally, but consider the complexity of the samples. In summary, the two methods we proposed are critical to the improvement of model performance. They can balance the accuracy of the model and the amount of calculation so that the model can be applied to various data sets.

5   Related Work

The related work of our work can be divided into two categories: (1) knowledge distillation, (2) self-distillation.

Knowledge Distillation. There have been many studies on knowledge distillation. The main idea of knowledge distillation is to train a complex teacher network to cultivate a compact student network to have considerable accuracy and efficiency. DistilBERT [18] distilled BERT in the pre-training stage. It used the triple loss to train the student model and achieved great results. TinyBERT [8] proposed a two-stage distillation framework, which performed Transformer distillation during pre-training and fine-tuning. Zhao et al. [28] proposed a new idea to improve the effectiveness of knowledge distillation, bringing down the model's size to several megabytes by reducing the vocabulary. Mirzadeh et al. [15] proved that when the gap between students and teachers is large, the performance of the student network will decrease, so they proposed the concept of assistant teachers. Sun et al. [21] proposed two patient learning strategies so that the student model can learn the intermediate layer of the teacher network. Yang et al. [26] proposed a method for multiple teachers to train a student together so that students can learn knowledge of different tasks. Li et al. [11] proposed a many-to-many mapping for the BERT compression method, namely BERT-EMD, which surpassed most methods in the accuracy of the model.

The general teacher-student framework of knowledge distillation is shown in Fig. 6. The predicted result of the teacher model is divided by the temperature [6], which is regarded as the soft target. The student model obtains knowledge through learning soft targets. However, knowledge distillation requires an additional small model whose performance depends entirely on the teacher model. Deploying additional models in the industry will undoubtedly cause a more significant burden. Moreover, the pre-training language model has proven to contain a lot of redundant calculations [9]. Although knowledge distillation reduces inference calculations, the fixed model structure does not solve the redundancy problem well. Aiming at multi-layer knowledge transfer, unlike BERT-EMD, our method completes knowledge transfer within the same model. And directly use the output distribution of the model to measure the distance. Relatively speaking, the calculation method of BERT-EMD is more complicated.

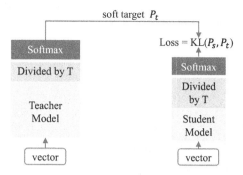

Fig. 6. A general teacher-student framework of knowledge distillation. T stands for temperature, which is used to amplify the knowledge contained in the soft target. The larger the T, the closer the values in the distribution.

Self-distillation. Self-distillation is a unique method of knowledge distillation, whose students and teachers are in the same framework. Liu et al. [12] proposed a FastBERT model, which combined sample adaptive mechanism and self-distillation for the first time. Xu et al. [25] proposed a method that combines self-distillation and self-ensemble to improve further the performance of the model in the fine-tuning stage, but it did not improve the inference speed. We found that the students often transfer knowledge from a specific layer of the teacher model in self-distillation. It will result in ignoring the knowledge contained in other layers of BERT. Because BERT is a multi-layer Transformer structure, different Transformer layers had different natural language features [7].

Different from the self-distillation method, we propose a self-distillation method to learn different levels of knowledge. Our model no longer requires additional external resources and avoids redundant calculations. In addition, it can effectively learn the knowledge contained in different layers of BERT for various NLP tasks.

6   Conclusion

This paper proposes MS-BERT, a multi-layer self-distillation method based on Earth Mover's Distance (EMD). Our model allows each student classifier to learn from all teacher layers in the self-distillation stage, which can reduce the omission of knowledge. Moreover, two student classifier splicing strategies are designed to further enhance the model's performance, thereby reducing the early output of excessive error samples in the adaptive inference stage. In addition, we propose a calculation method of top-K uncertainty to reduce the complexity of the samples. Experimental results conducted on four datasets show that our model has greater accuracy than FastBERT when the inference speed is similar. Compared with the traditional BERT-base model, it can accelerate 2 to 12 times under different accuracy losses. In industry, our model has strong practicality because of the adjustable inference speed. In the future, we will further study better knowledge transfer methods to improve the model's performance further.

Acknowledgements. This research was partially sponsored by the following funds: National Key R&D Program of China (2018YFB1402800), the Fundamental Research Funds for the Provincial Universities of Zhejiang (RF-A2020007) and Zhejiang Lab (2020AA3AB05).

References

1. Devlin, J., Chang, M.W., Lee, K., Toutanova, K.: BERT: pre-training of deep bidirectional transformers for language understanding. In: Proceedings of the 2019 Conference of the North American Chapter of the Association for Computational Linguistics: Human Language Technologies, Volume 1 (Long and Short Papers), Minneapolis, Minnesota, pp. 4171–4186. Association for Computational Linguistics, June 2019
2. Gordon, M., Duh, K., Andrews, N.: Compressing BERT: studying the effects of weight pruning on transfer learning. In: Proceedings of the 5th Workshop on Representation Learning for NLP, pp. 143–155. Association for Computational Linguistics, July 2020
3. Gou, J., Yu, B., Maybank, S.J., Tao, D.: Knowledge distillation: a survey. Int. J. Comput. Vis. **129**, 1789–1819 (2021)
4. Graves, A.: Adaptive computation time for recurrent neural networks. arXiv preprint arXiv:1603.08983 (2016)
5. Han, S., Pool, J., Tran, J., Dally, W.J.: Learning both weights and connections for efficient neural networks. CoRR arXiv:1506.02626 (2015)
6. Hinton, G., Vinyals, O., Dean, J.: Distilling the knowledge in a neural network. arXiv preprint arXiv:1503.02531 (2015)
7. Jawahar, G., Sagot, B., Seddah, D.: What does BERT learn about the structure of language? In: Proceedings of the 57th Annual Meeting of the Association for Computational Linguistics, Florence, Italy, pp. 3651–3657. Association for Computational Linguistics, July 2019
8. Jiao, X., et al.: TinyBERT: distilling BERT for natural language understanding. In: Findings of the Association for Computational Linguistics: EMNLP 2020, pp. 4163–4174. Association for Computational Linguistics, November 2020
9. Kovaleva, O., Romanov, A., Rogers, A., Rumshisky, A.: Revealing the dark secrets of BERT. In: Proceedings of the 2019 Conference on Empirical Methods in Natural Language Processing and the 9th International Joint Conference on Natural Language Processing (EMNLP-IJCNLP), Hong Kong, China, pp. 4365–4374. Association for Computational Linguistics, November 2019
10. Lan, Z., Chen, M., Goodman, S., Gimpel, K., Sharma, P., Soricut, R.: ALBERT: a lite BERT for self-supervised learning of language representations. CoRR arXiv:1909.11942 (2019)
11. Li, J., Liu, X., Zhao, H., Xu, R., Yang, M., Jin, Y.: BERT-EMD: many-to-many layer mapping for bert compression with earth mover's distance. arXiv preprint arXiv:2010.06133 (2020)
12. Liu, W., Zhou, P., Wang, Z., Zhao, Z., Deng, H., Ju, Q.: FastBERT: a self-distilling BERT with adaptive inference time. In: Proceedings of the 58th Annual Meeting of the Association for Computational Linguistics, pp. 6035–6044. Association for Computational Linguistics, July 2020

13. Liu, X., et al.: LCQMC: a large-scale Chinese question matching corpus. In: Proceedings of the 27th International Conference on Computational Linguistics, Santa Fe, New Mexico, USA, pp. 1952–1962. Association for Computational Linguistics, August 2018

14. McCarley, J., Chakravarti, R., Sil, A.: Structured pruning of a BERT-based question answering model. CoRR arXiv:1910.06360 (2019)

15. Mirzadeh, S.I., Farajtabar, M., Li, A., Levine, N., Matsukawa, A., Ghasemzadeh, H.: Improved knowledge distillation via teacher assistant. In: Proceedings of the AAAI Conference on Artificial Intelligence, vol. 34, pp. 5191–5198 (2020)

16. Pele, O., Werman, M.: Fast and robust earth mover's distances. In: 2009 IEEE 12th International Conference on Computer Vision, pp. 460–467. IEEE, September 2009

17. Radford, A., Wu, J., Child, R., Luan, D., Amodei, D., Sutskever, I.: Language models are unsupervised multitask learners. OpenAI Blog **1**(8), 9 (2019)

18. Sanh, V., Debut, L., Chaumond, J., Wolf, T.: DistilBERT, a distilled version of BERT: smaller, faster, cheaper and lighter. CoRR arXiv:1910.01108 (2019)

19. Schütze, H., Manning, C.D., Raghavan, P.: Introduction to Information Retrieval, vol. 39. Cambridge University Press, Cambridge (2008)

20. Shannon, C.E.: A symbolic analysis of relay and switching circuits. Electr. Eng. **57**(12), 713–723 (1938). https://doi.org/10.1109/EE.1938.6431064

21. Sun, S., Cheng, Y., Gan, Z., Liu, J.: Patient knowledge distillation for BERT model compression. In: Proceedings of the 2019 Conference on Empirical Methods in Natural Language Processing and the 9th International Joint Conference on Natural Language Processing (EMNLP-IJCNLP), Hong Kong, China, pp. 4323–4332. Association for Computational Linguistics, November 2019

22. Torregrossa, F., Claveau, V., Kooli, N., Gravier, G., Allesiardo, R.: On the correlation of word embedding evaluation metrics. In: Proceedings of the 12th Language Resources and Evaluation Conference, Marseille, France, pp. 4789–4797. European Language Resources Association, May 2020. https://www.aclweb.org/anthology/2020.lrec-1.589

23. Wang, A., Singh, A., Michael, J., Hill, F., Levy, O., Bowman, S.: GLUE: a multitask benchmark and analysis platform for natural language understanding. In: Proceedings of the 2018 EMNLP Workshop BlackboxNLP: Analyzing and Interpreting Neural Networks for NLP, Brussels, Belgium, pp. 353–355. Association for Computational Linguistics, November 2018

24. Wang, Y., Xu, C., Xu, C., Tao, D.: Packing convolutional neural networks in the frequency domain. IEEE Trans. Pattern Analy. Mach. Intell. **41**(10), 2495–2510 (2018)

25. Xu, Y., Qiu, X., Zhou, L., Huang, X.: Improving BERT fine-tuning via self-ensemble and self-distillation. arXiv preprint arXiv:2002.10345 (2020)

26. Yang, Z., Shou, L., Gong, M., Lin, W., Jiang, D.: Model compression with multitask knowledge distillation for web-scale question answering system. arXiv preprint arXiv:1904.09636 (2019)

27. Yang, Z., Dai, Z., Yang, Y., Carbonell, J.G., Salakhutdinov, R., Le, Q.V.: XLNet: generalized autoregressive pretraining for language understanding. CoRR arXiv:1906.08237 (2019)

28. Zhao, S., Gupta, R., Song, Y., Zhou, D.: Extreme language model compression with optimal subwords and shared projections. CoRR arXiv:1909.11687 (2019)

Smart Contract Vulnerability Detection Based on Dual Attention Graph Convolutional Network

Yuqi Fan[1,2(✉)], Siyuan Shang[1], and Xu Ding[3]

[1] School of Computer Science and Information Engineering,
Hefei University of Technology, Hefei 230601, Anhui, China
yuqi.fan@hfut.edu.cn, siyuan0102@mail.hfut.edu.cn
[2] Anhui Provincial Key Laboratory of Network and Information Security,
Anhui Normal Unviersity, Wuhu 241002, Anhui, China
[3] Institute of Industry and Equipment Technology, Hefei University of Technology,
Hefei 230009, Anhui, China
dingxu@hfut.edu.cn

Abstract. Smart contracts on blockchains have received increasing attention due to the decentralized, transparent, and immutable characteristics of blockchain. However, smart contracts are prone to security problems caused by critical vulnerabilities, which can lead to huge economic losses. Therefore, it is urgent to provide strong and robust security assurance for smart contracts. Most existing studies on smart contract vulnerability detection methods take heavy reliance on experts-defined rules, which are extremely time-consuming and labor-demanding. Moreover, the manually-set rules are limited to specific tasks and subject to errors. Although some studies explore the use of deep learning methods, they fail to represent both semantics and structural information. In this paper, we propose a novel model, Dual Attention Graph Convolutional Network (DA-GCN), to detect vulnerabilities in smart contracts on blockchains. Both control flow graph and opcode sequence extracted from smart contract bytecodes are fed into the feature extractor based on graph convolutional network and self-attention mechanism. Model DA-GCN then uses control flow level attention to focus on the more important nodes in the control flow graph and suppress useless information. Finally, a multi layer perceptron is used to identify whether the smart contract is vulnerable. Experimental results on the real-world smart contract data set containing two vulnerabilities of reentrancy and timestamp dependency demonstrate that our proposed model DA-GCN can effectively improve the performance of smart contract vulnerability detection.

Keywords: Smart contract · Vulnerability detection · Deep learning · Graph convolution · Dual attention

1 Introduction

Blockchain is widely used as an underlying programmable distributed infrastructure to support smart contract applications which can be seen as event-driven

H. Gao and X. Wang (Eds.): CollaborateCom 2021, LNICST 407, pp. 335–351, 2021.
https://doi.org/10.1007/978-3-030-92638-0_20

programs on the blockchain system. Once deployed on the blockchain, smart contracts are not allowed to be modified, due to the decentralized, transparent, and immutable characteristics of blockchain. However, serious vulnerability in smart contracts can be maliciously utilized, leading to huge financial losses. In June 2016, DAO, a large crowdfunding organization deployed on Ethereum, had $150 million worth of Ethereum digital currency stolen. In July 2017, Parity, a widely used multi-signature digital wallet was attacked, which directly resulted in a $30 million financial loss. Therefore, the smart contracts require strong security assurance, and there is an urgent need for effective vulnerability detection of smart contracts, such that we can remove the found vulnerabilities in the smart contracts before deploying them.

Current research on detecting smart contract vulnerability is mainly based on the traditional methods such as symbolic execution [15], fuzzy detection [7], etc. However, adopting traditional methodologies in vulnerability detection demands expert definition of logic rules, which takes heavy reliance on experience, capability of professionality, and understanding of domain knowledge. The design process of logical rules can also consume significant time. Besides, the manually set rules are often limited to specific tasks and prone to errors.

Deep learning methodologies have been used in software defect prediction or malware classification these years and achieved certain results. However, the research on smart contract vulnerability detection using deep learning has not received much attention. Some studies detect smart contracts vulnerabilities via deep learning approaches by taking either sequence-based [6,14,17] or graph-based [20] feature representations as input. Tann et al. [14] first converted the bytecode into an opcode sequence. The bytecode, represented by 32 bytes of hexadecimal numbers, is an intermediate form between high-level and machine languages. The authors then constructed a long short-term memory network (LSTM) model for vulnerability detection in smart contracts. Gogineni et al. [6] improved the work in [14] by using an encoder to predict the next instruction in the opcode sequence, such that the LSTM model continues to learn the parameters for the vulnerability classification task on the pre-trained layers of the encoder. Xing [17] proposed a feature extraction method named "slicing matrix" to divide smart contracts into a sequence of function blocks using jump instructions as the demarcation in the sequence of opcodes; the number of different opcodes within each function block is used as the input feature fed into the neural network for classification. To capture the structural information in smart contracts, Zhuang et al. [20] characterized the source code of smart contracts as a graph structure based on data and control dependencies of program statements, and then constructed a graph neural network and a temporal message propagation (TMP) framework to perform classification.

There is still room for improvement on the performance of smart contract vulnerability detection. The sequence-based methods [6,14] representing each smart contract as a one-dimensional opcode sequence cannot learn the control or dependency relations between instructions. The sequence-based method [17] defining the sequence at the scale of "function blocks" neglects the execution order of instructions within the function blocks. Graph-based method [20] characterizing the control dependencies of program statements via a graph works at the source code level or control flow level, failing to capture the information in the opcode level. In summary, neither sequence-based nor graph-based feature representations in the existing work can fully retain the rich structural or semantic information in the smart contracts and learn high-dimensional features effectively for classification.

In this paper, we propose a novel smart contract vulnerability detection method based on smart contract bytecodes using a hybrid feature representation by combining control flow and opcode sequence in the Ethereum virtual machine (EVM). The main contributions of this paper are as follows. We generate the attributes of the smart contracts, including the control flow graphs (CFGs) and the EVM opcode sequences. We also propose a Dual Attention Graph Convolutional Network (DA-GCN) to detect vulnerabilities in smart contracts. Model DA-GCN extracts the features from the generated CFGs and opcode sequences using two modules: graph convolutional module and dual-attention module. Graph convolutional module extracts the features of the graph structure using Graph Convolutional Network (GCN) at the scale of nodes of a CFG. The dual-attention module uses self-attention mechanism to extract sequential and associative features between opcode instructions, and further extracts the attention coefficients from a CFG, such that the model can better focus on the important parts of smart contracts in vulnerability detection and suppress useless information. Model DA-GCN then performs classification to identify whether the smart contract is vulnerable, using a Multilayer Perceptron (MLP) and the extracted features from the previous two modules. We obtain the dataset from Ethereum smart contracts containing two vulnerabilities of reentrancy and timestamp dependency, and conduct experiments on the obtained data set. Experimental results demonstrate that the proposed model DA-GCN achieves the accuracy of 91.2% and 87.5% in the two smart contract vulnerability detection task, respectively, and DA-GCN can effectively improve the performance in terms of accuracy, precision, recall, and F1-score on smart contract vulnerability detection.

The rest of the paper is organized as follows. Related works are presented in Sect. 2. The smart contract vulnerability detection problem is described in Sect. 3. Model DA-GCN is proposed in Sect. 4. We experimentally evaluate the proposed model in Sect. 5, and finally we conclude the paper in Sect. 6.

2   Related Works

Blockchain has been applied to various fields like industry, healthcare, supply chain, etc. The creation of smart contracts is a milestone in the history of blockchain. A smart contract, which can be seen as a program running on the blockchain system, automatically performs the execution of transactions once triggered by certain events. After being deployed on the blockchain system, the smart contract cannot be modified or reversed, so there are no remedies available to deal with code errors. However, attacks on smart contract vulnerabilities have become increasingly frequent and diverse in recent years. Therefore, vulnerability detection is one of the most fundamental tasks to ensure the reliability and security of smart contracts.

Some work on smart contract vulnerability detection relies on symbolic execution and formal verification methods such as Oyente [11] and Securify [15]. Luu et al. [11] proposed a static analysis tool for smart contract vulnerability detection. The tool takes bytecodes with the global state of Ethereum as input, constructs the CFG, and symbolically runs a contract to identify specific vulnerabilities through logical analysis. Tsankov et al. [15] proposed Securify which analyzes the smart contract in Ethereum to show whether the contract is secure in an automatic and scalable way. For each vulnerability property, Securify defines the corresponding secure or insecure smart contract behavior. To detect violation patterns, Securify symbolically analyzes the dependency graph of each contract, extracts attributes of semantic, and examines key code structures, using logical conditions and check for the presence of vulnerability properties. Feist et al. [4] proposed Slither, a multiple-vulnerability detector based on smart contract source code written in Solidity. Slither uses taint analysis to check vulnerabilities in relation to the input and data dependencies. Nikolić et al. [13] proposed a smart contract security tool which uses the runtime trace of a series of calls to capture vulnerabilities, targeting greedy, prodigal, and suicidal contracts. Jiang et al. [7] used fuzzy detection and runtime behavior monitoring to identify vulnerabilities during the execution of a contract. Liu et al. [9] proposed an analysis tool based on fuzzing method called Reguard, which finds reentrancy vulnerability in the contracts. The aforementioned works mainly apply traditional software analysis methods to detect smart contract vulnerabilities. However, vulnerability detection using these techniques demands expert definition of logic rules, which takes heavy reliance on experience, capability of professionality, and domain knowledge. The design of rules for logical statements takes significant time and is prone to errors. Moreover, the manually-set rules in most cases will only be used for specific tasks, which has significant limitations.

Deep learning methodologies have been showing great advantages in end-to-end automated feature learning, enabling better understanding of the intrinsic structure of complex data. There is limited research on smart contract vulnerability detection using deep learning. Tann et al. [14] extracted operand sequence from smart contract bytecodes and then used an LSTM model to detect vulnerabilities. Peng et al. [6] also used an LSTM model for learning sequence information, and used an auxiliary task for predicting operands as pre-training and fine-tuned the model on the vulnerability detection tasks, with an attention mechanism to tackle the problem of long-distance dependency in sequences. Considering that vulnerabilities in local code can show great impact on the overall code, Xing et al. [17] proposed a feature extraction method named "slice matrix". The bytecodes of smart contract are partitioned with RETURN instructions to form a series of matrices, and the number of instructions of each type within the matrix is used as features, which are fed into different classifiers such as CNN for classification. Ashizawa et al. [1] proposed Eth2Vec, which can learn the lexical and semantics features from the bytecode of a smart contract in the EVM, and they used similarity checking and code embedding to decide whether a smart contract is vulnerable. Zhuang et al. [20] represented the source code of smart contracts in the form of directed graphs and constructed a graph neural network DR-GCN and a time-based propagation framework for vulnerability detection. Liu et al. [10] designed specific patterns for different vulnerabilities and combined features learned from the graph neural network with the expert patterns to get the final analysis of the target smart contract.

Note that the sequence-based or graph-based feature representation methods introduced above lose certain structural and semantic information in the smart contract, and thus fail to learn high-dimensional features for vulnerability detection. In this paper, we use a hybrid feature representation and propose a novel model DA-GCN for smart contract vulnerability detection, which learn the features from both control flow graphs and opcode sequences.

3   Problem Description

In this paper, we study how to detect whether a smart contract is vulnerable based on the smart contract bytecode. Specifically, we investigate two types of vulnerabilities, i.e. Reentrancy and Timestamp Dependency.

Reentrancy is a vulnerability of great concern existing in Ethereum smart contracts, which was exploited by attackers in the DAO hack with a total loss beyond 60 million dollars. An Ethereum smart contract can call another smart contract during execution, and the smart contract being called must wait until the call is finished. The recipient of the call can exploit this intermediate status to steal digital currency. Example 1 shows a real-world attack event using reentrancy.

Example 1. There is a special mechanism in smart contract system called fallback function which has no function name and takes no arguments. The fallback function will be invoked in two scenarios when the function call does not match any functions in the called smart contract or the ether (the dedicated cryptocurrency used in Ethereum) is received by the caller. There are two contracts in Fig. 1. Contract Attacker attempts to steal the ether from contract Victim, a simplified version of digital wallet with a reentrancy vulnerability, by exploiting the fallback mechanism. To be specific, Attacker executes its attack() function to invoke withdraw() function in Victim. Victim will then transfer certain amount of ether to Attacker. Once the ether is received, the fallback function in Attacker will be executed. As we can see, the balance of Attacker's account has not yet been set to 0 by Victim at the time, the Attacker can hence repeatedly invoke the withdraw() method until the ether held by Victim drops to 0.

Timestamp dependency is another well-known Ethereum smart contract vulnerability which is related to timestamp in the blockchain system. When a smart contract takes the block timestamps as a dependency condition to trigger curtain critical operation like transfer ether, some malicious miners may manipulate it

```
1 contract Victim{                          1 contract Attacker{
2                                           2
3    mapping(address=>uint) userBalances;   3      function attack(address addr) {
4                                           4          victim(addr).withdraw();
5    function withdraw() {                   5      }
6      uint amount = userBalances[msg.sender]; 6
7      msg.sender.call.value(amountToWithdraw)(); 7      function () payable{
8      userBalances[msg.sender] = 0;        8          victim(addr).withdraw();
9    }                                       9      }
10 }                                        10 }
```

Fig. 1. Example of a smart contract with the reentrancy vulnerability.

to modify the timestamp for illegal benefits. Example 2 illustrates a real-world contract which suffers from the timestamp dependency vulnerability.

Example 2. Contract theRun, shown in Fig. 2, uses a set of rules based on the current block timestamp to choose who will win the bonus. In contract theRun, the variable h defined in line 7 is the hash value of a certain block in the blockchain, which is used to decide the winner. The selection of a block is determined by the variable seed defined in line 6. Three variables decide the seed value, including block number, last payout, and timestamp. Among them, block number and last payout are determined values recorded on the blockchain, while timestamp is decided by the miner. Normally, the timestamp is set as the current time of the miner's local system. However, the miner can vary the timestamp value by roughly 900 s, while still having other miners accept the block. Therefore, by choosing the timestamp, the miner can calculate the result in advance and manipulate the outcome of timestamp-dependent contracts to get the final bonus.

```
1    contract theRun {
2        uint private Last_Payout = 0;
3        uint256 salt = block.timestamp;
4        function random returns(uint256 result){
5            uint256 y = salt * block.number/(salt%5);
6            uint256 seed = block.number/3 + (salt%300) + Last_Payout + y;
7            uint256 h = uint256 (block.blockhash(seed));
8            return uint256 (h % 100) + 1;
9        }
10    }
```

Fig. 2. Example of a smart contract with the timestamp dependency vulnerability.

4   Smart Contract Vulnerability Detection Method

We first generate the attributes of smart contracts, including the CFGs and the EVM opcode sequences. We then propose a novel model, Dual Attention Graph Convolutional Network (DA-GCN), to detect vulnerabilities in smart contracts. Model DA-GCN extracts the features from the generated CFGs and opcode sequences, and identifies whether the smart contract is vulnerable by combining the extracted features.

4.1 Attributes Generation

To better express the rich semantic and structural information in smart contracts, we generate both control flow graphs and opcode sequences from smart contract bytecodes as attributes. The workflow of attributes generation process from smart contract bytecodes is shown in Fig. 3.

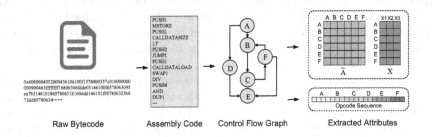

Raw Bytecode   Assembly Code   Control Flow Graph   Extracted Attributes

Fig. 3. Workflow of attributes generation process.

Control Flow Graph. We represent the smart contract bytecodes as CFGs. The reasons for using CFGs to characterize contracts are as follows. Firstly, CFGs use graph structures to explicitly express the logic of smart contracts. A CFG represents all the paths that can be traversed during the execution of a smart contract, which can well indicate the structural dependencies of smart contracts. We can also extract the CFGs from contract codes in different forms. Secondly, the CFG contains various information that can be used as attributes in deep learning-based smart contract vulnerability detection, e.g. n-grams, opcodes, and structural information [18].

We utilize the state-of-the-art tool evm-cfg-builder [2], which has been used in several applications including Ethersplay and Manticore [12], to extract CFGs from bytecodes. Every node in a CFG represents a basic-block consisting of a sequence of EVM opcodes. The basic blocks are independent of each other. That is, each basic block can only be entered at the first instruction and exited at the last instruction. Two neighboring basic blocks are connected by a directed edge. In this graph structure, we put the basic blocks in the order in which they appear in the EVM bytecode.

The complete EVM instruction set contains more than 150 instructions. Among them, we select totally 74 instructions, which can best reflect the logic and semantics of smart contract execution process and relate to the smart contract vulnerability detection tasks. For example, the jump instruction can indicate the switch from the current basic block to other basic blocks; the block, timestamp, call, callvalue instructions can relate to the critical part of vulnerable contracts as shown in Examples 1 and 2.

The selected instructions are categorized into 7 types: Arithmetic, Environment, Blockchain Information, Stack, System, Logic, and Cryptograph. We take the numbers of instructions in different instruction types as the attributes of each basic block, and the attributes will be fed into the neural network for feature extraction.

Opcode Sequence of Ethereum Virtual Machine. Considering that CFGs working at the basic block level cannot capture certain finer-grained information, we further extract the opcode sequences in each basic block and concatenate them together in the same order as the basic blocks appear. Different contracts may vary in the length of opcode sequences. To obtain the input of the neural network, the sequence lengths are fixed to the same value. Specifically, we pad 0 to the sequences shorter than the fixed-length and truncate the exceeding part of the sequences longer than the fixed-length. We randomly select 1000 Ethereum smart contracts and count the lengths of their opcode sequences, among them 91.5% of smart contracts are with the opcode sequence length within 2000. Therefore, we choose 2000 as the fixed-sequence length. Before feeding each fixed-length opcode sequence into the neural network, we map each opcode to a unique integer.

4.2   Construction of DA-GCN Model

The DA-GCN model shown in Fig. 4 consists of three modules: graph convolutional module, dual-attention module, and classification module. The graph convolutional module uses graph convolutional layers to extract features at the scale of basic blocks from the CFG. In the dual-attention module, we first use the self-attention mechanism to extract sequential and associative features between opcode instructions, and further extract attention coefficients from the CFG to better focus on the more important basic blocks in vulnerability detection task and suppress useless information. The final obtained high-dimensional features will be concatenated and fed into the classification module.

Graph Convolutional Module. We use graph convolutional layers at the control flow level to propagate each basic block's features to the neighbor blocks based on the structural connectivity, extract the features of the graphs, and learn the structural information in the smart contracts.

A CFG is a graph with directed edges. For a graph G with N nodes, we denote its corresponding adjacency matrix as $A \in \mathbf{R}^{N \times N}$. Since the features in a node cannot be propagated to itself using this adjacency matrix, we define an augmented adjacency matrix $\tilde{A} = A + I$. Accordingly, we denote this augmented diagonal degree matrix as $\tilde{D}$, which can be calculated from $\tilde{A}$:

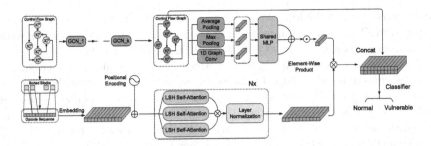

Fig. 4. Diagram of model DA-GCN.

$$\tilde{D}_{u,u} = \sum_v \tilde{A}_{u,v} \qquad (1)$$

where $\tilde{D}_{u,u}$ denotes the element (u, u) in augmented degree matrix $\tilde{D}$, and $\tilde{A}_{u,v}$ is the element (u, v) in augmented adjacency matrix $\tilde{A}$.

Assuming each node in graph G has c attributes, we denote the matrix of attributes for graph G as $X \in \mathbf{R}^{N \times c}$.

We use multiple staked graph convolutional layers in the graph convolutional module. The propagation formula of the graph convolutional layer [19] can be defined as follows:

$$Z^{t+1} = f(\tilde{D}^{-1}\tilde{A}Z^t W^t) \qquad (2)$$

where f denotes the activation function. $Z^t \in \mathbf{R}^{N \times c_t}$ is the output of the t-th graph convolutional layer, and $Z^0 = X$. c_t is the number of output channels of the t-th graph convolutional layer, and $W^t \in \mathbf{R}^{c_t \times c_{t+1}}$ denotes the parameters mapping from c_t channels to c_{t+1} channels.

Dual Attention Module. In this module, we calculate the attention coefficients at the opcode level and control flow level, respectively.

Extraction of Opcode Level Attention. We first apply word embedding to the opcode sequence so that the instructions mapped as different integers are transformed into fixed-size real value vectors. The parameters of word embedding are randomly initialized and will then be updated during the training process.

To exploit the ordering information of the opcode sequence, the position of each instruction is encoded in the sequence. The position encoding is added to the embedding vector and defined as:

$$\begin{cases} PE_{(i,2p)} = \sin(i/10000^{2p/d_{\text{embedding}}}) \\ PE_{(i,2p+1)} = \cos(i/10000^{2p/d_{\text{embedding}}}) \end{cases} \qquad (3)$$

where i denotes the i-th position in an opcode sequence. $2p$ and $2p+1$ represent the $2p$-th and $(2p + 1)$-th dimensions in the embedding vector of an opcode, respectively. $d_{\text{embedding}}$ is the dimension of the embedding vector of an opcode. $PE_{(i,2p)}$ and $PE_{(i,2p+1)}$ are the encoding values of the $2p$-th and $(2p + 1)$-th dimensions in the embedding vector of the i-th position in an opcode sequence, respectively. That is, every dimension in position encoding matches a sinusoidal signal whose wavelength grows geometrically from 2π to $20,000\pi$.

Long-distance dependency problem occurs when attention is used to process sequence-structured data. Transformer [16], a self-attention mechanism, uses the scaled dot-product attention to solve the long-distance dependency problem and also improves the computational speed of the model. However, Transformer will consume huge memory resources when dealing with long sequences. Locally Sensitive Hashing (LSH) self-attention mechanism [8] can address the memory-demanding problem of Transformer. LSH is a hashing scheme that can find nearest neighbors quickly in a high-dimensional space, where nearby vectors get the same hash value with high probability and distant ones do not. Therefore, we adopt LSH self-attention mechanism to extract the opcode level attention.

In order to use LSH self-attention, we write the attention equation in Transformer as:

$$\alpha_i = \sum_{j \in P_i} \frac{\exp(q_i \cdot k_j - z(i, P_i))v_j}{\sqrt{d}} \tag{4}$$

where i and j denote the i-th position and j-th position in an opcode sequence, respectively. α_i is the attention coefficient of position i. q_i, k_i, and v_i are query, key, and value vectors at position i, respectively. d is the dimension of each vector of q_i, k_i, and v_i. P_i denotes all the queries which the query at position i can attend to, and z denotes softmax which is used as the partition function.

We filter the keys into a hash bucket using a hash function $H(\bullet)$ from the queries which the query at position i can attend to:

$$P_i = \{j : H(q_i) = H(k_j)\} \tag{5}$$

The queries and keys at different positions are grouped into different hash buckets via Eq. (5). Note that the number of keys and queries may not be balanced in different buckets. Therefore, we set $k_j = \frac{q_j}{\|q_j\|}$.

We then sort the queries by the buckets which include the queries, and divide all the queries into several parts, each containing the same number of queries. We call each part a *chunk*. Obviously, the queries in the same bucket may fall into different chunks. Therefore, we repeat N^H rounds of hashing, each round with a different hash function H^r, where r denotes the r-th round of hash calculation:

$$P_i = \bigcup_{r=1}^{N^H} P_i^r \quad \text{where } P_i^r = \{j : H^r(q_i) = H^r(q_j)\} \tag{6}$$

Extraction of Control Flow Level Attention. Different from the self-attention mechanism between different opcodes, the control flow level attention, shown in Fig. 5, focuses on basic blocks that are more important for the vulnerability classification by assigning them greater weights.

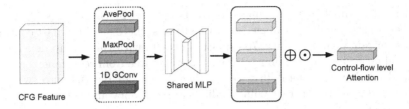

Fig. 5. Diagram of control flow level attention.

We take the CFG feature map obtained by performing m graph convolutional layers on the control flow graph as the input. We apply average-pooling and max-pooling on the channels of each node to better describe the relationship of c_m channel attributes. Moreover, to better aggregate the attributes of each node and its neighboring node, we apply a one-dimensional graph convolutional layer as follows:

$$V = f(\tilde{D}^{-1}\tilde{A}Z^m W^m) \tag{7}$$

where V is the output of the one-dimensional graph convolutional layer. $Z^m \in \mathbf{R}^{N \times c_m}$ denotes the output of the m-th graph convolutional layer, c_m represents the number of output channels of the m-th graph convolutional layer, and $W^m \in \mathbf{R}^{c_m \times 1}$ is a one-dimensional vector with c_m elements.

The features extracted from the average-pooling, max-pooling, and one-dimensional graph convolutional layer are then fed into a MLP with a hidden layer to produce the attention coefficients on the control flow level, which can be calculated as follows:

$$\begin{cases} \text{ATT}_{ave} = \sigma(W_1(W_0(\text{AvgPool}(Z^m)) + b_0) + b_1) \\ \text{ATT}_{max} = \sigma(W_1(W_0(\text{MaxPool}(Z^m)) + b_0) + b_1) \\ \text{ATT}_{gcn} = \sigma(W_1(W_0(\tilde{D}^{-1}\tilde{A}Z^m W^m) + b_0) + b_1) \\ \text{ATT}_{block} = \sigma(\text{ATT}_{ave} + \text{ATT}_{max} + \text{ATT}_{gcn}) \end{cases} \tag{8}$$

where $W_0 \in \mathbf{R}^{d_{hidden} \times c_m}$, $b_0 \in \mathbf{R}^{d_{hidden} \times 1}$, $W_1 \in \mathbf{R}^{c_m \times d_{hidden}}$, and $b_1 \in \mathbf{R}^{c_m \times 1}$. σ is the sigmoid function, and d_{hidden} denotes the dimensions of the hidden layer in MLP.

Classification Module. In this module, we concatenate the features extracted from the graph convolutional module and dual attention module, and then perform classification via convolutional layer, max pooling, fully connected layer, and softmax function to identify whether the smart contract is vulnerable.

5 Experiment

5.1 Experimental Settings

Dataset and Benchmarks. We integrate the real-world vulnerability smart contracts from three sources, including the dataset in SolidiFi [5], the dataset used in [20], and Ethereum smart contracts verified by SmartBugs [3]. In our dataset consisting of 2216 labeled smart contracts, there are 496 smart contracts with reentrancy vulnerability, 768 smart contracts with timestamp dependency vulnerability, and the remaining 952 contracts are free from reentrancy or timestamp dependency vulnerability. We further divide our dataset into two parts targeting the smart contract vulnerabilities of reentrancy and timestamp dependency, respectively.

In the experiments, we use cross-validation to evaluate our model. We first randomly divide the dataset into 10 folds, each containing 10% of the samples in the dataset. 9 of the 10 folds are used for training, and the remaining one is used as the test set. One fold in the training set is marked as the validation set. We use the validation set to validate the model after each epoch, and the model achieving the highest accuracy during the training process is saved and evaluated on the test set to obtain the final result.

The numbers of samples in training, validation, test, and total datasets on reentrancy and timestamp dependency are shown in Table 1 and Table 2, respectively.

Table 1. Dataset of reentrancy vulnerability.

	Training set	Validation set	Test set	Total
Reentrancy	396	50	50	496
Normal	760	91	91	952

Table 2. Dataset of timestamp dependency vulnerability.

	Training set	Validation set	Test set	Total
Timestamp	614	77	77	768
Normal	760	91	91	952

We compare the proposed model DA-GCN with the state-of-art smart contract detection vulnerability detection model TMP [20] and the state-of-art deep learning models dealing with sequences or graph structures, including BiLSTM-Attention (BLSTM-ATT), Transformer [16], and DGCNN [19]. BLSTM-ATT and Transformer learn the features from opcode sequences of smart contracts, while DGCNN learns from the control flow information of smart contracts.

For each method, 30 10-fold cross-validations are run and the average of the 30 results is taken as the final result.

Performance Metrics. We evaluate our proposed model DA-GCN in terms of 4 performance metrics: accuracy, recall, precision, and F1-score, assuming TP, FP, FN, and TN are the numbers of true positive samples, false positive samples, false negative samples, and true negative samples, respectively.

Accuracy: the ration of sum of TP and TN to the total number of samples.

$$\text{accuracy} = \frac{TP + TN}{TP + FP + TN + FN} \tag{9}$$

Precision: the proportion of all classified positive samples that are positive.

$$\text{precision} = \frac{TP}{TP + FP} \tag{10}$$

Recall: the proportion of positive samples that are classified as positive.

$$\text{recall} = \frac{TP}{TP + FN} \tag{11}$$

F1-score: a combination of precision and recall for the overall performance.

$$\text{F1} - \text{score} = \frac{2 \times \text{precison} \times \text{recall}}{\text{precison} + \text{recall}} \tag{12}$$

5.2 Experimental Results

Table 3 lists the accuracy, recall, precision, and F1-score performance of DA-GCN, BLSTM-ATT, Transformer, DGCNN, and TMP on reentrancy and timestamp dependency vulnerability detection tasks, respectively. The experimental results demonstrate that model DA-GCN achieves the best performance in terms of all the four evaluation metrics.

We first compare model DA-GCN with BLSTM-ATT, Transformer, and DGCNN. The classic LSTM model suffers from gradient disappearance and gradient explosion when propagating over long distances. Although BLSTM-ATT compensates the problem to a certain extent by using a bidirectional model and the attention mechanism, BLSTM-ATT still fails to achieve the ideal results when dealing with longer sequences. The experimental results show that Transformer can better capture the long-range association of sequences and achieve better results than BLSTM-ATT due to the distance between two arbitrary elements being 1, when applying self-attention mechanism in Transformer.

The control flow graph of a smart contract reflects the invocation relationship of basic blocks and the logical instruction structure of smart contracts, while the EVM opcode sequence focuses on the execution mode and the order

Table 3. Performance in terms of accuracy, recall, precision and F1-score on each vulnerability detection task.

Methods	Reentrancy				Methods	Timestamp dependency			
	Acc (%)	Recall (%)	Precision (%)	F1 (%)		Acc (%)	Recall (%)	Precision (%)	F1 (%)
BLSTM-ATT	83.92	71.25	74.41	72.80	BLSTM-ATT	78.69	72.09	80.52	76.07
Transformer	86.03	76.00	80.36	77.55	Transformer	83.72	78.96	82.41	80.13
DGCNN	88.89	82.86	74.36	78.38	DGCNN	84.25	76.29	76.88	76.44
TMP	89.87	80.80	87.46	83.46	TMP	85.33	80.27	85.50	82.81
DA-GCN	**91.15**	**82.00**	**89.84**	**85.43**	**DA-GCN**	**87.54**	**82.85**	**87.15**	**84.83**

of instructions in smart contracts at the opcode level. Both opcode sequences and control flows play an important role in smart contract vulnerability detection. Separate analyses of control flow graphs and opcode sequences may lose certain semantic and structural information. The proposed model DA-GCN uses a hybrid model to jointly learn the control flow graph and opcode sequence features. To be specific, the instructions are assembled in the form of basic blocks, resulting in opcodes within the same block and between different blocks have different associations. Model DA-GCN further implements attention at the scale of control flow level, which enables the network to focus on some basic blocks that are more useful for vulnerability detection and suppress information that is not useful for the classification tasks.

The experimental results in Table 3 also show that model DA-GCN that integrates the control flow level and opcode level features improves the accuracy by 3.25% and 3.82% on the two different detection tasks, respectively, compared to the best results achieved by DGCNN and Transformer, which only consider the features from either of the two levels.

We then compare model DA-GCN with TMP which is the state-of-the-art method used for smart contract vulnerability detection. As shown in Table 3, DA-GCN improves the accuracy by 1.28% and 2.21% on the two vulnerability detection tasks, respectively.

We also evaluate the effectiveness of each model using the receiver operating characteristic (ROC) curve. ROC is a plot regarding True Positive Rate (TPR) versus False Positive Rate (FPR) at different thresholds. To quantitatively measure the ROC curve and evaluate the performance of the classifier, we further adopt the area under the ROC curve (AUC) to measure the capability of the classifier to discriminate positive and negative samples. The range of AUC values is [0.5, 1]. The ROC curves and AUC values of different models targeting reentrancy and timestamp dependency vulnerabilities are shown in Fig. 6. It can be seen that the proposed model DA-GCN performs the best among the different models and achieves the AUC of 0.94 and 0.92 on the two vulnerability detection tasks, respectively.

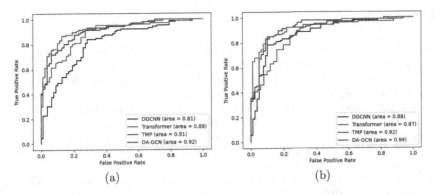

Fig. 6. (a) ROC curves for different methods on reentrancy vulnerability detection task. (b) ROC curves for different methods on timestamp dependency vulnerability detection task.

6 Conclusion

In this paper, we tackled the problem of smart contract vulnerability identification based on smart contract bytecodes. We generated the attributes of smart contracts, including the control flow graphs and the EVM opcode sequences. We also proposed a Dual Attention Graph Convolutional Network (DA-GCN) to detect vulnerabilities in smart contracts. Model DA-GCN extracts the features from the generated CFGs and opcode sequences using two modules: graph convolutional module and dual-attention module. Graph convolutional module extracts the features of the graph structure using graph convolutional network at the scale of basic blocks of a control flow graph. The dual-attention module uses self-attention mechanism to extract the sequential and associative features between opcode instructions, and further extracts the attention coefficients from a control flow graph, such that the model can better focus on the important basic blocks of smart contracts in vulnerability detection and suppress useless information. Model DA-GCN then performs classification to identify whether the smart contract is vulnerable, by combining the extracted features from the previous two modules and using a Multilayer Perceptron. We obtained the dataset from real-world Ethereum smart contracts containing two vulnerabilities: reentrancy and timestamp dependency. Experimental results demonstrated that the proposed model DA-GCN achieved an accuracy of 91.2% and 87.5% in the two smart contract vulnerability detection tasks, respectively, and DA-GCN could effectively improve the performance in terms of accuracy, precision, recall, and F1-score on smart contract vulnerability detection.

Acknowledgment. This work was partly supported by the open project of State Key Laboratory of Complex Electromagnetic Environment Effects on Electronics and Information System in China (CEMEE2018Z0102B), the Fundamental Research Funds for the Central Universities (PA2021GDSK0095), and the open fund of Intelligent Interconnected Systems Laboratory of Anhui Province (PA2021AKSK0114), Hefei University of Technology.

References

1. Ashizawa, N., Yanai, N., Cruz, J.P., Okamura, S.: Eth2Vec: learning contract-wide code representations for vulnerability detection on Ethereum smart contracts. In: Proceedings of the 3rd ACM International Symposium on Blockchain and Secure Critical Infrastructure, pp. 47–59 (2021)
2. evm-cfg builder (2017). https://github.com/crytic/evm_cfg_builder
3. Durieux, T., Ferreira, J.F., Abreu, R., Cruz, P.: Empirical review of automated analysis tools on 47,587 Ethereum smart contracts. In: Proceedings of the ACM/IEEE 42nd International Conference on Software Engineering, pp. 530–541 (2020)
4. Feist, J., Grieco, G., Groce, A.: Slither: a static analysis framework for smart contracts. In: 2019 IEEE/ACM 2nd International Workshop on Emerging Trends in Software Engineering for Blockchain (WETSEB), pp. 8–15. IEEE (2019)
5. Ghaleb, A., Pattabiraman, K.: How effective are smart contract analysis tools? Evaluating smart contract static analysis tools using bug injection. In: Proceedings of the 29th ACM SIGSOFT International Symposium on Software Testing and Analysis, pp. 415–427 (2020)
6. Gogineni, A.K., Swayamjyoti, S., Sahoo, D., Sahu, K.K., Kishore, R.: Multi-class classification of vulnerabilities in smart contracts using AWD-LSTM, with pretrained encoder inspired from natural language processing. IOP SciNotes 1(3), 035002 (2020)
7. Jiang, B., Liu, Y., Chan, W.: ContractFuzzer: fuzzing smart contracts for vulnerability detection. In: 2018 33rd IEEE/ACM International Conference on Automated Software Engineering (ASE), pp. 259–269. IEEE (2018)
8. Kitaev, N., Kaiser, L., Levskaya, A.: Reformer: the efficient Transformer. In: Proceedings of the International Conference on Learning Representations (2020)
9. Liu, C., Liu, H., Cao, Z., Chen, Z., Chen, B., Roscoe, B.: ReGuard: finding reentrancy bugs in smart contracts. In: 2018 IEEE/ACM 40th International Conference on Software Engineering: Companion (ICSE-Companion), pp. 65–68. IEEE (2018)
10. Liu, Z., Qian, P., Wang, X., Zhuang, Y., Qiu, L., Wang, X.: Combining graph neural networks with expert knowledge for smart contract vulnerability detection. IEEE Trans. Knowl. Data Eng. 1–1 (2021)
11. Luu, L., Chu, D.H., Olickel, H., Saxena, P., Hobor, A.: Making smart contracts smarter. In: Proceedings of the 2016 ACM SIGSAC Conference on Computer and Communications Security, pp. 254–269 (2016)
12. Mossberg, M., et al.: Manticore: a user-friendly symbolic execution framework for binaries and smart contracts. In: 2019 34th IEEE/ACM International Conference on Automated Software Engineering (ASE), pp. 1186–1189. IEEE (2019)
13. Nikolić, I., Kolluri, A., Sergey, I., Saxena, P., Hobor, A.: Finding the greedy, prodigal, and suicidal contracts at scale. In: Proceedings of the 34th Annual Computer Security Applications Conference, pp. 653–663 (2018)
14. Tann, W.J.W., Han, X.J., Gupta, S.S., Ong, Y.S.: Towards safer smart contracts: a sequence learning approach to detecting security threats. arXiv preprint arXiv:1811.06632 (2018)
15. Tsankov, P., Dan, A., Drachsler-Cohen, D., Gervais, A., Buenzli, F., Vechev, M.: Securify: practical security analysis of smart contracts. In: Proceedings of the 2018 ACM SIGSAC Conference on Computer and Communications Security, pp. 67–82 (2018)

16. Vaswani, A., et al.: Attention is all you need. In: Proceedings of the 31st International Conference on Neural Information Processing Systems, pp. 6000–6010 (2017)
17. Xing, C., Chen, Z., Chen, L., Guo, X., Zheng, Z., Li, J.: A new scheme of vulnerability analysis in smart contract with machine learning. Wirel. Netw., 1–10 (2020, in press)
18. Yan, J., Yan, G., Jin, D.: Classifying malware represented as control flow graphs using deep graph convolutional neural network. In: 2019 49th Annual IEEE/IFIP International Conference on Dependable Systems and Networks (DSN), pp. 52–63. IEEE (2019)
19. Zhang, M., Cui, Z., Neumann, M., Chen, Y.: An end-to-end deep learning architecture for graph classification. In: Proceedings of the AAAI Conference on Artificial Intelligence, vol. 32 (2018)
20. Zhuang, Y., Liu, Z., Qian, P., Liu, Q., Wang, X., He, Q.: Smart contract vulnerability detection using graph neural networks. In: Proceedings of the Twenty-Ninth International Joint Conference on Artificial Intelligence, pp. 3283–3290 (2020)

Crowdturfing Detection in Online Review System: A Graph-Based Modeling

Qilong Feng, Yue Zhang, and Li Kuang$^{(\boxtimes)}$

School of Computer Science and Engineering, Central South University,
Changsha 410075, HN, China
kuangli@csu.edu.cn

Abstract. With the widespread popularity of online reviews and crowd-sourcing, people may publish fake comments on online review system and get paid for crowdsourcing tasks. In order to identify these reviewers, machine learning methods are commonly used in traditional strategies and it is difficult to guarantee the accuracy of detection. In this work, we adopt a modeling method based on the graph structure and propose a novel aggregation method called CrowdDet. Therefore, two clear diagrams of Reviewer-to-Product and Co-Reviewer are constructed. Specifically, we first extract the node features and structure information in the graph, gaining the reviewers' features and neighborhood relations features. Secondly, we use an elaborate attention-based mechanism to aggregate the factors of reviewers in Review-space and Sociality-space, which comprehensively combines the representation of the reviewer factors from multiple dimensions. Thirdly, we get the classification results and optimize the original loss function by Focal loss to alleviate the impact of class imbalance. In the experiment, we verify the proposed scheme on a real dataset and compare it with other methods. The results show that our scheme has a significant effect under the real dataset, with a recall rate of 0.85+. Our research also provides a relevant foundation for resisting the malicious behavior from crowdsourcing.

Keywords: Crowdturfing detection · Graph-based modeling · Class imbalance solution · Online review system

1 Introduction

For e-commerce platforms or review sites such as Amazon, Yelp, or Taobao, user reviews can affect people's consumption choices and play an important role in people's decisions for purchasing. However, with the continuous development of crowdsourcing platforms such as Amazon Mechanical Turk and CrowdFlower, a large number of malicious reviews can be organized by merchants. Sellers post review tasks on the crowdsourcing platform, hiring crowdsourcing workers to promote products, or slander competitors [1]. Spam workers from crowdsourcing platforms are called crowdturfing. Crowdturfing is a word combines the "crowdsourcing" and "astroturfing". Unlike the original fake reviewers, crowdturfing can perform tasks alone, so it lacks concentrated

© ICST Institute for Computer Sciences, Social Informatics and Telecommunications Engineering 2021
Published by Springer Nature Switzerland AG 2021. All Rights Reserved
H. Gao and X. Wang (Eds.): CollaborateCom 2021, LNICST 407, pp. 352–369, 2021.
https://doi.org/10.1007/978-3-030-92638-0_21

behavior features and is more difficult to be detected. The fakers are divided into the following three categories [2] according to the different motivations of reviewers:

- Camouflage. They add links to ordinary reviews by adding special symbols, which creates confusion among normal reviews and pretends to be normal reviewers in this way.
- Spammer. They post irrelevant comments (e.g., advertisements, commodity promotion) in the review system, or even carry out illegal activities (e.g., selling contraband, sending sensitive words), and maliciously increase the popularity of the product through the above methods.
- Crowdturfing. The review task is published by the organizer on the crowdsourcing platforms (e.g., Rapidworkers, Amazon Mechanical Turk), and the crowdsourcing workers perform the task by reviewing for a fee.

Such behavior can easily mislead consumers' true judgments on product quality and cause unfair competition among merchants. On the other hand, it will reduce the credibility of product review content and violate the original intention of the crowd-sourcing strategy. We found that there are commonalities between crowdturfings, so how to identify them in an automated way is the goal of this research. In order to detect fake reviews or scoring behavior like this, many explorations have been carried out by researchers. The feature exploited in detection can be divided into review content features and reviewer behavior features.

1. Review Content Features. It refers to the description of the features of the review content, including both the analysis of the review text and the comment rating, such as review length, the proportion of special symbols, similarity of comments, review sentiment classification, etc.
2. Reviewer Behavior Features. It refers to the statistical features of the reviewer's comments, including the reviewer's attributes, relationships, and behavior, such as the number of reviews, product categories reviewed, the number of devices, or whether they are verified, etc.

Nitin and Liu [3] were the first to propose fake reviews or reviewer detection tasks. They regarded repeated or similar reviews as positive case, and the rest as negative case, and a logistic regression classifier is trained to distinguish fake reviewers from real reviewers. After that, the heterogeneous graph was used to model the relation among reviewers, reviews, and products, so as to explore the relationship among the credibility of the reviewer, the credibility of the review, and the credibility of the product [4, 5]. Recently, some researchers have constructed a homogeneous graph model based on the relationship among reviewers and obtained the possible labels of the current node [2, 6, 7] based on the state of neighboring nodes.

Although the association among reviewers, products and product reviews is considered in the above methods, the analysis of review text is limited to the statistical features of the review text, so it has great limitations in semantic understanding. In addition, taking into account that the data number of different classes is uneven, that is, the long tail problem still exists in reality. Oversampling, undersampling [19], and cost-sensitive learning [20, 21] are widely used to solve it. However, the solution of data imbalance in existing methods have not been applied in crowdsourced fake reviewer detection.

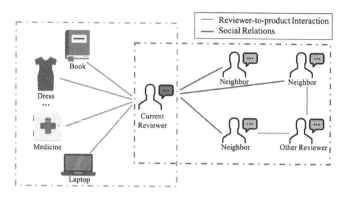

Fig. 1. Reviewer-to-product graph and co-reviewer graph.

In order to solve the above problems, inspired by the recommendation system method with graph modeling [22], we attempted to extract the common features of the crowdsourced fake reviewers from a small amount of category. Therefore, we modeled the current reviewer (see Fig. 1) and extracted the review content features and behavior features from the comment records. We assume that a user has only one comment record for a product, so there will be no conflicts and inconsistencies when modeling.

The representation of the reviewer in the review-space is obtained based on the attention aggregation, and the representation in the sociality-space is the aggregation of its neighbor nodes. Finally, based on the reviewer vector, the final predicted reviewer label is obtained through a three-layer multilayer perceptron (MLP). In reality, the number of normal reviewers is far greater than the number of fake reviewers, this paper optimizes the loss function of the detection model by specifying the weight of the cost-sensitive matrix or the weight of the cost-sensitive vector.

In the experiment, we used a high-quality online reviews dataset from the Amazon platform and compared our method with logistic regression (LR), random forest (RF), Deepwalk, and FdGars [2]. The results prove that our method is effective and has reached a high accuracy.

In this paper, we studied how to identify fake reviewers from crowdsourcing in online review platforms. Taking into account the particularity of reviewers from the crowdsourcing platform, we have established an effective detection model that is sensitive to cost and can aggregate multiple features. The main contributions of this article are summarized as follows:

1. This paper integrates the review content features and the reviewer behavior features, using attention to obtain factors of the reviewer in both review-space and sociality-space.
2. Because of the imbalance of reviewer classes in real-world scenarios, we apply a cost-sensitive method to optimize the loss function of the detection model.
3. We verified our model on a real Amazon dataset and proved the feasibility and effectiveness by comparing other methods.

2 Related Work

Crowdturfing is a new type of fake reviewer which has emerged with the rise of crowdsourcing services. Many researchers have accumulated a certain amount of research on identifying fake reviewers in social networks or comment systems. These methods can be roughly divided into three categories [3]: Content-based Detection Methods, Behavior-based Detection Methods, and Graph-based Detection Methods.

Content-Based Detection Methods. Researchers found that the content of the reviews may contain some advertising information or deceptive instructions. A lot of work is devoted to distinguishing fake reviews from numerous reviews by using text analysis or Natural Language Processing (NLP) models. For example, Mukherjee et al. [8] crawl 64,000 user reviews on the Yelp platform, they first extract the N-gram and part-of-speech features of the review text, and then use a Support Vector Machine (SVM)classifier for reviewer classification; Yao et al. [17] use recurrent neural network (RNN) to generated fake online reviews for products and services automatically, and then use the loss features in RNN training to distinguish real reviews from fake reviews; Ott et al. [9, 11], Shojaee et al. [12], and Li et al. [10] use N-gram and other NLP methods to detect fake reviewers from the perspective of text analysis in the dataset based on a crowdsourcing platform.

Behavior-Based Detection Methods. Since fake reviewers can organize their language normally and answer questions like normal users, the reviews of fake reviewers have similar attribute values to those of normal users. Therefore, in addition to the review text, some researchers mine the behavior characteristics of the reviewers to predict fake reviewers. For example, Fei et al. [13] believe that reviewers that emerge explosively are more likely to be fake commenters. Through time series analysis and loopy belief propagation (LBP) methods, it can be inferred whether the reviewers in the graph are fake reviewers; Jiang et al. [14] find that there is a clear difference between spammers and ordinary users in the attributes of their tracking networks, but the structure of the tracking networks among spammers is similar, so they provide an unsupervised method to model the link features, and then calculate the degree of suspiciousness by sending the features to downstream tasks.

Graph-Based Detection Methods. In order to further analyze the interrelationships among objects in real-world problems, the researchers model the interacting objects into a graph structure, and then identify fake reviewer nodes through matrix calculation or graph embedding. For example, Wang et al. [4, 15] use a method which is similar to hyperlink-induced topic search (HITS) to iteratively calculate the reliability of the reviewer, the authenticity of the review and the credibility of the product by constructing a heterogeneous graph model; Akoglu et al. [16] construct a bipartite graph for reviewers and products, and propose a FraudEagle model based on the hidden Markov model, and use the sIA algorithm based on the LBP cyclic belief propagation to calculate the user's credibility; Parisa [6] believes that reviewers have similar behaviors if they reviewed the same product. Therefore, a reviewer-reviewer graph is constructed, and then the graph propagation algorithm is used to calculate the suspiciousness of the reviewers are from the crowdsourcing task according to the reviewers with fake tags as seeds; Wang et al. [2] propose the FdGars that comprehensively considers the content of reviews and the behavior of reviewers. The model obtains the classification results through a two-layer graph convolutional networks (GCN). Then they propose a co-trained model to train the behavior-based model and the content-based model respectively for collaborative training [7]. Dou et al. [18, 23] designed the GNN-based model to against camouflages and solve the inconsistent problem in fraud detection. Besides, reinforcement learning was utilized to detect spammers [24].

All in all, the graph-based detection method takes into account the network topology among reviewers, reviewers and review products. However, in reality, there is a small proportion of critics from crowdsourcing in the comment area, and the existing methods rarely consider the problem of data imbalance. In addition, semantic feature in reviews is an important indicator for analyzing the characteristics of reviewers, while it has rarely been used in current methods. Therefore, it is worth studying that how to extract the common features of crowdturfing from a small number of categories and how to learn an unbiased model by using graph structure modeling.

3   Crowdturfing Detection Model

In the method, the strategy based on graph modeling is first introduced. In order to represent the node vector more accurately, the extraction and selection of review features are used. Then introduced a detection framework based on attention to aggregate reviewer vectors. Finally, considering the impact of unbalanced data on the detection, an improved cost-sensitive loss function method is introduced.

3.1   Modeling and Initialization

According to the previous content, one person can review multiple products, so there is a reviewer-to-product relationship diagram as shown in Fig. 2 between the reviewer and the product.

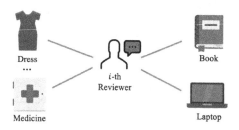

Fig. 2. The reviewer-to-product graph of the i-th reviewer.

Given that the crowdsourcing task is commodity-centric, users who have reviewed the same product may have similar characteristics. We assume that people who have reviewed the same product are neighbors, so a co-reviewer homogeneous sociality-space network can be built, as shown in Fig. 3.

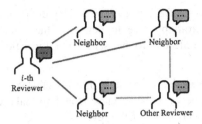

Fig. 3. Co-reviewer graph of all reviewers.

However, we found that the review information contains many features that can be mined, which can help distinguish fake reviewers from all reviewers. Therefore, the eigenvalues are used to replace the random vector representation when initializing the reviewers' embedding. Therefore, we extract and select the features from both the content of the reviews and the behavior of the reviewers.

Advertising information or deceptive indications may be included in the content of the review. Such features are called review content features. The detailed content features and description are shown in Table 1.

Table 1. The review content features and description.

Feature	Description
RL	Review Length
RSN	Review Symbol Number
RSR	Review Symbol Ratio
MCS	Max Content Similarity
RE	Review Emotion

- RL indicates the length of the review, represents the number of words in a review. It is found that the length of the fake reviews from the crowdsourced task is generally less than the normal reviews, and it is about half of the normal review. Therefore, the length of reviews can be used as an indicator to distinguish fake reviews from normal reviews.
- RSN indicates the number of special symbols in a review. There is existing that fake reviews will add special symbols to the text so as to avoid being recognized the same content or advertising information by the machine.
- RSR represents the proportion of special characters in the reviews. This value is the quotient of RSN and RL. RSR can explain the existence of special characters better compared to RSN and RSR.
- MCS represents the maximum content similarity of reviews, refers to the maximum similarity between the current review and the previous review of the reviewer. When a fake commenter writes a fake comment, it is very likely that he will copy the comment he has written before. So this indicator can be used for crowdturfing detection.

- RE indicates the emotional group of reviews. By dividing comment sentiment into multiple categories from positive to negative, the semantic information in the comment text can be reflected. Richer semantic information like this helps to detect fake reviewers.

In addition to analyzing the review text, the behavior of reviewers can also be used as a factor to distinguish between fake reviewers and normal reviewers. Table 2 lists the behavior features and descriptions of the reviewers.

Table 2. The reviewer behavior features and description.

Feature	Description
RN	Review Number
PN	Product Number
PCN	Product Category Number
PR	Praise Ratio
RD	Rate Deviation
WRN	Whether Real Name

- RN represents the number of reviews made by a user. Previous research has shown that fake reviewers generally post more reviews than ordinary reviewers, so the number of reviews can be used as one of the behavior features.
- PN represents the number of products that a user has reviewed.
- PCN represents the type's number of products a user has reviewed. Like RN and PN, it reflects user review behavior as a digital feature.
- PR represents good ratings. It's the number of five-star reviews a user rates as a percentage of the total. It is found that since the fake reviewers are mostly for the crowdsourced task of checking out positive or negative reviews, a user with either too high or too low a rating is likely to be a fake reviewer.
- RD represents the bias of rate. It is obtained by calculating the gap between the current reviewer and other reviewers for the same product. Because in general, there should not be a big gap in the ratings of the same product.
- WRN refers to whether a reviewer has verified his or her real name when registering for an account. Generally speaking, reviewers who have verified their real names are more credible and less likely to be fake reviewers.

The above is a summary of the features of the existing methods that are applicable to the current task. However, the applicable features may not be exactly the same, taking into account the differences between different datasets. Therefore, it is necessary to use a feature selection strategy to select the above features. By removing "Redundant" and "Irrelevant" features, the performance of the model can be improved.

Commonly used feature selection methods include filtering and packaging (e.g., Chi-Squared Test, Mutual Information). The selected features are used to initialize the embedding representations of reviewers and product reviews and contain more information than the random vectors.

3.2   CrowdDet Framework

The fake reviewer features extracted above can be used to initialize the reviewer node in Fig. 1. In order to integrate all the information to get the latent factor of the current reviewer, we propose an effective aggregation mechanism called CrowdDet.

The CrowdDet Framework. The overall structure is shown in Fig. 4. We can learn the latent vector of the reviewer from the review-space and the sociality-space by using this framework, and then combine the two to get the final classification prediction result. This scheme comprehensively considers the review content features and the reviewer behavior features, and the correlation among neighbors in the homogeneous graph is used to discover the spread of fake reviewer tags.

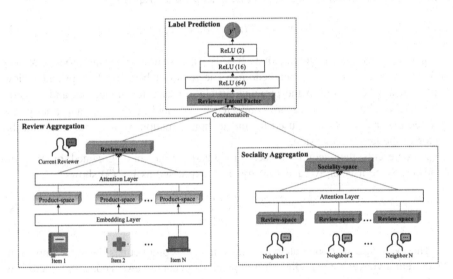

Fig. 4. The structure of the attention-based feature aggregation model CrowdDet.

It can be found from the figure that the CrowdDet framework contains three parts: review aggregation, sociality aggregation and label prediction. In review aggregation, the user's reviews are divided into products to obtain the user's embedding representation in the product-space, and the embedding of multiple product-spaces is aggregated through an attention layer to obtain the embedding in the review-space. Neighbors embedding in sociality aggregation is obtained from review aggregation, and through an attention layer to obtain sociality-space reviewer embedding. Then aggregating the output of the two aggregations to get the reviewer latent factor, and then input it into a three-layer MLP to get the prediction result. These are described in detail as follows.

Review Aggregation. It can be found from Fig. 2 that for the i-th reviewer, multiple products can be reviewed, and the edge of the graph is the corresponding comment. Therefore, we can formulate an aggregation rule to extract the potential factor $h_i^R \in R^d$

of the reviewer in the review-space from the reviewer-to-product graph, where d represents the potential dimension of the reviewer.

The general method is to obtain the review-space factor by learning the information in the product-space. The embedding in product-space is the aggregation of product embedding and comment information embedding, and the following function is needed, it is defined as Eq. (1) shows:

$$h_i^R = \sigma(W \cdot (\sum_{p \in P(i)} \alpha_i x_{ip}) + b) \tag{1}$$

Among them, $P(i)$ represents the set of products that are connected to the i-th reviewer in the reviewer-to-product graph. x_{ip} is the aggregated representation of commodity a in product-space, x_{ip} can be calculated by Eq. (2):

$$x_{ip} = RELU(u_i \oplus v_p \oplus e_p) \tag{2}$$

u_i represents the embedding of user i, v_p can be understood as product review embedding, and e_p is product embedding. The reviewer behavior feature and review content feature extracted in the previous article are used to initialize u_i and v_p here, respectively. These three parts are connected by channel merging $\oplus$, and finally, the rectified linear unit (ReLU)is used for linear transformation, which aims to obtain the vector of the target dimension.

α_i represents the weight of each product-space vector aggregated by the i-th reviewer. Since it is an average strategy, α_i is expressed as Eq. (3) shows:

$$\alpha_i = \frac{1}{|P(i)|} \tag{3}$$

The mean aggregation strategy assumes that each product has the same impact on the current reviewer's embedding. But in practice, when reviewers comment, there may be deviations in their attention to each product. For example, a person's comment may come from completing a crowdsourcing task, or it may be written spontaneously. Since the mean aggregator exhibits limitations, we hope to comprehensively consider the impact of different product reviews on the vector representation of reviewers. Inspired by the attention mechanism, limited attention can be focused on key products.

The calculation of the product-space vector is as shown as Eq. (2), the h_i^R function is shown as Eq. (4) shows:

$$h_i^R = \sigma(W \cdot (\sum_{p \in P(i)} \alpha_{ip} x_{ip}) + b) \tag{4}$$

In this case, α_{ip} can be adjusted according to different products, it is defined as Eq. (5) shows:

$$\alpha_{ip} = \frac{\exp(s(x_{ip}, u_i))}{\sum_{p \in P(i)} \exp(s(x_{ip}, u_i))} \tag{5}$$

Finally, the softmax function is used to normalize the above attention score to get the final attention weight. The attention scoring function $s(x_{ip}, u_i)$ is defined as Eq. (6) shows:

$$s(x_{ip}, u_i) = w_2^T \cdot \sigma(W_1 \cdot [x_{ip} \oplus u_i] + b_1) + b_2 \tag{6}$$

Social Aggregation. A reviewer will have neighbors. If they have reviewed the same product, the neighbor relationship is shown in Fig. 3. Due to the influence of neighbor nodes on the current reviewer, the potential representation $h_i^S \in R^d$ of the reviewer in sociality-space can be obtained by aggregating the embeddings of neighbor nodes.

For the i-th reviewer, the embedding of its neighbor node is the representation of his neighbor in review-space. The degree of attention to different neighbors is different during aggregation. For example, a product review may be written by crowdturfing or by ordinary users. Therefore, the correlation between a reviewer and its neighbors in the co-reviewer graph is different. The same attention mechanism is used to integrate the neighbor node vector with the attention weight of β_{in} to obtain h_i^S. From Eqs. (7)–(9), the specific operation is described:

$$h_i^S = \sigma(W \cdot (\sum\nolimits_{n \in N(i)} \beta_{in} h_n^R) + b) \tag{7}$$

$$\beta_{in} = \frac{\exp(s(h_n^R, u_i))}{\sum_{n \in N(i)} \exp(s(h_n^R, u_i))} \tag{8}$$

$$s(h_n^R, u_i) = w_2^T \cdot \sigma(W_1 \cdot [h_n^R \oplus u_i] + b_1) + b_2 \tag{9}$$

In the formula, h_n^R represents neighbors' vector of the current reviewer.

Label Prediction. When getting the node embedding of the product and review content, the potential representation h_i^R of the reviewer in the review-space is obtained by aggregating them. At the same time, by aggregating neighbors who have an interactive relationship with the current reviewer, the potential representation h_i^S of the reviewer in the sociality-space is obtained. At last, the potential expression of the reviewer needs to consider both the latent factor in review-space and it in sociality-space. Thus, after fusing the features, the two latent factors are combined into the final reviewer latent factor through a mapping. The definition of the reviewer latent factor h_i are represented as Eqs. (10) and (11) show:

$$c = [h_i^R \oplus h_i^S] \tag{10}$$

$$h_i = \sigma(W \cdot c + b) \tag{11}$$

After calculating the latent representation h_i of the user, the final prediction result y' is obtained through a standard MLP. In a mathematical method, the operation are described from Eqs. (12)–(14):

$$g_1 = \sigma(W_1 \cdot h_i + b_1)$$

(12)

$$\ldots$$

$$g_l = \sigma(W_l \cdot g_{l-1} + b_l)$$

(13)

$$y' = w^T \cdot g_l$$

(14)

In the formula, l represents the number of hidden layers of the MLP.

Our research problem can be regarded as a binary classification problem, so the output y' of the model is a two-dimensional result. The two values represent the probability of ordinary and crowdsourced. Then we calculate the loss based on the above probability and train the parameters in the model through the gradient descent method.

However, the positive and negative data is unbalanced in the real scenario. In order to achieve a better effect, we provide an optimization solution to this problem.

3.3   Improved Cost-Sensitive Loss Function

In order to deal with the sample imbalance problem from the algorithm level, we adopt a direct cost-sensitive learning method to alleviate the impact of class imbalance by specifying the misclassification weight of the cost-sensitive matrix or the cost-sensitive vector. Thus, this study intends to use cost-sensitive methods to optimize the loss function of the detection model and to train the model supervised. The cost information is embedded in the objective function of the learning model, and a cost-sensitive learning algorithm f is obtained by minimizing the expected loss. The general form of the training process is shown as Eq. (15) shows:

$$\min_f : loss(f, X, C)$$

(15)

X represents the training sample set, C is the misclassification cost matrix.

For the traditional cross-entropy loss, even if it is easy to classify (the probability of correct classification is greater than 0.5), there is a higher loss. In this study, a modulation factor $(1 - p_t)^{\gamma}$ is added to the original cross-entropy loss. We reduce the weight of easy-to-classify samples so that the model can focus more on difficult-to-classify samples during training. The definition of Focal loss and p_t are shown as Eqs. (16) and (17) show:

$$FL(p_t) = -(1 - p_t)^{\gamma} \log(p_t)$$

(16)

$$p_t = \begin{cases} p & if \ y' = 1 \\ 1 - p & otherwise \end{cases}$$

(17)

p_t represents the probability that the user is estimated to be positive or negative. γ is the focus parameter, and $\gamma > 0$. p represents the probability that user is regarded as a fake reviewer.

Considering the large gap in the number of positive and negative samples, adding weight to the positive and negative samples is a common strategy. The frequency of negative samples is high, so we reduce the weight of negative samples. Since the number of positive samples is small, the weight of positive samples should be relatively increased. The final focal loss function is shown as Eq. (18) shows:

$$FL(p_t) = -\alpha_t(1 - p_t)^\gamma \log(p_t) \tag{18}$$

$\alpha \in [0, 1]$ is the weight used to control the balance. We can control the shared weight to the total loss by setting the α value and take a relatively small value to reduce the weight of the negative sample (the one with more samples). Then take a smaller value of α to reduce the weight of negative samples (the one with more samples).

By adjusting the value of the weight α and the focus parameter γ, the model will be more concerned about the few samples and set a higher loss for the samples that are difficult to classify. So we can get a classifier that is sensitive to the cost of a small number of samples by optimizing the loss of the model.

4 Experiment

In this section, we use a real dataset from the Amazon platform for verification. Evaluation indicators, experimental settings and experimental results are also introduced.

4.1 Dataset and Evaluation Metrics

We use real datasets to conduct experiments, aims to verify the effectiveness of the model in identifying fake reviews created by crowdturfing platform organizations, and check the performance of the model in unbalanced data. Yao et al. [1] collected more than 110,000 high-quality online review data on the Amazon platform in 2017. The reviews of this dataset come from different categories and different reviewers. The reviewers with fake tags are all from the tasks posted by the crowdsourcing platform. The number of reviews, reviewers, and products in the dataset is shown in Table 3. Every review, reviewer and product have truthful and deceptive labels. The selected products are distributed in different product categories such as Books, Health, Electronics, Movies or Other, and the Other category is a mixture of multiple categories.

Table 3. Statistical data of reviews, reviewers and products.

	Deceptive	Truthful
Reviews	10114	101226
Reviewers	1524	18162
Products	994	72266

For the 19,686 reviewers in the dataset, we divided them into 11,812 as the training set, 1969 as the validation set, and 5,909 as the test set. The validation set was used to train the hyperparameters of the model.

Crowdturfing detection is essentially a binary classification task, so we can get a confusion matrix, as shown in Table 4. The positive cases are fake reviewers from crowdsourcing, and the negative cases are regular commenters. The horizontal header of the table represents the prediction result, and the vertical header represents the actual label.

Table 4. Confusion matrix of crowdturfing detection.

	Fake	Normal
Fake	TP (True Positive)	FP (False Positive)
Normal	FN (False Negative)	TN (True Negative)

Since the purpose of detection is to detect as many fake reviewers as possible, in the performance evaluation, recall is used as the main evaluation index. Its calculation process is defined as Eq. (19) shows:

$$Recall = \frac{TP}{TP + FN} \tag{19}$$

In addition, precision, F1, and accuracy are also important references that can be used to measure the detection effect, and the calculation process are defined as follows from Eqs. (20)–(22):

$$Precision = \frac{TP}{TP + FP} \tag{20}$$

$$F1 = \frac{2 \times Recall \times Precision}{Recall + Precision} \tag{21}$$

$$Accuracy = \frac{TP + TN}{TP + TN + FP + FN} \tag{22}$$

4.2   Baseline Methods

In order to verify the feasibility of the above theory, we verified the proposed method on an actual dataset. We selected several different types of algorithms that are commonly used as a classification task as the experimental baseline methods, including machine learning methods and graph-based methods.

- Logistic Regression. Based on the features of 19,686 reviewers in the Amazon dataset, an LR classifier is trained supervised. 70% of the data is used as the training set and 30% as the test set. Through this classifier, the reviewers in the test set are divided into real reviewers and fake reviewers.

- Random Forest. Similarly, the RF model is trained based on the features of the reviewer. When the tree is set to 1, the classifier is the decision tree (DT) model.
- Deepwalk. The nodes embedding is learned from the co-reviewer homogeneous graph. When training the DeepWalk model, the number of walks for each node is 80, the length of random walk is 10, and the length of node embedding is 128. Finally, the final result is obtained through an LR classifier.
- FdGars. The FdGars model is proposed by Wang et al. [2]. It is actually a two-layer GCN model. When initializing node embedding, we use review content features and reviewer behavior features in stand of random features. The length of node embedding is 50. The dataset is divided into the training set, validation set, and test set.

4.3 Data Preparation and Experiment Settings

According to the review records from Amazon, we constructed a reviewer-to-product diagram for each reviewer and a co-reviewer diagram that includes all reviewers. We extracted the node and the structural features of the graph based on the features of the comment data, then obtained a feature matrix containing the information in Table 5.

Table 5. Amazon dataset characteristics and description.

Feature	Description
RL	Review Length
RR	Review Rate
RE	Review Emotion
RP	Review Product
WP	Whether Purchase
WRN	Whether Real Name
NI	Neighbor's ID

Among them, RL, RR, and RE belong to the characteristics of the comment content. RP, WP, WRN, and NI belong to the characteristics of the commenter's comment behavior. This paper adopts filtering or encapsulation methods such as deleting Variance Threshold, Chi-Square Detection, L1 Regularization, and Decision Tree Strategies to filter the extracted features. The filtered features are integrated to initialize the embedding representation of reviewers, products, and product reviews instead of the random representation vector in the original strategy.

In order to explore the influence of the parameters of the focal loss function on the evaluation indicators, we fixed other influencing factors and modified γ values to obtain the experimental results shown in Table 6.

Table 6. The impact of changes in the parameters of the focal loss function on the classification results.

γ	Recall	Precision	F1	Accuracy
0.5	0.83	0.82	0.81	0.970
0.75	0.85	0.84	0.84	0.975
2	0.88	0.83	0.78	0.971

Recall, precision, F1 and accuracy of the entire test set classification are used as evaluation indicators. It can be found that the recall increases with the change of the γ. However, only when the value of γ is 0.75, the comprehensive index of the model is relatively high.

4.4 Performance Evaluation

To explore the effectiveness of the model for extracting review content and reviewer relations, we conducted ablation study on the two modules of the review aggregation and sociality aggregation. The results are shown in Table 7.

Table 7. Performance evaluation using different modules.

Method	Recall	Precision	F1	Accuracy
Review-only	0.47	0.71	0.56	0.94
Sociality-only	0.14	0.74	0.24	0.92
Review+Sociality	0.85	0.84	0.84	0.975

– Review-only. Only product and review features are considered in this method, without the neighbor relationship between user nodes.
– Sociality-only. This method only considers the features of the user's neighbors, without the features of products and reviews.
– Review + Sociality. This is the strategy we propose, taking into account the impact of products, comment features and neighbor relationships on user embedding.

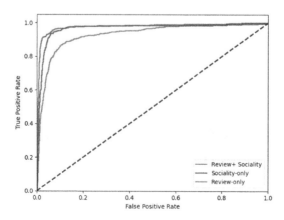

Fig. 5. Receiver operating characteristic (ROC) curve with different modules.

Figure 5 shows the ROC curve using different modules. The results show that the combined effect of the two aggregators is the best in terms of recall, accuracy, F1, accuracy, and area under curve (AUC) value, which is better than one aggregator. This is because the two dimensions of reviewer features are considered comprehensively, and richer information is integrated. It confirms that the model does not have redundancy and integrates the features of the reviewer effectively.

In addition, the proposed method needs to be compared with baseline methods. Table 8 shows the classification results of different methods for the Amazon dataset.

Table 8. The impact of the focal loss function's parameters on the classification results.

Method	Recall	Precision	F1	Accuracy
Logistic regression	0.13	0.73	0.22	0.93
Decision tree	0.41	0.55	0.47	0.93
Random forest	0.42	0.58	0.49	0.93
DeepWalk	0.82	0.80	0.81	0.968
FdGars	0.31	–	–	0.925
CrowdDet	0.85	0.84	0.84	0.975

From the experimental results, it can be found that the machine learning classification method has reached a high accuracy rate, which is caused by the imbalance amounts of positive and negative categories. In fact, the rate of recall is relatively low. When the method of graph embedding is adopted, the classification effect has been significantly improved, which shows that the structural information of the graph has a positive influence on the classification of reviewers. However, the solution of the FdGars model has not achieved good results in the current problem. The method we proposed obtained a good detection effect by extracting multiple features and using the CrowdDet method for fusion. The recall rate is 0.85, the precision is 0.84, the F1 is 0.84 and the accuracy is 0.975. Compared with the DeepWalk method, recall, precision, F1 and accuracy are increased by 0.03, 0.04, 0.03, 0.007, respectively.

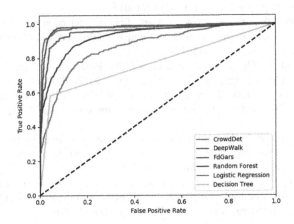

Fig. 6. ROC curve of different detection strategies.

Figure 6 shows the ROC curve of different strategies, the AUC values are 0.9784 for CrowdDet, 0.9783 for DeepWalk, 0.9557 for GCN, 0.9268 for RF, 0.8695 for LR, 0.7681 for DT. Although the curve of DeepWalk is close to the proposed method, its other indicators have not surpassed CrowdDet. It can be seen that we have verified the effectiveness of the proposed method on real datasets and achieved better classification results than other strategies.

5 Conclusion

In this paper, we studied a method for detecting fake reviewers from crowdsourcing. Considering the existing graph-based methods that have not achieved significant results. An attention-based strategy was used to integrate the representation of the review-space and the sociality-space. Firstly, we constructed two graphs and extracted the structural information and node features in the graphs. Not only the review features in the product review-space but also the impact of social interaction among reviewers was considered. Secondly, we calculated the reviewer latent factors through the neural network aggregation mechanism, using the focal loss to optimize the classifier. Finally, we validated the proposed method on the Amazon dataset. It is found that the proposed method can basically cover the fake reviewers among all reviewers, and the classification effect has been evaluated in the experiment. In the future, we plan to utilize the information of review groups and product clusters to further expand the detection methods of crowdturfing.

Acknowledgement. This work was supported by the National Natural Science Foundation of China (grant no. 61772560), and the Fundamental Research Funds for the Central Universities of Central South University (grant no. 2021zzts0747).

References

1. Yao, W., Dai, Z., Huang, R., et al.: Online deception detection refueled by real world data collection. arXiv preprint arXiv:1707.09406 (2017)
2. Wang, J., Wen, R., Wu, C., et al.: FdGars: fraudster detection via graph convolutional networks in online app review system. In: Companion Proceedings of the 2019 World Wide Web Conference, pp. 310–316 (2019)
3. Jindal, N., Liu, B.: Opinion spam and analysis. In: Proceedings of the 2008 International Conference on Web Search and Data Mining, pp. 219–230 (2008)
4. Wang, G., Xie, S., Liu, B., et al.: Review graph based online store review spammer detection. In: 2011 IEEE 11th International Conference on Data Mining, pp. 1242–1247. IEEE (2011)
5. Rayana, S., Akoglu, L.: Collective opinion spam detection: Bridging review networks and metadata. In: Proceedings of the 21th ACM SIGKDD International Conference on Knowledge Discovery and Data Mining, pp. 985–994 (2015)
6. Kaghazgaran, P., Caverlee, J., Squicciarini, A.: Combating crowdsourced review manipulators: a neighborhood-based approach. In: Proceedings of the Eleventh ACM International Conference on Web Search and Data Mining, pp. 306–314 (2018)

7. Wang, J., Wen, R., Wu, C., et al.: Analyzing and detecting adversarial spam on a large-scale online APP review system. In: Companion Proceedings of the Web Conference, pp. 409–417 (2020)
8. Mukherjee, A., Venkataraman, V., Liu, B., et al.: What yelp fake review filter might be doing? In: Proceedings of the International AAAI Conference on Web and Social Media, vol. 7(1) (2013)
9. Ott, M., Choi, Y., Cardie, C., et al.: Finding deceptive opinion spam by any stretch of the imagination. arXiv preprint arXiv:1107.4557 (2011)
10. Li, J., Ott, M., Cardie, C., et al.: Towards a general rule for identifying deceptive opinion spam. In: Proceedings of the 52nd Annual Meeting of the Association for Computational Linguistics (Volume 1: Long Papers), pp. 1566–1576 (2014)
11. Ott, M., Cardie, C., Hancock, J.T.: Negative deceptive opinion spam. In: Proceedings of the 2013 Conference of the North American Chapter of the Association for Computational Linguistics: Human Language Technologies, pp. 497–501 (2013)
12. Shojaee, S., Murad, M.A.A., Azman, A.B., et al.: Detecting deceptive reviews using lexical and syntactic features. In: 2013 13th International Conference on Intelligent Systems Design and Applications, pp. 53–58. IEEE (2013)
13. Fei, G., Mukherjee, A., Liu, B., et al.: Exploiting burstiness in reviews for review spammer detection. In: Proceedings of the International AAAI Conference on Web and Social Media, vol. 7(1), pp. 175–184 (2013)
14. Jiang, M., Cui, P., Beutel, A., et al.: Catching synchronized behaviors in large networks: a graph mining approach. ACM Trans. Knowl. Discovery Data (TKDD) 10(4), 1–27 (2016)
15. Wang, G., Xie, S., Liu, B., et al.: Identify online store review spammers via social review graph. ACM Trans. Intell. Syst. Technol. (TIST) 3(4), 1–21 (2012)
16. Akoglu, L., Chandy, R., Faloutsos, C.: Opinion fraud detection in online reviews by network effects. ICWSM 13(2–11), 29 (2013)
17. Yao, Y., Viswanath, B., Cryan, J., et al.: Automated crowdturfing attacks and defenses in online review systems. In: Proceedings of the ACM SIGSAC Conference on Computer and Communications Security, pp. 1143–1158 (2017)
18. Liu, Z., Dou, Y., Yu, P.S., et al.: Alleviating the inconsistency problem of applying graph neural network to fraud detection. In: Proceedings of the 43rd International ACM SIGIR Conference on Research and Development in Information Retrieval, pp. 1569–1572 (2020)
19. Moreno-Torres, J.G., Herrera, F.: A preliminary study on overlapping and data fracture in imbalanced domains by means of genetic programming-based feature extraction. In: 2010 10th International Conference on Intelligent Systems Design and Applications, pp. 501–506. IEEE (2010)
20. Zhou, Z.H., Liu, X.Y.: Training cost-sensitive neural networks with methods addressing the class imbalance problem. IEEE Trans. Knowl. Data Eng. 18(1), 63–77 (2005)
21. Lin, T.Y., Goyal, P., Girshick, R., et al.: Focal loss for dense object detection. In: Proceedings of the IEEE International Conference on Computer Vision, pp. 2980–2988 (2017)
22. Fan, W., Ma, Y., Li, Q., et al.: Graph neural networks for social recommendation. In: The World Wide Web Conference, pp. 417–426 (2019)
23. Dou, Y., Liu, Z., Sun, L., et al.: Enhancing graph neural network-based fraud detectors against camouflaged fraudsters. In: Proceedings of the 29th ACM International Conference on Information & Knowledge Management, pp. 315–324 (2020)
24. Dou, Y., Ma, G., Yu, P.S., et al.: Robust spammer detection by Nash reinforcement learning. In: Proceedings of the 26th ACM SIGKDD International Conference on Knowledge Discovery & Data Mining, pp. 924–933 (2020)

Attention-Aware Actor for Cooperative Multi-agent Reinforcement Learning

Chenran Zhao[1], Dianxi Shi[1,2,3(✉)], Yaowen Zhang[4], Yaqianwen Su[2], Yongjun Zhang[2], and Shaowu Yang[1]

[1] National University of Defense Technology, Changsha 410073, China
dxshi@nudt.edu.cn
[2] Artificial Intelligence Research Center (AIRC), National Innovation Institute of Defense Technology (NIIDT), Beijing 100166, China
[3] Tianjin Artificial Intelligence Innovation Center (TAIIC), Tianjin 300457, China
[4] Environment Information Support 32282 Research Institute, Jinan 250000, China

Abstract. In multi-agent environments, cooperation is crucially important, and the key is to understand the mutual interplay between agents. However, multi-agent environments are highly dynamic, where the complex relationships between agents cause great difficulty for policy learning, and it's costly to take all coagents into consideration. Besides, agents may not be allowed to share their information with other agents due to communication restrictions or privacy issues, making it more difficult to understand each other. To tackle these difficulties, we propose Attention-Aware Actor (Tri-A), where the graph-based attention mechanism adapts to the dynamics of the mutual interplay of the multi-agent environment. The graph kernels capture the relations between agents, including cooperation and confrontation, within local observation without information exchange between agents or centralized processing, promoting better decision-making of each coagent in a decentralized way. The refined observations produced by attention-aware actors are exploited to learn to focus more on surrounding agents, which makes Tri-A act as a plug for existing multi-agent reinforcement learning (MARL) methods to improve the learning performance. Empirically, we show that our method substantially achieves significant improvement in a variety of algorithms.

Keywords: Multi-agent cooperation · Graph · Attention mechanism · Multi-agent mutual interplay

1 Introduction

Cooperation is a widespread social behavior in nature, where humans tend to focus on the most relevant feature area such as objects [3] and faces [9] for understanding the mutual interplay between neighboring humans, allowing them to

This work was supported by the National Key Research and Development Program of China (2017YFB1001901).

H. Gao and X. Wang (Eds.): CollaborateCom 2021, LNICST 407, pp. 370–384, 2021.
https://doi.org/10.1007/978-3-030-92638-0_22

quickly process most relevant parts of the local observations during decentralized decision making [21]. This makes humans exceed all other species in terms of range and scale of cooperation.

Attention mechanism [20] has recently emerged as a successful approach in various fields. The main idea behind it is to select salient areas of interest which are more relevant to the current task from the numerous information according to the importance distribution of elements, and it has shown great success in mutual interplay understanding of MARL, examples include a wide range of approaches on designing effective attention-based MARL approaches, which can mainly be divided into two categories, exchanging local perceptual information on the field of view of each agent [6,7,18,23] and modeling how agents cooperate through a centralized critic with the attention mechanism [5,13]. However, most of these methods depend on either the existence of a communication message or the centralized attention mechanism which could access to the global information that contains the information of each agent on the field. Unfortunately, when the agents are independently deployed and communications are disabled or prohibitive, each agent has to predict its own action conditioning on its partial observation trajectory. Besides, typical attention-based approaches to MARL either consider all coagents at all time steps during the decentralized execution or take all these dynamics into account during the centralized training. It is costly and less helpful to take all other coagents into consideration whether in a decentralized or centralized manner, because receiving a large amount of information incurs high computational complexity.

To tackle these difficulties, we resort to the decentralized attention-based model that does not need to assume the existence of perfect communication or consider all agents all the time. Specifically, we are interested in building reinforcement learning (RL) agents, which learn representations guided by an understanding of what is important during multi-agent cooperation and confrontation for decision making. More importantly, since the reconstructed observation has the same form as that of the original observation, it is straightforward to plug in any existing MARL algorithms for decision making.

In this paper, we propose a graph-based attention module that is designed for understanding the mutual interplay between agents (including cooperation and confrontation) during the decentralized execution, called Attention-Aware Actor (Tri-A). Different from previous approaches, Tri-A learns an actor for each coagent that could selectively focus on neighboring agents from local observation, which helps achieve the cooperative goal with decentralized models. The intuition behind our idea comes from the fact that, in many real-world environments, each agent can observe other agents (both enemies and friends) in the field of view of each agent itself, and it is beneficial for each agent to know which one it should pay attention to or cooperate with at different stages of a complete trajectory of the battle. For example, a soccer attacker with the ball needs to pay attention to the opposing team's defenders as well as neighboring teammates, while she/he rarely needs to pay attention to her/his own team's goalkeeper. The specific players that the attacker is paying attention to varies over the complete trajectory of the game, depending on the situation on the field, especially the formation and strategy of the opponent team and its own team. By applying soft attention to the mutual interplay graph of each agent, our Tri-A is able to make decisions based on the situation on the field dynamically, such as selecting which coagents to attend to or avoiding attacks from enemies, improving performance in multi-agent domains with complex interactions.

We evaluate Tri-A on various MARL algorithms by replacing the original actor with the attention-aware actor (Tri-A). Our experiments on a range of unit micromanagement tasks built in StarCraftII [17] show that our method obtains significant improvement. The attention analysis shows that Tri-A can capture proper target agents that each coagent should pay more attention to as well as proper importance weight of each target agent at each time step t, which reveals the mutual interplay between agents, including cooperation and confrontation.

Our main contributions can be summarized as follows:

- **Attention-based graph structure.** We construct the multi-agent mutual interplay (including cooperation and confrontation) as a graph according to the local observation of each agent. It refines the local observations of each agent by applying the attention mechanism on the different parts of the local observations so as to make agents selectively and dynamically focus on the surrounding agents. Furthermore, it can solve the problem of high computational complexity which exists in the approaches that taking the perceived information from all agents into consideration.
- **Combining with actor under value decomposition architecture.** By combining the graph structure with actor, we propose a novel actor called Attention-Aware Actor (Tri-A) which could be used as a plug-in for any Value Decomposition (VD) architecture algorithms. Since the actor under the architecture of value decomposition is updated with the backpropagation of the upper network structure, we can replace the actor at will without having to design a loss function specifically for it. It improves the performance of making decisions in multi-agent domains with complex interactions.

The remainder of this paper is organized as follows. We first introduce the Markov games, attention mechanism, attnetion-based MARL algorithms and graph network in Sect. 2. Then in Sect. 3, we present the framework of Tri-A in details. Furthermore, we validate Tri-A in the challenging StarCraftII platform and give the specific analysis in Sect. 4. Finally, conclusions are provided in Sect. 5.

2   Background

A fully cooperative multi-agent task can be described as a Dec-POMDP [15] consisting of a tuple $G = \langle \mathcal{N}, S, A, P, Z, O, r, n, \gamma \rangle$. $s \in S$ describes the true state of the environment which contains the global information of all agents on the field. At each time step, each agent $i \in \mathcal{N} \equiv \{1, ..., n\}$ chooses an action $a^i \in A$, forming a joint action $\mathbf{a} \in \mathbf{A} \equiv A^n$. This causes a transition on the environment according to the state transition function $P(s'|s, \mathbf{a}) : S \times \mathbf{A} \times S \rightarrow [0, 1]$. All agents share the same reward function $r(s, \mathbf{a}) : S \times \mathbf{A} \rightarrow \mathbb{R}$ and $\gamma \in [0, 1)$ is a discount factor.

We specially consider a partially observable scenario in which each agent i draws local observations $o^i \in O$ instead of global state s according to the observation probability function $Z(o, a) : O \times A \rightarrow O$. Each agent i has an observation-action history $\tau^i \in T \equiv (Z \times A)^*$, on which it conditions a stochastic policy $\pi^i(a^i|\tau^i) : T \times A \rightarrow [0, 1]$, aiming at maximizing global rewards. The joint policy π has a joint action-value function: $Q^\pi(s_t, \mathbf{a}_t) = \mathbb{E}_{s_{t+1:\infty}, \mathbf{a}_{t+1:\infty}}[R_t|s_t, \mathbf{a}_t]$, where $R_t = \sum_{j=0}^{\infty} \gamma^j r_{t+j}$ is the discounted return.

2.1   Attention Mechanism

In recent years, attention mechanism [20] has made remarkable performance in various domains, including computer vision [1,14], NLP [2,10,20] and RL [4,8, 11]. More and more work relies on the idea of the attention to deal with challenges of multi-agent cooperation. An attention function can be described as mapping a query and a set of key-value pairs to an output, where the query V_Q, keys V_K^j, values and output are all vectors. The output is computed as a weighted sum of the values, where each weight w_j assigned to each value is computed by a compatibility function of the query with the corresponding key.

$$w_j = \frac{\exp(f(V_Q, V_K^j))}{\sum_k \exp(f(V_Q, V_K^k))}. \tag{1}$$

where $f(V_Q, V_K^j))$ is the user-defined function to measure the importance of the corresponding value and the scaled dot-product is a common one. In practice, the multi-head structure is usually employed to allow the model to focus on information from different representation sub-spaces.

2.2   Attention-Based Algorithms for MARL

ATOC [8] follows the alternative paradigm of centralizing policies while keeping the critics decentralized. Their focus is on learning an attention model for sharing information between the policies.

MAAC [5] applied the soft attention mechanism to the centralized critic so as to dynamically select which agents to attend to at each time step for each agent during the training, which improves the scalability and performance in multi-agent domains with complex interactions.

MADDPG [13] extends DDPG to multi-agent settings. It proposes a multi-agent policy-gradient algorithm using central critics. The centrally computed critic network takes the states and actions of all other agents as its input, and the actor network only relies on the local observation information of a given agent.

Compared with them, which assume the existence of effective communication or take all agents into consideration during the centralized training, our work applies the attention mechanism to the local observation of each coagent so that each coagent can pay more attention to neighboring agents when making decisions, which achieves the cooperative goal with decentralized models in the case of limited communication.

2.3   Graph Network

DGN [7] assumes a graph connection among the agents such that each node is an agent. A multi-head attention model is used as the convolution kernel to extract the connection weights to the neighbor nodes. Agents can share their observations and weights of all agents with their neighbors. In other words, each agent constructs a graph using the perceived information exchanged from others. It means each agent needs to process a large amount of information, which may incur high computational complexity.

G2ANET [12] represents all agents as a complete graph based on a two-stage attention network, where hard attention is used to cut the unrelated edges and soft attention is used to learn the importance weight of the edges. By combining the graph with the policy network, each agent considers the communication vectors of all other agents when making decisions. By combining the graph with the Q-value network, the critic of each agent considers the state and action information of all other agents when calculating the individual Q-value. However, both of them need to process a large amount of information received from other agents.

Different from them, we propose to construct a graph using only the local observations of each agent. In this way, the amount of information each agent needs to process is unchanged. Thus it may not incur high computational complexity. Besides, it explicitly models how agents cooperate and confront within local observations, thus promoting better decision-making.

3   Our Approach

In this section, we describe the proposed method Attention-Aware Actor (Tri-A) for learning actors in a graph-based manner. We construct the multi-agent mutual interplay as a graph according to the local observation of each agent and refine the local observation through a graph-based attention mechanism. It establishes connections between the individual agent and its surrounding agents so that each agent could focus on other agents in its vicinity selectively and dynamically, promoting better decision making of each agent in a decentralized way.

In order to figure out how Tri-A as a plug works in cooperative MARL, we choose a representative algorithm architecture called Value Decomposition (VD) for illustration, and the whole structure is shown in Fig. 1. Figure 1 provides a clear explanation that value decomposition is aimed at decomposing the global shared multi-agent Q-value Q^{tot} into individual Q-values Q^i to guide individuals' behaviors. Actors from the architecture of value decomposition make decisions based on local observations and generate the individual Q-value $Q^i(o^i, a^i)$ of the agent. More importantly, since the architecture of value decomposition takes the setting of end-to-end, we don't need to design a loss function for the attention-aware actor (Tri-A) because the backpropagation of value decomposition will update the attention-aware actor of each agent naturally.

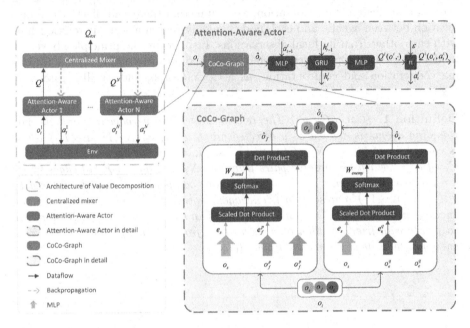

Fig. 1. The overall structure of Attention-Aware Actor. The Attention-Aware Actor is composed of CoCo-Graph architecture and RNN policy network. The left is the overall structure of value decomposition which mixes Q^i into Q^{tot}. The pink part is the CoCo-Graph architecture that reconstruct the local observations o_i into targeted observations $\hat{o}_i$ through soft attention mechanism. The green part is the RNN policy networks which receives last hidden states h_{t-1}^i, last action a_{t-1}^i and current reconstructed local observations $\hat{o}_i$ as inputs. The reconstructed local observation produced by CoCo-Graph architecture will be input into RNN policy networks for decision making or individual Q-value calculating. (Color figure online)

3.1 Multi-agent Mutual Interplay Graph Structure

We construct the multi-agent mutual interplay, including cooperation and confrontation, as a graph according to the local observation of each agent. Agents in the environment are represented by the nodes of the graph, and each node has a set of neighbors (including friends and enemies) which is determined by distance or other metrics, depending on the environment, and varies over time. The intuition behind it is that neighboring agents are more likely to interact with and affect each other. Thus each agent should adjust its strategy dynamically by observing the movements of the surrounding agents to promote better decision-making. Besides, as the number and position of agents vary over time, the cooperation relationship and confrontation relationship are changing continuously and violently during the battle, and it's vital for us to extract these relationships adaptively. Moreover, since it is costly and less helpful to take all agents on the field into consideration, we assume that there's no effective communication between agents, and each node can only reason about the relationships with each other from its local observations. Inspired by the principle above, we model the relationship between each coagent and its surrounding agents, including cooperation and confrontation, as a CoCo-Graph, and we illustrate it in Fig. 2.

Definition 1. *(CoCo-Graph) The relationship between coagent i and its surrounding agents is defined as a directed graph as $G_i = (N_f, N_e, E_f, E_e)$ which is consisting of the set N_f of friend nodes, the set N_e of enemy nodes, the set E_f of edges which are ordered pairs from i to N_f and the set E_e of edges which are ordered pairs from i to N_e. Each friend node p (for all friends indexed by $p \in \{1, ..., n-1\}$) represents a friend agent entry. Each enemy node q (for all enemies indexed by $q \in \{1, ..., m\}$) represents an enemy agent entry. If i tends to cooperate with friend p, then there is an edge from i to p. If i tends to confront enemy q, then there is an edge from i to q.*

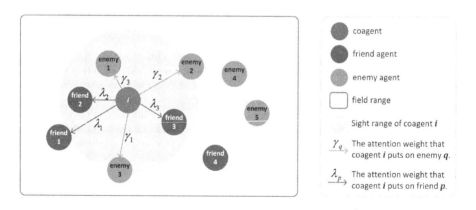

Fig. 2. CoCo-Graph G_i of coagent i

As illustrated in Fig. 2, each coagent i constructs a CoCo-Graph G_i based on its local observation at each time step t during the complete trajectory of game. The CoCo-Graph G_i is closely connected with agents within coagent i's sight range, and the agents out of sight affect coagent i little. By reconstructing the local observation of each coagent i through CoCo-Graph G_i, the observation is potentially simplified for understanding and reasoning, which is indeed helpful for understanding of the mutual interplay between agents. We then show how the connections between agents can be extracted by the designed attention architecture below.

3.2   Attention-Aware Actor Architecture

In this section, we show how Tri-A can be plugged in existing MARL methods to improve policy learning. Our aim is to learn a graph that indicates the mutual interplay between agents and the potential of each neighboring agent being the target to cooperate with or confront with. Based on the CoCo-Graph introduced above, we design a soft attention architecture to reconstruct local observations of each coagent, which could ideally differentiate between the interested agents and connected but less important agents. More specifically, we train a soft attention model to learn the weights of each coagent i focusing on neighboring agents according to its CoCo-Graph G_i at each time step t during the complete trajectory of the game.

Just like football players can observe the movements of other players on the field, each agent can observe other agents if they are both alive and located within the sight, including friends and enemies. Therefore we can use the information within local observation to help build the embedding vectors of both friends and enemies. First, we separate the local observation o of coagent i into three parts according to the prior knowledge: o_e represents enemy information, o_f represents friend information and o_s represents the information about coagent$i$ itself, as Eq. (2) shows (we drop the parameter dependence wherever its inferable for clarity of presentation).

$$o = (o_e, o_f, o_s). \tag{2}$$

where $\hat{o}_e = \sum_{q=1}^{m} \gamma_q \cdot e_a^q$ and $\hat{o}_f = \sum_{p=1}^{n} \mu_k \cdot e_f^p$, which means o_f is composed of n friends' information o_f^p (for all friends indexed by $p \in \{1, ..., n\}$) and o_e is composed of m enemies' information o_e^q (for all enemies indexed by $q \in \{1, ..., m\}$).

Then we encode the information about coagent i itself, friend agent p and enemy agent q in observation o into embedding vectors e_s, e_f^p and e_e^q respectively by MLP as shown in Fig. 1 at each time step t. Now we can use these embedding vectors to learn the weights of edges in CoCo-Graph G_i ($i \in \{1, ..., n\}$). We calculate and normalize the correlation between e_s and e_f^p, and between e_s and e_e^q within the local observations of each agent through soft attention mechanism according to Eq. (3) and Eq. (4) respectively. On the one hand, we hope that each agent could pay attention to surrounding agents, including both enemies and friends. On the other hand, we hope that agents could understand the mutual interplay between each other by holding targeted observations, and thereby promote cooperation.

$$\lambda_p = \frac{\exp(f(e_s, e_f^p))}{\sum_{k=1}^{n} \exp(f(e_s, e_f^k))}. \tag{3}$$

$$\gamma_q = \frac{\exp(f(e_s, e_e^q))}{\sum_{k=1}^{m} \exp(f(e_s, e_e^k))}. \tag{4}$$

Then we carry out the information integration by concatenating all parts of the local observations according to Eq. (5), where the friend information o_f and the enemy information are refined through CoCo-Graph. The reconstructed local observations are then fed into the RNN policy networks to strategize. The reconstructed local observations have considered the complex interaction between agents, which is indeed helpful for holding targeted observations and understanding the mutual interplay between agents, and thus promote better cooperation naturally.

$$\hat{o} = (\hat{o}_e, \hat{o}_a, o_s). \tag{5}$$

Since the reconstructed observation has the same form as that of the original observation, it is straightforward to plug it in any existing deep RL methods for decision making.

4   Experimental Evaluation

4.1   Settings

The StarCraft Multi-Agent Challenge (SMAC) environment [17] have a rich set of scenarios that allow complex interactions between agents including cooperation and confrontation, so we evaluate Tri-A in the SMAC environment to demonstrate the efficacy of our method. In this environment, each agent is a unit participating in combat against enemy units which is controlled by hand-crafted policies. Besides, agents receive individual local observation from the environment, containing distance, relative location, health, shield, and unit type of other allied and enemy units within their sight range. We consider SMAC maps with three different scenarios, here we briefly introduce the scenarios in Table 1. Training and evaluation schedules such as the testing episode number and training hyper-parameters are kept the same as QMIX [16] in SMAC. The percentage of episodes where the agents defeat all enemy units, i.e., test win rate, is reported as the performance of algorithms. All the results are averaged over 5 independent runs with different random seeds. We show that the RL agents equipped with Tri-A perform better in both convergence speed and the final test win rate than baseline algorithms. What's more, we demonstrate that Tri-A as a plug could be applied across different algorithms, showcasing the generalization ability.

Table 1. SMAC maps in three different scenarios.

Name	Ally Units	Enemy Units	Type
3s5z	3 Zealots 5 Stalkers	3 Zealots 5 Stalkers	Symmetric & Heterogeneous
1s3s5z	1 Colossi 3 Zealots	1 Colossi 3 Zealots	Symmetric & Heterogeneous
	5 Stalkers	5 Stalkers	
5m_vs_6m	5 Marines	6 Marines	Asymmetric & Homogeneous

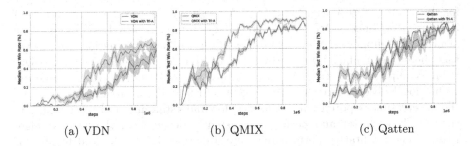

      (a) VDN   (b) QMIX   (c) Qatten

Fig. 3. Median test win rate on map 3s5z

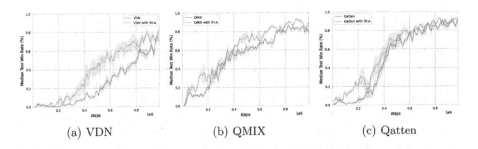

      (a) VDN   (b) QMIX   (c) Qatten

Fig. 4. Median test win rate on map 1c3s5z

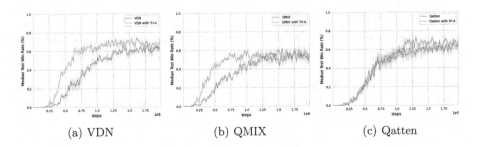

      (a) VDN   (b) QMIX   (c) Qatten

Fig. 5. Median test win rate on map 5m_vs_6m

4.2 Validation

We apply Tri-A on three centralized training with decentralized execution (CTDE) setting algorithms that adopts the architecture of Value Decomposition (VD), including VDN [19], QMIX [16] and Qatten [22], where agents make decisions based on local observations within decentralized actors. Since the actor under the architecture of value decomposition is updated with the backpropagation of the global shared multi-agent Q-value Q^{tot}, we can replace the actor of these algorithms at will without having to design a loss function specifically for the actor. Figure 3, Fig. 4 and Fig. 5 have shown the median test win rate of baseline algorithms (VDN, QMIX and Qatten) equipped with Tri-A and baseline algorithms equipped with original actors in three different scenarios. We observe that there is a significant gap between the baseline algorithms and baseline algorithms equipped with Tri-A in all scenarios. By constructing the CoCo-Graph within local observation for each coagent and focusing on neighboring agents, the observation is potentially simplified for understanding and reasoning, and coagents learn faster and perform consistently better than the baseline algorithms. The qualitative performance indicates that Tri-A is indeed helpful for the understanding of the mutual interplay between agents, and thus promotes better decision making for each coagent.

4.3 Attention Analysis

Next, we visualize the attention weights of each agent focusing on friends and enemies at each time step during a complete trajectory of battle to figure out what has been learned in the attention mechanism and how much effect the attention mechanism actually contributes to the decision making in Tri-A. For better understanding, we choose the 2s3z map to illustrate the attention weight heatmap of coagents focusing on other agents is shown in Fig. 6 and Fig. 8. We also attach some auxiliary snapshots in Fig. 7 to explain some interesting segments in the heatmaps. In all the snapshots, the red colored units indicate the agents controlled by Tri-A.

For 2s3z, the two armies are composed of the same units, 2 Zealots and 3 Stalkers, among which strong Stalkers are much more effective against enemies, so it is of great importance for Stalkers to learn to protect teammates that are vulnerable to certain enemies' attack, and the fragile little Zealots should learn to stick together and focus fire, ordering units to jointly attack and kill enemy units one after another. Besides, a very important technique is making enemy units give chase while maintaining enough distance so that little or no damage is incurred.

Attention Analysis of Attention-Aware Actor Focusing on Friends. For qualitative analysis, we visualize the attention weights (λ_i) of each coagent i focusing on other friend agents at each time step in a complete trajectory of 2s3z battle as shown in Fig. 6.

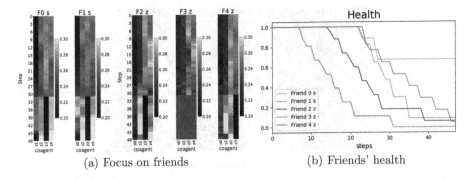

(a) Focus on friends   (b) Friends' health

Fig. 6. (a) The attention heatmap of coagents focusing on other friend agents during a complete trajectory of 2s3z battle. The head title of each heatmap indicates the unique mark of a specific agent A from our team, including agent camp (F means Friend), agent id (from 0 to 4) and agent type (s means Stalker, z means Zealot). Bottom horizontal ordination indicates the unique mark of other friend agents that A is focusing on, including agent id and agent type. Vertical ordination represents time steps that increase from top to bottom. (b) The health property of each coagent, which indicates the remaining blood.

Zealot has short range and short skill cool down, Stalker has a long range and long skill cool down. Therefore, it's beneficial for Zealot units to assemble into formations and fight at the front so that they can focus fire on enemies and destroy the enemy one by one, and it's proper for Stalker units to fight at the back to protect Zealot units from enemies' attack. As revealed by Fig. 6(a), Stalkers always pay more attention to fragile Zealots while Zealots also pay more attention to the other two friend Zealots, which exactly confirms what we have analyzed above.

Besides, as the health property shows in Fig. 6(b), friend Zealot 3 is dead at time step 31. We can tell that the attention weights in friend Zealot 3's heatmap in Fig. 6(a) no longer changes after time step 31, and friend Zealot 3's corresponding attention weights in other friend agents' heatmaps turn to be very dark after time step 31 compared to other living friend agents. What's more, those living agents' corresponding attention weights in others' heatmap turn to be brighter compared to the time step before 31, indicating that the living agents turn their attention to other friend agents after friend Zealot 3 is dead.

In order to illustrate the effectiveness of Attention-Aware Actor more intuitively, we attach an auxiliary snapshot of an appealing segment in Fig. 7, and we also extract the CoCo-Graph of an interesting agent (Friend 3) to explain the complex mutual interplay between agents. As revealed by the snapshot in Fig. 7, friend Zealot 3 helps friend Zealot 4 attack enemy Zealot 2. The CoCo-Graph of coagent 3 provides a clear explanation that these fragile Zealots (Friend 3, 4) have learned to stick together to form a formation so that they can focus fire on the enemy Zealot (Enemy 2) and achieve the goal of weakening the enemy

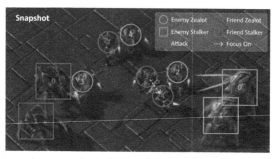

(a) Snapshot

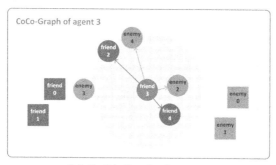

(b) CoCo-Graph of agent 3

Fig. 7. Snapshot and the surrounding CoCo-Graph of agent 3

combat power as soon as possible. Once the current target enemy is destroyed, friend Zealot 3 will focus on the target enemy (Enemy 4) that another friend Zealot (Friend 2) is attacking, and cooperate with that Zealot to attack the enemy, which is an effective way to win the battle.

Attention Analysis of Attention-Aware Actor Focusing on Enemies.
Figure 8 has shown the attention weights (γ_i) of each coagent i focusing on enemy agents at each time step in a complete trajectory of 2s3z battle.

One main tendency is that the corresponding part in heatmaps becomes completely dark after the corresponding enemy is dead, which means our coagents will pay no more attention to this dead enemy, and once an enemy is dead, the corresponding part of our coagents focusing on other living enemies' becomes brighter, indicating that our coagents turn their attention to other living enemies.

As we discussed in Sect. 3, the cooperation relationship and confrontation relationship are changing continuously, which means the attention weights within a complete trajectory of battle are changing violently. Under these circumstances, Tri-A could capture the mutual interplay between agents properly, and thus promote better understanding and decision-making as we analyzed above.

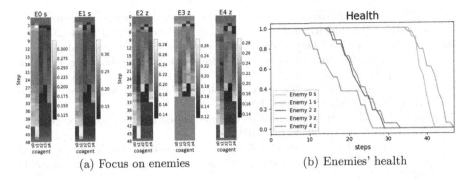

(a) Focus on enemies   (b) Enemies' health

Fig. 8. (a) The attention heatmap of coagents focusing on each enemy. The head title of each heatmap indicates the unique mark of a specific enemy agent B that our agents is focusing on, including agent camp (E means Enemy), agent id (from 0 to 4) and agent type (s means Stalker, z means Zealot). Bottom horizontal ordination indicates the unique mark of five agents from our team, including agent id and agent type. Vertical ordination represents time steps that increase from top to bottom. (b) The health property of each enemy, which indicates the remaining blood.

5 Conclusion

In this paper, we present Attention-Aware Actor (Tri-A), a plug designed for deep multi-agent reinforcement learning method, which learns a much more observant actor for each agent in a decentralized way by applying attention to the local observation of each coagent. Without taking all agents into consideration or centralized processing, our method is much more effective in the case of limited communication. Extensive experiments carried on a series of battle games in StarCraftII demonstrate that our method improves the performance on a number of baseline algorithms which adopts the architecture of value decomposition. Additionally, we perform the attention analysis to visualize the attention weights of each coagent focusing on neighboring friends and enemies, and the results provide intuitive explanations that Tri-A is indeed helpful for understanding the mutual interplay between agents and thus promote better cooperation.

References

1. Ba, J., Mnih, V., Kavukcuoglu, K.: Multiple object recognition with visual attention. arXiv preprint arXiv:1412.7755 (2014)
2. Bahdanau, D., Cho, K., Bengio, Y.: Neural machine translation by jointly learning to align and translate. arXiv preprint arXiv:1409.0473 (2014)
3. Borji, A., Cheng, M.M., Jiang, H., Li, J.: Salient object detection: a benchmark. IEEE Trans. Image Process. **24**(12), 5706–5722 (2015)
4. Iqbal, S., Sha, F.: Actor-attention-critic for multi-agent reinforcement learning. arXiv preprint arXiv:1810.02912 (2018)

5. Iqbal, S., Sha, F.: Actor-attention-critic for multi-agent reinforcement learning. In: International Conference on Machine Learning, pp. 2961–2970. PMLR (2019)
6. Jaques, N., et al.: Social influence as intrinsic motivation for multi-agent deep reinforcement learning. In: International Conference on Machine Learning, pp. 3040–3049. PMLR (2019)
7. Jiang, J., Dun, C., Huang, T., Lu, Z.: Graph convolutional reinforcement learning. arXiv preprint arXiv:1810.09202 (2018)
8. Jiang, J., Lu, Z.: Learning attentional communication for multi-agent cooperation. arXiv preprint arXiv:1805.07733 (2018)
9. Judd, T., Ehinger, K., Durand, F., Torralba, A.: Learning to predict where humans look. In: 2009 IEEE 12th International Conference on Computer Vision, pp. 2106–2113. IEEE (2009)
10. Lin, Z., et al.: A structured self-attentive sentence embedding. arXiv preprint arXiv:1703.03130 (2017)
11. Liu, Y., Wang, W., Hu, Y., Hao, J., Chen, X., Gao, Y.: Multi-agent game abstraction via graph attention neural network. arXiv preprint arXiv:1911.10715 (2019)
12. Liu, Y., Wang, W., Hu, Y., Hao, J., Chen, X., Gao, Y.: Multi-agent game abstraction via graph attention neural network. In: Proceedings of the AAAI Conference on Artificial Intelligence, vol. 34, pp. 7211–7218 (2020)
13. Lowe, R., Wu, Y., Tamar, A., Harb, J., Abbeel, P., Mordatch, I.: Multi-agent actor-critic for mixed cooperative-competitive environments. arXiv preprint arXiv:1706.02275 (2017)
14. Mnih, V., Heess, N., Graves, A., et al.: Recurrent models of visual attention. In: Advances in Neural Information Processing Systems, pp. 2204–2212 (2014)
15. Oliehoek, F.A., Amato, C.: A Concise Introduction to Decentralized POMDPs. Springer, Cham (2016). https://doi.org/10.1007/978-3-319-28929-8
16. Rashid, T., Samvelyan, M., Schroeder, C., Farquhar, G., Foerster, J., Whiteson, S.: QMIX: monotonic value function factorisation for deep multi-agent reinforcement learning. In: International Conference on Machine Learning, pp. 4295–4304. PMLR (2018)
17. Samvelyan, M., et al.: The starcraft multi-agent challenge. arXiv preprint arXiv:1902.04043 (2019)
18. Sukhbaatar, S., Szlam, A., Fergus, R.: Learning multiagent communication with backpropagation. arXiv preprint arXiv:1605.07736 (2016)
19. Sunehag, P., et al.: Value-decomposition networks for cooperative multi-agent learning. arXiv preprint arXiv:1706.05296 (2017)
20. Vaswani, A., et al.: Attention is all you need. arXiv preprint arXiv:1706.03762 (2017)
21. Wyart, V., Tallon-Baudry, C.: How ongoing fluctuations in human visual cortex predict perceptual awareness: baseline shift versus decision bias. J. Neurosci. **29**(27), 8715–8725 (2009)
22. Yang, Y., et al.: Qatten: a general framework for cooperative multiagent reinforcement learning. arXiv preprint arXiv:2002.03939 (2020)
23. Yang, Y., Luo, R., Li, M., Zhou, M., Zhang, W., Wang, J.: Mean field multi-agent reinforcement learning. In: International Conference on Machine Learning, pp. 5571–5580. PMLR (2018)

Geographic and Temporal Deep Learning Method for Traffic Flow Prediction in Highway Network

Tianpu Zhang[1,2] ⓘ, Weilong Ding[1,2(✉)] ⓘ, Mengda Xing[1,2], Jun Chen[1,2], Yongkang Du[1], and Ying Liang[3]

[1] School of Information Science and Technology,
North China University of Technology, Beijing 100144, China
dingweilong@ncut.edu.cn
[2] Beijing Key Laboratory on Integration and Analysis of Large-Scale Stream Data,
Beijing 100144, China
[3] Research Center for Ubiquitous Computing Systems,
Institute of Computing Technology, Chinese Academy of Science, Beijing, China

Abstract. Traffic congestion has become an inevitable situation faced by all countries and the prediction accuracy of traffic flow, as one of the means to solve this problem, still needs to be improved. Most studies lack the consideration of the influence of multiple factors such as spatial factors, time series factors and other external factors, which makes the prediction effect of traffic flow unsatisfactory. In this paper a method is proposed based on deep learning that can capture the geographic spatial relationship among toll stations, the dynamic temporal relationship of historical traffic flow, extreme weather and calendar types. On the three metrics of MAPE, MAE, and RMSE, the prediction effect of our model has increased by 30% compared with KNN, GBRT and LSTM models.

Keywords: Deep learning · Graph convolutional network · Long short-term memory · Traffic flow prediction · Spatio-temporal data

1 Introduction

With the growth of population and economy, many serious problems have been brought to modern cities, and traffic congestion has undoubtedly become one of the main problems faced by most countries in the world. Especially in the rush time of weekdays or holidays, the large number of vehicles brought huge challenges to the current capacity of highway. Therefore, it is indispensable to plan highway reasonably and provide correct guidance for people to travel. In recent years, with the development of artificial intelligence, more and more researchers are more inclined to use artificial intelligence technology to solve highway planning and guild people to travel. Intelligent transportation system (ITS) [2,37] is one of the important products brought about by the development of artificial intelligence. Among them, traffic flow prediction, as an important part of the

H. Gao and X. Wang (Eds.): CollaborateCom 2021, LNICST 407, pp. 385–400, 2021.
https://doi.org/10.1007/978-3-030-92638-0_23

intelligent transportation system and the basic index to solve traffic congestion problem, undoubtedly plays an important role. By analyzing and predicting the traffic flow, it is possible to learn about the distribution of vehicles in certain node at highway network, and then to regulate and divert the traffic flow so as to achieve the effect of alleviating traffic congestion. Traffic flow prediction is to predict the number of vehicles passing through the certain area in a certain periodic time. According to the length of periodic time, traffic flow prediction can be divided into two types, namely short-term traffic flow prediction that its time period is less than one day and long-term traffic flow prediction that its time period is more than one day. At the same time, according to the different spatial scopes, traffic flow prediction can be divided into single-site traffic flow prediction and the entire network traffic flow prediction.

Although traffic flow prediction has been developed for decades, in the actual situations, the traffic flow prediction at highway toll stations still has been facing many challenges. These problems can be divided into three points. The first point is the lack of consideration of the complex spatial dependence of traffic flow at highway toll stations. Because the highway is a kind of network structure where the vehicle in any toll station can reach the designated location, different toll stations have different influences on the predicted toll station. The second point is the lack of consideration of the temporal dependence of traffic flow at highway toll stations. Through analysis [1,39,40], the traffic flow at the same toll station shows a non-linear change over time. That means, different times of the same toll station have different effect on the moment to be predicted. The third point is the lack of consideration of the impact of extreme weather and calendar types on the prediction of traffic flow at highway toll stations. Under different weather conditions, the traffic flow will change differently. For example, in extreme weather conditions, highway may close for individual safety. By doing so, it may cause a sudden drop in traffic flow in this area. In addition, the date type is another influencing factor. According to our observation, there is a significant increase in traffic flow can on weekends and holidays.

In this paper, a GTM (Geographic and Temporal Model) is proposed, which based on deep learning method. Taking into account the spatial relationship among the toll stations, the historical temporal characteristics and the calendar types and the weather conditions of the toll stations, the GTM model can obtain a more accurate prediction of the traffic flow at the highway toll stations. The rest of this paper is organized as follows. At Sect. 2, we describe related work with our paper. Then at Sect. 3, we describe construction process of our prediction method of traffic flow at highway toll stations. At Sect. 4, we introduce two experiments to illustrate excellent effect of our method. Finally at Sect. 5, we conclude our work and discuss our future research direction.

2   Related Work

Nowadays, a large amount of work uses advanced technologies such as big data to process large amounts of historical traffic data to obtain useful information and functions, and then use artificial intelligence methods to obtain prediction results. We will introduce these methods from three aspects.

The first type of methods that is used to predict traffic flow at highway toll stations is traditional statistical manners. ARIMA (Autoregressive Integrated Moving Average model) [3,4,33], VAR (Vector autoregressive models) [5] and HA (Historical Average) [6] are all classical statistical methods that used to predict traffic flow. Definitely, it is the advantage of statistical methods to depend on single factor, easily implement and quickly compute result. In the early developing stage of intelligent transportation system, these methods are used to predict traffic flow. However, these methods have obvious weaknesses, that is, they only consider historical temporal factors without considering other influencing factors. Since, especially facing the problem of traffic flow prediction that affected by temporal, spatial and external factors, statistical methods can not get better prediction accuracy. The second type of methods that is used to predict traffic flow at highway toll stations is machine learning methods. These models are usually used to predict traffic flow including SVR (Support Vector Regression) [7], KNN (K-Nearest Neighbor) [1,8], Bayesian model [9,10] and GBRT (Gradient BoostRegression Tree) [32]. With the appearance of machine learning methods, the problem of single feature dependence has been successfully solved. These methods get final predicted result by analysing the inner relationship of temporal and other features. The ability to measure the weight relationship between different features is the advantage of machine learning. However, machine learning methods too depend on handcraft feature engineering to get better predicted accuracy, especially when face massive and complicated features, such as prediction traffic flow problem. The third type of methods that is used to predict traffic flow at highway toll stations is deep learning methods. Recently, as a branch of machine learning, deep learning methods have become state-of-the-art technology and have been applied to various fields [11–13]. At the same time, due to the characteristics of deep learning methods that are good at capturing temporal and spatial features, deep learning has also been widely used in traffic flow prediction problem [14,15]. Traffic flow prediction has been studied for decades as a common time series problem. In these studies [16–19], people have achieved better prediction results by using the ability of LSTM (long short-term memory) and GRU (Gated Recurrent Unit) to model complex functions and the characteristics of dynamically capturing time relationships. However, these studies ignore the fact that traffic flow prediction is not a simple time series problem. It is also affected by spatial relationship. Therefore, under the assumption of ignoring the impact of spatial relationship, the prediction results are often not very good. In response to this problem, related researchers use CNN (Convolutional Neural Network) to obtain spatial relationship. Researchers use grids to divide the highway network, and then use CNN to extract the spatial relationship between adjacent toll stations to obtain prediction results, such as these [20–23,38]. However, CNN always maps the traffic flow prediction problem in non-Euclidean space to Euclidean space, which leads to the loss of spatial information. More recently, with the popularity of GCN developed by [24,25], more researchers prefer to choose GCN to obtain spatial information, such as [15,26–31]. Because GCN extends the convolution operation to the non-Euclidean space, this operation is more in line with the real graph structure data.

Therefore, in this paper, we propose a geographic and temporal deep learning method that belongs to the third type of methods we mentioned above for traffic flow prediction in highway network. In order to overcome the shortcomings of the above models that lack multi-dimensional features considerations, our model uses the advantages of LSTM to capture temporal series features and GCN to capture spatial features, and fully considers the spatio-temporal factors, extreme weather features and calendar type to achieve more accurate prediction results in real cases.

3   Feature Pre-processing and Prediction Method

3.1   Feature Engineering

In order to acquire correlation among toll stations, we first need to construct highway graph. The graph definition as follow:

Definition 1 (Highway Graph). *A highway graph is represented by a undirected graph $G = (V, E)$. Where V is a collection representing all toll stations on highway graph. E is also a collection representing all the edges on the highway. $e_{ij} \in E$ represents correlation between toll station v_i and v_j, here $v_i, v_j \in V$ and i, j are a positive integer.*

In this paper, we constructed a highway graph from the perspective of geographic relations. Meanwhile, highway graph is undirected graph, because in actual situations any points in the highway road network is connected to other points. At the same time, the graph is constructed from a geographical perspective, which conform to the business logic, so that the final prediction results have better interpretability.

Definition 2 (Daily Traffic Flow of Highway Toll Stations). *For any toll station v_i, the daily traffic flow is expressed as $s_{v_i}^t$. It represent the total amount of vehicles that passed this toll station v_i, on the day t. Here, t represent current date, $v_i \in V$.*

From daily traffic flow, we construct historical traffic flow S_{v_i} of toll station v_i. It is represented by the formula (1). Here, d represents the length of the time window of historical data we need.

$$S_{v_i} = \begin{bmatrix} s_{v_i}^1 \\ s_{v_i}^2 \\ \cdots \\ s_{v_i}^d \\ \cdots \end{bmatrix}^{\mathrm{T}} \tag{1}$$

Definition 3 (External Factors). *We use $P_t^{vi} = (W_t^{vi}, D_t)$ to represent the external factors of the v_i toll station on the day t. Here, W_t^{vi} represents weather condition of the v_i toll station on the day t, D_t represents calendar type of the v_i toll stations on the day t.*

Firstly, we introduced extreme weather. Through analysis, we found that the traffic flow at highway toll stations fluctuates significantly under extreme weather conditions, while under good weather conditions, the traffic flow tends to stabilize. We use the label encoder method to divide the weather conditions into two types. The extreme weather conditions include heavy rain, heavy fog, and strong wind that we analysis from the raw data. We defined this factor as formula (2).

$$W_t^{vi} = \begin{cases} 0, & otherwise \\ 1, & extreme\,weather \end{cases} \tag{2}$$

Secondly, the calendar type plays an important role in the prediction of the traffic flow at the highway toll stations. We also use the label encoder method to divide the date types into three categories, namely holidays, weekends and others. During holidays, the charging mode of highway will be adjusted and people will have more leisure time to travel so that traffic flow can be effect by this factors. We define this feature as formula (3).

$$D_t = \begin{cases} 0, & otherwise \\ 1, & if\,t\,is\,a\,holiday \\ 2, & if\,t\,is\,a\,weekend \end{cases} \tag{3}$$

Definition 4 (Traffic Flow of Upstream Toll Stations). *In order to get better spatial relationship among toll stations, we use Vol^{v_it} that is a vector represents the traffic flow of upstream toll station related to vi on the day t. Upstream toll stations are generally considered to be toll stations where vehicles enter the highway. The specific analysis method can refer to our previous work [1]. This vector can be represented by the formula (4).*

$$Vol^{v_it} = \begin{bmatrix} vol_1^{v_it} \\ vol_2^{v_it} \\ \cdots \\ vol_k^{v_it} \\ \cdots \end{bmatrix}^T \tag{4}$$

3.2   Graph Construction

The creation of the highway graph is very important for us to extract the spatial correlation among toll stations. A reasonable graph construction method can greatly improve prediction accuracy of our model. Therefore, we created our highway topology graph based on three rules. The three rules are defined as follows.

Connectivity rule. This rule stipulates that the graph we construct is a connected graph. This rule is in line with the actual situation of China's highway, because in real situation, any point is connected to other points. At the same time, this rule also guarantees that we can achieve the traffic flow prediction for all toll stations in highway.

Neighborhood rules. This rule specifies how we choose toll stations adjacent to node v_j. This means that we will select adjacent toll stations based on the geographic topology of the highway.

Bidirection rules. This rule ensures that the highway graph we create is an undirected graph. This rule is in line with the actual Chinese highway scene, because any two toll stations are bidirection on the highway. You can reach v_j from v_i, and you can also reach v_i from v_j.

3.3   Traffic Flow Prediction

After the feature processing, the highway graph G we constructed, daily traffic flow $S_{v_i}^t$, external factors $P_t^{v_i}$ and upstream traffic flow $Vol^{v_i t}$ will be input into our model, the specific model structure can refer to the Fig. 1. This method is divided into four stages, namely feature engineering stage, feature extraction stage, feature concatenate stage and linear stage.

In the feature engineering stage, in order to obtain the spatial topological attributes of the highway, we create a highway graph G according to the rules specified above. In our work we use adjacency list to represent highway graph as shown in Fig. 2.

In this example, the stations that can be reached directly from Anyangbei toll station are connected by arrows, such as Anyang toll station. At the same time, in order to make better predictions, we also extract historical traffic flow features, traffic flow of upstream toll station and external features that include calendar types and extreme weather.

In the spatio-temporal feature extraction stage, we use GCN that is proposed by Kipf and Welling [36] to extract the spatial relationship of the highway graph and LSTM to extract the temporal relationship of daily traffic flow. In the GCN part, we use two layers of GCN, the formula is as follows.

$$X^{(1)} = Relu(\hat{D}^{-1/2}\hat{A}\hat{D}^{-1/2}XW) \tag{5}$$

$$X^{(2)} = Relu(\hat{D}^{-1/2}\hat{A}\hat{D}^{-1/2}X^{(1)}W) \tag{6}$$

Here, X represents the feature of toll stations in graph, including historical traffic flow S_{v_i} and $Vol^{v_i t}$ traffic flow of upstream toll stations mentioned in the definition 2 and definition 4 respectively. $\hat{A} = A + I_N$, A is the adjacency matrix of highway network G, I_N represents identity matrix of size N. And $\hat{D}_{ii} = \sum_j \hat{A}_{ij}, i, j \leq N$, $\hat{D}_{ii}$ represents the value of the i-th row and i-th column in $\hat{D}$. The weight matrix W is a learnable parameter. $X^{(1)}$ and $X^{(2)}$ represent the output of the first layer GCN and the second layer GCN respectively. They have the same feature count of 64.

At the same time, we input historical traffic flow data into the LSTM to obtain the temporal characteristics of the toll stations. As a kind of recurrent

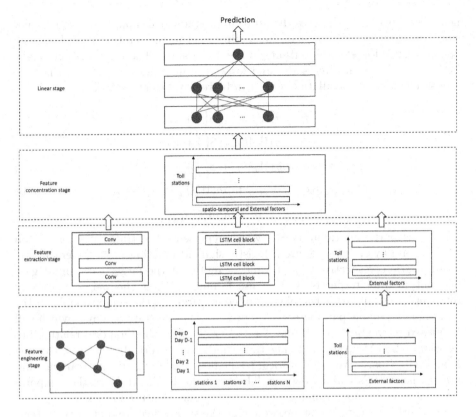

Fig. 1. Traffic flow predictoin method

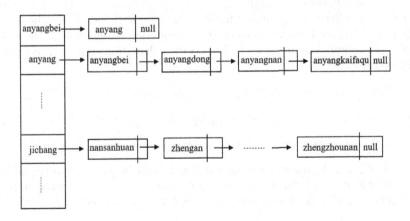

Fig. 2. Adjacency list of highway graph

neural network, LSTM solves the problem of gradient disappearance and explosion caused by too deep sequence by adding a gating mechanism. LSTM consists of input gate, forget gate, output gate and cell state. These components make LSTM memorize the time series and forget the unimportant parts of the time series. The specific calculation steps can be referred to as follows.

$$f_t = \sigma(W_f[h_{t-1}, S_V^t] + b_f) \tag{7}$$

$$i_t = \sigma(W_i[h_{t-1}, S_V^t] + b_i) \tag{8}$$

$$o_t = \sigma(W_o[h_{t-1}, S_V^t] + b_o) \tag{9}$$

$$C_t = f_t \odot C_{t-1} + i_t \odot tanh(W_c[h_{t-1}, S_V^t] + b_c) \tag{10}$$

$$h_t = o_t \odot tanh(C_t) \tag{11}$$

In this part, our input is S_V^t, which represents the traffic flow of all toll stations on day t. σ and $\odot$ are a logistic sigmoid function and an elementwise multiplication, respectively. f_t, i_t, and o_t represent the forget gate, input gate and output gate respectively. In these formulas, W_* is the weight matrix of different gates, and b_* is the bias of different gates. At the same time, both W_* and b_* are learnable parameters. C_t represents the cell state on day t, which will be passed to the next cell on day $t + 1$. h_t represents the temporal relationship learned by LSTM up to day t. The time window of historical traffic flow as same long as GCN part. We use historical traffic flow feature matrix for training, and use the next day's traffic flow as a label, to train LSTM to learn the temporal features of traffic flow. Finally, we get the temporal feature matrix h_t.

In feature concatenate stage, we merge the spatial feature matrix $X^{(2)}$, temporal feature matrix h_t and the external factor matrix P_t^V to form a new feature matrix M, and then enter the matrix into the linear stage. We use a three-layer fully connected network, including an input layer, a hidden layer, and an output layer to form a linear stage. In the input layer and the hidden layer, the number of neurons is 64. According to our task of predicting traffic flow in the output layer, the number of neurons is 1. The specific calculation steps can refer to the following.

$$M^{(1)} = Relu(MW_1 + b_1) \tag{12}$$

$$M^{(2)} = Relu(M^{(1)}W_2 + b_2) \tag{13}$$

$$M^{(3)} = M^{(2)}W_3 + b_3 \tag{14}$$

Here, W_* and b_* represent weighted matrix and bias respectively and both are learnable parameters. $M^{(*)}$ represents output of fully connected network. $M^{(3)}$ is the final traffic flow prediction of highway toll stations.

4   Evaluation

4.1   Settings

Our experimental data comes from real system Henan Highway Management System [34,35]. The system displays real-time traffic flow of highway toll stations in Henan Province. Based on this system, we collected traffic data, weather conditions, and calendar types at 269 toll stations from May 2017 to September 2017 to perform this traffic flow prediction task. For historical traffic flow S_{v_i}, we choose time window $d = 15$ and for $Vol^{v_i t}$ traffic flow of upstream toll stations, we choose $k = 3$. The system is built on a big data framework, and HBase 1.6.0 is a database for storing traffic flow data. We built the storage system with 3 servers each of witch server have 4 cores CPU, 22 GB RAM and 700 GB storage. Our method implementation is based on python 3.6 and the open source deep learning framework pytorch 1.7.0. The configuration of machine used to train our model is Intel (R) Core (TM) CPU i7-9750 2.59 GHz, 16 GB RAM, 1TB storage and one NVIDIA GeForce GTX 1660 Ti.

In order to evaluate the prediction effect of our model on traffic flow, we selected three evaluation indicators, namely root mean square error (RMSE), mean absolute percentage error (MAPE) and mean absolute error (MAE). Here, n is an integer, representing the number of all toll stations, $\hat{y}_i$ represents the traffic flow prediction for the v_i toll station and y_i represents the ground truth of traffic flow for the v_i toll station.

$$RMSE = \sqrt{\frac{1}{n}\sum_{i=1}^{n}(\hat{y}_i - y_i)^2} \tag{15}$$

$$MAPE = \frac{100\%}{n}\sum_{i=1}^{n}|\frac{\hat{y}_i - y_i}{y_i}| \tag{16}$$

$$MAE = \frac{1}{n}\sum_{i=1}^{n}|\hat{y}_i - y_i| \tag{17}$$

4.2   Experiments

We first evaluate the effect of temporal features in our proposed model GTM. We designed an experiment to compare the prediction result gained by our model with variant model without LSTM.

Experiment 1: The Effect of Temporal Characteristics. In this experiment, we used the GTM model and its variant model GTM$_{noL}$ to predict the traffic flow of 269 toll stations. We selected Xuchangdongqu from all the toll stations of Henan highway to compare and analyze the differences between the two models. Because the traffic flow of most toll stations is similar to this station, this station can represent other stations with generality. The comparison chart of prediction results can refer to Fig. 3.

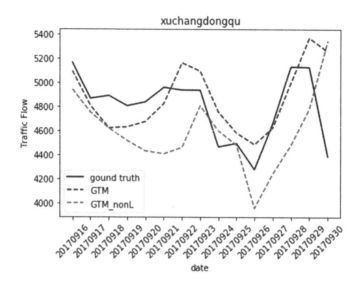

Fig. 3. The prediction traffic flow with GTM and its variant

GTM$_{noL}$ is a variant of our GTM model that does not use LSTM to obtain the temporal characteristics of the traffic flow at the toll station. In Fig. 3, it can be observed that our model GTM, represented by the blue line, is more in line with the real situation represented by the black line. At the same time, at the wave peaks and wave troughs of traffic flow, our model also has good learning ability and can accurately predict. In order to compare our models more closely, we have given a Table 1 and a Table 2.

Table 1. Prediction performances at Xuchangdonqu

	GTM	GTM$_{noL}$
RMSE	282.025	421.997
MAE	207.4274	351.864
MAPE(%)	4.437	7.369

Table 2. Prediction performances at all toll stations

	GTM	GTM$_{noL}$
RMSE	573.256	682.393
MAE	372.092	403.861
MAPE(%)	28.069	23.185

The Table 1 shows the prediction results of the GTM model and its variant model GTM$_{noL}$ for Xuchangdongqu. It can be seen from the table that the GTM model is higher than the GTM$_{noL}$ model in all three metrics. The GTM model is improved by 33.16% on the RMSE metric. Through this comparison, it can be shown that we have achieved better results using LSTM to extract temporal features. Therefore, the temporal feature is an important role in the prediction of the traffic flow of highway toll stations. At the same time, the Table 2 is the prediction average result for all toll stations. From the network-wide perspective, it also shows that the accuracy of the model GTM prediction is higher than GTM$_{noL}$ model. The GTM model is 15.99% higher than the GTM$_{noL}$ model on the RMSE metric. However, the MAPE metric did not improve as we expected to the RMSE and MAE metrics. We guess that the reason for this problem is that the model GTM$_{noL}$ without LSTM has a strong learning ability for toll stations that are more associated with other toll sites, because it mainly relies on GCN to obtain the spatial relationship of toll stations. For the GTM model, after adding LSTM to extract temporal feature, our model learns more comprehensively, thereby reducing the learning ability of toll stations that are more associated with other toll sites. In general, the MAPE metric of the two models still belong to same level. Therefore, from the three indicators and the line cart, it can be seen that the temporal features extracted by the LSTM model play an important role in predicting the traffic flow on the highway.

Experiment 2: Analysis of the Accuracy of Traffic Flow Prediction Results on Weekdays and Weekends. To show more clearly that our GTM model has obtained better results for the traffic flow prediction of highway toll stations, we further compared the traffic flow prediction results that are obtained by GTM with results that are obtained by variant GTM$_{noL}$ model under different calendar types. Since our testing set uses September 16, 2019 to September 30, 2019, which contains two weeks, we randomly selected two group weekdays and weekends from these two weeks. 20170916 and 20170920 belong to the weekday and weekend of the first week, and 20170928 and 20170930 belong to the weekday and weekend of the second week.

The traffic flow prediction results in highway toll stations that are obtained by GTM and its variant model GTM$_{noL}$ are illustrated in Fig. 4 and Table 3. From the scatter diagram, the GTM model can capture the real traffic flow of all toll stations well either on weekdays or on weekends. In addition, according to the metrics in the Table 3, we can observe that the GTM model obtains better results than the GTM$_{noL}$ model in RMSE metric. This phenomenon shows that it is very necessary to comprehensively consider the temporal characteristics and spatial characteristics of toll stations. However, the scores of the GTM model on the MAE and MAPE metrics are not consistently better than GTM$_{noL}$, but the scores of the two models are almost at the same level.

Table 3. Prediction performances in different calendar types

	GTM	GTM$_{noL}$	GTM	GTM$_{noL}$
	20170916		20170920	
RMSE	488.494	525.594	410.185	417.627
MAE	334.164	320.777	322.028	283.176
MAPE(%)	25.151	18.435	27.18	16.553
	20170928		20170930	
RMSE	588.093	658.360	1114.432	1578.820
MAE	333.209	420.355	322.028	283.176
MAPE(%)	22.021	20.553	39.266	58.505

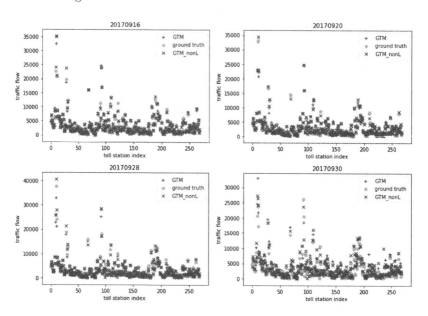

Fig. 4. The traffic flow prediction of toll stations in weekdays and weekends

Experiment 3: Prediction Effects Comparison with Other Models. In this experiment, we use the GTM model to compare with shallow machine learning models such as GBRT [32] and KNN [1], and deep model LSTM often used for time-series problem prediction. In order to clearly illustrate the superiority of our model, we selected two toll stations with a large difference in traffic flow and compared them. Refer to the Fig. 5.

We chose two toll stations, Luoyang and Zhengzhouxinqu. The daily traffic flow of their two stations is completely different. Luoyang's daily traffic flow is between 4000 and 7000, while Zhengzhouxinqu's daily traffic flow is between 15000 and 20000. By comparing the prediction results of these two stations, it can be seen that our model GTM has a good learning ability for all toll stations. At the same time, compared with other models, our model has the highest accuracy of prediction results. For detailed metrics comparison, please refer to the Table 4.

Table 4. Prediction performances of different models

	GTM	GBRT	KNN	LSTM	GTM	GBRT	KNN	LSTM
	Luoyang				Zhengzhouxinqu			
RMSE	208.854	385.904	428.284	522.572	884.770	1566.178	1979.314	1193.320
MAE	176.025	382.159	423.263	411.560	793.238	1556.606	1969.376	1061.904
MAPE(%)	3.475	7.504	8.291	7.669	4.363	8.688	10.985	5.919

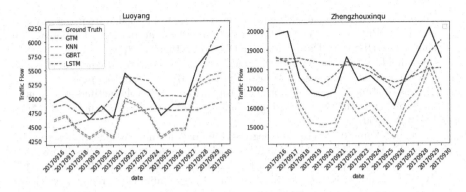

Fig. 5. Comparison of prediction accuracy of different traffic flow

From the Table 4, we can conclude that our model outperforms other algorithms in the three metrics of RMSE, MAE and MAPE. This also shows that our model can well capture the spatial and temporal characteristics of the traffic flow prediction problem at toll stations through the combination of GCN and LSTM.

5   Conclusion

In this paper, we proposed a deep learning method that can take into account spatio and temporal factors and has achieved good results in dealing with the prediction of highway toll stations. GTM is a model based on deep learning, combined with characteristics that GCN can capture the relationship between toll stations in the perspective non-Euclidean space and LSTM can capture the dynamic temporal factors of historical traffic flow. Experiments show that our model can capture the wave peaks and wave troughs of traffic flow at highway toll stations very well, and has improved three metrics compared with other models. Our model improves on the RMSE metric by an average of 30%. In future work, we will try to construct highway graoh from different perspectives to obtain spatial information from different perspectives.

Acknowledgments. This work was supported by National Natural Science Foundation of China (No. 61702014), Beijing Municipal Natural Science Foundation (No. 4192020) and 2020 "Shipei Plan" Project for the Cultivation of High-level Talents in Beijing Colleges and Universities (No. 21XN217).

References

1. Ding, W., Wang, X., Zhao, Z.: CO-STAR: a collaborative prediction service for short-term trends on continuous spatio-temporal data. Futur. Gener. Comput. Syst. **102**, 481–493 (2020)

2. Yuan, J., Zheng, Y., Xie, X., Sun, G.: Driving with knowledge from the physical world. In: Proceedings of the 17th ACM SIGKDD International Conference on Knowledge Discovery Data Mining (KDD), pp. 316–324 (2011)
3. Hamed, M.M., Al-Masaeid, H.R., Said, Z.M.B.: Short-term prediction of traffic volume in urban arterials. J. Transp. Eng. **121**(3), 249–254 (1995)
4. Lingras, P., Sharma, S.C., Osborne, P., Kalyar, I.: Traffic volume time-series analysis according to the type of road use. Comput.-Aided Civil Infrastruct. Eng. **15**(5), 365–373 (2000)
5. Zivot, E., Wang, J.: Vector autoregressive models for multivariate time series. In: Zivot, E., Wang, J. (eds.) Modeling Financial Time Series with S-Plus R, pp. 385–429. Springer, New York (2006). https://doi.org/10.1007/978-0-387-32348-0_11
6. Lv, Y., Duan, Y., Kang, W., Li, Z., Wang, F.Y.: Traffic flow prediction with big data: a deep learning approach. IEEE Trans. Intell. Transp. Syst. **16**(2), 865–873 (2015)
7. Wu, C.-H., Ho, J.-M., Lee, D.T.: Travel-time prediction with support vector regression. IEEE Trans. Intell. Transp. Syst. **5**(4), 276–281 (2004)
8. Zhang, X., He, G., Lu, H.: Short-term traffic flow forecasting based on K-nearest neighbors non-parametric regression. J. Syst. Eng. **24**(2), 178–183 (2009)
9. Sun, S., Zhang, C., Yu, G.: A Bayesian network approach to traffic flow forecasting. IEEE Trans. Intell. Transp. Syst. **7**(1), 124–132 (2006)
10. Anacleto, O., Queen, C., Albers, C.J.: Multivariate forecasting of road traffic flows in the presence of heteroscedasticity and measurement errors. J. Roy. Stat. Soc. Ser. C (Appl. Stat.) **62**(2), 251–270 (2013)
11. LeCun, Y., Bengio, Y., Hinton, G.: Deep learning. Nature **521**(7553), 436 (2015)
12. Krizhevsky, A., Sutskever, I., Hinton, G.E.: Imagenet classification with deep convolutional neural networks. In: Advances in Neural Information Processing Systems, pp. 1097–1105 (2012)
13. Larochelle, H., Bengio, Y., Louradour, J., Lamblin, P.: Exploring strategies for training deep neural networks. J. Mach. Learn. Res. **10**(Jan), 1–40 (2009)
14. Guo, S., Lin, Y., Feng, N., Song, C., Wan, H.: Attention based spatial-temporal graph convolutional networks for traffic flow forecasting. In: Proceedings of the AAAI Conference on Artificial Intelligence, vol. 33, pp. 922–929 (2019)
15. Cui, Z., Henrickson, K., Ke, R., Wang, Y.: Traffic graph convolutional recurrent neural network: a deep learning framework for network-scale traffic learning and forecasting. IEEE Trans. Intell. Transp. Syst. **21**(11), 4883–4894 (2019)
16. Luo, Y., Cai, X., Zhang, Y., Xu, J., et al.: Multivariate time series imputation with generative adversarial networks. In: Advances in Neural Information Processing Systems, pp. 1596–1607 (2018)
17. Rangapuram, S.S., Seeger, M.W., Gasthaus, J., Stella, L., Wang, Y., Januschowski, T.: Deep state space models for time series forecasting. In: Advances in Neural Information Processing Systems, pp. 7785–7794 (2018)
18. Cao, W., Wang, D., Li, J., Zhou, H., Li, L., Li, Y.: Brits: bidirectional recurrent imputation for time series. In: Advances in Neural Information Processing Systems, pp. 6775–6785 (2018)
19. Lai, G., Chang, W.-C., Yang, Y., Liu, H.: Modeling long-and short-term temporal patterns with deep neural networks. In: The 41st International ACM SIGIR Conference on Research & Development in Information Retrieval, pp. 95–104 (2018)
20. Zhang, J., Zheng, Y., Qi, D., Li, R., Yi, X.: DNN-based prediction model for spatio-temporal data. In: Proceedings of the 24th ACM SIGSPATIAL International Conference on Advances in Geographic Information Systems, pp. 1–4 (2016)

21. Zhang, J., Zheng, Y., Qi, D.: Deep spatio-temporal residual networks for citywide crowd flows prediction. In: Thirty-First AAAI Conference on Artificial Intelligence (2017)
22. Bai, L., Yao, L., Kanhere, S.S., Yang, Z., Chu, J., Wang, X.: Passenger demand forecasting with multi-task convolutional recurrent neural networks. In: Yang, Q., Zhou, Z.-H., Gong, Z., Zhang, M.-L., Huang, S.-J. (eds.) PAKDD 2019. LNCS (LNAI), vol. 11440, pp. 29–42. Springer, Cham (2019). https://doi.org/10.1007/978-3-030-16145-3_3
23. Yao, H., et al.: Deep multi-view spatial-temporal network for taxi demand prediction. In: Thirty-Second AAAI Conference on Artificial Intelligence (2018)
24. Defferrard, M., Bresson, X., Vandergheynst, P.: Convolutional neural networks on graphs with fast localized spectral filtering. In: Advances in Neural Information Processing Systems, pp. 3844–3852 (2016)
25. Kipf, T.N., Welling, M.: Semi-supervised classification with graph convolutional networks. arXiv preprint arXiv:1609.02907 (2016)
26. Chen, C., et al.: Gated residual recurrent graph neural networks for traffic prediction. In: Proceedings of the AAAI Conference on Artificial Intelligence, vol. 33, pp. 485–492 (2019)
27. Li, Y., Yu, R., Shahabi, C., Liu, Y.: Diffusion convolutional recurrent neural networks: data-driven traffic forecasting. In: Proceedings of the International Conference on Learning Representations (2018)
28. Song, C., Lin, Y., Guo, S., Wan, H.: Spatial-temporal sychronous graph convolutional networks: a new framework for spatial-temporal network data forecasting (2020). https://github.com/wanhuaiyu/STSGCN/blob/master/paper/AAAI2020-STSGCN.pdf
29. Wu, Z., Pan, S., Long, G., Jiang, J., Zhang, C.: Graph wavenet for deep spatial-temporal graph modeling. In: Proceedings of the 28th International Joint Conference on Artificial Intelligence, pp. 1907–1913. AAAI Press (2019)
30. Chen, W., Chen, L., Xie, Y., Cao, W., Gao, Y., Feng, X.: Multirange attentive bicomponent graph convolutional network for traffic forecasting. In: Proceedings of the AAAI Conference on Artificial Intelligence (2020)
31. Diao, Z., Wang, X., Zhang, D., Liu, Y., Xie, K., He, S.: Dynamic spatial-temporal graph convolutional neural networks for traffic forecasting. In: Proceedings of the AAAI Conference on Artificial Intelligence, vol. 33, pp. 890–897 (2019)
32. Ding, W., et al.: An ensemble-learning method for potential traffic hotspots detection on heterogeneous spatio-temporal data in highway domain. J. Cloud Comput. Adv. Syst. Appl. **9**, 1–11 (2020)
33. Ding, W., Zhao, Z.: DS-harmonizer: a harmonization service on spatiotemporal data stream in edge computing environment. Wirel. Commun. Mob. Comput. **2018**, Article ID 9354273, 12 p (2018). https://doi.org/10.1155/2018/9354273
34. Ding, W., Zou, J., Zhao, Z.: A multidimensional service template for data analysis in highway domain. Int. J. Internet Manuf. Serv. **7**(4), 290 (2020)
35. Zhou, J., Ding, W.: An evolutionary service solution for spatio-temporal data analysis in highway domain. Int. J. Intell. Internet Things Comput. **1**(1), 43–52 (2019)
36. Kip, F.T.N., Welling, M.: Semi-Supervised Classification with Graph Convolutional Networks (2016)
37. Zhou, J., Ding, W., Zhao, Z., Li, H.: SMART: a service-oriented statistical analysis framework on spatio-temporal big data (short paper). In: Wang, X., Gao, H., Iqbal, M., Min, G. (eds.) CollaborateCom 2019. LNICSSITE, vol. 292, pp. 91–100. Springer, Cham (2019). https://doi.org/10.1007/978-3-030-30146-0_7

38. Wang, Z., Ding, W., Wang, H.: A hybrid deep learning approach for traffic flow prediction in highway domain. In: Gao, H., Wang, X., Iqbal, M., Yin, Y., Yin, J., Gu, N. (eds.) CollaborateCom 2020. LNICSSITE, vol. 350, pp. 253–267. Springer, Cham (2021). https://doi.org/10.1007/978-3-030-67540-0_15
39. Ding, W., Wang, Z., Zhao, Z.: A platform service for passenger volume analysis on massive smart card data in public transportation domain. In: Wang, X., Gao, H., Iqbal, M., Min, G. (eds.) CollaborateCom 2019. LNICSSITE, vol. 292, pp. 681–697. Springer, Cham (2019). https://doi.org/10.1007/978-3-030-30146-0_46
40. Ding, W., Zhao, Z., Li, H., Cao, Y., Xu, Y.: A passenger flow analysis method through ride behaviors on massive smart card data. In: Romdhani, I., Shu, L., Takahiro, H., Zhou, Z., Gordon, T., Zeng, D. (eds.) CollaborateCom 2017. LNICSSITE, vol. 252, pp. 374–382. Springer, Cham (2018). https://doi.org/10.1007/978-3-030-00916-8_35

How are You Affected? A Structural Graph Neural Network Model Predicting Individual Social Influence Status

Jiajie Du[1] and Li Pan[1,2(✉)]

[1] School of Electronic Information and Electrical Engineering,
Shanghai Jiao Tong University, Shanghai, China
panli@sjtu.edu.cn
[2] National Engineering Laboratory for Information Content Analysis Technology,
Shanghai, China

Abstract. Human's daily life is now inextricably bound with online social networks like Weibo and Twitter, where user's opinions and emotions are delivered and get influenced by each other frequently. Therefore, predicting and understanding such phenomenon of social influence, especially on individuals, becomes crucial for applications like recommendation and advertising. Although recent studies achieve some predictions on individual social influence status (active or inactive), the complexity and diversity of the social structures have not been well solved, and such works also lack a deep understanding of the influence mechanism itself like how individuals are affected. Therefore, a structural graph neural network model (SGN) is proposed to learn the diverse relationships and quantify the propagated influence between users. The SGN model is consists of two special representation modules and some global layers. The two representation modules are based on two major social network structures: friendship structure and influence propagation structure. In the modules, the well-developed graph neural networks, GCN (Graph Convolutional Network) and GAT (Graph Attention Networks), are respectively applied to capture spatial correlations. Besides, the global attention mechanism then helps to quantify the relationships between influencers and influencees. Finally, experiments on two real-world social networks show that the proposed SGN not only outperforms other baselines on prediction metrics, but is also able to reveal the intermediate neighbors who affect the target most.

Keywords: Social influence status · Structure · Graph neural network

1 Introduction

Nowadays, social networks have aroused close and profound interactions between users than ever before. Such a phenomenon that a user's emotions or behaviors are affected by others is referred to as social influence. As social influence becomes ubiquitous and widespread among social networks, the related

H. Gao and X. Wang (Eds.): CollaborateCom 2021, LNICST 407, pp. 401–415, 2021.
https://doi.org/10.1007/978-3-030-92638-0_24

researches cover many areas including political election [1], advertising [9], public sentiment [11], academic collaboration [15] and so on. Therefore, a deep understanding towards the underlying dynamics mechanisms of social influence propagation is extremely valuable.

Previously, extensive works about social influence mainly aim to predict some global patterns like cascade size or the influence dynamics of the whole society [10,21,25]. But the differences between individuals and their personal information are ignored before, which turn out to be extremely important then. So recently, there are more user-level influence prediction works, Qiu et al. [24] achieve an automatic end-to-end approach to discover hidden signals and predict user's social influence actions (retweet). Tang et al. [26] take both friendship and temporal dynamics into consideration, and predict several categories of user behaviors jointly. However, these works do not focus a lot on the diversity and complexity of social influence structure itself, thus makes a need for us to analyze the structures and find some classic structural classifications.

Among the user-level prediction tasks of social influence, a core problem is: Given the local structure and some prior characteristic features of a user, how to predict his social influence status, according to [24]. In fact, due to complex user relationships in social networks [5], the cause of the influence is also diverse. As shown in Fig. 1, two typical causes from relationships and structures are friendship and historic influence propagation. Naturally, your friends in the real world also affect you on social platforms, and the netizens whom you interacted with before may also continue influencing you in retweets, comments or likes. Based on this division of the complex social structure, our exact aim is to predict the target u's influence status, which equals to identify whether he will be active about some social contents in the next timestamp.

Besides, the importance of neighbors in social networks is also our concern, as it could enhance our understanding of social influence. Tang et al. [26] used to quantify different importance between friends. But in our problem, the social structures contain not only friends but also some netizens from previous influence propagation records. And we use *neighbors* to refer to all these users who might have a relationship with the target. Then, a method is proposed to quantify the importance of different structures first and all the neighbors next. In this way, some vital neighbors would finally be identified to help us understand who is exactly influencing the targets.

To solve this user-level problem of prediction and identification, also inspired by the rapid development of graph neural networks, we propose an end-to-end individual social influence status prediction framework called SGN (structural graph neural network). Structural features are mined first based on the two structures mentioned above, and the predictions are accomplished next by using the features, finally, quantitative indicators of importance for structures and all the neighbors are calculated, making it reliable to figure out who affects the target's social influence status most. In particular, the proposed SGN contains: a) a friendship interacting module, b) an influence propagating module, c) global attention mechanism, d) outputs. The friendship interacting module captures

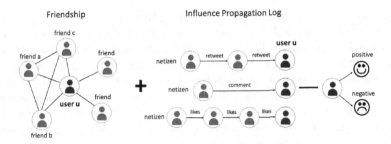

Fig. 1. Two typical relationships and their structures in social network: friendship and historic influence propagation. Friendship refers to the users who are friends in real-world, influence propagation refers to the netizens between whom some interactions have happened online, the interactions include retweets, comments, likes and so on. And the individual social influence status (positive or negative) is always decided by these two structures.

correlations between friends powered by attentioned-GCN, while the influence propagation module chooses multi-head graph attention network (GAT), as GAT is more suitable to the directional and dynamic influence propagation structure [28]. The global attention mechanism is in order to reveal the importance of different structures and aggregate the local attention indicators from the above two modules. Experiments conducted on two real-world social network datasets - Twitter and Weibo demonstrate that the proposed SGN not only outperforms the baselines on individual social influence status prediction, but also helps us identify the neighbors of a target who affect him most. To sum up, our contributions are:

- We present a study about the complexity and diversity of social influence structures and give a typical division: friendship and influence propagation.
- We propose an end-to-end user-level framework SGN, which compute the representation of each structure, predict the individual influence status, and figure out the topk important neighbors.
- Experiments conducted on two real-world datasets indicate that the proposed SGN not only outperform some baselines in prediction task, but also in neighbor importance identification task.

2 Related Work

2.1 Social Influence

Current social influence studies mainly aim to predict global patterns, cascade size is one of the major measurable indicators of social influence [11,34], and influence Maximization is another well-known problem, which David et al. [12] first solve it with famous independent cascade and linear threshold models.

Recently, there have been some efforts to solve these problems using deep learning technologies, e.g., a RNN based cascade prediction model DeepCas [17], a adversarial graph embeddings approach for fair influence maximization [13]. Besides, another major part of studies focuses on the underlying dynamic mechanism of influence propagation, there have been several models trying to explain this mechanism using reinforced [25] or nonhomogeneous [16] poisson processes, neural popularity prediction [2], or heavy tails [20]. However, researches about individual social influence and the explanations are inadequate, although [24] proposed an automatic predictive model, the diversity and homophily of structure raised from [5] is not solved yet.

2.2   Graph Neural Networks

Recently, graph convolutional network (GCN) [14] model and its variants have been widely studied and applied in many areas. GCN simplified from [14] aggregate the node features from their one-hop neighbors, Graph attention network (GAT) [28] introduces attention mechanism and solve the directional graph. GraphSAGE [7] aggregate features in neighborhood with mean/max/LSTM pooling. Graph neural networks are thus widely used in structural representation [30]. Furthermore, combined with LSTM or attention mechanism, these models are now applied in different areas such as disease-gene association identification [8], Traffic Forecasting [32], regional economy prediction [31] and so on.

Based on these contributions of fundamental models, graph neural networks now get evolved in some more specific and complicated areas. The Dynamic Graph Learning is one of the rising patterns [6,18,22], which use dynamic graph solve some time series prediction problems, as traditional GNN models only take static graphs as inputs. So [33] first uses the snapshots of graphs as inputs and demonstrates a ST-GCN model to take time as a dimension in previous CNN layers, and [27] combines the classic neighborhood embedding propagation with innovative self-propagation process in node aggregations, and [6] raised a new sampling method based on time series knowledge. Another interests is in solving some more complicated structures and using a deep model [3,19,23], like [3] introduces a new Generalized PageRank (GPR) GNN architecture to adaptively optimize node feature and topological information extraction and [19] proposes a new supplementary framework (CopulaGNN) which utilizes both representational and correlational information better.

3   Preliminaries

In this section, we define some important notations and problems. First, the *social networks* is a large-scale graph $G_{social} = (V, E)$ where V represents all the users and $E \subseteq V \times V$ could represent all kinds of the relationships between users. For a specific user u, if there is an undirected edge between him and another user v, they are friends to each other, if there is a directed edge from

u to v, it denotes u may retweet from, comment on or likes v, such directed relationship is defined as *social influence propagation*. For example, if u retweets from v, u also receives social influence from v. Besides, as mentioned in Section I, compared with some global information in the large-scale social network, we mainly focus on individual social influence status.

Definition 1. *Social Influence Status of a exact user u at timestamp t is defined as a binary status $s_t^u : \{0, 1\}$, where $s_t^u = 1$ indicates that user u is influenced to be active on timestamp t. Active users may have some actions such as retweet, comment or likes in Twitter. But if u is inactive and has no action, $s_t^u = 0$.*

Problem 1. Given the defination of social influence status, the problem of **predicting individual social influence status** is defined as: for a user u, we aim to compute the possibility of his influence status after a time interval Δt based on his current status s_t^u and his related social network subgraph G^u :

$$P\left(s_{t+\Delta t}^u \mid s_t^u, G^u\right).$$

Due to the diverse and complex relationships in social networks, We divide the structure into two major categories.

Definition 2. *Friendship Structure Graph G_f^u involves target user and his friends, and the edges indicate friendship or following relationship.*

Definition 3. *Propagation Structure Graph G_p^u is another major structure, which records the propagated users as nodes and retweeting process as directed edges.*

More concretely, given the user related social graph G_t^u, it is firstly divided into friendship structure graph G_f^u and influence propagation structure graph G_p^u, which denote friends and retweeting relationship respectively. The friendship structure graph is a triplet $G_f^u = \left\{V_f^u, E_f^u, H_f^u\right\}$, where $V_f^u = \{u \cup v \mid d(u, v) \leq 2\}$ consist of target user u and his two-hop friends. E_f^u is a set of edges denoting friendship relationship. $H_f^u \in \mathbb{R}^{n*h}$ is the characteristic feature matrix where each vector of h dimensions represents some basic information of a user. Similarly, in the propagation structure $G_p^u = \{V_p^u, E_p^u, H_p^u\}$, V_p^u denotes the users in influence propagation routines, the set of directed edges E_p^u represents the propagation paths, e.g., retweet, H_p^u demonstrates characteristic features of involved users in this structure.

Through the friendship and influence propagation structures, **the possibility of prediction** could be modified as:

$$P\left(s_{t+\Delta t}^u \mid s_t^u, G_{f,t}^u, G_{p,t}^u\right) \tag{1}$$

However, only predicting social influence status is inadequate for understanding propagation mechanism, thus we introduce the important intermediate neighbors identity: which is identifying the intermediate users who affect target user most.

Problem 2. (**Important Neighbors Identity**) For a target user u, given his social information G_t^u and all of his neighbors in both structures, compute importance indicators of each person I_u, and identify the top k important neighbors who make most difference on the future influence status of target user u.

4   Our Model: SGN

In this section, we will introduce our proposed model SGN for individual social influence prediction, the overall framework of SGN is shown in Fig. 2.

First in our proposed SGN, as mentioned before, to simplify the diversity and complexity of social network structure, we divide it into two structures: friendship structure and propagation structure, representing two major relationships between users respectively. Then inspired by the well-known graph neural network, two structural modules a) and b) are established taking the graphs of friendship and propagation structure as exact inputs and compute the related representations respectively. In the friendship interacting module, we take the different importance of friends into consideration and aggregate the impacts in the locality of target user u through attentioned-GCN. Meanwhile, the influence propagation module computes the representation by multi-head GAT which is more suitable to the dynamic and directional propagation graphs. Then, global attention c) is attached to learn the different importance of two modules and structures. Finally, the comprehensive attention mechanism through the framework help to predict the individual's social influence status and identify the intermediate users who affect the target most d). The details will be discussed in the following text.

4.1   Friendship Interacting Module

For the friendship interacting module, inspired by the rapidly developed graph convolutional networks where plenty of works have been done in graph representation [14,28,29], we choose the common GCN [14] and an attached neighbor attention mechanism [26] to learn structural information, compute representations, and finally figure out user's dependencies.

As shown in the top-left of Fig. 2, for each input of friendship structure graph G_f^u, GCN represents each node into its embedding vector. Concretely, GCN model is consist of several convolutional layers, and the node embedding matrix $H^{(l)}$ get updated using its structural information on each layer as:

$$H^{(l+1)} = \text{ReLU}\left(\widetilde{D_f}^{-\frac{1}{2}}\widetilde{A_f}\widetilde{D_f}^{-\frac{1}{2}}H^{(l)}W^{(l)}\right)$$
$$\widetilde{A_f} = A_f + I_f \tag{2}$$

where $W^{(l)}$ is a parameter matrix of each layer, *ReLU* is a nonlinear activation function. $H^{(l)} \in \mathbb{R}^{n*f^{(l)}}$ is the embedding matrix, where n is the number of nodes, $f^{(l)}$ denotes the dimensions of embedding vector on each layer, specially,

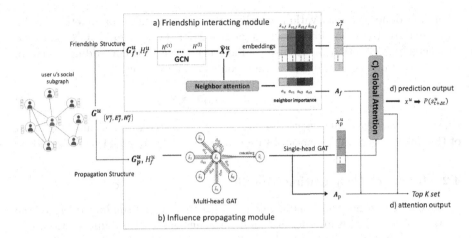

Fig. 2. The framework of Structural Graph Neural Network Model (SGN): each user's social subgraph G^u is framework input, and the exact inputs of each module are: for example, friendship subgraph G^u_f and the feature matrix H^u_f. The final outputs are the prediction possibility of status $P(s^u_{t+\Delta t})$ and the topk important neighbors set. For details, the SGN framework contains: a) a friendship interacting module which captures friendship structural embedding matrix $\hat{X}^u_f$ and output the embedding $\hat{x}_{u,f}$ of target u from GCN layers. Besides, neighbor attentions A^f are computed to demonstrate the importance of friends. b) an influence propagating module which uses multi-head GAT to get the attention matrix A^p, indicating how much different neighbors influence the target user u, the module also outputs an embedding $\hat{x}_{u,p}$. c) the global attention mechanism indicates the importance of two structures and computes the comprehensive embedding x^u. d) outputs.

$H^{(0)}$ is the characteristic feature matrix H^u_f of friendship structure G^u_f. Besides, $\widetilde{A}_f$ is the Laplaician matrix of graph G^u_f, where A_f and I_f denotes adjacency and degree matrix respectively. The final embedding matrix is $\hat{X}^u_f$ which contains the representations of each user in friendship structure $(\hat{x}_{u,f}, \hat{x}_{v_1,f}, ..., \hat{x}_{v_{n-1},f})$.

However, an obvious disadvantage of common GCN is that the information aggregation during convolution is equal and the differences between friends are ignored. But according to [26], 80% of users tend to contact with 20% of their friends frequently, which makes a need to quantify the exact impact from different friends to the target user on his individual influence status. Thus, we introduce the neighbor attentions mechanism, which, for each pair of friends, an attention factor is computed to indicate the clossness and importance of the friendship. For each friend $v \in N(u)$, the relative attention factor a_v is:

$$a_v = \frac{\exp\left(\phi\left(W\hat{x}_{v,f}\right)\right)}{\sum_{v\in N(u)}\left(\exp\left(\phi\left(W\hat{x}_{v,f}\right)\right)\right)} \tag{3}$$

where $\phi()$ denotes an activation function, W is the attention parameter matrix, $\hat{x}_{v,f}$ refers to the embedding vectors gained from the previous GCN. Through this neighbor attention mechanism, an averaged weighted embedding vector of target based on structural information could be denoted as:

$$x_f^u = \hat{x}_{u,f} \oplus \Sigma_{v \in N(u)} a_v * \hat{x}_{v,f} \tag{4}$$

where $\oplus$ indicates an aggregate operation, e.g., concatenation. Meanwhile, A set of the quantitative importance of target user's friends A_f could be collected.

4.2 Influence Propagating Module

As mentioned in Section I, influence propagation routine (mainly refers to the retweeting routines) is another crucial component of structural information. But the common GCN are not suitable enough as propagation data is often directed, dynamic and random. Besides, in this structure, intermediate users from higher-hop (not only one-hop neighbors) could have impact on the individual influence status of the target user. Therefore, we apply the state-of-the-art algorithm GAT on the propagation graph G_p^u. The details are shown in the bottom-left of Fig. 2. In fact, a main idea of GAT is to compute an attention coefficient between all the linked pair of nodes, thus for each node v_i, his attention $a_{i,j}$ to his propagation target v_j is:

$$a_{i,j} = \frac{\exp\left(\text{LeakyReLU}\left(a^T \left[Wh_i \| Wh_j\right]\right)\right)}{\sum_{v_j \in N(v_i)} \exp\left(\text{LeakyReLU}\left(a^T \left[Wh_i \| Wh_j\right]\right)\right)} \tag{5}$$

where $\|$ denotes concatenating operation between vectors, a^T and W are parameter vector and matrix, LeakyReLU is the activation function referred to [28]. Then, based on this attention martix $A_p = [a_{i,j}]_{n*n}$ and input of the characteristic feature matrix $H \in \mathbb{R}^{n*f}$ of propagation structure, the embedding matrix $\hat{H} \in \mathbb{R}^{n*f'}$ should be:

$$\hat{H} = \text{ReLU}\left(A_p H W'\right) \tag{6}$$

where $W' \in \mathbb{R}^{f*f'}$ is the embedding parameter matrix. To strengthen this process, we actually use the suggested multi-head GAT [28] which makes a parallel computation on K categories of attentions. For the set of parameters matrix $W' = \{W_1', W_2', \ldots W_K'\}$ and attention matrix $A_p = \{A_1, A_2, \ldots, A_K\}$, the output embedding matrix $\hat{H}$ is concatenated as:

$$\hat{H} = \text{ReLU}\left(A_1 H W_1' \| A_2 H W_2' \| \ldots \| A_K H W_K'\right) \tag{7}$$

In addition, as shown in bottom-right of Fig. 2, compared with the friendship interacting module, we further introduce another single-head GAT (which has only one kind of attention) as:

$$H = \text{ReLU}\left(A_{\text{out}} \hat{H} W_{\text{out}}'\right) \tag{8}$$

to obtain a same-dimentional embedding vector of target user x_p^u and the attention matrix A_{out}. As the attention matrix A_{out} only compute impact between direct neighbors, we use a breadth first search (bfs) algorithm to compute a similar set of quantitative importance A_p, which indicates the importance of all the nodes in propagation structure towards target user u.

4.3 Global Attention and Output

Given the embedding vector from friendship structure x_f^u and from propagation structure x_p^u. A global attention mechanism is introduced to differ the importance of the two structures. Take the attention coefficient of friendship structure a_f as an example:

$$a_f = \frac{\exp\left(W x_f^u\right)}{\exp\left(W x_p^u\right) + \exp\left(W x_f^u\right)} \tag{9}$$

and the structural representation x^u is:

$$x^u = a_f \cdot x_f^u + a_p \cdot x_p^u \tag{10}$$

Then, after a neural layer and softmax function, the model will finally output a two-dimentioned vector represent whether the user's individual social influence is active or not. The negative log-likelihood loss function will be optimized next.

$$\text{Loss} = -\sum \log \left(P\left(s_{t+\Delta t}^u \mid s_t^u, G_{f,t}^u, G_{p,t}^u\right)\right) \tag{11}$$

Besides, in order to identify the intermediate users who have most impact on target individual influence status, plenty of related attentions are learned in either module or globally. Based on these quantitative users attention set A_f, A_g and the relative global attention coefficient a_f and a_g, we could first obtain the final set of impact factors from target's friends in friendship structure I_f, and the set of impact factors from all the users who participate the influence propagation in propagation structure I_p. Then through concatenating and sort operation, we can final figure out the Top k important intermediate users who affect target user's individual social influence most as shown below:

$$\text{Top } K \left(\text{sorted}\left(\{I_f \mid I_f = a_f * A_f\} \oplus \{I_p \mid I_p = a_p * A_p\}\right)\right) \tag{12}$$

5 Experiment

5.1 Experiment Settings

Dataset. We use two real-world social network datasets to evaluate the proposed SGN framework on user-level social status prediction – Twitter and Weibo.

- **Twitter** [4] The Twitter dataset records the spreading processes on Twitter before, during, and after the announcement of the discovery of a new particle with the features of the elusive Higgs boson on 4th July 2012. The friendship and propagation structure refer to its follower network and retweet network respectively.
- **Weibo** Weibo is a famous large-scale Chinese microblogging network. The dataset here is from [34] and contains the directed following relationship and their retweets behaviour between 1,776,950 users from 28th July 2012 to 29th October 2012.

Data Preprocess: Following the practice in existing work [4,24], The users who are influenced in an extended period T_1 and be active in the next rather short T_2 are considered as positive samples, while the inactive ones are negative. Meanwhile, because of the imbalance in users' neighbors, we rebuilt the friendship and propagation structure with RWR(random walk with restart)

Baselines. We validate the effectiveness of SGN by comparison with some basic and state-of-the-art baselines as follow:

- **Logistic Regression (LR)** We use LR as a classic classification model. Some of the user's characteristics features are used as the input of the model which includes: Coreness, Pagerank, Hub score and authority score, Eigenvector Centrality, Clustering Coefficient, The number/ratio of active neighbors and Density of subnetwork induced by active neighbors.
- **Support Vector Machine (SVM)** SVM with linear kernel is another classic supervised classification model. And the same features as LR are the input of SVM.
- **Deepinf** [24] Deepinf is now the state-of-the-art model on user-level social influence prediction problems. Firstly, It maps each user to her D-dimensional representation through Deepwalk, then concatenates the representation and the characteristics features as an input of GCN/GAT layers, finally predicts the user's social influence status.
- **FATE** [26] FATE can predict different categories of behaviour of a user by modeling the friendship and user actions through an attentioned GCN and temporal dynamic through tLSTM. Here, we only predict one behaviour(retweet) and set the timestamp of tLSTM as 1.

Parameter Setting. First, the restart probability in random walk is set as 0.8, and the size of either structure graph is 50. Next, in SGN Framework, we trained two GCN layers with 32/8 hidden units, and two multi-head GAT layers consist of 8/1 attention heads and 16/16 hidden units. For the global attention mechanism, the hidden parameter dimension is 16 and then output 2 units for binary prediction. For detail, we adopted elu as the nonlinearity function and trained adam optimizer with learning rate 0.005, weight decay 1e-4, and dropout rate 0.2. In addition, We use 80%, 10%, 10% of the dataset for training, validation and test, respectively.

Table 1. Prediction performance between baselines on Twitter and Weibo (%)

Dataset	Module	Accuracy	Precision	Recall	F1-score
Twitter	LR	77.33	72.92	53.41	61.66
	SVM	78.15	76.48	54.49	63.64
	DeepInf	84.26	85.00	63.93	72.97
	FATE	83.95	85.30	63.27	72.67
	SGN	**85.78**	**89.36**	**65.90**	**75.86**
Weibo	LR	69.23	62.92	42.25	50.55
	SVM	71.34	55.24	44.14	49.07
	DeepInf	73.33	85.40	48.12	61.55
	FATE	73.73	88.68	48.61	62.80
	SGN	**74.86**	**94.84**	**49.85**	**65.35**

5.2 Experiment Result of Prediction Performances

The prediction performances between all the baselines on Twitter and Weibo datasets are compared in Table 1. The evaluation metrics are accuracy, precision, recall and F1-score. We have the following observations:

Our proposed model SGN achieves the best performance on all datasets and different evaluation metrics. Especially when compared with LR and SVM, SGN (Twitter) achieves about 10% improvement on AUC and 20% improvement on F1-score.

And it's obvious that graph neural networks related models Deepinf, FATE and SGN achieve significantly better performance compared with 2 classic ML models. It indicates that the structural features learned from GNN can be beneficial to user-level social influence status prediction. In addition, the better performances of SGN among GNN models also indicate the effectiveness of our division of structural graph from both friendship and influence propagation.

What's more, we can witness the significant improvement of GNN related models are mainly from Precision, which indicates that the structural features improve the classification ability especially on positive samples thus can identify users who will be more likely affected active in the future. It reveals the promoting effects of structural information and implies the existence of some important users either from friendship structure or propagation structure who effect the target user to be active. By contrast, the relatively poor correlation between negative samples and structural information may demonstrate the rather more complicated reasons for the formulation of negative attitudes. In fact, negative attitudes should not only come from the neighborhoods, but also be affected by various objective factors.

5.3 Attention Analysis

Global Attention. We compute the global attention of friendship and propagation structure in order to investigate their effectiveness and different importance. The Fig. 3 shows the attention values of propagation structure are higher than

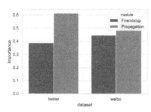
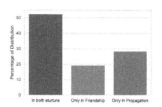

Fig. 3. The global attention importance between Friendship interacting module and Influence propagating module

Fig. 4. Distribution of Top 10 important intermediate neighbors who affect target user most

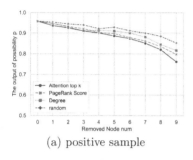
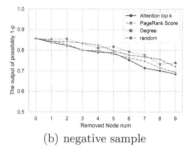

(a) positive sample

(b) negative sample

Fig. 5. The prediction possibility p after removing some nodes from original graph according to their importance computed by 4 methods

friendship after 20 training epochs. This implies that information in propagation structure should be more important, and incorporation with Table 1, positive users are affected by those from their influence propagation routines more.

User Attention. For each user, Their top 10 most important users are computed from the learned user attention mechanism in SGN framework. According to their belonging structure: friendship only, propagation only, or both, the distribution was shown in Fig. 4. The most important users are mainly from both structures, and again, propagation structure turns to be more crucial.

Further, in order to quantify the effectiveness of the attention mechanism and the top 10 most important users, we chose a positive and negative sample and output their predicted possibilities after removing part of his neighbors according to the top 10 list. By contrast, other three groups of nodes are established based on random, degree and PageRank score. For each group, neighbor nodes would be successively removed from the original graph according to its rank, then the model will output the new possibilities of the target user's status. As shown in Fig. 5, rather in positive or negative sample, prediction possibility p declines more when removing the users in our attention top10 list, which indicates the significant impact in target user's neighborhood structure. For details in the positive sample as an example, first, the head of each group which is removed in prior refers to important intermediate users selected by each method, thus the differences between random and others prove the effectiveness of this strategy; besides, our SGN attention even outperforms degree and pagerank which are commonly used in nodes importance ranking, this indicates the effectiveness of our neighbor attentions. Meanwhile, the decline range and trend of possibility p between two samples also imply that positive users suffer from their important intermediate neighbors more.

6 Conclusion

In this paper, we study the problem of individual social influence status prediction on diverse structures, and first introduce a division of the structural information which contains friendship and propagation structure respectively. Next, we propose an end-to-end prediction model SGN to learn representations from the two structures through attentioned-GCN and multi-head GAT. Besides, global and local attention mechanisms help to complete the predictions and to identify the most important intermediate neighbors who affect the target most. Experiments are conducted based on two real-world large-scale datasets, and the proposed SGN is compared with 4 baselines. The result shows SGN outperforms both the classic ml models and some current GNN models. Meanwhile, we validate the importance of the topk neighbors set by comparing our neighbor attention mechanism in SGN with some classic node ranking algorithms like degree and pagerank. What's more, those intermediate neighbors seem to be more important in positive samples, which means they are more likely to make target users active. For some future work, we would like to come up with some innovate graph encoders to substitute our model stack here, and also be able to get better representations of the complex social interaction graphs Besides, we'd also like to imply time as another important dimension in social networks and also the social influence prediction problems.

Acknowledgment. This work is supported by National Key Research and Development Plan in China (2018YFC0830500), and by National Natural Science Foundation of China (U1636105).

References

1. Allcott, H., Gentzkow, M.: Social media and fake news in the 2016 election. Social Science Electronic Publishing (2017)
2. Chen, G., Kong, Q., Xu, N., Mao, W.: NPP: a neural popularity prediction model for social media content. Neurocomputing **333**, 221–230 (2019)
3. Chien, E., Peng, J., Li, P., Milenkovic, O.: Adaptive universal generalized pagerank graph neural network. In: International Conference on Learning Representations (2021). https://openreview.net/forum?id=n6jl7fLxrP

4. De Domenico, M., Lima, A., Mougel, P., Musolesi, M.: The anatomy of a scientific rumor. Sci. Rep. **3**, 2980 (2013)
5. Dong, Y., Johnson, R.A., Xu, J., Chawla, N.V.: Structural diversity and homophily: a study across more than one hundred big networks. In: Proceedings of the 23rd ACM SIGKDD International Conference on Knowledge Discovery and Data Mining, pp. 807–816 (2017)
6. Goyal, P., Chhetri, S.R., Canedo, A.: dyngraph2vec: capturing network dynamics using dynamic graph representation learning. Knowl.-Based Syst. **187**, 104816 (2020)
7. Hamilton, W., Ying, Z., Leskovec, J.: Inductive representation learning on large graphs. In: Advances in Neural Information Processing Systems, pp. 1024–1034 (2017)
8. Han, P., et al.: GCN-MF: disease-gene association identification by graph convolutional networks and matrix factorization. In: Proceedings of the 25th ACM SIGKDD International Conference on Knowledge Discovery & Data Mining, pp. 705–713 (2019)
9. Hennig-Thurau, T., Wiertz, C., Feldhaus, F.: Does twitter matter? The impact of microblogging word of mouth on consumers' adoption of new movies. J. Acad. Mark. Sci. **43**(3), 375–394 (2015)
10. Hoang, T.B.N., Mothe, J.: Predicting information diffusion on twitter - analysis of predictive features. J. Comput. Sci. **28**(Sep), 257–264 (2018)
11. Jie, T., Sun, J., Chi, W., Zi, Y.: Social influence analysis in large-scale networks. In: ACM SIGKDD International Conference on Knowledge Discovery & Data Mining (2009)
12. Kempe, D., Kleinberg, J., Tardos, É.: Maximizing the spread of influence through a social network. In: Proceedings of the Ninth ACM SIGKDD International Conference on Knowledge Discovery and Data Mining, pp. 137–146 (2003)
13. Khajehnejad, M., Rezaei, A.A., Babaei, M., Hoffmann, J., Jalili, M., Weller, A.: Adversarial graph embeddings for fair influence maximization over social networks. arXiv preprint arXiv:2005.04074 (2020)
14. Kipf, T.N., Welling, M.: Semi-supervised classification with graph convolutional networks. In: ICLR (2017)
15. Kong, X., Shi, Y., Yu, S., Liu, J., Xia, F.: Academic social networks: modeling, analysis, mining and applications. J. Netw. Comput. Appl. **132**, 86–103 (2019)
16. Lee, C., Wilkinson, D.J.: A hierarchical model of nonhomogeneous poisson processes for twitter retweets. J. Am. Stat. Assoc. **115**(529), 1–15 (2020)
17. Li, C., Ma, J., Guo, X., Mei, Q.: Deepcas: an end-to-end predictor of information cascades. In: Proceedings of the 26th International Conference on World Wide Web, pp. 577–586 (2017)
18. Lu, Y., Wang, X., Shi, C., Yu, P.S., Ye, Y.: Temporal network embedding with micro-and macro-dynamics. In: Proceedings of the 28th ACM International Conference on Information and Knowledge Management, pp. 469–478 (2019)
19. Ma, J., Chang, B., Zhang, X., Mei, Q.: CopulaGNN: towards integrating representational and correlational roles of graphs in graph neural networks. In: International Conference on Learning Representations (2021). https://openreview.net/forum?id=XI-OJ5yyse
20. Mathews, P., Mitchell, L., Nguyen, G., Bean, N.: The nature and origin of heavy tails in retweet activity. In: Proceedings of the 26th International Conference on World Wide Web Companion, pp. 1493–1498 (2017)

21. Matsubara, Y., Sakurai, Y., Prakash, B.A., Li, L., Faloutsos, C.: Rise and fall patterns of information diffusion: model and implications. In: Proceedings of the 18th ACM SIGKDD International Conference on Knowledge Discovery and Data Mining, KDD 2012, pp. 6–14. Association for Computing Machinery, New York (2012). https://doi.org/10.1145/2339530.2339537
22. Pareja, A., et al.: Evolvegcn: evolving graph convolutional networks for dynamic graphs. In: Proceedings of the AAAI Conference on Artificial Intelligence, vol. 34, pp. 5363–5370 (2020)
23. Puny, O., Ben-Hamu, H., Lipman, Y.: Global attention improves graph networks generalization (2021). https://openreview.net/forum?id=H-BVtEaipej
24. Qiu, J., Tang, J., Ma, H., Dong, Y., Wang, K., Tang, J.: DeepInf: social influence prediction with deep learning. In: Proceedings of the 24th ACM SIGKDD International Conference on Knowledge Discovery amp; Data Mining, KDD 2018, pp. 2110–2119. Association for Computing Machinery, New York (2018). https://doi.org/10.1145/3219819.3220077
25. Shen, H., Wang, D., Song, C., Barabási, A.L.: Modeling and predicting popularity dynamics via reinforced poisson processes. In: Proceedings of the AAAI Conference on Artificial Intelligence, vol. 28 (2014)
26. Tang, X., Liu, Y., Shah, N., Shi, X., Mitra, P., Wang, S.: Knowing your fate: Friendship, action and temporal explanations for user engagement prediction on social apps. In: Proceedings of the 26th ACM SIGKDD International Conference on Knowledge Discovery & Data Mining, KDD 2020, pp. 2269–2279. Association for Computing Machinery, New York (2020). https://doi.org/10.1145/3394486.3403276
27. Trivedi, R., Farajtabar, M., Biswal, P., Zha, H.: DyRep: learning representations over dynamic graphs. In: International Conference on Learning Representations (2019)
28. Veličković, P., Cucurull, G., Casanova, A., Romero, A., Lio, P., Bengio, Y.: Graph attention networks. arXiv preprint arXiv:1710.10903 (2017)
29. Wang, X., Zhu, M., Bo, D., Cui, P., Shi, C., Pei, J.: AM-GCN: adaptive multi-channel graph convolutional networks. In: Proceedings of the 26th ACM SIGKDD International Conference on Knowledge Discovery & Data Mining, KDD 2020, pp. 1243–1253. Association for Computing Machinery, New York (2020). https://doi.org/10.1145/3394486.3403177
30. Xiong, H., Yan, J.: BTWalk: branching tree random walk for multi-order structured network embedding. IEEE Trans. Knowl. Data Eng. 1 (2020). https://doi.org/10.1109/TKDE.2020.3029061
31. Xu, F., Li, Y., Xu, S.: Attentional multi-graph convolutional network for regional economy prediction with open migration data. In: Proceedings of the 26th ACM SIGKDD International Conference on Knowledge Discovery & Data Mining, pp. 2225–2233 (2020)
32. Yu, B., Yin, H., Zhu, Z.: Spatio-temporal graph convolutional networks: a deep learning framework for traffic forecasting. In: Proceedings of the 27th International Joint Conference on Artificial Intelligence (IJCAI) (2018)
33. Yu, B., Yin, H., Zhu, Z.: Spatio-temporal graph convolutional networks: a deep learning framework for traffic forecasting. In: Proceedings of the 27th International Joint Conference on Artificial Intelligence, pp. 3634–3640 (2018)
34. Zhang, J., Liu, B., Tang, J., Chen, T., Li, J.: Social influence locality for modeling retweeting behaviors. In: IJCAI, vol. 13, pp. 2761–2767 (2013)

Multi-order Proximity Graph Structure Embedding

Wang Zhang[1,2], Lei Jiang[1], Huailiang Peng[1], Qiong Dai[1], and Xu Bai[1(✉)]

[1] Institute of Information Engineering, Chinese Academy of Sciences, Beijing, China
{zhangwang,jianglei,penghuailiang,daiqiong,baixu}@iie.ac.cn
[2] School of Cyber Security, University of Chinese Academy of Sciences,
Beijing, China

Abstract. Graph embedding methods convert the flexible graph structure into low-dimensional representations while maintaining the graph structure information. Most existing methods focus on learning low- or high-order graph information, and cause loss of information during the embedding process. We instead propose a new method that can learn low and high order graph information simultaneously. The method fuses structure-preserving model with random walk sampling, which learns multi-order graph structure information more efficiently. Our method also utilizes distance-based weighted negative samples to improve the representations learning. The experimental results indicate that our proposed method provides very competitive results on the node classification, node clustering and graph reconstruction tasks for four benchmark datasets, BlogCatalog, PPI, Wikipedia and email-Eu-core.

Keywords: Deep learning · Unsupervised learning · Graph embedding

1 Introduction

Graph structure widely exists in many scenarios of real world. For example, the connection between people in social networks, the interaction of proteins in organisms, and the communication between IP addresses in communication networks, etc. In the past few decades, many effective graph analysis methods have been proposed for many applications, such as node classification [2], node clustering [8], link prediction [14] and so on. Graph structure is very flexible and complex, many existing graph analytics methods may suffer the high computation and space cost, and graph embedding is an effective solution for the above problems [3]. Various graph embedding methods usually try to learn a vector representation for each node in the graph, thus it is easy to process these vectors using traditional analysis methods.

© ICST Institute for Computer Sciences, Social Informatics and Telecommunications Engineering 2021
Published by Springer Nature Switzerland AG 2021. All Rights Reserved
H. Gao and X. Wang (Eds.): CollaborateCom 2021, LNICST 407, pp. 416–431, 2021.
https://doi.org/10.1007/978-3-030-92638-0_25

Recently, there are many studies on learning representations from graph data. For example, DeepWalk model [19] treats nodes as words, random walk sequences as sentences, and embedded vectors through the skipgram model [16]. Node2vec [9] uses a biased random walk, which is considered as an improved DeepWalk model that combines DFS and BFS. Another famous model, SDNE [27], takes advantage of an autoencoder structure to optimize first and second order proximity. Although the above methods are very effective, there are still some disadvantages. DeepWalk tends to learn the context information of nodes but ignores the neighborhood information. Node2vec has been improved, but the above situation still exists. SDNE focuses on first and second order proximity but neglects higher order proximity. Thus, the methods might not learn multi-order graph structure information very efficiently. Figure 1 shows embedding examples of the same Karate club graph.

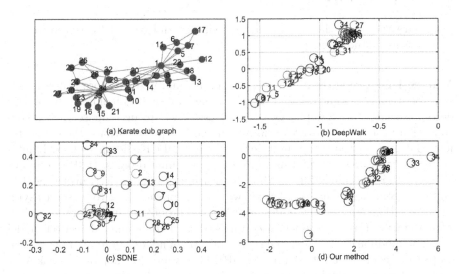

Fig. 1. Examples of three embedding methods on Karate club graph. It can be seen from the figure that the DeepWalk method effectively maintains the community structure, but ignores the low-order structure information within the community (e.g. node 2 and node 12 are very close). SDNE method ignores the community structure information, and the embedding representations are very scattered. Our method maintains not only community information, but also low-order structure.

To reduce loss of information in graph embedding, first, we introduce random walk sampling to structure-preserving model. Structure-preserving model can learn the low-order information of graph structure and generate embedding vectors containing the above information. Then, we sample the context of nodes in graph by random walk and force embedding vectors of nodes to learn their contextual information. Second, empirically, for a node, other nodes at different hop have different effects on it. Therefore, samples are weighted according to their distance from the starting node during negative sampling. Each node will stay away from the nodes that are relatively far away. The experimental results indicate the superiority of our proposed method. Our main contributions are listed as follows:

- We present a new method that fuses structure-preserving model with random walk sampling for learning multi-order graph structure information.
- We introduce distance-based weighted negative samples, which can improve the ability of learning representations.
- The proposed model is evaluated on four benchmark datasets and experimental results show that our method provides competitive results on the node classification, node clustering and graph reconstruction tasks.

2   Related Work

There are the researches on graph embedding, and we briefly introduce the representative studies here.

Matrix Decomposition. These methods use matrices to store the relationships between nodes and obtain the embedding representation of nodes by matrix decomposition. For example, GraRep [4] uses SVD to decompose each k-step transition probability matrix to obtain the node representations, then concatenates all these k-step representations and gets final embedding vectors. It integrates global structural information into the learning process. HOPE proposes a directed graph embedding method for learning asymmetric transitivity [17]. Different from other studies, it learns two vectors for each node to preserve asymmetric relationship between nodes. M-NMF [28] proposes a unified framework of representation learning model based on NMF and community detection model based on modularity, in which the representation of nodes can retain both microscopic and community structure. AROPE [32] is an arbitrary order proximity preserved graph embedding method. It is used to solve the problem that the existing methods can only learn fixed order proximity.

Random Walk. These methods convert graph to node sequences with graph properties by random walk sampling, then apply skipgram [16] or other model on the sampled sequences to get representations. DeepWalk [19] is one of the most famous work among them. It uses random walk to sample node path in the graph to capture co-occurrence information between nodes, and then apply skipgram model to learn the vector representation of nodes. Different from DeepWalk, Node2vec [9] uses a biased random walk with return parameter p and in-out parameter q, which combines DFS and BFS. To make full use of the auxiliary information in graph, TriDNR [18] uses information from three parties: graph structure, node content, and node labels to jointly learn node representations.

Deep Learning. Due to the superiority of deep learning methods, these models are adopted into the tasks of graph embedding. SDNE [27], take advantage of an autoencoder structure, that aims to minimize reconstruction errors between encoder and decoder, for optimizing first and second order proximity. It can preserve both the local and global graph structure effectively even though graph is very sparse. GCN [13] is a new neural network model designed for embedding graph data through local first-order approximation of spectral graph convolution. It can utilize information from graph structure and node features to learn node representations. GAT [26], a neural network framework that works on graph structured data, uses masked self-attentional layers to aggregate node neighborhood information to learn its representation. Many previous approaches are transductive, [10] proposed an inductive framework that can generalize to unseen nodes by aggregating local neighborhood information of a node.

Others. Line [23], optimize first and second order proximity by maximizing edge reconstruction probability through edge sampling. It can be extended to large-scale networks and suitable for directed, undirected, weighted graphs. Verse [24] method learns node representations that preserve the distributions of any selected similarity measure among nodes by optimizing Kullback-Leibler divergence from the given similarity distribution to embeddings. NodeSketch [29] proposes a computationally efficient graph embedding technique that can preserve the proximity of higher-order nodes through recursive sketching.

In general, most existing methods focus on learning low- or high-order graph information, and how to effectively learn multi-order graph information is still a valuable question. Inspired by previous work, we fuse structure-preserving model with random walk sampling, in which embeddings preserve low-level (first- and second-order) and high-level (community structure) graph information.

3 Proposed Method

3.1 Notation

We define a graph $G = (V, E)$, where V is the set of nodes and E is the set of edges. We use A to denote the adjacency matrix. For an unweighted graph, if there exists an edge from v_i to v_j, $A_{i,j}$ equals one, and $A_{i,j}$ equals zero otherwise. For a weighted graph, the value of $A_{i,j}$ is the weight of the edge between nodes i and j. $A_{i,:}$ represents the i-th row of the adjacency matrix, and $A_{:,j}$ stands for the j-th column of the adjacency matrix. Graph embedding aims to learn a mapping function $f : V \to Z \in \mathbb{R}^{N \times d}$ from nodes to the learning representations, where N is equal to the number of nodes, d is the specified number of dimensions of our embedding representations and $d << |V|$, Z is an embedding representation, and $\mathbf{z}_i$ is the embedding representation of node i. We define $N(u)$ as the neighborhood of node u. Let $N_{RW}(u)$ denote the context nodes of node u obtained by random walk sampling. $N_{neg}(u)$ is defined as the negative samples of node u.

3.2   Structure Preserving Model

We adopt the structure in SDNE [27], which can preserve low order graph structure effectively. Our main model is an autoencoder structure composed of an encoder and a decoder. The encoder consists of multiple fully connected layer and performs non-linear mapping. The input of k-th layer is defined as $\mathbf{x}_i^k$, and the output $\mathbf{y}_i^k$ is calculated as follows:

$$\mathbf{x}_i^0 = A_{:,i}, \quad \mathbf{x}_i^k = \mathbf{y}_i^{k-1}$$
$$\mathbf{y}_i^k = \mathbf{W}^k \mathbf{x}_i^k + \mathbf{b}^k, \quad k = 1, ..., K \tag{1}$$

The output of the encoder is $\mathbf{y}_i^K$, we take it as embedding representation $\mathbf{z}_i$ of the node i, and then restore it to the input of encoder through decoder. The calculation process of decoder is symmetric to encoder. Therefore, the autoencoder learns the second order proximity of graph by reducing the reconstruction loss. The reconstruction loss is defined as:

$$\mathcal{L}_{2nd} = \|(\hat{\mathbf{x}}_i - \mathbf{x}_i) \odot \mathbf{a}^i\|_2^2 \tag{2}$$

where $\hat{\mathbf{x}}_i$ is the output of decoder, $\mathbf{x}_i$ is equal to $A_{:,i}$, $\odot$ is the Hadamard product, and $\mathbf{a}_j^i = \beta$ if $A_{i,j} > 0$. The main function of the Hadamard product is to reconstruct the non-zero elements first. The loss of second order proximity guarantees that nodes with similar neighbors will be close to each other in embedding space.

The model also needs to learn first-order proximity, which means that if a pair of nodes i and j are connected, they should be close to each other. To preserve first-order proximity, a graph-based loss function is defined as:

$$\mathcal{L}_{1st} = -\frac{1}{|N(i)|} \sum_{j \in N(i)} log(\sigma(\mathbf{z}_i^\top \mathbf{z}_j)) \tag{3}$$

where σ is the sigmoid function ($\sigma(x) = \frac{1}{1+e^{-x}}$). The loss function of first order proximity also encourages nearby nodes to have similar representations in embedding space.

3.3   Random Walk Sampling

Although the structure-preserving model can effectively learn low-order graph structure information, it ignores high-order graph structure information. A graph can be represented as a set of information flows that contain community structure by random walk sampling [20]. We first randomly select a starting node, and uniformly sample a neighbor node of the last visited node until the maximum length is reached. The objective function of random walk sampling is as follows:

$$min_\Phi - logP(v_{i-\Delta}, ..., v_{i-1}, v_{i+1}, ..., v_{i+\Delta}|v_i)$$
$$= -log \prod_{-\Delta \leq j \leq \Delta} P(v_{i+j}|v_i)$$
$$= -log \prod_{-\Delta \leq j \leq \Delta} \frac{exp(\Phi^\top(v_{i+j})\Phi(v_i))}{\sum_{k=1}^{|V|} exp(\Phi^\top(v_k)\Phi(v_i))} \tag{4}$$

where the goal is to maximize the co-occurrence probability between nodes. However, due to softmax calculation is expensive, we do not use hierarchical softmax in DeepWalk, but use negative sampling. To preserve community proximity, loss function is defined as:

$$\mathcal{L}_{rw} = -\frac{1}{|N_{RW}(i)|} \sum_{j \in N_{RW}(i)} log(\sigma(\mathbf{z}_i^\top \mathbf{z}_j)) \tag{5}$$

3.4 Negative Sampling

In order to avoid the calculation of softmax, we introduce positive and negative samples. And we need to sample several nodes as negative samples for learning the ground truth effectively. Thus, we define a noise distribution $P_n(u)$ to pick negative samples for node u. Since many graphs are scale-free (the degree distribution of a graph follows the power law, as shown in Fig. 2), the noise distribution $P_n(u)$ we use here is actually a uniform distribution. And for each node, negative samples with different hops should have different weights. It is just like if the nodes in the graph are farther apart, then they should be "thrown" farther away in the embedding space. Therefore, we use the shortest distance between nodes as the weight of negative samples. The negative sample loss is defined as follows:

$$\mathcal{L}_n = -\frac{1}{|N_{neg}(i)|} \sum_{v_n \sim P_n(v_i)} s_{v_n} log(\sigma(-\mathbf{z}_i^\top \mathbf{z}_{v_n})) \tag{6}$$

where s_{v_n} is the distance between the negative sample v_n and the node v_i.

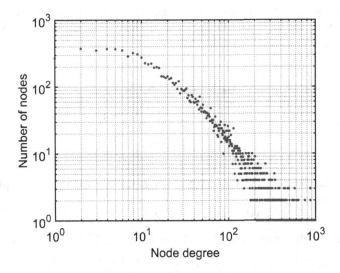

Fig. 2. Power law distribution of nodes in BlogCatalog dataset.

3.5 Algorithm

Objective Function. To learn low- or high-order graph information, and the final objective function is:

$$\mathcal{L} = \eta \mathcal{L}_{2nd} + \alpha \mathcal{L}_{1st} + \gamma \mathcal{L}_{rw} + \delta \mathcal{L}_n + \nu \mathcal{L}_{reg} \tag{7}$$

where $\mathcal{L}_{reg}$ is an L2-norm regularizer. Our proposed model only use one autoencoder structure with parameters $\boldsymbol{\theta}$ and does not introduce other structures. And we only adopt random walk strategy and negative sampling strategy. Our goal is to get reasonable parameters $\boldsymbol{\theta}$ by minimizing loss $\mathcal{L}$, and it is a weighted linear combination of per objective losses. Therefore, we introduce an efficient multi-objective optimization algorithm, MGDA-UB [22], to optimize $\mathcal{L}$. Because tuning these weights manually is very difficult. According to MGDA-UB, the resulting optimization problem is:

$$\min_{\alpha_1,\ldots,\alpha_T} \left\{ \left\| \sum_{t=1}^{T} \alpha_t \nabla_{\mathbf{Z}} \mathcal{L}_t(\boldsymbol{\theta}^{sh}, \boldsymbol{\theta}^{ta}) \right\|_2^2 \middle| \forall t, \sum_{t=1}^{T} \alpha_t = 1, \alpha_t \geq 0 \right\} \tag{8}$$

where $\boldsymbol{\theta}^{sh}$ are shared parameters, $\boldsymbol{\theta}^{ta}$ are task-specific parameters, $\mathbf{Z}$ denote the representations. In fact, the above optimization problem is equivalent to find a minimum-norm point in the convex hull of the set of input points [22]. MGDA-UB is computationally efficient, which requires only a single backward pass. After computing the gradient $\nabla_{\mathbf{Z}} \mathcal{L}_t(\boldsymbol{\theta}^{sh}, \boldsymbol{\theta}^{ta})$, the method uses Frank-Wolfe solver [12] to solve the optimization problem.

Optimization. To get the weights, we need to calculate the partial derivative $\nabla_{\mathbf{Z}} \mathcal{L}_t(\boldsymbol{\theta}^{sh}, \boldsymbol{\theta}^{ta})$. At first, we calculate the gradient $\nabla_{\mathbf{Z}} \mathcal{L}_{2nd}$, the detailed mathematical form is shown as follows:

$$\mathcal{L}_{2nd} = \|\beta(\hat{\mathbf{X}} - \mathbf{X})\|_2^2 \tag{9}$$

$$\frac{\partial \mathcal{L}_{2nd}}{\partial \hat{\mathbf{X}}} = 2\beta^2(\hat{\mathbf{X}} - \mathbf{X}) = \mathbf{H} \tag{10}$$

$$d\mathcal{L}_{2nd} = \mathrm{tr}((\frac{\partial \mathcal{L}_{2nd}}{\partial \hat{\mathbf{X}}})^\top d\hat{\mathbf{X}}) \tag{11}$$

The decoder here uses three fully connected layers. It can be phrased as follows:

$$\hat{\mathbf{X}} = \mathbf{W}_3 \sigma_2(\mathbf{W}_2 \sigma_1(\mathbf{W}_1 \mathbf{Z} + \mathbf{b}_1) + \mathbf{b}_2) + \mathbf{b}_3 \tag{12}$$

To simplify the expression of the formula, it can be rephrased as:

$$\mathbf{h}_2 = \mathbf{W}_1 \mathbf{Z} + \mathbf{b}_1, \mathbf{g}_1 = \sigma_1(\mathbf{h}_2)$$
$$\mathbf{h}_1 = \mathbf{W}_2 \mathbf{g}_1 + \mathbf{b}_2, \mathbf{g}_2 = \sigma_2(\mathbf{h}_1)$$
$$\hat{\mathbf{X}} = \mathbf{W}_3 \mathbf{g}_2 + \mathbf{b}_3 \tag{13}$$

Then the differential form of $\mathcal{L}_{2nd}$ can be expressed as follows:

$$
\begin{aligned}
d\mathcal{L}_{2nd} &= \text{tr}((\frac{\partial \mathcal{L}_{2nd}}{\partial \hat{\mathbf{X}}})^\top d\hat{\mathbf{X}}) = \text{tr}(\mathbf{H}^\top \mathbf{W}_3 dg_2) \\
&= \text{tr}(\mathbf{H}^\top \mathbf{W}_3(\sigma_2'(\mathbf{h}_1) \odot (\mathbf{W}_2 dg_1))) \\
&= \text{tr}((\underbrace{\mathbf{W}_3^\top \mathbf{H} \odot \sigma_2'(\mathbf{h}_1)}_{\mathbf{H}_1})^\top \mathbf{W}_2\, dg_1) \\
&= \text{tr}(\mathbf{H}_1(\sigma_1'(\mathbf{h}_2) \odot (\mathbf{W}_1 d\mathbf{Z}))) \\
&= \text{tr}((\underbrace{\mathbf{H}_1^\top \odot \sigma_1'(\mathbf{h}_2)}_{\mathbf{H}_2})^\top \mathbf{W}_1\, d\mathbf{Z}) \\
\frac{\partial \mathcal{L}_{2nd}}{\partial \mathbf{Z}} &= \mathbf{H}_2^\top
\end{aligned}
\tag{14}
$$

Then we can calculate the gradient $\nabla_{\mathbf{Z}} \mathcal{L}_{1st}$. From Eq. 3, it can be phrased as follows:

$$
\frac{\partial \mathcal{L}_{1st}}{\partial \mathbf{z}_i} = (-\frac{1}{|N(i)|} \sum_{j \in N(i)} \sigma_3'(\mathbf{z}_i^\top \mathbf{z}_j)\mathbf{z}_j^\top)^\top
\tag{15}
$$

Similarly, it is easy to calculate the gradient $\nabla_{\mathbf{Z}} \mathcal{L}_{rw}$ and $\nabla_{\mathbf{Z}} \mathcal{L}_{neg}$. And the above σ_1, σ_2 and σ_3 are element-wise functions. After obtaining these partial derivatives, we can make use of MGDA-UB method to get the weights of above objectives. Then the parameters θ can be optimized by using stochastic gradient descent. We present the our algorithm as follows (see Algorithm 1).

Algorithm 1: Multi-order graph embedding algorithm

Input: graph $G = (V, E)$, adjacency matrix A
Output: embedding representations Z

1 **while** *Parameter convergence* **do**
2   Walks = RandomWalkSampling(G);
3   Select nodes from V as a minibatch B;
4      $\mathbf{Z}_B, \hat{\mathbf{X}}_B = \text{Autoencoder}(\mathbf{X}_B; \theta)$;
5   **foreach** $v \in B$ **do**
6   Select the context nodes of node v as $N_{RW}(v)$ from Walks;
7   Select the neighbors of node v as $N(v)$;
8   Select the negative samples of node v as $N_{neg}(v)$;
9   **end**
10     $\alpha_1, ..., \alpha_T = \text{MGDA-UB}(\nabla_{\mathbf{Z}_B} \mathcal{L}_1, ..., \nabla_{\mathbf{Z}_B} \mathcal{L}_T)$;
11   Update parameters θ with stochastic gradient descent based on $\frac{\partial \mathcal{L}}{\partial \theta}$;
12 **end**
13 $\mathbf{Z}, \hat{\mathbf{X}} = \text{Autoencoder}(\mathbf{X}; \theta)$;
14 **return** embedding representations $\mathbf{Z}$;

---

4   Evaluation

4.1   Experimental Setup

Datasets. In order to evaluate the effectiveness of our method, we use four public graph datasets, including one social network, BlogCatalog,[1] one words co-occurrence network, Wikipedia,[2] a subgraph of the Protein-Protein Interactions network (Homo Sapiens),[3] and an email communication network between institution members (the core)[4] for node classification, graph reconstruction and node clustering tasks. The statistics of the above datasets can be summarized in Table 1.

Table 1. Statistics of the datasets

Datasets	#Node	#Edge	#Category	Note
BlogCatalog	10312	333983	39	Multi-label
Wikipedia	4777	92295	40	Multi-label
PPI	3890	37845	50	Multi-label
email-Eu-core	1005	25571	42	Single-label

Evaluation Metrics. We validated our method in three tasks. Specifically, we use Hamming Loss [7] in multi-label node classification task, which is often used in multi-label tasks [30,31]. And two well known F1 measures, Macro-F1 and Micro-F1 [25], were used to evaluate the performance in single-label node classification task. In graph reconstruction, we adopted Mean Average Precision (MAP) [27]. In node clustering, Normalized Mutual Information (NMI) [5] is often used in finding non-overlapping communities. However, we here used an improved Normalized Mutual Information (MGH-NMI) [15] to detect overlapping communities.

Baselines. In our experiments, we mainly verify the ability to maintain the structure information of undirected graphs. Thus, we compare our method with the following state-of-the-art methods: DeepWalk [19], Node2vec [9], GraRep [4], Line [23], SDNE [27], AROPE [32], M-NMF [28] and NodeSketch [29]. For the first five methods, we use the open source tool, OpenNE,[5] for experiments. The implementation of AROPE used in our experiments is available at https://github.com/ZW-ZHANG/AROPE. For M-NMF and NodeSketch, we use the open source tool, Karate Club [21] in our experiments.

---

[1] http://socialcomputing.asu.edu/datasets/BlogCatalog3.
[2] http://snap.stanford.edu/node2vec/POS.mat.
[3] http://snap.stanford.edu/node2vec/.
[4] http://snap.stanford.edu/data/email-Eu-core.html.
[5] https://github.com/thunlp/OpenNE.

4.2   Experimental Results

Node Classification. We used the multi-layer perceptron [11] without activation for multi-label node classification and use linear support vector machine [6] for single-label node classification. We also adopted 10-fold cross validation in this experiment. M-NMF and NodeSketch methods in Karate Club tool can not run on the disconnected graphs. Therefore, there are no experimental results on PPI and email-Eu-core. The experimental results of node classification are listed in Table 2. Our method provides competitive results in multi-label and single-label node classification tasks. And it shows that our method with MGDA-UB is always superior to the other methods. This also demonstrates that dynamic weights of multi-objective can help optimize the effect of node classification. SDNE or Line mainly preserves first and second order proximity of graph. Thus, DeepWalk or Node2vec always perform better than SDNE or Line, which indicates that the high-order graph structure information needs to be effectively learned. Overall, our method effectively learns the high-order graph structure information and provides competitive results in node classification tasks.

Table 2. Experimental results of node classification task.

	BlogCatalog	Wikipedia	PPI	email-Eu-core	
	Hamming loss	Hamming loss	Hamming loss	Macro-F1	Micro-F1
DeepWalk	0.0385 ± 0.0012	0.0414 ± 0.0009	0.0456 ± 0.0008	0.600 ± 0.061	0.752 ± 0.049
SDNE	0.0416 ± 0.0012	0.0394 ± 0.0011	0.0433 ± 0.0013	0.537 ± 0.057	0.694 ± 0.046
Node2vec	0.0392 ± 0.0008	0.0429 ± 0.0011	0.0454 ± 0.0010	0.593 ± 0.057	0.753 ± 0.039
Line	0.0441 ± 0.0010	0.0430 ± 0.0011	0.0543 ± 0.0015	0.522 ± 0.066	0.689 ± 0.063
GraRep	0.0349 ± 0.0010	0.0384 ± 0.0009	0.0419 ± 0.0010	0.593 ± 0.064	0.766 ± 0.048
AROPE	0.0409 ± 0.0011	0.0366 ± 0.0011	0.0402 ± 0.0013	0.593 ± 0.059	0.753 ± 0.051
M-NMF	0.0360 ± 0.0007	0.0343 ± 0.0011	–	–	–
NodeSketch	0.0417 ± 0.0020	0.0477 ± 0.0029	–	–	–
Our method[a]	0.0344 ± 0.0010	0.0377 ± 0.0011	0.0399 ± 0.0012	$\mathbf{0.609 \pm 0.081}$	0.774 ± 0.048
Our method-M[b]	$\mathbf{0.0333 \pm 0.0007}$	$\mathbf{0.0334 \pm 0.0009}$	$\mathbf{0.0368 \pm 0.0012}$	0.603 ± 0.034	$\mathbf{0.775 \pm 0.031}$

[a] This is the method with balanced weights of each objective.
[b] This is the method with dynamic weights of each objective.

Graph Reconstruction. In this experiment, we used inner products to measure the similarity of vectors. The performance results in Table 3 illustrate that our method is significantly superior to the other baselines on four benchmark datasets. In addition, compared to the second-ranked method, our method improved by 140%, 5.3%, 72.6% and 66.1%, respectively. In fact, the contribution mainly comes from the distance-based negative sampling method, and we will discuss in the section of ablation study. And it shows that our method with MGDA-UB performs not well. This is because it tries to reduce losses but does not effectively maintain the balance of tasks. In general, it also shows that our method can effectively learn low-order graph structure information.

Table 3. Experimental results of graph reconstruction task.

	BlogCatalog	Wikipedia	PPI	email-Eu-core
DeepWalk	0.138	0.416	0.224	0.340
SDNE	0.038	0.077	0.085	0.329
Node2vec	0.203	0.451	0.285	0.233
Line	0.013	0.085	0.126	0.276
GraRep	0.060	0.185	0.137	0.384
AROPE	0.199	0.348	0.151	0.218
M-NMF	0.004	0.336	–	–
NodeSketch	0.010	0.044	–	–
Our method	**0.488**	**0.475**	**0.492**	**0.638**
Our method-M	0.186	0.348	0.181	0.615

Node Clustering. K-means algorithm [1] was adopted to cluster nodes in this experiment. The performance results for node clustering task are shown in Table 4. PPI is a multi-graph data set and is not suitable for node clustering task. It can be seen that our method is superior to other methods in overlapping graphs. And it shows that our method with MGDA-UB performs not very well. It also shows that the experimental results of SDNE or Line are not very good because they mainly learn low-order structural information, and they are not suitable for the task. The performance results indicate that our method can effectively learn the high-order graph structure information.

Table 4. Experimental results of node clustering task.

	BlogCatalog	Wikipedia	email-Eu-core
	MGH-NMI	MGH-NMI	NMI
DeepWalk	0.0213	0.0017	0.700
SDNE	0.0	0.0040	0.575
Node2vec	0.0226	0.0024	0.702
Line	0.0	0.0022	0.665
GraRep	0.0264	0.0019	0.677
AROPE	0.0	0.0028	0.460
M-NMF	0.0049	0.0019	–
NodeSketch	0.0	0.0014	–
Our method	**0.0387**	0.0032	**0.708**
Our method-M	0.0097	**0.0041**	0.676

4.3   Ablation Study of Negative Sampling

Since we use distance-based negative sampling method to improve learning representations. In this section, we investigate the contributions of distance-based negative sampling to the performance. Some variants of our method are as follows:

- Variant-1: It learns low- or high-order graph information without negative sampling.
- Variant-2: Every negative sample has the same weight.
- Variant-3: It performs negative sampling based on the degree of nodes.

First, we conduct an experiment by removing negative sampling, where our method learns low and high order graph structure information with only positive sample. Then, we conduct an experiment where all negative samples have equal weight. The performance results in Table 5 illustrate that distance-based negative sampling can effectively improve the ability to learn representations. The method without negative sampling does not perform well, especially in node clustering and graph reconstruction tasks. This shows that we need not only positive samples in the training process, but also negative samples as noise to improve the model. And the experimental results of the method with equal weight negative samples have improved, but there is still a gap between the distance-based negative sampling method. If we do negative sampling based on the degree of nodes, it shows that does not perform well in node classification and node clustering. This is because negative sampling relies too much on nodes with large degrees and neglects most nodes with small degrees. These results demonstrate the contributions of distance-based negative sampling method.

Table 5. Experimental results about ablation study of negative sampling on BlogCatalog.

	Hamming loss	MGH-NMI	MAP
Our method	0.0344 ± 0.0010	0.0387	0.488
Variant-1	0.0371 ± 0.0009	0.0131	0.058
Variant-2	0.0348 ± 0.0011	0.0159	0.418
Variant-3	0.0363 ± 0.0009	0.0150	0.547

4.4   Study of Hyper Parameters

We investigate the how different hyper parameters affect the performance in this section. Specifically, we evaluate the results in terms of number of context, negative samples and embedding dimensions.

Performance on Different Number of Context. We first show how the number of context affects the performance in Table 6. We can see that it has little effect on node classification. In node clustering, results first increase with the growth of number of context and then remain stable. In graph reconstruction, results first increase and then drop, and it achieves the best performance of reconstruction at 24. This shows that learning too many context nodes at the same time is not good for identifying neighbors.

Performance on Different Number of Negative Samples. From Table 6, we can see that it has a little effect on node classification. However, it has a greater impact on graph reconstruction. The more negative samples, the better the results of graph reconstruction task. Too many negative samples will negatively affect node classification and clustering tasks, since this reduces the learning effect of context nodes.

Performance on Different Embedding Dimensions. At last, we show how different embedding dimensions affect performance. From Table 6, we can see that the results of our method become worse as the dimensions increase in node classification. In node clustering, when the dimensions increase, the performance initially gets better and then becomes worse. The reason is that too large dimensions will introduce noise, which has negative impact on performance. The influence on the task of graph reconstruction is volatile.

Table 6. Experimental results of different hyper parameters on BlogCatalog.

	Hamming loss	MGH-NMI	MAP
context = 8	0.0347 ± 0.0012	0.0252	0.473
context = 16	0.0344 ± 0.0010	0.0387	0.472
context = 24	0.0344 ± 0.0010	0.0388	0.488
context = 32	0.0345 ± 0.0006	0.0391	0.482
context = 48	0.0343 ± 0.0008	0.0392	0.444
neg = 8	0.0341 ± 0.0007	0.0393	0.427
neg = 16	0.0342 ± 0.0008	0.0384	0.459
neg = 24	0.0344 ± 0.0010	0.0388	0.488
neg = 32	0.0343 ± 0.0008	0.0388	0.486
neg = 48	0.0349 ± 0.0011	0.0378	0.497
dim = 32	0.0322 ± 0.0006	0.0334	0.403
dim = 64	0.0332 ± 0.0007	0.0331	0.472
dim = 96	0.0340 ± 0.0009	0.0390	0.453
dim = 128	0.0344 ± 0.0010	0.0388	0.488
dim = 256	0.0372 ± 0.0009	0.0278	0.494

5   Conclusion

In this paper, we present a new graph embedding method that focuses on learning low and high order graph structure information. Our method fuses structure-preserving model with random walk sampling, which can learn multi-order graph structure information simultaneously. Our method also introduces distance-based negative sampling method for improving the learning representations by collecting noise samples. It measures the importance of negative samples through the distance between nodes. We evaluate our embedding method in node classification, graph reconstruction and node clustering tasks. The experimental results demonstrate that our proposed method provides very competitive results compared with seven state-of-the-art baselines on four benchmark datasets.

Acknowledgement. This paper is Supported by National Key Research and Development Program of China (Grant No. 2017YFB0803003) and National Science Foundation for Young Scientists of China (Grant No. 61702507).

References

1. Arthur, D., Vassilvitskii, S.: k-means++: the advantages of careful seeding. Technical report, Stanford (2006)
2. Bhagat, S., Cormode, G., Muthukrishnan, S.: Node classification in social networks. In: Social Network Data Analytics, pp. 115–148. Springer, Boston (2011). https://doi.org/10.1007/978-1-4419-8462-3_5
3. Cai, H., Zheng, V.W., Chang, K.C.C.: A comprehensive survey of graph embedding: problems, techniques, and applications. IEEE Trans. Knowl. Data Eng. **30**(9), 1616–1637 (2018)
4. Cao, S., Lu, W., Xu, Q.: GraRep: learning graph representations with global structural information. In: Proceedings of the 24th ACM International on Conference on Information and Knowledge Management, pp. 891–900. ACM (2015)
5. Cavallari, S., Zheng, V.W., Cai, H., Chang, K.C.C., Cambria, E.: Learning community embedding with community detection and node embedding on graphs. In: Proceedings of the 2017 ACM on Conference on Information and Knowledge Management, pp. 377–386. ACM (2017)
6. Cortes, C., Vapnik, V.: Support-vector networks. Mach. Learn. **20**(3), 273–297 (1995)
7. Gibaja, E., Ventura, S.: A tutorial on multilabel learning. ACM Comput. Surv. (CSUR) **47**(3), 52 (2015)
8. Girvan, M., Newman, M.E.: Community structure in social and biological networks. Proc. Natl. Acad. Sci. **99**(12), 7821–7826 (2002)
9. Grover, A., Leskovec, J.: node2vec: scalable feature learning for networks. In: Proceedings of the 22nd ACM SIGKDD International Conference on Knowledge Discovery and Data Mining, pp. 855–864. ACM (2016)
10. Hamilton, W., Ying, Z., Leskovec, J.: Inductive representation learning on large graphs. In: Advances in Neural Information Processing Systems, pp. 1024–1034 (2017)
11. Hinton, G.E.: Connectionist learning procedures. In: Machine Learning, pp. 555–610. Elsevier (1990)

12. Jaggi, M.: Revisiting Frank-Wolfe: projection-free sparse convex optimization. In: Proceedings of the 30th International Conference on Machine Learning, pp. 427–435 (2013)
13. Kipf, T.N., Welling, M.: Semi-supervised classification with graph convolutional networks. In: 5th International Conference on Learning Representations, ICLR 2017 (2017). https://openreview.net/forum?id=SJU4ayYgl
14. Liben-Nowell, D., Kleinberg, J.: The link-prediction problem for social networks. J. Am. Soc. Inf. Sci. Technol. **58**(7), 1019–1031 (2007)
15. McDaid, A.F., Greene, D., Hurley, N.: Normalized mutual information to evaluate overlapping community finding algorithms. arXiv preprint arXiv:1110.2515 (2011)
16. Mikolov, T., Sutskever, I., Chen, K., Corrado, G.S., Dean, J.: Distributed representations of words and phrases and their compositionality. In: Advances in Neural Information Processing Systems, pp. 3111–3119 (2013)
17. Ou, M., Cui, P., Pei, J., Zhang, Z., Zhu, W.: Asymmetric transitivity preserving graph embedding. In: Proceedings of the 22nd ACM SIGKDD International Conference on Knowledge Discovery and Data Mining, pp. 1105–1114. ACM (2016)
18. Pan, S., Wu, J., Zhu, X., Zhang, C., Wang, Y.: Tri-party deep network representation. In: Proceedings of the Twenty-Fifth International Joint Conference on Artificial Intelligence, pp. 1895–1901. AAAI Press (2016)
19. Perozzi, B., Al-Rfou, R., Skiena, S.: DeepWalk: online learning of social representations. In: Proceedings of the 20th ACM SIGKDD International Conference on Knowledge Discovery and Data Mining, pp. 701–710. ACM (2014)
20. Rosvall, M., Bergstrom, C.T.: Maps of random walks on complex networks reveal community structure. Proc. Natl. Acad. Sci. **105**(4), 1118–1123 (2008)
21. Rozemberczki, B., Kiss, O., Sarkar, R.: An API oriented open-source python framework for unsupervised learning on graphs. arXiv preprint arXiv:2003.04819 (2020)
22. Sener, O., Koltun, V.: Multi-task learning as multi-objective optimization. In: Advances in Neural Information Processing Systems, pp. 527–538 (2018)
23. Tang, J., Qu, M., Wang, M., Zhang, M., Yan, J., Mei, Q.: LINE: large-scale information network embedding. In: Proceedings of the 24th International Conference on World Wide Web, pp. 1067–1077. International World Wide Web Conferences Steering Committee (2015)
24. Tsitsulin, A., Mottin, D., Karras, P., Müller, E.: VERSE: versatile graph embeddings from similarity measures. In: Proceedings of the 2018 World Wide Web Conference, pp. 539–548. International World Wide Web Conferences Steering Committee (2018)
25. Uysal, A.K., Gunal, S.: A novel probabilistic feature selection method for text classification. Knowl.-Based Syst. **36**, 226–235 (2012)
26. Velickovic, P., Cucurull, G., Casanova, A., Romero, A., Liò, P., Bengio, Y.: Graph attention networks. In: 6th International Conference on Learning Representations, ICLR 2018 (2018). https://openreview.net/forum?id=rJXMpikCZ
27. Wang, D., Cui, P., Zhu, W.: Structural deep network embedding. In: Proceedings of the 22nd ACM SIGKDD International Conference on Knowledge Discovery and Data Mining, pp. 1225–1234. ACM (2016)
28. Wang, X., Cui, P., Wang, J., Pei, J., Zhu, W., Yang, S.: Community preserving network embedding. In: Thirty-first AAAI Conference on Artificial Intelligence (2017)
29. Yang, D., Rosso, P., Li, B., Cudre-Mauroux, P.: NodeSketch: highly-efficient graph embeddings via recursive sketching. In: Proceedings of the 25th ACM SIGKDD International Conference on Knowledge Discovery & Data Mining, pp. 1162–1172 (2019)

30. Yang, P., Sun, X., Li, W., Ma, S., Wu, W., Wang, H.: SGM: sequence generation model for multi-label classification. In: Proceedings of the 27th International Conference on Computational Linguistics, pp. 3915–3926 (2018)
31. Yang, Y.Y., Lin, Y.A., Chu, H.M., Lin, H.T.: Deep learning with a rethinking structure for multi-label classification. arXiv preprint arXiv:1802.01697 (2018)
32. Zhang, Z., Cui, P., Wang, X., Pei, J., Yao, X., Zhu, W.: Arbitrary-order proximity preserved network embedding. In: Proceedings of the 24th ACM SIGKDD International Conference on Knowledge Discovery & Data Mining, pp. 2778–2786. ACM (2018)

Deep Learning and Application and UVA

PATR: A Novel Poisoning Attack Based on Triangle Relations Against Deep Learning-Based Recommender Systems

Meiling Chao[1,3], Min Gao[1,3(✉)], Junwei Zhang[1,3], Zongwei Wang[1,3], Quanwu Zhao[2,3], and Yulin He[3]

[1] School of Big Data and Software Engineering, Chongqing University, Chongqing, China
{meilingchao,gaomin,jw.zhang,zongwei}@cqu.edu.cn
[2] School of Economics and Business Administration, Chongqing University, Chongqing, China
zhaoquanwumx@cqu.edu.cn
[3] Chongqing Aerospace Polytechnic, Chongqing, China

Abstract. Recommender systems (RSs) have emerged as an effective way to deal with information overload and are very popular in e-commerce. However, because of the open nature of collaborative characteristics of the systems, RSs are susceptible to poisoning attacks, which inject fake user profiles into RSs to increase or decrease the recommended frequency of the target item. The traditional poisoning attack methods (such as random attack and average attack) are easy to be detected and lack of generality since they usually use global statistics, e.g., the number of each user's ratings and the average rating for filler items. Moreover, as deep learning (DL) becomes more widely used in RSs, attackers are likely to use related techniques to attack RSs. To explore the robustness of DL-based RSs under the possible attacks, we propose a novel poisoning attack with triangle relations (PATR). The triangle relations refer to the balance among a fake user and two real users, aiming to improve attack performance. We also present a novel fake & real sampling strategy, i.e., sampling a set of fake users from the real users, to decrease the possibility of being detected. Comprehensive experiments on three public datasets show that PATR outperforms traditional poisoning attacks on attack effectiveness and anti-detection capability.

Keywords: Deep learning · Poisoning attack · Recommender system · Triangle relation

1 Introduction

Recommender systems (RSs) are prevalent in e-commerce since they provide users with a critical discovery mode to mitigate the difficulties in finding items that users are interested in [1,2]. The ability to solve information overload has

H. Gao and X. Wang (Eds.): CollaborateCom 2021, LNICST 407, pp. 435–450, 2021.
https://doi.org/10.1007/978-3-030-92638-0_26

driven RSs be widely used in industries (e.g., Amazon, Netflix, and Facebook) [3]. RSs assist users in finding items and help merchants promote new products and increase retail sales. Unfortunately, due to the openness of the rating systems in RSs, malicious users unscrupulously attack RSs to achieve nefarious goals [4,5]. Since RSs have a profound impact on the e-commerce industry, researchers should take the initiative to consider the possible damages to RSs to protect customers' rights and interests better.

There is much effort has been devoted to studying how to spoof RSs to defend against malicious attacks. A variety of attacks such as sybil attack (i.e., illegally infer a user's preference) [6], unorganized attack (i.e., different attackers attack the RS without organization), and powerful user attack (i.e., select most powerful users who can impact RSs) [7] have been studied. In this paper, we focus on the poisoning attacks [8], which were initially referred to as shilling attacks [10,11], where malicious users inject fake user profiles (i.e., carefully crafted ratings) into RSs based on the statistical rating information during the training time. For example, the average attack is one of the poisoning attacks that assigns the highest rating to a target item to be promoted and assigns an average rating to a randomly sampled group of items [11]. Furthermore, we can divide the existing poisoning attacks into push attacks and nuke attacks according to the purpose. The push attacks assign the highest rating on the target item to improve the recommended frequency, and the nuke attacks do the opposite [8,11–13]. The poisoning attacks can be beneficial to unscrupulous merchants for increasing their retail sales and reducing their competitors' retail sales. Since the two types are similar, we only consider push attacks in this paper. Researchers have experimented successfully with poisoning attacks on real-world RSs, such as YouTube, Google search, Amazon, and Yelp [14]. Moreover, Large companies such as Sony, Amazon, and eBay have been attacked in real life [11]. Although all of these existing approaches have proved effective in some cases, they still have the following challenges:

(1) **Easy to be detected:** The generated user profiles lack personalized behavior patterns of real users, which are easily detected [15,16].
(2) **Low attack effectiveness:** According to the way the statistics are calculated, the traditional poisoning attacks are effective on some traditional collaborative filtering (CF) methods but do not do well on deep learning (DL) based RSs, which also means lack of generality [17,18].
(3) **Lack of effective metrics:** In the field of ranking-based recommender algorithms, the hit ratio (HK) is generally used to calculate the number of the target item recommended to real users, which cannot measure the disorder of top-K recommendation lists [10,12].

To address the above challenges and explore the potential security problems such as DL-based attacks of RSs, we propose a novel poisoning attack based on triangle relations (PATR), which includes two parts, a pre-training module, and a reconstruction module. For the pre-training module, we design triangle relations to generate more informative user embeddings to improve the anti-detection capability. As shown in Fig. 1, two cases are considered according to the

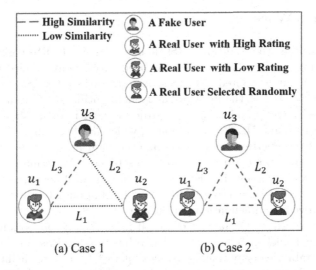

(a) Case 1   (b) Case 2

Fig. 1. Triangle relations are designed for the balance of three users. Two cases are considered according to the target item.

target item, where we focus on the balance of one fake user and two real users. We use Graph Convolutional Matrix Commissions (GCMC) [19] designed for recommendation scenarios to implement the pre-training module. We creatively propose a fake & real sampling strategy for the reconstruction module to generate the initial fake user representations. Then we use the convolutional auto-encoder (CAE) [20], which is easy to train and has a lower time cost, to reconstruct the enhanced fake user representations with the output of the pre-training module. We consider these deep learning (DL) techniques can help our model attack DL-based RSs. Our contributions are as follows:

(1) We propose a pre-training module based on triangle relations to assist in attacking RSs. The pre-training module can generate user embeddings with real user features, which reduce the probability of being detected; moreover, we apply CAE to the reconstruction module and combine the outputs of the pre-training module to reconstruct a set of enhanced fake users.

(2) According to heuristic learning, we present a novel fake & real sampling strategy to initialize fake user profiles. In addition to directly injecting fake users, we creatively sample a group of active users directly from real users. The ablation experiment proves that our sampling strategy is helpful for anti-detection capability.

(3) We present a new metric named top-K shift (TKS) to measure the disorder of the top-K recommendation lists affected. Our experimental results show that PATR can effectively attack DL-based RSs, and the anti-detection capability against two detectors is better.

2   Related Work

Generally speaking, the traditional RSs mainly refers to the RSs based on collaborative filtering (CFRSs) [21], which has been successfully applied to practical scenarios filter out unwanted resources. Among various CFRSs, matrix factor factorization (MF) [2] is the most popular one. It utilizes potential feature vectors to represent users and items and projects them into the shared potential space. In recent years, DL develops rapidly, which has been applied to RSs. The DL-based RSs have better performance than the traditional ones because the DL-based models are more consistent with the user-item interaction to improve the recommendation accuracy [17]. For example, adversarial networks (AN), CAE, and deep reinforcement learning (DRL) have been applied to recommender systems to improve recommendation performance [17,18].

As far as we know, O'Mahony et al. [4] first research on poisoning attacks (a.k.a shilling attacks). They define the robustness of RSs and demonstrate several vulnerabilities of poisoning attacks against CFRSs to facilitate specific advice [4,11]. Furthermore, Burke et al. [22] and Mobasher et al. [23] investigate some low-knowledge attack methods for pushing and reducing items, such as random, average, bandwagon, and segment attacks. They find that rating-based and ranking-based CFRSs are vulnerable to attack. Given more knowledge and budget, Wilson et al. [7] propose a powerful attack model that selects the most influential users or items to attack RSs. Fang et al. [24] study the poisoning attacks against graph-based RSs. Besides, Zhang et al. [25] utilize DRL to train the attack agent, which can generate user profiles for data poisoning. Xing et al. [14] conduct experiments on YouTube, Google, and Yelp. The experimental results show that manipulating RSs is possible.

Influenced by the popularity of the generative model in the field of image, some papers are using generative adversarial networks (GAN) [15,16]. Since the GAN mainly define the mini-max problem without loss function, which cannot fit well with the research of this paper, and the issues of long training time and difficult adjustment of parameters [26,27], we choose another generative model CAE [20]. As far as we know, we are the first to apply CAE to poisoning attacks. With the triangle relations and fake & real sampling strategy, our model has destructive attack effectiveness and good anti-detection capability.

3   Proposed Model

This section describes our proposed PATR, which includes a pre-training module and a reconstruction module.

3.1   Problem Formulation

We use $X \in \mathcal{R}^{N \times M}$ to represent the user-item rating matrix, where N is the number of all users, including real users and fake users, and M is the number of items. The user sets and item sets are denoted as $\mathcal{U}$ and $\mathcal{V}$, respectively. u_i

represents each user vector in $\mathcal{U}$, and v_j represents each item vector in $\mathcal{V}$, where $i, j \in \{1, 2, ..., N\}, \{1, 2, ..., M\}$, respectively. r_{ij} represents u_i's rating on v_j, and r_{max} is the highest rating. The fake user sets denote as $\mathcal{F}$, and $|\mathcal{F}|$ is the number of fake users. f_i and $\hat{f}_i$ denote each initial fake user vector and reconstructed fake user vector, where $i \in \{1, 2, ..., |\mathcal{F}|\}$. We use $\mathbf{u}_{iPre}$ and $\mathbf{v}_{jPre}$ to denote each fake user embedding and each item embedding generated by the pre-training module, where $j \in \{1, 2, ..., M\}$. $\mathbf{u}_{iE}$ denotes each fake user embedding generated by the reconstruction module.

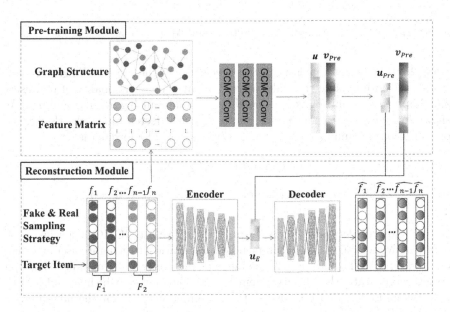

Fig. 2. The overall framework of PATR (Color figure online)

3.2   Pre-training Module

Problem Hypothesis. The traditional poisoning attack methods are easily detected and have a narrow application range due to simply using rating statistics without special designs. To enhance fake users' anti-detection capability and destructiveness, we first propose a pre-training module based on our elaborately designed triangle relations according to heuristic learning. The three nodes in the triangle relations represent three user embeddings of K dimensions, which are denoted as $\boldsymbol{u}_1 = [x_{11}, x_{12}, \ldots, x_{1K}]$, $\boldsymbol{u}_2 = [x_{21}, x_{22}, \ldots, x_{2K}]$, $\boldsymbol{u}_3 = [x_{31}, x_{32}, \ldots, x_{3K}]$, where x_i represents the i-th dimensional data. Each edge represents the similarity of two adjacent users, which is denoted as $L1$, $L2$, $L3$, where $L_1 = \sqrt{\sum_{i=1}^{K}(x_{1i} - x_{2i})^2}$, $L_2 = \sqrt{\sum_{i=1}^{K}(x_{2i} - x_{3i})^2}$, and $L_3 = \sqrt{\sum_{i=1}^{K}(x_{3i} - x_{1i})^2}$. As shown in Fig. 1, we consider the following two cases and use euclidean distance to calculate the similarity.

Case 1: If there are both positive ratings and negative ratings about the target item, we assume that fake users should be similar to real users who purchased the target item and rated it highly and stay away from users that rated it lowly. Moreover, the similarity of the two types of real users should be small. In Fig. 1 (a), u_1 is a real user embedding who rated high rating, and u_2 is a real user embedding who rated low rating, and u_3 is a fake user embedding. Hence, the corresponding optimization problem can be formulated as

$$\min L = \lambda_1 L_3 - \lambda_2 L_2 - \lambda_3 L_1 \tag{1}$$

where λ_1, λ_2 and λ_3 are hyperparameters, and $\lambda_1 + \lambda_2 + \lambda_3 = 1$.

Case 2: If the target item is a cold item, we consider the second triangle relation. In this case, we assume that fake users can learn the commonality of real users and improve the anti-detection capability by minimizing L_1, L_2, and L_3. As shown in Fig. 1 (b), u_1 and u_2 are two real users selected randomly. Hence, the optimization is minimizing the sum of three edges. The formula is

$$\min L = \lambda_4 L_1 + \lambda_5 L_2 + \lambda_6 L_3, \tag{2}$$

where λ_4, λ_5 and λ_6 are hyperparameters, and $\lambda_4 + \lambda_5 + \lambda_6 = 1$.

Graph Convolutional Matrix Completion. We use GCMC, a special graph neural network designed for recommendation scenarios, to generate user and item embeddings. As shown in Fig. 2, the input of the pre-training module is a graph structure generated by the user-item interaction matrix, which includes both real users and sampled fake users. The sampling strategy for the fake users is described in Sect. 3.3. In each iteration, we combine the triangle relations with GCMC for training. Specifically, we consider the user-item interaction matrix a weighted undirected graph $G = (\mathcal{W}, \mathcal{E}, \mathcal{R})$. The nodes consist of a collection of user nodes $u_i \in \mathcal{U}$ with $i \in \{1, \ldots, N\}$ and item nodes $v_j \in \mathcal{V}$ with $j \in \{1, \ldots, M\}$, and $\mathcal{U} \cup \mathcal{V} = \mathcal{W}$. The edges $(u_i, r_{ij}, v_j) \in \mathcal{E}$ tagged with labels represent ratings, where $r_{ij} \in \{r_1, \ldots, r_n\} = \mathcal{R}$.

GCMC assigns a specific transformation for each rating, resulting in edge-type specific messages $\delta_{j \to i, r}$, from items j to users i of the following form:

$$\delta_{j \to i, r} = \frac{1}{\varphi_{i,j}} W_r x_j^v, \tag{3}$$

where $\varphi_{i,j}$ is a normalization constant. W_r is an edge-type specific parameter matrix. x_j^v is the initial feature vector of item node j. Messages $\delta_{i \to j, r}$ from users to items are processed analogously. After the message passing step, we accumulate incoming messages at every node by summing over all neighbors $\mathcal{N}_i(u_i)$ connected by a specific edge-type r, and by accumulating the results for each edge type into a single vector representation:

$$h_i^u = \sigma \left[accum \left(\sum_{j \in \mathcal{N}_i(u_i)} \delta_{j \to i,1}, \cdots, \sum_{j \in \mathcal{N}_R(u_i)} \delta_{j \to i,R} \right) \right], \qquad (4)$$

where $accum()$ denotes an accumulation operation such as $sum()$, i.e., summation of all messages. $\sigma()$ represents an activation function such as ReLU. To arrive at the final embedding of user node i, we transform the intermediate output h_i as

$$z_i^u = \sigma\left(W h_i^u\right), \qquad (5)$$

where W is the same parameter matrix.

The outputs of GCMC are user embeddings and item embeddings. Because only the fake user embeddings are required, we pick them out from all the user embeddings according to the labels.

Algorithm 1. Pre-training Module

Input: The user-item interaction matrix (including fake users and real users) $\tilde{X}$.
Output: Powerful fake user embeddings u_{Pre} and item embeddings v_{Pre}.
1: Generate initialized user and item embeddings using Eq. (3) to Eq. (5).
2: **for** the number of training epochs **do**
3:　**for** the number of iterations **do**
4:　　**if** the target item belongs to Case 1 **then**
5:　　　Randomly select a fake user embedding $u_{iPre} \in \mathcal{F}$, a real user embedding $u_{jPre} \in \mathcal{U}_1$ and a real user embedding $u_{kPre} \in \mathcal{U}_2$ from u_{Pre}.
6:　　　Optimize the loss function according to Eq. (1).
7:　　**end if**
8:　**else**
9:　　Randomly select a fake user embedding $u_{Prei} \in \mathcal{F}$ and two real user embeddings.
10:　　Optimize the loss function according to Eq. (2).
11:　**end for**
12: **end for**

3.3 Reconstruction Module

In this part, we mainly describe the fake & real sampling strategy and the reconstruction module. With the outputs of the pre-training module, we apply CAE to reconstruct enhanced fake users.

Fake & Real Sampling Strategy. Since our goal is to reconstruct enhanced fake users, we first need to sample a batch of initial fake users. To improving the anti-detection capability, we design a unique sampling strategy including two steps, as shown in Fig. 2. In the first step, we consider the existing sampling strategies. In addition to the target item, a fake user needs ratings on other items (the dark blue circles in Fig. 2) to disguise, and these items are called filler items [10–12]. The sampling strategies are used for filler items. Among many sampling strategies, popularity sampling (i.e., sample filler items based on their popularity) performs well [12], so we consider generating a set of fake users $\mathcal{F}_1$ by popularity. In the second step, we directly sample a part of users $\mathcal{F}_2$ from real active users to enhance the anti-detection capability, and the light blue circles in Fig. 2 are the sampled real users' original ratings. Therefore, the initial fake users are denoted as $\mathcal{F}$, where $\mathcal{F} = \mathcal{F}_1 \cup \mathcal{F}_2$. We set the initial fake users' ratings on the target item (the red circles in Fig. 2) as r_{max} for attacking performance. The number of F1 and F2 is explained in parameter sensitivity experiments in Sect. 3.2.

Reconstructing Enhanced Fake Users. We use CAE to reconstruct the enhanced fake users. CAE is a fusion of an encoder and a decoder composed of convolutional networks and pooling layers. Convolution is a dot product between the filter and input data, described as

$$y_i^{l+1}(j) = K_i^l * x^l(j) + b_i^l, \tag{6}$$

where K_i^l and b_i^l denote the weights and bias of the i-th layer, and $x^l(j)$ is the j-th local region of the layer l. $*$ denotes a dot product operation, and $y_i^{l+1}(j)$ is the output of convolution operation, respectively. The activation function of the hidden layer is ReLU, and the activation function of the output layer is Sigmoid. Max pooling reduces the dimension of feature maps by taking the maximum among every window. By reducing the number of parameters, the feature dimension becomes smaller and manageable.

As shown in Fig. 2, the input is the sampled fake users vectors (i.e., the fake user-item rating matrix), and the encoder ultimately reduces input data into latent user embeddings $\boldsymbol{u}_E$. The user embeddings represent the lowest level space in which the input is reduced, with essential information preserved with a strong correlation between input features. To enhance the anti-detection capability of the fake users, we consider $\boldsymbol{u}_E$ generated by the encoder is similar to the fake user embeddings $\boldsymbol{u}_{Pre}$ generated by the pre-training module. Further, to maintain the destructiveness of fake users, we keep the ratings of fake users for the target item as high as possible. The optimization is described as

$$\mathcal{L}_{Encode} = \min_\theta \sum_{i=1}^{|F|} (Dist(u_{iE}, u_{iPre}) + \|r_{max} - u_{iE} \odot v_{tPre}\|), \tag{7}$$

where $\boldsymbol{u}_{iE}$ and $\boldsymbol{u}_{iPre}$ represent the fake user $\boldsymbol{u}_i$'s embedding generated by the encoder and pre-training module, respectively. $|F|$ is the number of fake users. $Dist()$ is the euclidean metric, $\boldsymbol{v}_{tPre}$ represents the target item embedding generated by the pre-training module, and $\boldsymbol{u}_{iE} \odot \boldsymbol{v}_{tPre}$ is $\boldsymbol{u}_i$'s rating on the target item. θ defines the parameters of the encoder.

The decoder acts as the mirror image of the encoder. The number of nodes in every layer increases and reconstructs the user embeddings to output as a similar input via transposed convolution. The process is described as

$$\mathcal{L}_{Decode} = \min_{\phi} \sum_{i=1}^{|F|} Dist(\hat{f}_i, f_i), \tag{8}$$

where $\hat{f}_i$ and f_i are the reconstructed and initialized fake user u_i's vector, respectively. ϕ represents the parameters of the decoder.

We combine two loss function as the final loss, which is

$$\mathcal{L} = \alpha \mathcal{L}_{Encode} + \beta \mathcal{L}_{Decode}, \tag{9}$$

where α and β are the hyperparameters, and $\alpha + \beta = 1$.

Algorithm 2. Reconstruction Module

Input: Initial fake users' rating matrix X_F (i.e., initial fake users' vectors).
Output: Reconstructed fake users' rating matrix $\hat{X}_F$, the parameter θ for the encoder.
　　　E and the parameter ϕ for the decoder D.
1: **for** number of training epochs **do**
2: 　**for** number of iterations **do**
3: 　　Uniformly sample a minibatch of fake users $\mathcal{F}'$.
4: 　　**for** each fake user $f'_i \in \mathcal{F}'$ **do**
5: 　　　Let the fake user embeddings u'_{iE} generated by the encoder be similar to
　　　　the fake user embeddings u'_{iPre} of the pre-training module using Eq. (7).
　　　　Set the rating of u'_{iE} for the target item to r_{max} using Eq. (7).
6: 　　　Let the reconstructed fake user vector $\hat{f}'_i$ generated by the decoder be similar
　　　　to the input f' using Eq. (8).
7: 　　**end for**
8: 　**end for**
9: **end for**

---

4   Experiments and Analysis

In this section, Experiments are conducted to verify the effectiveness of our model. We mainly focus on the following questions.

- **Q1:** Does our proposed model PATR have a significant attack effectiveness on DL-based RSs?
- **Q2:** Is PATR more likely to evade detection?
- **Q3:** Are our hypothesis and designs (the pre-training module and sampling strategy) conducive to PATR?

4.1   Experimental Setup

We use three benchmark datasets in our experiments: FilmTrust,[1] Ciao,[2] and ML-100K.[3] Each dataset is randomly split by 9:1 as training set and test set, respectively. Table 1 shows the details of the datasets. To avoid the cold start problem, we filter out users with fewer than ten ratings (They are too sensitive to attacks). Three layers of convolution with 512, 256, and 128 neurons are used in GCMC and CAE. The number of injecting fake users account for 5% of the number of real users, and the number of filler items for each fake user profile in $\mathcal{F}_1$ accounts for 1% of the number of real users.

Table 1. Dataset statistics

Dataset	Users	Items	Ratings	Sparsity
FilmTrust	1,058	2,071	35,497	98.86%
ML-100K	934	1,682	100,000	93,70%
Ciao	7,375	105,114	284,086	99.96%

Attack Models. In this paper, we choose the following four traditional poisoning attack methods as baseline methods.

(1) **Random Attack** [11]: Random attack is a naive attack model. The set of filler items are assigned to random ratings with a normal distribution around the mean rating value across the whole dataset, and the target item is given the maximum rating value r_{max}.

(2) **Average Attack** [11]: Average attack is a somewhat more sophisticated attack than random attack and requires knowledge of each item's average rating in the system. Each introduced user rates items not in the target set randomly on a normal distribution with a mean equal to the average rating of the rated item. The target item is assigned r_{max}.

(3) **Bandwagon Attack** [10]: Bandwagon attack, also known as popular attack, takes advantage of the items with high popularity in the dataset and calls these items selected items. These selected items and the target item are assigned the maximum rating value r_{max}. The ratings on the filler items are determined randomly in a similar manner as in average attack.

(4) **Unorganized Attack** [9]: unorganized malicious attacks allow the concurrence of various attack strategies, and the number of rated items, the target item, and the rating functions can be different. Each attacker produces a small number of attack profiles with their own strategies and preference.

---

[1] https://www.librec.net/datasets/filmtrust.zip.
[2] https://guoguibing.github.io/librec/datasets/CiaoDVD.zip.
[3] https://grouplens.org/datasets/movielens/100k/.

Recommender Algorithms. In this paper, we focus on two DL-based RSs, i.e., neural matrix factorization (NeuMF) [28] and deep matrix factorization model (DMF) [29]. NeuMF is a fusion of MF and multilayer perceptron (MLP), allowing two models to learn individual embeddings and combine them by connecting their final hidden layers. DMF takes the user-item interaction matrix as input and extracts the features of the users and items into a low-dimensional space through the novel loss function based on binary cross-entropy.

Table 2. Attack effectiveness against NeuMF.

RS	NeuMF					
Metric	TKS@10			HR@10		
Dataset	FilmTrust	Ciao	ML-100K	FilmTrust	Ciao	ML-100K
PATR	**0.542**	0.708	**0.627**	**0.0362**	**0.0823**	**0.0513**
Random	0.334	0.571	0.443	0.0072	0.0326	0.0027
Average	0.337	0.643	0.357	0.0064	0.0637	0.0025
Bandwagon	0.425	**0.750**	0.425	0.0141	0.0248	0.0033
Unorganized	0.375	0.689	0.378	0.0076	0.0523	0.0025
PATRt	0.418	0.530	0.569	0.0232	0.0635	0.0183
PATRs	0.501	0.665	0.424	0.0137	0.0687	0.0258

Table 3. Attack effectiveness against and DMF.

RS	DMF					
Metric	TKS@10			HR@10		
Dataset	FilmTrust	Ciao	ML-100K	FilmTrust	Ciao	ML-100K
PATR	**0.574**	**0.682**	**0.776**	0.164	**0.054**	**0.0479**
Random	0.457	0.486	0.329	0.0071	0.0025	0.0024
Average	0.407	0.535	0.305	0.0069	0.0025	0.0019
Bandwagon	0.519	0.682	0.563	0.0875	0.0208	0.0037
Unorganized	0.530	0.498	0.489	**0.191**	0.0231	0.0035
PATRt	0.389	0.635	0.403	0.087	0.042	0.0094
PATRs	0.530	0.678	0.730	0.073	0.0512	0.0154

Metrics. We propose a new metrics top-K shift (TKS) to measure how much the top-K recommendation lists affected after the attack. We assume that each user recommendation list without the attack is L, and the recommendation list after the attack is $\tilde{L}$. TKS calculates the number of items not in L after the attack. For example, if the top-K recommendation list of u_1 is $L_1 = \{23, 1, 5, 7, 34\}$ before attack and $\tilde{L}_1 = \{5, 1, 18, 22, 34\}$ after the attack, then the item 23 and item 7 that should have been recommended to user u_1 are missing in $\tilde{L}_1$. The bigger TKS indicates better attack effectiveness. Because there are some differences in the order of items among the top-K recommendation lists generated by the same RS, we do not consider the specific order bias for each item. TKS is defined as:

$$\text{TKS} = \frac{\sum_{i=1}^{N} |N_{absent}|_i}{K * N} \tag{10}$$

Where K is the length of each user's recommendation list, N is the number of the recommendation lists, N_{absent} is the number of items not in L after the attack.

Another metric is HR [10–12]. Let R_u be the set of top-K recommendations for user u and $H_{u,i}$ denotes whether the target item i is in the recommendation list of user u. For each target item i, $H_{u,i}$ is assigned to 1, where $i \in R_u$, otherwise $H_{u,i}$ is assigned to 0. As with TKS, the bigger HR indicates the better attack effectiveness. The metric is defined as:

$$\text{HR} = \frac{\sum_{u,i} H_{u,i}}{|U| * N} \tag{11}$$

In this work, the K in the top-K recommendation lists is set to 10, which means the metrics are TKS@10 and HR@10.

4.2 Experimental Results and Analysis

Attack Effectiveness. The researchers prefer to deliberately choose the long tail items in previous literature because the long tail items are more sensitive to attack methods, and reflect better attack effectiveness. To accurately reflect the effectiveness of our attack, we do not especially choose the long tail items and randomly select ten items that do not exist in top-K recommendation lists when RSs are not attacked. To verify the contribution of our proposed pre-training module and sampling strategy, we remove these two parts respectively for comparison. The way without the pre-training module (triangle relations) is denoted as PATR_t, and the method without fake & real sampling strategy (only use regular widespread sampling) is denoted as PATR_s. Table 2 and Table 3 show the average performance of attacking NeuMF algorithm and DMF algorithm, respectively, and we bold the data with the best performance. It can be seen PATR can achieve the best performance in most cases and the second-best occasionally. The average increases(compared to the second-best attack method and a negative growth if PATR is the second-best) of TKS@10 in NeuMF and DMF are 4.26% and 5.06%, respectively, proving that PATR can make recommendation lists more disordered. Meanwhile, the average increases of HR@10 are 98.84% and 67.46%, which means PATR pushes the target item to more real users. Neither PATR_t nor PATR_s performs as well as PATR, which proves that the triangle relations and fake & real sampling strategy are helpful to attack effectiveness. The experiments of attack effectiveness can answer the **Q1** and **Q3**.

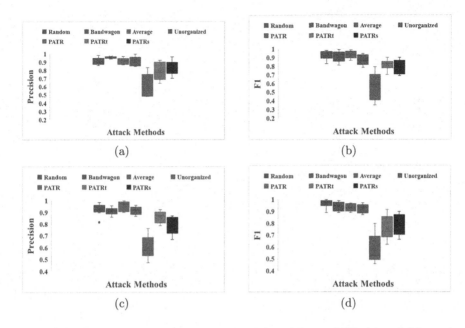

Fig. 3. Anti-detection capability against DLDRA and DegreeSAD. (a) and (b) are the results of DLDRA on the FilmTrust dataset. (c) and (d) are the results of DegreeSAD on the ML-100K dataset.

Anti-detection Capability. We apply two detectors, i.e., a state-of-the-art recommendation attack detector based on deep learning (DLDRA) [30] and a classic detector in recommender systems via selecting patterns analysis (DegreeSAD) [31] to verify the anti-detection capability of our attack. The metrics are precision and F1. The datasets are FilmTrust and ML-100K. The baseline attack models and the selection method of target items are the same as the attack effectiveness experiments. As shown in Fig. 3, we can observe clearly that the traditional poisoning attacks perform poorly, which means these attacks result in mission failure. The anti-detection capability of PATR is better than other methods. Specifically, both the precision and F1 are the smallest in the two datasets. Moreover, PATR makes the detector be the most unstable. Therefore, PATR has better anti-detection capability than baseline methods (answer the **Q2**). In ablation experiments, PATR$_t$ and PATR$_s$ are also better than the traditional poisoning attacks but less than PATR, which indicates that our proposed triangle relations and fake & real sampling strategy are conducive (answer the **Q3**).

Sensitivity Analysis. In this paper, we use some hyper-parameters and conduct experiments to determine the value of these hyper-parameters. We set λ_1 through λ_6 mentioned in Sect. 3.2 to 0.45, 0.45, 0.1, 0.35, 0.35, 0.3, respectively. In the sensitivity analysis, we focus on the encoder loss α, the decoder loss β,

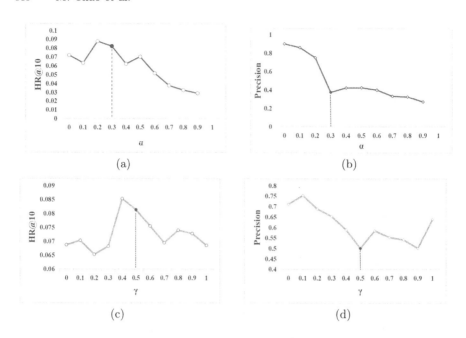

Fig. 4. Sensitivity analysis for β and γ. HR@10 measures the attack effectiveness, and precision measures the anti-detection capability.

and the ratio of user groups $\mathcal{F}_1$ and $\mathcal{F}_2$ in the sampling strategy for balancing our model's attack effectiveness and anti-detection capability. We use the Ciao dataset, and the metrics are HR@10 and precision, respectively. The higher the value of HR@10, the better the attack effectiveness. The smaller value of precision means the better anti-detection capability. We denote the ratio of $\mathcal{F}_1$ as γ. As shown in Fig. 4 (a) and (b), they are the sensitivity analysis of α. When α is 0.2, HR@10 is the best, while the anti-detection is poor. When α is 0.3, the attack effectiveness is the second best, and the anti-detection is the best. Therefore, we compromise by setting α to 0.3, while β is 0.7. Similarly, we set γ to 0.5, i.e., the number of $\mathcal{F}_1$ and $\mathcal{F}_2$ is the same.

5   Conclusion

In this paper, we focus on poisoning attacks. To reduce the probability of being detected, we optimize the sampling strategy for fake users by directly sampling a set of users from the real users. Furthermore, we adopt triangle relations and design a pre-training module. Finally, we propose a reconstruction module that combines CAE with the pre-training module's outputs to generate enhanced fake users. Our experiments on three real-world datasets show that our proposed model PATR outperforms baselines in attack effectiveness and anti-detection capability.

Acknowledgments. This study was supported by the National Key R&D Program of China (2018YFB1403602), Natural Science Foundation of Chongqing, China (cstc2020jcyj-msxmX0690), the Technological Innovation and Application Program of Chongqing (cstc2019jscx-mbdxX0008), the Fundamental Research Funds for the Central Universities of Chongqing University (2020CDJ-LHZZ-039), and the Overseas Returnees Innovation and Entrepreneurship Support Program of Chongqing (cx2020097).

References

1. Resnick, P., Varian, H.R.: Recommender systems. Commun. ACM **40**(3), 56–58 (1997)
2. Koren, Y., Bell, R., Volinsky, C.: Matrix factorization techniques for recommender systems. Computer **42**(8), 30–37 (2009)
3. Ricci, F., Rokach, L., Shapira, B.: Introduction to Recommender Systems Handbook. In: Ricci, F., Rokach, L., Shapira, B., Kantor, P.B. (eds.) Recommender Systems Handbook, pp. 1–35. Springer, Boston (2011). https://doi.org/10.1007/978-0-387-85820-3_1
4. O'Mahony, M., Hurley, N., Kushmerick, N., et al.: Collaborative recommendation: a robustness analysis. ACM Trans. Internet Technol. (TOIT) **4**(4), 344–377 (2004)
5. Hurley, N.J.: Robustness of recommender systems. In: Proceedings of the fifth ACM Conference on Recommender Systems, pp. 9–10 (2011)
6. Douceur, J.R.: The Sybil attack. In: Druschel, P., Kaashoek, F., Rowstron, A. (eds.) IPTPS 2002. LNCS, vol. 2429, pp. 251–260. Springer, Heidelberg (2002). https://doi.org/10.1007/3-540-45748-8_24
7. Wilson, D.C., Seminario, C.E.: When power users attack: assessing impacts in collaborative recommender systems. In: Proceedings of the 7th ACM Conference on Recommender Systems, pp. 427–430 (2013)
8. Li, B., Wang, Y., Singh, A., et al.: Data poisoning attacks on factorization-based collaborative filtering. In: Proceedings of the 30th International Conference on Neural Information Processing Systems, pp. 1893–1901 (2016)
9. Pang, M., Gao, W., Tao, M., et al.: Unorganized malicious attacks detection. In: Proceedings of the 32nd International Conference on Neural Information Processing Systems, pp. 6976–6985 (2018)
10. Gunes, I., Kaleli, C., Bilge, A., et al.: Shilling attacks against recommender systems: a comprehensive survey. Artif. Intell. Rev. **42**(4), 767–799 (2014)
11. Lam, S.K., Riedl, J.: Shilling recommender systems for fun and profit. In: Proceedings of the 13th International Conference on World Wide Web, pp. 393–402 (2004)
12. Si, M., Li, Q.: Shilling attacks against collaborative recommender systems: a review. Artif. Intell. Rev. **53**(1), 291–319 (2020)
13. Williams, C.A., Mobasher, B., Burke, R.: Defending recommender systems: detection of profile injection attacks. Serv. Oriented Comput. Appl. **1**(3), 157–170 (2007)
14. Meng, W., Xing, X., Sheth, A., et al.: Your online interests: Pwned! A pollution attack against targeted advertising. In: Proceedings of the ACM SIGSAC Conference on Computer and Communications Security, vol. 2014, pp. 129–140 (2014)
15. Lin, C., Chen, S., Li, H., et al.: Attacking recommender systems with augmented user profiles. In: Proceedings of the 29th ACM International Conference on Information & Knowledge Management, pp. 855–864 (2020)

16. Brendel, W., Rauber, J., Bethge, M.: Decision-based adversarial attacks: reliable attacks against black-box machine learning models. In: International Conference on Learning Representations (2018)
17. Zhang, S., Yao, L., Sun, A., et al.: Deep learning based recommender system: a survey and new perspectives. ACM Comput. Surv. (CSUR) **52**(1), 1–38 (2019)
18. Sahoo, A.K., Pradhan, C., Barik, R.K., et al.: DeepReco: deep learning based health recommender system using collaborative filtering. Computation **7**(2), 25 (2019)
19. van den Berg, R., Kipf, T.N., Welling, M.: Graph convolutional matrix completion (2017)
20. Masci, J., Meier, U., Cireşan, D., Schmidhuber, J.: Stacked convolutional auto-encoders for hierarchical feature extraction. In: Honkela, T., Duch, W., Girolami, M., Kaski, S. (eds.) ICANN 2011. LNCS, vol. 6791, pp. 52–59. Springer, Heidelberg (2011). https://doi.org/10.1007/978-3-642-21735-7_7
21. Herlocker, J.L., Konstan, J.A., Riedl, J.: Explaining collaborative filtering recommendations. In: Proceedings of the ACM Conference on Computer Supported Cooperative Work, vol. 2000, pp. 241–250 (2000)
22. Burke, R., Mobasher, B., Bhaumik, R., et al.: Segment-based injection attacks against collaborative filtering recommender systems. In: Fifth IEEE International Conference on Data Mining (ICDM'05). IEEE (2005)
23. Mobasher, B., Burke, R., Bhaumik, R., et al.: Toward trustworthy recommender systems: an analysis of attack models and algorithm robustness. ACM Trans. Internet Technol. (TOIT) **7**, 23-es (2007)
24. Fang, M., Yang, G., Gong, N.Z., et al.: Poisoning attacks to graph-based recommender systems. In: Proceedings of the 34th Annual Computer Security Applications Conference, pp. 381–392 (2018)
25. Zhang, H., Li, Y., Ding, B., et al.: Practical data poisoning attack against next-item recommendation. In: Proceedings of The Web Conference 2020, pp. 2458–2464 (2020)
26. Mescheder, L., Geiger, A., Nowozin, S.: Which training methods for GANs do actually converge? In: International Conference on Machine Learning, PMLR, pp. 3481–3490 (2018)
27. Hong, Y., Hwang, U., Yoo, J., et al.: How generative adversarial networks and their variants work: an overview. ACM Comput. Surv. (CSUR) **52**(1), 1–43 (2019)
28. He, X., Liao, L., Zhang, H., et al.: Neural collaborative filtering. In: Proceedings of the 26th International Conference on World Wide Web, pp. 173–182 (2017)
29. Xue, H.J., Dai, X., Zhang, J., et al.: Deep matrix factorization models for recommender systems. In: International Joint Conference on Artificial Intelligence, vol. 17, pp. 3203–3209 (2017)
30. Zhou, Q., Wu, J., Duan, L.: Recommendation attack detection based on deep learning. J. Inf. Secur. Appl. **52**, 102493 (2020)
31. Li, W., Gao, M., Li, H., et al.: Shilling attack detection in recommender systems via selecting patterns analysis. IEICE Trans. Inf. Syst. **99**(10), 2600–2611 (2016)

Low-Cost LiDAR-Based Vehicle Detection for Self-driving Container Trucks at Seaport

Changjie Zhang[2], Zhenchao Ouyang[1,3(✉)], Lu Ren[1,2], and Yu Liu[1,2]

[1] Hangzhou Innovation Institute, Hangzhou 31000, China
[2] State Key Laboratory of Software Development Environment, BeiHang University, Beijing 100191, China
ouyangkid@buaa.edu.cn
[3] Zhongfa Aviation University, Hangzhou 31000, Zhejiang, China

Abstract. The self-driving technology has been developed rapidly in the past decades, due to new sensors, and car manufacturers have become more open. However, fully self-driving vehicles for the public still has a long way to go. Most studies try to focus on self-driving in special scenes, such as park sightseeing car, express logistics vehicle, sweeper, indoor service robot, and special vehicles in the mining area or seaport area. One of the critical issues is that the cost of a self-driving vehicle should strictly be controlled for commercial uses. This paper presents a low-cost LiDAR-based moving obstacle detection and tracking for self-driving container trucks in the low-speed seaport area. We build a CNN model for obstacle detection with the bird's eye view (BEV) map generated from two low density LiDARs equipped at the head of a container truck. A boosting tracker is used to achieve real-time processing speed on the embedded module of Tx2. Simulation on the collected data shows that our Strided-Yolo model can achieve the highest mAP on the BEV projection map than other models.

Keywords: Obstacle detection and tracking · Autonomous truck · Multiple LiDAR · Deep learning · Seaport area

1 Introduction

In the past two decades, self-driving technologies have attracted interests from both academic researchers and commercial capital, especially from some IT giants, such as Waymo [32] from Google and Uber [1], who have published their self-driving passenger vehicles. However, besides many technical problems, the legal issues related also constrain the accessibility of self-driving vehicles to the public. Recent researches [6,16,19,23,31,35] begins to explore the applications of self-driving in specific scenarios, especially in the closed or semi-closed area with low speed, such as self-driving mine vehicles, container trucks and agricultural vehicles.

© ICST Institute for Computer Sciences, Social Informatics and Telecommunications Engineering 2021
Published by Springer Nature Switzerland AG 2021. All Rights Reserved
H. Gao and X. Wang (Eds.): CollaborateCom 2021, LNICST 407, pp. 451–466, 2021.
https://doi.org/10.1007/978-3-030-92638-0_27

Different from the research phase, a demo self-driving vehicle can be equipped with the best sensors for different targets [2,8]. Considering the commercial usage, the cost of the sensor solution is strictly constrained for large-scale deployment of self-driving vehicle. Selection of related equipment and sensors is a big challenge for container trucks. Moreover, different from normal vision-based detection tasks, the decision system in self-driving relies highly on accurate sensing data of the surrounding environment. Because the traditional camera-based front-view cannot offer accurate location information of on-road obstacles, almost all self-driving systems rely on the Light Detection And Ranging (LiDAR) data. Table 1 compares several of the reported solutions, it can be seen that research projects, such as KITTI, nuScenes and Argoverse use top mounting solutions for small vehicle. For commercial solutions, Waymo uses four short-range LiDAR on each side of the vehicle and a high resolution LiDAR on the top. Audi auto uses 5 Velodyne-16 on the top, and Tusimple highway solution uses two high resolution LiDAR on the each side of the truck head, and one static front-view LiDAR on the top. The mainstream solution is to install multiple LiDARs to ensure safety, but at the expense of sensor costs. Especially for large trucks, the blind area of a single LiDAR top installation scheme is too large.

Table 1. Comparison of the current reported LiDAR solutions.

Dataset/solution	Vehicle	Lidar	Position
KITTI [8]	VW Passat station wagon	Velodyne 64E	Top
nuScenes [2]	Renault Zoe electric car	Velodyne 32	Top
Waymo [15]	Waymo	1 Mid-range & 4 short-range	Top+side
Argoverse [3]	Ford Fusion Hybrids	Velodyne 32 * 2	Top
A2D2 [9]	Audi Car	Velodyne16*5	Top
Tusimple[a]	Truck	4 range LiDAR & 1 static LiDAR static	Top+side

[a] https://www.tusimple.com/

Although the price of current LiDAR sensors dropped quickly in the past several years, the cost for a redundant perception system still very high, especially when some dense LiDAR (such as Velodyne HDL-64E or HDL-32E) is used. Therefore, our system tries to reduce the cost by combining two low density LiDAR (Velodyne VLP-16) as the basic sensor module in our fully self-driving container truck.

This paper presents a deep learning-based CNN model for low-cost LiDAR 3D point cloud vehicle detection. With a series of point cloud pre-processing, such as distance filtering, frame accumulation, ground elimination and bird's eye view (BEV) projection, we can generate stable obstacle features for later detection and tracking. We build a new dataset with dual-LiDAR and GPS-RTK collected with our own self-driving container trucks in a seaport area in China. A well-designed lightweight CNN model is then trained based on this dataset. Both off-line and on-road tests show that our tracking system can achieve reliable results in real-time.

The contributions of this paper can be summarized as follows:

- A low-cost LiDAR-based obstacle detection and tracking system that uses only two low density LiDAR and GPS-RTK is designed. The system combines traditional point cloud process modules (ground removing and point cloud BEV projection) and CNN model together to achieve high accuracy. The total cost is also reduced.
- A lightweight CNN model is proposed to fulfill the real-time detection task based on the refined BEV map of LiDAR point cloud.
- A new dual-LiDAR based point cloud dataset in the seaport area is also presented based on a novel dataset collected from real seaport in Ningbo.

The rest of this paper is organized as follows. In Sect. 2, we review the LiDAR-based detection and related CNN architectures. We present our sensor solution and the low-cost LiDAR-based vehicle detection and tracking system in Sect. 3. In Sect. 4, we evaluate our system with a real LiDAR dataset collected from a seaport area in the east coast of China. Finally, we summarize the advantages and disadvantages of our system in Sect. 5.

2   Related Work

LiDAR-based obstacle detection in the self-driving area can be divided into two main categories: LiDAR 3D point cloud detection and LiDAR projection based detection.

2.1   LiDAR 3D Point Cloud Detection

The LiDAR 3D point cloud detection model often uses raw LiDAR point cloud or voxelized point cloud as the input to later deep learning models.

The 3D FCN [12] first changes the traditional 2D convolutional network module into 3D full convolutional network module to process the raw 3D point cloud from LiDAR. Therefore, the 3D FCN can use 3D bounding boxes as labels, and predict the target in a 3D manner. Simulation on Kitti dataset [7] shows that the 3D FCN can achieve better performance than traditional point cloud based detection approaches. In this way, the whole training process can be completed in an end-to-end way.

Due to the randomness of LiDAR point cloud, the representation of the same object is much disordered than pixel based pictures. Voxelization is commonly used to reduce this kind of randomness. The VoxelNet [40] first transfers raw point cloud into equally spaced 3D voxels, but the down-sampling process also reduces the features of the point cloud. A voxel feature encoding (VFE) [27] layer that combines with the region proposal network architecture is then presented for 3D object detection. This model can achieve effective representation of vehicles and human beings with a Velodyne HDL-64e.

Due to the huge computation of high dimensionality of point cloud and voxel, PIXOR [37] can achieve real-time 3D object detection through a proposal-free, single-stage detector that outputs oriented 3D object estimates decoded from pixel-wise neural network predictions. This model considers a series of optimization including feature representation, network architecture, time consumption and detection accuracy.

In [13], the authors present a 3D Backbone Network to solve the 3D feature extraction task. With this backbone, it is much easier to extract rich 3D feature maps by using sparse 3D CNN [34] operations, and benefit for later operation such as detection or classification. This module can transfer raw 3D point cloud into multiple 3D images efficiently way. Experiments on KITTI also show their model can achieve a reliable result in detection tasks.

In PointGrid [11], a full CNN of classification network and a U-Net segmentation network are presented for different tasks with raw point cloud input. Both of the two networks begin with a pointgrid [11] input layer that can encode the raw point cloud into multi-dimension matrix for later convolution. This model can achieve state-of-the-art performance in related tasks.

2.2   LiDAR Projection-Based Detection

Due to the huge computation needed for processing the 3D point cloud, reducing the 3D point cloud into 2D projection is a common way. Moreover, this kind of projection can be fused with camera images as multi-model-based algorithms.

Cristiano [21] proposed Bilateral Filter based upsampling to match the frontview of point cloud projection with related images. Different filter parameters are analyzed to match the field of view of both sensors (LiDAR and camera). Based on this work, different multiview [14,18,20,22] CNN models are proposed for related on-road obstacle detection, sense reconstruction [17,38] and segmentation [5,36] tasks for self-driving.

Xiaozhi Chen et al. [4] also proposed a multiview 3D object detection network that fused different fields of both the LiDAR projection maps and the camera image as input. In their model, both LiDAR-based frontview and BEV projections are used to generate region proposal along with the images.

Complex-YOLO [28] presented an Euler-Region-Proposal based on BEV projection of 3D LiDAR point cloud. This net can predict not only the bounding box of the obstacle, but also the heading angle with the 3D bounding box reconversion module. Simulation on the KITTI dataset shows that this model can achieve real-time detection at 50 frames per second (FPS) on an NVidia Titan X.

Most of the current LiDAR-based detection models are designed based on the dataset of KITTI and nuScenes with a single LiDAR mounted on the vehicle roof, this kind of setup is only suitable for small size vehicles. However, the container trucks are very large, the vehicle head and body will block most of the laser beams, and lead to blind spot. The mounting of the sensors has a great influence on the distribution of the point cloud; therefore, the deep learning model constructed based on the data collected by different solutions cannot be used on other systems. Moreover, the above mentioned models are only designed for high-performance GPU server and do not tested on vehicle environments.

3   Dual-LiDAR Perceptive System

However, as we mentioned above, most of current research works that utilize deep learning model [25] to process 3D point cloud are based on the KITTI dataset. This means that those works can only work with dense LiDAR such as Velodyne HDL-64E. This LiDAR sensor can offer 360° of 64 scan lines of the surrounding environment; however, the price of the sensor is too high. When using low-dense LiDAR such as Velodyne VLP-16 that can only offer 16 laser scan lines, the sampling information may drop to 1/4 of that of the Velodyne HDL-64E. Figure 1 shows the difference between our system and KITTI dataset. This means that we can get less stable sensing data for the later process. That is a big challenge for on-road obstacle detection and tracking for self-driving. Recent works rarely consider the sparse sampling of low-cost LiDAR and vehicle environment deployment as we do.

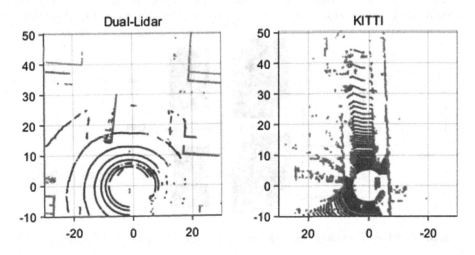

Fig. 1. The left figure shows a BEV LiDAR point cloud projection based on our system, and right one is based on the Velodyne HDL-64E of KITTI dataset.

Figure 2 shows the perception module of our sensor solution for the self-driving container truck. It can be seen that the two low density LiDARs are equipped on the corners of the vehicle head. Both of the two LiDARs' laser scan lines can reach the front area and can be combined as a 32 scan line. For the side areas, each LiDAR covers one side. This sensor deployment simulates the attention mechanism of human drivers.

Although our system has lower sensing performance than dense LiDAR, we investigate several refined modules together to enhance the raw point cloud feature. The vehicle has a maximum speed of 30 km/h in the seaport area. And most vehicles are container trucks with huge size, making them easier to be detected and tracked.

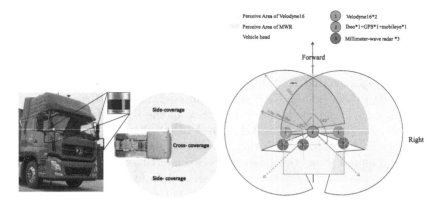

Fig. 2. Two low density LiDARs are equipped on the opposite side of the container truck head (left). The front sensing field (cross-coverage area) is covered by both LiDARs and can achieve double density, and the side-coverage areas are covered by one LiDAR (right). The bottom one is a full sensor scheme used in our self-driving truck.

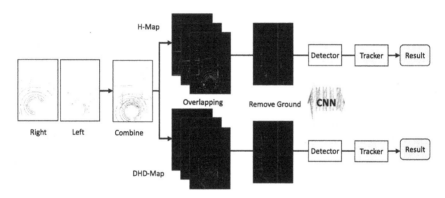

Fig. 3. Workflow of detection and tracking system for our dual-LiDAR container truck

Figure 3 illustrates the whole workflow of dual-LiDAR container truck detection and tracking system. We first calibrate the two LiDAR into the same vehicle body coordinate (with the RTK-GPS as the origin point). For LiDAR BEV projection, two kinds of maps are generated. The H-Map only considers the Height (z-axis) of each point, and the final H-Map contains only one channel (Gray). The HDD-Map considers the Height (z-axis), Depth (y-axis), and Density [39] values of point cloud as a three-channel-map. Equation 1 is the calculation of Density value at each point of i, where C_i is the total points in the local cell. And then, we merge each three successive frames according to the GPS into one to enhance the point cloud features. As the LiDAR sample frequency 10 Hz and installed as in Fig. 2, three-overlapped-frame for the side-view can achieve 48 scan lines, and for front-view can achieve 96 scan lines. We also propose a simple voxel-height-based algorithm to remove the scan lines on road surfaces. This also leads to clearer obstacle features for later detection.

$$Dense(i) = min(1.0, log\frac{C_i + 1}{64})$$ (1)

With the above pre-processing, the final BEV map will be fed into a lightweight CNN detection model and trained in an 'end-to-end' fashion with carefully labeled bounding boxes. A boosting tracker [10] is used for tracking the obstacles in each frame. We update the tracking items with the CNN detector each 0.5 s to reduce the time consumption of convolution.

3.1 Data Collection and BEV Map Projection

All the data used for model training and testing are collected from a seaport area with our self-driving trucks. Totally, there are three long sequences collected on both sunny and rainy days. The two Velodyne VLP-16 are equipped at the vehicle head of 1.7 m height, therefore, we filter the raw LiDAR point cloud with the following distances: $x \in [-30\,m, 30\,m]$, $y \in [-10\,m, 50\,m]$ and $z \in [-1.7\,m, 2.8\,m]$. In this way, each frame of the point cloud contains a 60 * 60 square with 4.5 m height. This height limitation can cover all the other trucks. Each frame of point cloud generates a 480 * 480 pixel image; therefore, 1 m equals 8 pixels in the image. Different from previous works that do not pay attention to the back view of the vehicle, our ego vehicle is in the back center of the BEV map. For safety reasons, about 10 m of the vehicle tailstock are also considered, because the container truck is nearly 7 m long.

For each long sequence, only the frame that contains obstacles is selected as the short sequence. Therefore, most of the short sequences contain 1 to 8 obstacles. And then, we label the BEV frames, and check the bounding boxes with several different people. The final dataset contains similar sequences of 4647 (sunny), 4594 (cloudy and small rain) and 3973 (sunny) frames, with each having two kinds of projection maps (based on BEV) and well labelled bounding boxes.

3.2 Lightweight CNN Detector

We combine a well designed lightweight convolutional neural network detector with the commonly used multi-target tracker to solve the obstacle tracking task for our self-driving vehicles. And the boosting tracker is used as the basic tracker in the multi-target tracking framework.

Considering the detection performance highly affects the later tracking, the key requirement is to detect all the obstacles efficiently. We combine a resized StridedNet [30] front-bone with the Yolo detection layer as the Strided-Yolo model. Figure 4 and Table 2 are the detailed CNN architecture of our detector model. Large kernel size of 7 * 7 convolutional layer is first used, followed by small kernel of 3 * 3 with a stride of 2 that can reduce the original image into 1/2 of the original size. Alternate stacking of 3 * 3 and 1 * 1 convolutional layers with different filters at 3–17 layers are used to extract the rich features. At the second last layer, we up-sample the map and combine it with layer 8. In this way, we use layers 18–23 to extract a two-layer-pyramid-feature at two different scales for Yolo layer.

For tracking stage, we eliminates the point cloud beyond the bounding boxes generated from the detection model. And then, the point cloud containing only the targets uses the same BEV projection to generate the feature maps. At last, the boosting tracker from Opencv is adopted for target matching of consecutive frames.

Strided-Yolo Architecture

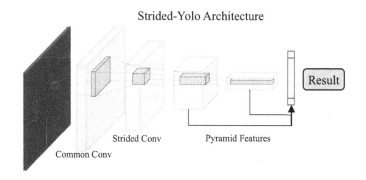

Fig. 4. The architecture of Strided-Yolo model.

Table 2. The detail architecture of Strided-Yolo model.

#	Layer	Parameter	Other OP
1	Conv	7 * 7 * 64/2	Maxpool (2 * 2/1)
2	Conv	3 * 3 * 128/2	Maxpool (2 * 2/1)
3	Conv	1 * 1 * 128/1	Maxpool (2 * 2/1)
4	Conv	3 * 3 * 256/2	Maxpool (2 * 2/1)
5	Conv	1 * 1 * 128/1	Maxpool (2 * 2/1)
6	Conv	3 * 3 * 256/1	Maxpool (2 * 2/1)
7	Conv	1 * 1 * 128/1	Maxpool (2 * 2/1)
8	Conv	3 * 3 * 512/2	Maxpool(2 * 2/1)
9	Conv	1 * 1 * 256/1	*4
10	Conv	3 * 3 * 512/1	
11	Conv	1 * 1 * 256/1	
18	Conv	3 * 3 * 1024/2	
19	Yolo		
20	Combine 8 + 18		
21	Yolo		

4   Experimental Study

4.1   Data Augmentation

Different from version-based image detection, the projection of LiDAR point cloud has more stable features than images. The commonly use projection algorithms mentioned in Sect. 3 use the distance values for sampling. And this kind of data will not be affected by the lighting conditions of the environment. Moreover, the commonly used data augmentation methods, such scale, flip and Gaussian Noise, also have very tiny effects during training. Therefore, we first test our dataset on the benchmark model the, tiny version of Yolo and Yolo-3l [26], on two kinds of projection maps (H-map and HDD-Map). Sequences 1 and 2 are used for training, and Sequence 3 is used for testing. For the random mode, we deployed the above mentioned augmentation methods on the dataset and use only the raw dataset for the non-random mode.

Table 3. Comparison of the training process with and without randomize for LiDAR projection data.

Model		Yolov3-tiny	Yolov3-tiny	Yolov3-tiny-3l	Yolov3-tiny-3l
Modality		H-Map	HDD-Map	H-Map	HDD-Map
FPS		**90.3**	84.5	79.5	75.0
BFLOPs		**7.12**	7.25	9.32	9.45
Random	RPs/Img	20.15	20.63	**14.7**	15.84
	IOU	60.17%	59.53%	59.61%	**63.52%**
	Recall	77.85%	77.26%	79.32%	**85.68%**
Non-random	RPs/Img	16.66	16.08	13.56	**13.19**
	IOU	60.27%	61.60%	62.83%	**64.22%**
	Recall	80.43%	82.5%	84.85%	**85.96%**

Table 3 illustrates the RPs per image, IOU and Recall of the two models trained and tested on our dataset. For H-Map based models, each frame contains only one channel of LiDAR BEV map, the FPS (Frame Per Second) and model sizes (Billion Float Operations Per Second, BFLOP) are slightly faster and smaller than the HDD-Map (three channels) based models, respectively. It can be seen easy that, the models achieve larger IOU and Recall when training without data augmentation methods. The Recall of Yolov3-tiny trained on H-Map increases by nearly 10% when shut down the random mode in training phase. However, this kind of difference is not so significant for Yolov3-tiny-3l models trained on HDD-Map. The RPs/image is the region proposal detected by the model per image, lower value means the model can reach similar or higher detection accuracy by generating less proposals. This means that when dealing with LiDAR point cloud projection maps, there is no need to use the traditional data augmentation method. The later training also shuts down the data augmentation function.

The H-Map contains only one channel of the LiDAR point cloud projection, and the models trained on the HDD-Map performs slightly better than the H-Map based models. However, the improvement of HDD-Map is still not very remarkable for it has triple scales of information. This also means that there is much redundant information in the HDD-Map.

4.2   Comparison of Models

We evaluate our model and compared with several state-of-the-arts CNN architectures. Three different kinds of enhanced LiDAR projection map are used: 1) $c1f3g1$: H-Map with the combination of three successive frames and elimination of the ground; 2) $c3f3g0$: HDD-Map with the combination of three successive frames and without elimination of the ground; 3) $c3f3g1$: HDD-Map with the combination of three successive frames and elimination of the ground. Figure 5 illustrates the related projection maps. It can be seen from Fig. 5(b) that simply combining three successive frames can increase the features of the obstacle; however, the scan lines on the ground also lead to noise. In Fig. 5(a) and Fig. 5(c), an H-Map and an HDD-Map with elimination of the ground are generated. Without the ground, the vehicle features are clearer and may help improve the later detection.

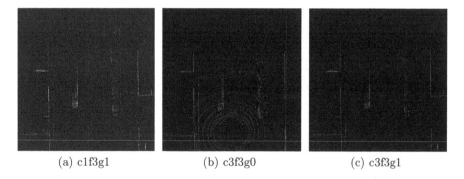

    (a) c1f3g1   (b) c3f3g0   (c) c3f3g1

Fig. 5. Difference between three different projection maps with a combination of three frames and elimination of the ground. ($c = channels$, $f = frames$, $g = ground$. PS. $c1f3g1 = 1$ channel of the projection map)

Along with the Strided-Yolo model, we also train 4 different detection models (i.e., Yolov3-tiny, Yolov3-tiny-3l, XNor [24], and HetConv [29]) on the three enhanced LiDAR projection maps (i.e., c1f3g1, c3f3g0, and c3f3g1) for comparison. Figure 6 illustrates the Precision-Recall curves of the five models on the three kinds of projection maps. The point where the line meets the curve is the break event point (BEP), where *precision = recall*. It can be seen easily that the PR curve of Strided-Yolo can cover all the other curves in Fig. 6(a) and Fig. 6(c). This means that our Strided-Yolo preforms the best on the two kinds of LiDAR projection maps. In Fig. 6(b), the Strided-Yolo and Yolov3-tiny show very similar values at the BEP. The XNor model performs the worst in all the cases, and cannot even converge when dealing with stacked point cloud.

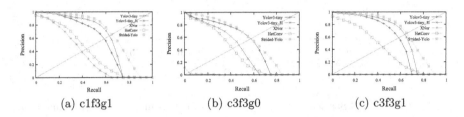

(a) c1f3g1   (b) c3f3g0   (c) c3f3g1

Fig. 6. Precision-Recall Curves of different CNN models with the three projection maps.

Figure 7 shows the PR curves of Strided-Yolo trained on the three stacked projection maps (i.e., c1f3g1, c3f3g0, and c3f3g1) and single frame maps (c1f1g0 and c3f1g0). It can be seen that with more frames, the model can achieve better performance. By eliminating the ground, the models (c1f3g1 and c3f3g1) can achieve higher performance. The models trained on HDD-Map (c3f3g1) and H-Map (c1f3g1) show very similar RP curves.

Table 4. Mean average precision (mAP) of the compared models under different IOU thresholds.

Map	IOU	Model				
		Yolov3-Tiny	Yolov3-Tiny_3l	XNor	HetConv	Strided-Yolo
c1f3g1	0.35	67.85%	71.21%	44.57%	46.90%	73.20%
	0.5	55.96%	60.70%	35.35%	40.14%	66.87%
	0.75	10.81%	10.97%	9.30%	5.17%	31.01%
c3f3g0	0.35	66.98%	62.64%	1.62%	44.45%	64.37%
	0.5	52.75%	41.78%	1.22%	37.37%	57.10%
	0.75	3.75%	6.06%	0.76%	4.91%	19.89%
c3f3g1	0.35	68.03%	71.16%	0.02%	46.06%	70.16%
	0.5	54.50%	61.50%	0.00%	39.60%	66.37%
	0.75	11.48%	9.37%	0.00%	5.02%	29.88%

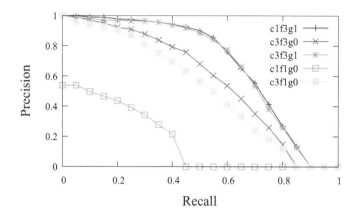

Fig. 7. PR curves of Strided-Yolo on the three projection maps vs. single frame maps.

In Table 4, the mean average precision (mAP) of each model at different intersections over the union (IOU) and LiDAR projection maps is listed. Three kinds of IOU (i.e., 0.35, 0.5 and 0.75) are calculated, and it can be seen that the Strided-Yolo model can achieve the highest mAP in most occasions. Even for $IOU = 0.75$, the Strided-Yolo can still remain about 30% of mAP when training with c1f3g1 and c3f3g1 projection maps, and the value is much higher than the rest of other models. This also means that our model is robust enough for real road conditions. For small IOU (0.35), the Strided-Yolo only performs slightly worse than Yolov3-Tiny and Yolov3-Tiny-3l when using c3f3g0 and c3f3g1, respectively.

Traditional LiDAR detection methods, such as the commonly used DBSCAN clustering [33], are not considered, because they are highly depend on manual tuning, and the robustness of the parameters is very poor. As we tested, the DBScan cannot learn the point cloud distribution of the target, and only relies on the point cloud distance features, which will introduce a large number of false detection results (such as stockade, container, portal crane, etc.), or detect the car head and body as two independent targets. Another disadvantage of the point cloud clustering algorithms is that they cannot provide an accurate target contour, and therefore cannot be used to predict the target size. This makes the quantitative evaluation of traditional algorithms very difficult.

Table 5. Time complexity of the final model with different input projection maps on Tx2.

Map	Preprocess	Detection	Tracking	Total
c1f3g1	0.105 s	0.008 s	0.0046 s	0.1176 s
c3f3g0	0.162 s	0.009 s	0.0046 s	0.1756 s
c3f3g1	0.108 s	0.009 s	0.0046 s	0.1216 s

4.3   Tracking Test

Although the stacked point cloud projection map of c1f3g1 has only one channel of the feature (with the elimination of the ground), it can achieve the highest mAP for Strided-Yolo. Therefore, we use it as our BEV projection map.

The detection and tracking are based CUDA and CNN model, and the processing speed is obtained based on the mean value of the point cloud for 500 consecutive frames, hence the speed. Therefore, the speed is an order of magnitude higher than Arm cpu-based preprocessing. Moreover, the number of dynamic targets in a single frame in the port area is generally about ten, and the matching speed of the boosting tracker is almost negligible. We stack each 3 successive frames of point cloud, and the average processing time for stacking and eliminating the round on Nvidia Jetson Tx2 is listed in Table 5. Most time consumption spends on pre-processing, and the detection and tracking time can be ignored. Moreover, as the Strided-Yolo can achieve very similar performance on the HDD-Map of c3f3g1 and H-Map of c1f3g1, their computational delays are also very close. We choose the c1f3g1 as our final projection map for it has better mAP on all IOU, as shown in Table 4. As the pre-processing module consume a large processing time of 0.1 s, we try to update the detection results for the tracker each 0.5 s. And the tracker will keep tracking for the next 5 frames (i.e., 0.5 s). This means that we stack each 3 continuous point cloud frames for detection, and use the next 5 single frames for tracking.

We also conduct an on-road test with our dual-LiDAR perceptive system on the Nvidia Jetson Tx2 along with other systems on a fully self-driving container truck. The total tracking accuracy can achieve about 87% (with IOU threshold as 0.35), and errors occur mostly when other trucks are driving out of the predefined sensing field of the ego-vehicle.

5   Conclusion

This paper has presented a novel deep learning-based vehicle detection system with two low-cost LiDAR for container trucks in the seaport area. Compare to other commercial solutions presented in Table 1, our sensor cost for low-speed truck is more than half lower than Tusimple. We employ the traditional LiDAR point cloud method to enhance the point cloud by merging continuous frames and eliminating the ground. This will help to maintain clearer vehicle features in BEV projection maps. Different kinds of projection maps are trained with a well-designed CNN model. A comparison with state-of-the-art models shows that our model can achieve the best performance on most occasions. We also test our system on the low-power embedded module of Tx2 with our self-driving system.

Acknowledgment. This work has been supported by China Postdoctoral Science Foundation (2020M681798), Qianjiang Excellent Post-Doctoral Program (2020Y4A001) and 2020 Zhejiang Postdoctoral Research Project (ZJ2020011). JITRI Suzhou Automotive Research Institute Project (CEC20190404). Chongqing Autonomous Unmanned

System Development Foundation and Key Technology Strategic Research Project (2020-XZ-CQ-3). The authors would like to thank Plusgo for their cooperation during data collection.

References

1. Bai, M., Mattyus, G., Homayounfar, N., Wang, S., Lakshmikanth, S.K., Urtasun, R.: Deep multi-sensor lane detection. In: 2018 IEEE/RSJ International Conference on Intelligent Robots and Systems (IROS), pp. 3102–3109. IEEE (2018)
2. Caesar, H., et al.: nuScenes: a multimodal dataset for autonomous driving. In: Proceedings of the IEEE/CVF Conference on Computer Vision and Pattern Recognition, pp. 11621–11631 (2020)
3. Chang, M.F., et al.: Argoverse: 3D tracking and forecasting with rich maps. In: Proceedings of the IEEE/CVF Conference on Computer Vision and Pattern Recognition, pp. 8748–8757 (2019)
4. Chen, X., Ma, H., Wan, J., Li, B., Xia, T.: Multi-view 3D object detection network for autonomous driving. In: Computer Vision and Pattern Recognition, pp. 6526–6534. IEEE (2017)
5. Dong, X., Niu, J., Cui, J., Fu, Z., Ouyang, Z.: Fast segmentation-based object tracking model for autonomous vehicles. In: Qiu, M. (ed.) ICA3PP 2020. LNCS, vol. 12453, pp. 259–273. Springer, Cham (2020). https://doi.org/10.1007/978-3-030-60239-0_18
6. Gao, J., Yan, W., Yin, S., Tian, D., Xing, L.: Research on the applicability of automated driving vehicle on the expressway system. Technical report, SAE Technical Paper (2020)
7. Geiger, A., Lenz, P., Stiller, C., Urtasun, R.: Vision meets robotics: the KITTI dataset. Int. J. Robot. Res. **32**(11), 1231–1237 (2013)
8. Geiger, A., Lenz, P., Urtasun, R.: Are we ready for autonomous driving? The KITTI vision benchmark suite. In: 2012 IEEE Conference on Computer Vision and Pattern Recognition, pp. 3354–3361. IEEE (2012)
9. Geyer, J., et al.: A2D2: Audi autonomous driving dataset. arXiv preprint arXiv:2004.06320 (2020)
10. Grabner, H., Grabner, M., Bischof, H.: Real-time tracking via on-line boosting. In: Proceedings of the British Machine Vision Conference (BMVC), vol. 1, pp. 1409–1422 (2006)
11. Le, T., Duan, Y.: PointGrid: a deep network for 3D shape understanding. In: Proceedings of the IEEE Conference on Computer Vision and Pattern Recognition, pp. 9204–9214 (2018)
12. Li, B.: 3D fully convolutional network for vehicle detection in point cloud. In: 2017 IEEE/RSJ International Conference on Intelligent Robots and Systems (IROS), pp. 1513–1518. IEEE (2017)
13. Li, X., Guivant, J.E., Kwok, N., Xu, Y.: 3D backbone network for 3D object detection. arXiv:1901.08373 (2019)
14. Li, Y., Niu, J., Ouyang, Z.: Fusion strategy of multi-sensor based object detection for self-driving vehicles. In: 2020 International Wireless Communications and Mobile Computing (IWCMC), pp. 1549–1554. IEEE (2020)
15. Sun, P., et al.: Scalability in Perception for Autonomous Driving: Waymo Open Dataset. arXiv:1912.04838 (2019)

16. Mokhtar, B., Azab, M., Fathalla, E., Ghourab, E.M., Magdy, M., Eltoweissy, M.: Reliable collaborative semi-infrastructure vehicle-to-vehicle communication for local file sharing. In: Wang, X., Gao, H., Iqbal, M., Min, G. (eds.) CollaborateCom 2019. LNICST, vol. 292, pp. 698–711. Springer, Cham (2019). https://doi.org/10.1007/978-3-030-30146-0_47
17. Ouyang, Z., et al.: A cGANs-based scene reconstruction model using lidar point cloud. In: IEEE International Symposium on Parallel and Distributed Processing with Applications. IEEE (2017)
18. Ouyang, Z., Cui, J., Dong, X., Li, Y., Niu, J.: SaccadeFork: a lightweight multi-sensor fusion-based target detector. Inf. Fusion 1, 1 (2021)
19. Ouyang, Z., Niu, J., Liu, Y., Guizani, M.: Deep CNN-based real-time traffic light detector for self-driving vehicles. IEEE Trans. Mob. Comput. 19(2), 300–313 (2019)
20. Ouyang, Z., Wang, C., Liu, Yu., Niu, J.: Multiview CNN model for sensor fusion based vehicle detection. In: Hong, R., Cheng, W.-H., Yamasaki, T., Wang, M., Ngo, C.-W. (eds.) PCM 2018. LNCS, vol. 11166, pp. 459–470. Springer, Cham (2018). https://doi.org/10.1007/978-3-030-00764-5_42
21. Premebida, C., Garrote, L., Asvadi, A., Ribeiro, A.P., Nunes, U.: High-resolution lidar-based depth mapping using bilateral filter. In: 2016 IEEE 19th International Conference on Intelligent Transportation Systems (ITSC), pp. 2469–2474. IEEE (2016)
22. Qi, C.R., Su, H., Nießner, M., Dai, A., Yan, M., Guibas, L.J.: Volumetric and multi-view CNNs for object classification on 3D data. In: Proceedings of the IEEE Conference on Computer Vision and Pattern Recognition, pp. 5648–5656 (2016)
23. Qin, K., Wang, B., Zhang, H., Ma, W., Yan, M., Wang, X.: Research on application and testing of autonomous driving in ports. Technical report, SAE Technical Paper (2020)
24. Rastegari, M., Ordonez, V., Redmon, J., Farhadi, A.: XNOR-Net: ImageNet classification using binary convolutional neural networks. In: Leibe, B., Matas, J., Sebe, N., Welling, M. (eds.) ECCV 2016. LNCS, vol. 9908, pp. 525–542. Springer, Cham (2016). https://doi.org/10.1007/978-3-319-46493-0_32
25. Redmon, J., Farhadi, A.: YOLO9000: better, faster, stronger. In: 2017 IEEE Conference on Computer Vision and Pattern Recognition. IEEE (2017)
26. Redmon, J., Farhadi, A.: YOLOv3: an incremental improvement. In: arXiv:1804.02767 (2018)
27. Shi, S., et al.: PV-RCNN: point-voxel feature set abstraction for 3D object detection. In: Proceedings of the IEEE/CVF Conference on Computer Vision and Pattern Recognition, pp. 10529–10538 (2020)
28. Simon, M., Milz, S., Amende, K., Gross, H.-M.: Complex-YOLO: an Euler-Region-Proposal for real-time 3D object detection on point clouds. In: Leal-Taixé, L., Roth, S. (eds.) ECCV 2018. LNCS, vol. 11129, pp. 197–209. Springer, Cham (2019). https://doi.org/10.1007/978-3-030-11009-3_11
29. Singh, P., Verma, V.K., Rai, P., Namboodiri, V.P.: HetConv: heterogeneous kernel-based convolutions for deep CNNs. In: Computer Vision and Pattern Recognition (CVPR) 2019. IEEE (2019)
30. Springenberg, J.T., Dosovitskiy, A., Brox, T., Riedmiller, M.: Striving for simplicity: the all convolutional net. arXiv preprint (2014)
31. Tang, X., Geng, Z., Chen, W.: Safety message propagation using vehicle-infrastructure cooperation in urban vehicular networks. In: Gao, H., Wang, X., Yin, Y., Iqbal, M. (eds.) CollaborateCom 2018. LNICST, vol. 268, pp. 235–251. Springer, Cham (2019). https://doi.org/10.1007/978-3-030-12981-1_17

32. Verghese, S.: Self-driving cars and lidar. In: CLEO: Applications and Technology, pp. AM3A-1. Optical Society of America (2017)
33. Wang, C., Ji, M., Wang, J., Wen, W., Li, T., Sun, Y.: An improved DBSCAN method for LiDAR data segmentation with automatic Eps estimation. Sensors **19**(1), 172 (2019)
34. Wang, P.S., Liu, Y., Guo, Y.X., Sun, C.Y., Tong, X.: O-CNN: octree-based convolutional neural networks for 3D shape analysis. ACM Trans. Graph. (TOG) **36**(4), 1–11 (2017)
35. Wang, X., Zhang, M., Meng, X., Xia, H., Wu, C., Luo, W.: Development conception and promotion strategy of bus system of the future. In: Proceedings of the 2020 5th International Conference on Cloud Computing and Internet of Things, pp. 63–68 (2020)
36. Wu, B., Li, P., Chen, J., Li, Y., Fan, Y.: 3D environment detection using multiview color images and lidar point clouds. In: 2018 IEEE International Conference on Consumer Electronics-Taiwan (ICCE-TW), pp. 1–2. IEEE (2018)
37. Yang, B., Luo, W., Urtasun, R.: PIXOR: real-time 3D object detection from point clouds. In: Proceedings of the IEEE Conference on Computer Vision and Pattern Recognition, pp. 7652–7660 (2018)
38. Yi, C., et al.: Urban building reconstruction from raw LiDAR point data. Comput. Aided Des. **93**, 1–14 (2017)
39. Zhao, J., Zhang, X.N., Gao, H., Yin, J., Zhou, M., Tan, C.: Object detection based on hierarchical multi-view proposal network for autonomous driving. In: 2018 International Joint Conference on Neural Networks (IJCNN), pp. 1–7. IEEE (2018)
40. Zhou, Y., Tuzel, O.: VoxelNet: end-to-end learning for point cloud based 3D object detection. In: Proceedings of the IEEE Conference on Computer Vision and Pattern Recognition, pp. 4490–4499 (2018)

Author Index

Ali, Sikandar   I-728, II-65

Bai, Xu   II-416
Bernard, Ngounou   I-20

Cai, Guanyu   II-276
Cai, Haini   I-318
Cao, Bin   II-316
Cao, Buqing   I-213
Cao, Chenhong   II-87
Cao, Zhihui   II-3
Chang, Mengmeng   I-299
Chang, Peng   I-575
Chao, Meiling   II-435
Chen, Dajiang   I-156
Chen, Dong   II-104
Chen, Gaojian   I-38
Chen, Jun   II-385
Chen, Junchang   I-554
Chen, Junjie   I-213
Chen, Kairun   I-678
Chen, Maojian   II-190
Chen, Peng   I-520
Chen, Rong   II-276
Chen, Xin   II-50, II-144
Chen, Yige   I-117, I-348
Chen, Yuqing   I-54
Chiu, Brian   II-104, II-124

Dai, Hong-Ning   I-368
Dai, Qiong   II-416
Deng, Zhidong   I-479
Ding, Bo   II-158
Ding, Weilong   II-385
Ding, Xu   I-99, II-335
Ding, Zhiming   I-299
Dong, Jing   I-642, I-661
Dou, Wanchun   II-33
Du, Bowen   II-104, II-124
Du, Jiajie   II-401
Du, Yongkang   II-385

Fan, Guijun   II-18
Fan, Guisheng   I-244, I-420

Fan, Hongfei   II-104, II-124
Fan, Jing   II-316
Fan, Yuqi   II-335
Fang, Mohan   I-20
Feng, Haodong   I-54
Feng, Meiqi   I-368
Feng, Qilong   II-352
Feng, Zhenni   I-554, II-87
Fu, Xiang   II-158

Gao, Honghao   II-87
Gao, Min   I-138, I-229, II-435
Ge, Weimin   I-479
Gu, Fei   I-713
Gu, Tianyi   I-259
Guo, Gengyuan   I-628
Guo, Xiao-Yong   I-498

Han, Jianmin   I-20
Han, Yanbo   I-38
He, Fei   II-175
He, Hui   I-608
He, Wen   I-697
He, Xin   I-678
He, Xionghui   II-206
He, Yulin   II-435
Hou, Yuexian   I-277
Hu, Rong   I-213
Huang, Hongyu   I-389, II-18
Huang, Jiahui   II-316
Huang, Jiwei   I-728, II-65
Huang, Kaiwen   I-259
Huang, Teng   I-244
Huang, Weiyi   I-534
Huang, Zijie   I-420
Huang, Ziyang   II-190
Huang, Zunfu   I-277

Ji, Cun   I-628
Jia, Weixing   I-171
Jia, Nannan   I-299
Jiang, Jinfeng   II-104, II-124
Jiang, Lei   II-416
Jiang, Ning   I-520

Jiang, Qinxue   I-277
Jiang, Xutong   II-33
Jiao, Boyang   I-38
Jiao, Libo   II-50, II-144
Jiao, Litao   I-368
Jin, Canghong   II-175
Jin, Hui   I-479

Ke, Yuxian   I-460
Kuang, Li   II-276, II-352

Li, Chengfan   II-87
Li, Dan   II-87
Li, Deyi   I-697
Li, Juanru   I-439
Li, Lutong   I-299
Li, Ning   I-191
Li, Peng   I-534
Li, Ping   I-259
Li, Qianwen   I-38
Li, Wei   I-661
Li, Wenxiong   II-241
Li, Xiaohong   I-479
Li, Yantao   I-389, II-18
Li, Yin   I-520
Li, Zhen   II-158
Liang, Jingyu   I-728
Liang, Yan   II-50
Liang, Ying   II-385
Lin, Liangliang   I-608
Liu, Bowen   II-33
Liu, Changzheng   II-261
Liu, Dianwen   I-642
Liu, Hongtao   I-277
Liu, Jian   I-368
Liu, Jianxiao   I-67
Liu, Jianxun   I-213
Liu, Junrong   I-439
Liu, Lin   I-498
Liu, Rui   I-642, I-661
Liu, Sihang   I-67
Liu, Tong   I-554, II-87
Liu, Yu   II-451
Liu, Zunhao   I-299
Lu, Jianfeng   I-20
Luo, Jie   II-158
Luo, Xiong   II-190
Lv, Qing   I-3
Lv, Xiang   II-3

Ma, Bowen   I-728
Ma, Shengcheng   II-50
Ma, Xiaoyu   I-608
Ma, Yifan   II-124
Mateen, Muhammad   I-318
Mu, Nankun   II-18

Nie, Lei   I-534
Niu, Jianwei   I-697

Ouyang, Zhenchao   I-697, II-451

Pan, Li   I-592, II-401
Panaousis, Emmanouil   I-368
Peng, Chengwei   I-575
Peng, Hao   I-20
Peng, Huailiang   II-416
Peng, Mi   I-213
Peng, Qiaojuan   II-190

Qi, Xiuxiu   II-241
Qian, Ye   I-592
Qin, Zhen   I-156

Ren, Lu   I-697, II-451
Ren, Yuheng   II-241

Sang, Yafei   I-575
Shang, Siyuan   II-335
Shen, Hailun   II-190
Sheng, Yu   II-276
Shi, Dianxi   II-370
Shu, Xiao   II-158
Su, Yaqianwen   II-206, II-370
Sun, Haifeng   II-3
Sun, Song   I-318

Tan, Jiefu   I-191, II-206
Tan, Yufu   II-65
Tang, Liangyao   I-520
Tian, Changbo   I-405

Wang, Bo   I-277
Wang, Ding   I-368
Wang, Guiling   I-171
Wang, Haotian   II-65
Wang, Huan   I-191
Wang, Jia   I-138
Wang, Jiahao   II-241
Wang, Jiaxing   II-316
Wang, Jing   I-38

Wang, Miao   I-3
Wang, Shiqi   I-138
Wang, Yang   I-99
Wang, Yifeng   II-297
Wang, Yipeng   I-348
Wang, Zongwei   I-138, II-435
Wang, Zuohua   I-83
Wei, Xiaopeng   I-642, I-661
Wen, Junhao   I-138, I-318
Wu, Bilian   II-144
Wu, Fan   I-138
Wu, Minghui   II-175
Wu, Wendi   I-191
Wu, Yingbo   II-225
Wu, Yunlong   I-191

Xi, Wei   I-608
Xia, Yunni   I-520
Xiao, Junlei   I-534
Xiao, Mengdi   I-534
Xie, Hong   I-520
Xie, Min   II-158
Xie, Yujian   I-460
Xing, Hai-Feng   I-498
Xing, Mengda   II-385
Xiong, Naixue   I-277
Xu, Chi   I-439
Xu, Guangquan   I-368
Xu, Huanhuan   I-713
Xu, Jiachi   I-191, II-206
Xu, Ruihong   I-67
Xu, Wenhua   II-104
Xue, Chao   II-206

Yang, Bowen   I-299
Yang, Chen   I-608
Yang, Huan   I-318
Yang, Jisong   I-575
Yang, Kang   I-420
Yang, Mengning   I-678
Yang, Peng   I-117, I-348
Yang, Ruilong   I-520
Yang, Senqiao   II-297
Yang, Shaowu   II-370
Yang, Xingguang   I-420
Yang, Xuankai   I-171
Yang, Yao   I-389
Yang, Yin   II-297
Yang, Zemeng   I-67
Yang, Zichao   II-124

Yao, Juan   II-225
Yao, Xin   I-20
Ye, Peng   I-333
Yi, Pengfei   I-642, I-661
Yin, Tao   I-405
Ying, Weizhi   I-83
Yu, Huiqun   I-244, I-420
Yu, Juan   I-20
Yu, Lei   I-54
Yu, Qing   I-83
Yu, Yang   I-229, II-225
Yuan, Lei   I-299
Yuan, Limengzi   I-460, II-261
Yuan, Yunjing   I-38

Zang, Tianning   I-117, I-348
Zeng, Jun   I-229, II-225
Zhang, Benzhuang   II-261
Zhang, Changjie   II-451
Zhang, Chaokui   I-333
Zhang, Fengquan   I-171
Zhang, Hanwen   I-156
Zhang, Junwei   II-435
Zhang, Mingzhe   I-628
Zhang, Ning   II-3
Zhang, Qiang   I-642, I-661
Zhang, Qingwang   I-67
Zhang, Shichao   I-628
Zhang, Song   II-33
Zhang, Tianpu   II-385
Zhang, Wang   II-416
Zhang, Xiang   I-333
Zhang, Yao   I-479
Zhang, Yaowen   II-370
Zhang, Yiteng   II-104, II-124
Zhang, Yongjun   II-206, II-370
Zhang, Yongzheng   I-117, I-348, I-405, I-575
Zhang, Yue   II-352
Zhao, Chenran   II-370
Zhao, Chong   I-99
Zhao, Jizhong   I-608
Zhao, Kun   I-608
Zhao, Qingzhan   I-460
Zhao, Quanwu   II-435
Zhao, Xingbiao   II-261
Zhao, Xuan   II-33
Zhao, Yizhu   I-229
Zheng, Hang   I-99
Zheng, Limin   I-3

Zheng, Xi   I-368
Zheng, Xiangwei   I-628
Zheng, Yuchen   I-460, II-261
Zhong, Zhenyang   I-333
Zhou, Dongsheng   I-642, I-661

Zhou, Jian-Tao   I-498
Zhou, Jingya   I-713
Zhou, Wei   I-229
Zhou, Yuan   I-117, I-348
Zhou, Ziyi   I-420

Printed in the United States
by Baker & Taylor Publisher Services